MW01406934

An Advocate for Women

The Public Life of
Emmeline B. Wells,
1870–1920

Biographies in Latter-day Saint History

An imprint of BYU Studies and
the Joseph Fielding Smith Institute for Latter-day Saint History

Brigham Young University
Provo, Utah

An Advocate for Women

The Public Life of Emmeline B. Wells, 1870–1920

Carol Cornwall Madsen

Brigham Young University Press
Provo, Utah

Deseret Book
Salt Lake City, Utah

This volume is part of the Smith Institute and BYU Studies series
Biographies in Latter-day Saint History

Other volumes in this series:
T. Edgar Lyon: A Teacher in Zion
"No Toil nor Labor Fear": The Story of William Clayton
Qualities That Count: Heber J. Grant as Businessman, Missionary, and Apostle

© 2006 Brigham Young University. All rights reserved.

Cover design by Kimberly Chen Pace
Cover image Emmeline B. Wells courtesy Church Archives

Opinions expressed in this publication are the opinions of the author and her views should not necessarily be attributed to The Church of Jesus Christ of Latter-day Saints, Brigham Young University, BYU Studies, or Deseret Book.

No part of this book may be reprinted or reproduced or utilized in any form or by any electronic, digital, mechanical or other means, now known or hereafter invented, including photocopying and recording or in an information storage or retrieval system, without permission in writing from the publisher. To contact BYU Studies, write to 403 CB, Brigham Young University, PO Box 24098, Provo, Utah 84602, or visit http://byustudies.byu.edu. To contact Deseret Book Company, write to P. O. Box 30178, Salt Lake City, Utah, 84130. This volume was prepared for publication by BYU Studies.

Library of Congress Cataloging-in-Publication Data

Madsen, Carol Cornwall, 1930–
 An advocate for women : the public life of Emmeline B. Wells, 1870–1920 / Carol Cornwall Madsen.
  p. cm. — (Biographies in Latter-day Saint history)
 Includes bibliographical references and index.
 ISBN 978-0-8425-2673-9 (hardcover : alk. paper)
 1. Wells, Emmeline B. (Emmeline Blanche), 1828–1921. 2. Mormons—United States—Biography. 3. Women—Suffrage—Utah—History. I. Title. II. Series.

BX8695.W45M33 2005
289.3092—dc22

2005026019

Printed in the United States of America
10 9 8 7 6 5 4 3 2

History tells us very little about women; judging from its pages, one would suppose their lives were insignificant and their opinions worthless.... Volumes of unwritten history yet remain, the sequel to the written lives of brave and heroic men. But although the historians of the past have been neglectful of woman, and it is the exception if she be mentioned at all; yet the future will deal more generously with womankind, and the historian of the present age will find it very embarrassing to ignore woman in the records of the nineteenth century.

Emmeline B. Wells, "Self-Made Women," *Woman's Exponent* 9 (March 1, 1881): 148.

Contents

Illustrations — ix
Acknowledgments — xi

1. Prologue: A Woman's Advocate — 1
2. "Granite and Old Lace," a Life Sketch — 15
3. "Remember the Women of Zion," the *Woman's Exponent* — 34
4. A "Strong-Minded Woman" — 67
5. "This Is Woman's Era" — 95
6. Utah and the Woman Question — 114
7. Wells Goes to Washington — 148
8. Diamond Cut Diamond — 182
9. Grace in Defeat — 212
10. The Politics of Woman Suffrage — 237
11. Strategies for Victory — 266
12. Schism in the Sisterhood — 293
13. The Perils of Partisan Politics — 321
14. The "Blessed Symbol" for All — 348
15. The Struggle for Inclusion — 376
16. The Power of Combination — 406

17 The Elusive Sisterhood	433
18 "A Fine Soul Who Served Us"	459
19 Epilogue	488
Abbreviations of Organizations	491
Index	492

Illustrations

Emmeline B. Wells, 1891	xiv
New Salem Academy, New Salem, Massachusetts	17
Newell K. Whitney	19
Daniel H. Wells	20
Emmeline's home in Salt Lake City	21
First page of *Woman's Exponent*	37
Edward L. Sloan	40
Susa Young Gates	44
Zina D. H. Young	47
Lucretia Mott	73
Eliza R. Snow	75
Margaret Fuller	79
S. M. Cullom	120
Charlotte Cobb Godbe	149
Belva Lockwood	156
Riggs House, Washington, D.C.	163
Lucy B. Hayes	167
Emily S. Richards	183
Ellen B. Ferguson	194

Romania Pratt Penrose	196
Elizabeth Cady Stanton and Susan B. Anthony	199
Frances Willard	213
John Randolph Tucker	224
Sarah M. Kimball	252
Delegates to National Council of Women convention, 1895	277
City and County Building, Salt Lake City	281
Anna Howard Shaw	294
Emily J. McVicker	295
Martha Hughes Cannon	300
Ruth May Fox	303
Rocky Mountain woman suffrage convention, 1895	320
Heber M. Wells	327
Grover Cleveland	328
Senate and staff of Utah's second legislature	338
Charlotte Perkins Gilman	352
Carrie Chapman Catt	353
Alice Paul	362
Lucy Stone	381
Utah Building at Columbian Exposition	384
Rachel Foster Avery	390
Delegates to Triennial National Council of Women, 1899	408
Reed Smoot	446
Bathsheba W. Smith	470
Bust of Emmeline B. Wells	480

Acknowledgments

It would have been impossible for me to produce this study of the public life of Emmeline B. Wells without the help of many people. Over the past twenty-five years I have slowly accumulated information and written short studies on her life, all with the help of mentors, colleagues, archival personnel, and research assistants.

I have had opportunity to gather material from the Schlesinger Library at Radcliffe College, Cambridge, Massachusetts; the Library of Congress in Washington, D.C.; the Fawcett Library of Women's History in London, England; as well as the British Library. A summer's study on British Women's History at Oxford University, England, produced important comparative and contextual information. The Mormon Collections in the Bancroft Library at the University of California at Berkeley and Huntington Library in San Marino, California, proved to be very useful. Most of all I came to know Emmeline Wells through numerous visits to Petersham and North New Salem, Massachusetts, Emmeline's childhood homes, where I had the great pleasure of meeting Carolyn Chouinard, a local historian, as devoted to Emmeline as I am. Funds for many of these travels have come from the following departments at Brigham Young University in Provo, Utah: the Joseph Fielding Smith Institute for Latter-day Saint History; the College of Family, Home, and Social Sciences; the Women's Research Institute; and the Kennedy Center for International Studies.

Local repositories of relevant materials have been the basis of my research. These include the L. Tom Perry Special Collections, Harold B.

Lee Library, Brigham Young University in Provo, Utah, which houses the diaries of Emmeline B. Wells; the Library and Archives of The Church of Jesus Christ of Latter-day Saints in Salt Lake City; the Utah State Historical Society; and the J. Willard Marriott Library, Special Collections Department, University of Utah, Salt Lake City.

My work on Emmeline Wells began under the tutelage of Brigham D. Madsen, Everett L. Cooley, and Davis Bitton, my graduate committee at the University of Utah. It has been long in coming, but this book reflects their interest in Utah history, their scholarly examples, and their encouragement in making the Emmeline Wells story available to all who share that interest. Though this book is only half her story, I hope it will justify their conviction that her story should be told. I want to acknowledge the value to my study of the pathbreaking work of Lola Van Wagenen's PhD dissertation, "Sister-Wives and Suffragists: Polygamy and the Politics of Woman Suffrage, 1870–1896" (New York University, 1994), reprinted by the Joseph Fielding Smith Institute for Latter-day Saint History and BYU Studies in 2003; and Joan Smyth Iversen's book, *The Antipolygamy Controversy in U.S. Women's Movements, 1880–1925* (New York: Garland, 1997). Both provided important insights and national context to the Utah suffrage story.

The collegiality, encouragement, and interest of my co-workers in the Smith Institute over the years have been enormously motivating. They have set a high standard of scholarship, which I have tried to attain in my own historical writing. For twenty-five years the Joseph Fielding Smith Institute has been my professional home base from which I have shared my colleagues' excitement in exploring our Mormon past. Our goal was to present our history honestly and wholly, rendering the past with faith, respect, and understanding. A special thanks goes to the institute's long-time secretary, Marilyn Rich Parks, for her supervision of the financial and material resources supporting this study, the clerical and research help she has provided, her computer expertise when desperately needed, and her interest in the project.

An inexpressible amount of gratitude is due to my two women colleagues in the institute who have shared my dedication to the pursuit of Latter-day Saint women's history: Maureen Ursenbach Beecher and

Jill Mulvay Derr. As deeply respected mentors, they have given me encouragement, knowledge, guidance, and inspiration to search out and tell the wondrous tales of our early Mormon foremothers. As well, I thank Jill Derr, Dawn Anderson, and all others who have read and made helpful suggestions for the manuscript, especially my husband, Gordon, for his keen and insightful comments.

The meticulous editing by Heather Seferovich and her assistance in making the manuscript clear and understandable and the citations full and accurate have been of immeasurable help. I also appreciate the careful diary editing of Sheree Maxwell Bench and her commitment to accuracy. As well, my thanks go to Marny K. Parkin for her careful work in typesetting and indexing. I do, however, take full responsibility for any lapses in these areas.

I have been favored with a steady stream of research assistants, too numerous to name individually, who have spent long hours in various archives and on the computer searching out obscure facts and elusive documents. These men and women have been absolutely essential in enabling this work to be published in my lifetime. Many have found an interest in Mormon women's history ignited by their research and some have contributed studies of their own to this field.

Most of all I am thankful to Emmeline B. Wells for providing the material for this book: her editorials and articles for the *Woman's Exponent* and other women's papers and her consistent diary entries. These, of course, have provided insight into both her public and private thoughts and are the basis for whatever assessments and conclusions expressed therein.

And to the interest and encouragement of my husband, Gordon, I owe the completion of this woman's story.

Emmeline B. Wells, women's rights advocate, by Charles Milton Bell, Washington, D.C., 1891.

Chapter 1

Prologue: A Woman's Advocate

*'I desire to do all in my power to help
elevate the condition of my people especially wom[e]n.*[1]

I was first introduced to Emmeline Blanche Wells while I was writing a thesis on the *Woman's Exponent*, a biweekly periodical for Mormon women that she edited from 1877 to 1914. I had nearly completed my study of its editorials, most of them written by Emmeline B. Wells, when I learned that Brigham Young University in Provo, Utah, had just acquired forty-seven volumes of her diaries. Time allowed me only a brief scanning of the diaries, but I knew then that I wanted Emmeline Wells to be part of my academic life.

As an 1842 convert to The Church of Jesus Christ of Latter-day Saints (LDS Church), Emmeline Wells followed the Church's western migration from Nauvoo, Illinois, to its final headquarters in Salt Lake City, Utah, which became her permanent home after 1848. A Massachusetts native, she did not return to her home state for more than forty years, but did return in 1885 as a dedicated suffragist, a well-known editor, a friend and co-worker of many of the national leaders of the controversial woman movement, and a plural wife of a prominent Mormon leader.

As my acquaintance with her deepened over the years, I became determined to write her biography. It was a daunting task to try to reduce this extraordinary woman's life to my words, since she left behind so many of her own. I am convinced, however, that her story needs telling, and I am committed to being one of the storytellers.

This volume is only part of Emmeline Wells's story. It is not a biographical narrative. Rather, it is a study meant to illuminate the motives, challenges, and achievements of a local worker in a national movement. It is also meant to show how a young girl from a small mill village in rural Massachusetts was able, through the strength of her convictions and determination, to transform herself into a self-confident, nationally known spokesperson for women and for her faith. This is the overall theme of the book. Experience was her teacher, and she brought to the task a voracious appetite for learning and an indefatigable energy. This book centers on Emmeline's social activism, a consuming passion and a major identifying quality in her adult years.

Like many of her contemporaries, she experienced both the security of marriage, home, and family life, as well as the uncertainties of widowhood and self-dependence. But unlike many nineteenth-century women, she was both socially aware and politically astute. Although she was not, strictly speaking, a renaissance woman, her interests did transcend geographic, ideological, and social boundaries. And her determination to advance women's status was deeply rooted. "I stand for the higher advancement of woman the world over," she explained in 1906, "for everything that will better her condition, mentally, morally, spiritually, temporally."[2] Her public work as an advocate for the "emancipation" of women from the arbitrary and constricting rule of custom and her role as a defender of the principles of her faith demonstrated her resolve.

Throughout the preparation of this volume, I was haunted by a warning to biographers to avoid the "fatal split between the private and public identities" of the subject.[3] Many scholars in women's history have questioned the delimitations that arise from conceptualizing the past in terms of distinct gender spheres that separate the private (women's sphere) from the public (men's sphere), finding women's lives more fluid than earlier perceived.[4] Indeed, that women created their own "public space" has been a premise of many historical studies.

A review of the autobiographical writings of women contemporary with Emmeline shows just how much their lives resisted the dichotomy of the private and the public that historians had initially imposed as a framework for studying woman's experience. A theme of "connectedness," literary critic Susan Cahill noted of women's accounts, placed the individual and those who comprised their world within what she called "a single web of life."[5]

Emmeline moved freely between the public and the private, their boundaries extremely permeable in her world and their values closely allied. She, and many women like her, created their own public spheres, a female domain of public activity that often overlapped but more often bordered the traditional public sphere of male institutions. Thus, my decision to separate the public from the private and proceed with this volume came after a long, internal debate. I concluded that the rhetorical duality I was imposing by writing two biographies of her, the public and the private, accommodated itself to a pattern of dualities that hyphenated, more than disconnected, the various elements of her complex life.

Emmeline was at once a very private and a very public person; a devoted, almost obsessive, family woman and a driven, ambitious professional; a poet of sentiment and nostalgic yearnings and a pragmatic, astute businesswoman; a woman of deep yet quiet faith and a public advocate of the principles of that faith; a thinker and a doer. Moreover, Emmeline created for herself a dual literary persona with accompanying pseudonyms: the sentimental "Aunt Em," who authored most of her poetry and nostalgic New England sketches, and the "strong-minded" Blanche Beechwood, an ideologically liberated equal rights advocate. The sheer volume of her public writings and the national and international scope of her political activities seemed to warrant this artificial biographical division. Extracting these sometimes contradictory elements for this study helps to situate her more clearly within a historical context beyond her Utah and Mormon environments. Thus, I have followed her lead and separated her two personae, with hyphens where necessary. This book is primarily Blanche Beechwood's story.

It is important to note that Emmeline imposed certain barriers around segments of her life, which, though they failed to prevent the public from intruding on the private, did firmly restrict much of her private life from encroaching on her public work. The very private agony she experienced as a neglected plural wife, for instance, never diminished her passionate, public defense of the practice of polygamy.[6] Similarly, neither age nor the weariness she felt at each day's end deterred her from agreeing to head committees, to serve as a patron of various organizations and as a member of civil and corporate boards, or to lecture, speak, or write for one cause or another. Known as a sympathetic listener and an encyclopedia of broad-ranging information, Emmeline was sought after for counsel and direction. A longtime widow, she was nonetheless included in the social gatherings of the leading families of the LDS Church and city for her wit and knowledge. Withal, she bore her personal disappointments, frustrations, and sorrows privately, a legacy from the stoicism of her New England background.

I am keenly aware, however, that the activist life Emmeline Wells made for herself cannot be totally disconnected from either her personal relationships or the religious institutional foundation that provided motivation, encouragement, assistance, and emotional support. Few women of her time functioned in the public sphere without the backing of a female network and a strong sense of female community. Emmeline's five daughters, her LDS Relief Society co-workers, and her expansive cluster of associates outside Utah provided a base that generated and supported her public service.

Traditional class and urban/rural social distinctions, though existing in some measure within the Mormon female community in Utah, generally yielded to the structured, pervasive, and unifying network of the women's Relief Society. This multileveled organization, which brought numerous women into leadership positions and linked its members through rounds of visits by the general officers from Salt Lake City and the semimonthly reports of their activities in the *Woman's Exponent*, collectivized the social service agenda of Latter-day Saint women. Economic, political, and benevolent social action was part of that agenda. Such public activism contributed to the politicization of Mormon women.[7]

These women were pioneers in the movement, not only in testing the waters of an often-alien world but also in evaluating their ability to cope with and eventually conquer their own self-doubts. The efforts of politically active Mormon women gave a feminine voice, style, and perspective to an otherwise male-defined social environment. Emmeline Wells and other Mormon activists functioned from the strength of this female collective. Emmeline was not, in other words, isolated from her social roots because of her public activism; indeed, she was nourished by them.

Another problem with which I grappled while writing this volume was to understand how Emmeline reconciled her feminist activism with what many non-Mormons felt was an oppressive religion. The historical context in which both lifestyles originated helped to provide an answer. Issues we would call "feminist" today fell under the rubric "the woman question" in her time, a social issue that divided Americans over the movement it generated for the equality and "emancipation" of women.[8] The cultural milieu in which the movement developed was principally immersed in the values, attitudes, and assumptions of American Victorianism, a social system that attempted to impose order on a society still basking in the heady atmosphere of the Revolution but facing the social and ideological dislocations generated by developments in industrialization, immigration, urbanization, and geographic expansion. Victorianism offered a value system that found fertile soil in the traditions of rural America and the verities of protestant evangelicalism. In this ambivalent social setting, the nineteenth-century woman movement was fostered.

Victorianism was essentially optimistic and progressive, but it resisted definition as a unified social philosophy. Its contradictions and inconsistencies derived from a society in flux. While this movement fostered the moral and philosophic values of a simpler time, it embraced the dramatic changes that were occurring in American life as evidence of an ineluctable move toward a preordained destiny. Victorianism was not only an ethnocentric social outlook—self-conscious and introspective—but it was also confident and self-righteous. Expressing itself in moral terms more than religious, Victorianism prescribed a set of behavioral standards that pervaded all segments of American society. These external indices of Victorianism comprise the popular understanding of the term.[9]

In America the conservative personal values associated with Victorianism—character traits such as self-denial, thrift, industry, self-improvement, and self-reliance—became stepping stones to economic and social advancement. Both the Revolutionary and Jacksonian periods propelled American democracy toward broader interpretations of that political philosophy and widely extended political and economic opportunities for men; but for women there was no corresponding change. Rather, such advances for men more visibly exposed the restricted opportunities for women, particularly as industrialization shifted the locus of production for many men from the home to the marketplace, creating separate and distinct male and female working domains with differentiated values.

The Victorian creation of an idealized domestic ethos was, to a large extent, a response to a redefinition of the home and woman's function within it. The home, as the traditional transmitter of society's values, became the focus of Victorian idealism, and woman, within her domestic sphere, became the custodian and mentor of the Victorian culture. She both derived this responsibility from and shared it with the clergy. Moreover, with the development of the popular press—especially the proliferating ladies' magazines and etiquette books—and the increasing popularity of the lecture circuit, these social values could be widely disseminated. Female editors, writers, and lecturers became the purveyors of Victorian values, while women were expected to serve as caretakers of the nation's moral probity.[10]

While never disavowing woman's domestic value, some women found domesticity limiting and the social constraints of Victorian "propriety" too restrictive. Some women also became more aware of their marginal role in the economic, political, and social processes of a burgeoning American society and rebelled against the excessive idealization of the domestic role of women as the rationale behind their peripheral public presence. Seeking greater autonomy and a wider field of social participation, women initiated a movement that would involve the imposing task of removing the psychological dominance of a male-defined social order to which many women, as well as men, subscribed. Those who sought for change encountered thickets of opposition. Tradition, especially, hedged in their efforts.

At issue were two contradictory worldviews of woman's place and function in society. These comprised the "woman question," which penetrated literature, religion, medicine, science, law, and politics, with the ballot ultimately symbolizing the goal of the emancipation effort.

Emmeline Wells personified the dilemma of women seeking to define American womanhood in the nineteenth century. From a traditional New England background but a participant in an untraditional marital practice, she interpreted the shifting circumstances of her own life within a larger social context and left a voluminous written record that reflects her response to the conflicting social currents of her time. Becoming one of the "strong-minded" women seeking to make change, she found her main impetus outside the evangelical or enlightenment arguments of her feminist peers. To the perplexity of many of her suffragist allies, her religion was a major wellspring of her activism.

The LDS Church's tenets of individual progression and free agency meshed with Romantic and feminist notions of the sovereignty of the individual and each person's need to grow and develop to its fullest potential, unfettered by arbitrary constraints. Moreover, by the latter part of the nineteenth century, Utah's social landscape included voting rights for women, property rights for married women, admission to institutions of higher learning, open career and economic opportunities, and leadership roles in a variety of religious and civic enterprises, all goals of the woman movement, enjoyed by few women elsewhere.

Several other factors engendered competence and initiative in Latter-day Saint women. Polygamy and the absence of husbands during long periods of missionary or other ecclesiastical service made Emmeline Wells and many of her peers both economic and spiritual heads of their households. "My husband is too much engrossed with public affairs to devote much time or even sympathy to his family," Emmeline wrote in 1875; "therefore the care and responsibility devolves upon the mother."[11] Moreover, most of her associates, like herself, were first-generation Latter-day Saints, who knew the privations and demands of conversion, repeated geographic relocations, and challenges of settlement. They were, willingly or not, models of female strength, endurance, and self-reliance. In that early labor-intensive period of Mormon history, the skills and talents of women were needed and highly valued. The genesis of Emmeline's arguments against passive, submissive women or arrogant, self-sufficient men is obvious. Since official LDS Church rhetoric did not dichtomize the educated, contributing, self-reliant woman and the dutiful wife and mother, her feminist discourse did not seem noticeably at odds with the Church's prevailing domestic ethos.

Emmeline Wells and other Latter-day Saint women leaders reminded the women in the Church, whom they called "sisters," of these realities in their editorials and speeches, hoping to unleash the power of conviction that had enabled women to join the LDS Church in the first place. Emmeline wanted to use that self-confidence to establish a Mormon presence in the world. She wanted to confront the critics, so adamantly opposed to the practice of plural marriage, and not cower or wither at their sly barbs and heated attacks.

As the impasse sharpened between Congress and women's reform groups on the one hand and the Mormons on the other, Emmeline Wells increasingly found herself in a mediating role. From the Victorian ethos into which she was born, Emmeline developed a strong fidelity to the notion of a common womanhood. Women's biological functions and nurturing capacities, she believed, drew them together in shared experiences that overrode any social differences. This foundational principle in her worldview enabled her to brave the ridicule, opprobrium, and pity leveled at Mormon women during her era of public activism. Emmeline was convinced that once their disparagers came to know them, what they held in common as women would diminish their condemnation of Mormonism. She acted on the assumption that female solidarity need not be equated with conformity and appealed for respect for individual differences.

Emmeline Wells became adept at personal diplomacy, and the friends she made among women not of her faith laid the groundwork for more congenial relations between Mormon and non-Mormon women generally. The role of mediator quietly settled on her, and for nearly forty years she bridged the chasm between the women of her faith and the women of the world. One of her close associates recognized her mediating mission and wrote of her in 1898: "The women of Utah should be ever grateful to Mrs. E. B. Wells for the glorious work she does and instigates in the interest of woman. She is doing the work of a veritable female Apostle Paul . . . and she occupies the difficult role of mediator between the different factions of woman's interests."[12]

Indeed, it was a difficult role. While the antagonisms that developed between Mormon and other women, especially in Utah, covered the social spectrum from religion and education to politics and economics, polygamy became the fulcrum around which the contentions revolved. Mormon opponents argued that plural marriage, as a vestige of orientalism, was not only immoral but also un-American and particularly demeaning to women. The practice, they claimed, robbed women of the trust Victorian society had placed in them as overseers of its code of moral behavior. Nonsense, retorted Mormon women. Polygamy offered all women opportunity for marriage and motherhood and cleansed society of the pernicious evils of prostitution, abandoned children, and other related social ills. It was a lopsided battle, however, and the combined power of convention and the federal government ultimately prevailed.

Though generally not a familiar name to later generations, Emmeline Wells was one of the best-known Latter-day Saint women of her time, both inside and outside Utah. Her breadth of service to women was noted at a public celebration of her eighty-second birthday:

> She has traveled tens of thousands of miles to render service in defense of her church and her sex and enjoys the respect—in many instances the intimate acquaintance and affection—of the leading women, not only of America but of the world.[13]

The focus of this volume is on the social activity that brought Emmeline Wells this kind of accolade. Not only was she deeply entrenched in the fight for civil rights for women, but she also traveled a variety of other avenues toward greater female expression and participation. She was a member of the National Woman Suffrage Association, the National and International Councils of Women, Daughters of the Revolution, the National and Utah Women's Press Associations, the Utah Federation of Women's Clubs, the Salt Lake City Library Committee, the Utah Kindergarten Association, the Deseret Hospital Board, and several literary clubs, two of which she organized. She was an active Republican, serving as an officer of Utah's Central Committee, and twice ran for office, though unsuccessfully.

Emmeline repeatedly lobbied the Utah legislature for various municipal improvements and social programs. From 1887 until her death in 1921, she also served in the general leadership of the LDS Relief Society, first as secretary (1892–1910) and later as president (1910–21). Her affiliations put her in contact with the major figures of the woman movement as well as members of Congress and United States presidents. Through her editorship of the *Woman's Exponent,* she became acquainted with many well-known authors, editors, and lecturers. Her circle of interests and influence was wide and varied.

Emmeline Wells left a large written legacy. The *Woman's Exponent,* the Latter-day Saint woman's newsletter that she edited for thirty-seven years, is only one route to her agile and perceptive mind. She also left letters, magazine articles, a volume of poetry, and more than forty-seven diaries from which we can discover something of her thoughts and motivations. The writings reveal a compulsive soul-searching and a persistent Puritan resignation threaded through the reflections of an intensely observant and introspective woman. Little happened in her wide world of interests that was not noted in one of these literary records. Both her public and private writings offer astute commentaries on her times. As an active agent in many of the historic events that were beginning to change the lives of women in the nineteenth century, she wrote from an insider's perspective. She was not an isolated westerner, a narrow religionist, or a naïve provincial in either outlook or experience. Her life's work was to move her Mormon sisters beyond the narrow provincialism to which constant harassment, isolation, and the drive for both physical and emotional survival had pushed them.

Emmeline's life was not the norm of her era. Born on the outer fringes of a rural society, she became an intellectual, a middle-class American, and a socially prominent Mormon. Though she was self-supporting for much of her life, she did not suffer the deprivations of the working-class woman. While still living beneath the financial security of the affluent, she was better educated than many women of her era and married at different times to two influential Church leaders. She enjoyed a position of prominence within her social setting from these relationships. The substance of her prominence, however, came from her own accomplishments within her church and community.

Emmeline Wells was first and foremost a Latter-day Saint. Her religion shaped her life and provided the premise from which she developed her thinking about the issues of her time. It was Emmeline's religion that lifted her out of the obscurity of rural New England and made it possible for her to return to the East as a noted and capable leader of women and an advocate for her people. From her Calvinist background, her adopted Latter-day Saint religion, and her Victorian environment, Emmeline carved an identity that reflected but ultimately transcended them all, for she was more than the product of the cultures in which she lived. She was an authentic original, quickened by an inimitable spirit. My hope is that this volume will give shape and pattern to Emmeline's ideas and to the public life she made for herself to promote them. I hope it will also give some insight into the intense and eventful times in which she lived.

Though there is a broad chronological pattern to the volume, it more closely follows a thematic and episodic path. The chapters are all related to these general themes but are also independent as they explore the various arenas of Wells's public service. The book begins with a brief sketch of her life to provide a personal context for the activities that are addressed in detail in succeeding chapters. An account of the *Woman's Exponent*, which was the medium that conveyed her into the public realm, follows. Since Emmeline Wells has sometimes been referenced as a prototype of a Mormon feminist, a discussion of her personal philosophy and the ideological streams that fed into it seemed a propitious topic.

While most of her Mormon contemporaries were of a more conservative nature than she, Emmeline Wells nonetheless enjoyed a strong support system at home and a supportive association with a prominent assemblage of women beyond Utah. Like most other activists of her time, she struggled to maintain a balance between attachment—her need to belong to someone and something beyond herself—and autonomy, an equally strong desire to be her own person, independent, individualistic, and free to make her own choices. One of those choices was to become an advocate for woman suffrage, a controversial issue of her time, and to be an active participant in Utah politics.

No story of woman suffrage in the United States is as intriguing, as overlaid with multiple issues, or as controversial as that which unfolded in Utah between 1870 and 1895. Given the vote in 1870, a dramatic and unexpected bestowal, Utah women lost it in 1887 with passage of the antipolygamy Edmunds-Tucker Act. The struggle to regain the vote at statehood in 1895 added a concluding chapter to the woman suffrage effort that proved to be neither redundant nor predictable. This historical episode is revisited in the next five chapters, the heart of the book, as experienced and observed by Emmeline Wells, a major player and recorder of the story. Her interest in the national and local suffrage movement led to her role in Utah's political drama as it shifted from local partisan issues and parties to the national two-party system and its respective platforms.

Once woman suffrage was reestablished in Utah law at statehood, celebrated in 1896, Emmeline Wells directed her energies toward the National and International Councils of Women and also to her numerous local associations. Her participation in these organizations comprises the concluding chapters of the book. She continued to attend national conventions until well into her eighties, but her appointment as LDS Relief Society General President at age eighty-two curtailed those excursions. She lived to see the Nineteenth Amendment passed in 1920, giving to all women of the United States the right to vote, and received special recognition at the local celebration of that historic moment.[14]

I hope this volume will introduce the modern reader not only to the events of a historic struggle to bring women into the political process of the nation but even more to the life of an articulate, intelligent, and dedicated Mormon woman who was an actor in that struggle. Retrieving her story from the margins of Mormon history should bring a new dimension to an understanding of the Mormon past and a broader perspective of the impact of the woman movement on the history of nineteenth-century America.

Notes

1. Emmeline B. Wells, Diary, January 4, 1878, L. Tom Perry Special Collections, Harold B. Lee Library, Brigham Young University, Provo, Utah.

2. Emmeline B. Wells, "Why a Woman Should Desire to be a Mormon," *Woman's Exponent* 36 (January 1908): 48.

3. Susan N. Cahill, *Writing Women's Lives: An Anthology of Autobiographical Narratives by Twentieth-Century American Women Writers* (New York: Harper Perennial, 1994), xi.

4. Linda K. Kerber, "Separate Spheres, Female Worlds, Woman's Place: The Rhetoric of Women's History," *Journal of American History* 75 (June 1988): 9–39.

5. Cahill, *Writing Women's Lives*, xi.

6. Polygamy, or more correctly polygyny, was initiated by the Church's founder and first prophet, Joseph Smith, in Nauvoo, Illinois, in 1843. It was not publicly announced as a religious principle until 1852, after the Church had moved to the Salt Lake Valley.

7. Lola Van Wagenen makes this claim in "In Their Own Behalf: The Politicization of Mormon Women and the 1870 Franchise," *Dialogue: A Journal of Mormon Thought* 24 (Winter 1991): 31–43.

8. Gerda Lerner has differentiated between the woman's rights movement, which focused on legal and political equality and has been most readily identified with the struggle for woman suffrage, and the concept of "emancipation," which she identifies as "freedom from oppressive restrictions imposed by sex: self-determination and autonomy." See Gerda Lerner, "Women's Rights and American Feminism," in *The Majority Finds Its Past: Placing Women in History*, ed. Gerda Lerner (New York: Oxford University Press, 1979), 49.

9. Three analyses of American Victorianism are Richard D. Altick, *Victorian People and Ideas* (New York: W. W. Norton, 1973); Daniel Walker Howe,

ed., *Victorian America* (Philadelphia: University of Pennsylvania Press, 1976); and Thomas Schlereth, *Victorian America: Transformations in Everyday Life, 1876-1915* (New York: HarperPerennial, 1991).

10. For information on female moral authority and its social use, see David J. Pivar, *Purity Crusade: Sexual Morality and Social Control, 1868-1900* (Westport, Conn.: Greenwood, 1973); Barbara Leslie Epstein, *The Politics of Domesticity: Women, Evangelism, and Temperance in Nineteenth-Century America* (Middletown, Conn.: Wesleyan University Press, 1981); Lori D. Ginzberg, *Women and the Work of Benevolence: Morality, Politics, and Class in the Nineteenth-Century United States* (New Haven, Conn.: Yale University Press, 1990); Peggy Pascoe, *Relations of Rescue: The Search for Female Moral Authority in the American West, 1874-1939* (New York: Oxford University Press, 1990).

11. Wells, Diary, October 22, 1875.

12. "With the Editor," *Young Woman's Journal* 9 (July 1898): 336.

13. "A Noble Woman," *Deseret Evening News,* March 5, 1910, 4.

14. Susa Young Gates, "Utah," in *History of Woman Suffrage,* vol. 6, ed. Ida Husted Harper (New York: National American Woman Suffrage Association, 1922), 650.

Chapter 2

"Granite and Old Lace," a Life Sketch

It is ardently hoped that future historians will remember the women of Zion when compiling the history of this Western land.[1]

In January 1879, when Emmeline Wells boarded the train that would take her from her home in Utah to the halls of Congress in Washington, D.C., to attend a convention of the National Woman Suffrage Association (NWSA), she had every reason to be apprehensive. She and her traveling companion, Zina Y. Williams, were braving the denigration and traducement that had been leveled against their people, members of the LDS Church, since Church leaders publicly announced the practice of plural marriage in 1852. Just four years after this announcement, the platform of the Republican Party combined polygamy with slavery as "the twin relics of barbarism," which the party was dedicated to eradicating. Since the 1850s, Congress had studied and debated a number of bills to end the practice. Only one bill, in 1862, had passed, but it was never enforced. A Supreme Court decision in 1879 would make a difference. Their commission to present a memorial to Congress and the President, seeking their support against these bills was now an even more urgent responsibility than attending the suffrage convention. Thus it was particularly distressing for them to learn just after they left on their journey that the United States Supreme Court had declared the practice unconstitutional.[2]

That experience in Washington was pivotal in Emmeline's public life. She had longed to become a player in the effort to advance women's status and to defend her Church and its principles, and she was now on public record in the pursuit of those goals. Many times this commitment would take her to Washington, D.C., where she would build bridges with national women's associations and meet with congressmen, senators, and even three United States presidents. At times she may have looked back wistfully on a more measured life in the safe environment of Utah Territory, but having entered the debate, she could not turn back. That 1879 journey proved to be a deciding moment in her long life, directing its course throughout the four decades ahead of her. It was a grand adventure, taking her outside the narrow boundaries of her home territory to the national and even international stages of the movement to improve the status of women and putting her in company with many of the most illustrious women of the period. Though she shared the same indomitable spirit of the pioneer woman, who trudged the path to a new home in the west, and the hardened settler who eked out a living in an often inhospitable environment, she little resembled either one. She was no stranger to hardship, but her days were lived in a different environment, both geographically and socially just as challenging and formidable.

Her beginnings hardly foretold the life she would one day lead. She was born in humble circumstances. Petersham, a small mill village situated in the wooded hill country of central Massachusetts, was the place of her birth. The date was auspicious, February 29, 1828, a rare day auguring an exceptional life for the seventh child and fifth daughter of David and Diadama Hare Woodward. The family was proud of their Woodward progenitors who had fought in the Revolutionary War as well as the War of 1812.

When Emmeline was about five or six years old, her father died, and soon the family moved to North New Salem when their mother remarried.[3] A child of nature, Emmeline was happiest roaming the surrounding fields and hillsides of the two villages or daydreaming under the hemlock trees, whose boughs swept the banks of the stream coursing its way past her home. Her nostalgic memories of these childhood scenes produced a lifelong tie to New England. In these outdoor settings, she wrote childish verses and recited stories to her nature friends and sometimes to her schoolmates. Her enduring ambition to write poetry was kindled by the natural beauties that surrounded her in the wooded hills and open meadows of her New England home. From those early years, she entertained a sense of destiny that continually pushed her to achieve beyond the expectations of her gender, time, and place.

Her evident talent was rewarded by an education that surpassed that of most of her brothers and sisters and indeed most of her North New Salem friends. Studying first at the common schools in the towns where she lived, she was eventually enrolled at the New Salem Academy, which she attended to the age of fifteen.[4]

In 1841, while thirteen-year-old Emmeline was attending classes at the academy, where she boarded during the school term, her mother and the three younger children of the family joined the LDS Church with several other North New Salem families. This new religion had been formally established in Fayette, New York, in 1830 under the leadership of its founding prophet, Joseph Smith. A vigorous proselytizing mission of the Church sent representatives throughout the Eastern seaboard and Canada, preaching the message of the restored gospel and gathering numerous followers in their travels.

None of Emmeline's older brothers and sisters joined the Church at that time, and conversion was a difficult choice for Emmeline who, with the

Carol Cornwall Madsen

New Salem Academy, New Salem, Massachusetts. Emmeline attended several terms here until the age of fifteen.

encouragement of her friends and mentors, looked forward to a teaching and literary career in her beloved New England. Her mother's entreaties and the persuasive preaching of Mormon missionary Eli P. Maginn altered Emmeline's plans, however, and she agreed to baptism, which occurred on the day her fourteenth birthday was celebrated, March 1, 1842. When she returned to school, she suffered intense ridicule and criticism along with many appeals to abandon her new faith for the promising future that awaited her.

Later, she looked back on those difficult days:

> As soon as Mormonism began to flourish were they not harassing me on every side did they not tear me from my beloved hom[e] and the arms of a tender parent to keep me from Mormonism and then the Good Spirit interposed and provided a way for me to be released from the hands of a cruel guardian who pretended so much respect for me that he did not wish me to associate with my own mother and sister because they were Saints of the Most High God.[5]

Emmeline resisted the importuning of her well-meaning friends, and after leaving the academy, she taught school. Then at age fifteen she married James Harvey Harris on July 29, 1843.[6] The marriage had been arranged by Emmeline's mother and James's parents, Elias and Lucy Stacy Harris, also members of the LDS Church.

In late spring 1844, the young couple, along with James's parents and his brother, left Massachusetts to join the Mormons in Nauvoo, Illinois, then the Church's headquarters. Her mother and younger siblings planned to join them later.

The Church's claims to divine revelation, to newly bestowed keys of authority, and to Joseph Smith's prophetic calling, along with a new book of scripture, the Book of Mormon—the source of the sect's nickname—aroused continual distrust and antagonism by its neighbors. The fledgling church was thus constantly on the move to find a place for peaceful settlement. The expulsion of Church members from Missouri in 1838 sent them eastward across the Mississippi River to the small river town of Commerce, Illinois, which they renamed Nauvoo and to which converts to the religion began to converge in large numbers. This was the city that Emmeline anticipated being her permanent home.

However, her dreams of a tranquil life in what was rapidly becoming a thriving, beautiful city rising above a curve in the river's flow were abruptly shattered. Only six weeks after her arrival in spring 1844, Joseph Smith and his brother Hyrum were murdered in the county jail in nearby Carthage. Once again Emmeline's life was dramatically altered. Amidst the disruption that followed their deaths, her newborn son, Eugene Henri, died, Emmeline's parents-in-law left the Church, and her husband James, hoping to find work, took a steamer down the Mississippi to St. Louis, promising to send for her when he was settled. The letter never came.[7] By November 1844, at the age of sixteen, Emmeline found herself alone, distraught, and despairing of a future of any stability or happiness. But she was also determined to stay the course she had set for herself at baptism and found refuge in the home of Olive Bishop, a fellow traveler to Nauvoo.

Emmeline's education rescued her from total dependency on others. She resumed school teaching. Among her students were the children of Elizabeth Ann and Newel K. Whitney, whom she had met through Olive Bishop, a cousin of Elizabeth Ann. Newel K. Whitney was a bishop of the Church in Nauvoo, and he was well known among the Mormons. Elizabeth Ann, many years Emmeline's senior, became not only her lifelong friend and surrogate mother after Emmeline's own mother died in 1846,[8] but also her sister-wife in the bonds of polygamy.[9] Marrying Newel K. Whitney on February 14, 1845, Emmeline traveled with the Whitneys when mobs forced Mormons to leave Nauvoo the

Church Archives, The Church of Jesus Christ of Latter-day Saints
Emmeline married Nauvoo bishop Newel K. Whitney on February 14, 1845. The couple had two children, Isabel and Melvina, before Newel died in 1850.

Church Archives, The Church of Jesus Christ of Latter-day Saints

In 1852 prominent Church leader Daniel H. Wells married Emmeline, his seventh and last wife. Daniel and Emmeline had three children: Emma, Elizabeth Ann, and Louisa.

next year. The Whitneys stayed for two years in Winter Quarters (now Florence), Nebraska, a way station for Mormons moving west, and then traveled on to Utah, arriving in fall 1848. Salt Lake City, the Church's new headquarters, would become her permanent home. There she gave birth to two daughters, Isabel and Melvina, before Newel Whitney's death in 1850.

Left again to her own resources at his untimely death, she once more took up teaching to support herself and her young daughters. She was relieved of that burden two years later, in 1852, when she became the seventh wife of Daniel H. Wells, a close friend of Newel K. Whitney.[10] Three daughters were born to this union over a nine-year period: Emma, Elizabeth Ann, and Louisa. Emmeline looked forward to a comfortable life with the prominent Church leader.

The prosperous Wells, besides serving as a counselor, or assistant, to LDS Church President Brigham Young, was also at various times mayor of Salt Lake City, superintendent of public works, chancellor of the University of Deseret, and lieutenant general of the Nauvoo Legion, reorganized in Utah with its original name. His other wives shared a large home on South Temple Street in Salt Lake City known as the "big house" (referring to its size), where Wells had his residence; Emmeline and her five daughters lived in a smaller home a few blocks away. She often lamented how little she saw of her husband, filling her diaries with expressions of longing.

Initially, Daniel Wells was able to provide a comfortable living for his large family. The early years of her marriage to him brought a level of security Emmeline had not known since leaving Massachusetts. Her home was well furnished, her garden well planted, and her larder well stocked. Her attractive and popular daughters made Emmeline's home a lively center of activity for the youth of Salt Lake City. The Wasatch Literary Association, made up of the young, educated, and energetic friends of her daughter Emmie, was organized in her home and often held its meetings there.[11] Excursions to Brighton Canyon and Saltair (at the lake), along with theater parties at the Salt Lake Theater, began and ended at the Emmeline Wells residence. She entertained a host of her own friends as well, many of them of faiths other than her own. Her interest in people motivated her to cross boundaries of all sorts when making friends and building alliances.

The good years, however, slowly dissipated. Some of Daniel Wells's financial ventures began to falter, necessitating changes in his family life. Without a son to whom she could look for support, as many plural

Church Archives, The Church of Jesus Christ of Latter-day Saints
Emmeline's house (ca. 1880s) on State Street and 300 South, Salt Lake City.

wives were able to do, Emmeline increasingly came to depend on her own resources to maintain a living for herself and her daughters. Learning to become both economically and emotionally self-reliant was a painful process for her, but one she eventually mastered, especially as she turned her thoughts and energy toward a public presence in defense of her religion and support of the woman movement.

But life held challenges even more anguishing for her. The death of her daughter Emmie, the belle of the Wasatch Literary Association, at age twenty-five, was followed a decade later by the death of her youngest daughter, Louisa, at about the same age. Her daughter Melvina's divorce and remarriage to a non-Mormon added to her distress. The deaths of several young grandchildren were additional burdens she quietly carried. One contemporary noted that her sense of humor, though never evident in her writing, "preserved her reason, in the midst of crushing trials" while making her a sought-after presence in public gatherings.[12] Moreover, each new tragedy and disappointment only strengthened her New England stoicism, though her diary belied the ease of this public demeanor. She brooded quietly and privately, and few people recognized the intense grip that sorrow held on this otherwise active and tireless woman.

Emmeline Wells had earlier shown her resilience when she suffered the hostility of her friends and mentors after her baptism in North New Salem and then the tragedies and turmoil in Nauvoo. That resilience, along with an unshakable commitment to her religion and the steady pursuit of her own individual goals, helped her shape a philosophy that would provide a base for her social activism. She was blessed with an innate curiosity about life and a desire to feel the pulse of the larger world—to connect with, rather than isolate herself from, people of varied backgrounds. These attributes she put to the service of her self-appointed mission to elevate the status and opinion of Mormon women in the eyes of the world. As far as her times and opportunities allowed, she became a woman of the world, not worldly, but world-wise.

To fulfill her greater ambitions, as well as simply meet the exigencies of her personal life, she learned the value of self-reliance. Her association with the *Woman's Exponent*, the Latter-day Saint woman's newspaper established in 1872, expedited that process. Her diaries throughout the 1870s are filled with feelings of inadequacy, loneliness, and constant longing for "the shelter and protection of a strong arm." Such entries became fewer, however, after she became editor of the paper in 1877, and they disappeared altogether within a few years. Her focus began to move outward; her attention transferred from the difficulties she, as a woman, felt in her own life to the limitations most women experienced in both family and public settings. Her interest in writing and her deep concern for the condition of women found expression in the pages of the *Woman's Exponent*.

First a contributor, later associate editor, and within five years editor, Emmeline Wells, over the thirty-seven years of her editorship, spoke clearly and boldly on issues of greatest concern to her as a Latter-day Saint woman and as a woman's activist. She often declared that "she was born a woman's rights advocate, inheriting [the trait] from her mother," who realized her own pressing need for educational and economic options when she became the sole support of her children at the death of her husband.[13] Emmeline's education and her single-minded drive to achieve equipped her for the labor that her mother had once said would bring "excellence to her ambition."[14] Emmeline's dominant characteristic, one contemporary wrote, was "her supreme will." What distinguished her from her colleagues, her friend continued, was her unique way of doing things because "her ambitions were high, her purposes lofty."[15]

Emmeline's tiny frame, measuring only five feet in height and scarcely a hundred pounds, belied the dynamic personality inhabiting it. The amethyst earrings and blue tulle neck scarf she frequently wore strikingly set off her black hair and forget-me-not blue eyes. Several rings adorned her fingers, and she usually wore a pocket watch on a chain around her neck. She was described as being "exquisitely delicate and dainty, in her writing, her living, and in her life."[16] The assessment, however, was only partially correct. The fragile exterior camouflaged her "exceedingly frank" nature that often found voice in her writings, both public and private.[17] She was also credited with being "sarcastic at times, not to say caustic," but this quality was softened, most agreed, by a show of repentance afterward.[18] Her highly acclaimed memory made her a living source for facts that others had forgotten about events in the early history of the Church as well as a popular speaker and conversationalist.

The *Woman's Exponent* was a natural outlet for Emmeline's creative and intellectual talents. Chided by her daughters for working so long at the *Exponent* office one day, "as if I had to earn my living," Emmeline, then associate editor, explained that she was "anxious to acquire a thorough knowledge of an Editor's duties."[19] It would be useful information when she became editor of the paper in 1877. Eventually she acquired full control of the publication, which in time did indeed become her major source of income. Widowed for the last thirty years of her life and dependent on her own resources even earlier, she knew firsthand the impediments to women's economic independence and was grateful for the editorship as a means of financially maintaining herself.

Mormonism became a significant impetus in her drive to better the condition of women. She believed that it offered unprecedented opportunity for female public activity, initiative, and leadership, especially through the economic and welfare programs Brigham Young outlined for the Relief Society before his death in 1877.[20] Her own life and those of her co-workers in the Relief Society and woman suffrage movement, one observer wrote, gave lie to the common assertion that Mormon women, because of their "isolation [in the West] and subservience to religious authority" were "repressed in [their] abilities and privileges."[21] To those not of the culture, Mormonism appeared to be a religious order offering little to women and consigning them to a degrading marital practice. Emmeline would be among the first to challenge this appraisal, her own life providing clear evidence that she could freely express both her thoughts and talents. Indeed, she had found innumerable occasions to exercise her own judgment and decision-making capability.

Admittedly, she, like other men and women who joined the LDS Church, willingly subjected herself to a patriarchal ecclesiastical hierarchy, a governing structure in most religions; but she also recognized that the institution's theology fostered the concept of free agency and individual progression and that the law of common consent was basic to Church doctrine and administration. Brigham Young's call to women to study skills beyond housekeeping, such as accounting, telegraphy, typesetting, even medicine and law, and to obtain an education at the highest level possible, along with the vote of confidence that the 1870 enfranchisement of Utah women represented, all reinforced Emmeline's assessment of the progressive attitude of Mormonism and what that meant to women.[22]

Though expressing her views on the equal rights of women as early as 1872 in the *Woman's Exponent* and in eastern woman suffrage publications with which she corresponded, Emmeline did not take an active public role in the national suffrage movement until 1879 when a member of the NWSA invited Mormon women to attend its annual convention in Washington, D.C. Emmeline Wells and Zina Young Williams were chosen to be the representatives. From outward appearances, Emmeline made an improbable choice, her diminutive stature and quaint apparel disguising the moral courage and strength of will that lay within. But her successful bridging on that occasion of the enormous gulf of misrepresentation and false perceptions of Mormon women ensured her welcome entree to national circles thereafter. Emmeline became a frequent delegate to national suffrage conventions, serving as vice president for Utah shortly after her return from her first convention and in various other offices during the next twenty years. She was the proud owner of a gold ring given to her by the grand dame of woman suffrage, Susan B. Anthony.[23]

At the triennial meetings of the National Council of Women (NCW), organized in 1888, which the LDS Relief Society and Young Ladies' Mutual Improvement Association (MIA) formally joined in 1891, Emmeline frequently represented the Relief Society with other Utah delegates. She held office in the NCW during one period, and with her fellow Mormon delegates presented papers on the Relief Society and life in Utah at its conventions. During the Columbian Exposition at the 1893 Chicago World's Fair, the International Council of Women (ICW) sponsored a special congress of representative women from around the world. Delegates from the Relief Society and the Young

Ladies' MIA attended, and Emmeline not only delivered a paper on Utah women but also presided at one of the plenary sessions. Her drive to unite women and demolish real and imagined barriers among them found local fruition in Utah's representation at this grand international exposition. She was credited with bringing together Jewish, Gentile (in this case, a non-Mormon), and Mormon women in Utah to provide a substantial contribution to both the Utah and the Woman's Buildings.

A highlight of her national work for women was attending the quinquennial meeting of the ICW held in London in 1899. Her first and only trip abroad allowed her to satisfy her literary interests, acquire genealogical information, visit local Relief Societies and Mormon missionaries, and even travel to Paris. She was awestruck at the great historical and architectural landmarks of England, and she found her way to as many homes of her literary idols as were open to the public at that time. She was pleased that in her work as assistant recording secretary of the NCW she met delegates from all the countries represented. She also had an opportunity to respond in one of the sessions of the Woman's Congress held in conjunction with the International Council's convention.

When Utah women were given the vote in 1870, Emmeline began her political career as a franchised woman. For many years she was a member of the Territorial Central Committee for the People's Party, the local political arm of the LDS Church, and she participated in the constitutional convention of 1882. She joined the Republican Party after the local political parties were dissolved in 1891 and served on the Republican Central Committee for several years. Twice she was nominated for legislative office but, disappointingly, never held elective office. However, she remained an active lobbyist on issues affecting the women of the state.

In October 1910, Emmeline Wells, nearing her eighty-third birthday, reached another milestone in her eventful life. She was appointed the Relief Society General President. Two years earlier, during a serious illness of then-President Bathsheba W. Smith, Emmeline had discussed possible successors in a letter to Dr. Romania Pratt Penrose, a close friend and Relief Society General Board member then in England serving a mission with her husband, Charles W. Penrose. Both Emmeline's daughter Annie Wells Cannon and Romania herself had been mentioned as possibilities by Bathsheba Smith, along with Clarissa Williams and Julina Smith, two other active Relief Society workers. Emmeline did not consider herself a candidate.[24] But when the time came, after Bathsheba Smith's death on September 20, 1910, Emmeline was the one selected.

Her appointment came on Sunday, October 2, 1910, at the conclusion of a worship service in the Salt Lake Temple, when President Anthon H. Lund, counselor to Church President Joseph F. Smith, told her she had been selected by the Relief Society General Board to be the new president, their decision then confirmed by President Smith.[25] She was totally surprised, fully expecting someone younger than eighty-two years old to fill the vacancy. The appointment proved to be the capstone to her work with women. Though she constantly struggled to maintain the emphasis on simpler personal charity and spirituality that marked the Relief Society at its founding in Nauvoo, Illinois, in 1842, she found herself presiding over an institution that had grown in numbers and responsibilities and had become ripe for some standardization and centralization of its programs. Standardized lessons outlined in the new publication the *Relief Society Magazine*, first issued in 1915, and systematization of the meeting schedule to correspond with other Church auxiliaries transformed the society that began in Nauvoo and its original benevolent objectives into a professional organization with a complexity of programs, lessons, and Church service.

Emmeline's initial venture in Relief Society work began in 1876 when Brigham Young gave her charge of a grain-saving program, which she implemented through the Relief Society and articles she wrote for the *Woman's Exponent*. Speaking of this assignment some years later, she recalled that she had been seriously ill in Nauvoo, Illinois, after the birth of her son. Eliza R. Snow, who was secretary of the Nauvoo Relief Society and already a prominent Mormon woman, promised her that she would "live to do a work that has never been done by any woman, since the Creation."[26] Emmeline believed that heading the grain-saving mission was the work Eliza Snow had envisioned for her. Her modest efforts in the beginning developed into an ambitious Relief Society venture that came to characterize the charitable thrust of the organization. Storing grain to sustain the poor at home and abroad soon became the group's major relief effort. During World War I, while Emmeline presided, the Relief Society sold its stored grain, more than 200,000 bushels, to the United States government for the military. After the war, when President Woodrow Wilson and his wife visited Salt Lake City, they called on Emmeline in her apartment at the former Hotel Utah, where she was recuperating from an illness. Going directly to her bedside, President Wilson shook hands with her and expressed his personal appreciation for "turning over the stored Relief Society grain to the nation in its hour of need."[27] It was her third visit with a U.S. President, the first in her own home.

On January 12, 1914, after thirty-seven years as editor, Emmeline closed her long association with the *Woman's Exponent*. It was a wrenching moment. The paper had been a compelling part of her life. It had been her voice to the world—a channel for her thoughts, opinions, memories, and emotions. But by 1914 the paper had become an anachronism, and Emmeline had long since been unable to carry the editorial burden alone. The causes that had given it life and relevance—woman suffrage and defense of polygamy—were part of a past that had quietly slipped away, as had many of the paper's devoted contributors and readers.

With the demise of the paper, Emmeline lost a trusted friend. It had been a major tie with women whom she admired and whose life's work she fully endorsed and tried to emulate. Since she was no longer able to travel as widely as before, the loss of the *Exponent* closed the doors on an eventful and purposeful activism that so many years earlier she had mapped out for herself. It had been a bridge to a world beyond the western boundaries that had defined her life and work. Her focus would now be closer to home, her remaining energies expended to serve exclusively the needs of her Latter-day Saint sisters.

Emmeline Wells's life bridged two centuries, and her later years bore the luster of many honors. Every birthday in those years was publicly noted, drawing hundreds of well wishers. Her book of poetry, *Musings and Memories*, was published in 1896; its popularity demanded a second edition in 1915. For her, the most signal honor came in 1912 when, at age eighty-four, she was selected to receive an honorary doctor of literature from Brigham Young University. It was an event "unique in Mormon history," she noted. In her acceptance speech to the large crowd assembled in the auditorium of the Salt Lake City Bishop's building, where the ceremony was held, her advocacy for women rose to the fore. Reporting on the occasion, the *Deseret News* stated that she said such an honor meant much to her, "not only as a personal tribute, but as a matter of honor to [her] sex." The article continued by saying she had always regretted that "great educational institutions had withheld this distinction from women, and she hoped that this [event] would have its influence in showing that Utah withheld nothing from the women of the state."[28]

That same year she was honored to unveil on Temple Square in Salt Lake City the Seagull Monument, a memorial to the birds that saved the crops of the early settlers from a devastating cricket infestation. In 1915 she received a bronze medal from the Genealogical Convention at the San Francisco World's Fair in behalf of the Relief Society, which had provided support and encouragement of genealogical research.

The last year of her life was largely shadow without substance. Her enormous energy had finally begun to wane. She had presided over the Relief Society for nearly eleven years, retaining a keen mind to the end. Long absences from her duties in spring 1921, however, prompted LDS Church President Heber J. Grant to reorganize the presidency of the Relief Society at the Church's April conference. Emmeline died three weeks later. At her death, flags were flown at half-mast in Salt Lake City and her funeral was held in the Salt Lake Tabernacle, a singular honor for a woman at that time, marking the occasion a unique and remarkable tribute to a woman.[29] Remembered as "one of the finest products of 'Mormonism,'" a woman who "had the mental force which caused her to be a pillar of strength perhaps more than has been given to any other woman of her day," she was noted as being as "unyielding as the granite of her native New England in her devotion to that which she considered her duty."[30] Her delicate and dainty exterior could not disguise the complex and dynamic woman within. Emmeline Wells had been a force in dispelling prejudice against Latter-day Saint women and in supporting the movement for women's advancement politically and socially.

During her long life, Emmeline Wells knew seven LDS Church presidents, and she was the last Relief Society General President whose Mormon experience included Nauvoo and a personal acquaintance with the Prophet Joseph Smith. For more than thirty years she served Latter-day Saint women through the Relief Society, holding the position of secretary for twenty-two of those years and as president until three weeks before her death in 1921. She was instrumental in creating links of mutual respect and friendship among women of all faiths.

A woman of limitless energy and drive, Emmeline Wells firmly set the course of her public work and lived to see many of her goals fulfilled. From her obscure beginnings in central Massachusetts, she became a nationally known woman's advocate whose name was linked with some of the most prominent women of her day. Mormonism, rather than being the deterrent her mentors and classmates feared it would be, opened unimagined doors of opportunity for her interests and talents. Though her life deviated from the path she originally envisioned, she never regretted her decision to become a Latter-day Saint nor doubted the importance of her work. She once wrote that she hoped historians would "remember the women of Zion when compiling the history of this Western land."[31] Emmeline Wells's life and writings insured that they will not be forgotten.

Notes

1. "The Fortieth Volume," *Woman's Exponent* 40 (July 1911): 4.

2. An interesting and well-researched study on the legal and political struggle between the federal government and the Mormons over the practice of plural marriage is exhaustively presented in Sarah Barringer Gordon, *The Mormon Question: Polygamy and Constitutional Conflict in Nineteenth-Century America* (Chapel Hill: University of North Carolina Press, 2002).

3. Diadama's remarriage, to Samuel Clark, resulted in one child, Hiram. Emmeline, age six at the time, never mentioned her stepfather in her diaries or letters, and little genealogical information is available for him. He evidently did not migrate to Nauvoo in 1845 with Diadama and her three youngest children, including Hiram.

4. Information on the early period of her life is taken primarily from Emmeline Wells's travel journal covering her first visit back to Massachusetts (after leaving in 1844), written in December–January 1885–86, L. Tom Perry Special Collections, Harold B. Lee Library, Brigham Young University, Provo, Utah. A more complete description of her New England life is in Carol Cornwall Madsen, "Emmeline B. Wells: A Mormon Woman in Victorian America" (PhD diss., University of Utah, 1986), chapters 1 and 2.

5. Emmeline B. Wells, Diary, February 20, 1845, Perry Special Collections. Who the "cruel guardian" was is unknown, but it may have been her stepfather, who did not join the LDS Church.

6. While marrying at such an early age was uncommon, it was not unheard of during this period. Arranging the marriage and removal to Nauvoo may have been Diadama's way of insuring that her precocious daughter would not be persuaded to leave her new religion.

7. Emmeline learned the following March that James had gone to sea. Wells, Diary, March 24, 1845. In 1859 James died at sea near Bombay, India.

8. Diadama Hare Woodward Clark, Emmeline's mother, and her younger sisters Maria and Ellen and brother Hiram, reached Nauvoo in 1845. Unable to leave Nauvoo in the earlier migrations, Diadama and her children were forced to leave Nauvoo in fall 1846 with the other remaining Church members. Diadama took ill and died in Iowa. The children were separated and traveled west with different families, although Hiram accompanied Emmeline with the Whitney family.

9. Very few members of the LDS Church had been introduced to the practice of polygamy during the brief period the Church was headquartered in Nauvoo. Family lore suggests that Emmeline believed at the outset that she was merely being adopted into the Whitney family, being thirty-three years Newel K. Whitney's junior. No issue of her marriage to Whitney occurred until November 1848, more than a year after James Harris's three-year absence, a period required before Massachusetts's law declared a spouse's absence was permanent.

10. Daniel H. Wells left a wife and son behind when he migrated to Utah. They had chosen not to join the Church nor to go west with him. Daniel and his first wife did not divorce until many years later. Emmeline is often referred to as Daniel's sixth and last wife, but in reality she was the seventh.

11. For more information on the Wasatch Literary Association, see Ronald W. Walker, "Growing up in Early Utah: The Wasatch Literary Association, 1874–1878," in *Qualities that Count: Heber J. Grant as Businessman, Missionary, and Apostle* (Provo, Utah: Brigham Young University Press, 2004), 61–79.

12. Susa Young Gates, "Emmeline B. Wells," in *History of the Young Ladies' Mutual Improvement Association* (Salt Lake City: Deseret News, 1911), 53.

13. "Aunt Em," *Young Woman's Journal* 26 (March 1, 1915): 141.

14. "The Old Garrett," *Woman's Exponent* 17 (October 1, 1888): 67.

15. Susa Young Gates, "President Emmeline B. Wells," *Improvement Era* 24 (June 1921): 719.

16. Gates, "Emmeline B. Wells," 53.

17. Augusta Joyce Crocheron, *Representative Women of Deseret: A Book of Biographical Sketches* (Salt Lake City: J. C. Graham, 1884), 67.

18. Gates, "Emmeline B. Wells," 53.

19. Wells, Diary, March 24, 1875.

20. For a full discussion of these activities, see Leonard J. Arrington, "The Economic Role of Pioneer Mormon Women," *Western Humanities Review* (Spring 1955): 145–64; see also Janath Russell Cannon, Jill Mulvay Derr, and Maureen Ursenbach Beecher, *Women of Covenant: The Story of Relief Society* (Salt Lake City: Deseret Book, 1993), 83–126.

21. Crocheron, *Women of Deseret*, 69.

22. See, for example, Brigham Young's statements in *Journal of Discourses*, 26 vols. (Liverpool, Eng.: F. D. Richards, 1855–86), 16:16 (April 7, 1873); 13:61 (July 18, 1869); 12:406–7 (April 8, 1867). See also *Millennial Star* 31 (April 24, 1869): 269; and Jill Mulvay Derr, "Woman's Place in Brigham Young's World," *BYU Studies* 18, no. 3 (1978): 377–95.

23. "Aunt Em," *Young Woman's Journal* 26 (March 1, 1915): 141; Ruth May Fox, "Emmeline B. Wells: A Tribute," *Young Woman's Journal* 32 (June 1921): 344–46.

24. Emmeline B. Wells to Romania Pratt Penrose, March 15, 1908, Emmeline B. Wells Papers, Church Archives, The Church of Jesus Christ of Latter-day Saints, Salt Lake City.

25. Wells, Diary, October 2, 1910.

26. Emmeline B. Wells, "The Mission of Saving Grain," *Relief Society Magazine* 2 (February 1915): 47–49.

27. "President and Mrs. Wilson Make Informal Call on Aged Leader, 'Aunt Em' Wells," *Deseret Evening News*, September 24, 1919.

28. The idea for this honor came from a number of "leading ladies of the city" from several different organizations. Their proposal was referred to BYU, which conferred the honor on her eighty-fourth birthday. Church Board of Education Minute Book, 1903–1918, February 1912, Church Archives. For a full account of the proceedings see "Emmeline B. Wells, Lit.D.," *Woman's Exponent* 40 (March 1912): 50–51, 54–55. The event was also noted in "Many Tributes to Mrs. E. B. Wells," *Deseret News*, March 1, 1912, 1; and "Emmeline B. Wells, Lit. D.," *Deseret News*, March 2, 1912, 5.

29. There were numerous accounts of her death, some of which are "Flags on Church Edifices at Half Mast in Honor of Mrs. Emmeline B. Wells," *Deseret News,* April 25, 1921, 2; "Life of Emmeline B. Wells Comes Peacefully to a Close," *Deseret News,* April 25, 1921, 1; "Emmeline B. Wells," and "Early Settler of State Dead," *Salt Lake Tribune,* April 26, 1921, 6, 20. Her death also was noted in the *New York Times*, April 27, 1921, 17.

30. "Glowing Tributes Paid at Bier of Beloved Woman," *Deseret News*, April 30, 1921, 10; "Mrs. Emmeline B. Wells," *Deseret News*, April 25, 1921, 4.

31. "Fortieth Volume," 4.

Chapter 3

"Remember the Women of Zion," the *Woman's Exponent*

Believe me ever ready to add all in my power in literary work for the advancement and culture of our people.[1]

From the time she first learned, as a child, that women could put their thoughts on paper, Emmeline Wells was destined to become a writer. Though she favored poetry and short fictional pieces as literary forms most compatible with her nature, life led her into a literary medium she could hardly have imagined adopting when she was just a child in her native New England. As an adult, she came to realize that the editorials and articles she wrote for more than forty years had an impact that few poets realize from verse. The demands of her journalism career, however, did not eliminate either her poetry or fiction writing. Moreover, all three mediums fully disclosed her wide range of interests and emotions. Emmeline expressed her opinions passionately and unequivocally in her editorials. As a foremost Latter-day Saint exponent of the woman movement, she brought the issues of debate clearly before her readers and unhesitatingly advocated more equitable relationships in marriage and in society as well as wider opportunities for women. Her life experiences gave force and validity to her claims in behalf of women.

When Emmeline Wells turned to fiction, she imitated the domestic novels popular in her day and also adopted the didactic mode of

Mormon "home literature."[2] The plot components, however, came from her own life: commitments that followed religious conversion; tragedies that threw women upon their own resources; letters that were miscarried or lost; misguided trust; and joy of genuine love. Like many women of her time, she favored poetry as the best literary medium to express the emotional quality of her experiences. From the evocations of her early life in Massachusetts to her reflections on lost loves and soulful memories, her poetry profiled her most deeply personal life. In all her literary efforts, Emmeline looked inward and wrote from what she found there.

As a female writer, Emmeline lived at a fortuitous time. For centuries writing had been a means of private self-definition for literate women and a way for them to relate to a world that had kept them at its margins. Their writings, personal and seldom published, were evidence of an inner life that had little opportunity for public expression. By the nineteenth century, however, women's writings were not only widely accepted, but their lives had moved from the periphery of social experience. As one examines Emmeline's life and prodigious literary outpourings, the boundaries of life and literature blur.

Her poetry was collected into a volume that was published in 1896 as *Musings and Memories*.[3] An expanded edition appeared in 1915. Her short stories, much to her disappointment, were never compiled and found occasional exposure only through the pages of the *Woman's Exponent* and several publications of the LDS Church. But for thirty-seven years the editorials she wrote for the *Woman's Exponent* appealed to an audience in numbers that neither her poetry nor her fiction could have ever matched. The *Exponent* gave Emmeline a public voice that opened a way of life for her that consumed nearly half a century of public activity.

The extent of the paper's influence cannot be measured by its subscription lists or revenues, which barely sustained the paper and its editor. The news of Mormon women, their defense of their religion, and the conversation they maintained with the women's issues of their day traveled far. The *Exponent* was carried to places and to people far beyond the boundaries of the Great Basin through a policy of exchange among national and regional publications. Editors borrowed freely from one another's columns, and *Woman's Exponent* articles and writers found their way into other journals and newspapers, particularly women's periodicals. The *Exponent* soon claimed a place for itself within the network of women's journalism.

When the first issue of the *Woman's Exponent* appeared, on June 1, 1872, women had already secured a firm place for themselves in the world of journalism. Many were on staff with major newspapers throughout the country, while others managed their own publications. Like numerous papers, the *Exponent* aspired to be more than a local newsletter and to publish more than traditional "womanly" topics or LDS Church news. Two months before its first edition was issued, the *Exponent* established its course: "As [the women of Utah] have long exercised the right to think and act for themselves, so they now claim the right to speak for themselves through the potent medium of the types."[4] And speak they did. By 1872 the public and federal outcry against polygamy included a barrage of ridicule, disparagement, and intolerance toward Mormon women by lecturers, novelists, clergymen, and national women's moral reform associations. A publication of their own provided a forum for Mormon women to respond.[5]

Before 1872, Mormon women had explained themselves and their views primarily in the columns of local newspapers. One of the earliest instances was a long poem by Eliza R. Snow, a highly regarded Latter-day Saint poet, printed, in 1852, in the *Deseret News*.[6] The poem was a strong denunciation of the budding woman's rights movement and reflected the newspaper and community's general position on the subject.

Poetry, however, was not the medium favored by the emerging contingent of women activists. As they gained popularity on the lecture circuit and editorialized in their own publications, these articulate and educated exponents of woman's rights borrowed the medium of the essay for their writings. In asserting their own voice and perspectives in a form traditionally dominated by men, women affirmed the validity of their own experience as well as their authority to offer commentary on the human condition. Most of their essays, particularly those on the

Woman's Exponent.

VOL. I.   SALT LAKE CITY, UTAH, JUNE 1, 1872.   No. 1.

NEWS AND VIEWS.

Women are now admitted to fifty American colleges.

Rev. De Witt Talmage is pronounced a success as a sensation preacher.

Theodore Tilton says the best brains in northern New York are wearing white hats. They might wear chapeaux of a more objectionable color.

Daniel W. Voorhees in one day destroyed the political record of a life-time, and that was when he became henchman to a judge with an ecclesiastical mission.

An Alabama editor writes "United State," and refuses to write "United States"—a straw to show how Southern sentiment runs. What a state he must be in?

The season of scattering intellectual filth has set in over the country. It occurs quadrennially in the United States, commencing a few months before the Presidentist election.

Dr. Newman failed to become a Bishop at the Methodist General Conference, and Dr. Newman mourns this second great defeat. He has remembrances of Salt Lake in connection with the previous one.

Great outcry is raised against the much marrying of the Latter-day Saints. The tendency of the age is to disregard marriage altogether, but there seems no indication of a desire to have the race die out.

The "Alabama" muddle like "confusion worse confounded" becomes worse mixed the more it is stirred. It stretches itself over the path of time, and "like a wounded snake drags its slow length along." The country has become heartily sick of it.

Some Eastern journals head their Utah news with "Deseret." With keen appreciation of the coming and inevitable, they accept the mellifluous name chosen for the region wrested by that industry which "the honey bee" represents, from the barren wilds of nature.

George Francis Train sends us a bundle of Train Ligues. The compliment is appreciated, but the act is like sweetness wasted. We can vote, but not for "the next President of America." Utah has not become Deseret yet, nor can it participate in President making.

The last week of May, 1872, will be memorable in American annals as the first time since the first ordinance of secession was passed in the South, that both houses of Congress had their full list of members. Statesmanship can retain a complete Federal legislature, but the article has grown somewhat scarce.

To pardon the worst class of criminals on condition that they emigrate to the United States, is growing in favor with European monarchies. Germany and Greece so far have done the largest business in this line, the latest batch of villains thus disposed of being the Marathon murderers from Greece. Orders have been forwarded by President Grant to New Orleans, to which port it is understood they have been sent, to prevent their landing. They should be captured, ironed, returned to Athens with Uncle Samuel's compliments, and a bill for direct and "consequential" damages presented.

News comes from France that trailing dresses for street wear are going out of fashion. So many absurd and ridiculous fashions come from Paris that the wonder is thinking American women do not, with honest republican spirit, reject them entirely. This latter one, however, is so sensible that its immediate adoption will be an evidence of good sense wisely directed.

The anti-Mormon bill of Judge Bingham seems to have fared no better in the judiciary committee of the House of Representatives than the one to which Mr. Voorhees stood sponsor. It is gratifying to think that a majority of that committee yet respect the antiquated and once revered instrument still occasionally referred to as the Constitution.

Rev. James Freeman Clark claims "that if it is an advantage to vote, women ought to have it; if a disadvantage men ought not to be obliged to bear it alone." Speaking from experience we feel safe in affirming that the Rev. gentleman is right, and we hope for a time when this immunity may be universally enjoyed by our pure-minded and light-loving sisters. We don't presume that those belonging to the opposite class care anything about it.

Mrs. Carrie F. Young, editor of the "Pacific Journal of Health," has been lecturing in Idaho on Temperance and Woman Suffrage. The editor of the "Idaho World" was not present, but did not regret his absence. He says, "We feel a most decided repugnance to the exhibition of a woman upon the rostrum, advocating such degrading theories as 'woman suffrage' and other cognate subjects." He omits to state whether "Temperance" is one of the "degrading theories" to which he refers.

Force is ever the argument of a bad cause. The principles which cannot be overcome except by the exercise of physical power, present a front that arrests the attention of thinking minds. Where argument fails and force is employed to overcome an opponent, the power of the principles to which opposition is made is admitted. Will those who urge repressive legislation against the people of Utah think of it? Witness the Voorhees bill as an illustration.

A notable event, as a result of the late terrible Franco-German war, is the opening of the German University in Strasbourg, which takes place June 1st—to-day. That famous city on the Rhine, after a siege memorable in the annals of warfare, passed into the hands of the Germans, and now they take the surest means to permanently consolidate their power, by establishing there one of those seats of learning for which Germany has become enviably famous.

Miss Susan B. Anthony, it is said, declared before the Cincinnati Convention met, that if it gave her cause "the cold shoulder," she would go to Philadelphia and pledge the ballots of the women of America to U. S. Grant. As the women of America are yet without ballots, and as it is very questionable, if they had them, whether they would authorize any single individual to pledge them for any candidate, the supposition is fair that Miss Anthony possesses too much good sense to have made any such declaration.

Rev. Mr. Peirce, a Methodist clergyman who has made Salt Lake his headquarters for some time, in lecturing east proposed the extinction of polygamy by the introduction here of vast quantities of expensive millinery goods, and by inducing "Gentile" women to dress in gorgeous style that "Mormon" women might imitate them and run up such heavy dry goods bills that it would be impossible for a man to support more than one wife, if even one. Mr. Peirce, no doubt, preaches modesty and humility occasionally, by way of variety ; now he recommends the encouragement of pride, vanity and extravagance to accomplish his "Christian" designs. The course he advises has been largely followed in many places, has tenanted brothels, aided to fill prisons, broken up families, hurled women of reputation and position down to degradation and infamy, and has met heavy denunciation from inspired men whom Mr. Peirce professes to revere. He would steal the livery of evil to serve religion in. There is not much of this reverend gentleman, and what little there is must be either very silly or very wicked.

The editor of "The Present Age" has been to a church and heard an orthodox sermon, in which the preacher took occasion to say that all religions "isms," including Mohammedanism, Mormonism and Spiritualism, rested their claims for being true "upon miracles." The "Age" is a Spiritualist and denies that his "ism" basis its claims to be true upon miracles. Latter-day Saints deny that Mormonism basis any claim for credence in it on miracles; the reverse is the truth. The "Age" defines a miracle to be "the setting aside for the time being of a natural law to meet an unexpected emergency." Had he said a miracle was the bringing into operation of certain natural laws not generally understood or comprehended, he would have been nearer correct. When somebody can tell how a natural law may be or can be set aside, except by the operation of some other natural law, his definition, which is the generally received one, may be entitled to more consideration. We imagine the working of the overland telegraph is as great a miracle to the Cheyenne Indians as any recorded miracle that the "Age" or the orthodox minister can quote.

Mrs. Laura De Force Gordon attended the Cincinnati Convention and claimed a seat as a delegate from California. Her claim was treated with hisses and laughter. She took a position in front of the stand and endeavored to speak, but her voice was drowned by a tumultuous discord. Her persistence in seeking to address an assemblage that treated her claim in such a manner was undignified; while the action of the Convention in receiving her with hisses and uproarious laughter, was disgraceful. The Liberal Republicans assembled in Cincinnati for a general work of purification and reform, evidently stood greatly in need of general reform themselves, in the matter of manners as well as in politics. Mrs. Gordon was as much entitled to a seat in that Convention as Carl Schurz himself, for we have yet to learn that the call for it specified that "male" Republicans only were admissible.

A new periodical in London is called "The Ladies."

First issue of the *Woman's Exponent.*

life of women, engaged the reader in a conversation on the social status of women that initiated responses beyond their printed boundaries.[7]

As the woman movement gained strength after the Civil War and numbers of women's newspapers began publishing, numerous Utah women subscribed to them, especially woman suffrage papers such as the short-lived *Revolution* and the long-lasting Boston *Woman's Journal*.[8] Contributions by enfranchised Mormon women on the subject of woman suffrage were welcomed. Besides Emmeline Wells, other Utah women—such as Mary, Annie, and Charlotte Godbe; Bathsheba W. Smith; and Sarah M. Kimball—are known to have corresponded with national papers during this period. Their comments ranged from the success of woman suffrage in Utah to the defense of plural marriage, a juxtaposing of seemingly contradictory social practices that baffled most Americans at the time. Utah newspapers also published women's literary submissions.[9] The poetry submitted to the *Salt Lake Herald* by Louisa (Lula) Greene, a young student from Smithfield, Utah, brought her the first editorship of the *Woman's Exponent*.[10] After 1872 the *Exponent* became the publisher of choice for Latter-day Saint women writers.[11] From its beginning, it served as an effective and long-lasting public voice of Mormon women.

Though the *Exponent's* first editorial naïvely absolved the paper from needing to contend against male privilege, champion any causes, or embroil itself in the woman suffrage question, since Utah women had been enfranchised for two years,[12] it turned out to be a major voice for woman's rights through the strong advocacy of its editors and many of its writers. Its first issue, in fact, included an article urging equal pay for men and women and supporting other economic and social reforms. This article was signed "E," which could well have been Emmeline Wells's early signature for her maiden journalistic effort. Five years and many women's rights articles later, the paper proudly noted that "Mormon women lead the van in the questions which are being agitated among the sex, whatever the world may think to the contrary."[13] The *Exponent* was not going to be a neutral voice.

Moreover, the *Exponent* became an assertive champion of the religious practices of Latter-day Saint women, especially plural marriage, which, the authors argued, was a fundamental woman's right.[14] The paper's aggressive policy did not begin when Emmeline Wells became editor in 1877; her predecessor, Louisa Greene, was equally forceful. But Emmeline augmented both the number and range of arguments on women's issues, combining ardent journalism with vigorous action.

While entertaining a variety of opinions on the woman question and balancing the *Exponent's* perspective between traditional and liberal ideas about women, Emmeline consistently kept its pages closed to those "who railed against principles honestly entertained by a whole community."[15] Differing viewpoints did not include antipolygamy sentiments.

Although the *Exponent* carried fiction, poetry, household advice, and reports of LDS Church activities, especially those of organizations headed by women,[16] the paper's reports of women's achievements throughout the world, its editorial content, and its advocacy of woman's advancement place it among woman suffrage publications. Over its forty-two-year history, nearly a third of its editorials spoke directly to issues of the movement, an even larger percentage if polygamy and its relevance to women's vote are included.[17] At its advent in 1872, it joined four other woman suffrage publications: the long-lived and similar *Woman's Journal* (1870–1914) of Boston; *Woodhull and Claflin's Weekly* (1870–76) of New York; the *Pioneer* (1854–55) of San Francisco (the first woman suffrage paper in the west); and the *New Northwest* (1871–87) of Portland.[18] These periodicals followed the lead set by the *Lily* (1849–56), a temperance paper that shifted to women's rights, and the *Una* (1853–77), which began and remained solely a woman's rights paper.[19]

Between 1870 and 1890, more than thirty-three suffrage papers supported the movement at one time or another. The *Revolution* (1868–70), the controversial organ of the National Woman Suffrage Association (NWSA), edited by Elizabeth Cady Stanton and Susan B. Anthony, was one of them and found a place in the home of several Latter-day Saint women, as other publications likely did as well. The editors of the *Woman's Exponent* included many articles and notices from these papers so that Mormon women who subscribed to the *Exponent* were fully informed on current issues relating to the woman question. Mormon women were thus not isolated from the movement that claimed the whole-hearted attention of many of them. Though the *Exponent* persisted for forty-two years, most of the other suffrage publications were fairly short-lived, and only a few remained after 1917. At that time, the mainstream press, rather belatedly, finally accepted the woman suffrage crusade as newsworthy. The alternative press had successfully served its mission.[20]

Ironically, the *Woman's Exponent* was not the brainchild of a woman. Edward L. Sloan, founder and editor of the *Salt Lake Herald* in 1870, both originated and named the journal just a year later.[21] The unenthusiastic response of his partner, W. C. Dunbar, to his suggestion of a woman's column in the *Herald* led Sloan to propose a separate woman's journal. Several other factors may have influenced his decision. As an editor, he was well aware of the popularity of the women's magazines and journals then circulating. A journal specifically for Mormon women was a timely journalistic move. Also, he was likely impressed, as were many others, by the effective public rally of Mormon women in 1870 against a very stringent antipolygamy bill that had nearly passed Congress shortly before.

The rally brought unexpected accolades to the women not only from local but also from New York papers for their "logic and rhetoric."[22] Passage of a woman suffrage bill by the

Church Archives, The Church of Jesus Christ of Latter-day Saints
Edward L. Sloan (ca. 1870s), editor and journalist, founded the *Woman's Exponent*.

Utah Territorial Legislature a month after the 1870 rally has been attributed to the effective presentation of the women. Sloan learned from this public demonstration and subsequent local rallies that Mormon women were articulate and persuasive in their own defense. Moreover, with their recent enfranchisement, Mormon women had become highly visible, particularly to Eastern suffragists. A forum to address these issues from their own perspective seemed propitious.

Additionally, Sloan may have wished to counter the influence of the Godbeites, especially Mary, Annie, and Charlotte Godbe, plural wives of William Godbe, founder in 1869 of a schismatic faction known as the New Movement.[23] These Mormon dissidents were ardent supporters of woman suffrage, and the three Godbe women were the first Utah women to connect with national suffrage leaders. Though originally supportive of woman suffrage, the movement soon disassociated itself with plural marriage and the leadership of Brigham Young and thus did not represent mainstream Mormonism.[24] Before Latter-day Saint women became members of the National Woman Suffrage Association, all three of the Godbes had at one time or another served as officers, and Charlotte, in particular, lectured in the East, submitting letters to the influential *Woman's Journal*, ostensibly as a representative of Mormon women. A publication of its own would enable the mainstream Latter-day Saint voice to be heard in a sympathetic medium.

Only months before the *Exponent* was first issued, the furor surrounding the 1872 attempt at statehood pitted local Mormon and non-Mormon women against each other for the first time in a petition campaign.[25] This fracas may well have prompted Sloan and his newly appointed *Exponent* editor to absolve their fledgling paper from engaging in controversy. However, before long, the *Exponent* was drawn into the debate on suffrage, polygamy, and statehood, and it became an influential voice and tool in ensuing confrontations.

Sloan's choice for editor, Lula Greene (Richards) took on the responsibility of the newspaper only after receiving sanction from Eliza R. Snow, leader of the LDS Relief Society, and endorsement from Brigham Young. Though she served only five years as editor, Greene set the paper's tone, direction, and policy, which varied little over the next forty-two years.[26] Though it enjoyed support from Church leaders, the paper was produced independently, sustained only by its subscriptions and, at various times, by a few advertisements.

Church President Brigham Young continually advised the sisters to subscribe, and Elder George A. Smith, in a conference address, encouraged the elders, bishops, and presiding officers of the Church to "return home, setting the example themselves, to solicit all the brethren, and especially the sisters, to become subscribers of the little sheet."[27] Issued semimonthly for the first twenty volumes and less frequently during its remaining years (undoubtedly because of the editor's numerous other activities), the *Exponent* did not claim many more than three thousand subscribers, though it circulated more widely. With a loyal but small band of literary contributors, it depended on its editors and reprints from other journals, letters from readers, and reports from Latter-day Saint auxiliaries headed by women: Relief Society, Young Ladies' Mutual Improvement Association, and the Primary Association to fill its pages.

When the new publication was announced in 1872, the two-year-old *Salt Lake Tribune* sneered at its prospects, wondering what kind of "woman character" the *Exponent* would possess. The *Tribune* assumed that this new women's publication would "be like Utah female suffrage—another polygamic institution."[28] After the *Exponent*'s first issue appeared, however, the *Tribune* conceded, declaring it to be "the greatest stride the Mormons have yet made in literature, being well edited and quite newsy."[29] Other newspapers also responded to the *Exponent*'s first issue, most of them with words of praise and encouragement.[30]

A decade later, Edward Tullidge, editor of a local publication, *Tullidge's Quarterly Magazine,* gave his own assessment of the *Exponent*. He explained that despite a few early favorable notices the *Woman's Exponent* did not evoke much widespread attention at the outset. In fact, he reported, "it was treated by some of the kindliest disposed brethren as a woman's whim—harmless to be sure, and therefore to be tolerated for 'their' dear sakes." Not so today, the column announced. Representing the political interest of "fifty thousand women at home, . . . it wields more real power in our politics than all the newspapers in

Utah put together." Moreover, the article enthusiastically added, as the "*authorized* exponent of the enfranchised women of Utah . . . it can call a million women of America to the help of its cause."[31] What a different story would have followed had it reached the number Tullidge so ebulliently declared!

Though functioning without a full complement of editors and reporters, the *Exponent* had the support of a business manager (Cornelia H. Horne), a standing Committee of Consultation, and a secretary. Eliza R. Snow, chief among the "leading sisters" of the Mormon community, presided over the thirteen-member committee. The committee appointed several correspondents and nine local agents or saleswomen under the direction of a general agent, Willmirth East. Though the *Exponent* seldom referred to actions of the committee, except for occasional notices to the sales agents, the committee "fulfilled President Brigham Young's counsel in relation to pursuits and employment of women," encouraging and training women in typesetting skills.[32]

In the November 1875 issue, Cornelia Horne's name was dropped as business manager and the name of Emmeline B. Wells appeared as associate editor. Emmeline was a propitious addition to the paper. She was forty-seven years old and had a cosmopolitan outlook. Her family was largely grown, and she was dedicated to making the *Exponent* a creditable newspaper. She clearly saw its usefulness in presenting Mormon women in a favorable setting as well as facilitating a direct connection between herself, as an editor and a western advocate for women's rights, and national women's leaders. Two years later, Emmeline assumed full editorship and in time became publisher, business manager, and owner. She remained as editor until cessation of the paper thirty-seven years later.

Aside from what was evidently a brief assignment for the Committee on Consultation, a record of whose duties has not been preserved, and the loosely associated group of sales agents and correspondents, the editors did not have the benefit of a regular working staff. All the editorials, many of the articles, most of the biographical sketches, and even some of the poetry and fiction were written by the editors themselves. Reader contributions were also a regular feature since editors constantly encouraged their readers to submit their thoughts in writing to develop their own literary skills and to make the paper truly representative.

In addition, with only occasional help, the editors handled the financial accounts, the correspondence, and the mailing.[33] "I never supposed when I commenced working on the paper," Wells confided to her diary in 1878, "that I should have to do everything for myself. I feel sometimes my burden is heavy."[34] Her full entry for March 28, 1881, was "Work! Work!" Her frequent protestations at having more than her share of work to do on the *Exponent* indicate the burden of editing and publishing the paper largely alone and the dedication necessary to keep it going.[35]

The overall appearance of the eight-page, folio-sized newspaper never quite satisfied its new editor. "It is not at all pretty," Emmeline admitted to her readers in 1879, "but remember," she added, "its dress is home manufacture."[36] Later, she hoped to redesign it as a journal suitable "for a lady's parlor or drawing room table," perhaps in the fashion of the popular annuals and gift books, although its contents hardly fit the scope of these "'ladies'" publications.[37] At the very least, her intent was to make it attractive to readers by giving it the "form and keeping of a magazine of literature."[38] Except for the addition of photos in its later years and some

Courtesy Lurene Gates Wilkinson

Susa Young Gates, founding editor of the *Young Woman's Journal,* developed a close relationship with Emmeline Wells. Gates and Wells represented Mormon women through their work with the National and International Councils of Women. Photo by Charles R. Savage, ca. 1875.

changes in its type, the *Exponent* remained consistent in appearance for its forty-two years.

Shouldering the editorial task alone until the last few years when her daughter Annie Wells Cannon assisted her, Emmeline Wells also served as sole proprietor and publisher. The *Exponent* became her public voice and her possession, as much a part of her life as her family. An offer in 1888 by the much younger Susa Young Gates to serve as an associate editor, willing to make numerous "possible improvements" relating to the "paper, cover, size & etc," and even to invest her own money in the enterprise, was soundly rejected.[39] Susa Gates went on to become the founding editor of the *Young Woman's Journal* the following year, but no rivalry seemed to exist between the two publications. Each one addressed a different audience. The two women became co-workers some years later in their support of Latter-day Saint membership in the National and International Councils of Women. It was Susa Gates who became editor of the *Relief Society Magazine* in 1915, when Emmeline's offer to give the *Exponent* to the Relief Society as its official organ was declined.[40]

Between 1872 and 1909, headquarters for the *Exponent* moved eight times before coming to rest in the newly constructed Bishop's Building, east of Temple Square in Salt Lake City, designed to house the offices of the woman-led organizations of the Church along with the Presiding Bishopric.[41] Heretofore, without headquarters of their own, the general officers of the women's organizations had used the *Exponent* office for their meetings, eventually helping with the paper's expenses by paying Emmeline rent for use of her office.[42] Her office also served as an informal gathering place where women expressed their private reactions to the volatile events of their time.

The Wells diary is filled with allusions to the numerous visitors who dropped by to talk, visitors who sometimes became an annoyance because of their interference with Emmeline's busy workdays. She seldom recorded the discussions in her diary, though occasionally noted the topic. Neither did Emmeline report these discussions in the pages of the *Exponent*, but they enabled her to take the pulse of women's ideas and responses to the events circling about them and undoubtedly influenced the contents of the paper.

During one brief period, the *Exponent* had its office in the Salt Lake Council House, sharing space with the territorial legislature and classes of the University of Deseret. The building also provided meeting space for several other religious and civic associations. Though it was a desirable location, putting the *Exponent* office in the mainstream of major civic and religious activity, the paper suffered disastrous losses while there. In January 1883 the building's water pipes burst, destroying much of the furniture as well as books and papers in the *Exponent* office. A few months later the water damage was repaired and new furnishings installed, but in June of that same year a fire broke out that destroyed the Council House and everything in the *Exponent* office: correspondence, account books, past issues, and all the business papers. Only the desk escaped irreparable damage. The material loss was valued at more than $300, but money could not replace the historical value of the lost items.[43]

Throughout its history, the *Exponent* attempted to fulfill its self-defined mission "to inculcate correct principles," and enable women "to help each other by the diffusion of knowledge and information."[44] It also promised to speak freely on every topic of interest to both the women of Utah and women the world over.[45] Emmeline Wells recognized that the pen in the hands of women, addressing literally thousands at once, could forward as well as record "the work of reformation" in which she was so fervently engaged. Women's papers, she believed, were essential features of the progressive elements of the nineteenth century. She was strongly committed to engaging the *Exponent* in that march of progress.

While the *Exponent* shared many features of other suffrage papers, such as format, uncertainties of funding, and limited circulation, it also differed from them in fundamental ways. The *Exponent*, as Emmeline fervently explained in an early editorial, was "actuated by the spirit of a religion embodying all the grandest and holiest principles that have ever been revealed from heaven."[46] Her fusion of the secular and the spiritual reflected the same linkage in Latter-day Saint doctrine. Providential history, or belief in the overruling presence of God in human affairs, informed the Latter-day Saint worldview in which the temporal and eternal are inescapably intertwined. Many Mormon women, like Emmeline, felt that the goals of the woman movement corresponded with ideals and elements of Church doctrine that gave women an enlarged temporal sphere and an essential role in salvation.[47] The nineteenth century, in Emmeline's words, was a long awaited "woman's era" by divine design. The *Exponent,* under the Wells editorship, reflected that philosophy. Moreover, unlike most other suffrage papers, the *Exponent* was supported by the men of its community and was regularly quoted and noted by other local newspapers. While the paper was exhortative and opinion making, it spoke to a largely sympathetic local audience even as it reached attentive readers beyond Utah's boundaries.

Nonetheless, despite local support from influential Church leaders, its circulation remained small. In her persistent drive to expand readership, Wells often reminded her subscribers how much the "little paper" facilitated the progress of woman's work in Utah, providing a channel of communication with one another and with other women of the world.[48] By subscribing, Relief Society General President and loyal supporter Zina D. H. Young added, "women could be posted upon the condition, growth, and progress of the various woman's organizations in Zion and elsewhere" and could be alerted to the great efforts expended for the "uplifting and advancement of all womankind." Furthermore, Emmeline noted, the paper's purpose was not simply to report. The *Exponent* always stood ready to advocate the woman's side of all "vexed questions," notably

Church Archives, The Church of Jesus Christ of Latter-day Saints

Zina D. H. Young, Relief Society General President (1888–1901), helped solicit subscribers to the *Woman's Exponent.*

suffrage, education, marriage, and other points of discussion included in the "woman question."[49]

Emmeline also reminded her readers of the good the paper did for them beyond Utah's borders. Not only was it the "champion of the suffrage cause," Emmeline wrote, but "by exchanging with women's papers of the United States and England it brought news of women in all parts of the world to those of Utah."[50] It had been "instrumental in removing much of the prejudice which has existed in regard to the condition of women in this Church," she editorialized in 1880. Yet she felt it remained unappreciated. "The prestige the *Exponent* has given the women of the Church in the outside world is little realized," she lamented in 1896.[51] She reminded readers that on several different occasions a set of the *Woman's Exponent* had been requested for display at national and international conferences, including the Columbian Exposition at the Chicago World's Fair in 1893, the Peace Conference at The Hague in 1898, and the World Exposition in Paris in 1900.[52] The urgency of Emmeline's appeal in this editorial was clearly symptomatic of her need to feel that her efforts in behalf of women were succeeding at home as well as abroad.

While the two standards it carried on its masthead for most of its forty-two-year history focused on woman's rights and linked it to other woman's rights papers, the *Woman's Exponent* served a multifaceted mission to meet the specific journalistic needs of its readership.[53] While it provided a medium for Mormon women to refute the diatribes against them, it also presented their views on all aspects of the woman question, published reports of their organizations and clubs, and offered descriptions of social and cultural events. Less often it addressed domestic issues, such as child-rearing and household efficiency.

Initially, during the period of antipolygamy agitation, many columns of the paper were devoted to defense of the practice. Although the primary justification for plural marriage was obedience to God's will, Latter-day Saints debated the question on the moral and social grounds argued by their detractors. Mormon women also explained the personal benefits of the practice and defended the irreproachable character of its adherents. One advantage, Emmeline explained, was that polygamy advanced woman's status by making her less subordinate and more independent than monogamy, with more opportunity for personal development and a share in the world's work.[54] It fostered personal qualities such as patience, generosity, tolerance, and sororal affection, she claimed. Significantly, she argued, it had the potential to eradicate the detested double moral standard and give more women a chance at marriage and motherhood with honorable men.[55] In other words, she maintained, it promoted Christian virtues and the qualities of selfless womanhood.[56]

Individual testimonials of these benefits filled the pages of the *Exponent* before polygamy was terminated in 1890, and *Exponent* writers turned to other topics. The antipolygamy movement had prompted a "circling of the wagons," a closing in to meet the attack, sometimes with defiance, other times with appeals for understanding, and finally, in the face of defeat, with resignation. Through it all, the pen had been the women's most forceful defense.

Because the movement to repeal woman suffrage in Utah became entwined with every federal threat against polygamy, maintaining woman's vote became another point of controversy. With suffrage as with polygamy, the political was deeply personal for Emmeline. An enfranchised woman, Emmeline Wells affirmed, "feels her political independence and that she is virtually part and parcel of the great body politic, not through her father or husband, but in her own vested right."[57] Latter-day Saint women had been psychologically as well as politically empowered by enfranchisement in 1870. When federal antipolygamy legislation was finally passed in 1882 and 1887—rescinding the right to vote from all polygamists and then from all Utah women—Mormon women were demoralized. Yet even as they submitted and adjusted their family and social life to meet the new federal guidelines, they mounted a grassroots effort to regain the vote whenever Utah finally became a state. Suffrage continued to be a topic addressed in the pages of the *Exponent* until that time, nine years after they had lost the vote.

A third and equally urgent level of editorializing included a whole range of woman-oriented issues. Emmeline admonished women to obtain as much education as possible, to eschew feminine artifices, and to seek an egalitarian relationship in marriage so that each spouse might have the freedom to develop individual capacities and interests.[58] Borrowing from other women's newspapers, the *Exponent* plugged into an international woman's network, reporting the progress of women's rights activists at home and abroad along with the achievements of noteworthy women around the world.

Wells also employed the *Exponent* as an unofficial newsletter to connect and coordinate the activities, programs, visits, reports, and conferences of the LDS women's Relief Society, the Young Ladies' Mutual Improvement Association, and the Primary Association as well as other groups such as the Senior Retrenchment Society and a variety of literary associations.[59] Notice of the meetings and often the minutes of other social, educational, and national women's groups such as the Daughters of the Revolution, Daughters of Utah Pioneers, and the National and International Councils of Women, along with the National Woman Suffrage Association found their way into the *Exponent*. It seemed that nothing involving Mormon women, including their birthdays, anniversaries, and deaths, was too insignificant for the paper. The *Exponent* is a repository of useful biographical, organizational, and historical information, which is exactly what Emmeline Wells intended it to be. "There has been no great work during these years commenced by women that has not been considered and helped by this little paper," she claimed in 1911, and for the length of her editorship she made sure this was true.[60] The *Exponent* abundantly fulfilled Emmeline's intent to include within its pages the wide range of ecclesiastical, political, economic, educational and social programs, activities, and interests that made up the lives of Mormon women during a dynamic period in their history.[61]

By 1877, when she became editor, Emmeline Wells had already contributed sixty-five articles or editorials to the paper. One of her first editorials was commissioned by the *Exponent*'s Committee of Consultation in August 1874 while Louisa Greene returned to her home in Smithfield. "This morning I commenced writing," Emmeline wrote in her diary. "I seem so concerned about the Editorial for fear I should not please the Committee—for my own part I would not be at all afraid, I love this kind of work."[62] Only nineteen of the sixty-five pieces carried her own name, however. These were mainly general articles or notices relating to Relief Society matters such as grain storage (which she was appointed to direct in 1876), the Centennial Commission stores, or visits of Relief Society officers to various wards and stakes. Thirty-two of these preeditorial articles appeared under the name Blanche Beechwood; the rest were signed "Aunt Em."

While feeling their way into the literary world, many women used the literary affectation of a nom de plume. Blanche Beechwood, like the authorial names of such prominent writers and lecturers as Fannie Fern, Grace Greenwood, and Jennie June, hid the identity of women whose experience, awareness, abilities, and character pushed them onto the public literary stage. The use of pseudonyms was not entirely a female artifice, however. Men, at times, also sought the anonymity they provided. After a decade's use, however, Emmeline abandoned them and urged her fellow writers to do the same.

In 1875, perhaps testing the anonymity of her pseudonym, Emmeline wrote a friend in Ogden, Hannah Pitcock, asking her to identify Emmeline's contributions to the *Exponent*, if she could, and how she would rate them. "I like to have the opinion of all good people," Emmeline assured her, "and more especially women."[63] The response, unfortunately, is unrecorded. On another occasion she noted in her diary that a piece she had written in the *Exponent* had caused "all sorts of comments, not altogether pleasant some of them." She did not seem unduly disturbed, however, and may well have been pleased to discover that her article had had an impact on the paper's readers.[64]

From the second to the eighth volume of the *Exponent* (1873–80), Blanche Beechwood contributed forty articles, the majority of them among the most forceful of her statements on three of her major themes: society's inequitable treatment of women, the need for women to assert themselves as contributing individuals in marriage and in society, and the religious rights of Latter-day Saint women. Behind these fervent declamations stood a double purpose: to empower women and to expose male hypocrisy.

Her consistent message to her Mormon sisters was to live up to their potential, to embrace the opportunities for development offered by their religion, and to shun the traditional but artificial dependencies that locked women into perpetual childhood. She urged them to seek the qualities of "real" womanhood: an active mind, common sense, knowledge for themselves, respect for individuality, and a desire to enlarge their experience.[65] As a spur to her Mormon readers, she boldly declared that though the world may think otherwise, "We are not restricted in our ideas of women's privileges. We are not in bondage as they suppose. We are perfectly capable of thinking for ourselves."[66] Women, she believed, were endowed "with more innate purity, grace [and] a more intuitive conception of divinity" than men, which obliged them to act as the "purifier[s] of the moral and religious atmospheres of society."[67] Women needed to recognize the strength of their own power, she urged, and move out of their contented indifference to confront life's challenges.

Blanche Beechwood advised her readers, "Women are what men have made them," reversing the familiar and falsely deferential adage. Men had defined the parameters of women's character, their nature, their sphere of action, and their mission in life, she complained. If men were "really superior to women," she added, "let them show themselves so." Real women desire someone worthy of the "reverence" men seem to want. Unfortunately, she concluded,

> Man, with all his boasted knowledge, and practical skill in reading character, is still in comparative ignorance of how women feel, or what they are. He regards them as toys, to be picked up and cast aside at will; very well for pastime playthings, or for housekeepers; but to consider them real, genuine, rational beings, is a novel idea; they are vain, frivolous, fickle and deceitful, incapable of performing any important part in life creditably.[68]

Her sorrow was that too many women accepted this false characterization.

In both chastising and complimenting women, Wells hoped these articles would motivate them to throw off the chains of custom and seek to develop what she was convinced were strong, innate abilities. Believing firmly in the power of "thinking women," she was delighted that her public life brought her in contact with many of the thinking women of her time.[69]

Several of Blanche Beechwood's articles were clearly ripostes to sharp attacks on polygamy, particularly from the *Woman's Journal*. She also refuted what she considered a weak attempt to find some redeeming aspect of plural marriage in one of her strongest assertions of the intelligence, rectitude, and conviction of Latter-day Saint women. In 1874 a male writer wrote that "polygamy makes comparatively respectable women, of girls who might otherwise have been prostitutes." Blanche Beechwood was irate. Though the writer may have thought he was "doing us such great honor," she exclaimed, "he knows nothing about it." The "goodness, purity, integrity and principle" that characterized women who accepted plural marriage and "endured to the end" were never the qualities of a potential prostitute, she heatedly declared.[70] Enumerating the womanly qualities and high moral convictions of plural wives, she wondered if such women as the writer described could have endured the "reproaches, slanders, and cruelties" heaped on them had they not had divine help and a firm conviction of the divine origin of the principle they lived. With more than thirty years of "trials, exposure and calumny," she asked, are plural wives to be "awarded this encomium of praise, 'they might otherwise have been prostitutes?'"[71] This was but the beginning of many refutations Emmeline would present over the next two decades of the derision endured by her Mormon sisters.

Many of Blanche Beechwood's articles echoed the rhetoric of the woman's rights movement, but she also voiced arguments from her own perspective. Though her primary audience was made up of women and men whom she knew well or who had shared with her the difficult experiences of early Mormonism and the struggle to build a community in the West, the persuasive tone of her articles seemed directed toward an extended and less sympathetic readership.

Sincerely, though somewhat ingratiatingly, she frequently lauded "the sharp-sighted, far-seeing and high-minded women" who were "beginning to seek out some remedy for the injustices done their sex."[72] By the end of the 1870s, Emmeline knew many of these women personally, women who would put forth tireless efforts and would later become her friends and co-workers in the woman movement. Perhaps justifying her own budding activism, Emmeline spoke out against women, including some of her Mormon peers, who would not support the efforts of those working "for the benefit of women," those who were ridiculed as being "strong-minded" and "unwomanly."

After boldly enunciating a broad platform of social equality, Blanche Beechwood disappeared from the *Exponent* in 1880, her arguments taken over by the editorial page. Fortunately, the demise of the Blanche Beechwood persona did not lessen or prevent Emmeline's passion and convictions from expression in her editorials and articles. Throughout her brief journalistic career, Blanche Beechwood had made a strong case for woman's rights—Mormons' and others—and had established Emmeline B. Wells as a forceful advocate for Mormonism and for women.

Emmeline's other literary persona was "Aunt Em." Aunt Em was the author of much of Emmeline's poetry and fiction, along with most of her nostalgic evocations of her New England years. Aunt Em was occasionally as outspoken as Blanche Beechwood on women's issues, just as Blanche Beechwood occasionally offered domestic advice and homely articles on "good manners."[73] But by and large, the two maintained distinctive voices, the feminine and the feminist, complementing rather than competing with one another.

Aunt Em's voice revealed the other side of Emmeline's complex personality so vividly expressed in her writing. Through this voice, Emmeline's early days in rural Massachusetts came to life. She wrote of Thanksgiving and Christmas services in the Congregational meetinghouse on Elm Street in North New Salem; of her schoolmates at the New Salem Academy; of the scenic beauties about her home, including the brook where she was baptized a Latter-day Saint; and of the hemlocks under which she wove fanciful stories for her woodland friends. Several visits to her childhood home revived old memories and replenished her store of memorabilia.

She wrote about the poet's task, the changing seasons, the influence of the home, and recorded midnight musings and thoughts in "desultory moments." "Reveries," "meditations," "soliloquies," "reminiscences," and "memories" figured frequently in the titles of Aunt Em's contributions. She seemed the serene, contemplative woman Emmeline might have become as the New England poetess she once appeared destined to be. The changes, challenges, and controversies that Mormonism brought into her life, however, fashioned a different kind of woman and unleashed talents, attitudes, and experiences unimagined by the introspective New England girl. Yet a certain longing for the earlier promise of a more pastoral life never wholly yielded to the reality of Emmeline's life as a Mormon woman and a woman's advocate.[74]

Toward the end of her editorship, Emmeline Wells gave stricter attention to a mandate given to her years earlier by Brigham Young. "I give you a mission to write brief sketches of the lives of the leading women of Zion, and publish them," he instructed in 1877 when she became editor.[75] By 1908, when many of the dramatic issues surrounding Mormon women had been tamed, she recalled that commission. She felt a strong desire, she noted in her diary, to be more devoted to collecting and publishing in the *Exponent* biographical sketches of women of the Church. "I am interested in writing of the women I have known in the past, and really feel I can keep their memory before the women of today, and in doing so leave a record of them for the coming generation," she wrote.[76] Enlisting the help of her contributors, she urged her readers to submit life sketches about others as well as themselves. "The columns of this paper are ever open to publish such sketches and incidents," she informed them and encouraged the submission of accounts "of their experiences and testimonies for the benefit of others and to leave them upon record."[77]

In addition to these individual life writings, Wells wrote and published numerous collective biographies of women in journalism, medicine, literature, politics, education, philanthropy, and other vocational and volunteer fields that women were beginning to enter. She also included brief obituaries submitted by friends and families of the deceased or written by herself. As a result of this commission, the *Exponent* contains nearly eight hundred obituaries and close to two hundred multicolumned biographical sketches of Emmeline's contemporaries. The paper serves as an impressive biographical dictionary of nineteenth-century Mormon women.[78]

Initially, the *Exponent* fairly burst with an enthusiasm to respond to the events that thrust Mormon women into the public spotlight: their enfranchisement; the escalating crusade against polygamy; the interest of national women's leaders; and the opportunity for Latter-day Saint women to express themselves in local rallies and events and to a national audience through the *Exponent*. Eager to exploit their enfranchisement and to explain their peculiar religious practices and the extraordinary opportunities the LDS Church offered women, *Exponent* writers unabashedly declared their political and social advantages. Nowhere else in the land, one woman wrote, "do women enjoy such freedom. Where are they looked upon by their husbands as their equal?" she asked. "The Gospel breaks the fetters wherewith woman is bound, takes her by the hand and says, 'Woman, know thyself.'"[79] Though such rhetoric may not have convinced a doubting public, it went far in building a self-image that helped sustain Mormon women against the flood of derision they experienced.

The proposed transformation of the ideal of womanhood, articulated by the woman movement and assured by a host of legal and educational changes, threatened the social order and unsettled both men and women bound to custom and tradition. In Utah, however, a long history of pioneering, which often blurred conventional role divisions and made uncustomary demands on women and men, as well as the need to establish legal protections for plural wives and their children, forced a consciousness and acceptance of women's legal and political rights in advance of many other sections of the country. These rights, along with the qualities developed in their defensive stand against the antipolygamy crusade, produced what Emmeline called "real" women. The real woman of Emmeline's pen was stoic and sure of her convictions, cultivating self-reliance, intellectuality, personal integrity, self-respect, and competence, while claiming equity with men in marriage and society.[80] As the "true" woman of the Victorian ethos—demure, passive, and complacent—gave way to the "new" woman of the post-Victorian period in American society, Wells found her to be remarkably like the Mormon woman and used the *Exponent* to introduce her to a curious audience.

The *Exponent* never provided a comfortable living for Emmeline, but she rebuffed any suggestions to give it up and accept Church assistance after the death of her husband, Daniel H. Wells, in 1891. Relinquishing her financial independence, however uncertain it had always been, was not an option for her. By 1914, however when her offer of two years' standing to oversee the transfer of the *Exponent* to the Relief Society had not materialized, she brought the forty-two-year enterprise to a close.[81] Through Emmeline's sheer determination, the *Exponent* had proved itself to be what Edward Sloan had envisioned so many years before.

Earlier, in 1905, she had informed her readers that its bound volumes, "extending back to 1872, contain many very able articles from the pen of the women pioneers and heroines of the early days of the Church, which are valuable history." She was proud to announce that not only had the paper served to inform Latter-day Saint women of women's work outside Utah but that its "pages have been read by hundreds of women outside the Church," informing them of the life and thought of Mormon women.[82] It had indeed chronicled the intellectual, religious, economic, and social history of Mormon women during those years and registered their responses to the events of their time. But the *Exponent* was more than an inanimate record. It was a major player, a viable advocate, illuminating the issues and participating in the debate.

The *Exponent* had begun as a medium through which Mormon women could defend their religious practices and beliefs, their integrity and morality, and their intelligence and ability. This they did with vigor while expressing their views and submitting articles on numerous other topics. In 1890, however, polygamy was officially proscribed by the Church, and in 1896 suffrage was reinstated in Utah at statehood, the two dominant issues to which the *Exponent* had addressed itself for nearly half of its life. The shifting focus of the *Exponent* to local and particularly Relief Society interests when Emmeline Wells became general president in 1910 did not rally the kind of impassioned support and advocacy that the controversial issues of polygamy and suffrage had evoked.

By 1914, like other suffrage papers, the *Exponent* had become an anachronism. Its editor was eighty-six years old. Most of her associates and supporters from earlier days were gone, and the women's reforms, which had energized so many of them, though by no means completely resolved, had somehow telescoped into the goal of equal suffrage, soon to be realized nationally through a constitutional amendment. Utah women continued to support suffrage until that time, but many of the newer generation lacked the fervor of their foremothers; the issues, the agitators, and their advocate, the *Woman's Exponent*, all belonged to a passing era.

For Emmeline Wells, the *Woman's Exponent* had been her passport to a life and work for which she proved to be well qualified and to which she was wholly dedicated. It gave her recognition, respect, and entry to the inner circles of female Mormon leadership and national women's associations. The experience she had gained after twenty-five years of association with the paper "cannot be told," she wrote, "but altogether it has been a labor of love; no matter how arduous the work or how numerous the fault finders never once has the writer been tempted to withdraw." The personal satisfaction of the long effort came from the "solace" and "relief" it gave her in troublesome times. "It has been a rare opportunity," she exclaimed, "and a happy service."[83] But it was more than her personal forum. Though she may have orchestrated its performance, the *Exponent* represented a multiple and united effort. Unencumbered by organizational ties, an overseer, or a narrow agenda, it gave its readers and contributors opportunity for an identity of their own making and through it a begrudging respect from a generally unsympathetic world.

Notes

1. Emmeline B. Wells to Susa Young Gates, January 11, 1887, Susa Young Gates Papers, Church Archives, The Church of Jesus Christ of Latter-day Saints, Salt Lake City.

2. The term was adopted among Mormons to designate the moralistic novels written by Latter-day Saint authors.

3. Emmeline B. Wells, *Musings and Memories: Poems by Emmeline B. Wells* (Salt Lake City: George Q. Cannon and Sons, 1896; 2d ed., Salt Lake City: Deseret News Press, 1915).

4. "The New Woman's Journal," *Salt Lake Herald*, April 10, 1872, 3.

5. Mormon women were encouraged to learn the skills of the publishing business. It was "the design of the authorities of the Church," as noted in the April 1874 semiannual general conference, "to establish a school to teach women typesetting and other aspects of the printing business" that "belonged to the women." The *Woman's Exponent* was produced almost exclusively by women. See "Conference Items," *Woman's Exponent* 2 (May 15, 1874): 188.

6. Eliza R. Snow, "The New Year, 1852," *Deseret News*, January 10, 1852, 17. Snow's position was that any lasting change for women would originate within the framework of the gospel, as promulgated by The Church of Jesus Christ of Latter-day Saints. She was opposed to woman's rights activists who castigated men as oppressors, disdaining any kind of "war between the sexes." Unity and complementary interests better characterized the relationship of Mormon men and women, Snow maintained, as did most of her peers.

7. This analysis of the female essay is given in detail in Eileen Boyd Sivert, "Flora Tristan: The Joining of Essay, Journal, Autobiography," in *The Politics of the Essay: Feminist Perspectives,* ed. Ruth-Ellen Boetcher Joeres and Elizabeth Mittman (Bloomington: Indiana University Press, 1993), 57–72. The introduction to this volume explains the history, usage, and value of the essay form to feminists. The authors report that the essay, as used by feminist advocates, moves beyond mere contemplation to expressing the conclusions of such contemplation with an aim of "reaching and connecting with a widely-based audience" (20). I am indebted to Sheree Maxwell Bench for bringing this work to my attention.

8. The *Revolution*, organ of the National Woman Suffrage Association, had limited funding and lasted only briefly from 1868 to 1870. The well-funded *Woman's Journal,* voice of the American Woman Suffrage Association, appeared in 1871 and continued publishing until 1914.

9. Sherilyn Cox Bennion identifies fourteen other women's publications by 1900 in "Enterprising Ladies: Utah's Nineteenth Century Women Editors," *Utah Historical Quarterly* 49 (Summer 1981): 291–304.

10. Lula Greene Richards, "How the Exponent Was Started," *Relief Society Magazine* 14 (December 1928): 604–7. The *Salt Lake Herald* editor Edward Sloan is credited with originating and naming the *Woman's Exponent*. He also

provided assistance in its production in the early years but not in its editorials or other content. Maureen Ursenbach Beecher also recites the founding of the *Woman's Exponent* in "Eliza R. Snow," in *Mormon Sisters: Women in Early Utah*, ed. Claudia L. Bushman (Cambridge, Mass.: Emmeline Press Limited, 1976), 25–26.

11. Phebe Clark Young was a typical contributor. In 1882 she decided to write out her thoughts about the intolerance toward the Mormons, prompted by passage of the Edmunds antipolygamy act, which disfranchised all polygamists. She tentatively took her article to Emmeline, the editor, and was delighted a week later to learn it had been accepted for publication. The editor urged her to write again in order "to cause the world to understand us better." See Phebe Clark Young, Journal, 1882–1901, January 21, February 3, 1882, Church Archives.

12. "Salutatary," *Woman's Exponent* 1 (June 1, 1872): 4.

13. "New Volume and Women of Utah," *Woman's Exponent* 6 (June 1, 1877): 4.

14. The Morrill Act of 1862 was the first of many items of legislation to outlaw polygamy, but the act proved to be unenforceable and was superseded by later Congressional measures. In 1890, after passage of the 1882 Edmunds Act and 1887 Edmunds-Tucker Act, which struck at the fiscal base of the Church and withdrew most of the civil rights of Latter-day Saints, Church President Wilford Woodruff issued a "Manifesto" suspending the practice and promising to abide by the law of the land. Sarah Barringer Gordon discusses these developments in *The Mormon Question: Polygamy and Constitutional Conflict in Nineteenth-Century America* (Chapel Hill: University of North Carolina Press, 2002).

15. "Salutatary," 4. Antipolygamists used the *Salt Lake Tribune* as their forum until publication of the *Anti-Polygamy Standard* in 1880.

16. These included the Relief Society (women), the Young Ladies' Mutual Improvement Association (teenage girls), and the Primary Association (children).

17. See Carol Cornwall Madsen, "Remember the Women of Zion: A Study of the Editorial Content of the *Woman's Exponent*, a Mormon Woman's Journal" (master's thesis, University of Utah, 1977).

18. The value of two western suffrage papers, the *Woman's Exponent* of Utah and the *New Northwest* of Oregon, is examined by Sherilyn Cox Bennion in "The *New Northwest* and *Woman's Exponent*: Early Voices for Suffrage," *Journalism Quarterly* 54 (Summer 1977): 286–92.

19. A brief history of the *Lily* is Edward A. Hinck, "*The Lily*, 1849–1856: From Temperance to Woman's Rights," in *A Voice of Their Own: The Woman Suffrage Press, 1840–1910*, ed. Martha M. Solomon (Tuscaloosa: University of Alabama Press, 1991), 30–47; Mari Boor Tonn surveys the *Una* in "The *Una*, 1853–1855, The Premiere of the Woman's Rights Press," in Solomon, *Voice of Their Own*, 48–70.

20. E. Claire Jerry argues that the "alternative" or women's press was essential to the movement by augmenting the audience of the women's conventions and lecture tours, creating a network of women with similar goals and values, and identifying and producing the movement's leaders. See Jerry, "The Role of Newspapers in the Nineteenth Century Woman's Movement," in Solomon, *Voice of Their Own*, 17–29.

21. Edward L. Sloan died unexpectedly at the age of forty-three in August 1874, just two years after founding the *Woman's Exponent*. He was born in County Down, Ireland, November 5, 1830, and joined the LDS Church at age eighteen. He immigrated to Utah in 1863. He began his career in journalism in England and assisted with the *Millennial Star*, a Church publication in Liverpool, England, after being baptized. In Utah he became assistant editor of the *Deseret News* and later of the *Daily Telegraph*. He co-founded the *Salt Lake Herald* with W. C. Dunbar in 1870. See "Biography of E. L. Sloan," *Tullidge's Quarterly Magazine* (1881): 590–91; "Death of Mr. E. L. Sloan," *Woman's Exponent* 3 (August 15, 1874): 45.

22. "Mormon Women in Council," *Deseret News*, February 16, 1870, 23. The *Deseret News* included quotes from the *New York Times* and the *New York Herald*, February 16, 1870 and March 8, 1870, all complimentary of Mormon women. Local rallies were held throughout Utah, also generating favorable responses. The Cullom Bill, against which they rallied, was ultimately defeated. See "Female Suffrage in Utah," *Deseret News*, February 16, 1870, 18; "Is Polygamy a Blessing," *Deseret News Weekly*, February 16, 1870, 23; "The Ladies' Mass Meetings—Their Significance," *Deseret News*, March 8, 1870, 49.

23. Under the leadership of William S. Godbe, this faction, which took its unofficial name from its founder, differed with LDS Church leader Brigham Young over a number of issues, particularly his insular economic policies that isolated Latter-day Saints from economic exchange with those outside the religion. Godbe's faction did not, however, renounce polygamy at the outset. A full discussion of the Godbeites can be found in Ronald W. Walker, *Wayward Saints: The Godbeites and Brigham Young* (Urbana: University of Illinois Press, 1998). Lola Van Wagenen also explores the relationship of the Godbe women to Mormon women and to the suffrage movement in "Sister-Wives

62   An Advocate for Women

and Suffragists, Polygamy and the Politics of Woman Suffrage, 1870–1896" (PhD diss., New York University, 1994; BYU Studies and Joseph Fielding Smith Institute for Latter-day Saint History, 2003), especially 1–151.

24. By the early 1870s, the New Movement had rejected polygamy as a religious principle, and William Godbe divorced Mary and Charlotte in 1879 (Annie was his first and legal wife). Charlotte had separated from him some time before that. Her ambiguous marital and religious status put her on the fringes of sisterhood with Latter-day Saint women, although it may have made her more appealing to eastern suffragists. Beverly Beeton has outlined Charlotte's suffragist activities in "'I Am an American Woman': Charlotte Ives Cobb Godbe Kirby," *Journal of the West* 27 (April 1988): 13–19; and "'A Feminist among the Mormons,' Charlotte Ives Cobb Godbe Kirby," *Utah Historical Quarterly* 59 (Winter 1991): 22–31. See also Van Wagenen, "Sister-Wives and Suffragists," 50–106. Chapter 6 gives more details.

25. Those outside the Church were opposed to statehood, fearing the loss of federal officials in Utah and a state controlled politically, legally, and economically by Mormons. They also wanted polygamy to be terminated before Congress yielded control of the territory to local state officers. Orson F. Whitney, *The History of Utah*, 4 vols. (Salt Lake City: George Q. Cannon and Sons, 1893), 3:691–705.

26. See Lula Greene Richards, "How the *Exponent* Was Started," *Relief Society Magazine* 14 (December 1928): 607. See also Emma R. Olsen and Beatrice B. Malouf, comps., "The *Woman's Exponent*," in *Chronicles of Courage*, 7 vols. (Salt Lake City: Daughters of Utah Pioneers, 1994), 5:184.

27. "The Woman's Paper," *Woman's Exponent* 18 (June 1, 1889): 4; "Interesting Extracts," *Woman's Exponent* 3 (June 15, 1874): 11.

28. "Woman's Exponent," *Salt Lake Tribune*, April 11, 1872, 338. Like most antipolygamists, the *Tribune* assumed that granting Utah women (mainly Mormon) the vote merely supported the practice of plural marriage.

29. "The Woman's Exponent," *Salt Lake Tribune*, June 10, 1872, 542. This proved to be a short-lived switch.

30. "Kind Words," *Woman's Exponent* 1 (August 1, 1872): 37.

31. "Emeline [*sic*] B. Wells," *Tullidge's Quarterly Magazine* 1 (January 1881): 252.

32. "Improvements," *Woman's Exponent* 2 (October 1, 1873): 68.

33. Emmeline B. Wells, Diary, July 3, 1881, January 30, 1883, March 10, 1883, L. Tom Perry Special Collections, Harold B. Lee Library, Brigham Young University, Provo, Utah.

34. Wells, Diary, January 18, 1878.

35. The burden never lifted until her daughter Annie Wells Cannon came aboard as an assistant editor a few years before the paper's demise.

36. "Home Affairs," *Woman's Exponent* 8 (September 15, 1879): 61. The paper on which the *Exponent* was printed was processed from rags contributed by its readers.

37. "Editorial Notes," *Woman's Exponent* 12 (June 1, 1883): 5.

38. "Home Affairs," *Woman's Exponent* 8 (June 1, 1880): 4.

39. Susa Young Gates to Emmeline B. Wells, May 5, 1888, Susa Young Gates Papers.

40. Though the paper was never officially connected with the LDS Church, Emmeline Wells used it to promote the women's organizations and in 1889 declared that it had been "the official organ of the women of Zion." It had reported on all of the women's activities, including suffrage, provided an outlet for Mormon women's opinions on the questions of the day, and presented biographical sketches of many of its readers. "Editorial Notes," *Woman's Exponent* 18 (November 15, 1889): 92.

41. The LDS Relief Society, with the help of the Young Ladies' Mutual Improvement Association and the Primary Association, had collected money to build a Woman's Building for the Relief Society, but the decision was made to enlarge the concept and house the offices of the three organizations with the office of the Presiding Bishopric of the Church. The three-man council oversaw all the material assets and welfare programs of the entire Church, supervising the work of the local bishoprics in their individual congregations. The Presiding Bishopric was thus a natural partner of the Relief Society General Presidency. Emmeline Wells became Relief Society General President in 1910, and this proximity facilitated the continuation of the *Exponent* in the new building.

42. Madsen, "Remember the Women of Zion," 21–26.

43. "Editorial Notes," *Woman's Exponent* 12 (May 15, 1884): 189; Wells, Diary, June 20, 21, 1883.

44. "Woman's Exponent, a Utah Ladies Journal," *Woman's Exponent* 1 (June 1, 1872): 8.

45. "Salutatary," 4.

46. "The New Volume," *Woman's Exponent* 7 (June 1, 1878): 4.

47. See Doctrine and Covenants section 132, especially verse 20.

48. "The Woman's Paper," *Woman's Exponent* 16 (May 15, 1888): 188; "Our Little Paper," *Woman's Exponent* 8 (May 15, 1880): 188.

49. "First General Conference of the Relief Society," *Woman's Exponent* 17 (April 15, 1889): 172; "Editorial Thoughts," *Woman's Exponent* 18 (November 15, 1889): 92.

50. Emmeline B. Wells, "Utah," in *History of Woman Suffrage,* vol. 4, ed. Susan B. Anthony and Ida H. Harper (Rochester: Susan B. Anthony, 1902), 936–56, reprinted in Carol Cornwall Madsen, ed., *Battle for the Ballot: Essays on Woman Suffrage in Utah, 1870–1896* (Logan: Utah State University Press, 1997), 33–51.

51. "Important to Women," *Woman's Exponent* 25 (November 1, 15, 1896): 68.

52. Madsen, "Remember the Women of Zion," 34.

53. From 1879 to 1896 the standard read, "The Rights of the Women of Zion, and the Rights of the Women of all Nations," and from 1896 to 1913 it read, "The Ballot in the Hands of the Women of Utah Should be a Power to Better the Home, the State, and the Nation."

54. See "Women Talkers and Women Writers," *Woman's Exponent* 5 (August 15, 1876): 44; and "Patriarchal Marriage," *Woman's Exponent* 6 (August 15, 1877): 44. Joan Iversen discusses the antipolygamy movement in national women's groups in *The Antipolygamy Controversy in U.S. Women's Movements, 1880–1925, A Debate on the American Home* (New York: Garland, 1997).

55. In 1879, after meeting Emmeline Wells and Zina Williams for the first time at the NWSA annual convention in January, Sarah Spencer, secretary of the association, defended the two women and plural marriage in her written report of the convention. "Those ladies were here," she reported, "not only because they were invited but because their rights had been wantonly assailed by unjust legislation." "For her part," she concluded "she would sooner see polygamy legislated in the District of Columbia than the social evil [prostitution] into Utah." *Woman's Words* 2 (February 1879): 347.

56. "The Position of Utah," *Woman's Exponent* 10 (January 1, 1882): 116.

57. "Sweet Is Liberty," *Woman's Exponent* 11 (March 15, 1883): 148.

58. See, for example, "Woman's Progression," *Woman's Exponent* 6 (February 15, 1878): 140.

59. These included two clubs she founded herself, the Reapers and the Utah Women's Press Club.

60. See "Fortieth Volume," *Woman's Exponent* 40 (July 1911): 4.

61. For an overview of the wide-ranging editorial content of the *Woman's Exponent,* see Madsen, "Remember the Women of Zion."

62. Wells, Diary, August 24, 1874.

63. Emmeline B. Wells to Mrs. Hannah Pitcock, January 21, 1875, Emmeline B. Wells Papers, Daughters of Utah Pioneers Museum, Salt Lake City, Utah.

64. Wells, Diary, September 19, 1874. The article was entitled "Our Fashionable Young Ladies," *Woman's Exponent* 3 (September 15, 1874): 58. It rebuked young women for bowing too much to fashions and the attention of men instead of developing themselves as intelligent, capable, and serious young women.

65. Blanche Beechwood, "Real Women," *Woman's Exponent* 2 (June 1, 1874): 118.

66. Blanche Beechwood, "Our Daughters," *Woman's Exponent* 2 (February 1, 1874): 131.

67. Blanche Beechwood, "Woman's Ambition," *Woman's Exponent* 4 (April 1, 1876): 166.

68. Blanche Beechwood, "Real Women," *Woman's Exponent* 2 (June 1, 1874): 118.

69. Blanche Beechwood, "Why, Ah! Why," *Woman's Exponent* 3 (October 1, 1874): 67.

70. Beechwood, "Why, Ah! Why," 67.

71. Beechwood, "Why, Ah! Why," 67.

72. Blanche Beechwood, "Impromptu Ideas of Home," *Woman's Exponent* 4 (May 15, 1876): 191.

73. Some examples are Blanche Beechwood, "Here and Hereafter," *Woman's Exponent* 3 (December 15, 1974): 114; and a series on good manners, beginning in 8 (July 15, 1880): 30; see Aunt Em, "After Long Years, Letter II," *Woman's Exponent* 6 (December 1, 1878): 97.

74. Her poems, seventy-one of which were first published in the *Woman's Exponent* under the names of both Aunt Em and Emmeline B. Wells, were compiled in a volume, *Musings and Memories*. Though she tried to do the same with her short stories, the *Exponent* proved to be their primary published outlet.

75. "The Jubilee Celebration, the Need of Press Representation," *Woman's Exponent* 20 (March 15, 1892): 132.

76. Wells, Diary, May 23, 1908.

77. "Editorial Thoughts," 92.

78. A brief study of Emmeline Wells as a historian and the *Exponent* as a historical repository is Carol Cornwall Madsen, "Telling the Untold Story: Emmeline B. Wells as Historian," in *Telling the Story of Mormon History, Proceedings of the 2002 Symposium of the Joseph Fielding Smith Institute for Latter-day Saint History at Brigham Young University*, ed. William G. Hartley (Provo, Utah: Joseph Fielding Smith Institute for Latter-day Saint History, 2004), 17–22.

79. "Woman's Voice," *Woman's Exponent* 16 (September 15, 1887): 63.

80. Madsen, "'Remember the Women of Zion,'" 148–150.

81. In 1912 the eighty-four-year-old Emmeline, then serving as Relief Society General President, offered the newspaper to the Relief Society as its official organ with herself as editor and her daughter Annie Wells Cannon as associate editor. No action was taken until two years later, when the Relief Society decided to launch an entirely new publication sponsored by the Church, which was to be called the *Relief Society Magazine,* with Susa Young Gates as editor.

82. "Helpful Suggestions," *Woman's Exponent* 33 (May 1905): 84.

83. "Editorial Work," *Woman's Exponent* 31 (July 1, 15, 1902): 12.

Chapter 4

A "Strong-Minded Woman"

*I believe in women,
especially thinking women.*[1]

Emmeline B. Wells was dispirited and anxious in the year that marked her fiftieth birthday. In 1878, at the midpoint of a life that would reach almost a century, she had slipped into an emotional nadir that drew her into a long period of despair. Her mind was plagued with unanswered questions: "What will be don in regard to Utah? What will be the end of the question on Universal Suffrage? What will be done in regulating church matters and are we to have a new prophet?"[2] She had also begun to feel the unrelenting pressures of her new position as editor of the *Woman's Exponent,* an occupation that both fueled her ambition and sapped her energies. She despaired over her daughter Melvina's divorce and remarriage to a man outside the faith,[3] and she worried over the illness, which all too soon proved fatal, of her daughter Emmie, then in the full bloom of young womanhood. Emmeline's husband's diminishing financial resources augured major changes in her circumstances and increased responsibility for her own material welfare. Moreover, living apart from her husband and his five other wives, who shared a large home, Emmeline was, in effect, head of her own household, the decision maker and counselor for her five daughters, and always in the demeaning position of petitioner for financial support from an absent husband.[4] But most of all that year, she was "heart hungry," aching for the conjugal attention that was so sparingly given. "No wonder I am forced to be strong-minded," she lamented to her diary one winter day in January 1878.

In the nineteenth century, "strong minded" was not a compliment. Even Eliza R. Snow, the center of Mormon female society, mentor of women's activities in the Church, co-worker with Emmeline, and, ironically, as strong-minded a woman as any other of her time, was among those who denigrated the trait in others, especially public activists. Strong-mindedness was not among the attributes of proper womanhood that she preached to her sister saints.[5] But there was a generation's difference and a chasm of experience and vicissitude that separated Eliza R. Snow—not burdened with domestic, family, or livelihood responsibilities while enjoying the esteem that came from marriage to two prophets[6]—and Emmeline—faced with the cares of her large family and the necessity to provide her own living for most of her adult life.[7] Though she embodied the characteristics of Mormon womanhood outlined by Eliza R. Snow, Emmeline expressed them in ways that fit her own life experience and areas of church service. The financial challenges she faced as a self-supporting mother of five and her call by LDS Church leaders to represent her sisters during the political crusade against the Mormons required a different interpretation of Snow's qualities of Mormon womanhood. Though in 1878 Emmeline had yet to be publicly numbered among those identified as "strong-minded," her own experiences had, unbidden, engrafted that characteristic on her. Rendering the kind of public service for the Church she was asked to do brought her into contact with other strong-minded women and engendered a lifelong respect for them.

Though Emmeline Wells did not consciously set out to be counted among strong-minded women, her own public activism soon made her one of the number and in time she was pleased to be so designated. As she began to experience for herself the criticism leveled against such women, she grew to admire those who were "willing to brave the storms, and stand fast for principle, though public opinion is against them, sacrificing the finest feelings and even allowing themselves to be deprecated by persons whose esteem they would fain retain."[8] Like all Latter-day Saints, Emmeline knew something about "standing fast for principle." Her firsthand experiences with harassment and ridicule made her capable of enduring the derogation that plagued those engaged in the woman movement. As she took on the personae of public defender of her religion and activist for women's advancement, she came to respect the strong-minded reformers for being thinking women who were not content to "sit and dream and wait for the good time coming," but were willing themselves "to open up the way for the advancement of others."[9] As Emmeline gradually took her place among them, she came to realize that this unsought trait of strong-mindedness was her best defense against the pressing responsibilities, unexpected disappointments, public derogation, and unabating sorrows that often shadowed her many achievements.

Emmeline did not derive her understanding of the legal, educational, and economic disabilities that characterized women's social status entirely from her own experience. Her mother, Diadama, who had twice been left on her own in the 1840s, first drew Emmeline's attention to the precarious economic position of women and the difficulties of being self-supporting. In addition to her mother's experience, Emmeline's early life in New England (the "seed-bed of reform"), her extensive reading of woman's rights literature, and her contact with eastern activists sensitized her to the social and legal constraints on women. Added to these feminist grounds was her own desire to measure up to the assessment of many in her youth that she was a prodigy—a "child of destiny," someone with a mission to perform. Her counsel to her daughters to be self-supporting and strong-minded sprang from the depths of her own private struggle to develop "habits of independence so that they never need to trust blindly but understand for themselves and have sufficient energy of purpose to carry out plans for their own welfare and happiness."[10] Her need to achieve economic and emotional self-determination set her apart from many of her Mormon peers and provided an ideological base for joining and promoting a conversation on the woman's issues of the day.

Emmeline's commitment to her personal goals and values and to the advancement of women never faltered or waned throughout her long life. Though probably unwilling to admit it, she was born to be a strong-minded woman. Like other such women, Emmeline developed early a feminist consciousness from her sensitivity to the social conventions that circumscribed women's individuality and self-expression. Laws denied them a legal identity upon marriage; tradition dictated their subordination in that relationship; both science and medicine questioned their intellectual capacity; and custom closed most educational and vocational avenues. The feminists' goal was to break the constraining chains that had bound them to a limited sphere of experience and social participation. Out of these social constraints arose Emmeline's focused drive to help women reach their highest potential.[11]

Emmeline and her nineteenth-century activist cohorts were not the first. For centuries, individual women had analyzed the barriers to their autonomy and initiated a social dialogue on what was known as the *querelles des femmes* in Europe and later in the United States as the "woman question."[12] But by the nineteenth century their isolated voices had become a united chorus as numbers more saw the discrepancies between the moral and spiritual superiority so often ascribed to women and their actual social inferiority. The demarcation between the domestically grounded moral values of the private sphere and the morally ambiguous values of the public sphere energized a concerted effort to bring public values into consonance with domestic virtues. Another impetus for action was the differing impact of postrevolutionary America on men and women. The heady idealism of the early Republic, which expressed itself in a more democratic political system, an expanding economy, and limitless opportunity for upward mobility through education, industrialization, and western expansion, seemed to a number of intelligent female social observers to have somehow eluded women; the newly written constitution had granted to them only a partial entitlement compared with the benefits and opportunities afforded to men.

While not all these thinking women became activists during this early period, they were outspoken in their derision of the limitations that contemporary ideas of femininity placed on women's mental, emotional, and social development. Drawing from several ideological strains, including the concepts of Romanticism, which swept through antebellum America as a new way of viewing the world, and with the strong sense of social responsibility and individual integrity of the evangelicals, these antebellum female intellectuals offered a nontraditional vision of "true womanhood" and of society itself. They eschewed the passive, submissive, and restrictive domestic qualities then in vogue and urged the removal of all constraints on woman's full realization of her identity as an individual. Some of these popular writers and journalists, such as Lydia Maria Child, Elizabeth Ellet, Elizabeth Oakes Smith, and Paulina Wright Davis, found that history had produced too many diverse and intellectual women for society to relegate all women to a single role, a narrow set of capabilities, and a circumscribed sphere of action. While the writers' names did not acquire the staying power in the manner of feminist theorists Mary Wollstonecraft of late eighteenth-century Great Britain or Margaret Fuller of early nineteenth-century United States, their arguments and analyses contributed toward the shaping of a feminist ideology.[13]

Theirs was not an ideology free from ambiguity and contradiction, however. Nor did all feminists express it in similar terms or with identical goals throughout the century. Even as nineteenth-century women activists argued, on the basis of their shared humanity, that women should have access to the social prerogatives that men had long enjoyed, activists also justified women's inclusion in the social order on the basis of their special female qualities. Society would be the beneficiary, they insisted, for lowering the barriers to women's participation in public life. "Woman's sphere," historian Nancy Cott explained, "was both the point of oppression and the point of departure for nineteenth-century feminists. 'Womanhood' was their hallmark, and they insisted it should be a human norm, too."[14]

According to Nancy Cott's analysis, the nineteenth-century woman movement expressed itself in three distinct ways. One impetus, most apparent early in the century, prompted the organization of charitable and benevolent societies and clubs designed to ameliorate society's ills, particularly those arising from the social changes that accompanied the rapid urbanization of American life and the dramatic influx of immigrants. Preserving the social order by addressing its problems best describes the aim of the benevolent work of these early social workers.

Other activists worked to reform society. The reform impulse that generated the abolitionist movement also propelled its female supporters to instigate a reform movement in their own behalf. Attacking discriminatory laws and constraining social customs, these activists hoped to reform rather than preserve the social structure. After they achieved some success in altering property laws and opening educational and employment opportunities by the end of the century, woman suffrage became the target of their campaign to reform society.

To ideologists, however, these achievements were merely cosmetic, begrudged gratuities that hid persistent discriminatory attitudes and conventions. A transformation in the ways men and women related to each other and of the assumptions by which the social order functioned was for them the ultimate objective.[15] The woman movement developed from and ultimately encompassed elements of these three ideologies.

From her reading of the *Lily: A Ladies' Journal Devoted to Temperance Literature* (1849–56), and the short-lived *Una: A Paper Devoted to the Elevation of Women* (1853–55), legal historian Elizabeth Clark concluded that many of the antebellum feminist theorists interpreted their concept of rights, equality, and freedom, within a religious framework. While employing much of the familiar rhetoric of the Enlightenment and the new republic, the reformers reinterpreted both the source and the meaning of women's rights within the context of human rights. They argued that the grantor of human rights was not the government but a divine source, and the rights to which these women made claim were those "which enabled the full realization of the human potential."[16] Thus, no rule of law should act as an impediment to this "natural right." Moreover, early theorists argued, these God-given rights were the avenues toward improving the lot of women and their children, both of whom suffered at the hands of a discriminatory legal and political system. Equal rights were the way to a greater realization of social justice. Equality to them meant equal access to all the entitlements of a democracy.[17]

After the hiatus imposed by the Civil War, the woman movement began in earnest, channeling its grievances into a constitutional claim to political equality. Emmeline Wells and others argued that the greater prize was the right to personal autonomy. Demolishing the gender boundaries erected by the concept of public (male) and private (female) spheres was a major step toward this fundamental transformation of the social order.[18]

The effort to gain political equality began with three hundred men and women who gathered in the Wesleyan Chapel in Seneca Falls, New York, in July 1848 to inaugurate the first woman's rights convention in the country. Spearheaded by Lucretia Mott and Elizabeth Cady Stanton, the woman movement that followed this auspicious beginning gained adherents and momentum in the antebellum East until suspended during the Civil War. The goal was to gain enough adherents that they could couple feminist theory with political action. The "Declaration of Rights and Sentiments," written by Elizabeth Cady Stanton for the 1848 convention, enumerated the limitations that women felt had restrained their full development as individuals and participation as citizens in a democratic society and expressed their desire to remedy these constraints.[19] Enthusiastic activists then began the long journey toward the "emancipation" of women that focused on gaining their enfranchisement, a crusade that would last nearly seventy-five years.[20]

Though this intellectual ferment took root and sprouted in the East, Mormons in the far western territory

Detail of Lucretia Mott from a collage titled "Representative Women" by L. Prang and Co., Boston, ca. 1870. Mott, along with Elizabeth Cady Stanton, helped spearhead the Seneca Falls Convention in 1848 and labored in the woman suffrage movement until her death in 1880.

of Utah were well informed on the issues it raised. Through the process of exchanging editions with eastern newspapers, the *Deseret News,* established in 1850, followed the movement throughout its factious history. It functioned like a barometer, which indicated the changes in the LDS Church leaders' readings of the woman movement. Besides articles reprinted from eastern papers, it published talks and articles by Church leaders and other contributors acting as a useful source to track the progress of the movement among Mormons. Viewing the antebellum woman movement primarily as a bid for extended political and legal rights, the *News* joined the chorus of naysayers who feared the movement's defeminization of women and its intrusion into the conventions of a long-established social order. Like public media elsewhere in the country, the *News* often ridiculed the so-called "modern woman," who agitated for equal rights, while praising the "true woman" for whom the movement for "rights" was irrelevant and outside her domestic interests. For many, the social activism of women bespoke a sharp departure from traditional values, and the *News* initially supported the latter.

In the early years, numerous articles invoked the familiar Victorian image of the "sturdy oak" and the "clinging vine" of popular verse and sermons that symbolized what was thought to be a desirable relationship of men and women.[21] In time, however, the *Deseret News* began to encourage the education of women, at first focusing on domestic skills but later stressing a wider range of learning, reflecting Church leader Brigham Young's own philosophy as expressed in an 1862 article: "Let our daughters be intellectually educated as highly as possible; let their moral and social nature receive the highest race of vigor and refinement." Many antebellum feminists would have applauded his liberal view of female education. Domestic values were not displaced, however, as the article concluded by asking that "along with these, let the domestic virtues find a prominent place," those womanly qualities that even some feminists believed would help to regenerate an acquisitive and dissolute society.[22]

While never advocating the subordination of marriage and family to other interests, Church leaders, through the *Deseret News* as well as

Eliza R. Snow served as Relief Society General President from 1880–87. She and Emmeline B. Wells visited local Relief Societies and other women's organizations throughout Utah Territory.

through their sermons at the pulpit, encouraged women to gain the education and learn the skills that would make them self-sufficient. Stressing the need for educated homemakers, the paper also urged women to use their talents and skills to help build the religious commonwealth envisioned by Brigham Young.

Though progressive in terms of female education and social participation, Latter-day Saint leaders were still cautious about other aspects of the woman movement. In 1852, just four years after the Seneca Falls meeting, Eliza R. Snow, a frequent contributor to the *Deseret News,* illustrated that restraint. All the exertion of woman's rights activists, she opined in a long poem, "were only making matters worse." In fact, she asserted,

> All the stars leaving their orbits,
> Contending for prerogatives, as well
> Might seek to change the laws that govern them
> As woman to transcend the sphere which God
> Thro' disobedience has assigned to her.[23]

Many women shared her sentiments, but as time went on the modern woman steadily gained ground, and by the late 1860s, the *News* reflected a decided shift away from the woman-as-clinging-vine image. Because gains had been made nationally in educational opportunities, legal rights, and employment options, the woman question had telescoped into a movement for woman suffrage, which became a topic for dialogue across the nation. Woman suffrage emerged as the primary symbol and major goal of the emancipation movement. What better symbol to borrow than the vote to show that Mormon women were not the subjugated, enslaved polygamous wives of popular fiction and the press? No longer disparaging the woman movement or the modern woman, the *Deseret News* touted Mormon women as self-reliant, intelligent, articulate, and perfectly capable of casting well-informed votes. The Utah legislature confirmed this confidence in women by enfranchising them in January 1870, long before any other women of the nation were so favored, except the few residing in Wyoming.[24] By 1870, when Utah women were given the vote, the *News* and most Church leaders were firmly in the camp of the suffragists.[25]

By the time Emmeline Wells came onto the public scene in 1876, two years before her fiftieth birthday, she had noted this shift in attitude within the Church and had already recognized her own feminist instincts. A subscriber to the *Revolution* (1869–71), the short-lived but influential organ of the National Woman Suffrage Association, under the direction of Susan B. Anthony and Elizabeth Cady Stanton, Emmeline Wells became heir to the intellectual tradition of Wollstonecraft, Fuller, and the early antebellum intellectuals as well as the feminist theories of Elizabeth Stanton published in the *Revolution*. Neither indifferent to nor isolated from the debate on women that followed the Civil War, Emmeline joined the conversation on this compelling issue and incorporated in her own writing many of the ideas and much of the rhetoric of these early theorists. In some regards more a transmitter or messenger than a creator of feminist ideas,[26] Wells wrote to stir women to study the woman question and to engage in some soul searching of their own.

That Emmeline's audience was chiefly her fellow Mormons—men as well as women—did not inhibit her critique of complacent women and insensitive men. Writing from within the framework of what critics derided as a male-dominated hierarchy, she distinguished between the demeaning attitude of individual men and what she believed were the enlightened and egalitarian teachings of her religion. She cleverly negotiated the paradox of the Latter-day Saints' liberating theology within a pervasive patriarchy and arrived at a personally satisfying ideology. Thus, though she leaned heavily on the writings of her feminist predecessors, Wells added her own theological dimension to her ideology that differed from the accommodation with religion made by other religious feminists.[27] Hers was not a solitary Mormon voice. Her bold stand in support of the woman movement and its denunciation of male hegemony elicited similar views from numerous readers, which she published in the *Woman's Exponent,* thereby assuring her reading public that she had colleagues among her fellow Mormons.[28]

The paper also provided Emmeline's eastern readers with an alternative view of Mormon women from that which they read in the popular press, a view that would prove of incalculable supportive value during the federal crusade against the LDS Church's practice of polygamy. By the time Wells made her first personal connection with leaders of the movement in 1879, she had established herself as a committed advocate for the expansion of women's rights. As for her contributions to the *Exponent,* the decade of the 1870s that brought her periods of disillusionment and unhappiness also produced some of her sharpest feminist critiques and opened a broad new avenue of experience for her. The private despair of her middle years gave way to heightened pleasures in her public life. Out of the depths of her own private battles, she created the feminist manifesto that initiated a lifelong commitment to the advancement of women.

Several ideological streams fed into Emmeline's approach to the woman question of her time. From the uncertainties of her private life, from the broad goals of a multifaceted feminism, from the doctrines of LDS theology, and also from a compelling sense of personal destiny, Emmeline Wells formulated her own worldview, a social cosmology encompassing her thoughts on individual human dignity, true compatibility in marriage, and the place of women in the work of the world, all of which assumed a fundamental reordering of the relationship of men and women.

Similar to the family claims on Elizabeth Stanton (a mother of seven), Wells's lively household of daughters, grandchildren, and streams of visitors and friends pressed hard against the ever-increasing demands of a full-time occupation and a growing public presence. But they also fed the intensity of Wells's public work. Each night she sifted through the activities of her day and formulated the ideas that gave perspective to her thoughts, which found eventual expression in the pages of the *Exponent*. Writing would indeed be her medium and the *Exponent* her forum, useful vehicles for expressing that "freedom of agency" so many women longed to have.[29] Shedding her pseudonym Blanche Beechwood in 1877 when she became editor, she showed no hesitancy in using her agency to present her views to the public.[30]

Like most feminist theorists of her time, Emmeline drew upon the egalitarian notions and focused on "educated reason" of the Enlightenment tradition, especially as enunciated by British writer Mary Wollstonecraft.[31] Emmeline's insistence on the inherent intellectual capabilities and natural rights of women echoed the Enlightenment notion as transmitted by Wollstonecraft that rationality, the ability to think and conceptualize, was a divine endowment to both sexes. "The nature of reason must be the same in all," Wollstonecraft explained, "if it be an emanation of divinity, the tie that connects the creature with the creator."[32] Her challenge, to "let the faculties of women unfold, and their virtue to gain strength" in order to "determine where the whole sex must stand on the intellectual side,"[33] became a basic article in the feminist canon and particularly informed the feminism of Emmeline Wells.

If, indeed, the nature of reason is the same in both men and women, Wollstonecraft further queried, "should woman be expected to believe that she was created only to submit to man—her equal—a being who, like her, was sent into the world to acquire virtue?"[34] The hegemony of patriarchy more than the hierarchical orientation of society stirred women's sense of injustice. Equivalence rather than equality, however, was the remedy, Wells believed. Equivalence skirted the problem of "sameness," which offended most nineteenth-century sensibilities, by positing a relationship between men and women defined by a complementariness of different natures and roles, a mutual respect for individuality, a reciprocity of interests, and an interdependence of rights and responsibilities.

Romanticism, particularly as articulated by Margaret Fuller, offered another base for nineteenth-century feminism. Emmeline Wells was probably more concordant with Fuller and her ideas than with other nineteenth-century feminists. Though Wells rarely mentioned Fuller in her extant diaries, never featured her in the *Woman's Exponent,* nor referred to either of Fuller's feminist tomes—the long article entitled "The Great Lawsuit" or her book-length study, *Woman of the Nineteenth Century*—Emmeline Wells demonstrated a familiarity with both Fuller and her literary works.[35] According to historian Susan Conrad, American romanticism, with its privileging of "imagination, empathy, and intuition," proved particularly felicitous to nineteenth-century feminism and narrowed the chasm between the feminine and the feminist.[36] These were, after all, traditional female qualities. Margaret Fuller, however, was quick to distinguish her idea of true womanhood from popular notions that defined passive and intellectually dormant women as typically feminine. Fuller claimed that the dual powers of reason (a traditional male attribute) and intuition (traditionally female) resided within both women and men, though she believed that women exhibited more of the intuitive power than did men.[37] The emphasis on intuition as a surer path to knowledge, however, did not diminish the focus on intellect as the tool for analyzing and synthesizing one's perception of the world.[38] As a path to truth, Wells also favored intuition, which, she felt, yielded "quicker perceptions" than "hard, cold reasoning." She also agreed that both qualities informed a woman's identity as much as a man's.[39] For her, as for Fuller, the thinking woman was the archetype of real womanhood and should be free to develop the divinely bestowed gifts of both reason and intuition.[40]

Margaret Fuller, a transcendentalist, articulated a new brand of feminism in the nineteenth century.

Library of Congress

Romanticism, as a system of thought and behavior, had given its early female adherents the impetus to seek out the "country of the mind" as a means of discovering their own individuality and identity.[41] Enshrining the individual and its self-realization as preeminent values, Romanticism emphasized individual growth and social diversity. But it also assumed a natural grouping of women as a class because of their exclusive biological characteristics and domestic orientation.[42] This concept allowed for a female "uniqueness," which served, though awkwardly at times, the goals of feminism throughout the nineteenth century.[43]

Latter-day Saint theology shared several philosophical strands with Romanticism, perhaps making Wells particularly susceptible to Fuller's theories and rendering Mormonism a comfortable matrix out of which Wells developed her own feminist philosophy.[44] Both Mormonism and Romanticism affirmed the basic goodness of individuals and their common destiny to grow and develop to their highest potential. Their optimism and hopeful approach to the human condition were a dramatic reversal of the enervating guilt and predestination of Calvinism, Emmeline's earliest religious indoctrination. The Latter-day Saint assertion of the divine origin of the spirit and the human potential of Godhood carried overtones of the transcendentalist focus on the preeminence of the individual soul, its divine emanation, its susceptibility to an intuitive path to truth, and its worthiness to progress naturally and freely with a concomitant moral accountability.[45] Romanticism's assertion that intuition or the "divine spark" within all humankind could impart knowledge that transcends the empirical paralleled the Latter-day Saint belief in the power of the Holy Spirit to prompt, instruct, and lead the individual toward understanding and proper action.

Mormonism offered other planks that supported Emmeline's feminism besides those it shared with Romanticism.[46] The principle of personal agency, so fundamental to the Church's doctrine and newly articulated by feminists, was primary.[47] As Erastus Snow, then a member of the Quorum of the Twelve Apostles, explained in 1878:

> We have come to the understanding that every soul of man, both male and female, high and low, is the offspring of God, that their

spirits are immortal, eternal, intelligent beings, and that their entity depends upon their agency and independent action, which is neither trammeled by God himself nor allowed to be restrained by any of His creatures with His action and approval.[48]

Using the *Woman's Exponent* almost exclusively as her debating forum, Emmeline extrapolated this religious concept to the social condition of women, fervently exclaiming that it was this "longing for freedom that is inspiring . . . women . . . to make war against the bondage with which they have been enslaved, and seek, by every available means, to inspire a universal feeling among men and women for equal rights and privileges in the sphere God has assigned them."[49] This concept of agency meant, however, that Christian feminists had to deal with the knotty problem of Eve's subordination to Adam, part of the "curse" she received for her disobedience in the Garden.[50] Some of them denounced biblical literalism, some reinterpreted sexist passages or refuted the timelessness or universality of the offending verses.[51] Some feminists, most notably Elizabeth Cady Stanton, rejected biblical authority and organized religion altogether for offering women "not one step of progress, or one new liberty."[52]

Though Eve was never castigated as a sinner or seducer in Latter-day Saint theology—indeed, she was honored for her courageous act in the Garden[53]—she nonetheless cast a long, debilitating shadow. Perhaps Emmeline's awareness of the centuries-long effects of that "curse" prompted her, along with many other Mormon women, to recognize that its historical dominance in earthly affairs would not be easily dismantled. Though she believed implicitly that woman's spiritual future, as did man's, lay within Christ's redemptive act, the earthly effects of Eve's punishment lingered, if only as a cultural phenomenon.

These effects, however, were in the province of women to ameliorate, Emmeline believed, by performing "redemptive acts" of their own.[54] She believed that all efforts to advance women were part of that process of redemption. As a fallen world would yet be redeemed from the effects of the Edenic transgression,[55] so also would women finally enjoy that equality that had been theirs before the Fall, Emmeline asserted. "Perfect equality then," she declared, "and so it must be when all things are restored as they were in the beginning. It is this spirit stirring within woman," she continued, "that is to bring her back again to that primeval state that existed in the Garden of Eden."[56] It was this spirit, she confidently believed, that animated the movement to reclaim that equality. The ultimate purpose of the restoration of Christ's gospel, which had been lost, LDS Church doctrine claimed, was to prepare a fallen world and its inhabitants to return to that paradisiacal glory.[57]

The promise of future spiritual equality spurred Emmeline toward efforts to reform a social structure that denied women temporal equality. In fact, Emmeline believed that full expression of the gift of agency in this life was a necessity for full equality in the next. To achieve this desired state required a united effort. "Woman's work in this day and age," she wrote, "is not only an individual work, but a universal work; a work for all her suffering sisterhood."[58] Building a group consciousness that transcended the boundaries of Mormondom and capitalized on the commonalities of women, despite their economic, regional, or religious differences, Emmeline believed, would create a power base from which change would be possible. "We are engaged in a stupendous work," she wrote in 1874, "view it in whatever light we may, and the work is increasing on every side. It is impossible to define its limits, or determine its magnitude." She assured her fellow workers in the LDS Relief Society that through this unified effort "the seed we sow will assuredly spring up, blossom and bear fruit in the future; having the same prize to obtain, the same goal to reach, aiming at the same great result, the regeneration of women."[59]

Though some of her Mormon sisters worried that the agitation created by "strong minded women" would result only in "a war of sexes," Emmeline Wells felt that the time had come for women to stand up in their own defense against the "usurpation of their inherited rights and privileges." Spiritual redemption was a handmaiden of secular redemption. Together they represented an undertaking that would transform not only laws and social policies but also attitudes and the tight grip of tradition.

Within the Church, Emmeline saw many opportunities for women to express their abilities and broaden their knowledge and understanding.

One door was opened when the women's Relief Society was organized in 1842 in Nauvoo, Illinois. At the sixth meeting of the Society, the Latter-day Saint prophet Joseph Smith announced to the members, "I now turn the key to you in the name of God and this Society shall rejoice and knowledge and intelligence shall flow down from this time—this is the beginning of better days to this Society."[60] That symbolic gesture not only opened the door to spiritual blessings but, later members asserted, also marked the beginning of the redemption of womankind and the restoration of primeval equality. Emmeline assured her readers that the bonds of female servitude began to loosen in 1842 and from that time on "men no longer held the same absolute sway."[61]

Since the beginning of this last gospel dispensation, she attested, "women have been developing powers and attributes which had previously lain dormant and also claiming independence and freedom in civil[,] political and religious matters unheard of before."[62] Thus, Latter-day Saint women attached a direct relationship between the organization of the Relief Society in Nauvoo in 1842, with its empowerment of women, and the first woman's rights convention of 1848. That the Relief Society was organized first was not a mere happenstance. As a result of that event, not only Mormon women, but women of the world, Emmeline insisted, were "acted upon by an influence many comprehend not which is working for their redemption from under the curse."[63] This was woman's era, she repeatedly exclaimed. "The very genius and spirit of the age is in keeping with the cry of woman for recognition of her position by the side of man. It is the consciousness in woman everywhere, if even a latent spark of her inherent divinity lingers, that the hour is hastening when the curse will be removed."[64]

The Relief Society was a major facilitator of this promised emancipation of women, promoting both their temporal and spiritual development. "The organization of the Relief Society," Emmeline Wells explained to her readers,

> opened one of the most important eras in the history of women. It presented the great woman-question to the Latter-day Saints previous to the woman's rights organizations which have created such extensive agitation since. . . . The question did not present itself in

any aggressive form as woman opposed to man but as a co-worker and help meet in all that relates to the well being and advancement of both, and mutual promoting of the best interests of the community at large. It has given to woman in its rise and progress, influence on almost all aspects that pertain to her welfare and happiness, and opportunities for expressing her own thoughts, views and opinions, all of which has had a tendency to make her intelligent in respect to matters which before were considered incompatible with "woman's sphere" and unintelligible to her "weaker" mind.[65]

Besides encouraging unprecedented intellectual and social development, the LDS Church offered avenues to individual spiritual growth and experience of special importance to women. From the earliest days of the Church, Joseph Smith had claimed that the exercise of spiritual gifts demonstrated the authenticity of the restoration of the pristine gospel and the presence of the Holy Spirit, and during the Church's first century members freely exercised spiritual gifts.[66] After Joseph Smith counseled the Nauvoo Relief Society in the use of these gifts, the exercise of one or more of them often marked the gatherings of women thereafter. Emmeline Wells recorded many such instances in the various Relief Society meetings she attended and in gatherings with her friends at home.[67] Manifesting these "signs of the believers," which were not necessarily unique to Latter-day Saints, gave women direct, rather than mediated, access to spiritual power and made *them* the vehicles through which God revealed his mind and will in their personal lives and organizational responsibilities. While men governed the Church as holders of priesthood authority, women had access to divine inspiration and the use of spiritual power for their own needs and obligations.

In addition to the ecclesiastical roles and charismatic functions that the Church afforded women, temple worship, a practice unique to Latter-day Saints, supported Emmeline's fundamentally religious feminism. This liturgical service allowed women to participate in the holiest rituals of the religion. As initiates in the temple ceremony, they received an "endowment," or "power from on high" (D&C 95:8–9). As officiators they were essential in administering specific priesthood ordinances necessary for salvation. This partnership in the most sacred of religious rites gave women an essential role in "building the kingdom" in this life and preparing themselves for the next. In sum, while men were ordained to individual priesthood offices and responsibilities, women expressed ecclesiastical and spiritual power in the governing of their own organizations, in their receipt and use of spiritual gifts, and in temple service.

Women, moreover, enjoyed direct benefits of priesthood in spiritually empowering ways that complemented the priesthood's governing purposes. Elder Franklin D. Richards explained this connection in a Relief Society conference address delivered in Ogden in 1888. "I ask any and everybody present who have received their endowments," he said to the mixed audience,

> whether he be a brother Apostle, Bishop, High Priest, Elder, or whatever office he may hold in the Church, "What blessings did you receive, what ordinance, what power, intelligence, sanctification or grace did you receive that your wife did not partake of with you?" I will answer, that there was one thing that our wives were not made special partakers of, and that was the ordination to the various orders of the priesthood which were conferred upon us. Aside from that, our sisters share with us any and all of the ordinances of the holy anointing, endowments, sealings, sanctifications and blessings that we have been made partakers of.

He concluded by asking:

> Is it possible that we have the holy priesthood and our wives have none of it? Do you not see, by what I have read, that Joseph [Smith] desired to confer these keys of power upon them in connection with their husbands? I hold that a faithful wife has certain blessings, powers and rights, and is made partaker of certain gifts and blessings and promises with her husband, which she cannot be deprived of, except by transgression of the holy order of God. They shall enjoy what God said they should.[68]

Emmeline Wells had long understood the nature of this endowment of spiritual power and prerogative. Ten years before Elder Richards spoke on the subject, she had explained her thoughts to the Gunnison,

Utah, ward Relief Society. "It is very hard for some people to believe that women are acknowledged of God as holding any Priesthood or power," she said. "But time will demonstrate the harmony which exists in [the sexes], . . . and prove to all that women are not an inferior race of beings. . . . To those who feel that there are prophetesses as well as prophets, we may speak of these things. To us, they are sacred truths."[69] She believed implicitly that her faith gave her exceptional opportunities for individual growth, for leadership and decision making, for participation in the Church's sacred rites, and for personal access to divine power. Her sense of partnership with men in both her secular and sacred pursuits was satisfying as well as enabling. She never expressed uncertainty about her own religious convictions even when organized religion was denounced by some of her admired sister suffragists. For Emmeline, Mormonism advanced rather than denied woman's full selfhood. It was both the foundation and motivation for her service to women.

Notes

1. Blanche Beechwood, "Why, Ah! Why," *Woman's Exponent* 3 (October 1, 1874): 67.

2. Emmeline B. Wells, Diary, January 2, 1878, L. Tom Perry Special Collections, Harold B. Lee Library, Brigham Young University, Provo, Utah.

3. In 1874, Melvina Whitney, daughter of Emmeline Wells and her second husband, Newel K. Whitney, married William Wells Woods, a nephew of her stepfather Daniel H. Wells. Woods was an attorney from Iowa who practiced law in Utah from about 1874 until he moved to the Coeur D'Alene area of Idaho in 1888, where he and Melvina lived until his death in 1920. He never joined the LDS Church, much to Emmeline's disappointment.

4. Through a series of financial misfortunes, her husband, the prominent Daniel H. Wells, could not provide the financial means his large family necessitated. The other wives all had sons who could assist them.

5. As early as 1857, Eliza R. Snow enunciated qualities of the model Mormon woman: submission, faith, constancy, and service. See Eliza R. Snow, "Woman," *Millennial Star* 19 (January 31, 1857): 79–80. Compare with Barbara Welter's identification of the virtues of "true womanhood" of the same period: submission, piety, purity, and domesticity. Barbara Welter, "The Cult of True

Womanhood, 1820–1860," *American Quarterly* 18 (Summer 1966): 151–74. See also Eliza R. Snow's talk under "Celebration of the Twenty-fourth at Ogden!" Journal History of the Church, July 24, 1871, 4–5, Church Archives, The Church of Jesus Christ of Latter-day Saints, Salt Lake City, also available on *Selected Collections from the Archives of The Church of Jesus Christ of Latter-day Saints,* 2 vols. (Provo, Utah: Brigham Young University Press, 2002), vol. 2, DVD 6, microfilm copy in Harold B. Lee Library.

6. Eliza R. Snow, who retained her maiden name until late in life, when she added the name Smith, was married first to founding prophet Joseph Smith and after his death to his successor Brigham Young.

7. This contrast in lifestyles was symbolic of the larger contrast and what was often a conflict between women who sought more expansive opportunities for their sex, either from their own necessity or from their commitment to an ideology of equality, and those whose life paths were more comfortable and secure.

8. "Women in Reform," *Woman's Exponent* 6 (November 15, 1877): 92.

9. "Belva Lockwood's Candidacy," *Woman's Exponent* 13 (September 15, 1884): 60.

10. Wells, Diary, January 7, 1878.

11. Though the term "feminism" was not employed by nineteenth-century female activists, and contemporary historical purists such as Nancy F. Cott discouraged its usage for them, the term will be applied in this volume as a shorthand description for what would later be labeled feminist theories and activities.

12. An overview of the long debate on women's place in the social order may be found in Susan Groag Bell and Karen M. Offen, eds., *Women, the Family, and Freedom: The Debate in Documents,* 2 vols. (Stanford: Stanford University Press, 1983). In 1884, Henry Stanton introduced the phrase "the woman question" to the woman's movement in the United States, no doubt borrowing it from the much earlier European labeling of the debate about women, as the "Querelles des Femmes." See Bonnie S. Anderson and Judith P. Zinsser, *A History of Their Own: Women in Europe from Prehistory to the Present,* 2 vols. (New York: Harper and Row 1988), 2:91–95; see also Bell and Offen, *Women, the Family, and Freedom,* 1:2n3.

13. Mary Wollstonecraft's theories on woman's rights, based largely on the ideology of the Enlightenment, are found in *The Vindication of the Rights of Women* (1792; New York: W. W. Norton, 1967). Margaret Fuller, a follower of Ralph Waldo Emerson and the transcendentalist movement and editor of

its publication, the *Dial,* expressed her feminist views in *Woman in the Nineteenth Century* (1845; repr., New York: W. W. Norton, 1971). Elizabeth Stanton attended a winter series of meetings of Fuller's famous "Conversation Club" in Boston and later wrote that the conversations "were in reality a vindication of woman's right to think." Much of Stanton's writing can be traced to ideas formulated by Fuller.

14. Nancy Cott, *The Grounding of Modern Feminism* (New Haven, Conn.: Yale University Press, 1987), 20.

15. Cott, *Grounding of Modern Feminism,* 16.

16. Elizabeth Clark elaborates the meaning of rights and entitlements as expressed by these early feminists in *Religion, Rights and Difference: The Origins of American Feminism, 1848–1860,* Legal History Program, Working Papers, Series 2 (Madison: University of Wisconsin Law School, Institute for Legal Studies, 1987), 24–34. Social justice was a logical cause in antebellum feminism since many feminists were also abolitionists and temperance workers. Besides slavery, they decried, especially in the *Lily,* the helpless status of women who had no legal protection from abusive husbands, especially alcoholics, at a time when the consumption of alcohol in the country was at its highest level. Legislative statutes and social norms made divorce an impossibility for most women.

17. Clark, *Religion, Rights and Difference,* 24–34.

18. Clark analyzed the nature of the antebellum feminist argument and its goal for "a transformative social change." See especially Clark, *Religion, Rights and Difference,* 34. The post–Civil War movement largely abandoned this goal in its single-minded effort to gain political and legal rights for women.

19. A complete copy of the Declaration is included in Elizabeth Cady Stanton, Susan B. Anthony, and Matilda Joslyn Gage, eds., *History of Woman Suffrage,* vol. 1 (New York: Fowler and Wells, 1881), 69–74, 809–10.

20. Numerous studies have been done on the origins of the woman movement, including Eleanor Flexner, *A Century of Struggle: The Woman's Rights Movement in America* (New York: Atheneum, 1974); Miriam Gurko, *The Ladies of Seneca Falls: The Birth of the Woman's Rights Movement* (New York: Schocken Books, 1976); Keith E. Melder, *Beginnings of Sisterhood: The American Woman's Rights Movement, 1800–1850* (New York: Schocken Books, 1977); Clark, *Religion, Rights and Difference*; Ellen Carol DuBois, *Feminism and Suffrage: The Emergence of an Independent Woman's Movement in America, 1848–1869* (Ithaca, N.Y.: Cornell University Press, 1978).

21. A January 1856 *Deseret News* article used the metaphor at length to show that just as the graceful vine, when a thunderbolt befalls the sturdy oak,

clings to it with "caressing tendrils," so should the woman, the dependent "ornament" of man, "wind herself into the rugged recesses of his nature" when he is smitten with sudden calamity. "Woman," *Deseret News* January 16, 1856, 353. A fable also based on the vine and oak metaphor depicted the calamity that the vine would encounter should it wish either to trade places with the oak or grow independently from it. By staying close, the oak promised, they would "grow and flourish happily together." "A Fable for Strong-Minded Women," *Deseret News,* May 14, 1856, 78. A thorough overview of articles on women in the *Deseret News,* official organ of the LDS Church, from which many of these references have been drawn, is Kami Wilson, "Women's Roles, the *Deseret News* and LDS Women in Utah, 1852–1870" (master's thesis, University of Nebraska, Omaha, 2001).

22. "Our Daughters," *Deseret News*, August 27, 1862, 66.

23. Snow, "Celebration of the Twenty-fourth at Ogden!" 4–5.

24. Wyoming women were enfranchised in December 1869, just two months before Utah women.

25. See for example "Miss Anna E. Dickinson," *Deseret News Semi-Weekly*, June 23, 1869, 236. Other articles favoring woman suffrage appeared in "Female Suffrage," *Deseret News Semi-Weekly*, December 5, 1868, 348; "Female Suffrage—Ends to be Gained by It," *Deseret News Semi-Weekly*, March 24, 1869, 78; "Female Suffrage in Utah," *Deseret News Semi-Weekly*, March 24, 1869, 78.

26. Susan P. Conrad identifies the true intellectual as one who creates rather than distributes or applies ideas. But she expands the meaning of "creator" to include those who "pursue and master a portion of their culture's extant body of knowledge which body is changed by their subsequent analyses, interpretations, revisions, and additions." One might include Emmeline Wells within this category. See Susan P. Conrad, *Perish the Thought, Intellectual Women in Romantic America, 1830–1860* (Secaucus, N.J.: Citadel Press, 1976), 6–7.

27. Donna A. Behnke examines the religious arguments relating to the woman question in *Religious Issues in Nineteenth Century Feminism* (Troy, N.Y.: Whitston, 1982).

28. Chief among those whose feminist ideas coincided with those of Wells was Lucinda (Lu) Dalton, one of the most consistent contributors to the *Woman's Exponent*. Former editor Lula Greene Richards, Susa Young Gates, Sarah M. Kimball, and Ellis Shipp were prominent among other supporters. For a detailed study on the feminist views of Lu Dalton, see Sheree Bench, "'Woman Arise!': Political Work in the Writings of Lu Dalton" (master's thesis,

Brigham Young University, 2002). In a slim volume entitled *the flight and the nest* (Salt Lake City: Bookcraft, 1975), Carol Lynn Pearson has collected numerous statements on the subject from a variety of Mormon publications. See also Judith Rasmussen Dushku, "Feminists," in *Mormon Studies,* ed. Claudia L. Bushman (Cambridge: Emmeline Press, 1976), 177–97.

29. Margaret Fuller made this observation in her major book, *Woman in the Nineteenth Century.* Eve Kornfeld quotes Fuller in *Margaret Fuller: A Brief Biography with Documents,* The Bedford Series in History and Culture (Boston: Bedford Books, 1997), 164. Fuller's book is an expanded version of her essay, "The Great Lawsuit, Man versus Men, Woman versus Women," originally published in *Dial* 4, no. 1 (July 1843): 1–47.

30. Emmeline Wells also used the pen name "Athena" for some of her poetry, but only for a brief period. As she became more caught up in the woman movement, she disdained the female use of pen names, urging women to be confident and proud enough of their efforts to attribute them to their own names.

31. Wollstonecraft's book for which she is remembered is entitled *The Vindication of the Rights of Women* and was originally published in 1792.

32. From Wollstonecraft, *Vindication of the Rights of Women,* as quoted in Eleanor Flexner, *Mary Wollstonecraft* (Baltimore: Penguin Books, 1973), 160. While her vocabulary was somewhat different, Wells frequently affirmed the same idea: "God has endowed woman with faculties and instincts, with the right of conscience inherent in her soul." See "Noble Work for Women," *Woman's Exponent* 7 (April 1, 1879): 218. Wollstonecraft, Fuller, and Wells all made the point that women were endowed with both reason and a moral sensibility and were therefore as accountable for their actions as men. It followed, then, they argued, that they needed the same experience to develop both endowments.

33. From Wollstonecraft, *Vindications of the Rights of Women,* as quoted in Alice Rossi, ed., *The Feminist Papers: From Adams to de Beauvoir* (New York: Columbia University Press, 1973), 53.

34. From Wollstonecraft, *Vindication of the Rights of Women,* as quoted in Flexner, *Mary Wollstonecraft,* 160–61.

35. She published only five notices of Margaret Fuller in the *Woman's Exponent.* Four are brief mentions of little more than her name in reprints from exchange papers. One is a eulogy by Mormon poet Hannah T. King. King had recently read a biography of Margaret Fuller and lauded her for helping "to awaken the world to the restoration of woman to the pedestal from which she had fallen . . . as the friend and co-partner of her brother

man." See "Margaret Fuller," *Woman's Exponent* 13 (November 15, 1884): 89. Margaret Fuller was living in Europe at the time of the Seneca Falls Women's Rights Convention of 1848. She unfortunately died in a shipwreck returning to America in 1850 with her husband and young son.

36. See Conrad, *Perish the Thought,* 9–13, 79.

37. While Fuller believed that men evidenced more of the rational and women showed more of the intuitive, only in a union of the two could either be perfectly whole. Most studies deal with Margaret Fuller as a literary rather than historical subject, but several offer insight into her feminist philosophy. Works consulted for this paper include Nancy M. Theriot, "Mary Wollstonecraft and Margaret Fuller: A Theoretical Comparison," *International Journal of Women's Studies* 2, no. 6, 560–74; Marie Olesen Urbanski, "The Genesis, Form, Tone, and Rhetorical Devices of Woman in the Nineteenth Century," in *Critical Essays on Margaret Fuller,* ed. Joel Myerson (Boston: G. K. Hall, 1980), 268–80; Paula Blanchard, *Margaret Fuller: From Transcendentalism to Revolution* (Cambridge: Delacorte Press/Seymour Lawrence, 1978); Margaret Vanderhaar Allen, *The Achievement of Margaret Fuller* (University Park: Pennsylvania State University Press, 1979).

38. Conrad, *Perish the Thought,* 20–27.

39. Blanche Beechwood, "Woman, a Subject," *Woman's Exponent* 3 (November 1, 1874): 82.

40. Not only Emmeline Wells but all feminists had a new vision of womanhood, one which combined the natural attributes of the feminine with those features associated with intellectuality. This is the substance of Susan Conrad's book *Perish the Thought* and has been discussed by other historians, especially those dealing with the suffrage movement.

41. Conrad, *Perish the Thought,* 11.

42. Conrad, *Perish the Thought,* 97.

43. Nancy Cott writes that "feminism posits that women perceive themselves not only as a biological sex but perhaps even more important, as a social grouping." This recognition of "shared ground," she claims, "enables the consciousness and the community of action among women to impel change." See Nancy Cott, *The Grounding of Modern Feminism* (New Haven, Conn.: Yale University Press, 1987), 5, 9.

44. In the late nineteenth century, both Mormonism and feminism were considered outside the norm of religious orthodoxy as was Romanticism.

45. In her article "Mystical Feminist, Margaret Fuller, a Woman of the Nineteenth Century," historian Barbara Welter describes Fuller's primary feminist themes as "the value of the individual, the free will, the enlightened

intellect, and the awakened sense of moral responsibility," values also highly regarded in Mormonism. See Barbara Welter, *Dimity Convictions: The American Woman in the Nineteenth Century* (Athens: Ohio University Press, 1976), 170.

46. Wells gave public hints of her theological views in her editorials and more fully in two published addresses: one presented at a meeting of the National Council of Women in 1902 and the other at a meeting of the Women's Clubs of New York in 1907. See Emmeline B. Wells, "The Age We Live In," in *The General Relief Society Officers, Objects and Status* (Salt Lake City: General Officers, 1902), 69–76; and "Why a Woman Should Desire to Be a Mormon," *Woman's Exponent* 36 (December 1907): 39–40; 36 (January 1908): 46–48.

47. Brigham Young asserted that "the actions of men [and women] . . . are left free; they are agents to themselves and must act freely on that agency." Wilford Woodruff declared that "with regard to the rights of the human family . . . God has given unto all of His children . . . individual agency." These and additional statements by Brigham Young, John Taylor, George Albert Smith, Joseph F. Smith, and Lorenzo Snow relating to individual agency can be found in Daniel H. Ludlow, ed., *Latter-day Prophets Speak* (Salt Lake City: Bookcraft, 1948), 155–58.

48. Erastus Snow, in *Journal of Discourses,* 26 vols. (Liverpool, Eng.: F. D. Richards, 1855–86), 24:69 (April 6, 1883).

49. "Special Life Missions," *Woman's Exponent* 6 (March 1, 1878): 148.

50. Genesis 2:22, relating Eve's creation after Adam's, and Genesis 3:16, pronouncing Eve's subservience to Adam because of her disobedience, were the primary passages from the Old Testament. Other scriptures used by antifeminists were 1 Corinthians 14:34–35, Paul's injunction against women speaking in the churches, 1 Timothy 2:11–15, and Ephesians 5:22–24, which also enjoin women to silence.

51. Feminists in the latter part of the nineteenth century who finally had access to advanced education were able to draw upon their own training in Greek and Hebrew as well as the methodology of the newly emerging higher criticism of the Bible, many of whose findings were compatible with their own views.

52. Elizabeth Cady Stanton, "Has Christianity Benefitted Woman?" *North American Review* 140, no. 342 (May 1885): 389–90, as quoted in Behnke, *Religious Issues in Nineteenth Century Feminism*, 165. Matilda Gage, Abby Morton Diaz, and other feminists were as vehement in their denial of Christianity's advantages to women as Stanton. See Behnke, *Religious Issues,* 159–80.

53. In the current Bible Dictionary in Latter-day Saint scriptures, Eve is identified as "the mother of all living" who will share eternal glory with Adam. "Eve's recognition of the necessity of the fall and the joys of redemption," it continues, "gives us an awareness of her nobility." The conclusion to Deborah F. Sawyer's article, "Resurrecting Eve? Feminist Critique of the Garden of Eden," in *A Walk in the Garden: Biblical, Iconographical and Literary Images of Eden*, ed. Paul Morris and Deborah Sawyer (Sheffield, Eng.: Sheffield Academic Press, 1992), 288, suggests a reading of Eve that corresponds with Latter-day Saint doctrine: "Eve . . . , created in the image of God, takes responsibility for human progress, liberates herself and her husband from the playground of paradise and engages with the real world."

54. For some, these redemptive acts that Emmeline Wells noted could be performed exclusively within the framework of the LDS Church. George Q. Cannon, a member of the Church's First Presidency, explained that women must redeem themselves by obedience to gospel principles, noting that accepting plural marriage as one of those principles would "exalt woman until she is redeemed from the effects of the Fall, and from that curse pronounced upon her in the beginning." *Juvenile Instructor* 19 (February 1, 1884), 38–39.

55. The Latter-day Saint position on the millennium is explained in Paul B. Pixton, "Millennium," in *Encyclopedia of Mormonism*, ed. Daniel H. Ludlow, 4 vols. (New York: Macmillan, 1992), 2:906–8.

56. Wells, "Age We Live In," 74–75.

57. The mythical and mystical as well as literal interpretations of the Eve story have invested it with perpetual currency in widely diverse cultures and eras. Time has proven the enormous religious, literary, and philosophical appeal of the notion of Paradise lost and regained. The Eve story in contemporary Christianity, however, has lost its religious force in defining Eve's disobedience as a basis for the relationship between men and women.

58. The dimensions of the world that Emmeline embraced were always more universal and ecumenical than many of her Mormon sisters. In the process of trying to advance her own sisters she hoped to be aiding all women. See "Woman's Work," *Woman's Exponent* 4 (November 15, 1875): 94.

59. Blanche Beechwood, "Bear Ye One Another's Burdens," *Woman's Exponent* 2 (March 1, 1874): 146.

60. Minutes of the Female Relief Society of Nauvoo, April 28, 1842. Two Apostles, besides numerous women, noted the universal changes that occurred for women following that significant pronouncement: Orson F. Whitney in 1906 and George Albert Smith in 1945. See Whitney, "Woman's Work and

Mormonism," *Young Woman's Journal* 17 (July 1906): 295; and Smith, "Relief Society," *Relief Society Magazine* 32 (December 1945): 717.

61. "A Wonderful Age," *Woman's Exponent* 27 (February 1, 1899): 100.

62. Wells, Diary, March 14, 1892. In her diary she inadvertently (and perhaps in a Freudian lapse) wrote "tree of knowledge" rather than "key of knowledge," in referring to that phrase, perhaps indicating her association of the two religious events.

63. "Self-Made Women," *Woman's Exponent* 9 (March 1, 1881): 148. Other Mormon women made the same observations. Some examples can be found in "Symposium, The Nineteenth and Twentieth Centuries," *Woman's Exponent* 29 (January 1, 1901): 69, and throughout various other issues of the *Exponent*.

64. "Patriarchal Marriage," *Woman's Exponent* 6 (August 15, 1877): 44.

65. "Women's Organizations," *Woman's Exponent* 8 (January 1, 1880): 122.

66. More discussion on this point can be found in Grant Underwood, *The Millenarian World of Early Mormonism* (Chicago: University of Illinois Press, 1993), 97–98.

67. Wells reminisces about these occasions in an article by her daughter Annie Wells Cannon entitled "Mothers in Israel," *Relief Society Magazine* 3 (February 1916): 70.

68. From "Memorial Anniversary," *Woman's Exponent* 17 (September 1, 1888): 52–54. Elder Richards read to them portions of a sermon by Joseph Smith to the Female Relief Society of Nauvoo delivered on April 28, 1842. Joseph Smith indicated in his journal that he met with the Relief Society on that day to show "how the Sisters would come in possession of the privileges & blessings & gifts of the priesthood." Wilford Woodruff, Diary, as quoted in Dean C. Jessee, ed., *The Papers of Joseph Smith,* 2 vols. (Salt Lake City: Deseret Book, 1992), 2:378–79. See Minutes of the Female Relief Society of Nauvoo, Church Archives. See also Joseph Smith Jr., *History of The Church of Jesus Christ of Latter-day Saints,* ed. B. H. Roberts, 2d ed., rev., 7 vols. (Salt Lake City: Deseret Book, 1971), 4:602.

69. Emmeline B. Wells to the Gunnison Ward Relief Society, February 15, 1877, a letter copied into the Minutes of the Gunnison Ward Relief Society, Gunnison Stake, February 1, 1877, Church Archives.

Chapter 5

"This Is Woman's Era"

*To woman has been opened
the great domain of the world.*[1]

Though it was not until the end of the century that social scientists reversed the assumption that women were inherently intellectually inferior to men, Emmeline Wells's editorials suggest that she had never entertained the notion of female inferiority. As women were gradually admitted to higher and graduate education, a number of them entered into the new field of sociology. Through their sociological studies they stressed the impact of "cultural conditioning" and "formulated theories about intelligence, personality development and sex roles that . . . affected the whole course of American social science."[2]

The differences between the sexes, beyond biological distinctions, could largely be laid at the feet of the different process of socialization of men and women, their studies showed. While Emmeline may have subscribed to distinctive social and familial roles for men and women and accepted male leadership in hierarchical institutions—government, law, religion, and education—these gendered functions did not imply lesser female capability. In 1874, after hearing popular lecturer Victoria Woodhull, at the Liberal Institute in Salt Lake City, rail against women, "classing them all together as weak, ignorant, vain and silly," Emmeline countered in the *Woman's Exponent*, "I believe in women, especially thinking women."[3]

This declaration was in effect her opening salvo for a decade of perorations on her conviction of women's innate intelligence and capacity, unused because of nothing more than untested assumptions that affirmed different capabilities of men and women. Using her pseudonym almost exclusively for her bold assertions on women during this debut decade of the '70s, she inadvertently, perhaps, revealed the frustration she felt in her own life. "This day is spoken of as woman's day," she wrote, "one in which woman is moving forward and claiming rights and privileges which have long been denied her." But however much they claimed these rights and privileges, she lamented, they were dependent on man's willingness to grant them and their willingness to receive them. Thus, she challenged, "Is it not absolutely essential that women should prepare themselves for the blessings of freedom and independence in thought and action, which they, some of them, claim and desire to enjoy as an inherent and God-given boon? We believe it is."[4]

Like Elizabeth Cady Stanton before her, Emmeline felt that the hard-won but often condescending reforms that had thus far been achieved only masked long-held assumptions about the nature of womanhood and woman's place within the social order. For too long, men had kept women from entering public life or participating in any of the professions, saying, "we attend to all these matters for them," thus ensuring that a woman would be "totally dependent on man's capabilities instead of developing her own."[5] Nothing more nearly characterized Wells's appeal for woman's emancipation than her oft-repeated phrase, "I want to know for myself," a desire she believed to be inherent in all individuals. Unfortunately, women, she found, had been so victimized by traditional notions of womanhood that "it will only be by small degrees that [they] themselves can comprehend the advantages rising from the progress of independence of thought and action, and a knowledge for themselves."[6]

In 1845, Margaret Fuller had averred that what a woman needed was not "to act or rule, but as a nature to grow, as an intellect to discern, as a soul to live freely and unimpeded, to unfold such powers as were given her when we left our common home."[7] This was the principle on which Wells envisioned the transformation of society, where each individual was valued and encouraged to magnify whatever abilities and talents he or she possessed. Such an ideal state, of course, required unrestricted education and broad experience as avenues essential to self-knowledge and fulfillment. To reach these lofty goals, Wells urged women to recognize their own divine nature, to utilize "the highest faculty" of that nature, "thought," and to accept responsibility for their own progress and salvation. "May it not be said of any of us," she cautioned, "that we neglected to improve the talent committed to our care."[8]

With access to channels of learning and experience that had long been closed to them, women could prove the truth of their claims that they had inherent but untapped talents. Feminists dared society to erase the social boundaries that imprisoned them. Margaret Fuller demanded that "every arbitrary barrier" that impedes woman's progress be thrown down. "We would have every path laid open to woman as freely as to man," she wrote.[9] Similarly, Emmeline Wells challenged men: "Let woman have all the same opportunities for an education, observation and experience in public and private for a successive number of years, and then see if they are not equally endowed with man and prepared to bear her part on all general questions socially, politically, industrially, and educationally as well as spiritually."[10] The argument was not aimed exclusively at men, since both men and women were bound by the conventions of an entrenched social order. But tradition had been especially limiting to women. "Why" Emmeline wondered, had such constraints been "set to their culture, or a boundary to their education."[11]

Another key feminist theme important to the development of the individual was self-reliance. As a true transcendentalist, Margaret Fuller made this quality a major issue in her advocacy for women. She enjoined them to resist living "too much in relations" lest one become "a stranger to the resources of [her] own nature."[12] She had found that "self-dependence" was woman's "sure anchor."[13] As Emmeline's personal circumstances pushed her closer to self-dependency she, however reluctantly, also came to value the power of self-reliance. But without some experience and education, self-reliance was not truly a viable option for women. "In the name of justice, reason and common sense," Emmeline urged in 1876, reflecting her own sense of inadequacy at that time, "let woman be fortified and strengthened by every possible advantage, that she may be adequately and thoroughly fitted not only to grace the drawing room, and manage every department of her household, but to perform with skill and wisdom the arduous and elaborate work of molding and fashioning the fabrics of which society is to be woven."[14] She counseled mothers to train their daughters to develop the attributes that would enable them to "live without leaning wholly on, or trusting blindly to another."[15] Taking a chapter from her own life history, she declared that "self-made women is a powerful term. It tells its own story, of struggles against fearful odds, with unpropitious circumstances, and a lack of the means of education and cultivation. But on the other hand," she wrote, again from firsthand knowledge, "it bespeaks self-help, self-denial, patient hopefulness and persistent determination."[16] Though from different circumstances, both Wells and Fuller came to value self-reliance as an instrument not only of self-discovery but of social equality.

Above all, Emmeline believed in "thinking women." This was the defining quality, she felt, of real women and the trait that distinguished them from the idealized "true woman" of popular Victorian imagery—passive and dependent. The associations she organized, the causes for which she labored, and the newspaper she kept afloat for thirty-seven years were her means of providing opportunity for women to develop and express that capacity. Though Emmeline was small and dainty like a "fragile Dresden figure," embodying the physical image of the "true woman" currently in vogue, she was inwardly the prototype of what she called a real woman. Both feminine and intellectual, she bridged the gulf between the "true" woman touted in the popular press and the "new" woman that emerged from the woman movement: educated, thinking, capable, and self-reliant. When she was in her ninetieth year, a contemporary expressed this duality in describing her as "our little, delicate, great-minded President [of the LDS Relief Society], walking softly, yet with fierce independence into the room."[17]

If the barriers to a woman's fully realizing and expressing her capabilities were removed, it would naturally follow, Emmeline Wells assumed, that her most personal relationship—marriage—would be the greatest beneficiary. "We can but deplore the condition of things that gives woman so little scope, so narrow compass, and accords to man all the space for his powers, and all the honors which the wife has helped him to attain," she complained.[18] Subscribing to Margaret Fuller's injunction to develop self-reliance by resisting living "too much in relations," an often undependable source of support, Emmeline counseled her readers to develop skills that would help them avoid such dependence, especially in marriage. In a series of letters entitled "After Long Years," published in the *Woman's Exponent,* Emmeline did not hide her thoughts in euphemisms. "Is it not time that after long years of bitter experience," she hoped, "some of us should learn that there is a better part for women than to be man's dupe, or slave, or drudge?" She may well have been voicing her own frustration during this difficult decade of "not having her home or means independent." Learning to live on the product of her own labor, Emmeline pitied those women who married primarily for a livelihood because they were not resourceful enough to earn their own bread. Far better off, she believed, were those women who were independent enough to "choose their partner to add to the sum of human happiness, and the higher development of womanhood."[19]

She was pleased to note that even "women of refinement and possessed of superior attainments [did] not feel quite satisfied to be dependent altogether upon the exertions of the 'men folks,'" but that "intelligent, cultivated women" were stepping out into avenues of employment and "actually earning money of their own."[20] Economic self-sufficiency, Emmeline had come to learn by 1883, removed one of the strongest pillars of woman's dependency.

Though women had heavy domestic duties, yet, she observed, "When the wheels of life's lumbering coach get clogged," and difficulties interrupt the road to prosperity, if the wife can help remove such impediments, "so much the better and easier are they overcome."[21] The needle and washboard had too long been the symbols of woman's economic bondage. All avenues of employment should be made available to women, Emmeline declared, so that they might offset the economic dependence too frequently ill placed.

Her fervent depictions of an ideal marriage betray the futility she felt in her own. Her longing for a partnership based on love and mutual respect and marriage as a journey of two individuals helping one another to reach his or her highest aspirations and potential seemed only Utopian dreams, especially in plural marriages. In many ways her dreams corresponded with Margaret Fuller's three-level design for marital happiness. The first level, as Fuller described it, was a practical "household partnership" that conjoined dutiful partners fulfilling traditional role expectations. Better than this, she noted, was a marriage of intellectual companionship, a true meeting of "mind partners," sympathetic and supportive, joined in common purpose but respectful of each other's individuality. Emmeline wrote often of this kind of marriage. But the higher level was a spiritual union of two souls. It encompassed the first two levels of marital companionship but rose high above them, reflecting a more exalted relationship and leading to nobler aims, a shared "pilgrimage to a common shrine."[22]

Companionship based on mutual respect as well as love, but especially shared aspirations, could lead two people to this elevated marital plane, Emmeline believed. Unevenly yoked partners could never hope to attain the intellectual and spiritual union that characterized a fulfilling marriage, one that gave wholeness to the relationship, as Fuller maintained.[23] Rather than "arrogating to himself the right to dictate in all things, saying, 'thus far shalt thou go and no farther,'" Emmeline challenged men to prove themselves "noble enough" to share with their wives "such laurels as either may be able to win in the battlefield of life." Though some would disagree at that time, a higher education would not render a woman incapable of loving, Emmeline knew, but would "qualify her to place her affections upon an object worthy of the best and truest affections of her womanly nature." A man who would stand in such a woman's favor must then make himself worthy of her affection.[24] That genuine love could inhibit the full expression of another being under the guise of protection was both demeaning and illogical to her. "Why is it not possible for man and woman to love each other truly, and dwell together in harmony," Emmeline wondered, "each according to the other all the freedom of thought, feeling, and expression they would grant to one who was not bound to them by indissoluble ties?" Margaret Fuller had envisioned the same ideal commitment in which "two persons love in one another the future good which they aid one another to unfold."[25] Custom had for too long dictated a relationship, Emmeline lamented, in which the wife gave all in order that she "may sit by his hearth, bear his children, preside at his table, and merge her life into his, to the extinguishing and crushing out of all desires, ambitions, tastes, or capabilities for anything save what he deems proper, or right, his wife should engage in."[26] While other activists critiqued the common law, which rendered married women virtual chattels of their husbands, Emmeline's argument transcended the limitation of law, placing the burden for an equitable relationship squarely on the shoulders of the participants.

The model marriage described by both Fuller and Wells did not easily fit the parameters of plural marriage, though Emmeline was quick to point out that plural marriage offered its own kind of advantage since it made "woman more the companion and much less the subordinate than any other form of marriage."[27] She also argued that it promoted self-reliance and a host of other admirable traits that compensated for the loss of exclusivity in the relationship. But these were only half-hearted arguments for a marriage pattern that could hardly yield the perfect relationship she so ardently envisioned. The sublime marriage that Emmeline continually described in her writings was certainly beyond the boundaries of her own marital experience and an illusion for many women of the time. Hidden beneath the nom de plume she chose for these heartfelt renderings and within the recesses of her diary was a woman longing for an elusive love.

It was not just custom or unthinking men, however, whom Emmeline Wells charged with preventing the development of a true marital partnership, however. Women, Emmeline submitted, had some obligation to create the environment in which such a relationship could flourish and to be the kind of wife who engendered the respect that could lead to genuine companionship. She urged women to act in marriage from a position of strength and capacity, not from one of weakness and subservience or empty idolatry. Women should not succumb to entreaties to be exclusively "domestic and submissive" by the "lords of creation" who were fearful that "if women are allowed to mingle more freely and their interests become more closely associated with man's they will lose their peculiar charms of modesty, grace and shyness." Unfortunately, Emmeline complained, men deemed these qualities "the strongest attraction (save beauty) which incites their admiration."[28] With this false ideal of womanhood, a man too often considered his wife as "simply a necessity in his establishment, to manage his house, cook his dinner, attend to his wardrobe, always on hand if she is wanted and always out of sight if not needed," Emmeline warned. "He doesn't mind kissing her occasionally, when it suits him," she added, "but he never thinks she has any thoughts of her own, any ideas which might be developed; she must not have even an opinion, or if she has she mustn't express it, it is entirely out of place." Her final words: "She is a subject, not a joint-partner in the domestic firm."[29]

If women did not assert themselves, she scolded, they must indeed bear some of the blame for, as well as the consequences of, this kind of male behavior. She assailed the willingness of women to succumb to the influences that made them reluctant to break the "silken cord" that bound them to the "proprieties and delicacies" of life, beyond which they dared not step. "From the first burst of incipient womanhood," she wrote, a woman's education and training has been to make her pleasing to a man who would be willing to "relieve her father and mother or guardians of her support," and take on that task himself. In being taught to look forward to this event "as the crowning point of her earthly existence," the young woman "neglects her own culture and training and becomes totally dependent and unschooled in life."[30]

Continuing her appeal to develop "real" womanhood, Emmeline dismissed the delicate, passive wife as untrue to herself. A real woman disregarded the customs of society and "dared to come and go alone," spurning the counterfeit emotions that passed for "true affection" in marriage. A real woman's highest incentive was "to attain to the most superior excellence in the disciplining and refining of the faculties of the soul." Men, she firmly believed, would learn to appreciate and seek after the real woman to marry, "a being of understanding, one who has pronounced opinions of her own, and who is free to choose, if need be, her own vocation, and can, when needful, 'eat her own bread and wear her own apparel.'"[31]

The irony of the prevailing concept of "true" womanhood, with its emphasis on fragility and deference, was its inherent falseness, the hypocrisy and artificiality it imposed upon the women it professed to honor. "How few there are," Emmeline regretted, who understand their own importance and "strive to preserve their own identity, their own individuality by being real; it is a very simple, commonplace word yet it comprises so much." Moreover, she explained, a real woman need not be a "distinguished" woman, one who excelled and was publicly renowned. The wife who attended only to her domestic duties but brought to them "strong common sense, and an active mind" was just as true to herself, displaying all the qualities of real womanhood, as one more favored by education and opportunity.[32]

By the time Emmeline Wells, as Blanche Beechwood, began her series of critiques on marriage she was only in her forties, but she had suffered the loss of two husbands and two children and was then experiencing the benign indifference of her current husband. A sense of betrayal by those meant to be her providers and protectors, through desertion, death, and finally neglect, may well have prompted these indictments of men and marriage and served as justification for her own strong ambitions. They may also have provided catharsis during a time when she felt vulnerable, inadequate, and very lonely. Only occasionally, after she had become a fixture in the woman suffrage movement, did she note that her husband expressed interest over her growing public activity. By the time he noticed, however, they were so distanced from one another that his words had little impact. It seemed that only in her carefully crafted written formula for the perfect marriage would Emmeline approximate it for herself.

While most of Emmeline's pronouncements on marriage appeared in the 1870s, when she was making the transition from an all-engrossing domestic life to the public world of the activist, many of her editorials and articles on women in public life were also written during that period, only a few of which used her pseudonym. The strong marital partnership she advocated was but a microcosm of the partnership she envisioned in the "world's work," a concept generated by her own experience in the public realm. In her editorial she argued that women would be an effective social force if given a chance to enlarge their sphere of usefulness, for "the great work of the world could never be done well by one-half of the human family."[33] "Has the world no claim upon women, and women no place in it except her home?" she asked. "Is she not a citizen of the world? Does she not possess some individuality? And is not her opinion of some weight and consequence to others besides her own immediate family?"[34] Women were not seeking for any independent power, she explained, but "only to become a co-worker in the future development of human progression, and mutual recognition of rights." She was convinced that if women were given an equal opportunity to "work with the same chance of success according to the labor performed without the consideration of sex," there would be a vast difference in society.[35] Once again she challenged men to recognize their own advantage in granting women opportunity to develop their latent abilities.

As in marriage, women were often unaware that they too created barriers to their social progress. Surrendering to custom kept many women resigned to their limited status. Like Susan B. Anthony and Elizabeth Stanton before her, Emmeline Wells deplored women who declared they had all the rights they wanted, for this admission merely demonstrated ignorance of their narrow and powerless condition. Besides their reluctance to disrupt the comfort zone to which so many of them were accustomed, women worried that ingress into the public sphere would "unsex" them. This possibility, posited by many educators of the day, deterred many men and women from wanting to seriously consider broadening woman's public participation. "The one strong point that opponents use," Emmeline complained, "is, that woman will lose her indefinable charm, designated womanliness, when she can discuss knotty questions, has strong opinions, can match herself with man in force of character, and intellectual ability, instead of sweetly assenting to whatever opinions he may hold, smiling all the while he is pitilessly crucifying all the finer feelings of her soul."[36]

Soon after becoming editor of the *Woman's Exponent,* Emmeline wrote a particularly strong assertion of women's determination to become more socially viable. By this time, 1877, she was a regular correspondent with eastern women's papers and had been exposed to the woman's rights doctrine of eastern activists. How much their forthrightness and advocacy for women emboldened her is unclear, but that she felt she was at least a peripheral player in the movement is evident. In language as forceful as that of her eastern cohorts, Emmeline wrote a polemic enumerating a list of injustices borrowed from the original Declaration of Sentiments drawn up at Seneca Falls, New York, nearly thirty years earlier. This editorial, "Woman's Expectations," also included an impassioned statement of the conviction that would carry her through the public work she was just then beginning to undertake.[37]

Though women had begun to enjoy broader opportunities, Emmeline recognized how much was left to be done. "Woman feels her servitude, her degradation," the editorial begins, "and she is determined to assert her rights, to attain to an equality with man, and to train herself to fill any position and place of trust and honor as appropriately and with as much dignity as her brother man." Then she itemized the objectives she and her fellow activists were committed to achieve. They hoped to create a more equitable social environment so

> that [woman] may not be compelled to conditions that are distasteful and objectionable in matrimony, that she shall have rights and privileges peculiarly her own and be able to protect herself in them; that she need not be held as goods and chattel at the mercy or brutality of man . . . and that her highest motive is that she may be recognized as a responsible being, capable of judging for and maintaining herself, and standing upon just as broad, grand and elevated a platform as man.[38]

She was, in effect, mapping out her own path to self-respect and autonomy.

Wells, like other women activists, did not envision women abandoning their domestic sphere for the "world outside." Rather, she looked to a reordering of the spheres, even their dissolution, in what would be a transformation of society, as historian Nancy Cott explained. The new society would not only allow but encourage women to pursue education and other paths to self-development with complete propriety. As women availed themselves of these options for individual achievement and growth, they would be prepared to act well in any circumstance in which they found themselves. "No home can be really attractive without intelligence," she wrote, "without a broader sympathy than that which confines itself to one's own family. Whatever efforts woman can make, whatever she may do that is not detrimental to home life, that she should be permitted to do without ridicule and without censure."[39]

Emmeline chided those women who did not partake of the advantages around them for their development nor realize that they could be contributing members of the communities in which they lived. "It is the opinion of many who are wise and learned," she wrote in 1875, "that woman's mission upon the earth is maternity, with its minor details, its accompanying cares, and needful exigencies; that these fill the measure of her creation; and when this is done, she should with becoming matronly dignity, retire from the sphere of active life and gracefully welcome old age." Emmeline's own life was her best refutation of this position. "That motherhood brings into a woman's life a richness, zest and tone that nothing else ever can I gladly grant you," she said, "but that her usefulness ends there, or that she has no other individual interests to serve I cannot so readily concede."[40] She also recognized that not all women were suited for nor desirous of maternity. "If there be some women in whom the love of learning extinguishes all other love, then the heaven-appointed sphere of that woman is not the nursery. It may be the library, the laboratory, the observatory."[41]

Women had a vested interest in society as much as in the home, Emmeline argued. Most of the important questions of the day, she informed her readers, such as moral reform, temperance, social welfare, and even the woman movement, all pointed significantly to the home. As new inventions lightened the load of men in all forms of employment and gave them more time to pursue other interests, so, too, she reasoned, had woman's labor been eased, allowing her more time to develop her talents and gifts. "Why, then," she asked, "should women allow themselves to be shaded by the towering oak to which so many of them cling," shut out from even a "rushlight of intelligence?"[42] She urged women to seek education, not as a privilege but as a duty, to themselves, to their children, and to their communities. Education was the primary means of developing one's latent capabilities, she believed. As one who had been well educated to the age of fourteen, an unusual achievement for a girl in early nineteenth-century rural New England, she recognized its value and urged her readers to take advantage of the educational opportunities available to them in Utah.[43] Through the advanced education of women, she declared, "the entire world could realize a higher civilization."[44] But, Emmeline affirmed, in order for women to exercise that uplifting influence, it was necessary that "the gates be thrown open by those who held the keys of power."[45]

Woman's Exponent readers had little reason to doubt Emmeline's confidence in the capabilities and intelligence of women, for there were role models in abundance in Mormon society. Mormon female leadership of the various women's organizations and clubs and in the woman's branches of home industry (that is, sericulture, the commission stores, and grain saving) enjoyed an enabling autonomy that left them free to plan and develop these enterprises. Much space in the *Exponent* was devoted to reports of the travels of editor Wells as she accompanied Eliza R. Snow, Zina D. H. Young, and Bathsheba W. Smith, her predecessors as Relief Society General President, to outlying settlements to organize Relief Societies, Primaries (children's organizations), and Retrenchment Societies for Young Women. The women planned and conducted conferences and territorial fairs, established a hospital, maintained nursing and obstetrical schools, executed a successful suffrage campaign, and spoke, presided, and preached in women's meetings and conferences throughout the territory. And many were polygamous wives who had raised, or were raising, large families, often alone. Thus, with complete impunity Emmeline could write, "It would be a deplorable thing if women who married and were rearing families settled down to think this was the end of their usefulness, that hereafter there were only meals to get, little children to wash and dress, sewing and knitting, and all the minor details of home-life to attend to."[46] Emmeline fervently believed in the power of women to stretch the boundaries of their usefulness and give the world the benefit of their minds, skills, and experience. Though the model she personified was unquestionably extraordinary, her life was a monument to her faith in the power of women *to be* and *to do*.

In her many discourses on the "new era" for women, Wells often borrowed from her poetic resources to elaborate her views. "Woman's sphere is widening," she wrote in one editorial, "her star is in the ascendant, resplendent, resplendent with light, that is shedding its effulgence abroad and penetrating the darkest corners with its glorious rays."[47] In "Special Life Missions," she employed other celestial allusions: "The struggle for a wider, higher and broader sphere is sure to result in good," she wrote, "though the dark cloud is not yet lifted, still it grows thinner and the faint dawn of the morning which shall usher in the era of woman's emancipation is becoming perceptible to the quick eye of the observer."[48]

One of her most poignant pleas for loosening the bands that restrained women was addressed to an anti-Mormon Christian newspaper, the *Watchman,* published in Boston, which had consistently urged the disfranchisement of all polygamists and particularly of the women in Utah, snidely claiming that "until women of culture and intelligence" became politically interested, "it would be dangerous" to enact universal suffrage. "We can forgive the *Watchman* for all its absurdities," Emmeline wrote in response, but "as for women everywhere, 'Watchman, what of the morning?'! Do you not see the morning star of woman's destiny in the ascendant. Why the whole civilized world is becoming enlightened with its beams. In America, lighting up the dark places, are some of its brightest rays becoming visible." Then, she pointedly concluded, "There are some wise men who recognize the star, and who even say 'peace and good will' to woman, and take her by the hand and welcome her to their circle, and would fain assign to her all that nature gave her intelligence and capacity to do, would lift her up to their level in education, and in science, and say there is room for us both, let us walk side by side."[49] Few passages expressed her hope for the future more poignantly than this chastisement of the *Watchman*.

By the end of the nineteenth century, time and the single-minded efforts of committed social activists had made a difference, Emmeline observed. In an 1899 editorial she looked back and declared the century a good one for women. She saw it as a new dispensation that had opened long-closed doors. Until she finally roused herself from complacency with the lot that society had thrust upon her, "the world wagged on," she wrote, "but when woman awoke to a consciousness of her own power," she was able to inquire about her rights and to do her own thinking on moral questions, social problems, economic issues, "and so on through the whole category of human affairs." At last, she was proud to say, "Has been opened [for women] the great domain of the world."[50]

That she had been a diligent advocate for women, those of her own faith and others—through her addresses, her editorials, her petitions, her organizations, and her relentless determination—was to her a source of great satisfaction. Always optimistic, often too idealistic, but with expectations generally infused with doses of reality, she invoked inner resources to match her unwavering will to succeed in every task. There was no moral ambiguity about her position that may have clouded her thinking or given her pause. Nor did she succumb to the feminine self-doubt. No amount of criticism or ridicule deflected her from the path she had set for herself. To the young women of the LDS Church, whom she hoped to inspire with a desire to assist in the cause of woman's advancement, she explained that they might well meet resistance similar to what she had experienced. "Some of our good sisters," she wrote in 1874, "will not sustain us in our efforts for the benefit of women" and "complain that we are 'strong-minded,' unwomanly, and so forth." Her admiration for those women who did not flinch at such epithets was evident even at that early date. Aware that many Mormon women had been bold enough to publicly defend themselves and their religion against the constant barrage of verbal assaults, she concluded, "Thank God that there are some women who have stamina enough to stand boldly forth in defence of right. . . . It matters little what name they give us, so long as our motives are pure, and our actions are honorable."[51]

Though Emmeline's "heart hunger" never left her and death took many family members and co-workers, work was her antidote to the sadness that counterpointed her life. By her own strength of will, she did not allow these private sorrows to penetrate her public life. She had too much hope and too compelling a conviction of her mission to sink into that enervating condition. Despite the set-backs, the disappointments, and the criticism that followed her efforts, she was yet able to say, "I love this work," an avowal that only a strong-minded woman could make.

Notes

1. "A Wonderful Age," *Woman's Exponent* 27 (February 1, 1899): 100.
2. Rosalind Rosenberg explains this educational and sociological breakthrough in "In Search of Woman's Nature, 1850–1920," in *Feminist Studies* 3 (Fall 1975): 141–54, and in "The Academic Prism: The New View of American Women," in *Women of America: A History*, ed. Carol Ruth Berkin and Mary Beth Norton (Boston: Houghton Mifflin, 1979), 319–41. Rosenberg includes portions of two studies done by two of these pioneer female scholars. One is Helen Thompson (Woolley), *The Mental Traits of Men and Women* (Chicago: The University of Chicago Press, 1903), 177–79; and Margaret Mead, *Sex and Temperament in Three Primitive Societies* (New York: William Morrow, 1935), 279–80. Nancy Woloch places these developments in the broad context of women's history in *Women and the American Experience*, 3rd ed. (Boston: McGraw Hill, 2000), 397–401.
3. Blanche Beechwood, "Why, Ah! Why," *Woman's Exponent* 3 (October 1, 1874): 67. Margaret Fuller had used a similar phrase in her book *Woman in the Nineteenth Century* (1845; repr., New York: W. W. Norton, 1971), 59: "Women are, often, the head of these institutions, but they have, as yet, seldom been thinking women, capable to organize a new whole for the wants of the time, and choose persons to officiate in the departments." Woodhull was both an advocate for woman suffrage and a notorious exponent of "free love." Her talk was delivered at the gentile Liberal Institute in Salt Lake City.
4. "Fitness for Practical Work," *Woman's Exponent* 6 (December 1, 1877): 100.
5. "Womanliness," *Woman's Exponent* 8 (December 1, 1879): 100.
6. "Woman's Progression," *Woman's Exponent* 6 (February 15, 1878): 140.
7. Margaret Fuller, *Woman in the Nineteenth Century* (1845; repr., Columbia: University of South Carolina Press, 1980), 27, as reprinted in Miriam

Scheir, ed., *Feminism: The Essential Historical Writings* (New York: Vintage, 1972), 68.

8. Blanche Beechwood, "Why, Ah! Why," 67. Joseph Smith instructed the members of the Nauvoo Relief Society that they were "responsible for their own salvation" and counseled them that "it was a privilege for them to be responsible for themselves." A Record of the Organization, and Proceedings of the Female Relief Society of Nauvoo, April 28, 1842, Church Archives, The Church of Jesus Christ of Latter-day Saints, Salt Lake City.

9. From Fuller, *Woman in the Nineteenth Century,* as quoted in Eve Kornfeld, *Margaret Fuller: A Brief Biography with Documents,* The Bedford Series in History and Culture (Boston: Bedford Books, 1997), 164.

10. Blanche Beechwood, "Action or Indifference," *Woman's Exponent* 5 (September 1, 1876): 54.

11. "Special Life Missions," *Woman's Exponent* 6 (March 1, 1878): 148.

12. As quoted in Kornfeld, *Margaret Fuller,* 178.

13. As quoted in Kornfeld, *Margaret Fuller,* 166.

14. Blanche Beechwood, "Impromptu Ideas of Home," *Woman's Exponent* 4 (May 15, 1876): 191. Elizabeth Cady Stanton, in what has been considered her finest speech, addressed this basic feminist issue. A portion of it reads: "The strongest reason why we ask for woman a voice in the government under which she lives; in the religion she is asked to believe; equality in social life, where she is the chief factor; a place in the trades and professions, where she may earn her bread, is because of her birthright to self-sovereignty; because, as an individual she must rely on herself." "The Solitude of Self," in *History of Woman Suffrage,* vol. 4, ed. Susan B. Anthony and Ida H. Harper (Rochester, N.Y.: Susan B. Anthony, 1902), 189–91.

15. Aunt Em, "After Long Years, Letter II," *Woman's Exponent* 6 (November 15, 1877): 89.

16. "Self-Made Women," *Woman's Exponent* 9 (March 1, 1881): 148.

17. Susa Young Gates, "Our Lovely Human Heritage, President Emmeline B. Wells," *Relief Society Magazine* 4, no. 2 (February 1917): 74.

18. "Special Life Missions," 148.

19. Aunt Em, "After Long Years, Letter II," 89.

20. "Women Self-Supporting," *Woman's Exponent* 11 (May 15, 1883): 188.

21. "Women Self-Supporting," 188.

22. From Margaret Fuller, "The Great Lawsuit: Man versus Men, Woman versus Women," as quoted in Alice Rossi, *Feminist Papers,* 171–74.

23. Kornfeld, *Margaret Fuller,* 190.

24. Blanche Beechwood, "Woman's Ambition," *Woman's Exponent* 4 (April 1, 1876): 166.

25. Beechwood, "Woman's Ambition," 166.

26. "Woman's Progression," *Woman's Exponent* 6 (February 15, 1878): 140.

27. Though the public announcement relating to the Latter-day Saint practice of polygamy was not made until 1852, Margaret Fuller, as early as 1845, expressed what became a frequent argument of Elizabeth Stanton and Susan B. Anthony regarding it. "It is idle to speak with contempt of the nations where polygamy is an institution . . . ," Fuller wrote, "when practices far more debasing haunt, well nigh fill, every city and every town." As quoted in Kornfeld, *Margaret Fuller*, 172. Though none of these women countenanced plural marriage, they judged those who indulged in extramarital affairs while denouncing polygamy to be hypocrites as well as adulterers.

28. "Women in the Legislature," *Woman's Exponent* 26 (January 15, 1899): 92; Blanche Beechwood, "Woman, A Subject," *Woman's Exponent* 3 (November 1, 1874): 82.

29. Blanche Beechwood, "Real Women," *Woman's Exponent* 2 (January 1, 1874): 118. Compare Margaret Fuller: "the same want of development . . . prevents his [man's] discerning the destiny of women. The boy wants no woman, but only a girl to play ball with him, and mark his pocket handkerchief." From Fuller, "The Great Lawsuit," as quoted in Rossi, *Feminist Papers*, 167.

30. Blanche Beechwood, "Something to Live For," *Woman's Exponent* 3 (December 1, 1874): 100.

31. "Self-Made Women," 148.

32. Beechwood, "Real Women," 118.

33. "Responsibility of Women Voters," *Woman's Exponent* 26 (September 15, October 1, 1897): 196.

34. "Woman's Relation to Home," *Woman's Exponent* 8 (August 30, 1879): 52.

35. Blanche Beechwood, "Action or Indifference," *Woman's Exponent* 5 (September 1, 1876): 54.

36. "Woman's Progression," *Woman's Exponent* 6 (February 15, 1878): 140.

37. "Woman's Expectations," *Woman's Exponent* 6 (July 1, 1877): 20.

38. "Woman's Expectations," 20.

39. "Woman's Relation to Home," 52.

40. Blanche Beechwood, "Life Lessons," *Woman's Exponent* 4 (October 2, 1875): 70. See also Carroll Smith-Rosenberg, "Puberty to Menopause: The Cycle of Femininity in Nineteenth Century America," in *Clio's Consciousness*

Raised, ed. Mary Hartman and Lois W. Banner (New York: Harper and Row, 1974), 31.

41. "Education of Women," *Woman's Exponent* 1 (April 1, 1873): 163.

42. "Noble Work for Women," *Woman's Exponent* 7 (April 1, 1879): 218.

43. Women had been admitted from the outset to the University of Deseret in 1850 and to the Brigham Young Academies in both Provo and Logan as well as the Agricultural College (now Utah State University) in Logan. They were also able to enter far more occupations without ridicule than many other women in the nation.

44. "Progress of Women in the Last Seventy Years," *Woman's Exponent* 40 (February 1912): 44.

45. "Looking Ahead," *Woman's Exponent* 19 (October 1, 1890): 60.

46. "Woman's Work," *Woman's Exponent* 4 (November 15, 1875): 94.

47. "Looking Ahead," 60.

48. "Special Life Missions," 148.

49. "Peace and Good Will," *Woman's Exponent* 7 (September 15, 1878): 60.

50. "A Wonderful Age," *Woman's Exponent* 27 (February 1, 1899): 100. See also "Progress of Women in the Last Seventy Years," 44.

51. Blanche Beechwood, "Our Daughters," *Woman's Exponent* 2 (February 1, 1874): 131.

Chapter 6

Utah and the Woman Question

Men will assuredly respect women's opinions more, when they know they can give them expression at the polls.[1]

Though Emmeline Wells was not directly associated with the founding of the *Woman's Exponent*, the date of its first publication, June 1, 1872, which was also Church President Brigham Young's seventy-first birthday, brought together two decisive elements in her public life. Both Brigham Young, in the five years remaining to him, and the *Woman's Exponent,* in its forty-two years, propelled Emmeline Wells into the public role that would consume the remainder of her life. She would soon be ineluctably drawn into the three-pronged challenge the LDS Church faced for the next two decades relating to polygamy, woman suffrage, and statehood.

In 1872, Emmeline Wells was forty-four years old. Her two older daughters, children of her marriage to Newel K. Whitney, were married. The three younger Wells daughters were still in their teens. She had been married for twenty years to the prominent Daniel H. Wells, who in 1872 was a counselor to Brigham Young in the LDS Church's First Presidency, chancellor of the University of Deseret, lieutenant general of the Nauvoo Militia, and head of the Endowment House (precursor to the Salt Lake Temple). Daniel had previously been mayor of Salt Lake City and superintendent of public works.[2] Despite her husband's prominence, Emmeline B. Wells is not listed among "leading sisters" of the community at that time.[3] The *Woman's Exponent*, however, would dramatically catapult her into their ranks. Emmeline's rise began in 1876 when Brigham Young appointed her to head the Church's grain-saving mission, an assignment that gave her organizational and leadership experience and her name recognition.[4] Young's early introduction to Emmeline's ability to rally the efforts of Mormon women also led him to enlist her in the defense of Latter-day Saint women and the Church, in partnership with Church leaders, against an escalating torrent of anti-Mormon sentiment. Young's support of the *Exponent* lent it a semi-official basis for its self-defined mission to refute the derogatory images of Mormon women. He also charged Emmeline to write the life stories of Latter-day Saint women and to keep their collective history, which transformed the *Exponent* into an indispensable witness of women's part in early Mormon history. As editor, Emmeline became both a facilitator and chronicler of that history.[5]

Perhaps its disclaimer at the outset of any need to debate woman suffrage (Utah women already had the vote) or to "champion any other causes" was disingenuous if not naïve.[6] Whatever the reason, the *Woman's Exponent*, soon after its inaugural issue, engaged in both. Acknowledging that Mormon women had been "grossly misrepresented through the press by active enemies who permit no opportunity to pass of maligning and slandering them, and with but limited opportunity of appealing to the intelligence and candor of their fellow country men and country women in reply," the paper could hardly remain silent or assume the neutral stance it was promising.[7] The inaugural issue was more realistic in stating, "It is better to represent ourselves than to be misrepresented by others."[8] Emmeline Wells, a writer and then editor of the *Exponent*, would be instrumental in staunching the flow of misrepresentation.

The decade that followed the launching of the *Woman's Exponent* proved to be a tumultuous period for the LDS Church and its members, especially women. Finding herself in the midst of it through her involvement with the *Exponent*, Emmeline Wells formulated the resolution that became her life's work: "I desire to do all in my power to help elevate the condition of my people especially wom[e]n."[9] Indeed the *Exponent* would be one of the agents she would use to achieve this goal. The events that led up to that necessity tested the strength of the federal government to compel conformity to a prevailing social consensus against the practice of unconventional religious beliefs.

Utah was an anomaly among its sister states and territories. Though governed by federally appointed officials as it awaited the self-rule of statehood, its people—more than 99 percent Mormon in the 1870s—gave political allegiance to their ecclesiastical leaders, with Brigham Young at the head. Mormons dominated the legislative assembly, the judiciary, and many of the elective offices, but Congress controlled the acts of the assembly and appointed the governor and the district judges, who also formed the territorial supreme court. As completion of the transcontinental railroad in 1869 brought an increasing number of non-Mormon ("Gentile") residents to the territory, the inevitable conflict of economic, political, and religious interests escalated in its reach and intensity. The Latter-day Saint practice of polygamy became the political scapegoat, especially as non-Mormon women in Utah confronted it firsthand.

The 1870 enfranchisement of Utah women complicated the "Utah problem" by adding another dimension to the status of Mormon women and drawing eastern suffragists into the controversy. For two decades Mormon women and their anti-Mormon critics fought a gender war of national proportions over the right to define the values and morals of American society.[10]

Even before Utah women confronted each other over polygamy, eastern suffragists were, ironically, waging a battle between themselves over the issue that had united them since antebellum days. Two distinct suffrage factions emerged after the Civil War, differing over Republican Reconstruction measures that placed the civil rights of the recently freed male slaves before those of women. The factions' divergent paths would figure decisively in the national crusade against polygamy.

As a visible and prominent Mormon woman, through her editorship of the *Woman's Exponent*, Emmeline Wells became a central player in the protracted struggle for the vote and in the Church's defense of plural marriage. When the campaign for woman suffrage began in 1848 in Seneca Falls, New York, however, Emmeline was traveling in the Mormon exodus from Nauvoo, Illinois, to the Salt Lake Valley, the LDS Church's new headquarters. At age twenty and far from the centers of reform, she was unaware of the crucial role she was destined to take in the woman's rights movement that followed the Seneca Falls meeting.[11]

The women activists who mounted this campaign for their rights, Elizabeth Cady Stanton and Lucretia Mott, both abolitionists, along with their activist cohorts, enjoyed the support of many of their male antislavery allies. At the conclusion of the Civil War, however, this coalition splintered. Though initially male abolitionists lobbied to include women in the proposed civil rights legislation for freed slaves, male abolitionists and a number of women activists, led by Lucy Stone and her husband Henry B. Blackwell,[12] agreed to support the Republican Reconstruction policy to secure civil rights only for freedmen, deferring the campaign for women's rights.

Another contingent of women activists, headed by Elizabeth Cady Stanton and Susan B. Anthony, convinced that a second window of opportunity for constitution amending would be far distant, continued to urge the inclusion of woman suffrage in Reconstruction legislation and bitterly opposed ratification of the Fifteenth Amendment when it did not include women's voting rights. It established, they claimed, "an aristocracy of sex" and would mean "male versus female, the land over."[13] The schism that developed between the two groups of former friends and co-workers was acrimonious and long lasting.[14]

Developing a feminist agenda of multiple objectives, including economic and marital reform as well as political, the Stanton-Anthony group formed the National Woman Suffrage Association (NWSA) in 1869, having launched a short-lived publication, the *Revolution,* a year earlier.[15] Restricting its officers to women, NWSA welcomed all who supported woman suffrage. While members campaigned to amend state and territorial constitutions, their primary focus was on securing a national amendment that would give to women the voting rights so recently guaranteed to black men. The NWSA earned the reputation for being "radical" for several unpopular actions, including opposition to the Fifteenth Amendment, and for associating with a number of unpopular bedfellows. Their initial embrace of racist George Train, who underwrote the *Revolution,* and their association with the disreputable free-love advocate Victoria Woodhull[16] and other socially marginal people—including Mormons—reinforced the epithet of radical. Additionally, Stanton's critique of marital laws and her advocacy of divorce put NWSA outside the pale of traditional American values.

To counter this negative view of suffragists, Lucy Stone and her followers, who supported the deferment of woman suffrage, organized the American Woman Suffrage Association (AWSA) a few months later. Leadership alternated between men and women, and members were recruited who shared the same "high moral tone" and middle-class values of its leaders.[17] Indeed, after initially promising to cooperate with the National, Lucy Stone eventually distanced the American as far as possible from the National to create a respectable, moderate, unthreatening image of woman suffrage.[18] The American placed its faith in Republican promises of support after Reconstruction in the South, only to be bitterly disappointed when Republicans gave woman suffrage short shrift in their 1872 platform and little concrete help thereafter. Though still hopeful for a national amendment, the American turned its attention to state referenda. When the expected Republican support did not materialize, AWSA members belatedly recognized what Anthony and Stanton had already concluded: the suffrage movement was going to have to rely on its own persuasive powers and would have to be a nonpartisan woman's movement, seeking constituents from both parties and genders and from all segments of society.

Mormonism's departures from the norm—its critique of monogamous marriage in favor of polygamy, its liberal policy toward divorce, its early renunciation of the common law (the basis of British and American jurisprudence, which disadvantaged married women), and the unconventional ideas of Brigham Young in urging college and professional training for women and their entry into a variety of fields of employment and public activities—aligned Mormon women more closely with the National's liberal position toward woman's rights than with the more conservative stance of the American.[19] The National's policy of campaigning at the federal level, where action against the Mormons was centered, also seemed advantageous to Mormons. Moreover, the American's public antipathy to polygamy, and to the Church in general, helped steer Mormon women into the National camp.

That woman suffrage and polygamy would become intertwined issues was hardly an expectation at the time the two suffrage organizations were asserting their policies. The *New York Times* is credited with creating a connection between these two volatile issues. In 1867, the *Times* suggested the possibility that woman suffrage might be the solution to the polygamy problem in Utah, allowing women to use the ballot to outlaw the practice.[20] That same year, Hamilton Wilcox of the Universal Franchise Association expanded on this idea and proposed granting suffrage to women in all the territories, but Congress did not respond. In February 1869, Indiana Representative George Washington Julian proposed an amendment enfranchising women to the House Committee on Territories, while Kansas Senator Samuel C. Pomeroy introduced a similar proposal to the Senate committee the following day,[21] but neither proposal passed.

A year later, Susan B. Anthony again raised the issue, declaring her belief that enfranchising the women of Utah was "the one safe, sure and swift means to abolish polygamy" in Utah Territory.[22] Both William Hooper, Utah's delegate to Congress, and the Salt Lake City *Deseret News,* in a series of three editorials published immediately after the measures were first proposed by Julian and Pomeroy, expressed their approval of enfranchising Utah women, much to the surprise of the proponents. Julian and Pomeroy fully expected a female electorate to vote out polygamy, which, they assumed, would undermine its religious sanction. The *Deseret News*, however, decided to call their bluff and challenged Congress to allow Utah to settle the question. "We like this suggestion," the *News* noted.

> If carried out, and if it should work as its originators hope it will, it would be a very easy method of settling this vexed question, and without the fuss and trouble which have heretofore attended the various schemes that have been proposed for that object; but if

the ladies should exercise the right of suffrage and yet not discourage nor break down polygamy, then members of congress would, perhaps, be satisfied to let the question rest.[23]

Though Congress did not pursue the proposals, the Utah legislative assembly did and enfranchised women in February 1870.

Even as the Julian and Pomeroy Bills were debated, other anti-Mormon legislation claimed the attention of Congress. Although the LDS Church had been subject to persecution since its founding in 1830, the public pronouncement of its acceptance of polygamy as a religious principle in 1852 brought national antagonism as well as federal legislation to abolish it. In 1856, Republicans had promised to eliminate the "twin relics of barbarism," polygamy and slavery, and in 1862 Congress passed the Morrill Act, criminalizing bigamy in the territories. This was followed by a series of bills designed to curtail Mormon dominance in Utah[24]: the Wade Bill of 1866; the Cragin and Ashley Bills of 1867, the latter proposing a radical solution to the Mormon problem—dismemberment of Utah territory; and the Cullom Bill of 1870, which, besides regulating marriage and divorce laws in Utah, removing a privileged tax exemption for the Church, and taking control of the local militia, also disfranchised and prescribed fines and imprisonment for those who practiced polygamy or cohabited with more than one woman. It also removed the right of jury duty from mere believers in plural marriage. Finally, the Cullom

Senator S. M. Cullom (ca. 1860–75) lent his name to the Cullom Bill of 1870.

Library of Congress

Bill included a drastic provision by which the U.S. President could send forty thousand troops to Utah to enforce these measures.[25]

The Cullom Bill, made public in January 1870, a month before suffrage was granted to Utah women and two years before the *Woman's Exponent* was established, unleashed a torrent of outrage not only from Utah but also around the country.[26] The most impassioned outrage, however, came from Mormon women. Their resentment seething, a group of Relief Society women[27] met in the Fifteenth Ward Relief Society hall in Salt Lake City on January 6 to plan a protest meeting.[28] "The ladies of Utah [have] too long remained silent while they [are] being so falsely represented to the world," declared Eliza R. Snow, the leader among the "leading sisters." Mormon women would finally respond publicly to the calumny they, their husbands, and the Church had experienced for nearly two decades.[29] Leading the dissension, Eliza R. Snow announced that the time had come "to rise up in the dignity of our calling and speak for ourselves." Another prominent woman in attendance, Sarah M. Kimball, a close friend and co-worker of Eliza R. Snow, added: "We would be unworthy of the names we bear and of the blood in our veins, should we longer remain silent." Plans were laid for a grand "indignation meeting" to be held in the Salt Lake Tabernacle the following week and replicated in the wards and branches throughout the territory.[30]

Besides these immediate plans for an all-woman rally, the women resolved on two further means to express their indignation toward the events in which they had such a large personal stake. One objective was to attain the vote and another was to send their own representatives to Washington to counteract the lobbying efforts of non-Mormons from Utah. The impetus for resolving to "demand the vote [for women] of the Governor" in order to have a voice in Utah's political affairs[31] can be easily traced to the widely publicized debate—in newspapers and forums and from reformers, Congress, and suffragists—over granting woman suffrage in Utah. Moreover, voting was not a radical notion for Latter-day Saint women, who had long voted on ecclesiastical and community issues in Utah. In fact, Brigham Young had gone on record in 1853 urging women to vote on church and public matters because

"Women are the characters that rule the ballot box."[32] In addition, several women in the planning meeting subscribed to the *Revolution* and the *Woman's Journal,* organs of the national suffrage associations, and most other women present had probably read articles in 1868 and 1869 in the *Deseret News,* praising women for their invaluable service in the "great cause of reform" and enthusiastically endorsing woman suffrage.[33] Certainly Mormon women had "proven" themselves to be loyal and capable co-workers in building and supporting the religious kingdom, a reality vigorously expressed by Elder George Q. Cannon in the *Deseret News* a few months prior to the women's meeting.[34] If this were not enough, only weeks earlier, the neighboring territory of Wyoming had granted women the right to vote.

By 1870 the idea of women voting in Utah was a natural response to the suffrage-charged environment surrounding them.[35] Moreover, "demanding" the vote of Stephen Mann merely reflected the opposition federal officials had persistently mounted to any measure increasing Mormon political control. However, for most Mormon women at that time, the vote was desirable more as a tool than as a right, which they would use as an expression of loyalty and unity to support the social and religious system to which they were committed, contrary to the initial expectations of Susan Anthony and several Congressmen.

The resolution to send Eliza R. Snow and Sarah M. Kimball to Washington, D.C., to plead the Mormon case was clearly motivated by the desire to counteract numerous anti-Mormon lobbyists from Utah who had already been urging Congressional legislation that would wreak havoc in Latter-day Saint families. Mormon women wanted to refute their arguments and make a personal appeal for the constitutionality of their religious practices as well as their beliefs. The resolution was an emotional rather than a rational reaction to the many voices in Washington arguing for their own interests in Utah territory.[36] As it turned out, this proposal proved extraneous. Numerous powerful non-Mormon economic and political factions as well as prominent newspaper editors around the country had weighed in with their own nonreligious objections to the detrimental effects of the Cullom Bill.[37] There was little doubt that economic and political arguments against its passage would carry more weight with Congress than religious ones. Moreover, Snow and Kimball, the two staid Mormon women appearing in Washington at that time, would probably have been regarded as social curiosities rather than serious activists, especially among hardened Mormon critics. It was better that the Cullom Bill be countered by others.

More effective than either of these measures might have been, if acted upon, was the indignation rally itself. Held a week after the planning meeting, it attracted five to six thousand women to the Salt Lake Tabernacle, and thousands of women in outlying communities held their own rallies.[38] It is very probable that Emmeline Wells attended the meeting. This gathering would be the only one in which she did not play a visible and influential role. Moreover, she and Zina Young Williams would be the women selected to plead the Mormon cause in Washington nine years later.

This large assembly of women was truly activism on a grand scale, "a scene upon which gentile civilization gazed with wide-eyed wonder," according to one ebullient historian.[39] With only a few reporters present, among whom was Colonel Finlay Anderson of the *New York Herald,* the all-woman assemblage elected twelve women to speak for the congregation. Seeking the vote was not the focus of this group of women. Theirs was a protest against the infringement of the First Amendment's protection of religion.[40] The "chief motives which have dictated our present action," Harriet Cook explained, were "not for the purpose of assuming any particular political power, nor to claim any special prerogative which may or may not belong to our sex; but to express our indignation at the unhallowed efforts of men, who . . . would force upon a religious community . . . either the course of apostasy, or the bitter alternative of fire and sword." This was a rally to demonstrate the indignation of an entire community and to show the women's loyalty to and unity with their men in defending their "sacred rights." As the assemblage's sixth resolution affirmed: "We are and shall be united with our brethren in sustaining them against each and every encroachment." "To suppose that we should not be aroused," said Eliza R. Snow, "when our brethren are threatened with fines and imprisonment, for their faith in, and obedience to, the laws of God, is an insult to our womanly natures."[41]

After a brief impassioned summary of the dire consequences of the bill, Phebe Woodruff concluded by warning the prosecutors of the law that if they should indeed imprison LDS Church elders for holding to their religious vows, the prisons should be made "large enough to hold their wives, for where they go we will go also." This bold and unequivocal announcement of the united interests of Mormon men and women undermined the efforts of suffragists and antipolygamists who acted on the assumption that Mormon women would willingly "throw off the yoke" of polygamy if given the opportunity.[42]

The rally was unusual and significant enough to attract the attention of several newspapers outside the territory, some of whose comments were republished in the *Deseret News*. They found the speakers articulate and intelligent, fully equal to the female suffrage workers such as Lucretia Mott, Elizabeth Stanton, and Susan B. Anthony in their ability to stir up public sentiment. The rally demonstrated qualities of Mormon women that had never before been noted in the gentile press or in any other non-Mormon public forum. There would be more rallies, but their purposes would be similar—a public defense of their religion and a show of unity with the men of their faith. In the ensuing struggle to hold onto the vote, religious, rather than political, rights claimed highest priority.[43]

Events moved rapidly after this first public rally. Mormon women had indeed broken their silence, and within a few years they would pursue additional means to defend and explain themselves to a censorious nation. Two weeks after the rally, the committee on elections in the newly assembled territorial legislature was instructed to look into the matter of granting women the vote, though no public demand had been made for it. A week later the committee recommended passage of a measure granting woman suffrage. By February 10 it had successfully passed both houses of the legislature, and two days later it was signed by Territorial Secretary Stephen A. Mann, acting governor in the absence of the newly appointed governor, J. Wilson Shaffer.[44] On February 14, at a municipal election, twenty-five women voted, the first women to vote in a general election in the United States.[45] That the decision to enfranchise Utah women was already in the making before the women's rally is quite probable. Church leaders did not need a public rally of women to assure them of their loyalty or political capabilities. Contrary to public opinion, extending the vote to women was motivated less by the need to increase political strength and more by the desire to show religious unity.

In response to their enfranchisement, women from around the city convened in the Fifteenth Ward Relief Society hall a week after receiving the vote to reflect on its impact. Their comments are an interesting mixture of political and religious rhetoric, all noting that their enfranchisement, in the words of historian Edward Tullidge, "had been marked out for [them] in the economy of divine providence." While a politically astute Sarah Kimball hailed the legislation for allowing her to openly admit that she had long been a "woman's rights woman," she also remarked that "the interests of man and woman cannot be separated, for the man is not without the woman nor the woman without the man in the Lord." Prescindia Kimball saw the vote as a means "to accomplish what is required at our hands" and was glad the time had come "when our vote will assist our leaders, and redeem ourselves." Bathsheba W. Smith, who had raised the question of suffrage in the January 6 planning meeting, declared a sense of weakness as she contemplated "the greater responsibilities which now rested upon them."[46]

Eliza R. Snow read from a favorable account of the indignation meeting and proposed an "expression of gratitude to Stephen Mann," for concurring with the wishes of the legislature. She then suggested that Bathsheba W. Smith be appointed to preach retrenchment "and woman's rights, if she wished."[47] Though Eliza Snow disdained the manner of those "who are strenuously and unflinchingly advocating 'woman's rights,'"[48] she encouraged Mormon women to use the ballot, explaining that it was as necessary for them "to vote as to pray."[49] Always supportive of the enfranchisement of Mormon women, she explained to the sisters that "[God] has given us the right of franchise," and that right should not be taken lightly. Woman suffrage in Utah, she believed, was born of a different power than women's agitation, and had a different purpose than what most feminists argued. "Unless we maintain our rights," she warned, "we will be driven from place to place," reminding them of their history of repeated impotence in claiming government protection.[50] Their enfranchisement was primarily to unite the Church in shoring up what they fervently believed were their religious rights.[51] Of course, this was exactly what non-Mormons feared. That women took their enfranchisement seriously was noted by one observer in 1872. "If the matter on which your vote was required was one which might decide the question whether you were your husband's wife, and your children legitimate," she wrote to a friend, "you would be apt to entertain a determined opinion on the subject."[52]

Emmeline Wells's name is absent from any public record of these events, but her later comments show that she was well aware of and likely participated in much that transpired during these transforming years. She was certainly as eager as everyone else to meet Elizabeth Cady Stanton and Susan B. Anthony when they visited Utah little more than a year later, in July 1871.

Several compelling reasons motivated Stanton and Anthony to make the long journey across the continent that year. Competing with AWSA for adherents, NWSA was eager to affiliate western suffragists with their organization and to extend their lecture circuit into new and fertile fields. Completion of the transcontinental railroad two years earlier made coast-to-coast travel feasible, fast, and relatively comfortable. Though their destination was California and the Northwest, Stanton and Anthony were interested in meeting the enfranchised women of Wyoming and Utah. They were also curious, like most Americans, about Mormons, and they wished to make a judgment about them for themselves. And finally, Stanton and Anthony had been invited by a group of Mormon dissenters who had started a "new movement" with a reform agenda that Easterners hoped might overthrow polygamy.

William Godbe, a leader of the New Movement, met Stanton and Anthony at the railroad depot in Salt Lake City and escorted them to their hotel. Two years earlier, in 1869, William Godbe and several other prominent merchants and journalists had led a number of dissenters from the Mormon fold who disagreed with Brigham Young primarily on his trade policies, his authoritarian rule, and his inordinate intervention as a spiritual leader in the material affairs of his people. The completion of the transcontinental railroad put Utah on the highway of the nation. In anticipation of an influx of non-Mormon merchants and commercial entrepreneurs, Brigham Young, devoted to the principle of self-sufficiency that had helped the Church survive its troubled beginnings, initiated a number of economic programs designed to insulate the Saints economically. Denouncing trade with non-Mormons, creating a cooperative mercantile system among Mormons throughout the territory, and encouraging lower wages for producers of home-manufactured items to keep prices lower than those of imported goods, Brigham Young appeared to be retrenching at the very moment that economic development and prosperity seemed imminent. Using their journal, the *Utah Magazine*, Godbe and his followers attacked Brigham Young, his program, and his "one-man rule." Moreover, on their business visits to the East, some of the Godbeites found a new religious philosophy that fed their discontent. Spiritualism, a system that denied all forms of authoritarianism and institutionalized religion, reinforced their revolt against Brigham Young.[53]

The disaffection of these economically successful and socially influential Mormons brought them excommunication from the LDS Church and into political and economic association with Utah Gentiles. Together they established a local political party in 1870, the Liberal Party, and organized the Liberal Institute, which offered a public platform for a diversity of ideas and lecturers who spoke to enthusiastic crowds in a handsome, newly constructed building.[54] Mormons, including Emmeline Wells, often attended the lectures. The *Mormon Tribune*, also founded in 1870 and later named the *Salt Lake Tribune*, with the *Utah Magazine*, served as forums for the Liberal Party. The affiliation of these dissidents with non-Mormons in the community created a small but influential cadre of men and women who developed a well-orchestrated, persistent, and eventually successful anti-Mormon agenda. Moreover, as the non-Mormon population grew in Utah, gentile women became highly visible, their ranks swelled by estranged Mormon women. Three of their number, in fact, were the first to make contact with the eastern suffrage movement. All three were also wives of William Godbe: Annie Thompson, Mary Hampton, and Charlotte Ives Cobb.

Charlotte, the most politically active of the three, married William in 1869 before his excommunication. She was the daughter of Augusta Adams Cobb of Boston, who left her husband and five of her children in 1843 to join the Mormons in Nauvoo. Augusta took only her six-year-old daughter Charlotte with her. Augusta later became a plural wife of Brigham Young. Augusta counted Lucy Stone as a Boston friend, and sometime before Charlotte's marriage, Augusta and Charlotte went east, where Charlotte was introduced to a number of activist women.[55] During subsequent visits, Charlotte spoke at woman suffrage gatherings and later claimed to have been influential in helping the suffrage bill to pass in Utah through "the letters I wrote to leading papers, & words I spoke at conventions of W[oman].S[uffrage]. Meetings" as well as by "personal influence used among my relatives and friends in Washington, New York, & Boston."[56] The vigorous suffrage activity of these former Mormon women might well, as Charlotte claimed, have influenced the Mormon legislature to see advantages in granting woman suffrage. Eastern suffragists, who were under the false impression that members of the New Movement in Utah had seceded from the Church because of polygamy, welcomed the Godbe women as harbingers of a reformed Utah.

While LDS Relief Societies introduced lessons on the political process to initiate Latter-day Saint women into politics, Annie Godbe did the same for gentile women. Charlotte and Annie eventually became NWSA vice presidents for Utah, and Charlotte also served as a delegate to the association's education committee. Though members of the National, these sister-wives maintained their ties with the American through personal friendships and their letters on Utah affairs submitted to its publication, the *Woman's Journal*.

During the week that Elizabeth Stanton and Susan Anthony spent in Utah, they divided their time between members of the New Movement and the Mormons. Mary and Annie Godbe entertained them in their homes, and they gave several lectures at the Liberal Institute for the newly organized Young Ladies' Mutual Improvement Society.[57]

The old Tabernacle was the setting for Anthony and Stanton's lecture to the Mormon audience. Nearly a thousand men and newly enfranchised women attended the initial lecture by Elizabeth Stanton. She was introduced by Daniel H. Wells, and few Salt Lake City women, including Emmeline Wells, would have missed such an event. Among other benefits of woman suffrage, Elizabeth Stanton pointed out to her large audience, was the possibility that "if there were henceforth any slavery among Utah women" or if "any social institution degrading to women" continued, "they held the power to rid themselves of it." Her point could hardly have been missed by her eager listeners. She added, contrary to critics' claims, that woman suffrage would improve marriage: "Man will gain as much as women by an equal companionship in the nearest and holiest relations of life."[58]

Later in the week, Stanton held four hundred Mormon women enthralled for five hours, discoursing not only on woman suffrage and the controversial subject of "voluntary motherhood," or birth control, but also on a topic she deemed of equal importance: the inferior status of women in marriage and the necessity for women to have easier access to divorce.[59] In the "full and free discussion" that followed, neither Stanton nor her listeners referred to the fact that Stanton was in a territory that had one of the most lenient divorce statutes in the country. Ironically, while antipolygamists agitated for legislation to free polygamist wives from their "marital bondage," Utah had provided both religious and legal remedies to do so. Brigham Young held the authority to dissolve plural marriages,[60] and first or legal wives could receive divorces just as easily through the Mormon-governed probate courts.[61] For a period in the mid-1870s, Utah acquired the dubious distinction of being a divorce mecca, attracting migratory applicants who met the lenient residency requirements. Neither the political power of the vote nor the leniency of the law, however, induced Mormon women in any collective sense to leave their polygamous marriages. Moreover, the legal, social, and ecclesiastical freedom to exit an unhappy marriage in Utah undermined the necessity of the vote to extricate individual women from the controversial practice. Except for the rhetoric of the deeply committed reformers, the campaign against plural marriage was much more political than altruistic. The vote in the hands of disillusioned polygamous wives was not their only way out of an impossible marriage.[62]

Into this maelstrom of politics, religion, and women's rights, the *Woman's Exponent* made its bold appearance, and Emmeline B. Wells began her journey into public life. From its beginning in June 1872, the *Exponent* addressed the issues arising from the "contending forces" that were part of the Utah social environment.[63] The battle lines were, in effect, drawn just three months earlier, when Utah attempted for the fourth time to become a state. It had been ten years since the third unsuccessful bid, a time when few Gentiles resided in Utah and were thus unable to mount a major local opposition to the statehood effort.[64] Completion of the transcontinental railroad, however, had brought an influx of non-Mormons into Utah, women as well as men. Now there was a small, vocal, and influential contingent of non-Mormons and their ex-Mormon allies.[65] Statehood meant something different to these new residents than it did to Mormons. The self-rule that Mormons desired worried the Gentiles, who depended on their territorial status with its federally appointed officials to offset Mormon numerical dominance and control of the probate courts.

In 1872, though gentile residents were beginning to enjoy growing economic power, political parity was far distant and political imbalance remained a major source of discontent. Suspicions about the patriotism of Mormons was also a concern. The *Salt Lake Tribune* explained that the chief worry was that Mormons were "not a republican people" because they eagerly anticipated the downfall of "man-made kingdoms and governments" and their replacement with the "kingdom of God," which, alleged the *Tribune* writer, was Mormonism itself.[66] That Mormons were disloyal to the U.S. government was a charge frequently expressed in anti-Mormon rhetoric. The Mormons' unswerving allegiance to Brigham Young as both their spiritual and temporal leader strengthened this claim. Yet the "social blight" of polygamy rankled even more, particularly among gentile women. Until polygamy was terminated, Gentiles would oppose every effort toward statehood, and until the Edmunds Bill of 1882 was enacted, denial of statehood was

Congress's primary weapon against polygamy. However, the 1872 bid for statehood faced, for the first time, formidable opposition *within* Utah. Also for the first time, four women, as voting residents, were appointed as delegates to the nominating committee, and all women were eligible to vote in the ratification election.[67]

Among the most active opponents of the 1872 try for statehood were gentile women. New to the territory, some of them found the novelty of becoming voters less compelling than their animus toward polygamy. Moreover, the territorial legislature's approval, just as the convention convened, of a Married Persons Property Act, which removed the long-held common law protection of the dower right, only exacerbated their antagonism.[68] The provision was enacted to avoid the anomaly of granting multiple one-third dower interests to wives in plural marriages should their husbands die intestate, but its removal left legal wives dependent on other legal protections in such an event.[69] Schuyler Colfax, former United States Vice President and a relentless critic of Mormons, argued that abolishing the right of dower rendered a woman who chose to go into polygamy "slavishly dependent on the husband's favor for any share of his property that they held after his death for herself or her children." Urging reinstatement of dower, he explained that it would "carefully guard the legal wife, who, in polygamy is not the favorite as a general rule. This would greatly discourage women from marrying a polygamist."[70] Emmeline Wells, as the seventh wife of Daniel H. Wells, had reason to favor the legislative act removing dower and argued in the pages of the *Woman's Exponent* that the liberal provisions of the statute, which also allowed married women to retain or convey property that they held in their own name, something many states did not yet permit, were "far in advance of the right of dower." She viewed dower as "a sort of vassalage, and a relic of the old common law of England," causing references to widows as "relicts."[71] The 1872 Act renouncing dower would be one of the last pieces of Utah legislation passed in an effort to protect the inheritance rights of plural wives and their children, and the dower was immediately reinstated with the Edmunds-Tucker Act of 1887.[72]

The constitution that eventually derived from the 1872 convention also generated controversy and rancorous debate, not because it included a provision enfranchising women, but because of a clause that asked Congress to set the terms of admittance—thereby implying an expedient surrender of polygamy in exchange for statehood and self-rule. While the former provision validated women's possession of the vote and caused Mormon women to rejoice, Gentiles believed the latter provision seemed too politically motivated to be sincere.[73] Non-Mormon and ex-Mormon women presented their own objections in a petition to Congress that carried the names of four hundred Utah women. In response, Mormon women submitted a petition of their own. This initial and dramatic female confrontation clearly marked the political boundaries between Mormon and gentile women in Utah and established a pattern of political action that would prevail for another decade.[74]

While Congress deliberated, support for statehood came from an unlikely source. Thomas L. Kane, a non-Mormon friend of Brigham Young and an intermediary between the Church and the federal government on several occasions, traveled with his wife, Elizabeth, from their home in Pennsylvania to Utah during this same contentious year. The couple and their two young sons, at Brigham Young's invitation, spent several weeks with him in St. George, Utah, Young's winter home. A fervent antipolygamist, Elizabeth Kane evidently acquired a measure of empathy for polygamists through this experience. Before leaving Utah, she wrote a series of letters to her senator Simon Cameron, urging him to admit Utah as a state with polygamy intact. "I assure you," she wrote, "the United States will have no more admirable citizens than these Mormons." She, as did others, believed that polygamy would die of attrition if Utah were included rather than excluded from the community of states and their "civilizing" influence.[75] Like Susan B. Anthony and Elizabeth Stanton, Elizabeth Kane believed that the men in Congress were not quite fit to throw stones at the Mormons in the interest of "Virtue."

Unconvinced, Congress not only rejected this fourth attempt at statehood but continued to entertain antipolygamy bills, each time garnering more support for eventual passage. The strongest antipolygamy furor, however, began in Utah with the Protestant clergy and several influential women.

Under the forceful leadership of gentile Cornelia Paddock and the impassioned writing and lecturing of former Latter-day Saint Fannie Stenhouse, whose antipolygamy book went through a second edition in 1872,[76] a woman's antipolygamy movement began to take shape in Utah, eventually embracing women's groups throughout the nation. The women's 1872 petition to defeat statehood showed the strength of women's organized agitation against polygamy and introduced an antisuffrage sentiment among most of Utah's non-Mormon women because they realized that woman suffrage virtually doubled the Mormon voting power while making little difference among the gentile population. After the events of 1872, both federal legislators and national moral reformers were convinced of the necessity to rescind woman suffrage in Utah and encouraged inclusion of this proposal in antipolygamy legislation. In response to this nascent female antipolygamy movement, the *Woman's Exponent* served as a small but forceful voice to counter the crusade. The *Exponent* would have had little or no impact had it not been for the support of eastern suffragists, who fought every attempt to disfranchise Utah women. The ensuing crusade would pit the suffragists against the moral reformers, each group making Utah central to their campaigns.

Thus, woman suffrage, polygamy, and Utah statehood became permanently entwined as each contending party struggled for its own special interest. The battle lines were curiously drawn. Antipolygamy proposals that disfranchised Utah women met stiff resistance from those who stringently opposed polygamy but favored woman suffrage. A number of suffragists noted the illogic of disfranchising Mormon women while allowing Mormon men to vote. Some Congressmen, opposed to both woman suffrage and polygamy, refused to support antipolygamy measures, recognizing the constitutional questions they raised. Some antipolygamy suffragists urged the repeal of woman suffrage, viewing it as a prop for polygamy. Even the sedate *Boston*

Woman's Journal, an inveterate foe of polygamy and polygamists, separated its support of Mormon woman's vote from its antipathy to plural marriage.[77] Meanwhile, as Congressional committees were bombarded by the antipolygamy, antiwoman suffrage vitriol of ex-Mormon Fannie Stenhouse on the one hand, and the defense of woman suffrage by New Movement women Annie, Mary, and Charlotte Godbe on the other, mainstream Latter-day Saint women were gradually establishing a solid connection between themselves and the national suffrage movement and would soon take their case in person to Congress.

During this pivotal year the *Woman's Exponent* proved to be more than a forum for Mormon women to express their views. It also channeled information to Utah women about developments in the suffrage movement and anti-Mormon activity. Since several Mormon women had also subscribed to the *Revolution* during its brief existence, and others were regular subscribers to the *Woman's Journal,* the *Exponent* simply augmented the information found in these periodicals. It also repudiated the "downtrodden" image attached to Mormon women, as the unexpected need to defend their enfranchisement elicited reasoned, articulate articles and editorials. It was in very deed Mormon women's voice to the world. Other aspects of the woman's rights movement would also find consistent coverage in the semimonthly paper. The *Exponent* was beginning to prove its important role in the battle to retain the ballot.

Like Susan B. Anthony and Elizabeth Stanton, Emmeline Wells fashioned her own pantheon of women's rights, incorporating a wider range of goals than simply woman suffrage. But Emmeline began to center her attention on suffrage as it became increasingly endangered in Utah with each new antipolygamy bill. She argued for woman suffrage on every level: as a constitutional right, as a simple act of justice, as a means to defend her religion, and as a social instrument to protect the home and society.[78] Her advocacy began in earnest, however, after her first attendance at a national suffrage convention in 1879 in Washington, D.C. For two decades, Utah would be the centerpiece of the woman's rights campaign and the debate over woman suffrage.

Notes

1. "Address to W. S. A. at Ogden," *Woman's Exponent* 18 (July 15, 1889): 30.
2. Bryant S. Hinckley, *Daniel H. Wells and Events of His Time* (Salt Lake City: Deseret News Press, 1942). For dates and details of his public experience see Orson F. Whitney, "Daniel Hanmer Wells," in *History of Utah*, 4 vols. (Salt Lake City: George Q. Cannon and Sons, 1904), 4:175–79.
3. Maureen Ursenbach Beecher identified the women and their credentials for fitting the category in "The 'Leading Sisters': A Female Hierarchy in Nineteenth-Century Mormon Society," *Journal of Mormon History* 9 (1982): 25–40. Although many were included in this category by virtue of their own accomplishments, others were wives of LDS Church leaders.
4. There are several accounts on the grain-saving program of the Relief Society. See Wells's own account, "The Mission of Saving Grain," *Relief Society Magazine* 2 (February 1915): 47–58; E. Cecil McGavin, "Grain Saving among the Latter-day Saints," *Improvement Era* 44 (March 1941): 141–44, 180; and Jessie Embry, "Relief Society Grain Storage Program 1876–1940" (master's thesis, Brigham Young University, 1974).
5. Emmeline's husband's approval of her entry into the world of journalism was mixed at first, but in an 1875 diary entry, Emmeline noted that he "seemed proud of my literary acquirements for once in his life." Emmeline B. Wells, Diary, June 3, 1875, L. Tom Perry Special Collections, Harold B. Lee Library, Brigham Young University, Provo, Utah. Whether he was aware of her writings under a pseudonym in the *Woman's Exponent* or of her poetic contributions to the *Deseret News* and other publications is not clear, but Emmeline was pleased with this recognition.
6. "Salutatory," *Woman's Exponent* 1 (June 1, 1872): 4.
7. "Woman's Exponent, Utah Ladies Journal," *Woman's Exponent* 1 (June 1, 1872): 8.
8. "Woman's Exponent, Utah Ladies Journal," 8.
9. Wells, Diary, January 4, 1878.
10. The deviance of polygamy from traditional American social norms provoked a national campaign to end the practice, spearheaded by women's religious and reform associations. This universalizing of social values has been defined as a means of asserting the "moral authority" of women, evident in their role as watchdogs of the moral well being of American society. Peggy Pascoe illustrated this concept in *Relations of Rescue: The Search for Moral Authority in the American West, 1847–1939* (New York: Oxford University Press, 1990).

11. The woman movement, which claimed the public energies of Emmeline Wells for nearly three decades, began modestly but courageously with a convention of three hundred men and women at Seneca Falls, New York. The societal limitations women experienced in their public activism against slavery generated within them a profound discontent with the social, religious, political, and legal constraints that identified their own relationship to family and society, and set in motion the movement that would permanently change women's lives. Elizabeth Cady Stanton was the author of the Declaration of Rights and Sentiments that enumerated their many grievances. Details of the convention can be found in Miriam Gurko, *The Ladies of Seneca Falls: The Birth of the Woman's Rights Movement* (New York: Schocken Books, 1976); Ellen Carol DuBois, *Feminism and Suffrage: The Emergence of an Independent Women's Movement in America, 1848–1869* (Ithaca, N.Y.: Cornell University Press, 1978), 21–52; Ellen Carol DuBois, ed. *Elizabeth Cady Stanton, Susan B. Anthony, Correspondence, Writings, Speeches* (New York: Schocken Books, 1981), 2–35; Elizabeth Cady Stanton, Susan B. Anthony, and Matilda Joslyn Gage, *History of Woman Suffrage,* vol. 1 (New York: Fowler and Wells, 1881), chapter 4; Mari Jo and Paul Buhle, *The Concise History of Woman Suffrage* (Urbana: University of Illinois Press, 1978); and Judith Wellman, "The Seneca Falls Women's Rights Convention: A Study of Social Networks," *Journal of Women's History* 3 (Spring 1991): 9–37.

12. Lucy Stone retained her maiden name after marrying Henry B. Blackwell.

13. Elizabeth Stanton, "Drawing the Lines," *Revolution,* March 11, 1869, quoted in DuBois, *Feminism and Suffrage,* 175.

14. Ellen DuBois details this split in the suffrage movement in *Feminism and Suffrage,* chapters 4, 5, and 6. Stanton and Anthony believed that the best hope for woman suffrage was while Republican Reconstruction was in motion, and they refused to support the Fifteenth Amendment unless it offered the same protection from disfranchisement for women as for blacks, openly advocating defeat of the bill during ratification when it did not. Their lack of support for the amendment proved to be another wedge between female suffragists and led to the charge of racism against Stanton and Anthony. See DuBois, *Feminism and Suffrage,* 171–72.

15. Elizabeth Cady Stanton used the *Revolution* to express her views on marriage reform, divorce, prostitution, and birth control while Susan B. Anthony took up the problems of workingwomen along with their joint advocacy of woman suffrage. Martha M. Solomon analyzes the founding, funding, content and demise of the *Revolution* in *A Voice of Their Own: The Woman*

Suffrage Press, 1840–1910 (Tuscaloosa: University of Alabama Press, 1991). See also Lynne Masel-Walters, "Their Rights and Nothing More: A History of *The Revolution*," *Journalism Quarterly* 53 (Summer 1978): 251. Ellen Carol DuBois discusses the almost militant stance of the *Revolution* in *Elizabeth Cady Stanton, Susan B. Anthony, Correspondence, Writings, Speeches*, 92–101.

16. Victoria Claflin Woodhull was an unconventional reformer who found her impetus in nineteenth-century spiritualism. She and her sister established a brokerage firm in New York before she ventured into supporting a utopian community scheme of "free love" and community care of children and property. Woman suffrage was another cause she advocated, and in 1872 she ran for the United States presidency. Her association with the NWSA deepened the schism between the two suffrage groups. For more details of her unconventional life, see Geoffrey Blodgett, "Victoria Claflin Woodhull," in *Notable American Women, 1607–1950: A Biographical Dictionary*, ed. Edward T. James, Janet Wilson James, and Paul S. Boyer, 3 vols. (Cambridge: Belknap Press of Harvard University Press, 1971), 652–55.

17. DuBois, *Feminism and Suffrage*, 168. Julia Ward Howe, a well-known Bostonian, was elected president and Lucy Stone a member of the executive committee. Stone was the heart and de facto head of the organization, though other men and women held the presidency.

18. DuBois, *Feminism and Suffrage*, 172–82; DuBois, *Elizabeth Cady Stanton, Susan B. Anthony, Correspondence, Writings, Speeches*, 90–92; Elisabeth Griffith details the personal and philosophical conflicts of the two associations in *In Her Own Right: The Life of Elizabeth Cady Stanton* (New York: Oxford University Press, 1984), 133–43, as does Andrea Moore Kerr in *Lucy Stone: Speaking Out for Equality* (New Brunswick, N.J.: Rutgers University Press, 1992), 130–47. All studies of the women involved and histories of the woman suffrage movement provide information on this bitter cleavage in the suffrage movement.

19. Brigham Young encouraged women to learn to speak in public, to manage their own enterprises, and to study all branches of learning, including law, medicine, and business. See, for example, *Journal of Discourses*, 26 vols. (Liverpool, Eng.: F. D. Richards, 1855–86), 12:31–32 (April 8, 1867); 12:111–16 (December 8, 1867); 13:56–62 (July 18, 1869); "An Address to the Female Relief Society, Delivered by Brigham Young in the Fifteenth Ward Meeting House, Feb. 4, 1869," *Millennial Star* 31 (April 24, 1869): 267–70.

20. Two years later the *Times* did an about-face and noted that Utah women would not use the vote to eliminate polygamy. See "The Women of Utah," *New York Times*, March 5, 1869, 6–7; and "The Mormon Question," *New*

York Times, March 17, 1869, 6. See also "The Female Suffrage Question," Journal History of the Church, January 9, 1868, 2, Church Archives, The Church of Jesus Christ of Latter-day Saints, Salt Lake City, also available on *Selected Collections from the Archives of The Church of Jesus Christ of Latter-day Saints,* 2 vols. (Provo, Utah: Brigham Young University Press, 2002), vol. 2, DVD 6, microfilm copy in Harold B. Lee Library. Numerous other *Deseret News* articles followed in 1869 and 1870.

21. Hamilton Wilcox of the Universal Franchise Association is credited with having initiated the idea for proposing woman suffrage in the territories. Six western territories acted on Wilcox's proposal: Colorado, Dakota, Idaho, New Mexico, Wyoming, and Utah. Only the latter two actually succeeded in acquiring the vote for their women. For more details about these proposals see B. H. Roberts, *A Comprehensive History of The Church of Jesus Christ of Latter-day Saints, Century One,* 6 vols. (Provo, Utah: Corporation of the President, The Church of Jesus Christ of Latter-day Saints, 1965), 5:323–24; T. A. Larson, "Woman Suffrage in Western America," *Utah Historical Quarterly* 38 (Winter 1970): 9–10; Beverly Beeton, "Woman Suffrage in Territorial Utah," *Utah Historical Quarterly* 46 (Spring 1978): 100–20, reprinted in Carol Cornwall Madsen, ed., *Battle for the Ballot: Essays on Woman Suffrage in Utah, 1870–1896* (Logan: Utah State University Press, 1997), 117. See also Ellen Carol DuBois, *Feminism and Suffrage: The Emergence of An Independent Women's Movement in America* (Ithaca: Cornell University Press, 1978), 170–73.

22. Quoted from the *National Republican,* January 19, 1870. Clippings from this newspaper and others can be found in the Scrapbook of Susan B. Anthony, located in the Library of Congress, and in the collection of materials by Patricia G. Holland and Ann D. Gordon, eds., *Papers of Elizabeth Cady Stanton and Susan B. Anthony* (Wilmington, Del.: Scholarly Resources, 1991).

23. "A New Plan," *Deseret News Weekly,* March 24, 1869, 78.

24. Though polygamy set the pace in anti-Mormon sentiment, many non-Mormons found the political and economic dominance of Mormons in Utah to be even more egregious. The general "un-American" insularity, cohesiveness, and theocratic leadership that seemed disloyal, even treasonous to some, fueled the intense anti-Mormon crusade of the 1870s and 1880s. The Morrill Act of 1862 was the first major piece of legislation to suppress polygamy. Its provisions included outlawing bigamy, disincorporating the LDS Church, and confiscating Church property over $50,000. Since the probate courts, which controlled domestic litigation, were primarily headed by Mormon men, the Morrill Act proved to be unenforceable. The Poland Bill of 1874 curtailed the jurisdiction of the probate courts. The Edmunds and Edmunds-Tucker Acts of 1882 and 1887, which contained the provisions of the Morrill Act, were

enforceable after the U.S. Supreme Court ruled in 1879 that polygamy was not protected by the Constitution. The legal nuances of the Morrill Act are discussed in Sarah Barringer Gordon, *The Mormon Question: Polygamy and Constitutional Conflict in Nineteenth-Century America* (Chapel Hill: University of North Carolina Press, 2002), esp. 81–83.

25. See Gustive O. Larson, *Outline History of Territorial Utah* (1958; repr., Provo, Utah: Brigham Young University, 1972), 225–26; Richard D. Poll, Thomas G. Alexander, Eugene E. Campbell, and David E. Miller, eds., *Utah's History* (Provo, Utah: Brigham Young University Press, 1978), 250–52; Roberts, *Comprehensive History*, 5:311–16. A precedent for sending troops to supervise voting procedures occurred earlier when U.S. President Ulysses S. Grant sent troops to Louisiana, a move that outraged many in Congress. See Davis Bitton, *George Q. Cannon, A Biography* (Salt Lake City: Deseret Book, 1999), 202. Noted in James A. Henretta, ed., *America's History* (Chicago: Dorsey Press, 1987), 495–96.

26. Roberts includes a number of press statements expressing the outrage of many non-Mormons to the excesses of the Cullom Bill. See Roberts, *Comprehensive History*, 5:314–17. Many individuals saw that the economic liabilities inherent in the bill would prove costly to more people than Mormons.

27. Many were "leading sisters," a phrase not of historians' making but used frequently to designate those women who headed local ward Relief Societies or who were publicly visible in other ways. Eliza R. Snow and Zina D. H. Young were among the most prominent at that time, since they had recently taken on the task of reorganizing the Relief Society at Brigham Young's request. Both were wives of Brigham Young. Emmeline B. Wells was not among the women so designated at that time, since she had not yet taken a public role.

28. Minutes of the Fifteenth Ward Relief Society, 1868–73, January 6, 1870. Besides the original minutes of the meeting, numerous printed sources recount the events transpiring immediately before and after. See Jill Mulvay Derr, Janath Russell Cannon, and Maureen Ursenbach Beecher, *Women of Covenant: The Story of Relief Society* (Salt Lake City: Deseret Book, 1992), 110–13; Beverly Beeton, *Women Vote in the West: The Woman Suffrage Movement, 1869–1896* (New York: Garland, 1986); T. A. Larson, "Woman Suffrage in Western America," *Utah Historical Quarterly* 38 (Winter 1970): 7–19; Thomas G. Alexander, "An Experiment in Progressive Legislation: The Granting of Woman Suffrage in Utah in 1870," *Utah Historical Quarterly* 38 (Winter 1979): 20–30; Maureen Ursenbach Beecher, Carol Cornwall Madsen, and Jill Mulvay Derr, "The Latter-day Saints and Women's Rights, 1870–1920: A Brief History," *Task Papers in LDS History*, no. 29 (Salt Lake City: Historical

140   An Advocate for Women

Department of the Church of Jesus Christ of Latter-day Saints, 1978); Lola Van Wagenen, "In Their Own Behalf: The Politicization of Mormon Women and the 1870 Franchise," *Dialogue: A Journal of Mormon Thought* 24 (Winter 1991): 31–43, reprinted in Madsen, *Battle for the Ballot*, 60–73.

29. Although the Church had been subject to persecution since its founding in 1830, the public pronouncement of its practice of polygamy as a religious principle in 1852 brought national antagonism as well as federal legislation to abolish the practice.

30. Minutes of the Fifteenth Ward Relief Society, Church Archives, January 6, 1870.

31. Ironically, there was no governor in residence in Utah in January 1870. Territorial Secretaries Stephen A. Mann and Edwin Higgins filled interim positions as Acting Governors between January 1869 and March 1870. Stephen Mann, who eventually signed the woman suffrage bill after a unanimous vote of the legislature, was the acting governor in February 1870. The newly appointed governor, J. Wilson Shaffer, expected since January, had tarried in Washington, D.C., to await the outcome of the Cullom Bill, whose passage would have greatly strengthened his power as governor of the territory. He was extremely perturbed that Acting Governor Mann had allowed the suffrage bill to become law by his signature.

32. Women's indirect influence on political affairs was often noted, both in favor of and against granting women the vote. Brigham Young here was referring to the actual voting power of women in LDS Church affairs. *Journal of Discourses*, 1:218 (October 9, 1852).

33. See for example "Female Suffrage," *Deseret News*, December 9, 1868, 348; "Female Suffrage in Utah," and "Female Suffrage—Ends to be Gained by It," *Deseret News Weekly*, March 24, 1869, 78; "Woman and Her Mission," *Deseret News Weekly*, May 26, 1869, 186. See also "Women's Sphere in Utah," *Utah Magazine* 2 (February 13, 1869): 252; and E. W. Tullidge, "Woman and Her Sphere," *Utah Magazine* 3 (June 26, 1869): 119.

34. See "Woman and Her Mission," 186.

35. Lola Van Wagenen has delineated many of the public activities in which Mormon women were engaged from the days of Nauvoo to their enfranchisement to show their "politicization" before receiving the vote in 1870. See Van Wagenen, "In Their Own Behalf," 31–43. In her article, Van Wagenen also claims that the resolution to demand the vote of the governor was a radical notion. I would argue only that demanding the vote of the governor, sparked as it was by the intensity of their outrage at the Cullom Bill, simply reflected an idea that was already well established and not as radical a resolution as

it might seem. If it represented political activity "in their own behalf," their interests could not be defined as their own political independence but rather as the preservation of the religion and its principles to which they were deeply committed in union with their husbands, fathers, and sons.

36. The published report of the meeting some days later by Sarah Kimball, as Lola Van Wagenen has pointed out, did not include mention of either of these two resolutions. Until the indignation rally, these progressive planners could not be certain of the support of such actions. "Great Indignation Meeting," *Deseret News,* January 19, 1870, 2. However, the seriousness of the women's intent, as evident by the resolutions, was undoubtedly perceived by LDS Church leaders, many of whom were members of the legislature, since several of the women in attendance at the January 6 meeting were married to members of the First Presidency and Quorum of the Twelve Apostles.

37. The Cullom Bill of 1869, proposed by Senator Shelby M. Cullom, generated opposition not only from Latter-day Saints but from members of Congress and others throughout the nation who believed its passage would "incur, not the certainty, but the liability, of the destruction of a vast and growing trade and business which it would require twenty years to repair and restore." Others feared its stringent measures would provoke "violence, war, and the certain destruction of great interests." Congress was advised that the bill was unnecessary for "the pacific forces are now in action that will make it impossible for polygamy to exist any great length of time." This notion could have meant that there was hope that the New Movement in Utah, comprised of disaffected Latter-day Saints who also opposed the Cullom Bill, would bring reform to the Church, or that the railroad would in time bring "civilizing" elements into the territory. B. H. Roberts enumerates and quotes many of these sources, such as the *New York Sun, New York Times, New York Herald, New York World, Cincinnati Times, Springfield Republican, Missouri Republican, Chicago Times, Chicago Tribune,* and *New York Journal of Commerce* in *Comprehensive History of the Church*, 5:316. Roberts also quotes from the *Omaha Herald,* April 2, 1870, and *New York World,* in *Comprehensive History of the Church,* 5:316. The statements originally appeared in the *Deseret News Weekly,* April 20, 1870, and under "What They Say of Us," *Millennial Star* 32 (1870): 181, 142–45, 230–31, 243–44.

38. "Great Indignation Meeting (continued)," *Deseret News,* January 15, 1870, 2. The *Millennial Star* also reported on the women's mass meetings in "Indignation Meeting of the Ladies of Utah," *Millennial Star* 32 (April 12, 1870): 225–28; "Con't," *Millennial Star* 32 (April 26, 1870): 263; "Con't," *Millennial Star* 32 (May 24, 1870): 324–26.

142   An Advocate for Women

39. Orson F. Whitney, *History of Utah*, 4 vols. (Salt Lake City: G. Q. Cannon and Sons, 1892–1904), 2:395. Whitney describes the rally in detail on pages 395–401.

40. See Doctrine and Covenants section 134 for a long statement of Latter-day Saint political beliefs.

41. "Grand Mass Meeting of the Women of Utah on Polygamy and the Cullom Bill," as reported in Edward W. Tullidge, *The Women of Mormondom* (New York: Tullidge and Crandall, 1877), 379–402. See also Whitney, *History of Utah*, 395–401.

42. Tullidge, *Women of Mormondom*, 379–402. See also Whitney, *History of Utah*, 395–401.

43. This does not mean that many women did not employ the rhetoric of individual rights, justice, and equality, or also argue for the instrumental value of the vote in the hands of women. But during the period when the Church was under siege, the vote was seen as a visible symbol of unity with the men of the Church.

44. Thomas G. Alexander details the passage of the bill in "An Experiment in Progressive Legislation," 25–26. Despite his expressed reservations in signing the bill, Acting Governor Mann received a resolution of warm appreciation signed by fourteen prominent Mormon women, to which he graciously replied. See "To His Excellency, the Acting Governor of the Territory, S. A. Mann," *Deseret News*, March 2, 1870, 37; and "Female Suffrage," *Salt Lake Tribune*, February 19, 1870, 57.

45. Noted in a letter from Brigham Young to Heber Young, February 16, 1870, in Dean C. Jessee, ed., *Brigham Young's Letters to His Sons* (Salt Lake City: Deseret Book, 1974), 140.

46. Tullidge, *Women of Mormondom*, 500.

47. Minutes of the Fifteenth Ward Relief Society, February 19, 1870; Tullidge, *Women of Mormondom*, 501–6. The retrenchment movement, designed to diminish reliance on imported goods by the development of "home industries," had its beginning about this time.

48. Eliza R. Snow, "Celebration of the Twenty-fourth at Ogden!" *Journal History*, July 24, 1871, 4–5. Her comments were likely a reaction to the visit just two weeks earlier of Susan B. Anthony and Elizabeth Cady Stanton, the two major figures in the national suffrage movement.

49. Weber Stake, Ogden City Wards Joint Session [Relief Society] Minutes, 1879–88, February 6, 1879, quoted in Jill Mulvay Derr, "Eliza R. Snow and the Woman Question," *BYU Studies* 16 (Winter 1976): 250–64, reprinted in Madsen, *Battle for the Ballot*, 77–78. Uncharacteristically, Eliza even called women

together to urge support for the Anthony Amendment guaranteeing the right of suffrage to all United States women. Derr in Madsen, *Battle for the Ballot*, 78.

50. Weber Stake, Ogden City Wards Joint Session [Relief Society] Minutes 1879–88, February 6, 1879.

51. A *Deseret News Weekly* editorial concurred. "As for ourselves," it reported, "we have no doubt as to the result [of women voting], and are satisfied that it will strengthen the cause of Zion, polygamy included. . . . In every other way it cannot but result also in good." Quoted in Roberts, *Comprehensive History*, 5:325–26.

52. Elizabeth D. Kane, *Twelve Mormon Homes Visited in Succession on a Journey through Utah and Arizona* (Salt Lake City: Tanner Trust Fund, University of Utah Library, 1974), 70.

53. A thoroughgoing analysis of the New Movement is Ronald W. Walker, *Wayward Saints: The Godbeites and Brigham Young* (Urbana: University of Illinois Press, 1998). See also Roberts, *Comprehensive History*, 5:259–71, 285–87, 305–12; and Whitney, *History of Utah*, 2:328–35. While leaders of the Godbeites sometimes differed with their non-Mormon allies over various issues, most did not rejoin the LDS Church. The New Movement's open acceptance of spiritualism, according to some writers, deterred other more secular sympathizers from supporting their cause, and the loss of its paper, the *Utah Magazine*, and its lecture hall, the Liberal Institute, accelerated the group's demise. See Walker, *Wayward Saints*, 343–59.

54. Among the noted speakers were Phoebe Couzins, admitted to the Utah Bar in 1872, and the well-known and notorious Victoria Woodhull, a suffragist, lecturer, and publisher. Her advocacy of "free love" radicalized her reputation and that of NWSA during the short period she was prominent in the organization.

55. Additional information about Charlotte Godbe can be found in Beverly Beeton, "'I Am an American Woman:' Charlotte Ives Cobb Godbe Kirby," *Journal of the West* 27 (April 1988): 13–19; Beverly Beeton, "A Feminist among the Mormons: Charlotte Ives Cobb Godbe Kirby," *Utah Historical Quarterly* 59 (Winter 1991): 22–31; Mary Cable, "She Who Shall be Nameless," *American Heritage* 16 (February 1965): 50–55; Beeton, *Women Vote in the West: The Woman Suffrage Movement, 1869–1896* (New York: Garland, 1986); Lola Van Wagenen, "Sister-Wives and Suffragists: Polygamy and the Politics of Woman Suffrage, 1870–1896" (PhD diss., New York University, 1994; Provo, Utah: BYU Studies and Joseph Fielding Smith Institute for Latter-day Saint History, 2003), 1–23.

144   An Advocate for Women

56. From a letter to President Wilford Woodruff, February 5, 1889, Wilford Woodruff Papers, Church Archives, quoted in Beeton, "Feminist among the Mormons," 24–25. She does not explain exactly how her public appearances in the East influenced the decisions of Utah lawmakers in the West, but her advocacy of suffrage undoubtedly helped to keep suffrage in the political forefront in Utah.

57. See "Society for the Improvement of Women," *Salt Lake Herald*, July 8, 1871, 3; and Susan B. Anthony, "Susan B. Anthony at Salt Lake," *Salt Lake Tribune*, July 19, 1871, 4. Elizabeth Stanton's speech on voluntary motherhood is reviewed in "Local Items," *Salt Lake Tribune*, July 1, 1871, 3. The *Salt Lake Tribune* indicated that a "very small audience" of Gentiles attended Susan B. Anthony's lecture at the Liberal Institute, where she spoke primarily on the value of the vote to working-class women (July 3, 1871), 3. Elizabeth Stanton seemed to be the more popular speaker whenever the two women appeared together, a fact that understandably disturbed Anthony.

58. "Woman Suffrage," *Salt Lake Tribune*, July 1, 1871, 3.

59. Introducing a reprint of a *Salt Lake Tribune* article in her paper, the *Revolution*, Anthony noted that she and Stanton had evidently "thrown into the polygamic camp the bombshell of woman's individual sovereignty and direct inspiration from the heart of God equally with that of man." Stanton felt that this and her remarks on motherhood made her an unwelcome guest in Utah thereafter. See *Revolution*, July 13, 20, and 27, 1871. Additional accounts of their visit are Theodore Stanton and Harriot Stanton Blatch, eds. *Elizabeth Cady Stanton as Revealed in Her Letters, Diary, and Reminiscences*, 2 vols. (New York: Harper and Brothers, 1922), 1:237–40; Alma Lutz, in *Susan B. Anthony: Rebel, Crusader, Humanitarian* (Boston: Beacon Press, 1959), 186–87, briefly mentions the visit. Kathleen Barry in *Susan B. Anthony: A Biography of a Singular Feminist* (New York: New York University Press, 1988), skips any mention of Utah in describing their western trip (237–38). Other biographers give more or less attention to the Utah visit.

60. Extant records show that at least sixteen hundred applicants, most of them women, received ecclesiastical divorces before polygamy was suspended in 1890. An analysis of these certificates of divorce is found in Eugene E. Campbell and Bruce L. Campbell, "Divorce among Mormon Polygamists: Extent and Explanations," *Utah Historical Quarterly* 46 (Winter 1978): 4–23. Utah was among the 20 percent of states and territories with the highest divorce rate (granted in its territorial courts) for this period, though it was lower than nearly all its western neighbors. Divorce, however, was anathema to conventional women, including most Mormon women.

61. The statute, passed the same year that plural marriage was publicly announced as a Latter-day Saint practice (1852), provided that divorces could be obtained "when it shall be made to appear to the satisfaction and conviction of the court, that the parties cannot live in peace and union together, and that their welfare requires a separation," a grounds comparable to "incompatibility" in today's law. The residency requirement was particularly lenient. Anyone who was or "wished to become" a resident of Utah could invoke the jurisdiction of the court. See An Act in Relation to Bills of Divorce, Sections 2, 3, 1851–52, *Laws of Utah* 82. Several other states and territories had similar provisions but did not include both an incompatibility clause and an open residency requirement as did Utah. For a more complete analysis see Carol Cornwall Madsen, "'At Their Peril': Utah Law and the Case of Plural Wives, 1850–1900," *Western Historical Quarterly* 21 (November 1990): 425–44. It should be noted that though divorce was relatively easy to obtain in Utah, Church leaders counseled against it and an article in the second issue of the *Woman's Exponent,* less than a year after Stanton and Anthony's visit, expressed dismay that "certain advocates of women's rights . . . claim the privilege to set natural laws and sound social regulations at defiance" that would destroy the family circle. See "Dangerous Excesses," *Woman's Exponent* 1 (June 15, 1972): 12.

62. The number of divorces granted in Utah tripled between 1875 and 1878, but records show that only a small minority during that period were granted to bona fide Utah residents. To stem the deluge of migratory divorces, the Mormon legislature reluctantly agreed to alter the statute. The Mormon-owned *Deseret News* explained the hesitation: "Polygamy would be considered a system of bondage, if women desiring to sever their relations with a husband having other wives, were refused the liberty they might demand." "Divorce," *Deseret News Weekly,* October 3, 1877, 552. The national antipathy toward divorce, however, foreclosed the possibility of suffragists and moral crusaders accepting the dissolution of existing polygamous marriages as a means of eventually eliminating the practice. Rather, they viewed the ease of Utah divorces as an unfortunate correlative of polygamy, both considered immoral practices that destroyed the traditional Christian marriage and family. Thus, the practice itself needed to be outlawed. See Sarah Barringer Gordon, "'The Liberty of Self-Degradation': Polygamy, Woman Suffrage and Consent in Nineteenth-Century America," *Journal of American History* 83 (December 1996): 832–47.

63. See "Our Position" and "Statehood," *Woman's Exponent* 1 (June 1, 1872): 4.

64. Congress not only rejected Utah's bid in 1862, it handily passed the Morrill Act, which prohibited bigamy in the territories, disincorporated the LDS Church, and restricted its property ownership to $50,000, measures that proved unenforceable at the time but would later be successfully incorporated in the Edmunds-Tucker Act of 1887.

65. The non-Mormon population in Utah during the 1860s and 1870s has been estimated between 10 and 15 percent. See Gustive O. Larson, "Government, Politics, and Conflict," in Poll and others, *Utah's History*, 247.

66. "Mormon Delegates," *Salt Lake Tribune*, January 23, 1872, 2.

67. The four women were Sarah M. Kimball, Bathsheba W. Smith, Elizabeth Howard, and Willmirth East. Information on the controversy surrounding the convention can be found in Robert Joseph Dwyer, *The Gentile Comes to Utah: A Study in Religious and Social Conflict, 1862–1890* (Salt Lake City: Western Epics, 1971), 126–27; Beeton, *Women Vote in the West: The Woman Suffrage Movement, 1869–1896* (New York: Garland, 1987), 45–46; Whitney, *History of Utah*, 2:692–704; Van Wagenen, "Sister-Wives," 93–106.

68. Dower, a provision of the common law, provides the widow with a one-third interest in her deceased husband's estate if he dies intestate (without a will) and one-third interest during his lifetime. The latter is an inchoate interest, meaning it is not hers to convey, sell, or will during her husband's lifetime, nor can her husband do so without her consent.

69. After signing the bill, Governor George L. Woods reconsidered and urged the legislature to repeal it at the next session. This was not done, and the lack of dower in Utah Territory, though not anomalous, became a focal point in the growing antipolygamy campaign.

70. Schuyler Colfax, "The Mormon Defiance to the Nation: Suggestions As to How It Should be Met," *Chicago Advance*, December 22, 1881, microform 299, no. 6, also reprinted in Jennie Froiseth, *The Women of Mormonism or the Story of Polygamy* (Detroit: C. G. G. Paine, 1882), 360–61.

71. "Woman's Right of Dower," *Woman's Exponent* 11 (December 1, 1882): 106.

72. More information concerning the legal rights of plural wives can be found in Madsen, "At Their Peril," 425–44.

73. The inclusion of woman suffrage was insured by the Enabling Act, sponsored by Representative Aaron A. Sargent of California. Henry Blackwell of the *Woman's Journal* acknowledged the convention delegates as being the first to be elected by "the united suffrage of men and women," and the *New York Times* found the constitution to be very "liberal, perfectly republic, and eminently progressive," as quoted in Beeton, *Woman Vote in the West*, 67.

Mormon leaders insisted that asking Congress to set the terms for admittance was primarily to learn what the expectations were for admitting Utah rather than suggesting any surrender of polygamy. See Roberts, *Comprehensive History*, 5:462–63.

74. See Whitney, *History of Utah*, 2:703; Beeton, "Woman Suffrage in the American West," 46; Van Wagenen, "Sister-Wives," 102–5. Records show that 25,160 people voted in favor of ratification and 365 against. Either the tallies are incorrect or some of the four hundred women and all the men opposed to statehood did not vote. See Whitney, *History of Utah*, 2:704.

75. Elizabeth Kane to Simon Cameron, December 29, 1872, Thomas L. Kane Collection, Perry Special Collections.

76. Mrs. T. B. H. Stenhouse, *Expose of Polygamy in Utah: A Lady's Life among the Mormons,* 2d ed. (New York: American News Company, 1872).

77. Henry Blackwell of awsa commented several times in the *Woman's Journal* that the Republican platform, which had vowed to eradicate polygamy along with slavery, had proven to be less committed to its 1872 pledge to support women's rights. Congress, he said, seemed "utterly indifferent" to the rights of Utah women compared to an "almost morbid sensitiveness to the rights of colored men." See, for example, "Senator Frelinghuysen and the Utah Bill," *Woman's Journal* 5 (January 10, 1874): 12; and "Another Utah Bill," *Woman's Journal* 5 (January 10, 1874): 12.

78. See for example Blanche Beechwood, "Why, Ah! Why?" *Woman's Exponent* 3 (October 1, 1874): 67; and "A Mormon Woman's View of Marriage," *Woman's Exponent* 6 (September 1, 1877): 54.

Chapter 7

Wells Goes to Washington

*I thank God I was the first
to represent our women in the Halls of Congress.*[1]

For most of the decade following the enfranchisement of Utah women in 1870, the three Godbe wives (Annie, Mary, and Charlotte) were the primary Utah representatives in the national suffrage movement, maintaining ties with both the National and American Woman Suffrage Associations. But Emmeline Wells, whose experience with the *Woman's Exponent* drew her ineluctably into awareness of the national movement, increased her public exposure among suffrage circles in other ways and gained confidence in her own abilities by fulfilling assignments to speak in religious meetings and to preside at women's gatherings.[2] As she became a regular contributor to the *Woman's Exponent*, she also began submitting letters and articles to other women's journals.[3] This foray into journalism was not necessarily self-serving. Though she was protecting her own interests as a plural wife, Emmeline Wells was primarily bent on persuading her readers that the beliefs and practices of her religion neither demeaned nor subjugated women.

Woman's Words, a Philadelphia-based suffrage paper with which Emmeline corresponded, proved to be most sympathetic to her position. In 1877 she wrote a letter, by way of introduction, and thereafter submitted three articles offering a glimpse of Mormon society. The first lauded the achievements of Mormon youth. In others she explained the successful economic activities of Mormon women, commended the enterprising work of the women's retrenchment societies in promoting home industries, and touted the community service of the Relief Society.[4]

It was in the Boston *Woman's Journal,* published by the American Woman Suffrage Association (AWSA), however, that Emmeline waged a brief skirmish with Charlotte Cobb Godbe. Charlotte was in the anomalous position of being the stepdaughter of Brigham Young and the plural wife of Mormon dissident William Godbe. At first defensive of plural marriage, William took Charlotte as his fourth wife in 1869. Just two years later, he began to deny polygamy's divine origin, claiming it to be nothing more than "a superstition."[5] Dissolution by mutual consent, rather than federal mandate, however, was his solution for suppressing the practice, and by 1873 he had separated amicably from all but his first wife, Annie.[6] Charlotte and William did not formalize their separation by divorce until 1879. Charlotte later admitted that during this period she had "wobbled around in the faith," never wholly leaving the LDS Church, but not convincingly a true believer.[7]

Charlotte Cobb Godbe, stepdaughter of Brigham Young and wife of Mormon dissident William Godbe, was a prominent Utah suffragist.

Utah State Historical Society

During the late 1870s, Charlotte and Emmeline engaged

in a literary sparring match over who was the "true" representative of Mormon women in national suffrage circles. The friendly terms that characterized their relationship prior to this time quickly gave way to a contest of accusations and finally disdain.[8] While it is uncertain to which Mrs. Godbe Emmeline is referring when she uses only the married name in her diary, she does make specific reference to visits with Charlotte on May 18 and 30, 1875. While Charlotte had a ten-year edge on Emmeline in terms of her personal connection with suffragists in both national associations, Emmeline had a publication that enabled her voice to be heard authoritatively as she exchanged her paper with other women's publications throughout the country. Charlotte's and Emmeline's differing views on polygamy, however, would prove to be the most decisive element of their respective credentials.

Although Charlotte had been well into her thirties when she entered into what observers called an impassioned "love match"[9] with William Godbe as his fourth wife, she surprisingly disparaged the practice of polygamy. In December 1870, a little more than a year after her marriage to William, Charlotte wrote to the *Revolution* to defend Brigham Young against a critical attack, but she also obliquely introduced a theme that she would elaborate frequently in following years. The "Mormon problem," she opined, would be solved not by national lawmakers, but by the young ladies of Utah when their "womanly instincts" were "freed from all religious constraint, [and] let loose from priestly fear."[10] Natural attrition, her solution to this knotty problem, preceded her husband's similar suggestion by nearly a year, which, like his, offered an alternative to federal intervention. Whether she was excusing her own participation in the practice or confident the next generation would be less susceptible is unclear. Her benign solution, however, suggests her own self-interest at that time in proposing that existing plural marriages be left intact and free from prosecution.

During the 1870s, three of the Godbe wives attended the annual convention of the National Woman Suffrage Association (NWSA) in Washington, D.C., served on its board, spoke at suffrage gatherings, and corresponded with suffrage newspapers. In September 1876, three years after her separation from William, Charlotte wrote a letter to the

Woman's Journal.[11] In her lengthy letter, written while she was in California, Charlotte was more condemning of polygamy than previously and invited sympathy for Mormon women who, she claimed, were in subjection to male influence, expressing her "emphatic desire" to see "a discontinuance of the practice of plural marriage." She once again predicted, as she had done six years earlier, that the strong aversion to polygamy that she detected among Mormon youth eventually would eradicate the practice, eliminating the need for a federal act.[12]

Accompanying Charlotte's letter was one from Caroline Severance, a friend of Lucy Stone and the AWSA. Caroline and a traveling companion had visited Utah in 1875 and been entertained by Emmeline Wells. They had enjoyed a pleasant conversation about women's work and publishing, and Emmeline found the two women to be "very pleasing ladies."[13] She was not surprised, however, when Caroline's letter to the *Journal* endorsed Charlotte Godbe as a spokesperson for Utah women and praised Charlotte's effort in seeking a bill providing for the equal division of the property of convicted polygamists among their wives and children.[14] Usually sympathetic to any level of anti-Mormon sentiment, the *Salt Lake Tribune* nevertheless mildly chastised Charlotte and her California admirer for their "maudlin sentiment" and benevolent approach to ending polygamy.[15]

These letters from Charlotte and Caroline prompted Emmeline's first contribution to the *Woman's Journal.* Her rebuttal, written after she had become associate editor of the *Woman's Exponent* in 1875 and a familiar figure in women's journalism, was immediate and forceful. Both Charlotte's and Caroline's letters had been ambiguous about Charlotte's own marital status, but Emmeline, correctly but somewhat acidly, informed the *Journal*'s readers that Charlotte had chosen plural marriage, even though shortly before marrying she had claimed publicly that the lives of her Boston friends were "higher, holier and happier than that obtained through plural marriage." Emmeline capitalized on the duplicity of Charlotte's position; she also disclosed the fact that Charlotte's husband no longer acknowledged his plural wives, leaving Charlotte in a state of social limbo.[16] Emmeline's disclosure of this information, which Charlotte had chosen not to mention, clearly chafed.

Still smarting from the attack thirteen years later, Charlotte complained in a self-aggrandizing letter to LDS Church President Wilford Woodruff that Emmeline had "so cruelly [given] to the world . . . my painful domestic experience in polygamy, adding that I was not now an advocate for this principle of the Church, hence could not be a representative for the women here."[17] Emmeline herself had not been above currying favor with Church leaders. In 1876 she sent copies of her *Journal* letters to Brigham Young, perhaps at his request, expressing hope that her response to Charlotte answered his "expectations or wishes upon the subject" and indicating her willingness to confer with him in the future "on matters of a general nature . . . in the best interests of the sisters."[18]

Alongside Emmeline's response to Godbe and Severance was another article by Charlotte entitled "Life among the Mormons," which Emmeline refuted two months later in "Another Version of Mormon Life."[19] In answer to Emmeline's rebuttal, Charlotte lauded the younger Mormons who already had freed themselves from the "superstitions of their parents" and described Eliza R. Snow, perhaps the best loved and respected woman in the LDS Church at that time, as "an old lady on the shady side of seventy." Both Eliza and Brigham Young, Charlotte's stepfather, were, she asserted, among the "antiquarians too old to change."[20] In an effort to belittle the credibility of the *Woman's Exponent*, Charlotte also claimed that Brigham Young supervised the "little sheet" and alleged that "it did not represent the views of the most influential class among Mormon women."[21] These statements not only estranged her from the women she claimed to represent but also deepened the rift between the maverick Charlotte and the orthodox Emmeline.

Early on, Charlotte Godbe had opened the door for Utah women to enter national politics. She had, as she claimed, made influential friends, "beat down the b[ar]riers & made it possible for those women who followed [her], to speak at these conventions."[22] But despite her professed Mormon ties at the time, she lacked a following and a forum in Utah, organizational support, and the confidence of LDS Church leaders. She may have been Brigham Young's stepdaughter, but throughout this period she was still the wife of dissident William

Godbe. Her undefined allegiances in these two relationships, as well as her own religious vacillation, gave her an indeterminate identity. Only once, in 1881, was Charlotte considered as a possible representative at a suffrage convention, mainly because of her nonpolygamous status by then and her personal acquaintance with women suffragists who were lobbying against the antipolygamy measures that included the repeal of woman suffrage. That year, LDS Church President John Taylor proposed sending a memorial[23] to Congress hopefully to counteract the proposed Edmunds Bill. He also suggested that Charlotte Godbe attend the NWSA's annual convention. George Q. Cannon, however, felt the time inauspicious, and neither Charlotte nor the memorial was sent.[24]

Emmeline Wells had all the accoutrements that Charlotte lacked. Emmeline also had an impeccable record of loyalty to the Church, beginning with her decision to resist the importuning of her in-laws in Nauvoo when they left the Church, her faithfulness following the desertion of her first husband, her participation in two plural marriages, and her subsequent defense of the practice despite her own painful experience in polygamy. Few plural wives, including Emmeline, found polygamy compatible with their desire for the constant contact and exclusive companionship of their husbands, for which the sisterly bonds that developed among them could not quite compensate. However, renouncing any part of her religious faith was not an option for Emmeline. Her experience and the depth of her belief had firmly committed her to the divine origin and the constitutionality of plural marriage.

While this journalistic contest ran its course, Emmeline attended to her new duties as editor of the "little sheet" Charlotte had disdained. Emmeline had begun working in the *Exponent* office on a daily basis when she was appointed associate editor in 1875, but in 1877 she shouldered the whole editorial responsibility herself. Other activities crowded in to make it a portentous year for her. Not only did she take over the reins of the *Exponent,* she also was heavily engaged in her commission from Brigham Young to develop a grain-saving program. In addition, she began traveling with Eliza R. Snow, head of the women's Relief Society, to visit local Relief Societies and other women's organizations throughout the territory. Emmeline gradually became well known to her Mormon sisters and highly regarded.[25] She also continued to enlarge her readership beyond that of the *Woman's Exponent.* Along with correspondence to *Woman's Words* and the *Woman's Journal,* Emmeline contributed letters and articles to the *Ballot Box* (later the *National Citizen and Ballot Box,* 1876–81), another influential eastern suffrage paper edited in Syracuse, New York, by Matilda Joslyn Gage.

Latter-day Saint women's formal entry into the national suffrage movement began when Emmeline Wells wrote a letter to the *Ballot Box* in 1877 just as she was taking charge of the *Woman's Exponent.* Noting a call in the *Deseret Evening News* from NWSA for support of a petition for a constitutional amendment guaranteeing woman's vote, Emmeline wrote to the *Ballot Box,* then the voice for NWSA, and volunteered the services of Mormon women. She explained that she had entertained a similar plan for gathering petitions but had been hesitant to propose it on a national scale. Emmeline expressed the "ardent" desire of the women of Utah "to be one with the women of America in this grand movement."[26] Moreover, she explained that Latter-day Saints "do not believe man has the right to deter women from enjoying the God-given privilege of free agency." Rather, they believe "that man and woman are created free and equal to act in unison on all subjects and interests to both."[27] Utah's successful petition campaign helped to create a contingent of Mormon men and women who were eager to support those who were working in their behalf.

The emphasis on a campaign for a constitutional amendment in 1877 came as a result of NWSA's failed attempt five years earlier to secure woman suffrage under the "immunities clause" of the Fourteenth Amendment.[28] In 1872, Missouri attorney Francis Minor, an active suffragist along with his wife, Virginia, had broadly interpreted the first clause of the Fourteenth Amendment as establishing the power of the federal government to protect individual rights. He argued that national citizenship was preeminent and concluded that "the benefits of national citizenship were equally the rights of all . . . and that the right to vote was one of the basic privileges and immunities of national citizenship."[29] All citizens, women as well as men, were protected by the immunities clause of the Fourteenth Amendment by this interpretation.

This "new departure" in strategy, as it was called, served as the basis for urging hundreds of women to vote in 1872 to test the validity of Minor's interpretation. Their efforts culminated in the well-publicized trial of Susan B. Anthony in Rochester, New York, and the U.S. Supreme Court case *Minor v. Happersett*, brought by Virginia Minor. The Court had already ruled four years earlier that the Fourteenth Amendment did not elevate national over state jurisdiction in matters of civil rights, and in 1875 the Court ruled in the Minor case that "the Constitution does not confer the right of suffrage upon any one."[30] With the defeat of the new legal strategy, suffragists recognized that only a national amendment specifically guaranteeing the voting rights of women would secure their enfranchisement.

This new legal strategy, however, proved to be another divisive element in the ongoing competition between the National and American associations. While the National was focusing its energies on this new approach, the American, in a continuing effort to differentiate the two organizations, first urged a new constitutional amendment and then returned to its earlier drive to amend state constitutions. The National resumed its focus on a constitutional amendment after defeat in the Minor case.[31]

Another impetus for the National to move in the direction of a new amendment was the increasing pressure to take the vote away from Utah women. Editorials in the influential *Woman's Journal* condemned the illegal and discriminatory base of such legislation; speakers at the American association's meetings also declaimed against it, one area in which the two associations were harmonious.[32] Ironically, Utah delegate George Q. Cannon was "rather pleased" with the efforts to remove Utah women's right to vote in the various proposals to end polygamy "only because it will call the women suffragists to our aid," thereby impeding the rush toward punitive legislation, he optimistically declared.[33] The National did, in fact, appoint three women to "memorialize Congress and otherwise to watch over the rights of the women of Utah." The appointed women were Belva A. Lockwood,

Belva Lockwood (ca. 1865–80) championed Mormon women on the national suffrage scene. As a lawyer, Lockwood questioned the constitutionality of the 1882 Edmunds Act, legislation that punished polygamists and removed existing officers in the Utah territorial government.

Library of Congress

Sara Andrews Spencer, and Ellen C. Sargent.[34] There was little doubt that woman suffrage in Utah had become a political football. It also became ever more clear that only a constitutional amendment could protect this political right for women.

Woman's Words sent Wells the information she requested to mount a petition drive in Utah, and in December 1877 at her *Woman's Exponent* office, "some of the most prominent [female] leaders of the City" met to organize a campaign. Emmeline was elected chair. Plans were made to canvass the city and later the entire territory.[35] The *Deseret News* supported the women's efforts and editorialized on the value of woman suffrage as well as the absurdity of denying women the right to vote "in a nation that boasts of universal liberty, and under a system which admits the principle of general equality."[36] Emmeline exhausted herself in supervising the campaign, preparing the petitions, collecting the signatures, and sending them to Washington early in 1878. But she enjoyed the rewards of her efforts. The Utah campaign yielded nearly seven thousand signatures, more than from any other state or territory.[37] It garnered more than signatures, however. It brought notoriety and respect to Emmeline Wells and admiration, however qualified, for the women who participated. Though she had yet to attend a single suffrage convention, Emmeline was appointed to the Advisory Board of the National Association.[38]

The *Woman's Exponent,* with its practice of exchange with other papers, was proving to be a valuable tool in representing Mormon women to the world beyond Utah. One enthusiastic reader from Philadelphia, liking what she read in its pages, believed that "it well deserves to take its place, side by side" with the other suffrage papers of the time. She admitted she had been "in the dark" and then "deceived" as to the condition of the women in Utah and felt that "the women of the States have jumped at very unjust conclusions in regards to their sisters in Utah." Too many in the East, she found, believed a Mormon woman to be "either an oriental dolt or a domestic drudge." "May the able little Exponent," she hoped, "do the work of disproving what I now truly believe to be erroneous in the highest degree."[39] Emmeline herself, in a continuing effort to boost circulation, consistently reminded her local readers of the good the paper did abroad and at home in bringing the news of women throughout the world to Utah.[40]

While altering the opinion of some of its non-Mormon readers like the Philadelphia woman, the *Exponent* also carried Emmeline Wells into the collegiality of an elite circle of intellectual women journalists. Her name and work were therefore familiar to eastern suffragists even before the successful petition campaign. The petition drive, the *Exponent,* and her contributions to *Woman's Words* and the *Woman's Journal* elicited an admiring letter from Sara Andrews Spencer, Washington correspondent for *Woman's Words* and secretary of the NWSA. "Surely my day-star is rising," Emmeline joyfully recorded in her diary. "I consider this one of the events of my life."[41]

Spencer's interest was manifest publicly a few months later when she invited Mormon women to the annual suffrage convention: "Let us by all means invite one or more of the enterprising, public spirited, women of Utah to be present at the next Washington convention. If we mistake not," she continued, "our Gentile sisters have much to learn from these heroic women. What we read of their business ability, courage, and patriotism, is an inspiration to us."[42] From her personal correspondence with Emmeline to the public invitation to Mormon women, Spencer effectively cleared the way for connecting Mormon women with their eastern supporters. Spencer remained a loyal advocate throughout the difficult years ahead.

Spencer also inadvertently brought to fruition a proposal Brigham Young made in 1877, shortly before his death. Seeing the value of an alliance with Easterners, he proposed sending several women, including two of his daughters—Zina Young Williams and Susa Young—to the East to lecture on Mormonism, acknowledging that it would be "an experiment," but one he hoped to see tried.[43] A more precipitous inducement to send Mormon women east at the time than Spencer's invitation, however, was the formation of a local antipolygamy society. It represented the growing political strength of the non-Mormon female community in Utah and became the hub in a national network of anti-Mormon agitation.

Following their protests during the 1872 constitutional convention, Utah's antipolygamy women had begun to coalesce into a small but discernible entity, one in which Jennie Froiseth was a leading agitator. The group attracted both non-Mormon and disillusioned Latter-day Saint women. An organizing meeting held in November 1878 drew two hundred women and was extensive enough in its effect to spread across the nation. The Utah Anti-Polygamy Society, as the group called itself, acquired a nationally prestigious advocate when it sent a letter to Lucy B. Hayes, wife of U.S. President Rutherford B. Hayes, and found her to be a serious sympathizer. It also sent thirty thousand copies of the same letter to American clergymen throughout the country, voicing its appeal for support against the "moral evil" of plural marriage.[44]

In the Mormon rally hastily called immediately after, Emmeline Wells was among the speakers. Her usual optimism in the supporting ties of a universal sisterhood had begun to waver in light of the growing female agitation against polygamy. "I love woman," she began. "It is one of my sentiments," but "the time has come when we can no longer be silent, as we are assailed, and that too by our own sex. . . . We have been attacked in a way we never anticipated. We never thought that woman could rise up against woman."[45] A decade later the *Woman's Exponent* regretfully recalled that "the first blow against Woman's Rights in Utah" had been struck by women.[46]

The struggle over moral and social values that dominated the 1870s and 1880s among women's organizations presented the eastern suffragists with a dilemma that was never fully resolved until woman suffrage was repealed in Utah in 1887: whether to align themselves with Mormon women—who defended woman suffrage along with polygamy—or with gentile women—who were willing to surrender support of suffrage in exchange for federal legislation against polygamy.

The years of female confrontation that followed this organized display of opposition continually distressed Emmeline. She could not easily surrender her core faith in what was rapidly becoming only a utopian dream of the solidarity of women who, she had hoped, would value rather than disparage class, regional, or religious differences.[47] Like Elizabeth Cady Stanton, Emmeline regarded "the rights and duties of a woman as an individual" to be more telling in a woman's experience and identity than her "incidental relations of mother, wife, sister, daughter," some of which, Stanton noted, many women never experience.[48] It was their shared gender, Emmeline believed, more than their social roles or relationships that bonded women into a female collective that she felt should supercede, not oppose, these varied identities. She readily agreed with the sentiment Stanton expressed in a letter to her friend Lucretia Mott: "Men mock us with the fact and say we are ever cruel to each other. Let us end this ignoble record and henceforth stand by womanhood."[49] Wells believed womanhood was transcendent and all-encompassing in its claims and was a unifying bond that had the power to transform society.

Emmeline used the *Woman's Exponent* to express this fundamental belief. "Woman's work in this day and age," she wrote in 1875, "is not only an individual work, but a universal work for all her suffering sisterhood."[50] Woman's nature made her particularly suitable to succor the poor, the weak, or the downtrodden, she claimed. How logical then, "that we should love one another, that we may the more readily aid, comfort, strengthen, encourage and truly sympathize with each other."[51] Stanton later expressed a similar sentiment. Complaining of women who "crucified" those who were different, she wrote, "To me there is a sacredness in individual experiences which it seems like profanation to search into or expose."[52] Marriage, Emmeline Wells argued, was just such an individual experience. That plural marriage should be such a persistent target of reformers seemed inexplicable to her. "The wrongs of women betrayed and abandoned, and the neglected progeny that swarm the cities of the United States, these are the evils of modern society" that should demand the attention of women, she argued, "not plural marriage." "Let Mormon women alone," she pleaded. "They know how to take care of themselves and their children."[53]

However naïve, Emmeline believed that the strength of sisterhood, if properly focused, would erase the gentile antipathy to polygamy. "Many think we are little less than barbarians," she wrote in a brief statement to *Woman's Words*, "but woman's charity will sustain each other, feel for one another's sorrows, and extend the hand of fellowship to all who are striving for the elevation of the sex, even though they may not see alike. I do not think it is the nature of women to crush each other," she hopefully added. "Women are most all universally peace makers," she wrote.[54] But the woman's antipolygamy crusade, which would last nearly two decades, proved otherwise.[55] It effectively polarized women across the country, and none felt the sharp divisiveness more than the women of Utah.

With the escalation of federally initiated antipolygamy proposals throughout the 1870s, women's vote in Utah was jeopardized. Considering it a prop to the LDS Church's dominance in Utah, and thus a support of polygamy, antipolygamists urged Congress to overturn the territorial statute of 1870 that had enfranchised Utah women. Though many of the gentile women of Utah supported the proposal, eastern suffragists were adamant in their opposition to what seemed to them to be a blatantly discriminatory and unconstitutional measure. "In order to abolish polygamy," Lillie Devereux Blake complained, "Congress is asked to pass a law to disfranchise—the women! . . . Surely common sense and common justice would dictate that the bill should be so drawn as to disfranchise all polygamists, both men and women, [sic] there would then be some reason in this suggestion."[56] Some argued that since "Congress has repeatedly refused to interfere with State or Territorial governments to grant suffrage to women, it should not interfere to take it away when local authorities have conferred it."[57] Even the *Boston Woman's Journal* condemned the movement to disfranchise Utah women.

None were more supportive of the Mormon's side than Sara Spencer and Belva Lockwood, the NWSA's appointed overseers of Utah women.[58] Spencer was not only instrumental in bringing Latter-day Saint women into the national suffrage fold, but even before accepting responsibility to support the Mormon representatives to NWSA, she had lent a strong voice against removing the vote from Utah women. "The sisters should not forget her kindness and courage," Emmeline reminded her readers, "It requires nobility of character and heroism to face opposition and speak boldly in defense of a principle that is not popular."[59] The truth of those words and the importance of that support would become dramatically personal a year later when Emmeline made her first foray into national politics. Spencer's friendship with the Mormons warranted a life sketch in the *Woman's Exponent,* a distinction afforded only a few national suffragists.[60]

To avert the possibility of such capricious acts by Congress or state legislatures as to arbitrarily rescind the voting rights of citizens was another motive for the NWSA to focus its attention on a constitutional amendment.[61] The NWSA was as determined to maintain this outpost of enfranchised women as these Utah women were to retain NWSA's support.

The strength of woman's voice, even in the aggregate, raised against Mormonism may have seemed negligible beside the Congressional measures gathering force in Washington. Nevertheless, the voices proved effective in arousing public indignation. Moral reform organizations, particularly the Woman's Christian Temperance Union, joined the anti-Mormon bandwagon with alacrity and by 1878 rejoiced that "the whole country is now alive to the Mormon evil."[62] The time seemed propitious for Mormon women to carry their dual cause to Washington in person, not only to defend their voting rights but also to ask for repeal of the 1862 Morrill Act, which outlawed bigamy and imposed numerous sanctions. Though Brigham Young had proposed that two of his daughters go to Washington as emissaries, only one,

Zina Young Williams, made the trip.[63] Emmeline Wells, a friend and neighbor, would be her companion.

Amidst mocking statements from the *Salt Lake Tribune,* which maligned the two women as "cackling hens," "Zion's roosters," and "Mormon concubines"[64] and burdened with their own anxieties about the reception awaiting them, the two women left Salt Lake City on January 3, 1879. Emmeline Wells was then fifty-one and Zina Williams was twenty-eight. Traversing the land by train that she had crossed on foot thirty years earlier, Emmeline succumbed to an engulfing nostalgia. Could she possibly have imagined in 1848, as she trudged westward with the other Mormon outcasts on their western journey, that her return to the East would take her to the highest level of government? And what kind of response would she receive to her plea for tolerance of the religion that had transformed her life? These two women acutely felt the responsibility that this journey represented.

Through a coincidence of timing, as the two women traveled eastward, the United States Supreme Court issued its decision on *George Reynolds v. the United States,* litigation designed to test the constitutionality of the Morrill Act.[65] To the dismay of Church members, it upheld the constitutionality of the antibigamy clause of the act and swept away Latter-day Saints' claim on the First Amendment protection of their religious liberty. The two Mormon representatives could now plead only for the forbearance of Congress in passing means to enforce the act.

Once in Washington, Emmeline and Zina were markedly impressed with the Riggs House, headquarters of the NWSA, where they resided during their time in Washington. Several senators and other prominent visitors, as well as many of the convention delegates, made the Riggs House their temporary home. Emmeline was delighted to be surrounded by such distinguished individuals and ensconced in such luxurious accommodations.[66]

Once among the suffragists, the two women found their way had been considerably eased by Emmeline's correspondence acquaintances.[67] They also met their champion, Sara Andrews Spencer. "Our heart went forth in great waves of love to her for her courageous defense of the

Detail of the Riggs House (ca. 1882–1900) in Washington, D.C., which housed the headquarters of the National Woman Suffrage Association. Emmeline Wells and many others who visited the NWSA headquarters found lodging at the Riggs House.

women of Utah here in the Congress of the National Capitol," Emmeline wrote. They also were delighted to meet the hostess of Riggs House, the distinguished Jane Spofford, who similarly extended a gracious welcome to the two provincial guests.[68] They were nonetheless a curiosity to many of the delegates and Washingtonians alike and drew large crowds wherever they went. "Dear me," Zina noted, "what an awful thing to be an Elephant. The ladies all look at me so queer."[69]

A planning meeting at the residence of Belva Lockwood to determine the agenda for the NWSA annual convention took place the night before the opening session. At that preliminary meeting, Emmeline was appointed to the committee on resolutions and Zina to the committee on finance. The next day both were pleased to be invited to ride to the opening session with Elizabeth Stanton, Susan B. Anthony, and Jane Spofford, where they were invited to sit on the platform and later to address the convention.[70] This was a reception far beyond their expectations. Emmeline was scheduled to speak at the evening session on January 9, but notice had not been posted so the crowd was small. Both Emmeline and Zina were then scheduled to speak the following day, and advance notice helped fill Lincoln Hall to capacity.[71] As curiosities, "their fame and personal appearance became so well known that they are the observed of all observers on the street," attracting more attention even than George Q. Cannon, the Mormon delegate to Congress, according to a *Salt Lake Tribune* story.[72]

Emmeline used this speaking opportunity to chastise Congress for seeking to remove the ballot from Utah women. "Congress had better heed what wrong is contemplated to be done by taking away the only safety they enjoy," she warned. "The women of Utah have never broken any law of that Territory, and it would be unjust as well as impolitic to deprive them of this right." Zina Williams followed, reinforcing Emmeline's message, and asked the women of the convention to aid them in their fight to retain the ballot. In support, Sara Spencer then reminded the audience that the women had been invited to the convention and added that polygamy was "preferable to the licensed social evil, which is being advocated by many of our bloated public men." Moreover, she added, many Gentiles had hoped that the women of Utah would use the vote "to discourage the plurality of wives. . . . Now that the women do not vote to suit the Gentiles," she concluded, "they want to disfranchise them."[73]

Emmeline's words evidently struck a responsive chord. The convention reacted by including among its resolutions for U.S. President Rutherford B. Hayes one reproving the government for not only refusing "to exercise federal power to protect women in their citizen's right to vote in the various States and Territories" but allowing the "exercise of federal power to disfranchise the women of Utah."[74] At the conclusion of the convention, officers of the National appointed the two Utah women to join Matilda Joslyn Gage and Sara Spencer in presenting the NWSA resolutions to President Hayes.

The *Woman's Journal,* as expected, ridiculed the National for admitting the two Mormon women. But Elizabeth Stanton defended their presence and chided Lucy Stone for not refuting the *Journal* article. "If George Q. Cannon can sit in the Congress of the United States without compromising that body on the question of Polygamy," Stanton retorted, "I should think Mormon women might sit on our platform without making us responsible for their religious faith. . . . When the women of a whole Territory are threatened with disfranchisement where should they go to make their complaint but to the platform of the National Suffrage Association?"[75]

Matilda Gage, editor of the *National Citizen and Ballot Box,* also chose to defend Emmeline and Zina's attendance. "We have only pity for those women who turn and rend their sister women working differently from themselves," she wrote. Moreover, she continued, "it ill becomes the *Woman's Journal* to cast a slur upon those women whose married life is not in accord with its ideas of right, for Lucy Stone's own married life . . . is a protest against the laws of marriage as recognized by the *Christian Church* and the Commonwealth of Massachusetts."[76] This kind of journalistic sniping fueled the dissension between the two associations and their leaders. While they generally differed over tactics, policies, and procedures, polygamy and its proponents remained major divisive factors between these two national organizations.

Before presenting the NWSA's resolutions to President Hayes, Zina Williams and Emmeline Wells turned their attention to the second purpose of their Washington trip: to present their own memorial to the President and Congress in behalf of the Latter-day Saints. For the next three weeks, the two women visited senators and congressional committee members and prepared a memorial to be read in both houses of Congress. The memorial asked Congress to repeal the Morrill Act but short of that to "enact such legislation as will securely legitimize our children and protect our names from dishonor by preserving unbroken the existing relationships of families."[77] With little hope that Congress would overturn the Supreme Court's ruling on the Morrill Act, the women focused their argument on the legal retention of existing plural marriages, a compromise with which many antipolygamists concurred—but not all. Senator Allen G. Thurman "refused to put their petition before the Senate," when they appealed to him, and Senator George F. Edmunds gave them "no particular encouragement." When they met with a similar response from Attorney General Charles Devens, Zina Williams judged him to be "a crusty old bad man." But, she added, "he got some wholesome truths from us."[78]

Emmeline and Zina also pled their case before the House Judiciary Committee and "met all their furie [sic] with coolness," according to Zina's account.[79] Sara Spencer introduced them and reminded the committee members that it had heard "large numbers of gentlemen upon this question, asking you for legislation, which will work terrible hardships upon women and children. Will you not hear these women in their own behalf?"[80] Asking primarily for protection from the effects of the Supreme Court decision, Emmeline and Zina presented an emotionally charged argument for legislation that would ameliorate the obvious consequences of enforcement of the Morrill Act.[81]

The response of the Judiciary Committee was to draft a bill "legitimatizing the offspring of plural marriages to a certain date; also authorizing the president to grant amnesty for past offenses against the law of 1862."[82] Although this concession to plural wives and their children was encouraging, LDS Church President John Taylor advised Delegate Cannon to refrain from urging passage of the bill since it implied acceptance of the constitutionality of the Morrill Act, which Taylor was not yet ready to do despite the Supreme Court ruling. As it turned out, however, some of the mitigating provisions of the bill were incorporated in the 1882 antipolygamy act, authored by Senator George Edmunds, which provided some relief for plural wives and their children.[83]

After lobbying Congress on behalf of their own interests, Emmeline Wells and Zina Williams joined Sara Spencer and Matilda Gage in carrying to President Hayes the memorial drawn up by the suffrage convention. After listing their grievances, the memorial charged the President with neglecting the women of the country in his annual messages. He promised the women to consider their complaints and to "act according to the dictates of [his] conscience and the best light [he had]" in his next message.[84]

Immediately afterward, the two Latter-day Saint women were granted time to present their own memorial inviting the president "to extend a fatherly care over an oppressed people" and to use his influence to avert legislation that would be injurious to the women and children of Utah.[85] The memorial petitioned the President to repeal the 1862 Morrill Act and consider, in any further legislation, "the rights and the conscience of the women to be affected by such legislation." It also asked him to consider "the permanent care and welfare of children as the sure foundation of the state."[86]

While the *Salt Lake Tribune* was outraged at the idea of these two "celestial spouses" pleading their case before the president of the United States, a sympathetic eastern reporter delighted in the emotional drama of the scene in the president's library. The president "showed such kindly sympathy with them," the reporter wrote, "when they proved what misery would follow in Utah if the 1862 Act were enforced," that Hayes invited his wife, Lucy, to come and meet the two beleaguered women. Mrs. Hayes, the writer observed, "listened and spoke to them in a sisterly manner that aroused in all present a feeling of reverence for her noble, womanly nature."[87]

Both Emmeline and Zina commented on the gracious reception they received and found Lucy Hayes to be "a lovely woman." "Her sympathy seemed to be with us," Zina observed.[88] Mrs. Hayes's cordiality, however, as well as her husband's, masked their shared aversion to polygamy and her subrosa support of the Anti-Polygamy Society in Utah.[89] At that time, however, the two women were encouraged when the president requested that they put their appeal in writing for distribution to other officials. In reality their written plea provided President Hayes with information for his address to Congress later that year in opposing the women's appeal. After a visit to Utah the next year (in 1880), he urged even more stringently the removal of the right to vote or hold office from all men and women who had entered the practice of polygamy.[90]

First Lady Lucy B. Hayes (ca. 1877) met with Emmeline Wells and Zina Williams in January 1879 when they attended the NWSA convention in Washington, D.C. Photograph by Charles Milton Bell. Library of Congress

Before the end of this, her first presidential visit, Emmeline presented the First Lady with a copy of Edward Tullidge's eulogistic *Women of Mormondom*, which she wryly inscribed, "Please accept this token of the esteem of a Mormon wife, E. B. Wells."[91] Impressed by the graciousness of their hosts, the two women had every reason to believe that some good must come of it. Despite this error in judgment, Emmeline was beginning to hone her communication skills and would soon become expert at winning genuine friends for herself and building bridges for her Latter-day Saint sisters. Her inherent optimism would continue to cloud reality, but it never failed to be a spur to her persistent drive to serve the interests of women.

No date was set for Wells and Williams to return to Utah. As late as January 28, 1879, LDS Church President John Taylor noted in a letter to Wilford Woodruff, a fellow Apostle, that "our Sisters remain in [Washington], doing all the good they can, and will remain there as long as Bro. Cannon thinks they can be of use to the cause."[92] When the two women finally returned to Salt Lake City early in February, they had not changed any votes regarding the Morrill Act, but they had found sympathetic friends who urged that some form of amnesty be granted protecting the status of plural marriages that existed before enforcement of the act.

The Washington visit evoked a wide range of response and national attention. As expected, in its penchant for name-calling, the *Salt Lake Tribune* declared the mission of "the roosters who have been strutting around Washington" a complete failure. It attacked Emmeline through her husband, Daniel, who, it claimed, was experiencing "the retribution of his descent into polygamy" in the "bankruptcy of his business, discord in his household, profligate sons and betrayed daughters." It absolved the NWSA convention and "managers of that gathering" of any culpability for the speeches of Emmeline and Zina, crediting them "with better sense than countenancing a defense and exposition of Utah polygamy from a platform in the Capital City."[93] Nor was Emmeline exempt from the anger of Charlotte Godbe, who did not want this intrusion on territory she had claimed for herself. "Charlotte Cobb Godbe struck at me with a serpent's fangs today," Emmeline wrote shortly after returning home; "I must pray for strength."[94] On the other hand, the *Deseret News* lauded the women's achievement and declared that "the ladies are doing a good work in representing their causes in the great political center."[95]

Emmeline Wells and Zina Williams were delighted that their work had not gone unnoticed by their Mormon sisters at home. One local

Relief Society president effused, "We hold in high esteem our sisters . . . who have so ably represented us in the Capitol of the Nation."[96] Another wrote to the *Woman's Exponent* to express her opinion of the work in Washington:

> I heard you say at one of our meetings that if the sisters thought you had a good time while absent they were very much mistaken. I for one can readily believe you in this: to me it appears the most arduous mission any of our sisters (as yet) have been called upon to perform. It must have been a trial for two plural wives to meet the talented and worthy ladies of the Convention at a time when prejudice towards us as a people abounds to such an extent.[97]

An understanding voice at home expressed the kind of support that would be necessary in the years to come.

More important, perhaps, was the degree of satisfaction the two women felt in knowing that they had been helpful in influencing the thinking of at least a few of the lawmakers and especially the suffragists whom they met in Washington. A number of newspapers' sympathetic response to their Washington appeals was also heartening. The *San Francisco Mission Mirror* argued that the devastation resulting from enforcement of the Morrill Act would be "an evil worse than polygamy" and that the act should be made effective only when declared constitutional.[98] The *New York Graphic,* moved by the "plea of the lady delegates from Utah," declared,

> Now we see the question of putting down polygamy is not a simple question of putting down a crime. A whole society is based upon this custom, which has existed for more than a generation. Endeavor to root it out with fire and sword and you break the bonds of society, you make paupers of industrious, wealthy and self-supporting persons; you declare thousands of women who are innocent of any intentional wrong to be common harlots, and you condemn innocent children to bear the infamous brand of illegitimacy. Granting that polygamy is now and has been a crime, is not this too great a price to pay for its suppression?[99]

The *Washington Capitol* also weighed in with a word of caution to Congress. After rehearsing the scene that took place in President Hayes's library, the reporter noted that "the polygamy of Utah is doing no harm to the United States.... There are many and important issues to be considered, and there are not a few of the best observers who think that the best thing that can be done in the matter is not to legislate on it at all."[100] Despite criticism from the *Tribune* and other sources, the women's words had definitely made an impact.

Her first Washington experience was a personal achievement for Emmeline. "I thank God I was the first to represent our women in the Halls of Congress," she confided to her diary.[101] Zina, however, returned less confident, expressing some trepidation about her performance in Washington. "I hope I have said nothing wrong," she repeatedly confessed to her diary, and seemed reassured when many friends congratulated her on her representation. She worried because both Emmeline and "Aunt Eliza" R. Snow seemed somewhat "cold" to her after her return but was heartened by the warm welcome others extended to her.[102] Emmeline's restraint, and perhaps Eliza's, too, might be explained by Emmeline's growing concern over the "lethargy" she detected at home, which appeared incongruent with the escalating tension she had experienced in Washington over the Mormon question.

To the satisfaction of both Emmeline Wells and Zina Williams, however, LDS Church President John Taylor expressed his own appreciation for their work. Indeed, it had not been easy, as one writer observed, but it had indeed been a fruitful trip, for both the Church and for Emmeline personally. The experience was pivotal in her life and self-defined mission. She had gained friends, supporters, confidence, influence, and especially knowledge that would provide the foundation for her future labors in behalf of women. She was beginning to shed the homegrown provincialism with which her isolated Utah life had cloaked her and was finding her own place among the influential women in the national struggle for equal rights.

An earlier version of this chapter was published as "Emmeline B. Wells Goes to Washington: The Search for Mormon Legitimacy," Journal of Mormon History 26, no. 2 (2000): 140–78.

Notes

1. Emmeline B. Wells, Diary, February 20, 1879, L. Tom Perry Special Collections, Harold B. Lee Library, Brigham Young University, Provo, Utah.

2. Her diary records that on February 4, 1875, she "went . . . to the Teachers Meeting [Relief Society] at which I presided for the first time in my life, got on excellently well." A month later she attended a meeting of the Retrenchment society, which was organized to promote less dependence on imported goods and more reliance on home products. "I rose and tried to speak for a few minutes, the first time in my life that I ever spoke in public before men." Wells, Diary, March 15, 1875.

3. Even before Emmeline sent letters and articles to the *Woman's Journal* and *Woman's Words,* a fellow Latter-day Saint, Bathsheba W. Smith, already had written to the *Woman's Journal,* published by the American Woman Suffrage Association. Smith took it upon herself in 1872 to answer criticism of the voting procedures at the fall election in Utah that year, and she described the order at the polling places where women voted. She also disputed claims that young boys and girls had voted. In three letters she informed readers of the *Journal* of the orderly voting procedures and the value of women's voting rights in Utah. See "The Utah Election—Woman Suffrage Vindicated," *Woman's Journal,* March 23, 1872, 96; Bathsheba W. Smith, "Woman Suffrage in Utah," *Woman's Journal,* March 30, 1872, 104; and Bathsheba W. Smith, "The Result in Utah," *Woman's Journal,* April 6, 1872, 106.

4. Emmeline B. Wells, "The Young People of Utah," *Woman's Words* 1 (July 1877): 53; Emmeline B. Wells, "Home Industries in Utah," *Woman's Words* 1 (August 1877): 67; Emmeline B. Wells, "Retrenchment Associations," *Woman's Words* 1 (October 1877): 101–2.

5. Ronald W. Walker, *Wayward Saints: The Godbeites and Brigham Young* (Urbana: University of Illinois Press, 1998), 327.

6. Walker, *Wayward Saints,* 329.

7. Walker, *Wayward Saints,* 330.

8. Emmeline B. Wells to Brigham Young, November 13, 1876, Emmeline B. Wells Papers, Church Archives, The Church of Jesus Christ of Latter-day Saints, Salt Lake City.

9. Walker, *Wayward Saints,* 138.

10. "A Mormon Lady on the Mormon Leader, Mrs. Godbe's Views of Brigham Young," *Revolution,* December 15, 1870, 2.

11. The Boston *Woman's Journal* was founded by Lucy Stone of the AWSA and had the distinction of being the major and most enduring of the eastern suffrage papers.

172   An Advocate for Women

12. Charlotte Ives Godbe, "Polygamy in Utah," *Woman's Journal*, September 9, 1876, 296.

13. Wells, Diary, May 30, 1875.

14. "Letter from Mrs. Severance," *Woman's Journal*, September 9, 1876. Caroline's suggestion seems to imply a permanent separation of a polygamist from all his wives and children while leaving him also bereft of any material possessions, or she may have meant at his death. For biographical information, see "Caroline Maria Seymour Severance," in *Notable American Women, 1607–1950: A Biographical Dictionary*, ed. Edward T. James, Janet Wilson James, and Paul S. Boyer, 3 vols. (Cambridge: Belknap Press of Harvard University Press, 1971), 3:265–67.

15. "Polygamy in Utah," *Salt Lake Tribune*, September 16, 1876, 2.

16. "Answer to Polygamy in Utah," *Woman's Journal*, October 29, 1876, 352. A second article by Charlotte Godbe was printed next to Emmeline's, titled "Life among the Mormons," in which Charlotte corrected some errors in Caroline's glowing introduction and further emphasized her belief that time rather than legislation would be the best solution to the polygamy problem.

17. Charlotte Godbe to President Wilford Woodruff, February 5, 1889, in Wilford Woodruff Papers, Church Archives, quoted in Beverly Beeton, "A Feminist among the Mormons: Charlotte Ives Cobb Godbe Kirby," *Utah Historical Quarterly* 59 (Winter 1991): 25–28.

18. Emmeline B. Wells to Brigham Young, November 13, 1876, Wells Papers.

19. Emmeline Wells, "Another Version of Mormon Life," *Woman's Journal*, December 23, 1876, 413.

20. Charlotte Ives Godbe, "Polygamy Condemned by Mormon Women," *Woman's Journal*, February 17, 1877, 52. The article's title is misleading.

21. Godbe, "Polygamy Condemned by Mormon Women," 52. Charlotte, in disparaging the value of the *Woman's Exponent*, did not reveal the fact that its editor, Emmeline Wells, was the wife of a member of the First Presidency of the LDS Church and that Eliza R. Snow, "presidentess of all Mormon women," was the wife of Brigham Young, and that other prominent women of the community were on its board and also made regular literary contributions to the *Exponent*. Her motive in making the assertion seems to have been a desire to discredit the paper as a legitimate representative of Mormon women's sentiment. Utah congressional delegate George Q. Cannon, conversant with the correspondence of Mormon women with the national suffrage papers, indicated to President John Taylor in 1878 that he felt that the *Woman's Exponent* had helped the Mormon cause. George Q. Cannon to John Taylor, January 28, 1878, George Q. Cannon Letterbook, Church Archives.

22. Godbe to Woodruff, 26.

23. A memorial in this context is a petition or a written statement of facts to be presented to a legislative body, such as Congress.

24. Beverly Beeton, *Women Vote in the West: The Woman Suffrage Movement, 1869–1890* (New York: Garland, 1987), 66–67; and Wells, Diary, December 30, 1881; January 6, February 19, 1882.

25. The LDS women's Relief Society was originally organized in Nauvoo, Illinois. The process of reorganizing in Utah began in 1867, and in 1868 Brigham Young appointed Eliza R. Snow, with Zina D. H. Young as her assistant, to organize a society in all local congregations. Emmeline Wells and others often accompanied Snow as she made visits to encourage and unify the sisters in their charitable and religious service. For details about the reorganization, see Jill Mulvay Derr, Janath Russell Cannon and Maureen Ursenbach Beecher, *Women of Covenant* (Salt Lake City: Deseret Book Company, 1992), 86–98.

26. Emmeline B. Wells, "Convention Letters," *National Citizen and Ballot Box* 2 (July 1877): 1.

27. Wells, "Convention Letters," 1.

28. The Fourteenth Amendment guaranteed all citizens equal protection under the law. As Ellen Carol DuBois explains in "Taking the Law into Our Own Hands: *Bradwell, Minor,* and Suffrage Militance in the 1870s," in *Visible Women: New Essays on American Activism,* ed. Nancy A. Hewitt and Suzanne Lebsock (Urbana: University of Illinois Press, 1993), 35n5, Elizabeth Cady Stanton proposed a sixteenth amendment in 1869 primarily in reaction to the "manhood suffrage" of the Fifteenth Amendment, which gave emancipated male slaves the right to vote.

29. Ellen Carol DuBois details this new strategy in "Taking the Law into Our Own Hands," 22–23. In 1871 the infamous Victoria Woodhull entered the constitutional debate to argue for the Minor interpretation. Gaining a hearing before the House Judiciary Committee, she asked Congress to pass legislation clarifying women's right to vote on the basis of the Fourteenth and Fifteenth Amendments. She looked to Congress to resolve the matter while the Minors had turned to the courts. See DuBois, "Taking the Law into Our Own Hands," 26. DuBois further elaborates the effects of this new strategy in "Outgrowing the Compact of the Fathers: Equal Rights, Woman Suffrage, and the U.S. Constitution, 1820–1878," *Journal of American History* 74 (December 1987): 836–62, esp. 852–62. Additional information is in Albie Sachs and Joan Hoff Wilson, *Sexism and the Law: A Study of Male Beliefs and Legal Bias in Britain and the United States* (New York: Free Press, 1979), 85–109.

174   An Advocate for Women

30. See *Minor v. Happersett*, 88 U.S. 162 (1875). The earlier cases were *Bradwell v. The State* and the well-publicized Slaughter House cases. An earlier case based on the Fourteenth Amendment, also negatively affecting women, was *Bradwell v. Illinois* 83 U.S. 130 (1873), which ruled that the rights referred to in that amendment were those "belonging to a citizen of the United States and not as a citizen of a State." Myra Bradwell had been denied admission to the Illinois State Bar and had then appealed her case to the U.S. Supreme Court, which ruled against her.

31. See DuBois, "Taking the Law into Our Own Hands," 35n5.

32. Journal History of the Church, October 13, 1874, 5, Church Archives, also available on *Selected Collections from the Archives of The Church of Jesus Christ of Latter-day Saints*, 2 vols. (Provo, Utah: Brigham Young University Press, 2002), vol. 2, DVD 6, microfilm copy in Harold B. Lee Library. The American association's support at this point did not go beyond what the columns of the *Woman's Journal* could do. See also Andrea Moore Kerr, *Lucy Stone, Speaking Out for Equality* (New Brunswick, N.J.: Rutgers University Press, 1992), 197.

33. George Q. Cannon to John Taylor, March 19, 1878, George Q. Cannon Letterbook. While Cannon understood that the suffragists had no tolerance for plural marriage, he knew that their resolve to maintain woman suffrage in Utah would naturally draw their opposition toward any antipolygamy bills that outlawed suffrage. Their "support" was thus inadvertent and ancillary to their primary goal.

34. Journal History of the Church, February 3, 1876.

35. "Woman Suffrage," *Deseret News*, December 19, 1877, 728; "Woman Suffrage in Utah," *Deseret News*, December 13, 1877, 2; "Woman Suffrage," *Deseret News*, December 14, 1877, 1.

36. Editorial, *Deseret News*, January 11, 1878, 4.

37. As reported in "Petitions," *Ballot Box* 2 (March 1878): 3; and "Sixteenth Amendment Workers," *Ballot Box* 3 (April 1878): 2. The articles include a description of the presentation of the petitions to the Committee on Privileges and Elections and an entire listing of the workers from the states and territories. Emmeline B. Wells and George Q. Cannon personally contributed funds to the National. "Treasurer's Report," *National Citizen and Ballot Box* 5 (August 1878): 3 (the name change occurred in April 1878). Records of later years show Wells's continuous financial support.

38. Under "Officers of the National Woman Suffrage Association, for 1878–9," the *National Citizen and Ballot Box* 3 (September 1878): 3 lists Emmeline's name as a member of the Advisory Committee.

39. Virginia Barnhurst, "Correspondence," *Woman's Exponent* 6 (September 1, 1877): 49.

40. Emmeline B. Wells, "Utah," in *History of Woman Suffrage*, vol. 4, ed. Susan B. Anthony and Ida H. Harper (Rochester: Susan B. Anthony, 1902), 937. See also Carol Cornwall Madsen, ed., *Battle for the Ballot: Essays on Woman Suffrage in Utah, 1870–1896* (Logan: Utah State University Press, 1997), 34.

41. Wells, Diary, February 15, 1878.

42. Sara Andrews Spencer, "From Utah," *Woman's Words* 2 (October 18, 1878): 282. Much of what she read came from Emmeline's pen.

43. Orson F. Whitney, *History of Utah*, 4 vols. (Salt Lake City: George Q. Cannon and Sons, 1893), 2:845.

44. Whitney, *History of Utah*, 3:61–62. See also Barbara Hayward, "Utah's Anti-Polygamy Society, 1878–1884" (master's thesis, Brigham Young University, 1980), 19–21. The society also memorialized Congress.

45. "Woman's Mass Meeting," *Woman's Exponent* 7 (December 1, 1878): 103.

46. "The Women of Utah," *Woman's Exponent* 17 (June 15, 1888): 10. The unsigned article rehearsed the history of women in Utah politics from 1870 to 1888.

47. Catharine Beecher, nineteenth-century educator and lecturer, promoted the concept of a universal domesticity in which women were the chief actors. She generally eschewed the fight for suffrage or other political or legal changes, accepting male authority and dominance in both the home and society. For the sake of order and efficiency, certain dependencies had to be maintained, such as children on parents, and wives on husbands. Her popular *Treatise on Domestic Economy* (first issued in Boston in 1841 by Marsh, Capen, Lyon and Web, publishers) outlined this social theory, which is analyzed in more detail by Kathryn Kish Sklar, *Catharine Beecher: A Study in American Domesticity* (New York: W. W. Norton, 1976), 151–67. Emmeline Wells and her sister activists, however, opposed Beecher's theory of "voluntary servitude" and argued that the concept of "universal domesticity" exposed the limitations on their autonomy imposed by the legal and political systems that excluded them.

48. From Stanton's 1892 valedictory address to the newly merged National American Woman Suffrage Association and published as "The Solitude of Self," extracts found in Ellen Carol DuBois, ed., *Elizabeth Cady Stanton, Susan B. Anthony, Correspondence, Writings, Speeches* (New York: Schocken Books, 1981), 246–54.

176   An Advocate for Women

49. Quoted in Theodore Stanton and Harriot Stanton Blatch, eds. *Elizabeth Cady Stanton as Revealed in Her Letters, Diary, and Reminiscences*, 2 vols. (New York: Harper and Brothers, 1922), 2:137. While Elizabeth Stanton, like other suffragists, did not endorse polygamy, she did not disparage polygamous women and instead defended their right to participate in the national suffrage movement against the objections of Lucy Stone and others of AWSA.

50. "Woman's Work," *Woman's Exponent* 4 (November 15, 1875): 94.

51. Blanche Beechwood, "Bear Ye One Another's Burdens," *Woman's Exponent* 2 (March 1, 1874): 146.

52. Stanton and Blatch, *Elizabeth Cady Stanton*, 137.

53. "The New Crusade," *Woman's Exponent* 7 (November 15, 1878): 92.

54. Emmeline B. Wells, "A Few Extracts from Letters," *Woman's Words* 1 (May 1, 1877): 23.

55. Female antipolygamists not only sought to preserve what they perceived to be a national consensus on moral behavior but also to express their own personal aversion to the notion of husband-sharing and loss of domestic independence in sharing their households with sister-wives. The home, in Victorian America, was woman's domain, in which she exerted a degree of influence unavailable to her in more public pursuits. It was the one area in which she had a measure of control and from which she exercised her public moral authority. How best to utilize her influence and responsibilities in the well being of her household is examined in Catherine Beecher's book, *A Treatise on Domestic Economy*.

56. As quoted in "The Proposition to Disfranchise the Women of Utah," *Woman's Exponent* 7 (June 15, 1878): 15.

57. From the "Philadelphia Times," as reported in "Mormon Ladies Calling at the White House," *Woman's Exponent* 7 (March 15, 1879): 212.

58. The third member of the committee, Ellen C. Sargent, wife of Congressman Aaron Sargent, a strong suffrage supporter, was not as publicly visible in her association with Mormon women as the other two. See Journal History of the Church, October 13, 1874; February 3, 1876.

59. "Woman Suffrage and the Coming Convention," *Woman's Exponent* 6 (December 15, 1877): 108.

60. "Sketch of Mrs. Sara J. Andrews Spencer," *Woman's Exponent* 6 (March 15, 1878): 158.

61. It was not only polygamy that Congress aimed to suppress by such measures. The cohesiveness of the Latter-day Saints, their allegiance to Brigham Young as both their spiritual and temporal leader, their political dominance in Utah, and their expansion throughout the Mountain West were also viewed

as un-American or threatening. Other contributions to the negative image of Mormons (and particularly of Brigham Young) during this decade were the 1875 divorce suit of Ann Eliza Webb, Brigham Young's plural wife; her subsequent lecture tour; and the 1877 trial and execution of Mormon John D. Lee in connection with the Mountain Meadows Massacre, in which an entire emigrant party was killed in southern Utah twenty years earlier for which the Mormons were blamed.

62. "The Women's Movement," *Salt Lake Tribune,* November 8, 1878, 2.

63. Zina Young Williams had been a widow since 1874 but would become the fourth wife of Charles O. Card in 1884.

64. Mormon women generally, and Emmeline Wells in particular, were the subjects of the *Salt Lake Tribune*'s name-calling for many years. See, for example, "City Jottings," *Tribune,* January 4, 1879, which reported "one of the One-Eyed Pirate's concubines is going to Washington to-day to attend a Hen Convention" (Emmeline's husband, Daniel H. Wells, had one defective eye). The next day it reported that "Two of Zion's Female Roosters are now on their way to Washington to crow for polygamy. Fit representation for a nasty cause." The paper was equally demeaning of suffragists and the movement for woman suffrage.

65. See "Home Affairs," *Woman's Exponent* 7 (January 15, 1879): 12. The conviction of polygamist George Reynolds, who voluntarily agreed to a trial in 1874 and to a second one in 1875, led to an appeal before the U.S. Supreme Court. On January 6, 1879, the Court sustained the decision of the lower court outlawing polygamy, holding that "it was within the legitimate scope of the power of civil government to determine whether polygamy or monogamy should be the law of social life within its domain." The Court thus took a position that few Latter-day Saints expected and one they resisted for another decade. See Sarah Barringer Gordon, *The Mormon Question: Polygamy and Constitutional Conflict in Nineteenth-Century America* (Chapel Hill: University of North Carolina Press, 2002), 113–16.

66. The Riggs House, a small but elegant hotel, was built in 1856 and owned and managed by Jane Spofford and her husband since 1876. Susan B. Anthony often made it her home when she was in Washington, and Jane Spofford, an active suffragist, usually entertained the annual convention delegates with a reception. In 1891 the Spoffords closed the House, but friends urged them to buy another "hostelry," which they hoped would be called "The Spofford House." These plans never materialized, however. See "The Announcement of the Closing of the Riggs House," *Woman's Exponent* 19 (June 1, 1891): 179.

67. Delegate George Q. Cannon noted in a letter to John Taylor on January 28, 1879, that "the correspondence of Emmeline B. Wells had done good for the women's favorable reception." See George Q. Cannon Letterbooks.

68. "Over the Hills and Far Away," *Woman's Exponent* 7 (February 1, 1879): 186.

69. Zina Young Williams, Diary, January 26, 1879, Church Archives.

70. "Over the Hills and Far Away," 186; "The Washington Convention," *Woman's Exponent* 7 (March 1, 1879): 202.

71. A Washington correspondent for the *Salt Lake Tribune* ridiculed the women's speeches, claiming that people began to leave the hall when the women mentioned polygamy and dismissed their efforts as impertinent and ineffectual. He concluded that their Washington appearance was far more damaging to their cause than had they remained at home. See "Pablo", "Washington," *Salt Lake Tribune,* January 18, 1879, 4; "Trotting the Utah Roosters Along," *Salt Lake Tribune,* January 18, 1879, 1; "Our Utah Delegates," *Salt Lake Tribune,* January 19, 1879, 2; "Polygamy and Woman Suffrage," *Salt Lake Tribune,* January 22, 1879, 2.

72. "Washington," *Salt Lake Tribune,* January 18, 1879, 4. The paper also reported that Eliza R. Snow, "the chief cackler," had advised the two "hens" to "wear the plainest kind of homespun clothes" to represent the modesty and decorum of Mormon women, but her idea was vetoed by George Q. Cannon, who wanted the women to dress in their "best bib and tucker," which the two women were more inclined to do anyway. "The Hens," *Salt Lake Tribune,* January 16, 1879, 4.

73. An abridged account of this session of the convention can be found in "The Utah Ladies in Washington," *Deseret News,* January 18, 1879, 808–9. Additional descriptions of the convention can be found in Elizabeth Cady Stanton, Susan B. Anthony, and Matilda Joslyn Gage, eds., *History of Woman Suffrage,* vol. 3 (New York: Susan B. Anthony, 1887), 128–29; "Over the Hills and Far Away," *Woman's Exponent* 7 (February 1, 1879): 186; "Visit to Washington," *Woman's Exponent* 7 (February 15, 1879): 194; "The Washington Convention," *Woman's Exponent* 7 (March 1, 1879): 202; "Washington Convention, Continued," *Woman's Exponent* 7 (March 15, 1879): 210; "Women in Council—Their Recent Convention," "Memorial, Anti-Polygamy Law," and "Mormon Women before the House Judiciary Committee," *National Citizen and Ballot Box* 3 (February 1879): 11; "The Brand of the Slave," *National Citizen and Ballot Box* 4 (May 1879): 2; "Report from Utah," *National Citizen and Ballot Box* 4 (July 1879): 6; "Suffrage Convention in Washington," *Woman's Journal* 1 (January 18, 1879): 24; "Suffrage Convention at Washington (continued)," *Woman's*

Journal 1 (January 25, 1879): 29; "A Compromise Proposed," *Woman's Journal* 1 (February 8, 1879): 41, 54; "Memorial of Mormon Women," *Woman's Journal* 1 (February 15, 1879): 54; "Woman's Rights Convention," *Deseret Evening News,* January 11, 1879, 2; "Woman Suffrage Festivities," *Deseret Evening News,* January 14, 1879, 1; "Eastern—Woman's Suffrage Convention—Mrs. Wells and Mrs. Williams call on President Hayes," *Deseret Evening News,* January 14, 1879, 1; "The Utah Ladies in Washington," *Deseret Evening News,* January 18, 1879, 2; "Mrs. Wells and Mrs. Williams before the Committee," *Deseret Evening News,* January 18, 1879, 1; "The Mormon Question," *Deseret Evening News,* January 28, 1879, 2; "Memorial of the Mormon Women," *Deseret Evening News,* January 31, 1879, 2; "Mrs. President Hayes," *Deseret Evening News,* March 15, 1879, 2. For their personal accounts see Wells, Diary, January 1–February 5, 1879; and Williams, Diary, January 3–February 1879.

74. "Resolutions," *Woman's Exponent* 7 (February 15, 1879): 196–97.

75. "The Brand of the Slave," *National Citizen and Ballot Box* 4 (May 1879): 2. See also "Mrs. Stanton and Mormon Women," *Woman's Exponent* 7 (May 15, 1879): 240. Cannon was Utah's delegate to Congress (1874–82), and after 1880 he also served as First Counselor to John Taylor and later to Wilford Woodruff in the First Presidency of the LDS Church.

76. "The Brand of the Slave," 2. Lucy Stone and Henry Blackwell wrote their own marriage covenant (eliminating the word "obey"), and Stone added six articles protesting the legal status of women as prescribed by both civil and religious law. Her refusal to take her husband's name created numerous legal complications and sometimes moral ambiguities about their life together.

77. "Memorial to the 'Mormon' Women," *Deseret News,* January 31, 1879, 2. A printed copy resides in the Perry Special Collections. A copy of the memorial was included in the Jubilee Box of Zina Williams's mother, Zina D. H. Young. The LDS Church celebrated its fiftieth Jubilee year in 1880. Numerous individuals collected keepsakes in Jubilee boxes to be opened at the centenary of the Church. See Derr, Cannon, and Beecher, *Women of Covenant,* 261–62.

78. See Williams, Diary, January 9, 20, 23, 29, 30, 1879, for these and other comments about the officials they met.

79. Williams, Diary, January 16, 1879.

80. "Mormon Women before the House Judiciary Committee," 11. Delegate Cannon reported to LDS Church President John Taylor in 1880 that the suffragists had become such an influential power in Washington that they were allowed to appear before the House Judiciary Committee, "a mark of respect almost unprecedented." The remarks were to be printed as well. George Q. Cannon to John Taylor, February 7, 1880, George Q. Cannon Letterbook.

81. "By Telegraph, Eastern Women's Suffrage Delegation," *Deseret Evening News,* January 17, 1879, 2.

82. Stanton, Anthony, and Gage, *History of Woman Suffrage,* 3:130. See also "Mormon Women before the House Judiciary Committee," 11; and "Editorial Notes, the Following from the *Mission Mirror,*" *Deseret Evening News,* January 24, 1879, 2.

83. Provisions of the Edmunds Act are outlined in Gustive O. Larson, *Outline History of Territorial Utah* (Salt Lake City: Deseret Book, 1965), 267–68. See also Sarah Barringer Gordon, *The Mormon Question: Polygamy and Constitutional Conflict in Nineteenth-Century America* (Chapel Hill: University of North Carolina Press, 2002), 152–53. For a history of inheritance and other laws relating to wives and children of polygamous marriages following the Edmunds-Tucker Act, see Carol Cornwall Madsen, "'At Their Peril': Utah Law and the Case of Plural Wives, 1850–1900," *Western Historical Quarterly* 21 (November 1990): 425–44.

84. "The Old Hens," *Salt Lake Tribune,* January 14, 1879, 1.

85. "Memorial of Emmeline B. Wells and Zina Young Williams of Salt Lake City, Utah Territory to the President of the United States," Washington, 1879, Church Archives.

86. Parts of the memorial are reprinted in Stanton, Anthony, and Gage, *History of Woman Suffrage,* 3:179.

87. From the *Philadelphia Times,* January 10, 1879, Miss Grundy, "Mormon Ladies Calling at the White House," *Woman's Exponent* 7 (March 15, 1879): 212. A biting response to the two women's activities in Washington, published in the *Chicago Advance,* was reprinted in the *Woman's Journal* under "Injudicious Agitation," 10 (February 15, 1879): 51. It claimed that the presence of these women and their interview with President Hayes could only hurt the cause. "Was ever such a scene witnessed before in a Christian land!" it exclaimed. The two women's appearance in Washington was clearly a newsworthy event beyond Utah and Washington.

88. Williams, Diary, January 13, 1879.

89. A year after this interview, Lucy Hayes founded the Methodist-Episcopal Home Mission Society. Under its auspices, numerous women, including Angelia (Angie) Thurston Newman, a vociferous foe of polygamy, worked with the Anti-Polygamy Society of Utah.

90. Gustive O. Larsen, "The Crusade and the Manifesto," in *Utah's History,* ed. Richard D. Poll, Thomas G. Alexander, Eugene E. Campbell, and David E. Miller (Provo, Utah: Brigham Young University Press, 1978), 257–58.

91. Wells, Diary, January 18, 1879. The book—Edward W. Tullidge, *The Women of Mormondom* (New York: Tullidge and Crandall, 1877)—was preserved with Lucy Hayes's papers and housed in the Hayes Library in Ohio. I am grateful to Patricia Lyn Scott for providing me with a copy of the inscription.

92. John Taylor to Wilford Woodruff, January 28, 1879, John Taylor Family Papers, Manuscript Division, Special Collections, J. Willard Marriott Library, University of Utah, Salt Lake City. John Taylor, as President of the Quorum of Twelve Apostles, had presided over the Church since the death of Brigham Young in 1877 and was formally sustained as Church President in October 1880.

93. "Our Women Delegates," *Salt Lake Tribune,* January 18, 1879, 2.

94. Wells, Diary, March 8, 1879.

95. "At Washington Still," *Deseret Evening News,* January 28, 1879, 3.

96. "Correspondence," *Woman's Exponent* 7 (May 1, 1879): 235.

97. "Correspondence," *Woman's Exponent* 7 (April 15, 1879): 228.

98. Reprinted in "Editorial Notes: The Following from the *Mission Mirror*," *Deseret Evening News,* January 24, 1879, 2.

99. Reprinted in "The Mormon Question in Congress," *Deseret Evening News*, January 27, 1879, 2.

100. Reprinted in "The Mormon Question," *Deseret Evening News*, January 28, 1879, 2.

101. Wells, Diary, February 20, 1879.

102. Williams, Diary, February 5, 6, 7, 1879.

Chapter 8

Diamond Cut Diamond

*'We never thought that
woman could rise up against woman.'*[1]

It would be seven years before Emmeline Wells returned to Washington, D.C. A change in the political climate of the nation's capital discouraged the kind of personal appeal, especially from a plural wife, that Emmeline had presented in 1879. The nation's attitude toward polygamy coalesced around government action in January of that year when the United States Supreme Court upheld the constitutionality of the Morrill Act, and while "laws cannot interfere with mere religious belief and opinions," it ruled, "they can with practices."[2]

In his message to Congress in December of that same year, President Rutherford B. Hayes disclosed his intent to implement the Morrill Act. "If necessary to secure obedience to the law," he said, "the enjoyment and exercise of the rights and privileges of citizenship in the Territories . . . may be withheld or withdrawn from those who violate or oppose the enforcement of the law."[3] This would be the basis of the anti-Mormon legislation that followed. To what extent his personal feelings were influenced by the petitions sent to his wife, Lucy, by the Anti-Polygamy Society of Utah and her own feelings about the practice is undetermined, but this address and his farewell speech in December 1880, which reiterated his stance, opened the gates to a flood of petitions urging legislation to abolish polygamy.

Although she served only sporadically as a vice president for the Utah chapter of the National Woman Suffrage Association (NWSA) during the next few years, attended only one executive committee meeting in Omaha (in 1882), and lobbied in Washington in 1886, Emmeline Wells did not attend another Washington NWSA convention until 1891. Mormon representation at its annual meetings was assumed by two women who resided in Washington: Emily S. Richards, wife of the attorney for the LDS Church Franklin S. Richards, and Margaret N. Caine, wife of John T. Caine, Utah's delegate to Congress after 1882. Both women were monogamist. Together the two attended the 1885 convention, and in 1888 Emily Richards attended the fortieth anniversary of the 1848 Seneca Falls woman's rights convention, accompanied by Isabel Cameron Brown, a non-Mormon Utah suffragist, who was not linked to the antipolygamy movement.[4]

Emily S. Richards represented Mormon women on the national suffrage scene. Living with her husband, Franklin, in Washington D.C., Emily served as chair of the executive committee for Utah of the National Woman Suffrage Association and vice president of the Utah Territorial Woman Suffrage Association.

But these were not the only Utah representatives. Also attending the annual conventions during this time were the Godbe wives and other non-Mormon women, namely Sarah A. Cooke (a former member of the LDS Church), Cornelia Paddock, and Jennie Froiseth, who served at various times as the NWSA's vice president for Utah. The reports Emmeline sent from Utah, however, consistently kept her name, if not her person, before her suffrage colleagues. She also maintained a lively correspondence with Henry B. Blackwell (Lucy Stone's husband), Susan B. Anthony, Sara Spencer, Belva Lockwood, and even Elizabeth Cady Stanton's son Theo, who shared his mother's interest in women's issues and authored a book, *The Woman Question in Europe,* in 1883, while living in Paris with his French wife.[5]

Following her first experience at personal diplomacy in 1879, Emmeline departed from her focus on marriage relationships, which comprised her articles for the *Woman's Exponent* under the name of Blanche Beechwood, and as editor since 1877 shifted to woman's rights and the defense of woman suffrage in Utah.[6] This new interest was most evident in 1879 when she added to the masthead of the *Exponent* the phrase, "The Rights of the Women of Zion and the Rights of the Women of All Nations," a statement that remained until statehood in 1896. Thereafter, reflecting not only a fait accompli in Utah but also a philosophical change in the national movement, the masthead read "The Ballot in the Hands of the Women of Utah Should be a Power to Better the Home, the State, and the Nation."[7] The potential social usefulness of woman's vote formed a readier acceptance than its political significance.

Emmeline was not idle during her hiatus from national conventions. She enjoyed the prestige of traveling with Eliza R. Snow, newly elected president of all the LDS Relief Societies in 1880, to visit the various units throughout the territory, expanding Emmeline's circle of acquaintances and developing her speaking and organizational skills. Another public duty, hosting the interesting and interested visitors to Utah, gave her opportunity to meet a widely diverse group of western travelers, which included politicians, writers, foreign dignitaries, and popular lecturers, along with curious tourists, all of whom found a firsthand look at the Mormons irresistible.[8] Emmeline was also busy implementing the Church's grain-saving program, the monumental responsibility that Brigham Young had given to her in 1876.[9] In addition, she served throughout the decade of the 1880s as secretary of the Deseret Hospital board, a charitable institution founded in 1882 by Relief Society women. She was beginning to feel the burden of public responsibilities and an increasing demand on her developing leadership and influence.

Deeply attached to both the Newel K. Whitney and Daniel H. Wells families, she found little time for yearly sojourns to Washington, D.C. Most pressing, however, were the unrelenting publishing deadlines of the *Woman's Exponent*, which she faced twice each month. She often complained of too much to do and too little time to do it.[10] But she never declined invitations to serve in any capacity, enjoying rather than resenting the many diverse claims on her abilities.

Her own ambition had received a decided boost from her attendance at the 1879 NWSA convention, and she relished the accolades she often received from her other civic contributions. When writer Augusta Joyce Crocheron dedicated her book, *Representative Women of Deseret*, to Emmeline in 1881, she confessed her pleasure in her growing fame. "Never was one [day] more auspicious," she noted in her diary after the public tribute, "for fame and friendship are better than riches,"[11] and definitely more accessible to her. A surprise birthday party that same year brought seventy-five guests, including LDS Church President John Taylor, several Apostles, and many other friends who declared that the honor shown her on that occasion "was a well deserved token of the esteem in which herself [sic] and her useful labors are held by a large and steadily increasing circle of friends."[12] Her life was changing, as she had hoped, from the backstage defender of the Church of the 1870s to a well-known, highly vocal, and visible advocate for women in the 1880s.

But neither journalism nor politics, though bringing her notoriety and respect, was her desired route to fame. While the *Exponent* carried her writings well beyond the boundaries of Utah territory and made her name familiar in suffrage and political circles, she regretted that her poetry and fiction had received so little recognition. No editorial on woman's rights, no matter how passionately conceived, no fervent appeal to Congress, no matter how eloquently presented, quite revealed the part of her nature and the talent for which she most wanted public acclaim. "Once before the world in the hands of readers," she wrote of these literary efforts, "I feel I should be known for what I am. Now I am comparatively unknown."[13] In a retrospective moment, however, musing on the unexpected events that had so recently altered her expectations, she conceded that "there may be honors yet in store for me."[14] To her dismay, her advocacy of Mormon women and defense of her religious beliefs overshadowed her poetic efforts.

Prospects for her personal life, however, did not seem as promising. Like many other plural wives, she had learned to curtail her emotional and financial dependence on her husband.[15] Being obliged to earn her own living brought her rewards but also evoked her resentment. Her growing dependence on the *Woman's Exponent* as her principal means of livelihood, though never fully adequate, required ceaseless attention to marketing as well as editing the paper. As a result, her literary contributions to other publications and her poetry were generally suspended during this time. The emotional distancing from her husband was achieved less easily, but she threw herself into her public work as a catharsis and substitute for the long-term companionship that eluded her in three marriages.

These personal concerns, however, gave form to a nascent feminism enlivening her editorials and energizing her political activism. Her first political action after returning from Washington was to lobby for an amendment to the 1870 woman suffrage statute to include the right to hold office, a provision the Wyoming legislature had included in its 1869 grant of woman suffrage. She had a vested interest in this effort. In 1878 she had been nominated for county treasurer by the People's Party, the political arm of the LDS Church that had been formed as a response to organization of the Liberal Party by Gentiles and ex-Mormons in 1870.[16] Her ineligibility to accept the nomination was the catalyst for the campaign to amend the law when the legislature met in 1879. Accompanied by suffragist Sarah M. Kimball, Emmeline visited Governor George Emery, hoping to persuade him to support their petition, but the women found him opposed not only to female candidates but also to women voters "on general principles," and their efforts failed.[17]

In 1880, Wells drew up another petition from the "ladies of Salt Lake County" and asked Charles W. Penrose, an LDS Church Apostle and a territorial legislator, to carry it to the legislative assembly. The women of several other counties also submitted petitions.[18] As their standard bearer, Penrose introduced a bill that struck the word "male" from all references to office holding and added the phrase, "All laws or parts of laws which disqualify any citizen from holding office on account of sex are hereby repealed." He appealed to the legislative assembly to "Give to the women of Utah . . . full, perfect and complete political liberty. . . . Having done so much for woman's cause," he challenged the assembly, "why halt in timid hesitation before the last barrier to her political freedom?"[19]

When the bill attracted controversy among Utah voters, Wells was not dismayed. Rather, she applauded the interest and the debate it engendered, responding with an editorial entitled, "Agitation is Educational." "People are beginning to think upon the woman question," she wrote. "When people begin to study a theme in earnest they generally improve, and gradually light dawns upon them, and the mists disperse and shadows are dispelled." Discovering that for many women, as well as men, the move from woman voter to woman candidate was too large a step, she argued that "whatever privilege is given [woman], man is benefited and ennobled by." The desire to hold office, she explained "is not an aggressive act on the part of women but a progressive one which will remove the discrimination that exists among equal citizens." Many offices, she confidently asserted, would be well served by women, who were presently denied the opportunity to bring their intelligence and abilities to the good of the community.[20]

Endorsing Emmeline's position, Louisa King Spencer, an *Exponent* reader, made a personal appeal to the members of the legislative assembly through Emmeline's paper. By extending this political privilege to women, she wrote, they would be showing the world their fair-mindedness. What respect the members would realize, she surmised, if they could say,

> "Behold! These our wives, daughters and sisters are women of God; they stand side by side with us." How noble they would prove themselves if they could say to the world, "These are they who in the midst of denunciation, calumny and ostracism . . . have proved themselves worthy to become the mothers of a race of free men, and lo! We

present them to you free women, free to vote, free to hold office, free to honor virtue, and to take part in legislating for its protection."[21]

Emmeline had an enthusiastic and articulate ally.

Other voices also made themselves known in the pages of the *Exponent*. In response to the report of one community opposed to the bill, despite the fact that "all the most intelligent ladies voted for it," an *Exponent* reader from Morgan, Utah, wrote to object to the gratuitous insult and to fervently defend the intelligence and the opinion of those who had voted against it. She appealed to her "sisters in the Gospel" not to "snap at one another because we cannot all see alike."[22] More representative was the opinion of Emmeline's friend and fellow suffragist, Lucinda Dalton of St. George, Utah. In a letter to the *Exponent*, she explained that though she herself neither "expected nor wished to hold any office whatever," she did not relish "being forbidden." Moreover, she knew some offices that she wanted to see filled by women.[23]

Since removing the vote from Utah women was a key element in proposed antipolygamy legislation, Church leaders were uncertain whether extending the political status of women might be helpful in gaining favorable notice and support of the suffragists or whether it might instead become the decisive factor in the repeal of women's vote. Acknowledging the "good results" from enfranchising Mormon women a decade earlier, LDS Church President John Taylor advised delegate George Q. Cannon that he thought the women's campaign to extend their political rights might add to the favorable response already enjoyed from women's rights activists "if," he cautioned, "our National Legislature would not take matters into their own hands, and place them in a worse position . . . by repealing both the former law, as also that which may be passed."[24]

Cannon concurred with Taylor as to the potential risk of a reversal of the 1870 suffrage act. Cannon doubted, however, that the governor would sign the 1880 bill, thus obviating any congressional action. Cannon was certain, however, that such a legislative attempt would have "the moral effect. . . . It would be a good stroke of policy in giving us influence and placing us in the van of this movement." An early supporter of equal suffrage, Cannon noted that removing this disability would let the world see that "we recognize them [the women] as our sisters, and in a certain sense our equals, and that we are willing that they shall not be handicapped in the race of life."[25]

Besides his strong support for woman's rights on its merits and as a value to the Mormon community, Cannon worked as a Congressional delegate to preserve the Church and its practices and to maintain the unity of Latter-day Saints. That unity, of course, which demonstrated itself politically, economically, and socially as well as religiously, was the craw in the government's throat. Thus, Cannon cautiously weighed the support Utah legislative action might draw from suffragists against the possible rejection by Congress. With opposition coming from all quarters, giving full political equality to women was a means of showing, as well as shoring up, the unity he so valued. Any favorable attention or action was no small consideration. When the federal government was considering legislation that would virtually dismantle the Church and with so little support coming from any other source, Cannon, as well as Mormon women, could well appreciate the importance of suffrage leaders as "a powerful element in sympathy with us."[26]

To the delight of its proponents, Utah's legislative assembly passed the political disability bill in February 1880. But, as anticipated, it met a formidable foe in the newly appointed governor, Eli H. Murray, who upon his arrival in Utah a month earlier, had joined the "clique of Liberals most hostile to the Latter-day Saints." He began, with that bill, a policy of frequently vetoing measures enacted by the legislature, predominantly made up of Mormons.[27] Thus, when the bill reached the governor for signature he "treated it with silent contempt, as he did a similar bill two years ago" and refused to sign it into law, the *Exponent* reported.[28] The congressional legislation that followed in 1882, disfranchising polygamists, forestalled any further attempt to amend the statute.

Meanwhile, Susan B. Anthony, commiserating with Utah women over their unsuccessful campaign to win the right to public office, remarked that the lack of interest in either holding office or in supporting efforts to gain that privilege was undoubtedly due to women's "utter hopelessness of making any changes, however much they may desire them," even as voters. "Men have so long had absolute control," she lamented, "that every activity of woman to shape matters in the primary meetings and nominating conventions is still deemed an intrusion on her part."[29]

Though usually in accord with Anthony in such assertions, Emmeline Wells was quick to defend her fellow Mormons from the accusation. In Utah, she retorted, "every office open to woman, she has been allowed to occupy," including membership on nominating committees and as delegates to county and territorial conventions, where women have always "been most politely treated, invited to speak and express opinion." It is the "*statutes*" of Utah which still exclude woman from offices of trust or emolument," she explained. Failure to amend these statutes cannot be placed at the feet of Mormon legislators, she noted, but solely at the hands of the gentile governor, who thus far has refused "to extend the courtesy of his signature."[30] Neither the women nor the men of her Church, Emmeline made clear, could be held accountable for the impediments to women's political liberties in Utah.

The bill's defeat was a bitter blow to Emmeline Wells, one of many political setbacks she would experience, but when asked "What are you going to do now?" by her readers, she optimistically answered, "We are going to do just as we did before, only better if we can. . . . We are going to labor in the interests of humanity, in the education and elevation of women and children; we are going to help promote the interests of Zion with all the energy and ability we possess."[31] Time would show that these were not empty words. Emmeline had become the consummate advocate.

In 1880, encouraged by defeat of the political disability bill and unwilling to wait while Congress vacillated over a new antipolygamy measure by Senator George Edmunds that would disfranchise all polygamists, local anti-Mormons initiated a move of their own to disfranchise Utah women.[32] On September 25, 1880, with an eye to the coming November election in which the Liberal Party hoped to unseat Cannon as Utah delegate to Congress, George R. Maxwell, who had been a federal marshal, a registrar of the federal land office in Utah, and a member of the gentile Liberal Party, secured a writ of mandamus to compel Robert T. Burton, assessor and voter registrar, to strike from the voting list of Salt Lake County the names of Emmeline B. Wells, Maria M. Blythe, Mrs. A. G. Paddock, and all other women registered to vote in the county, claiming that the voting qualifications for women differed from those for men and thus invalidated the 1870 statute that had enfranchised them.[33] Emmeline printed the entire writ in the *Woman's Exponent,* while expressing her dismay at such action.[34]

There followed numerous indignant letters to the *Exponent,* including one from Isabella Horne, president of the Salt Lake Stake Relief Society and a vocal suffragist. Horne reflected a widespread reaction to the claim that women, as non–tax payers, were not lawful voters. "I claim that women do pay taxes with their husbands," she retorted, "as they are partners in the property which they hold; for if the man dies, the woman is called on to pay taxes on the property, the same as before. Now you see it is not the individual that is taxed, but the property, whether owned by man or woman."[35] The claim that women had representation but were not taxed appeared to many Utah women to be an inaccurate and specious excuse to rescind women's voting rights, Horne declared.

Eastern suffrage papers also offered their objections as they joined the chorus against this local disfranchisement attempt. *Woman's Words* editor Mrs. Juan Lewis confidently asserted that the move would not succeed. "Liberty takes no step backward," she declared, "and when the elective franchise is once exercised, no power can take it away without a revolution." Matilda Joslyn Gage, more realistically, acknowledged that only passage of a constitutional amendment would make woman's ballot unassailable.[36] The question was ultimately resolved when the territorial supreme court denied the writ on procedural grounds, ruling that the law could not be collaterally challenged in a mandamus proceeding, which could be used only to compel a person to do what the law required him to do.[37]

Victory only intensified Emmeline's resolve to turn women into active voters and to inspire them to a stronger sense of political responsibility. "Show by good works," she implored her *Exponent* readers, "that the ballot is not lightly held, or ignorantly handled. Study to become better informed upon all the subjects of law and government, that the influence of woman may at all times and in all places be that which will tell for good."[38] But she and all other polygamous wives had only two years to put that advice into action before the privilege of voting was taken from them.

Though denied the right to hold office, Wells remained active in the People's Party. She delighted in local politics, keeping herself and her readers informed of all developments, particularly in the continuing effort to gain statehood. She was a welcome participant. In July 1881 she was chosen as a delegate to the Salt Lake County convention and later selected to be a member of the county central committee. The next year she urged a delegation of women to attend the mass convention at city hall where she, Sarah M. Kimball, and Elizabeth Howard were among the fifteen Salt Lake County delegates to the territorial convention, which, for the fifth time, would prepare a constitution for statehood.[39] Intrigued by the work of the convention and showing her usual political optimism, Emmeline believed that "the consequences will be significant as regards Zion." She was pleased to be appointed to the committee on education as well as the committee on schedule and election. "Both have important work in hand," she observed. "I enjoy it very much indeed. It suits me admirably and all are quite polite to me."[40]

The meetings were frequent and lengthy, but her interest in them never flagged. She could not help being amused at the "pretty speech" by a young male delegate from Nephi who "argued that women should not labor but be protected and when they assumed duties which belonged to men they were no longer women."[41] Strains of this Victorian sentiment must have echoed in her ears when she left the convention hall and returned to her office, laboring late into the night to meet her publication deadline, or again when she attended to the needs of her family or organized meetings of the Grain Committee or Deseret Hospital Board. They may have resounded even more loudly during the rare visits of her oft-absent husband, whose responsibility it was to provide the "strong arm to lean on," that she had learned to live without.[42]

She was delighted, however, to find that several women were interested in attending the proceedings, though she lamented the fact that there were only a few who desired to "step forward and make some progress" in understanding and participating in political affairs.[43] In May 1882, at the end of the convention, the constitution was submitted to and approved by a majority of Utahns and a petition for statehood drawn up the following month. Anti-statehood lobbyists, however, succeeded in convincing Congress to reject the petition. For the fifth time, the statehood effort failed.[44]

In the meantime, with the U.S. Supreme Court's ruling on the constitutionality of the Morrill Act and its endorsement by three Republican presidents in little more than a year's time,[45] measures to enforce the act were gaining ground in Congress. Anti-Mormon efforts originating in Utah and supported by Governor Murray were also making rapid headway in Washington. To assist the Mormon effort to win friends and supporters, Emmeline not only used the *Exponent* but also proposed sending several Mormon women on a goodwill mission to the East. In July 1881, still remembering the warm reception she had received in 1879, Emmeline visited Congressman George Q. Cannon at his home in Salt Lake City. Cannon, the husband of four wives, was at that time concerned about retaining his congressional seat in view of impending legislation that would prohibit his serving in Congress. Wells and Cannon discussed the tenuous political situation for the Church, after which Cannon agreed with Wells's proposal that a lecture tour might be advantageous.[46]

She suggested Zina D. H. Young, who was a counselor in the presidency of the LDS Relief Society and already planning a trip to her native New York to gather genealogical information. A widow of Brigham Young, she was affable and articulate, kindly and approachable, a solid example of Mormon womanhood.[47] Dr. Ellen Ferguson, who had been an active suffragist in the East prior to moving to Utah, with many Eastern friends, was another likely choice, especially since she was also intending to return to the East for some additional medical training. She was a monogamist, recently widowed, and had joined the LDS Church after settling in Utah five years earlier.[48]

Two days after her meeting with Cannon, Emmeline repeated the suggestion to Church President John Taylor, who was "very favorably disposed about the sisters going East."[49] The next month, August 1881, the two women, accompanied by Willard Young, Zina's foster son, who was returning to New York to teach at West Point, embarked on their eastward journey. In September, Dr. Romania B. Pratt, also returning to the East for additional medical training, joined them for part of their tour. All were single women; both Zina and Ellen were widows and Romania had divorced her husband shortly before leaving.[50]

Ellen B. Ferguson, medical doctor and suffragist, was president of the Salt Lake County Woman Suffrage Association.

While the two doctors spent most of their East Coast trip attending medical clinics and lectures and Zina Young gathered genealogical information and visited friends and relatives, they also sought opportunities to publicly refute the accusations and misrepresentations made by antipolygamy lecturers. Zina Young spoke briefly at the Vermont Woman Temperance Convention while Dr. Ferguson, who was a friend of Isabella Beecher Hooker, a noted suffragist and member of the NWSA, lectured with Hooker at a memorial service for the recently assassinated U.S. President James Garfield at the Unity Church in Hartford, Connecticut.[51] While there, she did all she could "to present a reasonable and correct view of our faith and practice," she reported to the *Woman's Exponent*.[52] Before leaving Hartford she also met Harriet Beecher Stowe, Isabella's sister, and received an invitation to address the subject "Can Women Organize?" at the forthcoming national Woman's Congress in Buffalo, New York.

Both Dr. Ferguson and Zina Young attended the congress, which was sponsored by the American Association for the Advancement of Women (AAAW).[53] Though they had been invited by Harriet Beecher Stowe and were introduced by Sara Andrews Spencer, who remained a congenial supporter to Mormon women and was at that time a member of AAAW, they were denied the platform on the grounds that the speakers already had been selected. Julia Ward Howe, leader of the association, was a vocal antipolygamist, and under her direction the conservative AAAW remained unalterably opposed to permitting Mormon women to address its convention.[54]

Being the only enfranchised women at this convention of conservative but largely prosuffrage women, they found some irony in their silencing. The incident proved to be an early indicator of the direction the suffrage movement was taking toward Mormon suffragists, a stance that would soon become even more evident as the movement broadened its base of support to include many other anti-Mormon reformers. Antipolygamy had begun to echo louder than prosuffrage sentiment among many women in the movement, and Mormon women were beginning to sense the strong reverberations.

In February 1882, all three Utah women attended a convention of the New York Woman Suffrage Association. Also denied the platform there, a disheartening turn of events since the national platform still welcomed Mormon women, the Utah women nonetheless were able to speak personally with Susan B. Anthony, though even this turned out to be an awkward and uncomfortable encounter. Anthony expressed her concern that Mormon women had made only one effort to attend the national conventions since 1879, implying there had been an open invitation to return. She then explained that she was deeply engrossed in writing the history of woman suffrage and asked them who should write the chapter on Utah. They all agreed that Emmeline Wells was the logical choice, to which she assented. Anthony's next inquiry, however, rankled Romania Pratt. Who, Anthony wondered, should write the anti-Mormon viewpoint? Not so much in awe of the stately leader as to hedge her indignation, Romania retorted, "If you were always

Dr. Romania Pratt (Penrose) participated in the Woman Suffrage Association meeting in New York in 1882, where she championed Mormon women.

so eager to hear our side on all matters of dispute concerning us as you are the anti-side, we would suffer a great deal less from misrepresentation than we now do." The self-possessed Anthony "for a moment seemed a little non-plussed," Dr. Pratt reported, "but soon rallied to explain the need to protect their 'cause' by shunning even the appearance of evil," especially in "the present feverish state of society, an insulting characterization of the women's religion." Anthony did, however, reaffirm her commitment to defending their voting rights and noted that Mormon women would continue to be welcome on the speakers' platform at the annual suffrage conventions.[55]

Another disappointment came from the pen of Matilda Gage, whom they had visited at the New York suffrage convention and who had always been a strong supporter of woman suffrage in Utah. In her paper, the *National Citizen and Ballot Box,* Gage deemed the lecture tour of the women extremely unbecoming. She was surprised, she wrote, that such gifted and capable women "should lend themselves to the propagation of a system, which under the name of religion, degrades woman."[56] It was one thing to befriend polygamists when they were advocating suffrage, but quite another to befriend suffragists when they were defending polygamy.

Attendance at the January 1882 NWSA convention had not been on the original agenda of the three emissaries. Cannon and Wells had discussed the advisability of their participation shortly after the women left for their eastern tour but decided to wait on a decision until Cannon returned to Washington and could sense the mood there. Meanwhile, in Salt Lake City a growing demand for action against the pending Edmunds Bill prompted the First Presidency of the Church to explore the usefulness of submitting another petition to Congress. President Taylor was also eager to have the women submit a memorial.[57] While awaiting Cannon's appraisal of the situation, Emmeline, at President Taylor's request, prepared credentials for the women, proposed a mass meeting in Salt Lake City as a show of support, and began writing a memorial for the women to present to Congress.[58] All preparations were abandoned, however, when Cannon discouraged the three women from continuing their journey to the convention. This was not a good year for Mormons in Washington.[59] Passage of the long-debated Edmunds Bill in March made clear that neither petitions nor memorials could have halted its progress.

Disappointed in the reception the emissaries received from women who had treated her with such courtesy, Emmeline rightfully concluded, "Everything seems unfavorable towards our people at present."[60] While the three women completed all their individual goals, spoke at LDS Church meetings, and organized a Relief Society in New York, their six-month tour clearly missed its mark in winning sympathy for the women of the Church. The tide of public opinion, fueled by the growing strength of female opposition, and the ambivalence of former allies among the suffragists, was simply too strong to reverse.

The sporadic attendance of Mormon representatives at the NWSA conventions during the next few years was primarily their own decision rather than a result of deliberate estrangement by suffrage leaders. Susan B. Anthony's remark to Zina Young and Romania Pratt indicated an open door, and Zina Young, then a counselor in the Relief Society presidency, was specifically invited in 1883.[61] As noted, Emily Richards and Margaret N. Caine, both in Washington with their husbands, attended the 1885 convention, and Richards and Isabel Brown attended the 1888 meeting that followed the fortieth anniversary celebration of the Seneca Falls Convention. NWSA members Jennie Froiseth and Cornelia Paddock, together with Sarah Cooke and Annie Godbe, however, not only attended each convention during these years but also served as vice presidents for Utah. They superseded Mormon representation during this uncertain decade and remained the only voting delegates from Utah.

The NWSA executive committee meeting scheduled for Omaha, Nebraska, in September 1882, seemed less forbidding to Emmeline than the Washington conventions, and she decided to attend. Unfortunately, she did not record her feelings in returning, after thirty-four years, to the Missouri River town situated near the remains of the early Mormon settlement known as Winter Quarters, where she had spent two harsh winters in 1846 and 1847, waiting to continue her westward journey to the Salt Lake Valley. Omaha little resembled that early Mormon outpost where thousands of uprooted Latter-day Saints like Emmeline had encamped while collecting the necessary supplies and equipment to complete the long trek to Utah.

At the convention, Emmeline renewed her association with Susan B. Anthony, whom she had not seen for three years. Anthony's warm greeting pleased Emmeline immensely, their friendship consistently surmounting Anthony's aversion to Emmeline's lifestyle. Emmeline also began a long, close, and fruitful acquaintance with May Wright Sewall, president of the Executive Committee and later to be an officer in both the National and International Councils of Women. Emmeline also met Mrs. E. L. Saxon of Louisville, Mrs. Clara Bewick Colby of Nebraska, and Rachel G. Foster of Philadelphia; these new acquaintances would play a role in events yet to unfold. Emmeline returned home at the close of the convention, invigorated from the trip and pleased to renew friendships she had carefully cultivated in the suffrage association.[62]

Besides passage of antipolygamy legislation, the new decade brought changes in the suffrage movement, which Emmeline already sensed, that made Mormon membership in the NWSA problematic. In 1881 and 1882, Elizabeth Stanton and Susan B. Anthony, two of Utah women's most dependable friends, gave their full attention to writing the first two volumes of the weighty *History of Woman Suffrage* and were not present to encourage the acceptance of Mormon delegates at the annual conventions. When these two volumes were published, with favorable reviews, both women retreated to Europe to recuperate their energies and health, Stanton leaving in 1882 and Anthony joining her the following year.[63] Anthony's nine-month sojourn solidified her desire to expand the suffrage movement, which seemed to be making little progress, by enlarging its constituency at home and uniting national suffrage associations into an international alliance, a move that would dramatically affect the NWSA's relationship with Mormon women.

Elizabeth Cady Stanton *(seated)* and Susan B. Anthony *(standing)* (ca. 1880–1902) worked tirelessly for woman suffrage. Emmeline Wells corresponded with these national leaders, met with them at conventions, and hosted them when they visited Utah.

Consolidating the two national suffrage organizations seemed a logical beginning point. Both Anthony and Stanton had spoken of it before leaving for England. In fact, as early as 1880 Elizabeth Stanton, in a letter to Isabella Beecher Hooker, a strong advocate for unification, noted that she agreed with Hooker that a "union of the suffrage forces would be a move in the right direction."[64] Other suffragists also looked toward merger. They were convinced that only personal differences and resentments, particularly those between Lucy Stone and Susan B. Anthony, kept the two organizations apart, especially since Congress had finally addressed the polygamy problem with passage of the Edmunds Bill.

In the meantime, another kind of merger began to take shape, fostered by Anthony's goal to enlarge the NWSA's membership by reaching out to the proliferating and mainly antisuffrage moral and reform associations and the home mission organizations.[65] It was an unlikely partnership, which estranged some of the NWSA's strongest supporters, including Sara Andrews Spencer, and dismayed Elizabeth Stanton, who returned to England in 1886 after a brief visit to the states. It also required Anthony to accommodate herself to a much more conservative view of women's role in society.[66]

This informal merger began with Susan B. Anthony's admiration for the leadership and organizational skills of Frances Willard, who assumed the presidency of the Woman's Christian Temperance Union (WCTU) in 1879.[67] "Home protection" was the union's motto and was thus closely allied with, though far more ambitious than other "home mission" or "social purity" organizations of evangelical Christian women or the philanthropic work of the women's clubs. Acting from the Victorian assumption of female moral superiority, the home mission societies targeted practices that invaded the sanctity of the Christian home, as they defined it. Polygamy, along with intemperance, prostitution, and divorce, headed their agenda of moral reform.[68]

Frances Willard's recognition of the value of the ballot to her temperance crusade greatly facilitated the merger. Having developed a close working relationship with Susan B. Anthony, Willard publicly announced in 1881 the WCTU's support of woman suffrage. Moral suasion and prayer, she had concluded, could not accomplish what the ballot promised. Though a vocal minority of home mission workers distrusted Anthony, fearing she lacked "proper Christian credentials," others agreed to endorse the movement she headed.[69] As moral reformer Sarah M. Perkins explained at the 1885 NWSA convention: "The WCTU had by a prayer been brought to espouse the cause of woman's suffrage . . . for the reason that the Temperance [Union] could never hope to accomplish any permanent good until woman, by the ballot could say that the dram shop 'round the corner . . . should be forever closed."[70]

There was no question that this merger painted the character of the National with hues of the American, which included a number of reform leaders in its membership. Anthony herself admitted that the only difference that then existed was the American's policy to permit men to be officers of the organization, a concession the National had vowed never to make.[71] Moreover, Anthony, with an eye to the future, courted a younger generation of suffragists, more conservative and conciliatory than were her contemporaries. Among them was the devoted Rachel Foster, who relieved the aging Anthony of much of the administrative work of the campaign.[72] Thus, with their most welcoming allies either away or preoccupied in writing the history of the movement, along with the assimilation of Mormon women's most relentless enemies by the National, it is little wonder Mormon women no longer felt comfortable at the conventions. Nonetheless, Emmeline never failed to send a letter or report to be read at each annual meeting. They might be out of sight, but Mormon women were determined not to be out of mind.

Nor were they. Interest in Utah woman suffrage had not waned among the National's older suffragists, despite the changing nature of the association. Woman suffrage papers continued to rail against every proposal to divest Utah women of the vote.[73] During the final months of debate over the Edmunds Bill, national suffragists waged a strong campaign against the section repealing woman suffrage. In their conventions and journals, they urged sympathizers to show disapproval by writing their Congressmen to defeat the bill. Some Congressmen, already ambivalent about its legality, voiced their own disapproval of removing suffrage from Utah women or from any qualified voter because of religious belief. They were joined by other legal experts who feared that federal legislation against polygamy represented a major incursion of the state into religious beliefs and practices, and the wholesale removal of the voting rights of a class of citizens based on their religious convictions was arbitrary at best and unconstitutional at worst. Suffragists Phoebe Cousins and particularly Belva Lockwood, who were also lawyers, publicly questioned the constitutionality of the Edmunds Bill.[74] Moreover, it seemed illogical to many individuals besides suffragists that only women and not men were to be deprived of this civil right, especially, some argued, since men were the "true polygamists" (plural wives, after all, were married to only one man, they noted).[75] Suffragists also strongly resisted local attempts to rescind women's voting rights in Utah.

But all arguments proved fruitless. When Congress finally succeeded in passing the Edmunds Bill in March 1882, it became law with a disfranchisement clause. But instead of disfranchising Utah women, as expected, it debarred from voting, holding office, or sitting on juries both men and women who were then practicing or had entered plural marriage since 1862. It was a logical penalty even to suffragists.[76]

Emmeline's usual optimism was betrayed by the realities of Congress's oversight of the LDS Church and the changes that followed passage of the Edmunds Bill. Many public offices became vacant as polygamists, including George Q. Cannon, were obliged to give up their elected positions as well as voting rights under terms of the bill. With Utah elections now under supervision of a newly created Utah Commission, a group of five men appointed by the U.S. President to oversee all electoral processes in Utah, the political topography of Utah was beginning to change and the balance of power would undergo a major alteration in the ensuing years. Emmeline Wells, an avid voter for twelve years, was determined that she would one day vote again and that she would be instrumental in regaining that right.

Notes

1. "Woman's Mass Meeting," *Woman's Exponent* 7 (December 1, 1878): 103.

2. Gustive O. Larson, "Government, Politics, and Conflict," in *Utah's History*, ed. Richard Poll, Thomas G. Alexander, Eugene E. Campbell, and David E. Miller (Provo, Utah: Brigham Young University Press, 1978), 254. See also Sarah Barringer Gordon, *The Mormon Question: Polygamy and Constitutional Conflict in Nineteenth-Century America* (Chapel Hill: University of North Carolina Press, 2002), 119–45.

3. As quoted in Larson, "The Crusade and the Manifesto," in Poll and others, *Utah's History*, 257–58. See also Orson F. Whitney, *History of Utah*, 4 vols. (George Q. Cannon and Sons, 1895), 3:140. Both President James Garfield and President Chester A. Arthur reiterated President Rutherford B. Hayes's position on the Mormons.

4. Isabel Cameron Brown was the second wife of Arthur Brown, a lawyer from Michigan who settled in Utah in 1879. He represented Utah in the U.S. Senate in 1896, after Utah acquired statehood. Isabel's father was a state senator in Michigan, where she ran a newsstand for a short time in Kalamazoo.

Isabel was a sister-in-law to Olympia Brown, a reverend as well as a suffragist and likely influential in Isabel's own suffrage interests and attendance at the 1888 anniversary celebration of the Seneca Falls convention. See Linda Thatcher, "The 'Gentile Polygamist': Arthur Brown, Ex-Sentaor from Utah," *Utah Historical Quarterly* 52 (Summer 1984): 231.

5. Elizabeth Stanton delightedly exclaimed that Theo "was heart and soul . . . interested in my work." He gave up the practice of law to become a journalist and reformer and worked with his sister Harriot in publishing their mother's papers. See Elisabeth Griffith, *In Her Own Right: The Life of Elizabeth Cady Stanton* (New York: Oxford University Press, 1984), 173–74.

6. Of the 109 editorials appearing between 1872 and 1896 on woman suffrage, Emmeline wrote 94 of them. This number does not include the regular editorial reports of both national and local suffrage conventions, suffrage talks, and summaries of suffrage activities that filled the editorial and other columns of the *Exponent*. Polygamy drew 143 editorials between 1872 and 1893, the highpoint being between 1883 and 1885. Both editors of the *Exponent* also contributed articles of their own writing to these numbers. See Carol Cornwall Madsen, "'Remember the Women of Zion': A Study of the Editorial Content of the *Woman's Exponent*" (master's thesis, University of Utah, 1977).

7. Aileen S. Kraditor explores this shift in ideology in *The Ideas of the Woman Suffrage Movement, 1890–1920* (New York: Columbia University Press, 1965).

8. During one year, 1886, Emmeline was host to Annie Wittmeyer, president of the Women's Christian Temperance Union; Jennie June of the Grand Army of the Republic; Prince Wittgenstein of Russia; and several other members of European royal families. These were in addition to national suffrage workers who visited, as well as women from the national purity movement. See, for example, "Some People We Have Met," *Woman's Exponent* 15 (October 10, 1886): 67.

9. Her primary networks in facilitating this new program were the Relief Society and the *Woman's Exponent*. Information on the grain-saving program can be found in several sources: Emmeline B. Wells, "The Mission of Saving Grain," *Relief Society Magazine* 2 (February 1915): 47–48; Annie Wells Cannon, Emily S. Richards, Rebecca E. Little, Harriet B. Harker, "Grain Saving in the Relief Society," *Relief Society Magazine* 2 (February 1915): 54–55; "Relief Society Reports," *Woman's Exponent* 7 (October 15, 1878): 74. See also Carol Cornwall Madsen, "Emmeline B. Wells: A Mormon Woman in Victorian America" (PhD diss., University of Utah, 1986), 331–39. Other studies include Jessie L. Embry, "Relief Society Grain Storage Program, 1876–1940" (master's

thesis, Brigham Young University, 1974); and E. Cecil McGavin, "Grain Storage among the Latter-day Saints," *Improvement Era* 44 (March 1941): 142–44, 181–86.

10. Such complaints begin to dot her diaries in the 1880s and increased over time. See, for example, October 13, 1881: "Between writing visiting the sick answering everybody's questions, keeping up correspondence & trying to please all parties I find myself pretty well used up and weary in the extreme." Emmeline B. Wells, Diary, L. Tom Perry Special Collections, Harold B. Lee Library, Brigham Young University, Provo, Utah.

11. Wells, Diary, July 15, 1881.

12. "Local and Other Matters—a Pleasant Occasion," *Deseret Evening News,* March 1, 1881, 3.

13. Wells, Diary, February 26, 1881. She did not consider her editorials and *Exponent* articles most representative of her literary skills. Poetry was her first love, and she consistently yearned for more time to write it.

14. Wells, Diary, March 2, 1881. By 1890, however, she had achieved a certain amount of public acclaim for her poetry. Her picture, a short life sketch, and several poems are included in Thomas W. Herringshaw's book, *Poets of America* (Chicago: American Publishers' Association, 1890), 805, featuring over one thousand living American poets. Her own collected volume of poetry, *Musings and Memories: Poems by Emmeline B. Wells* (Salt Lake City: George Q. Cannon and Sons, 1896; 2d ed., Salt Lake City: Deseret News Press, 1915), did not appear until six years later.

15. Although she did not lose her home to pay her husband's mounting debts until 1888, hints that such a move would take place began as early as 1881. See, for example, her diary for March 11, 1881, and her emotional wish to have her means and home independent rather than subject to the fortunes or desires of someone else, December 9, 1881.

16. Thomas G. Alexander and James B. Allen, *Mormons and Gentiles, A History of Salt Lake City,* The Western Urban History Series, 5 vols. (Boulder, Colo.: Pruett, 1984), 5:92. These two local parties were in lieu of the national party system, which was not adopted in Utah until 1891.

17. Report to the 1880 Annual Convention of the NWSA from Emmeline B. Wells, clipping in the Papers of Elizabeth Cady Stanton and Susan B. Anthony, Library of Congress, Washington, D.C.

18. The Salt Lake County petition was signed by Eliza R. Snow, Sarah M. Kimball, Emmeline B. Wells, and fourteen other women. See "The Legislature," *Woman's Exponent* 8 (January 15, 1880): 125. The petition of the citizens of Beaver, signed by Louisa Barnes Pratt and 382 others, is printed in

"Petition of Citizens of Beaver and Other Places," *Woman's Exponent* 8 (February 1, 1880): 133. A petition was also submitted by the women of Juab County but was evidently not read to the assembly.

19. References to his speech are in "The Legislature," *Woman's Exponent* 8 (January 15, 1880): 124; "Home Affairs," *Woman's Exponent* 8 (February 1, 1880): 133. For a full text of Penrose's speech, see "Speech of Hon. C. W. Penrose," *Woman's Exponent* 8 (February 1, 1880): 130. See also Journal History of the Church, February 4, 1880, 1, Church Archives, The Church of Jesus Christ of Latter-day Saints, Salt Lake City, also available on *Selected Collections from the Archives of The Church of Jesus Christ of Latter-day Saints,* 2 vols. (Provo, Utah: Brigham Young University Press, 2002), vol. 2, DVD 8, microfilm copy in Harold B. Lee Library.

20. "Agitation Is Educational," *Woman's Exponent* 8 (February 1, 1880): 132.

21. Louisa King Spencer, "A Woman on the Woman's Bill," *Woman's Exponent* 8 (February 15, 1880): 139, originally published as by Louisa Spencer in *Deseret News*, January 19, 1880, 3.

22. C. E. F., "Correspondence," *Woman's Exponent* 8 (March 1, 1880): 147.

23. L. L. Dalton, "Our Opinion," *Woman's Exponent* 8 (February 15, 1880): 138.

24. John Taylor to George Q. Cannon, January 31, 1880, George Q. Cannon Papers, Church Archives.

25. George Q. Cannon to John Taylor, February 7, 1880, George Q. Cannon Letterbook, Church Archives.

26. George Q. Cannon to John Taylor, February 7, 1880.

27. Edward Leo Lyman, *Political Deliverance: The Mormon Quest for Utah Statehood* (Urbana: University of Illinois Press, 1986), 21.

28. "Legislative Proceedings," *Woman's Exponent* 8 (March 1, 1880): 145. See also Journal History of the Church, February 4, 11, and 21, 1880. It is unclear whether Governor George W. Emery or Governor Eli H. Murray actually vetoed the bill, since the dates of their service in Utah do not seem to coincide with the events described.

29. From an 1881 clipping of an article (no date or source) in the Papers of Elizabeth Cady Stanton and Susan B. Anthony.

30. "Woman Suffrage in Utah," clipping in Papers of Elizabeth Cady Stanton and Susan B. Anthony.

31. "Work and Wait," *Woman's Exponent* 8 (March 1, 1880): 148.

32. Though antipolygamy legislation had been proposed since 1869, the Supreme Court decision of 1879, validating the constitutionality of the Morrill Act, led to a renewed effort to pass enforcement legislation. Senator George F.

Edmunds led the action, which caused considerable debate in Congress. This bill eventually passed as the Edmunds Act in March 1882.

33. Journal History of the Church, September 30, 1880; "Attempt to Disfranchise Women," *Woman's Exponent* 9 (October 1, 1880): 68–69. George Q. Cannon had served as Utah's delegate to Congress since 1872.

34. "Woman's Right to Vote in Utah Contested," *Woman's Exponent* 9 (October 1, 1880): 68–69. See also "To Disfranchise Woman," *Salt Lake Daily Herald*, September 26, 1880, 3.

35. M. Isabella Horne, "Pertinent Question," *Woman's Exponent* 9 (October 1, 1880): 69.

36. "Attack upon Vested Rights," *National Citizen and Ballot Box* 5 (October 1880): 2. See also "The Coming Election," *Woman's Exponent* 9 (November 1, 1880): 84.

37. A full text of the proceedings appears in "Decisions of the Supreme Court in the Mandamus Case," *Woman's Exponent* 9 (October 15, 1880): 77–79; see also "Woman Suffrage in Pioneer Days," lesson pamphlet for February 1977 (Salt Lake City: Daughters of Utah Pioneers), 283–84; Journal History of the Church, October 1, 1880. For a more detailed discussion of the disfranchisement efforts see Joseph H. Groberg, "The Mormon Disfranchisements of 1882 to 1892," *BYU Studies* 16 (Spring 1976): 399–408. See also Davis Bitton, *George Q. Cannon: A Biography* (Salt Lake City: Deseret Book, 1999), 248–62.

38. "The Coming Election," *Woman's Exponent* 9 (November 1, 1880): 84. Wells was also making a plea for votes to return George Q. Cannon as congressional delegate. His election, overturned by Governor Murray, became a major political battle in both Utah and Congress until passage of the Edmunds Act, which barred polygamists from holding office, ended Cannon's decade in Congress. He was replaced in 1882 by John T. Caine, a monogamist. For more details, see Whitney, *History of Utah*, 3:130; and Gustive O. Larsen, "The Crusade and the Manifesto," in Poll and others, *Utah's History*, 258.

39. Wells, Diary, April 1, 1882. Not only were women included as delegates, but for the first time non-Mormons were among the delegates.

40. Wells, Diary, April 10, 12, 1882.

41. Wells, Diary, April 26, 1882.

42. Wells, Diary, June 27, 1876. She once wrote, "O, I am so weary and I long so much for the leisure some women enjoy." Wells, Diary, April 28, 1882.

43. Wells, Diary, April 11, 1882.

44. Whitney, *History of Utah*, 3:203–6; see also Larson, "The Crusade and the Manifesto," 258.

45. Rutherford B. Hayes served from 1877 to 1881. James A. Garfield took office in 1881 but was assassinated in July of that year, elevating his vice president, Chester A. Arthur, to president.

46. Wells, Diary, July 5, 1881.

47. From "Zina D. H. Young," by Ora Jacobs Cannon, typescript copy in possession of author. At one of Young's public appearances during her trip to the East, a woman who had eyed her from afar and seemed to be examining her with intense curiosity was heard to exclaim with surprise, "Why, you do not look very degraded!" Reported by Romania Pratt in "Woman's Suffrage Convention," *Woman's Exponent* 10 (March 1, 1882): 146.

48. Information on Dr. Ferguson is taken from Ann Gardner Stone, "Dr. Ellen Brooke Ferguson: Nineteenth-Century Renaissance Woman," in *Sister Saints,* Vicky Burgess-Olson (Provo, Utah: Brigham Young University Press, 1978), 325–39. See also "Dr. Ferguson's Letter," *Woman's Exponent* 10 (November 15, 1881): 90.

49. Wells, Diary, July 7, 1881.

50. Romania Pratt's first marriage was to Parley P. Pratt Jr. Four years after their 1881 divorce, she married Elder Charles W. Penrose, a strong champion of women's rights. Romania, a popular doctor in Utah, was a close friend of Emmeline's and a tireless worker in behalf of Latter-day Saint women. See Christine Croft Waters, "Dr. Romania Pratt Penrose: To Brave the World," in Burgess-Olson, *Sister Saints,* 341–360. See also Romania Pratt, "Woman's Suffrage Convention," *Woman's Exponent* 10 (February 15, 1882): 143; Romania Pratt, "Woman's Suffrage Convention," *Woman's Exponent* 10 (March 1, 1882): 146.

51. Stone, "Dr. Ellen Brooke Ferguson," 331. Isabella Hooker was a sister to Harriet Beecher Stowe and Catherine Beecher, both of whom were opposed to woman suffrage. Dr. Ferguson's friendship with Hooker, an avid fan of spiritualism, may well have been instrumental in drawing Ferguson, in the 1890s, into the system known as Theosophy, closely connected to Spiritualism. More information on Hooker can be found in Alice Felt Tyler, "Isabella Beecher Hooker," in *Notable American Women, 1607–1950: A Biographical Dictionary,* ed. Edward T. James, Janet Wilson James, and Paul S. Boyer, 3 vols. (Cambridge: Belknap Press of Harvard University Press, 1971), 2:212–14.

52. See "Dr. Ferguson's Letter," 90.

53. Members of both the New England Women's Club and the New York Sorosis, reputed to be the first women's clubs in the United States, organized this association in 1873. It was established to encourage the formation of other

women's clubs whose agendas would be conservative and "home based." Julia Ward Howe, an officer of the AWSA, was a moving party in its organization. Emmeline Wells describes its organization and functions in an article "Julia Ward Howe," *Woman's Exponent* 17 (July 1, 1888): 17–18. For more information on Howe's life, see Paul S. Boyer, "Julia Ward Howe," in James, James, and Boyer, *Notable American Women,* 2:225–29. A more intimate study is Valarie H. Ziegler, *Diva Julia: The Public Romance and Private Agony of Julia Ward Howe* (New York: Trinity Press International, 2003). Ziegler discusses the disconnect between Howe's private and public life.

54. A chapter of the American association was organized in Utah under the direction of the editor of the *Anti-Polygamy Standard,* Jennie Froiseth, a long-time friend of Julia Ward Howe. Howe had assisted Froiseth a decade earlier in organizing a social club for non-Mormon women, the Blue Tea Club. For more information on this club see Patricia Lyn Scott, "Jennie Anderson Froiseth and the Blue Tea," *Utah Historical Quarterly* 71 (Winter 2003): 20–35.

55. Anthony limited her fairly consistent support of Mormon women to protect her own reputation. Romania B. Pratt, "Woman Suffrage Convention," *Woman's Exponent* 10 (March 1, 1882): 146. Some years later, Emmeline Wells did indeed write one of the chapters on Utah, Susa Young Gates writing a second. See Emmeline B. Wells, "Utah," in *History of Woman Suffrage,* vol. 4, ed. Susan B. Anthony and Ida H. Harper (New York: Susan B. Anthony, 1902), 936–56; and Susa Young Gates, "Utah," in *History of Woman Suffrage,* ed. Ida Husted Harper, vol. 6 (New York: National American Woman Suffrage Association, 1922), 644–50.

56. "Mormon Women Missionaries," *National Citizen and Ballot Box* 6 (September 1881): 3.

57. L. John Nuttall (Secretary to the First Presidency) to George Q. Cannon, January 1, 1882, John Taylor Family Collection, Manuscript Division, Special Collections, J. Willard Marriott Library, University of Utah, Salt Lake City. See also Wells, Diary, December 30, 1881.

58. Wells, Diary, November 22, 1881. Emmeline's relationship with George Q. Cannon had taken on a personal dimension when her daughter Annie married his son John Q. the previous year.

59. George Q. Cannon, a member of the LDS Church's First Presidency, had served as Utah's delegate to Congress since 1872. His reelection in 1882 was nullified in March of that year by the Edmunds Act, which prohibited polygamists from voting or holding office. His replacement, John T. Caine,

was a monogamist; his wife, Margaret Nightingale Caine, was an active suffragist. One historian, who has studied this volatile period and Cannon's role during his decade of representing Utah, has characterized him as the LDS Church's "most astute political strategist." Whatever his personal ambitions, his primary effort in Congress always centered on protecting the Church and maintaining the viability of its principles and practices. See Bitton, *George Q. Cannon: A Biography,* 248–62.

60. Wells, Diary, December 2, 1881.

61. See "Home Affairs," *Woman's Exponent* 11 (January 15, 1883): 124.

62. "Convention of the National Woman Suffrage Association at Omaha," *Woman's Exponent* 11 (October 15, 1882): 76; "From Omaha to Atcheson," *Woman's Exponent* 11 (October 15, 1882): 79; and "Lady Speakers at Omaha," *Woman's Exponent* 11 (November 1, 1882): 87–88.

63. The two women, along with Matilda Joslyn Gage, finished the first two volumes in just two years, working together in Stanton's New Jersey home. Stanton found the process a welcome relief from twelve years of lecturing "from Maine to Texas." For her part, Anthony found the work tedious and was eager to get back into the crusade. "My large room with a bay-window is the literary workshop," Stanton wrote, "and there Susan and I sit vis-a-vis, laughing, talking, squabbling, day in and day out, buried in illegible manuscript, old newspapers and reams of yellow sheets. . . . My only regret is that we have not more experience in book-making." Theodore Stanton and Harriot Stanton Blatch, eds., *Elizabeth Cady Stanton as Revealed in Her Letters, Diary, and Reminiscences,* 2 vols. (New York: Harper and Brothers, 1922), 2:181, 187.

64. Stanton and Blatch, *Elizabeth Cady Stanton,* 169.

65. Anthony had long explored ways to enlarge the suffrage constituency. Even a decade later, when she had built a strong coalition of women's associations, she lamented the small number of women belonging to the national suffrage association (seventeen thousand) compared with forty thousand in the National Federation of Women's Clubs and half a million in the Women's Christian Temperance Union. See "Organization among Women as an Instrument in Promoting the Interests of Political Liberty," in *The World Congress of Representative Women,* ed. May Wright Sewall (Chicago: Rand, McNally, 1894), 463–66, as quoted in Ellen Carol DuBois, ed., *Elizabeth Cady Stanton, Susan B. Anthony, Correspondence, Writings, Speeches* (New York: Schocken Books, 1981), 176–77, also 196n21.

66. Stanton and many other first-generation suffragists feared a religious domination of the organization by the new members and a blurring of the

religious and political separation they had been careful to maintain. Moreover, they had assiduously dissociated themselves from the temperance movement as a matter of political expedience. See Kathleen Barry, *Susan B. Anthony: A Biography of a Singular Feminist* (New York: New York University Press, 1988), 292–96.

67. Joan Smyth Iversen discusses this growing alliance with moral reformers in *The Anti-Polygamy Controversy in U.S. Woman's Movements, 1880–1925: A Debate on the American Home* (New York: Garland, 1997), 159–84.

68. Peggy Pascoe analyzes the work of these women in *Relations of Rescue: The Search for Female Moral Authority in the American West, 1874–1939* (New York: Oxford University Press, 1990). See also Iversen, *Anti-Polygamy Controversy*, 104–5.

69. Katharine Anthony details these developments in *Susan B. Anthony: Her Personal History and Her Era* (Garden City, N.Y.: Doubleday, 1954), 351–52. See also DuBois, *Elizabeth Cady Stanton, Susan B. Anthony, Correspondence, Writings, Speeches*, 170–75. It is somewhat ironic that these conservative societies allied themselves with the National rather than the more conservative American suffrage association, especially given the feelings some members had toward Anthony and Stanton, who seemed too radical to them. It is to Anthony's credit that her powers of persuasion won them over.

70. As quoted in Anthony, *Susan B. Anthony: Her Personal History and Her Era*, 351–52.

71. Susan B. Anthony to Elizabeth Harbert, July 7, 1880, as quoted in Barry, *Susan B. Anthony: A Biography*, 288.

72. Rachel Foster (Avery), an active suffragist since 1879, was a companion to Susan B. Anthony for twenty-five years. She helped to organize the 1888 meeting at which the International Council of Women was organized and served for five years as its corresponding secretary. She was instrumental in the merger of the American and National Woman Suffrage Associations and continued to be active in various capacities in the suffrage movement. Avery, May Wright Sewall, and Carrie Chapman Catt were star players among the second-generation suffragists. See Christopher Lasch, "Rachel G. Foster Avery," in James, James, and Boyer, *Notable American Women*, 1:71–72.

73. An opposing voice is noted by Joan Iversen, who recounts a debate at the 1881 suffrage convention in Omaha, in which an Edward Rosewater, using Emmeline Wells's statement of belief in polygamy as a divine principle, discredited the argument that suffrage advanced woman's position since woman's vote in Utah was supporting a practice degrading to women. From the

Nebraska Constitutional Amendment Campaign, Debate, *Omaha Bee,* October 18, 1882, clipping in Stanton-Anthony Papers, Library of Congress. See Iversen, *Anti-Polygamy Controversy,* 100–131.

 74. In the 1882 and 1884 NWSA conventions, Lockwood had claimed the illegality of the Edmunds Act and the proposed new Edmunds Bill, noting the constitutional implications of limiting the voting rights of a particular class of people. Her speech drew the ire of Susan B. Anthony, who felt she had stepped beyond the movement's legitimate concerns. Lockwood nonetheless continued to be a champion of the Mormons, receiving their accolades even as she lost the confidence of her suffrage sisters. Her speeches were reprinted in the *Woman's Exponent.*

 75. See, for example, Matilda Joslyn Gage, "Utah Letter," *National Citizen and Ballot Box* 5 (August 1880): 3.

 76. "The Test Case," *Woman's Exponent* 11 (October 1, 1882): 65, 66, 68.

Chapter 9

Grace in Defeat

*It is the time of proving
and to those who can endure the reward will be sure.*[1]

Passage of the Edmunds Bill in 1882 marked an important victory for antipolygamists, particularly members of the Anti-Polygamy Society of Utah, their national associates, and their male allies in Utah and Washington.[2] Working in partnership with the non-Mormon clergy and federal officials in Utah, their agents and attorneys in Washington, and women of the home mission movement, the Anti-Polygamy Society had achieved its two-fold mission: to arouse public attention to the problem of polygamy and to move Congress to legislate against it. Moral and political arguments proved to be more convincing than constitutional or religious appeals.

While the disfranchisement of polygamists by the Edmunds Act, passed a few months before the 1882 Omaha meeting of the National Woman Suffrage Association's (NWSA) executive committee, lessened the stigma of supporting woman's vote in Utah, the new relationship of NWSA with social reform organizations, especially the Women's Christian Temperance Union (WCTU) and its dynamic leader Frances Willard, had begun to weaken the association with Mormon women.[3] During a trip to Salt Lake City soon after the Edmunds Bill had passed, Frances Willard recorded in her diary that she had visited with "three

Mormon ladies," who happened to be Emmeline Wells, Zina D. H. Young, and Romania Pratt, all of whom she did not realize were Mormons. After learning who they were, Willard declared that "all were bright women, leaders of their church."[4]

Since the visit happened to occur on election day, both Emmeline and Zina Young mentioned to Willard that they were unable to vote because they were plural wives. To this unsolicited comment, she quickly retorted, "On that question I have my own opinion, but the temperance work is the only reform about which I care to express myself in Utah."[5] She made no mention of her written endorsement of Jennie Froiseth's antipolygamy book, *The Women of Mormonism,* published that same year. Because of Willard's influential position, her personal aversion toward polygamy and polygamists, despite passage of the Edmunds Act, easily perpetuated anti-Mormon sentiment not only within the NWSA but also within the National Council of Women (NCW), which she headed after it was organized a few years later.

Frances Willard, president of the Woman's Christian Temperance Union (1879–92) and head of the National Council of Women in the United States (1888–91), was an outspoken critic of polygamy. Willard visited Emmeline Wells and others during her visit to Salt Lake City in 1882.

The successful passage of the Edmunds Bill in 1882 prompted the Anti-Polygamy Society to disband and to terminate publication of its organ, the *Anti-Polygamy Standard,* published since 1880.[6] But antipolygamy sentiment was hardly dead. Utahns Jennie Froiseth and Cornelia Paddock, both of them authors of best-selling antipolygamy novels, began lecturing around the country, promoting their books.[7] They capitalized on the topic already exploited by Ann Eliza Webb, divorced wife of Brigham Young, whose titillating tales of her life in polygamy attracted large audiences.[8]

Kate Field was probably one of the most popular lecturers on this topic on the Chautauqua circuit, which sponsored traveling lecturers on issues of the day. Field visited Utah in 1884–85 to make her own assessments of polygamy and the Mormons. Her subsequent career confirmed Ann Eliza Webb's experience that both fame and fortune could be made on the lecture circuit, particularly with a topic as sensational as plural marriage.[9] Her first contact in Utah was with Emmeline Wells. Field carried with her a letter of introduction from popular author Helen Hunt Jackson, a previous visitor, who had written favorably of her visit among the Mormons and of Emmeline Wells.[10] Wells introduced Field to most of the leading sisters in the city, arranged social entertainments among a variety of Mormons, and included her in an intimate family birthday party for Emmeline's husband, Daniel. Field also attended Sunday services in the Tabernacle, collected and read numerous books on Mormonism, and discussed the Church at length with Elder Charles W. Penrose. She interviewed hundreds of Latter-day Saint women during her eight-month visit. Before leaving, Field assured Emmeline that she had no intention of lecturing on the religion or culture; rather, she said, she simply wanted to make her own appraisal of Mormon life. During those eight months, however, she had also spent time with Governor Eli Murray, Cornelia Paddock, and other non-Mormons whose viewpoints more closely corresponded with her own preconceived opinions.

To Emmeline's chagrin, Field lost little time in turning her experience among the Mormons into a verbal exposé that captivated her audiences. In a letter to Emmeline, she apologized for breaking her promise, explaining that "because of the intercessions of the people she had consented to give one or two lectures."[11] Those "one or two" talks were merely the beginning of a wildly successful lecture tour in which Field denounced women's culpability in their own "degradation," and berated woman suffrage as a prop for Mormon political control. While

Emmeline nursed her sense of betrayal, Kate Field became one of the nation's most famous anti-Mormon lecturers. The Edmunds Act had severely curtailed the political activities of Latter-day Saint polygamists but had neither eliminated the practice nor its popularity as a lecture topic.

Antipolygamists could not complain that the Edmunds Act had been ineffectual since it clearly enabled the law to punish both male and female polygamists by withholding the vote and public office. But the other smarting issue was Mormon political dominance in Utah territory and what many perceived as the establishment of a theocracy within a democratic society. Even the removal of twelve thousand names from the voting lists did not seriously diminish Mormon political power.[12] The repeal of woman suffrage, a means of further reducing that political hegemony, continued to be the target of anti-Mormons.

At the 1884 NWSA convention, Utah was still on the agenda. Though neither Annie Godbe nor Emmeline Wells attended, they both sent letters at Susan B. Anthony's request to explain their versions of conditions in Utah following the Edmunds Act. For Annie Godbe, the Act had been ineffective and was only a token measure at suppressing plural marriage or the Church's political control. Women still constituted nearly half of the Mormon electorate, a political reality Annie found oppressive. Although she was herself a suffragist, she favored removing the vote from Utah women to secure better political equity.[13] This quietly accelerating position—by a small contingent of women reformers, including some suffragists—was acquiring more vocal adherents.

Emmeline's report, as expected, condemned the Edmunds Act, refuted claims that women dared not vote their own conscience, and reemphasized the fact that secret ballots enabled women to vote independently. Asserting the intelligence and political astuteness of Mormon women, she emphatically denied that they were the political clones of their husbands or fathers.[14] But many antipolygamists, including the newly appointed Utah Commission, charged with overseeing Utah elections, continued to argue that Mormon women voted only as Church leaders dictated. Emmeline particularly resented that claim. "Intelligent, consistent women will naturally vote for those, who maintain the institutions which they believe to be for the highest elevation of the human race," she countered. "Mormon women vote for their own highest interest, and the men who they believe will best subserve that interest." Would they actually be expected "to vote for men who persecute and denounce them, and who are continually urging upon Congress the necessity of severe measures in dealing with [them]?" she wondered.[15] Moreover, could not non-Mormon women, or indeed anyone, be charged with the same self-serving voting behavior?

Annie Godbe, however, found many compatriots in her quest to rescind woman's vote in Utah. One such woman, Angelina (Angie) Newman, head of the Woman's Home Mission Society (WHMS) of the Methodist-Episcopal Church and well-known lecturer, made her first visit to Utah that same year, 1884. While there, she and Cornelia Paddock drew up a formal petition calling for the disfranchisement of Utah women. Convinced that woman suffrage was meant to "neutralize the voices of non-Mormons" and "to perpetuate the religious bondage and domestic slavery of the women so enfranchised," Newman and WHMS enlisted the support of Republican Senator George F. Hoar to present their petition to Congress recommending removal of the vote from all Utah women.[16] Explaining the petition in a May issue of the *Woman's Journal,* Paddock exclaimed: "The entire Gentile population, both men and women, are willing to be disfranchised, and to have the Territory governed by a commission."[17]

Emmeline Wells was quick to report to her readers that Paddock's assertion evoked immediate rebuttals from Sarah A. Cooke, of the Anti-Polygamy Society, and Jennie Froiseth, who both remained committed to woman suffrage.[18] The petition drew the ire of national suffragists and caused a rift among non-Mormon suffragists in Utah.

After 1884, Emmeline was no longer a vice president of NWSA for Utah. She was replaced at different times by Cornelia Paddock, Jennie Froiseth, Sarah Cooke, and Annie Godbe, but Sarah Cooke's death in 1885 and Cornelia Paddock's campaign to disfranchise Utah women removed their names from the executive roster. In 1899, a year before the two suffrage associations merged, Jennie Froiseth and Cornelia

Paddock left NWSA and joined the American Woman Suffrage Association (AWSA).

Meanwhile, Emmeline faced some disruptions of her own. The first was the loss of her files and office furniture when the water pipes in the building that housed the *Woman's Exponent* office burst. Then, within days of returning to her rehabilitated office, a fire broke out and again created havoc, destroying more of her papers, correspondence, and copies of the *Exponent*.[19]

But work had long served as her emotional crutch, and even amidst the loss occasioned by these two disasters, she continued to passionately decry the withdrawal of political liberties. "The persecution of a people because of their religion," Emmeline wrote soon after the Edmunds Bill passed, "in a land of free thought and 'the birthplace of free religious liberty' plainly proves 'the times are out of joint.'"[20] The strengthening anti-Mormon movement was beginning to erode her natural optimism.

Emmeline repeatedly reminded her readers that Latter-day Saints "are having daily manifestations to convince them that the Lord meant what He said when He declared that He would have a tried people."[21] And tried they were as they faced the revocation of many of their civil liberties, the breakup of their families, the imprisonment of their fathers and husbands, and ultimately the confiscation of the Church's financial underpinnings. But she nonetheless offered hope to her readers, as she had expressed it earlier for herself. "Disappointment cometh not in vain," one of her poems promised. "Life's richest treasures oft are bought with pain."[22] To her *Exponent* readers, Emmeline declared that their suffering, individually and collectively, would not go unheeded, and she reassuringly declared that "these are good times for Zion, even if severe tests have come, it is the time of proving, and to those who can endure the reward will be sure."[23] Emmeline Wells was a survivor and her optimism for the future was never wholly extinguished, despite her own and the Church's trials.

The antipolygamy struggle and the need to defend and provide a rationale for a religious principle, when religious reasons failed to convince their detractors, developed in Mormon women a self-image that defied the belittling comments from the press, pulpit, and rostrum.[24] They had faithfully and unitedly resisted the forceful power of the state to regulate their religious lives; they had become articulate and confident advocates for their religious beliefs; and they had long before proven the strength of their convictions as they left homes and families to join this new religious movement, for which they could sacrifice again. They were, if anything, martyrs to their cause, nourished by the self-vindication that suffering for a belief yields to its adherents. They had lost the battle for woman's vote, but they felt certain that they would rise triumphant from their trials.

Despite her own loss of the ballot, Emmeline continued to argue for woman suffrage, not only on the basis of justice but also for its social usefulness. "It is not alone because of unjust taxation and a desire to stand equal with their husbands and brothers," she wrote in 1884, "but it is for the better protection of the home, the foundation of all good government that women are asking and interceding for political rights."[25] With twelve years experience as an enfranchised woman, she could write with authority that "a woman who goes to the polls and deposits a ballot, feels her political independence and that she is virtually part and parcel of the great body politic, not through her father or husband, but in her own vested right."[26] It was a bitter blow, psychologically as well as politically, to lose that sense of individual identity and political accountability when the Edmunds Act deprived her of the vote.

In November 1885, Emmeline decided to take a long-postponed nostalgic journey to her native Massachusetts to visit relatives she had not seen since leaving as a young bride more than forty years earlier. During her trip, she made time to interview writers such as John Greenleaf Whittier, whom she was fond of quoting; Elizabeth Stuart Phelps, who dismissed her after learning she was a Latter-day Saint; and Charlotte Fowler Wells, editor of the *Phrenological Journal,* who had elicited Emmeline's admiration by managing her publishing house so successfully.[27]

After visiting her family in North New Salem, still a small rural hamlet, Emmeline traveled to Boston, hoping to meet Lucy Stone and her husband, Henry Blackwell, despite their fervent anti-Mormon feelings. She also wanted to meet their daughter, Alice Stone Blackwell, who had visited Utah in 1883 but had been hosted by only gentile women. Thus, with equal amounts of determination and trepidation, she visited the office of the *Woman's Journal*. Henry Blackwell, who assisted at various times in editing the *Journal,* happened to be in the office and greeted Emmeline, who found him to be "very cordial in his manner." Even more surprising, he invited her to dinner with his family.[28] He was probably as curious to visit with this Mormon woman with whom he had so long sparred in their respective papers, as she was to meet him and his illustrious wife. The invitation to their home, however, was far more than Emmeline had expected, and she eagerly accepted.

At the Stone-Blackwell home in Naponset, a short train ride from Boston, Emmeline found her hosts congenial and gracious. They discussed the pending new Edmunds Bill, which had recently passed the Senate, agreeing that the sections confiscating LDS Church property and disfranchising all Utah women were "unjust and unconstitutional."[29] Had polygamy not been such a divisive element between the two women, they might have become fast friends. In their conversation they discovered many things that would easily have engendered an enduring relationship. Their love of New England gave them much in common, and it was satisfying to Emmeline to learn that Lucy and Emmeline's mother shared Brookfield, Massachusetts, as their birthplace. Both Lucy and Emmeline were single-minded in the causes they pursued; both were self-supporting despite their married status; both stood firm in unconventional marriages; and both were articulate and persuasive speakers and writers. Lucy and Emmeline commanded the forum of their own newspapers, and both were unyielding in their convictions.[30]

The conviviality of the evening, however, did not temper the Stone-Blackwell view toward polygamy, and Emmeline remained to them a public symbol of the offensive practice. This became evident two years later in May 1888 when Emmeline, thinking the power of personal contact had softened their anti-Mormon attitude, wrote a glowing tribute to Lucy Stone and AWSA in the *Woman's Exponent*. "I fell in love with her the moment I saw her," Emmeline confessed to her readers, "and shall never forget how my heart went out to her."[31]

Though Lucy Stone undoubtedly read the complimentary words, they did not deter her from expressing her unabated disdain for Mormonism. Three months later, in a private letter to Frances Willard, newly elected president of the National Council of Women (NCW), Lucy Stone admitted that she had resisted allowing AWSA to join the newly organized council because it had permitted Mormon women to attend its organizing meeting. Moreover, it had allowed a "particular Mormon woman," identified as Emmeline, to become a life member, assuring that her name "stands secured in the [Executive] Committee for the Council."[32] Perhaps unaware of Lucy Stone's personal antagonism toward her, Emmeline never ceased to admire her as an unflinching pioneer and advocate of woman's rights.[33]

In January 1886, following her New England visit, Emmeline traveled to Washington, D.C. Congress was debating a new bill sponsored by Senator George Edmunds, already passed by the Senate. Anti-Mormon sentiment was rampant in Washington. Emmeline chose not to attend the annual convention of the NWSA in such a hostile environment, but she did meet with Susan B. Anthony, whom she had not seen since 1882. Emmeline was no longer certain of her relationship with her longtime co-worker, given the strong anti-Mormon bias of the new members of the NWSA. She was thus relieved to find that Anthony had no intention of withdrawing her support from what was rapidly becoming a hopeless struggle to maintain woman suffrage in Utah. Emmeline also met long-time suffragist Hamilton Wilcox, who gave her "much advice."[34]

Two other meetings consumed her time in Washington, one with John T. Caine, Utah's delegate to Congress, with whom she discussed the pending legislation, and the other with Rose Cleveland, President Grover Cleveland's sister, then acting as his official hostess. The two women discovered a shared love of the writings of George Eliot, the subject of a book Rose Cleveland had recently authored.[35] Emmeline also hoped to influence the new president through Rose, as she had hoped to do with Lucy Hayes, seven years earlier. Wells reportedly gave Rose Cleveland "the whole theory and principle, lock, stock and barrel, of the Mormon religion, waxing quite eloquent." But Miss Cleveland was unimpressed. "It is very beautiful, the way you regard it," she was reputed to have said, "but of course I do not agree with you or regard it as you do."[36] Emmeline was learning that her style of personal politics went a long way in establishing friendships and instilling respect but it could not alter the course of events nor the aversion to polygamy, as she had so earnestly hoped. The good it did, however, was not as evident to her then as it later proved to be.

With little more to be done in Washington, Emmeline looked homeward, anticipating stopping at sites along the way that were important in LDS Church history, such as Kirtland, Ohio, and Nauvoo, Illinois, her home for two years. From Cleveland, she wearily acknowledged in a letter to her grandnephew Orson F. Whitney, "I am beginning to long for home and a sight of the loved ones there more and more." She felt she had once more done the best she could to help her people. "While in Washington (and making an effort at least,) to do something for our people, that I might prove loyal to the cause I so devotedly love," she explained, "I felt that I could endure absence from home and even privation, [had it] been necessary, at any rate scorn and ridicule for the sake of vindicating principle, and proclaiming truth."[37] But she was returning far less sanguine than she ever had been before.

Meanwhile, as Emmeline retraced the westward journey of the Mormons, Utahns Isabella Horne, Sarah Kimball, and Romania Pratt expressed their desire to Church President John Taylor to "publicly protest against the indignities inflicted on plural wives in the district courts."[38] In the mass meeting that followed, the three women vented their indignation. "Women are arrested and forcibly taken before sixteen men and plied with questions that no decent woman can hear without a blush," ran their protest. "If they decline to answer, they are imprisoned in the Penitentiary as though they were criminals." The three women cited cases where their Mormon sisters had been incarcerated and recounted the humiliating treatment to which plural wives had been subjected.[39] The three women also protested against the movement to deprive them of the vote. "What have we done that we should thus be treated as felons?" they asked. Acknowledging that no woman "living with a bigamist, polygamist, or person cohabiting with more than one woman," was then able to vote, why, they wondered, should those women "against whom nothing can be charged," also be disfranchised?[40] The Latter-day Saint women put their protests in a memorial, hopefully to counteract the efforts of Angie Newman and others then lobbying Congress on behalf of Senator Edmunds's new bill, which was much more punitive than his 1882 bill. Not only did it propose rescinding the vote of all Utah women, it struck at the financial foundation of the Church, severely crippling its ability to function. The final resolution of the memorial reasserted the female bond, a theme that sang out in all their appeals for relief: "Resolved: That we will call upon the wives and mothers of the United States to come to our help in resisting these encroachments upon our liberties and these outrages upon our peaceful homes and family relations."[41] Such an appeal had long met only silence, since most American wives and mothers believed Latter-day Saint women had brought these outrages upon themselves when they agreed to become plural wives. That attitude did not deter Latter-day Saint women from appealing to the compassion of other women. But always to no avail. Emmeline learned of the women's rally in Salt Lake City, and after reaching Chicago she sent a letter home, expressing her own indignation at Senator Edmunds's new proposal to revoke women's right to vote and denounce the arbitrary methods of federal officials.[42]

At the conclusion of the rally, Salt Lake City stake president Angus M. Cannon, likely at the instigation of the rally's leaders, most of whom lived in his stake, suggested to Church President John Taylor that he send two women to Washington with the memorial. President Taylor thought that Emmeline Wells might be persuaded to return to Washington and present the memorial to Congress along with Dr. Ellen Ferguson, who had entree to a number of influential eastern women.[43] Hoping to intercept Emmeline, he sent a telegram, which reached her in Kansas City. She loyally, if reluctantly, agreed to return to Washington, where she met Dr. Ferguson as well as Emily Richards and Emily's sister-in-law Josephine West, who were in Washington with their husbands.

Once again Emmeline would strive to temper the provisions of the pending legislation, including the revocation of woman suffrage. She also hoped to contravene the petition by Angie Newman for means to establish a home of refuge for plural wives in Utah, a proposal viewed by Latter-day Saints as a waste of federal money and an insulting gesture. Emmeline Wells's response to Newman's efforts showed a growing exasperation with the proposals made by a virtual army of antipolygamy women. "Is it not time," she wearily wrote, "that woman as a rational being aroused herself to the imperative duties of the age and by every exertion possible maintain the rights of women as a class to self protection? Is there not work enough for women to do among their sisters in the world without reaching away over to Utah to hunt out a few plural wives, who have homes and children around them honorably born?"[44]

Congress's rapid response to Newman's petition, in the form of a $40,000 allocation to build the home, followed by generous stipends to furnish and maintain it, not only showed polygamy's high priority as a congressional issue, but might also be construed as a salve to the nation's conscience for the decimation of Latter-day Saint families. This had already begun with the Edmunds Act and would become even more invasive with legislation passing in 1887 as the Edmunds-Tucker Act.

The situation, Emmeline saw, was deeply ironic. Even as Newman and her associates petitioned for this compassionate use of federal funds, they continued to apply every strategy available to them to pass legislation that would disrupt polygamous families, thus creating the "terrible exigencies" the petition for a home was designed to assuage.[45] For Emmeline, the petition was an offensive measure, and she predicted, with remarkable accuracy, that there would be few residents in the new home.[46]

Emmeline Wells and Ellen Ferguson presented the Mormon women's memorial to President Cleveland who, Emmeline reported, read it all the way through.[47] Senator William Blair of New Hampshire then presented it to the Senate and requested that it be printed in full in the Congressional Record. Representative Long of Massachusetts presented it to the House. "The wrongs and grievances have been heard, but the redress asked for may be very slow in coming," Emmeline presciently reported to her readers. "The prejudice is exceedingly strong."[48]

Most important was the hearing before the Judiciary Committee, chaired by John Randolph Tucker, whom Emmeline found to be "a very kindly and wise man—a southern gentleman, largehearted and full of that chivalry towards women which seems so thoroughly natural to the 'old Virginians.'" Besides LDS Church attorney Franklin S. Richards, Joseph A. West and John T. Caine (Utah's congressional delegate) spoke against the proposed new Edmunds Bill, citing its unconstitutionality as well as the familial and social disruption it would impose. Robert N. Baskin, a notable non-Mormon from Utah, who was a major lobbyist for anti-Mormon legislation, spoke in its favor. Throughout the long hearing, Emmeline was impressed with Chairman Tucker and informed her readers that "he deserves gratitude for the unprejudicial and unbiased spirit he manifested throughout the entire proceedings."[49] Because of his sympathetic manner and earlier opposition on constitutional grounds to the original Edmunds Act of 1882, she was stunned when he shepherded the new bill through the House and allowed his name to be coupled with Senator Edmunds's in its final version the following year.[50]

John Randolph Tucker (ca. 1870–80), senator from Virginia, lent his name to the Edmunds-Tucker Bill in 1887. This bill disfranchised women in Utah and confiscated LDS Church property, among other punitive measures.

Library of Congress

While Emmeline was in Washington she took time to meet Caleb W. West, newly appointed governor of Utah Territory, then awaiting Senate confirmation. She was rather hopeful about his approach to Utah politics and the possibility of his being a helpful antidote to the strong anti-Mormonism of former Governor Eli Murray. She and her companions also attended Elder Lorenzo Snow's appeal in the Supreme Court, which had extensive implications for plural-wife families. Convicted on three separate instances of unlawful cohabitation, a legal distinction known as "segregation" that tripled the punishment originally allocated for that criminal offense, Snow was seeking a decision on the action's legality. A year earlier the Court had dismissed the case on the grounds that it did not have appropriate jurisdiction. However, this second appeal, brought on a writ of habeas corpus, was successful in getting a hearing and, to the delight of the appellant, a favorable verdict. The Supreme Court ruled that only a single indictment of unlawful cohabitation could be brought against any one defendant, a small concession in the ongoing prosecution of polygamists.[51]

Emmeline Wells was under no illusions after this second foray into Washington politics. "Everything done here in presenting facts and seeking to remove prejudice," she wrote to her readers at home, "seems only a drop in the ocean of public sentiment arrayed against a people struggling with the effects of falsehood and misrepresentation."[52] For some time she had seen little probability of forestalling new antipolygamy legislation and thus focused her energies on preserving woman suffrage and especially legal protection for plural wives and their children.

She was somewhat encouraged in this effort by a renewed outcry against the motion to rescind Utah women's voting rights. The *Woman's Tribune,* the organ of NWSA, consistently voiced its opposition and even reported favorably on the mass rally in Utah, reprinting its resolutions.[53] The Executive Session of the NWSA convention drafted resolutions condemning the action of Congress in unjustly "punishing Gentile and non-polygamous Mormon women for crimes never committed."[54] Clara Colby, editor of the *Woman's Tribune,* attacked Angie Newman personally, asking her, "On what tenable and safe grounds can the proposed disfranchisement be brought about? Is it because they hold opinions which are different from those of these petitioners that they are to be disfranchised?"[55] Colby was joined by Matilda Gage, Lillie Devereux Blake, Belva Lockwood, and even Henry Blackwell, who pointed out the discriminatory basis of the bill. Letters submitted to the *Woman's Tribune* added more voices to the denunciation of the proposed legislation.[56]

Several Washington newspapers also proved to be sympathetic. The *Christian Union* called for an investigation into the sufferings of Utah women and their families already sustained from the 1882 Edmunds Act before enacting any further punitive legislation. The *Washington Critic* published a letter from a one-time admirer of Kate Field, the popular lecture circuit speaker, which expressed his disillusionment with Field and declared his belief that the Mormon women then in Washington "are better qualified to determine their own fate than anyone else." The *National Republican* published an interview with Emmeline and her companions, finding the four women to be "well-favored, agreeable and intelligent women."[57] All of the answers to the reporter's questions were printed in full, allowing the women an opportunity to dispel some of the myths and misunderstandings about Latter-day Saint women. Their presence caused "not a little comment," according to one account, and the newspapers took full advantage of the public interest they aroused.[58]

Emmeline returned home on May 17, 1886, having been gone since December of the previous year. It had been an extremely eventful trip, and she was elated by the visits she had made to her family and literary friends but discouraged and resigned to the fate of her people. As she had done repeatedly before, she reminded her readers that "again and again in ancient and modern revelation has the Lord said He would have a tried people . . . therefore, the Saints should not murmur as did Ancient Israel lest they lose sight of 'the prize of the high calling.'"[59] And of those who mounted the unrelenting battle against the Mormons she opined, "Those who live longest will see in the finale of the present controversy and persecutions now raging, ostensibly in consequence of the practice of a principle that was taught and practiced by holy men of old, that it will appear that office-seeking, political place and power, and mammon were the real motives that caused the raid against the 'Mormons.'"[60] In her denunciation, Emmeline departed from the moral and constitutional defense she had always mounted in hinting at a more sinister motive to the campaign.

The assignment of ulterior motives reflects that of the *Washington Capital* in 1879, which facetiously suggested that polygamists would continue to be prosecuted, "for they are guilty of owning some rich silver mines in Utah, and we Christians want them. Therefore we cannot abide [their] polygamous conduct. Our pious souls are filled with wrath, and will so continue until we dispossess these sinners of their ill-gotten wealth and many wives."[61]

Finally, in March 1887, without President Cleveland's signature, the Edmunds-Tucker Bill became law. Utah women lost the vote; the material base of the LDS Church was impaired; and plural marriage was essentially doomed as a Latter-day Saint religious practice.[62] John Randolph Tucker, the southern gentleman whom Emmeline had so admired, having reversed his earlier position against the Edmunds Bill, gave strength to the new bill by supporting all of its provisions, giving it his name, and even going so far as to suggest another bill providing for a constitutional amendment outlawing polygamy. While they warranted admiration from many quarters for this final legislative step in bringing the LDS Church in line with American society, for Mormons George F. Edmunds and John Randolph Tucker would always carry a badge of opprobrium.

The long battle over polygamy and woman suffrage had been waged on many fronts. The challenge posed by the LDS Church encompassed the political, judicial, legislative, religious, and social arenas of American life and brought into question constitutional issues of individual rights, Congressional power, separation of church and state, state rights, and the guarantees of the First Amendment. The battle had given prominence to lawyers, judges, politicians, and clergymen, whose names would otherwise have been peripheral to nineteenth-century history. It had prompted a debate on the extent of legal and judicial authority over the private lives of individuals. It also had opened up fields of expression to women as writers, journalists, and lecturers, on both sides of the Mormon question, and fostered a genre of sensational literary fiction. The practice of plural marriage had been a primary target for a national "purity" campaign, engaging the interest and efforts of thousands of women across the country. Moreover, the battle had kept woman suffrage on the Congressional agenda with far more consistency and immediacy than it may otherwise have had.

The fallout for Latter-day Saints, however, was deeply personal, striking at the most sacred of their institutions: their religion and their families. The adjustment that necessarily followed was long lasting and replete with long-foreseen difficulties. As a benediction to the intense and troublesome fray, the two most visible exponents of polygamy, Church President John Taylor and Relief Society General President Eliza R. Snow, both died in 1887, sharing the death knell of a principle that had been central to their lives.

Though some modern historians have levied criticism that LDS Church leaders manipulated both their own women and gentile suffragists in their confrontation with the government over polygamy, neither national nor local suffragists could be construed as pawns, maneuvered by the stratagem of religious leaders. Plural wives were no less committed to the Church and plural marriage than their husbands or Church leaders. Mormon women were inseparable partners in defense of what they persistently maintained was a divine mandate and a constitutional guarantee. Realistically, women had far more to lose than men if their marriages were invalidated and their children illegitimatized. Mormon women's defense of the practice was thus fervent and personal. Most of all, these were men and women inextricably bound by the shared uprooting that conversion to the Latter-day Saint religion had required. Church members knew the wrenching feeling of repeated removals, including a thousand-mile westward journey in search of a hospitable environment. They had suffered from the lack of protection from an indifferent government, including a state government in whose protective custody the religion's founding prophet had been murdered. This was but one more provocation to "circle the wagons."

When Emmeline Wells approached Church Presidents Brigham Young, John Taylor, or Wilford Woodruff, she respected them as prophets and heeded their authority and counsel, but she also recognized them, and they her, as fellow travelers who had proven themselves physical, emotional, and spiritual equals in allegiance to the cause that had brought them together. Mormon women were not only willing but also essential partners in this long-standing confrontation. Their presence, their petitions, their writings, their lectures all assisted in arousing public empathy, in finding allies, and in building bridges.

As for the national suffragists, indeed, none could ever be characterized as puppets in a power struggle of two equally determined forces, as one historian has claimed.[63] Members of NWSA, particularly, had resisted the Republican Party, their abolitionist associates, and their closest allies when these former suffrage friends put woman suffrage on hold during Reconstruction. They had already risked their reputations for accepting Mormon women and felt the sting of public ridicule. NWSA members could hardly be unwittingly drawn into an alliance with a principle they emphatically disdained. Their eye was always on the prize—woman suffrage—and holding on to it in Utah.

Throughout the long controversy, the NWSA never withdrew its support. Whatever the women in the organization thought had been the reason for granting woman suffrage to Utah women in the first place, and even when the connection to Mormon suffragists became awkward and embarrassing, its support of this stronghold of women voters, though publicly less vocal at times, never ceased. Suffrage was its single concern, and despite the long controversy and years of argument rationalizing the repeal of woman suffrage in Utah, its leaders never capitulated beyond the terms of the Edmunds Act. And they were aware that whatever difficulties it created for the suffrage movement, the "Mormon problem" had brought woman suffrage to the forefront of national debate.

Unable to represent themselves in Congress and with only the power of persuasion available to them in this national struggle, women on both sides of the conflict depended on their ability to convince male lawmakers of the validity of their arguments. Dealing a severe blow, the Edmunds-Tucker Act intensified the drive to embed woman suffrage within the protective folds of the nation's Constitution.

For Emmeline Wells, the long struggle had brought her into partnership with three LDS Church presidents and two Utah congressional delegates. It also forced her to confront senators, congressmen, and even presidents of the United States. The passage of the Edmunds-Tucker Act was not only the ending of an era but also the beginning of a new chapter in her public life, one which showcased all her organizational skills and promised a brighter, more satisfying conclusion.

Notes

1. "Christmas 1888," *Woman's Exponent* 17 (December 15, 1888): 108.
2. Joan Smyth Iversen provides details of the Anti-Polygamy Society's effective mobilization of men and women in the antipolygamy cause in *The Anti-Polygamy Controversy in U.S. Women's Movements, 1880–1925: Debate on the American Home* (New York: Garland, 1997), 108–12.
3. Both Joan Iversen and Lola Van Wagenen discuss this period of transition in their respective studies. See especially Lola Van Wagenen, "Sister-Wives and Suffragists: Polygamy and the Politics of Woman Suffrage, 1870–1896" (PhD diss., New York University, 1994; Provo, Utah: BYU Studies and Joseph Fielding Smith Institute for Latter-day Saint History, 2003), 119–44.
4. The visit is recorded in Frances E. Willard, *Glimpses of Fifty Years: The Autobiography of an American Woman* (Columbus, Ohio: William G. Hubbard, 1890), 326.
5. Willard, *Glimpses of Fifty Years*, 326.
6. Appeals were made to the *Woman's Tribune*, a popular suffrage paper, and endorsed by Utah Governor Eli H. Murray in August 1883 to raise funds to continue publication, but the appeals were unavailing.
7. These Utah novelists were only two among many writers who wrote lurid and sensational best-selling novels about polygamy. Several scholars have identified and analyzed this fiction. See Leonard Arrington and Jon Haupt, "Intolerable Zion: The Image of Mormonism in Nineteenth-Century American Literature," *Western Humanities Review* 22 (Summer 1968): 243–60; Davis Bitton and Gary Bunker, "Double Jeopardy: Visual Images of Mormon Women," *Utah Historical Quarterly* 46 (Spring 1978): 184–202; Karen Lynn (Davidson), "Sensational Virtue: Nineteenth-Century Mormon Fiction and American Popular Taste," *Dialogue: A Journal of Mormon Thought* 14

(Autumn 1981): 102–6; Craig L. Foster, "Victorian Pornographic Imagery in Anti-Mormon Literature," *Journal of Mormon History* 19 (Spring 1993): 115–32. See also Iversen, *Anti-Polygamy Controversy*, 133–57, for a discussion on the discourse of antipolygamists in lectures, sermons, and fiction.

8. See Ann Eliza Young, *Wife No. 19, or The Story of a Life in Bondage, Being a Complete Expose of Mormonism, and Revealing the Sorrows, Sacrifices and Sufferings of Women in Polygamy* (Hartford, Conn.: Dustin, Gilman, 1876). Several studies have been done on Ann Eliza Webb Young. Irving Wallace, *The Twenty-Seventh Wife* (New York: Simon and Schuster, 1961) is the best known; Fawn M. Brodie wrote a short biographical sketch "Ann Eliza Young" in *Notable American Women, 1607–1950: A Biographical Dictionary,* ed. Edward T. James, Janet Wilson James, and Paul S. Boyer, 3 vols. (Cambridge: Belknap Press of Harvard University Press, 1971), 3:696–97.

9. Mary Katherine (Kate) Keemle Field was a journalist, a would-be actress, and a well-known lyceum lecturer on many topics. While disparaging the practice of polygamy, she also declaimed against the ease with which Utah granted divorce, both ecclesiastical and legal, which she declared to be as morally reprehensible as "polygamic marriages." This position put her at odds with Elizabeth Cady Stanton and others who argued that easier egress from debilitating relationships was a woman's rights issue. More information on this volatile and intriguing woman is found in David Baldwin, "Kate Field," in James, James, and Boyer, *Notable American Women*, 1:612–14. Field's lectures on the disgrace of Mormon marriage and divorce is noted in Sarah Barringer Gordon, *The Mormon Question: Polygamy and Constitutional Conflict in Nineteenth-Century America* (Chapel Hill: University of North Carolina Press, 2002), 164–68.

10. Helen Hunt Jackson, "The Women of the Bee-Hive," *Century Magazine* 6 (May 1884): 114–22, esp. 120.

11. A popular lecture of Kate Field's entitled "The Mormon Monster" given in December 1886 was reported by John Irvine of Salt Lake City. A year previous he had enquired of Emmeline about her impressions of Kate Field, since she had been her official hostess during much of her stay in Salt Lake City. This information comes from Emmeline B. Wells's response in a letter to John Irvine, November 11, 1885, Church Archives, The Church of Jesus Christ of Latter-day Saints, Salt Lake City.

12. George Q. Cannon learned that Senator Edmunds was not "seeking so much to put down polygamy as to break down the 'Mormon' system of theocracy." The public furor against polygamy was a convenient tool by which to do so. See Mark W. Cannon, "The Mormon Issue in Congress, 1872–1882:

Drawing on the Experience of Territorial Delegate George Q. Cannon" (PhD diss., Harvard University, 1960), 269, as quoted in Edward Leo Lyman, *Political Deliverance: The Quest for Utah Statehood* (Urbana: University of Illinois Press, 1986), 23, 38n42.

13. *Report of the Sixteenth Washington Convention of the National Woman Suffrage Association* (Rochester, N.Y.: Charles Mann, 1884), 80–81.

14. *Report of the Sixteenth Washington Convention*, 80–81.

15. Emmeline B. Wells, "Woman Suffrage in Utah," *Woman's Exponent* 10 (November 15, 1881): 92.

16. "Petition to Disfranchise Women," *Woman's Exponent* 13 (June 15, 1884): 11.

17. As quoted in "Petition to Disfranchise Women," 11.

18. "Petition to Disfranchise Women," 11.

19. "Editorial Notes," *Woman's Exponent* 12 (May 15, 1884): 189.

20. "The Times Are Out of Joint," *Woman's Exponent* 10 (May 15, 1882): 188.

21. "Retrospective," *Woman's Exponent* 14 (April 15, 1886): 173.

22. "A Glance Backward," in Emmeline B. Wells, *Musings and Memories: Poetry by Emmeline B. Wells* (Salt Lake City: George Q. Cannon and Sons, 1896), 167.

23. "Christmas 1888," *Woman's Exponent* 17 (December 15, 1888): 108.

24. The concept of a developing self-image through the long polygamy conflict is detailed in Gail Casterline, "'In the Toils' or 'Onward to Zion': Images of the Mormon Woman" (master's thesis, Utah State University, 1974).

25. "Suffrage in Utah," *Woman's Exponent* 12 (December 1, 1883): 124.

26. "Sweet Is Liberty," *Woman's Exponent* 11 (March 1, 1883): 148.

27. Emmeline Wells ran an article describing Charlotte Wells's business experiences and success in "Mrs. C. Fowler Wells," *Woman's Exponent* 7 (March 1, 1879): 204. It is doubtful that this Mrs. Wells and Emmeline were related.

28. Emmeline B. Wells, Diary, January 12, 1886, L. Tom Perry Special Collections, Harold B. Lee Library, Brigham Young University, Provo, Utah; see also "A Tribute to Lucy Stone," *Woman's Exponent* 22 (November 15, 1893): 60.

29. Wells, Diary, January 13, 1886.

30. A good biography of Lucy Stone with a description of her unusual relationship with Henry Blackwell is Andrea Moore Kerr, *Lucy Stone: Speaking Out for Equality* (New Brunswick, N.J.: Rutgers University Press, 1992).

31. "American Woman Suffrage Association," *Woman's Exponent* 16 (May 1, 1888): 177. See also "A Tribute to Lucy Stone," *Woman's Exponent* 22 (November 15, 1893): 60.

32. Lucy Stone to Frances Willard, President of the National Council of Women, August 23, 1888, in Leslie Wheeler, ed., *Loving Warriors: Selected Letters of Lucy Stone and Henry B. Blackwell, 1853–1893* (New York: Dial Press, 1981), 314–15, and 393 for identification of Emmeline as the "Mormon woman." Though she did not attend the organizing meeting in 1888, Emmeline later became a patron or life member of NCW by making an initial financial contribution.

33. Emmeline wrote an impressive tribute to Lucy Stone at her death in 1893. See "A Tribute to Lucy Stone," 60. She had been in personal contact with her that summer at the World's Congress of Representative Women, held in conjunction with the Columbian Exposition at the 1893 Chicago World's Fair.

34. Wells, "My Trip East," Diary, January 28, 1886.

35. Rose Cleveland's book, *George Eliot's Poetry, and Other Studies* (New York: Funk and Wagnalls) was published in 1885.

36. Emma Janes, "Washington Gossip," *Philadelphia Press,* May 2, 1886, 6. The *Woman's Exponent* carried a brief article about the manner of receiving guests at Rose Cleveland's regular afternoon receptions. Whether this was the occasion for Emmeline's visit with her is unclear. She may have requested a private interview. "Miss Cleveland's Reception," *Woman's Exponent* 14 (March 1, 1886): 151.

37. Emmeline B. Wells to Bishop Orson F. Whitney, March 2, 1886, Orson F. Whitney Collection, Church Archives.

38. Acknowledged in a letter from John Taylor to Mrs. M. I. Horne, S. M. Kimball, and R. B. Pratt, February 20, 1886, John Taylor Family Collection, Manuscript Division, Special Collections, J. Willard Marriott Library, University of Utah, Salt Lake City.

39. Orson F. Whitney, *History of Utah,* 4 vols. (Salt Lake City: George Q. Cannon and Sons, 1895), 3:492–93. Worse treatment was yet to come. Sarah Gordon notes that the Edmunds-Tucker Act of 1887 gave federal officials another tool to prosecute plural wives in the form of a new statute outlawing adultery and fornication, indicting polygamist men for adultery and their plural wives for fornication. Almost two hundred women were indicted under this statute between 1887 and 1890. See Gordon, *Mormon Question,* 166, 180–81.

40. Whitney, *History of Utah,* 3:495.

41. "The Ladies' Mass Meeting," *Woman's Exponent* 14 (March 1, 1886): 148–49. The rally was held on March 6 but reported in this issue. An added note indicated the paper was issued late in order to report the proceedings of the mass meeting in that particular issue. "Editorial Notes," *Woman's Exponent* 14 (March 1, 1886): 149. During all her trips, Emmeline continued to write her editorials for the *Exponent*. In later years, her daughter Annie occasionally substituted for her.

42. "Letter to the Sisters at Home," *Woman's Exponent* 14 (April 1, 1886): 164.

43. John Taylor to Angus M. Cannon, March 17, 1886, John Taylor Family Papers. Taylor was hopeful that "the presence of two industrious persevering workers of our sisters would be attended with good results."

44. "Notes from Washington," *Woman's Exponent* 14 (May 1, 1886): 181. In Charles Dickens's words, this would be called "telescopic philanthropy" (*Bleak House*). Working under the auspices of the Woman's Home Mission Society of the Methodist-Episcopal Church, founded by Lucy Hayes, as well as the "Mormon Department" of the WCTU, Angie Newman directed her efforts toward the "rescue" of plural wives, persuading Congress to allocate money for what would be called the Industrial Christian Home in Salt Lake City to serve as a refuge and rehabilitation center for them. For more information on Angelia Newman (Angie Newman), see Theodore L. Agnew, "Angelia Louise French Thurston Kilgore," in James, James, and Boyer, *Notable American Women*, 2:620–22. The home never attracted many residents, and to the dismay of Newman and the members of the Home Mission associations who contributed to it, the government appointed a board of directors made up of federal officials in Utah.

45. From a letter by Cornelia Paddock and Mrs. Jacob Boreman to the Senate, quoted in Jeanette Ferry, *Industrial Christian Home Association of Utah* (Salt Lake City: n.p., 1893), 6–11.

46. "Notes from Washington," 181. Besides Ferry's book, see Gustive O. Larson, "An Industrial Home for Polygamous Wives," *Utah Historical Quarterly* 38 (Summer 1970): 263–75. Peggy Pascoe also treats the genesis and demise of the home in *Relations of Rescue: The Search for Female Moral Authority in the American West, 1874–1939* (New York: New York University Press, 1970), 22, 23–26, 28, 29–30, 89–90. Pascoe estimates that no more than 150 residents ever occupied the home before its demise in 1893 with only twenty women and their children living there at any one time. After an initial flurry of interest, applications dwindled, some women citing the difficulties they had with the Matron, Ruth Woods. Pascoe, *Relations of Rescue*, 100–102.

47. "'The Rotunda'—Kirtland—the Memorial," *Woman's Exponent* 14 (April 15, 1886): 169. Emily Richards and Josephine Richards West temporarily joined the two women in their lobbying efforts, but Dr. Ferguson and Emmeline Wells remained until May, meeting with the President and various congressional committees. See Whitney, *History of Utah,* 4:589.

48. "Notes from Washington," 180.

49. "Washington Jottings," *Woman's Exponent* 14 (May 15, 1886): 188.

50. In a letter to the *Woman's Journal,* reprinted in the *Woman's Exponent* 14 (March 1, 1886): 150–51, Hamilton Wilcox, head of the Universal Suffrage Association, urged readers to write in opposition to the revocation of woman suffrage in Utah. He also enumerated Senator Edmunds's positions on a number of current issues including his personal opposition to woman suffrage on the basis that it was degrading to women, his campaign to remove the vote from enfranchised women, and his effort to prevent women from practicing law.

51. Details about the conviction, trials, and appeals of Lorenzo Snow are in Whitney, *History of Utah,* 3:459–77, 537–546. See also Gordon, *Mormon Question,* 159–60.

52. "Notes from Washington," 180.

53. "Mormon Women Protest," *Woman's Tribune* 3 (May 1886): 2.

54. "Report of Executive Sessions of the National Convention," *Woman's Tribune* 3 (April 1886): 2.

55. "The Edmunds Bill," *Woman's Tribune* 3 (July 1886): 2.

56. See, for example, Letter from Mrs. Almedia B. Gray from Schofield, Wisconsin, in "Extracts from Letters to the N.W.S. Convention," *Woman's Tribune* 3 (March 1886): 4; and Letter from Lucinda B. Chandler, "The Declaration of Independence and the Fourteenth Amendment," *Woman's Tribune* 3 (June 1886): 1.

57. As reported in "Mormon Women in Washington," *Deseret Evening News,* May 7, 1886, 4.

58. See "Mormon Women in Washington," 4. See also "The Ladies' Memorial," *Deseret Evening News,* March 13, 1886, 1. A heavily biased verbal caricature of Emmeline, Ellen Ferguson, and Emily Richards appeared in an unidentified article pasted in a scrapbook collection of newspaper accounts of Emmeline and her Washington activities. "Apparently here were the three types of Mormon women," the article explained, "the one so strong-minded that she could not find a husband in the states; the second of the fortune-telling variety, who if they wed at all always wed with cranks or fanatics, and the third an unintelligent being, who could be influenced or led by those with

whom she might happen to be associated." It is difficult to determine which description was intended to fit which woman. Copy in possession of author.

59. "Fear Not for Zion," *Woman's Exponent* 20 (November 15, 1891): 76.

60. "Thoughts on the Times," *Woman's Exponent* 14 (September 1, 1885): 52.

61. Quoted in "The Mormon Question," *Deseret Evening News*, January 28, 1879, 2.

62. These and other provisions of the Edmunds-Tucker Act are detailed in Gustive O. Larson, *Outline History of Territorial Utah* (Provo, Utah: Brigham Young University, 1972), 276–77.

63. The conclusion of Beverly Beeton's study on woman suffrage in the West is that both Mormon and gentile suffragists were in effect "pawns" of the Mormon leadership, who used them to effect their own aims to protect polygamy at all costs. This characterization also ignores the tremendous personal investment Mormon women had in the principle as well as in the right to vote.

Chapter 10

The Politics of Woman Suffrage

'I do feel so interested in political movements.[1]

"It is election day and so much depends upon the results," Emmeline Wells wrote in her diary on August 1, 1887. "I do feel so interested in political movements. The sisters are not called upon to act in this movement but if they were we should certainly be sure of success." Utah was making its sixth bid for statehood, but after twelve years of enjoying the franchise women would not be able to vote at the forthcoming election because of the Edmunds-Tucker Act, passed earlier that year. Emmeline Wells, nevertheless, attended the Territorial Central Committee meeting, where there were "nineteen gentlemen present and only one lady," she noted. "It does take some courage," she admitted, "but I [was] determined to attend and do my best to understand how things were going."[2]

The newly written constitution for the proposed state, prohibiting any form of union of church and state as well as the practice of either bigamy or polygamy, also excluded woman suffrage. Although the constitution passed the all-male electorate by a heavy majority, the provisions it made were unsettling to Emmeline and many of her fellow Latter-day Saints. Recognizing that "such sentiments should be embodied as would be acceptable to the head of the nation," she nonetheless worried over them. "This is a great step to take in the opposite direction from our former position," she commented.[3] Despite the many apparent concessions, this attempt at statehood also met defeat in Congress.[4] "There is nothing lost in such a vigorous contest as has been made for the right," Emmeline philosophically responded to the continual congressional rebuffs of statehood. "By and by . . . the great men of the nation . . . will be ready and willing as well as anxious to acknowledge them [the Mormons] as a part of the great body politic," she promised, and she advised her readers "to submit with grace . . . to the persistent refusal of Congress to acknowledge their rights to a state government."[5]

Utah had already adopted several new laws respecting marriage, as mandated by the Edmunds-Tucker Act earlier that year, including the requirement that all marriages be a matter of public record.[6] Moreover, that year the election brought five Gentiles into the legislative assembly, and within three years Gentiles would control the municipal governments of both Ogden and Salt Lake City. Even more telling was the razing of the Endowment House in 1889, the site of plural marriages, a symbolic as well as logistical action since the Salt Lake Temple neared completion.[7] The intrusion of federal officials, imprisonment of polygamists, the confiscation of property owned by the Church so painstakingly acquired over the years, and the loss of civil liberties made deep inroads into Mormon society.

Despite these recent political incursions, Mormons maintained their sense of cohesiveness and community, but they did so under a mantle of martyrdom. The Church was at a crossroads. How long, many wondered, could it endure the tightening grip of Congress and still function as an institution? "It seems to me that there is soon to be a great change in the general affairs of the Church," Wells sadly noted. "Things cannot go on long as they are now."[8]

These changes took on a personal dimension when Emmeline's husband returned from England, where he had presided over the European Mission of the Church. To see him now meant clandestine visits, which Emmeline found irksome and ridiculous. What might have been pleasant visits after his long absence were furtive and spoiled, she wrote, "by having to steal away under cover of night for fear of the deputies under the Edmund's law—such humbug."[9] The two Edmunds Acts were clearly taking a toll on Mormon family life.

Though the pages of the *Woman's Exponent* showed Emmeline's keen interest in the historical changes taking place around her, she was privately working her way through a series of personal struggles. In 1888, as her husband's financial condition worsened with the declining value of his investments, she finally heard the news she had been dreading for years. Her home of more than thirty years, situated in the heart of the city (now Main Street and Third South), was needed to settle his mounting debts. She would have to move so the valuable city property on which it stood could be sold.[10]

A year earlier, in April 1887, her youngest daughter, Louisa, became the third of her children to die, a tragedy Emmeline faced alone, since her husband Daniel was in England at the time. The next year, these losses were accompanied by the decision of two of her other daughters to relocate; Melvina moved to Idaho with her husband, William Woods, and Annie moved to Ogden when her husband, John Q. Cannon, took on the editorship of the Ogden *Commercial.* Her only other daughter, Belle, was then residing in San Francisco with her husband, Septimus Sears. Later that year, Emmeline's brooding grief increased when another choice grandchild, Melvina's son Percival, succumbed to diphtheria.

As Emmeline watched her familiar world unravel around her in the late 1880s, gloomy thoughts shrouded her usual hopeful attitude, and she allowed herself, in private, to give way to her despair. "O, how lonely are the days and nights, nothing seems the same, all has changed for me and my heart is almost frozen in my body."[11] A lingering melancholy settled over her, a malaise that matched the general restiveness of Latter-day Saints trying to maintain some sense of equilibrium amidst the volatile circumstances created by the Edmunds-Tucker Act. With enormous effort, she continued to write her editorials and attend to her Relief Society commitments. As much to herself as to her readers, Emmeline used the *Woman's Exponent* to assuage the uncertainty and disruption that had beset the members of her religion. She told her readers "this is indeed an interesting period in the history of this people, and those who have been looking forward for a great change to transpire that Zion might be liberated from bondage, ought to take into consideration, how often it has been repeated to the Saints, that the Lord's ways are not man's ways, and that great things never come about as even wise men anticipate."[12] Her present unhappiness turned her thoughts to the past, and she frequently drew on her nostalgic 1885 journey to New England to write sketches of the places, the friends of her childhood, and the comforting sameness of the wooded hill country, all so deeply embedded in her memory.

While Emmeline attempted to deal with these emotional upheavals in her personal life, events in the national suffrage movement foreshadowed difficulties in her public life. The officers of the National Woman Suffrage Association (NWSA) were planning an innovative eight-day gathering of women with the intent of organizing an international woman's council to be held prior to their own annual suffrage convention. This event, they hoped, would be followed by the organization of individual national councils that in turn would collectivize women's associations in each nation. Only representatives of national women's organizations were invited to attend or become members. Ostensibly to celebrate the fortieth anniversary of the Seneca Falls woman's rights convention of 1848, the council was also meant to be a step toward consolidating the interest of all representative groups in achieving woman suffrage while also supporting the special interests of individual member organizations. Invitations were sent to women's associations throughout the world.[13]

Though not actually the first incident of internationalizing women's social concerns, the international organization that came from the celebration was one of the earliest and most successful, claiming to represent thirty-six million women by 1925.[14] Woman suffrage, however, did not become its rallying cause, social welfare being a more pressing universal interest. But the association did collect a global conglomerate of women's groups to consider a wide range of issues, and in time a close symbiosis developed between the national suffrage associations and the National and International Councils of Women.

In January 1888, Emmeline wrote an editorial announcing the March gathering, expressing her approval and hopeful expectations of the new association.[15] Mormon women, already organized in the Relief Society and heading both the Young Ladies' Mutual Improvement Association and Primary Association, with units in many parts of the United States as well as in Europe, were potential members eager to continue their national connections. They were concerned, however, and rightly so, that their membership in the new council as well as in the NWSA, with its altered, more reform-minded constituency, might be rejected. The strong influence of the Woman's Christian Temperance Union (WCTU) and other reform groups, along with a relentless overt antagonism toward polygamists, were formidable obstacles. Emmeline correctly observed that it would probably take "money and wire pulling" to make women's membership happen.[16] She had learned the rules of politics. Letters from Emmeline to Susan B. Anthony and others of the NWSA, personal interviews between Utah's congressional delegate John T. Caine and officers of the NWSA, along with generous donations to the NWSA from Margaret N. Caine and Jane S. Richards, did indeed open the way for consideration of Mormon membership.[17] Four women were selected to attend the auspicious meeting, all then residing in the East with their husbands: Emily S. Richards (Jane's daughter-in-law), Luella Cobb Young, Margaret Nightingale Caine, and Nettie Young Snell.[18] Whether their presence would lead to membership was the burning question.

Also interested in attending the international convention were non-Mormon women in Utah. Though the Anti-Polygamy Society had long been dissolved, the Industrial Christian Home Association, which supervised the refuge home sponsored by Angie Newman, served as the requisite "organization," and Dr. Ruth Woods, superintendent of the home, was to be its representative. Evidently intending to speak at the convention as a representative of women's organizations in Utah, Dr. Wood visited Emmeline late in February to solicit information, much to Emmeline's chagrin.[19] "Dr. Wood called on me for items, statistics etc. to give her lectures in Kansas and at the International Council at Washington D.C.," Emmeline wrote in her diary. "She evidently thinks she can do more towards our cause than any Mormon woman can do. After being here 15 months she knows more than we know ourselves." Finding "her manner and her discourse . . . equally repulsive," Emmeline was instinctively wary of a non-Mormon representing Utah at the convention.[20]

    Emmeline Wells did not intend to travel to the two meetings herself. Even the anniversary of a cause that gave so much vitality and purpose to her life could not overrule the continual need to solicit funding but more so the relentless grip of sorrow that continued to afflict her. Emmeline was deeply immersed in the confusion and heartache of dismantling her home, bowed by the emotional and physical strain of moving into a temporary residence, and still almost immobilized by grief from Louisa's death, a grief intensified by the memories of the death of another daughter, Emmie, at the same age a decade earlier. Emmeline found it hard enough just to prepare the credentials for the LDS women who would represent Utah. It was a laborious, tedious task made more difficult, she found, in having to please all who felt they had authority as to how the credentials were to be written.

    Emmeline was urged on all sides to join the women in Washington, but her desultory mood and the compelling claims on her thoughts and energies at home militated against her going.[21] Only once, shortly after the convention commenced, did she feel any regret at not making the "exertion" necessary to go herself. She had, however, laid the groundwork for Mormon representation through her correspondence with national leaders and the preparation of the credentials that would justify attendance by the representatives at both conventions. She also kept her readers informed of the Washington meetings through the reports she wrote for Salt Lake newspapers as well as for her own paper.[22]

    Though the convention was called by NWSA to commemorate the beginning of the drive for woman suffrage in 1848, most of the fifty-one organizations represented at the Washington convention did not put suffrage at the top of their agenda. Besides the peace movement, many were more interested in measures to suppress moral vices that degraded or abused women, such as prostitution (the double standard), and sexual slavery and trafficking.[23] United States delegates added polygamy to this list.

Unexpectedly, the organizers of the convention invited Emily Richards rather than Ruth Woods to report on women's associations in Utah.[24] At the time, Utah statehood was a topic of debate in Washington papers, generating negative reports by Senate and House committees because of Mormons' unwillingness to abandon polygamy despite federal legislation and creating an environment that made the Mormon representatives objects of suspicion and derision. Emily Richards, though a monogamist herself, thus faced an unsympathetic audience when she delivered her speech. But she was buoyed by the complimentary and enthusiastic introduction given her by Harriet Shattuck, chair of the session, who was especially effusive when she discovered that she had inadvertently failed to announce Emily initially as a speaker. According to reports of the convention, Emily touched her audience with her demure ways and her interesting report on the work accomplished by Latter-day Saint women's associations in Utah.[25]

The convention closed with the organization of both an International and a National Council of Women (NCW), with Frances Willard, president of the WCTU, chosen to head the National Council in the United States. Emmeline Wells, in absentia, was invited to be a member of the press committee of the National Council of Women. Though they had enjoyed acceptance at this first meeting, Mormon women's organizations were not formally affiliated until the first triennial convention of the NCW in 1891.[26]

With one hurdle behind them, the Mormon representatives faced another at NWSA's annual convention, which convened directly afterward. Overtones of the conservative mode of the international convention lingered throughout the NWSA meeting. Added to this influence was the overt opposition of Lucy Stone and her American Woman Suffrage Association (AWSA) to admitting Mormon women to a merged suffrage association, an important item on the meeting's agenda. Continuing affiliation of the LDS Relief Society and Young Ladies' Mutual Improvement Association (MIA) was thus far from assured.

Anticipating a merger with the AWSA, officers of the NWSA revamped the structure of their organization, allowing only fully organized suffrage associations to send authorized delegates to the annual conventions, rather than unaffiliated individuals as before. Although the Relief Society and Young Ladies' MIA were not officially woman suffrage organizations, politics and woman suffrage informed many of the discussions and lessons in their meetings, and the network the societies offered for petitioning, rallying, fundraising, and other suffrage support made them quasi–suffrage associations and thus eligible for membership. However, early the next year (1889) Mormon women organized a territorial association with county affiliates to be in explicit accord with the guidelines for membership and to promote their own retrieval of the vote. The current makeup of the NWSA, however, with the WCTU a major force in the opposition of antipolygamists, did not augur well for the Mormon delegates. "It is noticeable in almost every instance," Emmeline Wells observed, "that whenever 'Mormons' are to be admitted, a question arises as to the feasibility of the matter."[27]

Once again they found an advocate, this time in the person of Harriet H. Robinson, a suffragist from Massachusetts,[28] who reminded the convention that the NWSA "knows no North, no South, no East, no West but is cosmopolitan, and welcomes to its membership women of all classes, all races and all religions." Her appeal superseded the arguments of antipolygamists, and the executive committee not only accepted the LDS Church's organizations as members but appointed two new representatives for Utah: Emily Richards, who was nominated by a "Mrs. Slautter of Dakota," and non-Mormon Isabel Cameron Brown, who was nominated by Dr. Ruth Woods and whose sister-in-law was a well-known national suffragist, Olympia Brown. Although Jennie Froiseth remained a vice president for Utah, the convention commissioned the two new representatives to organize a territorial association in Utah.[29]

Just how tenuous the relationship of Mormon women with the suffrage associations was, especially in the event of a merger of the two organizations, became apparent the following June, when prominent club woman Julia Ward Howe, author of the popular "Battle Hymn of the Republic," and longtime friend of Jennie Froiseth, visited Utah. As an influential member of AWSA, the founder and president of the conservative Association for the Advancement of Women, and an outspoken enemy of polygamy, she had little reason to spend time with Mormon women.[30] Recognizing the importance of Howe's visit to Utah and wanting to meet the grand lady herself, Emmeline repeatedly sent messages to Howe's hotel, inviting her to meet with some of the prominent Latter-day Saint women of the community.[31] All requests remained unanswered.

In the meantime, Howe, who was sponsored by the women of the Grand Army of the Republic (GAR), spent her time at Saltair and other scenic spots with Jennie Froiseth and the forty members of the Women's Relief Corps of the GAR, when she was not otherwise occupied giving lectures at the Congregational Church and the Grand Army Hall.[32] Emmeline was invited by friends to attend the lecture at the Congregational Church but chose not to go, feeling that "it would be too conspicuous for me, knowing the enmity they have towards me as a representative Mormon."[33] She preferred a private meeting, but after three days of silence from Howe, Emmeline "gave her up."[34]

It had been a decade since Emmeline had realized that a united sisterhood could be little more than a hope, but even then she did not anticipate how deep or how widespread the animus toward Mormon women and toward herself as a prominent defender would eventually become. Howe's pointed indifference confirmed her disillusionment. Emmeline was thus totally surprised when Howe finally agreed to a brief visit. Emmeline was accompanied by Dr. Romania Pratt, their arms laden with flowers. They were granted an hour with the acclaimed woman in her room at the Continental Hotel. "We had a pleasant call," Emmeline noted, "and I hope made an agreeable impression."[35] But the famous poet remained unmoved by their solicitations and continued her public crusade against them.

Three months later, Emmeline received more compatible visitors: Elizabeth Lyle Saxon of Memphis, who had visited Utah in 1882; and Clara Bewick Colby of Beatrice, Nebraska, who was editor of the *Woman's Tribune,* a journal of the NWSA. Both active members of the organization, the two women represented the faction within the association that favored the participation of Mormon women.[36] Saxon and Colby's visit established them as sympathizers. Meeting them at the depot, where they arrived from a similar tour in the Northwest, were several Utah suffragists, including Isabel Brown, one of the few non-Mormon women who participated in their visit. While not ignoring gentile women during the time they spent in Utah, Saxon and Colby spent most of their visit with their Mormon hosts. The visitors spoke in the Salt Lake Theater and the LDS Church's Assembly Hall on social reform, suffrage, and other pertinent topics, sharing the pulpit on one occasion with Relief Society General President Zina D. H. Young and Charlotte Cobb Godbe, now Kirby, who was once more on the Utah suffrage scene.[37]

Saxon and Colby also visited Angie Newman's Industrial Home, surprised to find that only one woman and nine children currently occupied the large multistoried edifice. The visitors listened attentively to the brief talk given by the matron of the home, a Mrs. Campbell. They were particularly impressed with the joint sponsorship by Mormon, Catholic, and Protestant women of a day nursery, a rare cooperation at that time.[38] Borrowing a carriage, Emmeline Wells, Jane Richards, and Amelia Young took the visitors on a tour of the city that included Prospect Hill, Liberty Park, and the fair grounds. A reception was held that evening in the Gardo House, residence of Amelia Young, who served as hostess in the large, lovely home built for the purpose of entertaining important visitors to the city.[39] Colby's report of the visit painted a favorable picture of her Mormon hosts, which helped dispel the affront they had felt from Julia Ward Howe. Their visit encouraged Mormon suffragists to maintain their association with the national movement and to take steps to organize suffrage societies throughout the territory.

When learning of Clara Colby's intent to speak in behalf of Mormon women at the November 1888 meeting of the Association for the Advancement of Women in Detroit, Jennie Froiseth arranged to attend the convention herself. With the help of her friend Julia Ward Howe, who presided, Froiseth, rather than Clara Colby, was given the platform to present a report on the women of Utah. According to the *Salt Lake Tribune*, she was successful in "checkmating all that Mrs. Colby and Mrs. Saxon hoped to do."[40] As long as Latter-day Saint members continued to engage in plural marriage, neither the demise of the Anti-Polygamy Society nor the Edmunds-Tucker Act diminished anti-Mormon sentiment.

Meanwhile, in Utah, neither Emily Richards nor Isabel Brown acted on their charge to organize a suffrage association. They had no experience with organizing groups, and a suffrage association was clearly an innovative move for Utah women. The two women deferred to the LDS Relief Society, which had been connected to the suffrage movement since 1870. It had been instrumental in sending delegates to the national conventions and providing most of the funding for the trips to Washington. Thus, in November 1888, newly appointed Relief Society General President Zina D. H. Young, her counselor Jane Richards, an avid suffragist, and Jane's daughter-in-law Emily Richards met with L. John Nuttall, secretary to Wilford Woodruff, to arrange a meeting with Church leaders about the proposed organization. Most Church leaders were as interested in retrieving the vote for women as were the women themselves.

The meeting took place in January 1889. In attendance were Wilford Woodruff, President of the Quorum of the Twelve and acting President of the Church since John Taylor's death in 1887;[41] Elders Franklin D. Richards (husband to Jane), Brigham Young Jr., John Henry Smith, Heber J. Grant, L. John Nuttall, and Zina Young, Jane and Emily Richards, Relief Society counselor Bathsheba W. Smith, and secretaries Sarah M. Kimball and Emmeline B. Wells. All parties were agreeable to the formation of a territorial suffrage association, which the women hoped to organize the following week.

President Woodruff suggested that Emily Richards represent the association at the annual suffrage convention later that month, since she was "posted in these matters and has previously reported the labors of the Ladies of this Territory at Washington."[42] Emily's part-time residence in Washington, D.C., made her a logical choice to attend, and having been authorized to organize an association with Isabel Brown just the year before, Emily seemed the appropriate person to report on the new organization in Utah.

Recognizing the importance of Jennie Froiseth's position as vice president for Utah, Emily Richards and Isabel Brown visited Froiseth the day following the meeting with Church leaders and invited her to participate in organizing a local suffrage association.[43] At their request, Emmeline Wells joined them.[44] Since Froiseth, who found it impossible to cooperate "in any cause with women who believed in the rightfulness and propriety of polygamy," had already made clear her feelings about woman suffrage in Utah, the women hardly expected her to be supportive. But she would not stand in the way, she explained, if they were determined to organize as instructed by NWSA.[45] This Mormon initiative, as well as Froiseth's friendship with Julia Ward Howe, may well have spurred Froiseth's decision to join the American Woman Suffrage Association later that year, an unmistakable gesture of protest.

A week later, on January 10, 1889, the Utah Territorial Woman Suffrage Association (UTWSA) came into being. While the constitution and bylaws of the association did not so designate, a conscious effort to minimize polygamy and maximize cooperation with Gentiles determined the policies that developed as Utah suffragists prepared to regain the vote. In preparation for the meeting, Emmeline complained that she had been "besieged on all hands to assist in organizing a woman suffrage Association and yet none who have ever been in plural marriage can have any [leadership] position in it."[46] She did assist, but she found the UTWSA capitulation to social norms in stark contrast to her own indifference to public opinion of a decade earlier and especially to her determined and successful efforts to be accepted despite her polygamous status.

The call to meeting was issued by Emily Richards, chair of the executive committee of the NWSA for Utah, and by the presidency of the LDS Relief Society, Zina D. H. Young, Jane S. Richards, and Bathsheba W. Smith. They were joined by Josephine West, president of the Primary Association of Weber County; Dr. Ellen Ferguson; Elizabeth Howard; Dr. Romania B. Pratt; and Emmeline Wells. The response was extremely satisfying. As planned, all the new officers elected at the organizational meeting were monogamous. Margaret N. Caine was elected president.[47] Her fellow officers included Lydia D. Alder, Nellie Webber, Priscilla Jennings Riter, Cornelia H. Clayton, Margie Dwyer, and Charlotte I. Kirby, who addressed the meeting.

Wells, who had actually carried the major responsibility for organizing, could not help bristling at being relegated to backstage, especially in light of the service she had rendered for more than a decade. In the absence of Emily Richards, who was sick during the preparatory period, Emmeline had spearheaded the effort to solicit the names of suffrage supporters, requiring sixty yards of paper for the 8,393 signatures, three thousand of them male, to add to the national enrollment.[48] She had written the articles and bylaws for the UTWSA the morning before the meeting and prepared the credentials for the two delegates to the national convention, Emily Richards and Margaret Caine.[49] It is not surprising that Emmeline "felt very unpleasant about the work." She was pleased, however, that monogamous wives, whom she called "the free women of Utah" in an 1888 editorial, had joined the effort to regain the vote after being noticeably quiet when losing the franchise with the Edmunds-Tucker Act in 1887.[50]

The credentials, the rapid success in organizing, the large enrollment, and the revenue that enrollment promised confirmed the value of Mormon membership in the NWSA despite the opposition of some of its members. At NWSA's annual convention in 1889, Emily Richards was able to report that Utah's newly organized auxiliary to the national association brought two hundred dues-paying members who had enrolled within a week's time.[51] Four months later, fourteen county associations came into the territorial association. While maintaining a regular correspondence with suffrage leaders, including Lucy Stone, and writing occasional articles for the *Woman's Journal,* Emmeline added to her already burdensome workload the task of organizing county associations, speaking at their meetings, writing and distributing suffrage literature, and generally advancing the work of woman suffrage in Utah. Support for woman suffrage in the territory, she soon discovered, could not be assumed.

The strength of the opposition was reinforced when several women who had attended the 1889 Denver meeting of the Association for the Advancement of Women visited Utah in October of that year, hosted by Jennie Froiseth. Emmeline's experience with Julia Ward Howe gave her little hope that these guests would have any interest in meeting Mormon women. However, the three visitors called at Emmeline's office, and the next day she and Zina Young, along with Jennie Froiseth, met the visitors at their hotel and presented them with various pieces of LDS Church literature, copies of the *Woman's Exponent,* and an edition of Emmeline's published poetry. That "Mrs. Froiseth was very insulting to us" could be expected, but their inclusion in the visit meant much to the two Mormon women, convinced, as they always were, that personal contact would diminish the disdain they so regularly received.[52]

Until statehood was achieved, which reenfranchised women seven years later, Emmeline Wells's public life was spent in organizing and promoting woman suffrage. A popular speaker, she was much in demand throughout the territory. In her addresses, she focused on both the use of the vote to promote women's social goals and its symbolic value in affirming women as independent citizens capable of expressing their voices in the governance of their communities as well as the nation. "Women have a right to use their influence toward making the laws that are to govern them and their children," she asserted in a talk to the members of the Ogden Woman Suffrage Association, "and should have the privilege of having a voice as to who shall execute the laws of the land, and how the taxes shall be applied." Moreover, she stated, enfranchisement "gave a feeling of independence, that [is] itself an elevating power." Men, she was certain, "will assuredly respect women's opinions more, when they know they can give them expression at the polls."[53] Utah women, she reminded her listeners, had enjoyed the franchise for seventeen years and had proven that it neither "unsexed" them nor resulted in neglected families and cold suppers. She had little patience with the argument that women's voice expressed itself through their husbands' vote, noting that many women spent either part or all their adult lives single and were thus totally disfranchised. Her ideas took form in nearly a hundred editorials in the *Woman's Exponent*.

While women naturally carried primary responsibility for garnering territorial support for woman suffrage, they were ably aided by a host of influential men, some of them Church leaders. Many of the Salt Lake County and Territorial conventions were addressed by high-ranking Apostles and bishops, notably Bishop Orson F. Whitney, Apostle Heber J. Grant, and Joseph F. Smith of the First Presidency. This support would continue throughout the vigorous campaign to restore the vote to women at statehood.

Although its bid for membership in the NWSA was successful, a berth for the UTWSA was less than secure if the AWSA and NWSA merged. That possibility consumed the attention of the delegates at the 1889 NWSA convention. Though other considerations, such as the unconventional notions of Elizabeth Cady Stanton on divorce and religion, underpinned the AWSA resistance to a merger, Mormon membership in the association was also a formidable deterrent. On the other hand, some NWSA members feared that the conservative stance and multifaceted goals of the AWSA, when joined with those of the moral reformers who had already become a prominent voice in the NWSA, would diffuse that organization's single-minded effort toward acquiring the vote.

Susan B. Anthony, architect of the merger, appealed to the members of the committee on merger to keep an open door policy that allowed "every woman to come upon our platform to plead for her freedom." She urged the members to keep the suffrage platform "as broad as the universe, that upon it may stand the representatives of all creeds and no creeds—Jew or Christian, Protestant or Catholic, Gentile or Mormon, pagan or atheist."[54] Such a policy made room for both Mormons and social reformers in the merged association, though it could not promise amity in their new relationship with one another.

Finally, the members voted, the motion for merger prevailed, and in February 1890, the National American Woman Suffrage Association (NAWSA) held its first convention. The controversial Elizabeth Cady Stanton, with the helping vote of the Mormon delegates (pertinently noted by Lucy Stone), was elected president.[55] Just prior to the national meeting, the Utah Territorial Woman Suffrage Association,

Sarah M. Kimball, a prominent Latter-day Saint involved with the woman suffrage movement, became the first president of the Utah Territorial Woman Suffrage Association in 1890.

still abiding by its policy to elect only nonpolygamous officers, held its first annual convention and chose the aging Sarah M. Kimball as president. Emily Richards was elected vice president.[56] Sarah Kimball, along with Maria Young Dougall, represented Utah at the initial convention of the newly merged national suffrage associations. "It will not be all roses," Emmeline Wells noted as they left. "They will find many thorns I fear."[57]

By courting the social purity activists, especially the popular WCTU, Anthony was broadening the suffrage constituency along a wide range of women otherwise unsupportive of the vote for women.[58] She also recognized that getting the support of the WCTU meant risking the powerful opposition of the liquor interests, a risk she was evidently willing to take. Frances Willard, head of the WCTU and an early suffragist, had the task of bringing her membership on board the suffrage bandwagon. She did so by astutely developing a concept that she called the "Home Protection Ballot," tying the goals of WCTU directly to the power of the ballot, thereby giving the two movements an organizational affinity.[59] This focus also redirected women's possession of the ballot from a democratic to a social imperative, which suffrage rhetoric reflected.

Meanwhile events were culminating in another exciting scenario that would dramatically affect the suffrage movement in Utah as well as the territory's religious, political, and social landscape. The successful mobilization of women into the local suffrage campaign alerted LDS

Church leaders to the value of their participation in the escalating political drama in Utah. Not only was the effective network of LDS Relief Societies already in place, but there was now a political network of local suffrage units functioning under direction of a territorial association. They turned to Emmeline for assistance. "Complications in politics seem to have assumed considerable strength," she wrote in November 1889. "It will be a problem, local perhaps and it may be national. I have been advised to speak to the sisters about women taking an active part in the movement and to urge it in the sisters meetings."[60]

The complications that had arisen were related to the increased political strength of Utah Gentiles, since the Edmunds-Tucker Law had removed the franchise from all women, further diminishing the strength of the Mormon electorate. For the first time, Gentiles had carried a municipal election, sweeping their candidates into office in Ogden in the 1889 election. The loss of Ogden, a major railroad terminal populated largely by non-Mormons, to the Liberal Party was disturbing but not devastating. However, when the Liberal Party set its sights on winning the February 1890 election in Salt Lake City, Church officials were gravely concerned and employed a variety of measures to increase the Mormon vote.[61] Unable to vote themselves, women could be counted on only to urge their nonpolygamous male relatives and friends to vote.

Both the Liberal and People's Parties staged massive parades shortly before the election. "There has never before been so much ado over one as this time," observed Emmeline. But much was at stake in this election. Despite a cold and windy snowstorm, the "bands were out and excitement ran high," noted Emmeline, and she lamented that the "Liberals . . . were so well assured of success that they were making considerable demonstrations and speeches and shouts."[62] When the Liberal Party won all the offices in the election, accusations of illegal voting were voiced by both sides, but the results stood. It was clear to Church members that Salt Lake City was no longer theirs to control despite their long history of governing. But the Church was also facing the possibility of disfranchisement of all its members as well as extreme political pressure to publicly renounce plural marriage.[63]

Moreover, the Church was in the throes of adjusting to the escheatment of its property and facing the moral dilemma of maintaining family relationships and responsibilities while yielding to the stipulations of the Edmunds-Tucker Act.[64] The difficulties of the present brought all "the wrongs of the past" to Emmeline's mind and made her feel "heart-sick" and "low-spirited." Having lived through most stages of the Mormons' tumultuous history, she could only regret that the refuge that the Great Basin had once offered the Church no longer existed. Times had changed once again, and at age sixty-two she would have to adapt, as would the Church.

The inevitable had finally arrived. By the end of summer 1890, Church President Wilford Woodruff had reached a time of decision and revealed to the Church the result of his long struggle over subjecting a deeply held religious principle to an overriding temporal law. On September 24, he announced that he was suspending any new plural marriages, advising Church members to obey the law of the land. Though his announcement was a shock to many and a surrender of a long-held principle, the congregation responded with a sustaining vote. Emmeline Wells observed that some "will be very much tried over the affair" and later noted that "there is a class who do not relish it at all," but she felt that most people willingly accepted the "manifesto" and arranged their lives to accommodate the requirements of the law.[65]

She was aware, however, of the legal disabilities that fell upon plural wives.[66] "The law places so many restrictions upon them and the social claim is very indistinct and indefinite," Emmeline protested, recognizing the social and financial vulnerability of plural families. Her personal response, however, was tempered by a fatalistic belief that such a pronouncement had been inevitable and that Latter-day Saints would adjust, despite the unavoidable personal hardships. As for herself, she had already created emotional and financial shields and was thus less vulnerable than many others to the tremendous personal alterations that would accompany this capitulation.

The Woodruff Manifesto was a benchmark in Mormon history. Not only did it disestablish a basic tenet of LDS Church doctrine, but it also required years of extensive legal adjustment to give plural wives and their children some legal recognition.[67] Community activities underwent slow but remarkable transitions as businessmen, religious leaders, politicians, and women began the search for common meeting grounds. Some few areas of cooperation had actually begun earlier with the organization of Chambers of Commerce and Boards of Trade in both Ogden and Salt Lake City. A state-funded school system was established in 1890, breaking the educational barriers that had separated Latter-day Saint schools from the denominational schools that had attracted numbers of Mormon students.[68]

Politics, a major divisive factor, required a dramatic reconfiguration of loyalties as the territory found it desirable as well as advisable, with statehood the goal, to adopt the national party system, a suggestion made by the *Salt Lake Tribune* as early as 1888. Thus, serious efforts to dissolve the People's Party and realign Church members with the national political parties began early in 1891.[69]

Since virtually all repressive measures against the Church had been initiated by Republicans, beginning with their 1856 vow to obliterate slavery and polygamy and their role in passing the Morrill, Poland, and Edmunds Bills, most Mormons favored the more sympathetic Democratic Party. By 1890, however, Republicans, who were then in power, actively campaigned to win favor with Utahns by promising support for statehood efforts. This campaign altered the political persuasion of numerous Mormons, including LDS Church President Wilford Woodruff, his counselors Joseph F. Smith and George Q. Cannon, and several other ecclesiastical leaders. They urged members who leaned toward the Republican Party's philosophy to recruit others toward their preference in order to create political balance among the heretofore politically unified Mormons.[70] By May 1891 both Democrats and Republicans had effected organizations in Salt Lake City, and in June the People's Party formally disbanded.[71]

To what extent women would take part in the business of the new political system in Utah remained unclear at this date. Emmeline petulantly noted, "It is possible, to be sure, for women to decide in their own minds whether they lean more to the Republican or Democratic party . . . and as neither one of these organizations seemed disposed to recognize women in any positive way, women are not very likely to do more than to look on and see those who have it in their own hands appreciate all the golden opportunities to benefit themselves."[72]

The new political divisions created "considerable feeling and some pettiness," Emmeline Wells observed.[73] After the loss of plural marriage, the "division in politics is another trial to many," she lamented, "and hard to comprehend."[74] John Nuttall also noted the anxiety felt by so many: "I fear the results of these measures of unity on party lines as some of our people will carry their party feelings into their church membership."[75] It was a time of tremendous political, emotional, and psychological adjustment for Mormons, and the separation of church and state, a topic that dominated politics in territorial Utah, continued to be a convoluted one, even within a new political and social framework.

Notes

1. Emmeline B. Wells, Diary, August 1, 1887, L. Tom Perry Special Collections, Harold B. Lee Library, Brigham Young University, Provo, Utah.
2. Wells, Diary, June 11, 1887.
3. Wells, Diary, June 16, 1887.
4. The machinations required to produce these concessions and the general continuing disbelief in the sincerity of LDS Church leaders to abandon polygamy led, once again, to congressional rejection of this effort toward statehood. See Edward Leo Lyman, *Political Deliverance: The Mormon Quest for Statehood* (Urbana: University of Illinois Press, 1986), 41–64, esp. 60–64. A letter from Franklin S. Richards to his Washington legal associate, Judge George Ticknor Curtis, explains the rationale for these concessions: "I hope the Constitution will meet your approval. The Convention tried to meet the real issues and meet them squarely. We did not think it wise or expedient to define the status of plural wives, or say anything on the subject of marriage or divorce, but leave that whole matter to the legislature. Although in favor of female suffrage, the Convention were of the opinion that it would rather diminish than increase our chances of success to incorporate it in the Constitution, because the most of our friends in Congress are from the South and are strongly opposed to women voting." Franklin S. Richards Letterbooks, 1886–90, Utah State Historical Society, Salt Lake City. On a later occasion he also explained the rationale for prohibiting the practice of plural marriage: "The

provision of the revelation [on plural marriage]," he said, "was simply permissive, the language used being that 'if a man having a wife espoused another then is he justified' [with the conditions noted in the revelation], pointing out clearly that this language was not mandatory and could not fairly be so construed." Franklin S. Richards, "Statehood," n.d., typescript copy, Church Archives, The Church of Jesus Christ of Latter-day Saints, Salt Lake City.

5. "A Noble Endeavor," *Woman's Exponent* 17 (February 15, 1889): 140.

6. The territorial legislative assembly of 1852 had authorized officers of the LDS Church and other denominations to solemnize marriages and to keep a registry of marriages in every branch or stake (ecclesiastical unit). At that time no provision was made for civil recording of marriages. Civil marriages and marriages of people of other religions were permitted and performed, but they were similarly not subject to civil registration or licensing. See An Ordinance, Incorporating The Church of Jesus Christ of Latter-day Saints (February 6, 1851), *1851 Laws of Deseret*, 66. Evidence of these marriages came from personal records of judges and justices of the peace, church records, diaries and journals, and from signature books of Latter-day Saint temples. Lyman D. Platt has reclaimed many of these records, which formed the basis for his article "The History of Marriage in Utah, 1847–1905," *Genealogical Journal* 12 (Spring 1983): 32–33. A record of marriages compiled from various sources is the *Utah Territorial Vital Records Index, 1847–1905*, published by the Genealogical Society in Salt Lake City. This index also includes records of divorce, naturalization, and probate as well as other vital statistics.

7. Gustive O. Larsen, "The Crusade and the Manifesto," in *Utah's History*, ed. Richard D. Poll, Thomas G. Alexander, Eugene E. Campbell, and David E. Miller (Provo, Utah: Brigham Young University Press, 1978), 268–71. See also Lyman, *Political Deliverance*, 113. The Salt Lake Temple was nearing completion, the St. George Temple had been functioning since 1877, the Logan Temple since 1884, and the Manti Temple since 1888. The Endowment House had clearly outlived its usefulness.

8. Wells, Diary, May 24, 1887.

9. Wells, Diary, August 13, 1888.

10. Salt Lake City real estate doubled in value between 1886 and 1891. Thomas G. Alexander and James B. Allen, *Mormons and Gentiles: A History of Salt Lake City*, The Western Urban History Series, vol. 5 (Boulder, Colo.: Pruett, 1984), 87.

11. Wells, Diary, May 31, 1887.

12. "Fear Not for Zion," *Woman's Exponent* 20 (November 15, 1891): 76.

13. For a thorough study of women's international associations, see Leila J.

Rupp, *Worlds of Women: The Making of an International Women's Movement* (Princeton: Princeton University Press, 1997). A condensed account is Leila J. Rupp, "Constructing Internationalism: The Case of Transnational Women's Organizations, 1888–1945," *American Historical Review* 99 (December 1994): 1571–1600.

14. See Rupp, *Worlds of Women;* and Rupp, "Constructing Internationalism," 1571–1600.

15. "International Council of Women," *Woman's Exponent* 16 (January 15, 1888): 124.

16. Wells, Diary, March 10, 1888. A more detailed account of the interest taken by both the women and Church leaders in Mormon representation at the council can be found in Lola Van Wagenen, "Sister-Wives and Suffragists, Polygamy and the Politics of Woman Suffrage, 1870–1896" (PhD diss., New York University, 1994; BYU Studies and Joseph Fielding Smith Institute for Latter-day Saint History, 2003), 129–31.

17. The account in Susan B. Anthony and Ida H. Harper, eds., *History of Woman Suffrage,* vol. 4 (Rochester: Susan B. Anthony, 1902), 126–27, of the founding of the International Council of Women lists both Jane S. Richards and Margaret N. Caine as giving $100 to help defray the costs of the convention. The money was probably the same $100 sent by the Church to its Washington agents and given to the International Council in the name of the two delegates. According to Leo Lyman, quoting Joseph F. Smith, it was donated "with the express understanding that they did not want to pay money to be misrepresented and maligned." Lyman, *Political Deliverance,* 87–88. Emmeline sent $5.00. Anthony and Harper, *History of Woman Suffrage,* 4:126–27. The interest of Church leaders in the meetings attest to their continuing concern about the acceptance of Mormon women among their peers since they were no longer voting citizens. After the Edmunds-Tucker Act there was little national suffragists could do to help Mormon women beyond maintaining a cordial relationship with them, which they hoped to secure.

18. Emily Richards was the wife of Church attorney Franklin S. Richards, and Margaret Caine was the wife of Utah's congressional delegate, John T. Caine. Luella Cobb Young, wife of John W. Young, a New York railroad promoter and son of Brigham Young, was the granddaughter of Augusta Cobb Young, one of Brigham Young's wives, and was also the niece of Augusta's daughter Charlotte Cobb Godbe. Luella's father was James T. Cobb, Augusta Cobb's son whom she had left behind in Massachusetts when she joined the LDS Church and married Brigham Young. As an adult, James traveled to Utah, where he met and married Mary Van Cott. They had one daughter, Luella,

before divorcing. Mary then married Brigham Young, and James married Camilla Meith and joined the LDS Church. Luella eventually left John Young, became a Christian Scientist, and settled in the Northwest. James was active in the woman suffrage movement with his sister Charlotte, and eventually left the LDS Church. Nettie (Jeanette) Young, a daughter of Brigham Young and Clarissa Decker, was first married to George Henry Snell before divorcing and marrying Robert Easton, making her permanent home with him in New York City. For many years she wrote a regular column for the *Deseret News* on life in New York. My thanks to Jeffery O. Johnson for this information.

19. It is uncertain whether Dr. Woods was invited to speak or simply assumed she would speak as a delegate to the convention. The original notice, which Emmeline reported in a *Woman's Exponent* editorial on February 15, 1888, two weeks before Dr. Woods visited her, specifically indicated that invitations were sent only to "nationally organized bodies of women," with some personal invitations extended to "distinguished women," particularly those in the professions of medicine, law, and journalism, which were largely unorganized. "Fortieth Anniversary of the Woman Suffrage Movement," *Woman's Exponent* 16 (February 15, 1888): 140.

20. Wells, Diary, February 28, 1888.

21. Wells, Diary, March 6, 1888. Lamenting the loss of her daughter Louisa, who would have shared her pleasure at the invitation and who acted as a confidante and adviser in the absence of Emmeline's husband, she evidently wrote to Church President Wilford Woodruff seeking his counsel on responding to the invitation to serve on the press committee of the NCW. He advised her to accept. Wells, Diary, February 16, 1888. A letter by Lucy Stone to Frances Willard, newly elected president of the council, suggests that Emmeline was made a life-member of the NCW at this time. Lucy Stone to Frances Willard, August 23, 1888, in *Loving Warriors: Selected Letters of Lucy Stone and Henry B. Blackwell, 1853–1893*, ed. Leslie Wheeler (New York: Dial Press, 1981), 314, 393, but a diary note indicates that that honor did not come to Emmeline until 1894. See Wells, Diary, January 25, 1894.

22. The *Deseret Evening News,* the *Salt Lake Herald,* and the *Salt Lake Tribune* all ran several articles on the events in Washington. See, for example, E. B. Wells, "An International Council of Women," *Deseret Evening News,* March 8, 1888, 3; "Council of Women," *Salt Lake Tribune,* March 27, 1888, 1; "The Council of Women," *Salt Lake Tribune,* March 28, 1888, 1; "The Women Still Talking," *Salt Lake Tribune,* March 30, 1888, 1; "Elizabeth C. Stanton," *Salt Lake Tribune,* April 3, 1888, 1; "Woman Suffragists," *Salt Lake Tribune,* April 4, 1888, 1. See also E. B. Wells, "A Women's Jubilee," *Salt Lake Herald,* March 25, 1888, 6.

260   An Advocate for Women

23. Kathi L. Kern, in recounting the founding of the International Council of Women, examines the competing claims of woman suffrage and social purity as its flagship issues in "'The Cornerstone of a New Civilization': The First International Council of Women and the Campaign for 'Social Purity,'" *Kentucky Law Journal* 84 (1995–96): 1235. Original minutes and proceedings can be found in May Wright Sewall, comp., *Genesis of the International Council of Women and the Story of Its Growth, 1888–1892* (n.p., n.d.); and in *Report of the International Council of Women* (Washington, D.C.: National Woman Suffrage Association, 1888).

24. Emily Richards was not new to the platform and had previously reported at the annual conventions of NWSA. Her talk is reported favorably in correspondence from Mack Smith to Wilford Woodruff and George Q. Cannon, March 30 and April 6, 1888, as noted in Lyman, *Political Deliverance*, 95n50. For more information on the council meeting, see "The Women's Council," *New York Times*, March 26, 1888, 1; "For Woman's Rights," *New York Times*, March 27, 1888, 3; "Women in Council," *New York Times*, March 29, 1888, 5; "Speaking for Women," *New York Times*, March 30, 1888, 3.

25. See C. A. L. in the *Woman's Exponent* 16 (April 15, 1888): 169–70, for a report of this incident and a favorable review of Richards's talk. Emily's husband, Franklin S. Richards, in his description of his wife's performance, failed to include the names of any of the other women who also represented the Church at the meeting. See "Appendix to Address Delivered by President Franklin S. Richards to the high priests quorum of Ensign Stake, Sunday, November 13, 1932," typescript copy, Church Archives.

26. The AWSA hesitated to join the newly organized NCW because of Lucy Stone's concern that the Council had demeaned itself in asking to be received by Grover Cleveland, whom she called "a male prostitute," passing judgment on his private life. She was also upset that a Mormon, "and not the Gentile from Utah," spoke for the territory. She could not put her association in the position of having to welcome Mormon women into the Council when they continued to support polygamy. Lucy Stone to Frances Willard, August 23, 1888, in Wheeler, *Loving Warriors*, 314–15.

27. "Editorial Thoughts," *Woman's Exponent* 16 (May 1, 1888): 180.

28. For more information on Harriet H. Robinson, see Claudia L. Bushman, *A Good Poor Man's Wife* (Hanover, N.H.: University Press of New England, 1981).

29. "N.W.S.A. Convention," *Woman's Exponent* 16 (April 15, 1888): 172; "The Women," *Salt Lake Herald*, April 3, 1888, 1.

30. In 1871, Howe presided over the New England Woman's Club, one of the country's first woman's clubs, and helped found the General Federation of Women's Clubs in 1889, serving as a director from 1893 to 1898. In 1875, at Howe's suggestion, Jennie Froiseth organized non-Mormon women in Utah into the Blue Tea Club, which later merged with a break-off group that called itself the Ladies Literary Club. Patricia Lyn Scott, "Jennie Anderson Froiseth and the Blue Tea," *Utah Historical Quarterly* 71 (Winter 2003): 20–35. Interestingly Froiseth, Cornelia Paddock, and Sarah Cooke, all instrumental in organizing the Anti-Polygamy Society, did not affiliate with the other Blue Tea members in the Ladies Literary Club. This club is known as the first woman's club in Utah. See Katherine B. Parsons, *History of Fifty Years: Ladies Literary Club, Salt Lake City, Utah, 1877–1927* (Salt Lake City: Arrow Press, 1927), 22–24.

31. Wells, Diary, June 23, 1888.

32. "Mrs. Howe's Reception," *Salt Lake Tribune*, June 23, 1888, 4, and "Julia Ward Howe's Lecture," *Salt Lake Tribune*, June 24, 1888, 4, give a full account of her visit to Salt Lake City.

33. Wells, Diary, June 24, 1888.

34. Wells, Diary, June 25, 1888.

35. Wells, Diary, June 26, 1888. The *Salt Lake Tribune* carried an article regarding Howe's visit, noting that at the recent "woman's congress in Washington," non-Mormon women were not given a hearing (referring to the omission of Dr. Woods from the program) and erroneously reporting that "Mrs. Froiseth was set aside from the Vice-Presidency and Mrs. Emeline [sic] B. Wells was substituted in her stead." The *Tribune* urged Howe to investigate the matter to see "how wicked a mistake her sister women made when they made that change." Froiseth did, however, continue for another year as vice president, before joining the AWSA just a year before it merged with the NWSA. "For Mrs. Howe to Investigate," *Salt Lake Tribune*, June 24, 1888, 2; see also "Mrs. Howe's Reception," 4, reporting Howe's visit.

36. Most notable among the faction that was supportive of Mormon membership were Elizabeth Stanton and Matilda Gage. Both women resisted NWSA's alliance with conservative moral reform associations and the merger of the two suffrage organizations because of the reformers' less tolerant attitude toward membership as well as their basic philosophical differences. Though Stanton reluctantly remained a member of the new association after the merger, even taking on the presidency, at Anthony's maneuvering, Gage left the movement and attempted to organize a separate, more radical organization, The Woman's National Liberal Union. For details of Gage's life, see Elizabeth B. Warbasse, "Matilda Joslyn Gage," in *Notable American Women*,

1607–1950: A Biographical Dictionary, ed. Edward T. James, Janet Wilson James, and Paul S. Boyer, 3 vols. (Cambridge, Mass: Belknap Press of Harvard University Press, 1971), 2:4–6.

37. Charlotte Godbe Kirby had married John Kirby, a non-Mormon and successful mine owner, after her divorce from William Godbe and had made her home in California for a period, all the while maintaining her activism in behalf of woman suffrage. For more details about her life, see Beverly Beeton, "'I Am an American Woman': Charlotte Ives Cobb Godbe Kirby," *Journal of the West* 27 (April 1988): 13–19.

38. Details of their visit can be found in "Visit of Mrs. Saxon and Mrs. Colby," *Woman's Exponent* 17 (October 1, 1888): 68; and "Comments," *Woman's Exponent* 17 (October 15, 1888): 76.

39. Wells, Diary, September 24, 1888.

40. "Utah Seen by the East," *Salt Lake Tribune,* November 23, 1888, 4. See also Papers of the Association of American Women, Sophia Smith Collection, Smith College, Northampton, Mass.

41. Wilford Woodruff was sustained as Church President three months later at the semi-annual general conference of the Church in April 1889.

42. Reference to the meeting can be found in Wells, Diary, January 3, 1889 (recounting the previous night's events); Zina D. H. Young, Diary, January 2, 1889, Church Archives; L. John Nuttall, Journal, January 2, 1889, also November 14 and December 31, 1888, Church Archives; and Franklin D. Richards, Journal, January 2, 10, 24, 1889, Church Archives.

43. Beyond her appointment to organize a local association and her attempt to enroll Jennie Froiseth in the effort, Isabel Brown does not appear to have played a particular role in the movement to organize a suffrage association in Utah. She was one of several non-Mormon women who supported woman suffrage, including Margaret Blaine Salisbury, Lillie Pardee, Emma J. McVicker, and Corinne Allen. An article by Linda Thatcher, "The 'Gentile Polygamist': Arthur Brown, Ex-Senator from Utah," *Utah Historical Quarterly* 52 (Summer 1984): 231–45, briefly discusses Isabel, who died in 1905.

44. Wells, Diary, January 2, 3, 1889.

45. "The Sister Suffragists," *Salt Lake Tribune,* January 8, 1889, 4, carried a disparaging article about the attempt of the women to enlist the support of Jennie Froiseth, referring to Wells and Richards as "Mormon Sisteren," "holy matrons," and "celestial queens," but ignoring the presence of Isabel Brown.

46. Wells, Diary, January 8, 1889. See also Susa Young Gates, "Woman Suffrage in Utah," Susan Young Gates Papers, Utah State Historical Society; and "Woman Suffrage Meeting," *Woman's Exponent* 17 (January 15, 1889): 121.

47. Margaret Nightingale Caine, wife of Congressional delegate John T. Caine, should not be confused with Margaret Ann Mitchell Caine, wife of Alfred Caine. Margaret A. Caine was a dedicated sericulturist and was prominent in the preparation of silk items for the Columbian Exposition in 1893. Margaret N. Caine served as president of the suffrage association only from January to July of that year. Sarah Kimball followed her, serving until Emmeline Wells picked up the reins in 1893.

48. "Woman Suffrage Meeting," 122. Emmeline's friend Romania Pratt along with Zina D. H. Young and several others assisted in gathering the signatures. Wells, Diary, January 10, 11, 12, 1889.

49. As wives of the LDS Church's Washington attorney, Franklin S. Richards, and Utah's delegate to Congress, John T. Caine, both of whom met frequently with women's leaders and congressional representatives, these two women were obvious choices to represent Mormon women's interest in the national suffrage convention. After Margaret Caine resigned her position as president of Utah's suffrage association a few months after her election, first vice president Lydia Alder served as interim president for the remainder of the year. "W. S. A. Meeting," *Woman's Exponent* 18 (August 15, 1889): 46.

50. "The Women of Utah," *Woman's Exponent* 17 (June 15, 1888): 10.

51. "Utah's Lady Delegate," *Woman's Exponent* 17 (February 15, 1889): 137.

52. Wells, Diary, October 22, 1889.

53. "Address to W. S. A. at Ogden," *Woman's Exponent* 18 (July 15, 1889): 30.

54. "Some of Miss Anthony's Views," *Woman's Exponent* 17 (March 1, 1890): 150.

55. Details of the final steps toward merger are addressed in Katharine Anthony, *Susan B. Anthony: Her Personal History and Her Era* (Garden City, New York: Doubleday, 1954), 388–97.

56. Wells, Diary, January 11, 1890.

57. Wells, Diary, February 8, 1890.

58. A discussion of Anthony's strategy in bringing into NWSA a broad spectrum of conservative women's groups, and with it a younger, even more conservative generation of suffragists, is found in Ellen Carol DuBois, ed., *Elizabeth Cady Stanton, Susan B. Anthony, Correspondence, Writing, Speeches* (New York: Schocken Books, 1981), 172–81.

59. Erin M. Masson briefly discusses this concept in "The Woman's Christian Temperance Society, 1874–1898: Combating Domestic Violence," *William and Mary Journal of Women and the Law* 3 (Spring 1997): 163. See also Aileen S.

Kraditor, *The Ideas of the Woman Suffrage Movement, 1890–1920* (New York: Columbia University Press, 1965).

60. Wells, Diary, November 8, 1889.

61. These developments are addressed in Lyman, *Political Deliverance*, 110–20. See also Orson F. Whitney, *History of Utah*, 4 vols. (Salt Lake City: George Q. Cannon and Sons, 1893), 3:679–711.

62. Wells, Diary, February 9, 10, 1890.

63. Once again Congress was debating an anti-Mormon bill, this time the Cullom-Struble Bill, which prohibited all participants, believers or members of organizations that condoned polygamy, from political participation. Not all non-Mormons supported this extreme measure, including many who lived in Utah. See Whitney, *History of Utah*, 3:736–39, 743. During this same period, numbers of non-Mormon Utah women refrained from the anti-Mormon activities of their gentile sisters.

64. Lyman, *Political Deliverance*, 114–20.

65. Wells, Diary, September 29 and October 9, 1890. It became evident soon after the 1890 Manifesto was issued that some who opposed it would continue to perform and practice plural marriage, requiring a second manifesto in 1904. See D. Michael Quinn, "LDS Church Authority and New Plural Marriages, 1890–1904," *Dialogue: A Journal of Mormon Thought* 18 (Spring 1985): 4–105; B. Carmon Hardy, *Solemn Covenant: The Mormon Polygamous Passage* (Urbana: University of Illinois Press, 1992).

66. Details concerning how the provisions of the Edmunds-Tucker Act affecting plural families were interpreted are found in Carol Cornwall Madsen, "'At Their Peril': Utah Law and the Case of Plural Wives, 1850–1900," *Western Historical Quarterly* 21 (November 1990): 425–43.

67. Some of these legal entanglements are discussed in Madsen, "'At Their Peril,'" 425–43.

68. Jean Bickmore White briefly examines the conditions leading to statehood in "Prelude to Statehood: Coming Together in the 1890s," *Utah Historical Quarterly* 62 (Fall 1994): 300–315. For women's efforts at shared community activity, see Carol Cornwall Madsen, "Decade of Detente: The Mormon-Gentile Female Relationship in Nineteenth-Century Utah," *Utah Historical Quarterly* 63 (Fall 1995): 298–319.

69. Nuttall, Journal, February 25, 1891.

70. A number of political factors were involved in the Democratic preference of most Church members as well as the shift to Republican sympathy by some of the ecclesiastical leaders. This process has been outlined in several studies including Lyman, *Political Deliverance*, 150–84; Gustive O. Larson

and Richard D. Poll, "The Forty-fifth State," in Poll and others, *Utah's History*, 387–404; White, "Prelude to Statehood," 300–315.

71. "An Important Political Movement," *Deseret Evening News,* May 7, 1891, 4; "Central Democratic Club," *Deseret Evening News,* May 7, 1891, 8; B. H. Roberts, *A Comprehensive History of The Church of Jesus Christ of Latter-day Saints, Century One,* 6 vols. (Provo, Utah: Corporation of the President, The Church of Jesus Christ of Latter-day Saints, 1965), 6:299–301.

72. "Women in Politics," *Woman's Exponent* 20 (August 15, 1891): 28.

73. Wells, Diary, June 9, 1891.

74. Wells, Diary, November 12, 1891.

75. Nuttall, Journal, May 21, 1891.

Chapter 11

Strategies for Victory

*A woman who goes to the polls and deposits a ballot,
feels her political independence and
that she is virtually part and parcel of the great body politic,
not through her father or husband, but in her own vested right.*[1]

The next few years took Emmeline Wells into social and political paths she had little reason to anticipate yet which fulfilled her desire to be "about the world's work." In February 1891 she returned to Washington, D.C., after an absence of five years. She went to attend the first triennial meeting of the National Council of Women (NCW) and to assist in the Mormon bid for membership. Since her last visit to Washington in 1886, the Edmunds-Tucker Bill had become law, Utah women had lost the franchise, the two national suffrage associations had merged, and President Wilford Woodruff of the LDS Church had issued his manifesto forbidding further plural marriages. Though she was no longer either a voting woman or an impassioned advocate for a suspect religious practice, she nevertheless attracted press attention. The *Woman's Tribune* agreed with Emily Richards that Emmeline was "one of the most interesting women at the Council," and the *Washington Post* recalled her prior work and reported that "her advocacy of wronged women and the equality of the sex has been particularly fearless."[2]

While the accolades were pleasing, her primary concern was whether the antipolygamy members had mellowed enough with all the change that had transpired to allow the Latter-day Saint women's organizations to become members of the NCW. Meeting with May Wright Sewall, the NCW's corresponding secretary, Sarah Kimball, Emily Richards, Caroline Thomas, and Emmeline Wells submitted their credentials and "made a clear statement of the case." Left to themselves, these strong-willed women prepared the content of their written application. Emmeline noted that "there was some misunderstanding of how we should present the matters and what part of the work we should state as it must necessarily be brief." When finally completed, Emmeline gave the report to May Sewall, who submitted it first to the committee on credentials and then to the executive committee. "We were left in suspense," Wells noted. But finally, to their surprise and great relief, Susan B. Anthony herself brought "the good news that we were admitted without a dissenting vote." This time there were no donations and no wire pulling. Mormon women were admitted on the basis of their reputation as loyal organization women. It was a crucial juncture, undoubtedly facilitated by the Woodruff Manifesto but also, on a personal level, by the carefully nurtured friendship of Wells and Richards with Anthony, Sewall, and other NCW officers. From that point on, the Utah delegates participated in NCW sessions and made friends among many of the council members.[3]

Finally relieved of the anxieties and frustrations endured during her 1886 Washington trip, Emmeline enjoyed a sense of amiability with many of the other delegates. She was openly admiring of these women who were "laboring to unite, in a grand band of sisterhood, the several great organizations" represented at the convention, an objective that coincided with her own efforts toward unity and accord among women.[4] The organizing of both the National and International Councils of Women convinced Emmeline that "the increase of love toward one another through these united efforts is one of the most hopeful signs of the age. . . . It proves conclusively that there is a power and influence binding women together, such as has not been heretofore."[5] Perhaps the disfranchisement of Mormon women actually strengthened, rather than weakened, their connection with eastern suffragists; all now endured the same political disability.

Upon returning home, Wells was immediately inundated with celebration plans for the 1892 jubilee of the founding of the Relief Society, which as corresponding secretary she was called on to coordinate. This was an important occasion for her. From the time of its organization, she believed, "women have been developing powers and attributes which had previously lain dormant and also claiming independence and freedom in civil political and religious matters unheard of before."[6] This conviction had been a foundation for her enthusiastic participation in the woman movement of her time and she believed the Relief Society facilitated these advances. She was also immediately caught up in her work as president of the Salt Lake County branch of the World's Fair Committee, assisting to organize the Utah women's exhibit at Chicago's forthcoming Columbian Exposition in 1893, celebrating the 400th anniversary of Columbus's arrival in the Americas. This was but one civic enterprise that united the formerly hostile Mormon and gentile women during the last decade of the century.

Emmeline was elated to see that the unity of women she had so long advocated was now a possibility in her own home territory. The formerly divided women had begun to pool their time, efforts, and resources toward combining their separate interests in the fashionable kindergarten movement; in establishing a Utah branch of the General Federation of Women's Clubs that brought Mormon and gentile women's clubs together in mutually shared civic betterment campaigns;[7] and in supporting a newly organized committee on charity that crossed denominational lines. While woman suffrage remained a divisive issue until after Utah statehood, it would eventually unite Mormon and gentile women in political associations and in the Utah Council of Women (UCW), a nonpartisan forerunner of the League of Women Voters in Utah. But regaining suffrage was the immediate task at hand for Emmeline Wells.[8]

Observing the rapidly changing political scene, she found that the new political alignments in Utah created an ambiguous future for woman suffrage. "Which party will recognize women?" she queried in a *Woman's Exponent* article in June 1891. Perhaps neither, she feared, for "wherever suffrage for woman is spoken of in public gatherings, there are only a few who dare speak for Utah upon this question."[9] With suffrage still a controversial issue even in Utah, the newly organized parties were understandably reluctant to champion a cause that might be detrimental either in obtaining statehood or winning office. The diverse makeup of the Utah legislature in the 1890s was measurably different from the homogeneous legislative body of 1870, which had originally granted the vote to Utah women. Moreover, Wells observed, "It does not yet appear to be the time of women's choosing in political issues until further developments of difficult questions now pending are made in the Territory."[10] Women's exclusion from the restoration of the vote to male polygamists by the Utah Commission in July 1893, following a presidential pardon the previous January, intensified her resolve to regain the vote for women at statehood.[11]

At this time, most women had not publicly declared a party preference, nor had they been invited to join either of the national parties recently organized in Utah.[12] Instead, they focused on keeping woman suffrage a bipartisan issue, as they had been advised by national suffrage leaders. Moreover, most women, like Ruth May Fox, who later became an active Republican supporter, preferred to do "further study of the parties" to determine their choice. But it was not easy to avoid following the tide of political excitement and dickering over the potential membership and success of the newly organized parties. At the regular monthly meeting of the Utah Women's Press Club, president (and founder) Emmeline Wells, wary of the divisive influence of partisan politics, set the limits of political expression. "These meetings," she announced, "are simply for literary improvement and devoted to the press and similar things, and not for the discussion of religion or politics as we can secure these things in other places. No subject should be presented here upon which we are likely to conflict or that will create unpleasantness."[13]

Occasional infractions occurred, however. Shortly before the ratification election of the new state constitution of 1895, Ruth May Fox, giving a paper on current political affairs to the Reaper's Club, a popular literary club organized by Wells, criticized a statement of prominent Democrat (and non-Mormon) Judge Orlando Powers.

She "immediately withdrew it," as the club was "divided in politics and some of the ladies thought we should take no note of it on that account." At the next meeting, however, a Democratic member of the club found opportunity to defend Judge Powers, before she was presumably silenced also.[14]

Unexpectedly, in October 1893, Sarah Kimball resigned as president of the Utah Territorial Woman Suffrage Association (UTWSA); Emmeline Wells, a widow since 1891 and thus eligible for office, was elected in Kimball's place. Emmeline was pleased finally to have a title that in some measure reflected the work she expended for the association. She frequently noted that, though she was usually exhausted from the demands of her varied activities, she enjoyed politics. She expanded coverage on woman suffrage in the *Woman's Exponent* and published detailed accounts of the county meetings and particularly the semiannual conventions of the UTWSA. She intensified her arguments for woman suffrage in her paper's editorial column while also printing similar appeals by contributors to the paper. "The women of Utah had the ballot wrested from them without adjudication," she reminded her readers, "and no redress has ever been offered for that wrong. It would be but a simple act of justice for that wrong done in the past to restore that right of franchise."[15]

Another unexpected event occurred a few months later when Emmeline received word that she had been made a patron of the NCW, "an honor which I should never have anticipated," she wrote, "and if any one had given me a quantity of gold I could not have been much more astonished. It was certainly a very handsome compliment." Though the title did not confer the right to vote (unless she was also a delegate), it did confer lifetime membership.[16]

A long-awaited major step toward statehood was taken on July 16, 1894, when U.S. President Grover Cleveland approved the Enabling Act, which permitted the people of Utah to form a constitution and state government and to be admitted into the union "on an equal footing with Original States." A constitutional convention was authorized for the following March. Emmeline immediately used her paper to pressure the soon-to-be elected delegates to the forthcoming convention to restore the voting rights of women. "Let us all rejoice in the prospect statehood offers, more especially if it makes all citizens equal irrespective of sex. Only a simple act of justice to one half of the community who are taxed without representation," she exclaimed.[17]

Susan B. Anthony had advice of her own to pass on to the women of Utah. In a lengthy letter to Emmeline Wells, which she had printed in the *Deseret News* and the *Woman's Exponent,* Anthony warned Utah women to insure that woman suffrage would be included in the constitution and not left to a later time. "I am sure that you, my dear sisters," she wrote, "who have not only tasted the sweets of liberty, but also the bitterness, the humiliation of the loss of the blessed symbol, will not allow the organic law of your state to be framed on the barbarism that makes women the political slaves of men." Expressing her dismay at eastern suffragists' lack of success to add woman suffrage to their state constitutions, she urged Utah women to take strong action to avoid that situation, knowing that only two states had thus far been successful in granting suffrage to their women. "Now in the formative period of your constitution is the time to establish justice and equality to all the people," Anthony wrote. "That adjective 'male' once admitted into your organic law, will remain there. . . . No, no! Don't be deluded by any specious reasoning, but demand justice now. Once ignored in your constitution—you'll be as powerless to secure recognition as are we in the older states."[18] Her words would ring loudly in the ears of Utah suffragists a few short months later when woman suffrage became a major point of discussion at the constitutional convention.

As the national political parties began to take a firm hold in Utah, the divisiveness that Emmeline and others feared began to encroach on the unity of the suffrage association. By 1894, when the road to statehood had been cleared of obstacles, most politically minded women had begun to indicate their party preference. Thus the surface unity of the association began to ripple with small waves of dissension as individual party differences and personal aspirations began to appear. Both Margaret Caine and Sarah Kimball had served only brief terms as president of the UTWSA, but newly elected president Emmeline Wells and her vice president Emily Richards were still active participants in the movement. Both were capable leaders, both had had extensive experience in the national suffrage associations, and both quietly nurtured their own political views and goals. Despite party differences, Wells and Richards would retain leadership of the UTWSA until after statehood.

It did not take long for the women's differences to surface. A small power struggle erupted when Emmeline urged Ruth May Fox, a young woman new to public affairs and a devoted follower of Emmeline, to allow Ruth's name to be nominated as chair of the county organizational meeting. But Emmeline had to leave the meeting before nominations were made, and Ruth and another political novice, Ella Hyde, were left to make nominations. Feeling inadequate, Fox, joined by Hyde, decided that Dr. Ellen Ferguson, a long-time suffragist with political ambitions of her own, was much more experienced and thus a better candidate than Ruth, so they nominated Ferguson for chair.[19]

Ferguson's chairmanship of the organizational meeting led to her election as president of the Salt Lake County Association. In this capacity, Dr. Ferguson marshaled the force of her county organization two months later and held a private meeting to which Ruth and others were invited. The ladies met, according to Fox, "to complain of the way they had been treated by the Ter. Board of U.W.S.A [Territorial Board of the Utah Woman Suffrage Association] under Emmeline's leadership." The ladies also debated the legality of the election of officers in the convention at which Emmeline Wells was elected president, and so they drafted a letter asking for another convention. Besides failing to secure her nomination as chair of the county organizational meeting, Fox also admitted making a mistake in signing the letter, having done so, she said later, "with the best of feeling toward Sister Wells." Ironically, Ruth May Fox and Emily Richards, who also had signed the letter, were asked to deliver it to Emmeline.[20] When Emmeline received it, she quietly dismissed it as originating with "persons who wish to make trouble. No one," she commented in her diary, "could misunderstand the spirit of envy and jealousy in the communication."[21] Confident and ambitious herself, she was not above belittling the motives of others at critical times. Though her relationship with Ruth May Fox remained unchanged, the rivalry between Emmeline Wells and her younger colleague Emily Richards, as well as with her friend Dr. Ferguson, became more acute when they all declared their party allegiances later that year.

Other developments were more distressful. Shortly before the constitutional convention convened in March 1895, Emmeline Wells worried about a potential fissure in the territorial association that might derail the suffrage momentum. In a letter to Mary A. White of the Beaver County Association, Emmeline warned about "some unwise women who would push the Association to the extreme and antagonize all the men in the country." She explained that three or four unnamed women were "trying to form a League," and had said to her "they would write to the County Associations and get them to join in this League." Emmeline hoped to foil their plan and gather her own allies by warning county members in advance. Evidently dissatisfied with the moderate strategies of the UTWSA under Emmeline, these suffragists, she acknowledged, were "smart women who are very dangerous and have to be guided if they will submit, and if not then one must be on the watch for breakers." She further advised against joining either of the political parties, which could possibly create a divide in the campaign. While her letter expressed her fear that five years of careful spadework might be jeopardized by the creation of another, more aggressive suffrage organization, similar to the split in the national movement twenty-five years earlier, she was clearly worried as well about her own standing in the movement. Her forceful manner, her desire to control, and her overt ambition sometimes bred resentment and opposition to her leadership. She nonetheless attracted a devoted following who recognized the impact of her involvement in community as well as women's affairs. More than others in the movement, she had confidence in the men who controlled the political future of the women in the state. "I rather trust men than distrust them by far," she wrote. "Most of our leading brethren I believe think the woman element in politics at this present crisis will be a saving power."[22]

That woman suffrage was developing into a major political issue became evident soon after the two political parties were established in

Utah. Even before the Enabling Act had been issued, the inclusion of woman suffrage in the proposed state constitution had become a public topic of debate. One contrary voice, whose opposition would make an impressive impact on the delegates to the constitutional convention, registered his disapproval early and publicly. After a Sunday service in the Salt Lake Tabernacle on March 20, 1892, Emmeline reflected on comments by Brigham H. (B. H.) Roberts, a member of the Church's Quorum of Seventy, who spoke at the meeting. "He speaks well on the Gospel," she conceded, "but is not quite broad enough on some matters pertaining to women. . . . He has prejudiced many against the suffrage question and kept some back who believe in it from taking active part."[23] He was countered three weeks later by Elder Francis M. Lyman, who urged an assembly of young women in Farmington to "take hold of this woman suffrage movement," affirming that it is "according to the mind and will of the Lord as manifested by the First Presidency" of the Church. "Every Latter-day Saint woman should join in and use her influence for good," Lyman concluded.[24] The divisiveness of contemporary politics was changing the political scene in Utah.

In addition to her suffrage responsibilities, Wells spent much of her time petitioning the legislative assembly on other matters. Representing the Silk Committee, which had been formed six years earlier,[25] Emmeline prepared a petition for a payment or bounty on cocoons and the creation of a territorial board to manage the industry. Granted a hearing, members of the committee successfully made a case for presentation before the assembly, which resulted in the requested bounty.[26] Wells also petitioned the legislators in behalf of the Relief Society to allow Angie Newman's abandoned Industrial Christian Home to be used for a hospital under direction of the Relief Society, an ironic conclusion to a misguided venture. She was not successful in this effort, however. An appeal to appoint women to school boards and other territorial boards was similarly unsuccessful until statehood.[27]

Emmeline Wells became well acquainted with the legislative process during these years, and she developed well-defined goals regarding other legislation, beyond the vote, that would benefit women. Besides the education such activity provided her, the experience expanded her sphere of influence and her coterie of co-workers. Her time was spent almost as much with her non-Mormon friends as with her co-religionists, and she relished the public work that seemed to proliferate before her. Unfortunately, her enthusiasm and sense of purpose could not always offset the fatigue that so much activity created for the sixty-five-year-old woman. "I am very weary tonight," she wrote in February 1894, although it could have been any night. "Yet [I] feel but little has as yet been accomplished by me—I am so anxious to do more than is possible."[28] When her daughter Annie complained of the immense amount of work Emmeline was doing and implied that somehow it was improper, Emmeline was hurt but not persuaded to change her course. "I feel that I must do some public duty," she confided to her diary, "and that will give me development in the direction of the pursuits I am working in as well as influence." Her strong iterations of the noble work in which she was engaged may well have disguised, even to herself, her personal ambition to make a name in the political, if not the literary, world. Whatever the motivation, it was clearly an energizing force. "One cannot work for the elevation and uplifting of humanity," she reasoned, "unless there is some public encouragement as well as personal effort."[29] The public acclaim she garnered from time to time, which increased as she aged, massaged her sense of accomplishment as it spurred her to continue her work.

In the meantime, Utah suffragists held rallies, meetings, and socials and they lobbied the party conventions at which party platforms were determined and delegates to the constitutional convention were elected. Emmeline was eager to keep woman suffrage at the forefront of the politician's minds as they prepared for statehood. Thus the delegates to the constitutional convention found themselves under her watchful eye well before the convention convened. As the delegates were being elected, she was quick to challenge their intent. "How will the delegates to the Constitutional Convention consider the interest of the sex who have no representation save through them?" she queried. "Will their claim to citizenship be guaranteed to them through these great, grand, noble hearted sons of the soil?" she coyly added.[30] Surely, they could not resist such a trust.

Success seemed assured when both parties included a woman suffrage plank in their political platforms, despite the fact that not all of the delegates were supportive.[31] Lurking below the surface, however, were cautious voices sounding warnings that the time was not propitious to press woman's political rights. Favorable reports from the governors of Wyoming and Colorado of the success of woman suffrage in their states, however, helped to reassure some of the doubters.[32] On the eve of the constitutional convention, which convened in March 1895, suffragists, LDS Church leaders, and most convention delegates anticipated successful passage of woman suffrage into the new state constitution.[33]

During this period of local political activity, Emmeline Wells spent the early weeks of January 1895 preparing materials and raising money for dues to submit to the forthcoming meetings of the National American Woman Suffrage Association (NAWSA) and NCW, which she planned to attend later that month. Before leaving she hoped to reinforce the necessity for maintaining unity in the county suffrage associations.[34] Now that the moment of decision had come in the impending constitutional convention, she did not want anything unexpected to upset the precarious support the women had been able to elicit. Theirs was not to be a militant display of feminist belligerence. They were to conduct their campaign with intelligence and decorum. Thus she urged her co-workers to quietly and unobtrusively "try and convert people, and educate and prepare" themselves. "We must be ready when developments are made that show the time has come," she wrote. "Both parties are pledged," she reminded them, "but if great opposition is brought to bear they may succumb."[35]

That year Atlanta, Georgia, was selected as the site of the national suffrage convention.[36] Emmeline's companions were Aurelia Spencer Rogers of Farmington and Marilla Daniels of Provo, who were attending a national convention for the first time. At the meeting, Emmeline once again was pleased to be singled out by Susan B. Anthony, who invited her to sit by her side at an informal delegates' meeting prior to the official opening of the convention. Emmeline's appointment to the committee on the plan of work kept her in subcommittee meetings

E. S. Taylor E. B. Wells L. Stevens Mrs. Bagley M. W. Sewell R. F. Avery I. C. Davis S. B. Anthony Mrs. Howland Mrs. Dickenson

Delegates to the National Council of Women convention in Washington, D.C., February 1895.

Young Woman's Journal 6 (June 1895): 390.

during much of the conference. Marilla Daniels, along with Emmeline, was appointed to the executive committee, and Aurelia Rogers to the committee on resolutions, the first experience for Rogers and Daniels to work alongside other national delegates. On the third day of the conference, Emmeline was asked to report on the work in Utah. She reviewed the years of preparation for statehood and for the restoration of the vote to women and expressed confidence in a favorable vote by the delegates to the constitutional convention. As a final measure, she told her audience, plans were made for a delegation of women to be on hand "watching carefully any and every measure calculated to infringe upon the full freedom and liberty of women to present petitions, if needful, should emergencies unlooked for arise."[37] When Emmeline concluded her brief talk, according to a newspaper account, "President Anthony came forward and putting her arm around her gave her endorsement to the speaker. As she told of the work being done in Utah she kept her arms around the delegate and the audience was visibly affected at this exhibition of affection." It was not only a "tribute of personal affection," Emmeline noted in her diary, but "a flattering compliment to the Territory."[38] The two committed suffragists must have made a striking picture with the tall, slender Anthony standing next to the tiny, delicate Emmeline Wells.

After the NAWSA convention, the three Utah women traveled to Washington, D.C., to await the opening of the triennial meeting of the NCW. While Marilla Daniels and Aurelia Rogers spent their time sight-seeing, escorted by a relative of Emmeline's whom she called to assist them, Emmeline wrote letters, prepared for the council meetings, and eagerly awaited other delegates from Utah. She had urged Relief Society General President Zina D. H. Young, the group's official representative, to attend but had little hope of seeing her, aware of Young's commitment to her service in the recently dedicated Salt Lake City Temple along with her other Relief Society duties. Finally, seven Utah women assembled in Washington—Elmina S. Taylor, Ellis B. Shipp, Minnie J. Snow, and Susa Young Gates, who joined Emmeline and her two companions. The women made individual arrangements for lodging, Susa Gates and Ellis Shipp staying with national suffragist

Belva Lockwood at her home, and Emmeline, Elmina Taylor, and Minnie Snow, lodging at the Ebbit House, NCW headquarters during the convention.

All the women participated in the various sessions, presenting papers on aspects of Latter-day Saint women's lives and community service. As a member of the resolutions committee, Emmeline was busy during the convention but took time to accept an invitation to the elegant Philadelphia home of Rachel Foster Avery (NCW treasurer), along with Lucy Anthony (Susan's niece), the Reverend Anna Howard Shaw, and Louise Barnum Robbins (the new corresponding secretary). Emmeline was aware of the significance of her inclusion in such an auspicious group and was duly impressed with the sophistication of the women and their gracious lifestyle.[39] Later, the whole Utah contingent was invited to attend a banquet in honor of Susan B. Anthony's seventy-fifth birthday. The two delegates, Emmeline Wells (as proxy for Zina Young), and Elmina Taylor (president of the Young Ladies' Mutual Improvement Association), were seated at the head table to the right of Anthony. Both Mormon women were invited to speak.[40] Several other speakers praised Utah, and the Utah delegation received five invitations to additional receptions. "They crowd around us and seem very anxious to vie with each other in the attention we receive," Susa Gates enthusiastically reported.[41] They could not have failed to observe the reversal of their experience at the 1891 triennial convention!

On her journey home, Emmeline continued to be fêted, this time at the Indianapolis home of May Wright Sewall, president of the NCW. "She welcomed me like a queen," Emmeline observed, returning the favor in designating Sewall "a queen of hearts." Their friendship blossomed on this particular visit, and Emmeline added Sewall to many other acquaintances that she transformed into solid friendships during this eastern journey.

The organizations drawn to the NCW reflected middle-class American women of widely divergent political and religious views but united in their concern for women's advancement. Their leadership was usually comprised of women with the means and leisure that enabled them to devote their lives to organizational work.[42] Emmeline always felt the financial disability that impeded a larger role for most Utah women in the council, though convinced that they were more than equal to any assignment.

After a month of travel, Wells returned to Utah just days before the constitutional convention was to convene. She was interviewed by the *Salt Lake Tribune*, which referred to her as "the noted woman suffrage leader of Utah," a far cry from the epithets it had used to describe her on her first trip to Washington sixteen years earlier. The social climate in Utah had indeed changed. In the interview, Emmeline expressed her pleasure at being back to work for woman suffrage in the state's constitution, and then, once more, as she had repeatedly done in the editorial columns of the *Woman's Exponent*, she explained her practical views on suffrage. She reminded her interviewer that Utah women had been granted the vote by their territorial legislature, that they had exercised it responsibly for seventeen years, and that it had been taken from them as an expedient "political measure." Drawing on remarks she had made at the Atlanta convention, she argued the injustice of "taxation without representation," citing the number of Utah women who had been made virtual heads of their families by congressional enactments (imprisonment of polygamists) while others owned their own homes and paid taxes, if only minimally.[43]

Within a week her arguments surged with intensity as woman suffrage became an open question in the convention and antisuffragists made their voices heard. Responding to an invitation to attend an antisuffrage meeting in Utah, the popular antipolygamy lecturer Kate Field unexpectedly refused. Explaining that she had helped put Utah "in harmony with the Union" (perhaps thinking her lectures had helped resolve the polygamy issue), she felt it was "an outrage" for antisuffragists to expect Mormons, who constituted the majority of convention delegates, to deny women the vote at this time. "With woman suffrage," she concluded, "even I might be induced to become a citizen of Utah."[44] Many Mormons besides Emmeline Wells may have wondered if this was the same Kate Field who had so maligned the Mormons in her popular lectures. It was indeed a remarkable turnabout.

Of the 107 convention delegates, twenty-eight were not Mormons, including C. C. Goodwin, editor of the *Salt Lake Tribune;* George P. Miller, a Methodist Episcopal minister; and Charles Varian, an attorney who had earlier prosecuted polygamists. Fifty-nine of the delegates were Republicans; forty-eight were Democrats. Both parties had pledged to support woman suffrage.

The City and County Building (ca. 1895) in Salt Lake City was the site of the state's constitutional convention.

Thus, when Emily Richards and Nellie Little informed Emmeline upon her return of their misgivings about the fate of suffrage in the convention, Emmeline was not unduly distressed. Their worries may have found their source in a *Salt Lake Tribune* editorial warning the convention delegates that the constitution might well be rejected if woman suffrage and prohibition were included. Reports that members of the committee on elections and suffrage were themselves divided on the issue also undermined the women's confidence. Though remaining optimistic about the ultimate outcome, Emmeline decided not to leave matters entirely in the hands of those delegates on whom she counted, so she brought her considerable leadership skills to the fore. She called a meeting of suffragists on March 18, 1895, in the probate court room next to the convention hall to prepare a memorial. Emily Richards carried the finished document to the convention, which had already entertained memorials from Weber and Utah Counties. Commenting on the large delegation of women, more than seventy-five, the *Salt Lake Tribune* observed that "the invasion did not have the serious aspect that it might have worn had it not been pretty well established that the convention is strongly in favor of woman suffrage."[45] A few days later, Emmeline called another meeting to prepare a second memorial, which was introduced by delegate Franklin S. Richards, Emily's husband. Several women were then invited to speak before the committee on elections and suffrage. Some had prepared their talk beforehand, but Emmeline, exhausted and pressed for time, later complained at not being able to write her talk and thus had to rely on her ability to speak rapidly and extemporaneously on a subject for which she undoubtedly lacked no words.[46] Even as the women spoke, memorials continued to flow into the convention from the county suffrage organizations.

The majority report of the committee on elections and suffrage revealed a favorable response to woman suffrage, indicating no reason to deny women the vote and citing the success of woman suffrage in Wyoming. However, recognizing that woman suffrage was still an outrageous concept to most Americans, if not to some Utahns, the *Salt Lake Tribune* served as a cautionary voice and joined those who favored submitting the question as a separate measure to the voters.[47] "Utah will join the small group of freak states," it warned, appropriating a common antisuffrage epithet. Some of the members of the election and suffrage committee used the warning to issue a minority report based, however, not on the political expedience of separate submissions but on the merits of woman suffrage itself. The report also raised the specter of the recent past when Mormons dominated Utah politics and resurrected the oft-used argument that Mormon women voted only as they were directed. The former political imbalance, they claimed, would be perpetuated by LDS Church leaders "working upon the generous impulses and religious instincts of women, which would result in political, if not social and business ostracism of the minority."[48]

In light of this report, assurance of the passage of woman suffrage wavered. When the two reports were presented to the convention on March 28, they opened the door to a long and emotional debate on the advisability of incorporating woman suffrage into the constitution or offering it to the voters as a separate issue. One of the first speakers was B. H. Roberts, a member of the Church's Quorum of Seventy and a Democratic delegate from Davis County, who had already announced his opposition to woman suffrage. Long regarded as a gripping orator, he spoke to a packed house, including suffragists and other observers. All seemed enthralled by his oratory. The *Salt Lake Herald,* voice of the Democrats, wrote: "A stream of language, potent and pleasing, flowed from his lips and caught his listeners until even those who were most bitterly opposed to him were compelled to pay compliment to his power with rapturous applause."[49] His rhetorical skills, aided by the voices of several other delegates, both Mormons and non-Mormons, Democrats and Republicans, lent considerable strength to the arguments of the minority report and extended discussion on the topic for nearly two weeks. Disclaiming any part in preparing the minority report or any need for arguing the issue on its merits, Roberts questioned only the advisability of adopting woman suffrage at that time. Statehood, he argued, superseded suffrage and no chance should be taken to encumber the constitution with controversial measures. Though Roberts had been advised by the LDS Church First Presidency not to impede the passage of a woman suffrage clause, he ventured to act on his own initiative. Woman suffrage sympathizers, not anticipating the need for defense, nonetheless, rose to the occasion. Among them were two fellow Democrats, Franklin S. Richards and Orson F. Whitney, whose persuasive oratory rivaled that of Roberts.

Emmeline Wells and her co-workers immediately sent a "Resolution of Thanks" to Whitney and to majority members of the committee on elections and suffrage. The women arranged to have both Whitney's and Richards's speeches printed in a pamphlet for the utwsa. But the discussion was far from over. Within a few days, as the debate continued, the argument shifted as Roberts again took the floor. He moved from arguing the political advantage of separate submission to the propriety of woman suffrage. Declaring his high regard for women, he explained that for him their influence did not come from public platforms but rather from the hearthside and that the political arena could do nothing but debase them. Seemingly ignoring the fact that women in the territory had voted for seventeen years, he contended that only the most shameless women would sully themselves by going to the polls.[50]

Roberts met his rhetorical match in Whitney. Point by point he answered Roberts's arguments and added his own conviction that a woman was not made "merely for a wife, a mother, a cook, and a housekeeper." Regardless of the importance of these roles, "they are not the sum of her capabilities," he asserted. In fact, he stated, the woman's movement that had so pricked the national conscience "means something more than that certain women are ambitious to vote and hold office. I regard it," he argued, "as one of the great levers by which the Almighty is lifting up this fallen world, lifting it nearer to the throne of its Creator."[51] So the debate continued with most of the delegates registering their own positions on the issue. Eventually, a motion to submit the question to the voters as a separate measure from the constitution was discussed with a final word by Roberts scheduled for the following day.

Emmeline's dismay at this troubling turn of events found voice in an *Exponent* editorial:

> It is pitiful to see how men opposed to woman suffrage try to make the women believe it is because they worship them so, and think them far too good, and one would really think to hear those eloquent orators talk, that laws were all framed purposely to protect women in their rights, and men stood ready to defend them with their lives.... We can only say they have been bold and must answer to their own consciences; they are no doubt honest in their convictions and let us hope the practical experience that will come with the ballot may convince even them that good may follow and they and their children receive the benefit of what they could not discern in the future progress of the world.[52]

The delegates failed to pass the motion for separate submission, despite Roberts's stirring closing argument, though the vote showed enough support to encourage proponents of the measure to press for reconsideration. One group agreed with Roberts that the controversial issue would doom this seventh attempt at statehood. Others, still worried that woman suffrage would continue Mormon political dominance in the state, also supported separate submission. These groups organized rallies, submitted petitions, and stirred the populace in both

Salt Lake City and Ogden to join with them. Gentile women joined in by calling a meeting in Salt Lake City at the Grand Opera House for "those who do not hold suffrage above statehood."[53] This frenzy of political activity played out, ironically, against the backdrop of the LDS Church's semiannual conference.

It was thus with reluctance that Latter-day Saint suffrage leaders requested several Relief Society women to miss conference to attend the meeting in the Opera House, where they could personally refute the arguments for separate submission. One of them, Mary Ann Freeze, explained that it was "much against my natural inclinations, but [I] soon learned that it was necessary."[54] Ultimately, only twenty-nine women, one of whom was Jennie Froiseth, signed a resolution calling for separate submission. Conspicuously absent were the signatures of prominent gentile women: Corinne Allen, Emma J. McVicker, Isabella Bennett, Lillie R. Pardee, and Margaret Blaine Salisbury.[55]

On April 4, following the conclusion of the LDS Church's semi-annual conference, the general Relief Society conference convened. After reports of the society's activities were presented, Emmeline, the corresponding secretary, in her own report turned the theme of the meeting from Relief Society business to the proceedings of the constitutional convention. She affirmed her conviction that despite the strong move to prevent woman suffrage from being inserted into the constitution, it would ultimately be included. Emily Richards followed, pressing the Society to stand united and firm and concluding her remarks with a request that all who favored equal suffrage in the constitution to stand. "Every woman in that large congregation was on her feet immediately," the minutes reported.[56]

While the women were assembled in their conference, the First Presidency of the Church joined with the Apostles in their own meeting, where the subject of woman suffrage was discussed for more than two hours. Wilford Woodruff expressed his fear that the constitution would not pass the voters if woman suffrage were *not* a part of it. First Counselor Joseph F. Smith supported him in that view; Second Counselor George Q. Cannon, however, favored separate submission and argued so strongly for it that he succeeded in changing the mind of

President Woodruff, though not that of Joseph F. Smith.[57] However, there was no Church action on the measure.

Although the new developments were disturbing, Emmeline did not seem to feel as "gloomy" as many other women and was buoyed by the talk that Joseph F. Smith gave at the evening session of the Relief Society conference. "I have felt impressed all day with a desire that I or some one or more of the brethren might be present with you during this conference," he said, understanding the anxiety the women were experiencing over the unexpected political developments. Then he delivered a strong oration on woman's rights, chastising those women who were "careless and indifferent to their rights" and tended to "rest content and seek no changes, however much for the better a change might be." While he deplored this attitude, he nevertheless preferred these women to those who would "not only make no exertion themselves to progress, but would and did exert themselves to prevent the progression of others." He regarded them as "enemies to society." For his part, he said, he wanted women to enjoy "every blessing, privilege, right or liberty which he himself enjoyed in the legitimate pursuit of happiness in this world or in the world to come. . . . God never did design that a woman should receive less for the produce of her labor, whether of hand or brain, skilled or meniel [sic] than a man should receive for the same labor no better executed than hers." The question of the day, he went on to say, is:

> Shall women be as free as men or not, shall the male citizen have a voice in civil government because he is a male and a female citizen be denied the same privilege simply because she is a female . . . ? Why shall one enjoy civil rights and the other be denied them? Why shall one be admitted to all the avenues of mental and physical progress and prosperity and the other be prohibited, and prescribed within certain narrow limits, to her material abridgment and detriment . . . ? Strange to say, women may be found who seem to glory in their enthralled condition, and who caress and fondle the very chains and manacles which fetter and enslave them! Let those who love this helpless dependent condition and prefer to remain in it . . . enjoy it; but for conscience and for mercy's sake let them not stand in the way of those of their sisters who would be, and of right ought to

be *free*. . . . Let them who will not enter into the door of equal rights and impartial suffrage step aside, and leave the passage clear to those who desire to enter.[58]

It was a powerful statement on the rights of women and it gave the suffragists an energizing boost to face the final hurdles to success. Moreover, at the following evening session of the Relief Society conference, Apostles Heber J. Grant, Franklin D. Richards, and Charles W. Penrose, expressed their desire to see the franchise returned to the women of Utah. Armed with this support, the Relief Society women mobilized to counter the growing tide of "separate submission" sympathy.[59]

On April 5, the Utah Women's Press Club abandoned its planned program in order to talk about suffrage and voted to aid the cause by circulating petitions against separate submission. Emmeline coordinated the petition campaign, enlisting the help of the county suffrage organizations.[60] They were heartened to learn, according to a *Tribune* tally, that all the petitions received by the convention ultimately numbered 24,801 signatures against separate submission and just 15,366 signatures in favor.[61]

Throughout the days of such frenzied political machinations, Emmeline worked day and night. She wrote letters to suffragists in every county, drew up petitions, solicited signatures, attended meetings, wrote editorials and articles for her paper, corresponded with national suffrage leaders, and when asked to speak in a session of the Relief Society conference, gave only a short speech, unable to "say half that was in my heart of the present needs of the time." This moment was the culmination of nearly twenty years of labor. She had lost the battle to retain the vote; she could not lose the fight to regain it. On April 18, nearly three weeks after the first intimations of the struggle emerged, Emmeline was once again preparing new lists of signatures to rush to the convention. On her way to deliver them she met one of the supportive delegates, Samuel R. Thurman, and found him "confident of the result." "He is one who reassures you when in doubt," she noted.[62]

When the delegates finally voted on April 18, 1895, woman suffrage passed with a large majority, but it would be superseded if the motion for separate submission resulted in a majority vote. By the time Emmeline arrived at the convention, she learned that the motion had failed, allowing the earlier vote to stand. Woman suffrage had become part of Utah's organic law. Women would once more vote in Utah. Emmeline rejoiced at the good news. "A little bitterness was manifest from Roberts," she noticed, "but altogether it was smooth sailing." The women who attended this final session were "very quiet and made no demonstration," despite their joy, but Emmeline could hardly wait to send a telegram to Susan B. Anthony with the good news. Anthony promptly wrote back: "Hurrah for Utah, No. 3 State—that establishes a genuine 'Republican form of Government.'"[63]

Notes

1. "Sweet Is Liberty," *Woman's Exponent* 11 (March 1, 1883): 148.
2. "National Council of Women," *Woman's Tribune* 8 (March 4, 1891): 75; *Washington Post,* February 23, 1891, clippings from Susan B. Anthony, Scrapbook, Library of Congress, Washington, D.C.
3. Emmeline B. Wells, Diary, February 21–25, 1891, L. Tom Perry Special Collections, Harold B. Lee Library, Brigham Young University, Provo, Utah.
4. "A Glimpse of Washington," *Woman's Exponent* 19 (March 1, 1891): 133.
5. "Women in Politics," *Woman's Exponent* 20 (August 15, 1891): 28.
6. Wells, Diary, March 14, 1892.
7. Emmeline Wells was instrumental in establishing two of the clubs that eventually became members of the Utah Federation: the Reapers Club and the Utah Women's Press Club, the latter organized in 1891, the same year that Emmeline became a member of the National Woman's Press Club.
8. For more detail on this period of rapprochement, see Carol Cornwall Madsen, "Decade of Detente: The Mormon-Gentile Female Relationship in Nineteenth-Century Utah," *Utah Historical Quarterly* 63 (Fall 1995): 298–319.
9. "Which Party Will Recognize Women?" *Woman's Exponent* 19 (June 15, 1891): 188.
10. "Women in Politics," *Woman's Exponent* 20 (August 15, 1891): 28.
11. Unlike polygamous men, plural wives did not come under the Presidential pardons of either 1893 or 1894. See Gustive O. Larson and Richard D. Poll, "The Forty-fifth State," in *Utah's History,* ed. Richard D. Poll, Thomas G. Alexander, Eugene E. Campbell, and David E. Miller (Provo, Utah: Brigham Young University Press, 1978), 392. As Wells explained, since a Congressio-

nal law disfranchised Utah women, the legislature was powerless to restore it until or unless the law was revoked or Utah became a state. "Utah," *Woman's Exponent* 23 (December 15, 1894): 221.

12. "An Appeal to Women," *Woman's Exponent* 23 (November 1, 15, 1894): 204.

13. See "Minutes of the Utah Woman's Press Club," *Woman's Exponent* 23 (August 15, 1893): 21.

14. Ruth May Fox, Diary, October 12, 28, 1895 , typescript copy, Church Archives, The Church of Jesus Christ of Latter-day Saints, Salt Lake City.

15. "Appeal to Women," 204.

16. Wells, Diary, January 25, 1894.

17. "Utah and Statehood," *Woman's Exponent* 23 (August 15, 1894): 172.

18. "Susan B. Anthony's Letter," *Woman's Exponent* 23 (August 1, 15, 1894): 169.

19. Ruth May Fox, "My Story," typescript copy, 25, Utah State Historical Society, Salt Lake City. In the same autobiographical account, Fox noted, "It is appropriate to acknowledge my great indebtedness to Emmeline B. Wells. No other woman had so great an influence as she in shaping my life. I became her devoted disciple and she in turn loved me as a daughter. I named after her my last child, Emmeline Blanche, born September 14, 1896, when Sister Wells was the center of my orbit of public activities. For many years subsequently she had much to do with my progress." Fox, "My Story," 24.

20. Fox, Diary, December 30, 1894, January 9, 1895.

21. Wells, Diary, December 31, 1894.

22. Emmeline B. Wells to Mary A. White, January 14, 1895, Papers of the Beaver County Woman Suffrage Association, Perry Special Collections.

23. Wells, Diary, March 20, 1892.

24. Minutes of Conjoint Meeting of the Relief Society and the Young Ladies' Mutual Improvement Association of the Farmington Ward, April 13, 1892, Church Archives.

25. The silk industry, which had lain moribund since Brigham Young's time, was revived in 1888 by both Mormon and gentile women. A silk committee was formed that included Zina D. H. Young, Emmeline Wells, and Margaret A. Caine, all Mormons, along with non-Mormons Margaret Salisbury, Isabella Bennett, and Corinne Allen. These women supervised the successful silk exhibit at the 1893 Chicago World's Fair. Chris Rigby Arrington discusses the beginnings of the silk industry in Utah in "The Finest of Fabrics: Mormon Women and the Silk Industry in Early Utah," *Utah Historical Quarterly* 46 (Fall 1978): 376–96.

26. Wells, Diary, February 16, 1894.
27. Wells, Diary, January 29, 1894.
28. Wells, Diary, February 1, 1894.
29. Wells, Diary, January 12, 1894.
30. "The Need of the Hour," *Woman's Exponent* 23 (September 1, 1894): 180.
31. "Woman Suffrage Column, Utah W.S.A.," *Woman's Exponent* 23 (February 1, 15, 1895): 233; Fox, Diary, February 22, 1895.
32. Journal History of the Church, February 21, March 19, April 5, 1895, Church Archives, also available on *Selected Collections from the Archives of The Church of Jesus Christ of Latter-day Saints*, 2 vols. (Provo, Utah: Brigham Young University Press, 2002), vol. 2, DVD 19, microfilm copy in Harold B. Lee Library.
33. "Equal Suffrage Department," *Young Woman's Journal* 6 (February 1895): 225–32 and 6 (March 1895): 280–86; "State Builders at Work: Among the Committees," *Salt Lake Tribune*, March 12, 1895, 1–3.
34. Wells, Diary, January 2, 10, 11, 13, 19, 1895.
35. Emmeline B. Wells to Mary A. White, January 14, 1895, Papers of the Beaver County Woman Suffrage Association.
36. This southern city was selected, in place of the usual Washington, D.C., location, to generate more southern interest in the suffrage movement and to support the suffrage workers already energized by NCW membership.
37. "Utah W.S.A.," *Woman's Exponent* 23 (February 1, 15, 1895): 233–34.
38. "Convention in Atlanta," *Atlanta Evening Journal* and "Utah WSA," *Atlanta Evening Journal,* reprinted in *Woman's Exponent* 23 (February 1, 15, 1895): 237; Wells, Diary, February 2, 1895. Aurelia Rogers also kept a diary account of their attendance at the convention but focused more on the people and places visited than on the meetings. See Aurelia Spencer Rogers, *Life Sketches of Orson Spencer and Others and History of Primary Work* (Salt Lake City: George Q. Cannon and Sons, 1898), 301–22.
39. Wells, Diary, March 5, 1895.
40. Susa Young Gates, "Utah Women at the National Council of Women," *Young Woman's Journal* 6 (June 1895): 392. Also, "The Women's Councils," *Deseret News,* March 14, 1895, 5; and "Addresses by Utah Women," *Salt Lake Tribune,* February 21, 1895, 2; "Utah Women to the Fore," *Salt Lake Tribune,* February 22, 1895, 3. A detailed account of the convention and the speeches made by Utah women is in "National Council in Washington," *Woman's Journal,* March 2, 1895, 65–72; "National Council in Washington," *Woman's Journal,* March 9, 1895, 77.

41. Susa Young Gates to Family, February 17, 1895, Washington, D.C., Susa Young Gates Papers, Church Archives.

42. Gates, "Utah Women at the National Council of Women," 396.

43. "Utah's Woman Suffragists," *Salt Lake Tribune,* March 15, 1895, 8.

44. "Kate Field's Opinion," *Woman's Exponent* 23 (May 1, 1895): 261. Field died just a year later.

45. "God Bless the Ladies," *Salt Lake Tribune,* March 19, 1895, 5. See also Fox, Diary, March 18, 1895.

46. Wells, Diary, March 26, 1895.

47. "The Article on Elections," *Salt Lake Tribune,* March 23, 1895, 4. A more detailed analysis of this aspect of the constitutional convention is Jean Bickmore White, "Woman's Place Is in the Constitution: The Struggle for Equal Rights in Utah in 1895," *Utah Historical Quarterly* 42 (Fall 1974): 344–69, see especially 353. White's article is taken from her dissertation, "Utah State Elections, 1895–1899" (PhD diss., University of Utah, 1968).

48. Utah, Constitutional Convention, 1895, *Official Report of the Proceedings and Debates,* 2 vols. (Salt Lake City, 1898), 1:407, as quoted in White, "Woman's Place Is in the Constitution," 354.

49. "Women and the Ballot," *Salt Lake Herald,* March 29, 1895, 1; "Woman Suffrage Again," *Deseret News,* April 5, 1895, 1; and "Created a Breeze," *Deseret News,* April 10, 1895, 1, all of which give accounts of the separate submission discussion.

50. As quoted in White, "Woman's Place Is in the Constitution," 358–59.

51. Utah, Constitutional Convention, 1895, *Official Report of the Proceedings and Debates,* 1:508, as quoted in Jean Bickmore White, "Woman's Place Is in the Constitution," 359.

52. "Woman Suffrage," *Woman's Exponent* 23 (April 1, 1895): 244.

53. The antisuffragists were encouraged by the support of the *Ogden Standard* and the *Salt Lake Tribune,* both Republican papers, as well as by the Salt Lake Chamber of Commerce. "More Oratory," *Ogden Standard,* March 30, 1895, 1; "The Proceedings of the Constitutional Convention," *Ogden Standard,* March 30, 1895, 2; "Two to One Against It," *Salt Lake Tribune,* March 31, 1895, 5; "Shall the Women be Voters," *Salt Lake Tribune,* April 1, 1895, 5; "Plain Talk," *Salt Lake Tribune,* April 2, 1895, 1; "A Scorcher," *Salt Lake Tribune,* April 3, 1895, 1; "Bring in the Remonstrances," *Salt Lake Tribune,* April 3, 1895, 4; "Separate Submission Must Win," *Salt Lake Tribune,* April 3, 1895, 4.

54. Mary Ann Freeze, Diary, April 5, 1895, Perry Special Collections.

55. "Two More Articles," *Salt Lake Tribune,* April 4, 1895, 4. See also "To Still the Theme," *Deseret Evening News,* April 5, 1895, 1. In the same issue is an

article submitted by Charlotte Godbe Kirby, former corresponding secretary of the Utah Woman Suffrage Association, supporting both woman suffrage and separate submission. While disclaiming the validity of Roberts's arguments against the value of woman suffrage, she supported his arguments on expedience.

56. Wells, Diary, April 4, 1895; "Relief Society Conference," *Woman's Exponent* 23 (May 1, 1895): 262. See also Minutes of the Relief Society Conference, April 4, 1895, in Emmeline B. Wells Record Book, 1892–96, Church Archives.

57. Franklin D. Richards, Journal, April 4, 1895, Church Archives; Abraham H. Cannon, Journal, April 4, 1895, Perry Special Collections. A few days later President Woodruff returned to his original position. Cannon, Journal, April 12, 1895.

58. As quoted in "Relief Society Conference," *Woman's Exponent* 24 (August 15, 1895): 45–46; and Minutes of the Relief Society Conference, April 5, 1895.

59. See Fox, Diary, April 3, 4, 9, 1895; Freeze, Diary, April 4, 5, 9, 1895; Wells, Diary, April 6, 7, 11, 1895. Mary Ann Freeze noted that Margaret Roberts, wife of B. H. Roberts, frequently accompanied her to the convention when woman suffrage was first introduced. After Roberts's speeches on March 28 and 29, however, she no longer attended nor was she visibly present in the political campaigns that followed.

60. Minutes of the Utah Women's Press Club, April 5, 1895; for a humorous account of the name-gathering effort, see Cactus, a suffragist in St. George, "Cactus Papers No. 2," *Woman's Exponent* 23 (May 15, 1895): 267, 271–72.

61. "Settled It," *Salt Lake Tribune*, April 19, 1895, 1.

62. Wells, Diary, April 8, 18, 1895.

63. Wells, Diary, April 18, 1895; "Equal Suffrage in the Constitution," *Woman's Exponent* 23 (May 1, 1895): 260. Utah followed Wyoming and Colorado as the third woman suffrage state. Included in the equal suffrage clause of the new state constitution is wording that could be construed as an early "equal rights" declaration. It reads: "The rights of the citizens of the State of Utah to vote and hold office shall not be denied or abridged on account of sex. Both male and female citizens of this State shall enjoy equally all civil, political and religious rights and privileges."

Chapter 12

Schism in the Sisterhood

*What an experience this has been for me—
really one could scarcely credit what I have done this year.*[1]

Emmeline Wells and her sister suffragists hardly had time to savor their success in the constitutional convention when they turned their attention to the upcoming visit of Susan B. Anthony and the Reverend Anna Howard Shaw.[2] As officers of the National American Woman Suffrage Association (NAWSA), Anthony and Reverend Shaw were traveling to California to attend the California Woman's Congress. They allowed time to make stops along the way, receiving accolades and large crowds everywhere they went, unlike Anthony and Elizabeth Cady Stanton's western campaign nearly twenty-five years earlier.[3] Salt Lake City had changed as well. On this visit Anthony found it had become a thriving metropolis, complete with electricity, commercial enterprises, hotels, the Salt Lake Temple's command of the city skyline, and a system of public transportation. Their visit, according to Reverend Shaw, was like a "triumphal progress. . . . The men as well as the women in Missouri, Utah, Wyoming, Colorado and Nevada have been simply devoted to Aunt Susan and I."[4] In Utah they were to be the featured guests at a special western convention of the NAWSA that celebrated the return of the ballot to Utah women. Everyone assumed

Dr. Anna Howard Shaw (ca. 1923) served as president of the National American Woman Suffrage Association from 1904 to 1915. She and Susan B. Anthony visited Utah in May 1895.

Photograph copyrighted by Underwood and Underwood (Keystone View Co.). Library of Congress

the newly framed Utah constitution would win acceptance at the November ratification election.

Once again, as president of the Utah Territorial Woman Suffrage Association (UTWSA), Emmeline became responsible for organizing a major event. She selected the convention hall, so recently the venue of the constitutional convention, as a "neutral" meeting place and began inviting guests and writing articles for the *Deseret News* about the NAWSA convention plans. She also hired the "Utah Drag" (sometimes called the "Big Utah"), a large omnibus that seated thirty, to convey guests on a sightseeing tour of the city before the convention. Among those invited were the governor and secretary of state (lieutenant governor), who also were asked to introduce the guests at the opening session, and Mary C. C. Bradford and Lyle Meridith Stansbury, suffragists from Colorado, a state that had recently amended its constitution to give women the vote. While Emmeline continued her planning, notices appeared in Salt Lake City papers days before the arrival of Anthony and Shaw, heralding them as figures of national prominence and international acclaim.

The women arrived early on a Sunday morning, May 12, 1895. They were welcomed at the depot by seventy-two women riding in the Big Utah and several other carriages. Forty of the women hosted the guests at breakfast at the Templeton Hotel, and after a ride through the city and lunch, the party proceeded to the Tabernacle, which was filled with

Emma J. McVicker was an educator, a prominent Utah suffragist, and a non-Mormon. She and other Utah suffragists helped host Susan B. Anthony and Reverend Anna Shaw during their May 1895 visit to Utah to attend the Rocky Mountain convention of the NAWSA.

Utah State Historical Society

more than six thousand eager listeners. There Anthony and Shaw were joined on the stand by Mrs. Emma J. McVicker (a non-Mormon educator) and several officers of the Relief Society: Zina D. H. Young, Sarah M. Kimball, Bathsheba W. Smith, and Jane S. Richards, along with Emily S. Richards, Electa Bullock, Josephine B. Hardy, and Emmeline Wells. According to one account, that afternoon the Reverend Anna Shaw "preached in the great Tabernacle, Bishops [Orson F.] Whitney and Richards assisting."[5] Each of the various clergymen of the city, including the two Mormons, congratulated Reverend Shaw for preaching doctrine of their own religious persuasion, "so she concluded she had made a politic sermon."[6] It was the largest audience she had ever addressed, Shaw later reported. "It was the easiest audience too," she added, "for Utah people are accustomed to go to church and listen." She was also pleased that in Ogden, a town thirty-five miles north of Salt Lake City, two buildings were needed to contain the large crowd that had gathered to hear her. She proved to be a mesmerizing lecturer to her Utah audiences.

Susan B. Anthony was also invited to speak that day. She recalled her first visit to Utah years earlier in 1871 when she attended a Fourth of July celebration in the Tabernacle. After nearly a quarter century, she told her audience, "They were about to pass from the childhood of government to the full responsibility of statehood." She rejoiced that "in the Constitution they had shown a sense of justice and generosity to the women of Utah." Utah, she predicted, "would go on and become the greatest of the mountain States."[7]

Both Anthony and Shaw noted the absence of overt criticism from the people of Utah, so noticeable in the previous few years. The "condemnatory character," marked almost from settlement, had been changed "to that in which the brightness, the liberality and the progress exhibited in the accomplishments and condition of the people here are held up in commendatory form to the world," Anna Shaw was pleased to report.[8] The two suffragists received much local praise for their positive and complimentary remarks.

The following morning, Emmeline Wells conducted the opening session of the convention. The hall was draped with red, white, and blue banners, and portraits of Lincoln, Anthony, and Elizabeth Cady Stanton hung above the stage.[9] For many of the women assembled, this was their first opportunity to meet the great woman suffrage leader, and her long opening address was met by frequent interruptions for applause. After the morning session, the convention delegates and friends were treated to an elegant reception at the home of Emily Richards. The dresses of the serving girls as well as the flowers and other decorations, the newspapers observantly reported, all displayed "the significant yellow," the official color of the woman suffrage associations. The next day, the popularity of the noted guests drew far more to the convention hall than could be accommodated, so the session was moved to the Assembly Hall on Temple Square, a venue Emmeline originally rejected to avoid any complaints from the non-Mormon community.[10]

At both the Monday evening and Tuesday morning sessions, B. H. Roberts was the object of humorous derision by several speakers. Susan B. Anthony, Reverend Anna Shaw, Mrs. Mary C. C. Bradford of Colorado, Dr. Ellen Ferguson, and several other local Utah women chided him for regarding women as too delicate, too reluctant, or too refined to vote. They also disparaged his prediction that home life would be disrupted if women became politically involved. All was said with humor, spiced with a pinch of sarcasm, which brought repeated rounds of laughter and applause from the audience.[11]

The final event was a trip to Saltair, the Great Salt Lake resort, after which the convention officially concluded. Though Emmeline was extremely reluctant to see it come to an end, she was also exhausted from orchestrating the proceedings. Her reward was the exhilaration she felt in the presence of prominent women and the energizing acknowledgment that she had played a central role in the movement that brought them together. She thus rallied the next morning to have her picture taken with Anthony and Reverend Shaw, "a sort of fad," she remarked, and finally, with some difficulty, to wrest a few moments alone in her own home with the two prominent women. During that time she was pleased to present them with a modest honorarium, collected from members of the UTWSA.[12] Emmeline and her co-workers had done their best to involve politicians, clerics, and suffragists from all religious faiths, making the affair as ecumenical as possible. It was a triumph of good will and rapprochement that had eluded Utah for nearly fifty years.

Thus concluded one act in the unique political drama of Mormon women. It had been challenging and enlightening, but the play was not yet over. The constitutional convention, with all its unexpected developments, and the suffrage convention afterward proved to be only preambles to the political imbroglio that followed, with Emmeline once again a key figure. It began during the constitutional convention when delegates Franklin S. Richards and Samuel Thurman, both Democrats, proposed that women be permitted to vote at the November election, in which the constitution would be ratified or rejected and the new state officers elected.[13] Denounced as a political trick, the motion was voted down, but the two men promised to raise the issue again. In fact, it became the major focus of the political attention throughout the ensuing months as both parties, aided by the local newspapers, voiced their opinions on the issue.

The controversy centered on the legal interpretation of the voting qualifications described in the Enabling Act, which clearly indicated that only male citizens who met the proper age and residence requirements could vote on the constitution. Moreover, the Edmunds-Tucker Act's proscription on woman suffrage would legally remain in effect until statehood was officially achieved. But there seemed to be a legal possibility that women could vote at least for the new state officials, since the newly written constitution provided women the right to vote.[14] Differences of opinion regarding the issue seemed to divide along party lines. Most suffragists, however, initially chose to be politically neutral, including Wells who, when approached by a newspaper reporter to give her views on the proposal, refused to respond. "I was very unwilling to talk to him," she wrote, "as I hold very different views from many of the ladies on the question of voting on the Constitution."[15] Time would unfold a variety of political interpretations, but only the courts could give a decisive ruling.

In June, recognizing the political potential of a female electorate in this important election, the Democrats issued a formal call to women to join their party. Their invitation, as expressed in the Democratic-leaning *Daily Herald,* was appealing:

> [The] party now leads out in welcoming the women of Utah . . . to a voice in choosing delegates to the county and territorial conventions, and also to act as delegates themselves. . . . Whether women may vote or not at the first election . . . they have an interest in the choice of the proper persons for office in the new state.[16]

Having remained publicly nonpartisan during the six-year campaign to regain the vote, women were concerned about the advisability and propriety of publicly affiliating with the political parties before the constitution was approved. This was also a concern to leaders of the Church, who were then debating the wisdom of sanctioning the political activity of other ecclesiastical leaders. Four years earlier, it had been necessary to resort to some political maneuvering, albeit quietly, to bring numerical balance to the two parties. But they were not unanimous about whether members in high ecclesiastical positions, male or female, should engage in politics, as either candidates or party advocates.

Thus, early in the morning of June 15, 1895, Relief Society General President Zina D. H. Young decided to meet with her counselor Jane Richards and Jane's husband, Franklin D., at the home of their son Franklin S. and his wife Emily for clarification. All were Democrats.

The younger Franklin explained to the group their party's plan to include women in the political societies, caucuses, and conventions and to involve them in the party on the precinct, city, county, and territorial levels. The Democrats, he said, wanted women to be part of the nominating process and to vote in the election. The meeting evidently emboldened the women, all Democrats, to make their party loyalty public. At the quarterly woman's conference of the Salt Lake Stake in session later that day, much of the discussion centered on steps for women to take in dividing on party lines. At the conference, Zina Young, Jane Richards, and Salt Lake Stake Relief Society President Isabella Horne all declared for the Democratic Party.[17]

Before the month was over, five women had been appointed to the Salt Lake County Democratic executive committee, and a move to add women to executive committees in all the counties was well under way.[18] When Bathsheba W. Smith, second counselor in the Relief Society General Presidency, also joined the Democrats, along with three prominent women doctors and suffragists—Martha Hughes Cannon, Ellen Ferguson, and Romania Pratt Penrose—the Democrats had reason to feel secure in the woman's vote. These were all influential women.[19] Emmeline, also a general officer of the Relief Society, had not yet made public her own party preference but noted the activity of her Relief Society co-workers. "The Democratic party are doing all in their power to help the women of the Territory forward," she observed; "they are speaking here and there in Wards and districts. Aunt Zina [Young] made the first speech at Taylorsville and Dr. Ferguson in the 10th Ward. Mattie H. Cannon is in the field."[20] The political activity of these respected women and the *Herald*'s assurance that political participation would not require anything "offensive to their true womanhood," that, indeed, government was "a great household and women [could] do much to keep it clean," helped assuage the fears of many other women that their womanliness would be compromised by political involvement.[21]

Through most of June, the *Herald* chided Republicans for failing to take the initiative in bringing women into their party's ranks and criticized them for waiting until the courts decided whether women could vote. The Democrats, the *Herald* was quick to point out, had wanted women in the party ever since they had been given the right to vote by the state's yet unratified constitution. Moreover, it claimed, there were many "leading and influential" women who wanted to help the party carry the state elections in November. Its recital of the party's program to include women concluded with a challenge for Republicans to do the same.[22]

The conservative *Salt Lake Tribune* countered with the question, "Who will care for mother now?" But the *Herald* had an answer: "The Democratic societies; so long as she has a vote and they a chance to get it." The *Herald* reminded the *Tribune* of the Republican doubts of the legality of women's vote but snidely suggested that the party would be quite willing to change its position if there were any possibility that women would be able to vote in the fall.[23]

Medical doctor and suffragist Martha Hughes Cannon won a seat in the Utah State Senate in 1896 on the Democratic ticket. Not only was it highly unusual for a woman to be running for a political office, but for her to run against her husband, Agnus M. Cannon, and win was truly a novelty.

Though the *Tribune* had frequently expressed its opinion that women would lose some of their womanliness if they joined in political activities, it noted, for the *Herald*'s benefit, that a woman had been chosen a delegate to the convention of the National Republican League and that Republican women had organized their own national league. The *Herald* merely pointed out the *Tribune*'s inconsistency, suggesting that it had added one more change to its "chameleon journalistic colors."[24]

As the Democratic drive to enlist women gathered momentum, the Republicans finally recognized the political necessity to follow suit. Reminded by the persistent *Herald* that the Republican-controlled convention had created the problem by defeating the Richards proposal, allowing women to vote by legislative decree, the Republicans reiterated their view that women were not eligible before the constitution was ratified. The *Herald* claimed that Republicans, who "in their hearts are opposed to this act of justice," were merely hiding their antisuffragist views under a legal argument. The paper further criticized Republicans for not joining the growing consensus favoring the eligibility of women to vote in November. At the core of the Republican opposition, the *Herald* rightly asserted, was the fear that if women were permitted to vote in November, their party would be "swamped" and the Democrats would carry the day.[25]

The Republicans, as represented by the *Tribune*, had indeed been opposed to woman suffrage, and many of the Republicans present at the constitutional convention had championed the "separate submission proposal." They did, however, acknowledge that political reality made it necessary to include women in the party. Initially discouraging women from registering, the Republicans soon decided to "fight the thing out on the lines proposed by the Democrats." The Republicans' original argument had been that the rush to get women to the polls was contrary to the provisions of the Edmunds-Tucker Act, and if the state constitution were rejected, the Act would still be in force. However, they were political realists and admitted that it would be wise to plan for any eventuality. To that end, they decided to organize Republican women's clubs throughout the territory, modeled after the National Woman's Republican League.[26] Restating their concern that registering women to vote was not only illegal but might jeopardize statehood, Republicans conceded that whatever the outcome, organizing women into political clubs would be useful for the time when they could vote.[27]

The greatest advantage of the Republicans in this effort was Emmeline Wells's decision to join their party in early July. Her decision came after long political discussions with her gentile friends Isabella Bennett,

Corinne Allen, and especially Margaret Salisbury, who was fast becoming one of Emmeline's closest associates. Visits from Judge Charles Bennett, Mrs. Isaac Trumbo, Charles Crane, George M. Cannon, and Judge J. A. Miner and his wife also helped Emmeline make her decision. Church Apostle John Henry Evans added his voice to the others, eventually convincing her to join their party. By July 3, after hours of discussing politics and studying books on political science, Emmeline made her decision to become a Republican. Three days later she attended a meeting with Republican leaders, both men and women, where the majority voted to organize separate women's organizations, which she would later head.[28] Party politics would consume much of her time in the next few years as she became a solid party worker, candidate, and campaigner. She did not use the *Woman's Exponent,* however, as a partisan newsletter. She reported on political events and on the burning question of women's participation in the November election, but to her credit she did not tout the Republican Party, chide her Democrat friends, or wage a journalistic campaign as the local newspapers continued to do.

Wells was not the only Mormon woman to join the party. Sarah M. Kimball, though growing old and becoming less active in public life, lent her support, and Elmina Taylor, president of the Young Ladies' Mutual Improvement Association, seemed to Emmeline to be sympathetic to the Republicans. Many Latter-day Saint women were reluctant to join the party because of its large gentile membership, but Emmeline had associated with many non-Mormon women for several years and had built strong and lasting friendships. Two young converts to the Republican Party were Clarissa Spencer Williams, who later became a counselor to Emmeline Wells in the Relief Society General Presidency, and Ruth May Fox, Emmeline's supporter during the last years of the suffrage campaign. Fox's reason for becoming a Republican was unique: "When the women who had been ardently working for suffrage arrayed themselves for the political battle, most of them [Mormons] seemed to be Democrats while Aunt Em stood almost alone, a Republican," she observed. "To even things up a bit, I joined hands with that great leader."[29]

Ruth May Fox, a prominent Utah Republican worker, represented a younger generation of women who were political activists. Fox later served as the Young Ladies' Mutual Improvement Association General President (1929–37).

Though she indicated in a political speech that she had "turned from a Democrat to a Republican" (as many other Mormon Democrats had done), Emmeline did not articulate her reasons for politically separating herself from so many of her Mormon associates. The male political influence of her family was varied. Without a living husband or son, she did not have the immediate political persuasion that the Richards women had. Moreover, one son-in-law, John Q. Cannon, was a strong Democrat (though his father George Q. was a Republican), and another, Septimus Sears, was an ardent Republican. Her "surrogate son," Orson F. Whitney, was a champion of woman suffrage, was a Democrat. But Daniel H. Wells, her late husband, was considered "the father of Republicanism" in Utah, and his political influence may have lingered.[30] Perhaps Joseph F. Smith, another fervent supporter of woman's rights and a declared Republican, may have influenced her. More likely, she eschewed male suasion and calculated where her own interests would best be served and which political philosophy best suited her own. Even her daughter Annie's disappointment in her choice did not dissuade her.[31] Emmeline had always been an independent thinker and was familiar with the repercussions of making unpopular decisions.

Just days after joining the party, Emmeline was chosen permanent chairman of the Territorial Republican Women's League. Her friend Margaret Salisbury served with her as vice chairman. At its organizational meeting in Salt Lake City on July 13, 1896, she prepared a paper, signed by Lillie R. Pardee and Mrs. C. E. (Corinne) Allen, two non-Mormon civic leaders, explaining Republican support for the protection of home industries, for bounties to encourage struggling industries, and for bimetallism.[32] It also claimed that Republicanism was more progressive in its outlook toward the future. It urged women to consider these and other Republican-supported measures and make their pledge for the Republican Party.[33]

Emmeline and her Republican co-workers then began organizing branches in Salt Lake City, Ogden, Provo, and other cities throughout the territory, usually traveling once or twice a week. Wells quickly learned how to make political speeches, some lasting an hour. As the organizing efforts began to succeed, the *Herald* ridiculed the decision to organize women's political clubs. "It is easy to see the reason for this," the paper explained: "It would not take a month to split the Republican party wide open in this city if the women were allowed to participate this fall. The feeling within the ranks on that subject is already pretty high and the women would be received with ill grace."[34] The *Herald* continued its diatribe two days later:

> While the Democratic women are thus enjoying equal political privileges in the great convention a handful of Republican women will be endeavoring to devise some means of carrying on a sort of afternoon tea and sewing circle style of politics separate from the regular organization, which does not want them and is content that they shall get off in one corner and do what they like so long as they do not interfere with the plans of the men. What a spectacle for gods and men.[35]

Not one to leave a challenge unanswered, Emmeline responded to the *Herald* article while being busily engaged in forming a Republican woman's club in Provo a few days later. "One of the newspapers in Salt Lake," she wrote, "has called the Republican movement a sort of tea party." She reminded the paper what kind of tea party was once held in Boston, "in which women led in the creation of public opinion. Perhaps this tea party in Utah may also grow into prominence."[36]

In reality, women were included in the party organizations as well as in their own clubs. Both Emmeline Wells and Corinne Allen were appointed to the territorial executive committee, and Lillie Pardee was elected as permanent secretary. The double political burden took its toll in energy and time, but Emmeline was acknowledged as one of a few women with experience in organizing and addressing new associations. Contrary to her party's position, her message to women was to prepare "at once for the possible exercise of your franchise in November 1895." She was more hopeful of a positive outcome than either her party or the *Tribune,* which supported the move to organize women's clubs but continued to assert its position that "under the law women have no more right to vote this year than have boys of twenty years of age."[37]

Throughout summer 1895, the *Herald* continued to attack Republicans for their hesitance to admit women, their reluctance to support the woman's vote in November, and their decision to organize separate women's clubs. The *Tribune* continued to justify the party's caution and its separate organizations. However, as membership grew in the Republican women's league, the *Herald* warned of the impending contest: "Now the Democratic women have a foe in sight. They see that the game of politics for them has begun in real earnest."[38] If the women themselves did not yet perceive the political schism in military terms, the warring "morning contemporaries," as the two newspapers were known, kept the battle cry ringing from their columns throughout the political campaign.[39]

While Republicans continued organizing separate women's clubs, the extent to which women had been rapidly absorbed into the Democratic Party was evident at the third annual convention of the Democratic societies, held in the Salt Lake Theater on July 13, 1895. Three days before, the *Herald* trumpeted the news that women would be a part of all the convention's deliberations. Many delegates were leading ladies of the community, it commented, and others would attend "to see how their sisters comport themselves in a public political meeting."[40] Some of these "leading ladies" were from the fourteenth political ward in Salt Lake City, which elected Amelia Folsom Young (a widow of Brigham

Young) and seven other women as delegates, creating a female majority of the fifteen-member delegation from that ward. Four women were named to the executive committee of the ward, also comprising a majority.[41] Other wards and precincts elected women to various party committees. "The ladies are better hustlers" than the men, one Democrat reported, and he wanted them "on all the committees."[42]

At the Democratic convention an estimated one-third of the delegates were women. Featured on the stage, besides Governor Caleb West, Congressional delegate J. L. Rawlins, former delegate John T. Caine, and other prominent Democrats, were Zina D. H. Young, Jane S. Richards, Bathsheba W. Smith, Isabella Horne, Dr. Martha Hughes Cannon, and "others not known to the Newsman." Judge H. P. Henderson of the Federal District Court, who presided, congratulated the convention on the fact that "women had been taken in as an auxiliary aid, to mingle their wisdom and advice with the men." He opined that if they were allowed to vote in November, they "would aid in giving party principles clearness and strength."[43]

At the convention, women were assigned to a variety of positions and lent their names for whatever political or social value they afforded. Zina Young was elected first vice president of the party's executive committee, and Eurethe K. LaBarthe and Electa Bullock, both non-Mormon women, were elected secretaries. Several women were appointed to the committee on resolutions, and Zina Young, Eurethe K. LaBarthe, and Isabella Horne were invited to address the twelve hundred delegates. Notice also was made of Bathsheba Smith, whose husband, it was mentioned, had, in earlier years, been one of the few Republicans in the territory and regarded as "a sort of curiosity on that account." The convention endorsed the right of women to vote in November if the Enabling Act permitted.[44] If the "leading women of the territory" were not quite on "an equal footing with their male colleagues" in the party, as the *Herald* claimed, neither was their "true womanhood compromised."[45]

However much the *Herald* ridiculed the organization of Republican women's clubs, Democrat women were not above forming their own separate organizations. A number of Salt Lake City women, under the chairmanship of Eurethe LaBarthe, combined into a special political education and work society with the intention of meeting regularly for their own political edification and assistance to the party. Other groups followed, which eventually included most of the prominent women Democrats in the city.[46]

Throughout July and August 1895, Emmeline Wells organized Republican clubs, spoke at political gatherings, and attended party meetings. She was pleased that Mary Ann Freeze, well-regarded president of the Salt Lake Stake Young Ladies' Mutual Improvement Association, had agreed to speak for the Republicans, and that Louie B. Felt, general president of the Primary Association, was "about half converted." She was also delighted to learn that Felt's counselor May Anderson had converted to Republicanism.[47]

While taxing, the round of political meetings intrigued Emmeline. In Tooele she was serenaded by a brass band, guitars, and the Mandolin Club and successfully organized two women's clubs. In nearby Grantsville, a large audience welcomed her with flowers and decorations. She succeeded in organizing clubs there as well.[48] The rest of August took her to Heber City, Park City, and other communities in Utah, organizing clubs in every place. "We are having so much work to do and so few workers or speakers that we scarcely know how all is to be accomplished," she noted midway through the month.[49] But her political work was not the only demand on her time. She also attended Relief Society conferences with Zina Young and continued to publish regular issues of the *Exponent*. Her correspondence was legion: she wrote letters for the party, for the Relief Society, for the UTWSA, which was still very active in seeking grass roots support for a constitutional amendment, and she also exchanged letters with officers of the NCW.

Fatigue, understandably, continued to plague her. "Newspaper work is not done by looking on," she lamented, "and really I do as much work as seven other women I firmly believe. I have answered some letters today and have tried to [d]o my very best in all the interests with which I am connected or associated." Then, justifying her labors with the nobility of the goal, she wrote, "I have desired with all my heart to do those things that would advance women in moral and spiritual as well as educational work and tend to the rolling on of the work of God upon the earth."[50] This was the motivating vision that enabled her to confront the unrelenting pressure of each day.

Though she enjoyed her organizing forays into nearby cities, Emmeline often came home depressed and dispirited from the executive meetings where she occasionally found "some men uncouth with the ladies." It was indeed a time of adjustment as women began entering long-held male domains. At a meeting of the County Republican Committee, to which seven women had recently been added, a move that made Emmeline and Jennie Froiseth political comrades, the infighting over the ballot form for the primaries and whether women should be allowed to vote in the meetings evoked a heated response from Emmeline: "It looked as though some of the gentlemen present . . . appeared not to desire to give the women a fair chance."

As a new convert to the party, Emmeline warned the committee that their present attitudes "would drive the women into the Democratic party." The opposing men offered their apologies, and Ruth May Fox attempted to ease the tension by assuring the women present that the men meant no offense.[51]

Three days later at an executive committee meeting in the *Woman's Exponent* office, discussion focused on the advisability of appointing at least one female election judge in each precinct, or possibly even appointing one on each board of judges. Again, dissension arose in the meeting. Committeeman Sam Hill worried about women "staying out until 1:00 a.m.," as was often required, and explained that he objected to woman suffrage itself. His remarks drew another emphatic response from Emmeline, who commented that he "need not be afraid that women would thrust themselves forward." She was convinced "that no woman in either party would ask for any office which she could not fit." It was clear to everyone that Wells would be far from a silent worker, and her comment managed to silence Hill. Annie Atkins of Provo, another member of the committee, also voiced her opinion in the meetings. The politicians whose wives were active in the party, she noted, were far more sympathetic to female participation than those men who did not have politically active wives.[52] They were all learning that the adjustment to a new political order required patience.

As she was discovering how demanding the actual business of politics could be, Emmeline attempted to stay informed about the questions confronting the party. She wrote to her former nemesis, Kate Field—who had become an active supporter of many civic causes and a recent and enthusiastic convert to woman suffrage until her death the following year—for political literature. Emmeline also studied the issues so she would "not be at a loss when conversing with those who are up in everything, and not appear ridiculous."[53] By September 1895, she found that she had to speak nearly every evening, and, as chairman of the Women's Republican League, she knew "something bright" was expected of her on all occasions.[54] Though she preferred preliminary preparation and "time to reflect," before speaking at the various chapters of the Republican League, her suffrage experience had given her the ability to "say what comes uppermost in my mind" and express herself coherently with little or no preparation.[55]

While the campaign marched on to November, Emmeline temporarily shifted her attention to preparing for the National Editorial Convention taking place in Salt Lake City that summer, which included meetings, dinners, and a parade. She arranged for three wagons to carry the members of the Utah Women's Press Club, which she had founded in 1891, along the Main Street route of the parade. She also was obliged to divide her time between the Editorial Convention meetings and the Republican convention scheduled for the same time.[56] Like a roller-coaster ride, her emotions rose and fell from the excitement and intrigue of party politics to the frustration she felt from the increasing demands on her time and energy. By the end of the summer she was amazed at what she had managed to accomplish. "What an experience this has been for me," she wrote. "Really one could scarcely credit what I have done this year."[57]

On July 30, 1895, the expanding political activity of the "leading sisters" of Mormon society, most of whom were Democrats, prompted a meeting called by leading Mormon Democrats to determine the propriety of women's participation in party politics. In attendance, besides the First Presidency of the Church, were five Apostles, the Salt Lake Stake presidency, and John T. Caine, Franklin S. Richards, Samuel R.

Thurman, Judge William H. King, and George F. Gibbs, the latter four all influential Democrats.

The LDS Church had not yet established a firm policy regarding the political activity of either its male or female leaders, and separating the Church from politics at this juncture became a two-edged sword. The dilemma was that if Church leaders restricted the political actions of women, it would be seen as interfering. But if they did not, John Caine reported, Gentiles, most of whom were Republicans, would accuse the Church of using women to accomplish its political aims. Responding to that concern, Salt Lake Stake President Angus Cannon (a Republican) indicated that he had asked the prominent women leaders in his stake "to resign their [Church] offices or cease mixing in politics."[58] However, Caine clearly saw the disadvantages to the Democratic Party of Cannon's ultimatum and complained that such Church interference as Cannon's dictum would reinforce the popular belief that the Church had not recused itself from politics. President Cannon defended his stake directive as being nonpartisan and applicable to both men and women (though he himself would run for office the following year). Partisan politics clearly informed the discussion. The problem affected everyone. Caine, therefore, wanted a statement from the First Presidency concerning the extent to which officers of the Church would be permitted to engage in politics. The discussion that followed made clear the lack of consensus on the question. While Democrats Caine, Thurman, Richards, Taylor, and Penrose all believed in allowing members freedom to accept nominations and actively work for their party, the others at the meeting, most of whom were Republicans, believed that those in highly visible Church positions should not participate in politics beyond voting. No firm decision resulted.

Another concern was raised by George Q. Cannon, a counselor in the First Presidency and brother of Angus, which had been prompted by the impassioned public addresses of Democrats Isabella Horne and Amelia Folsom Young invoking the "democratic political beliefs" of Church founder Joseph Smith. Cannon suggested that the sisters and all others should at least be restrained from declaring the politics of "our dead leaders" and urged both parties to cease circulating political literature making similar assertions in support of their political beliefs.[59] After a lengthy discussion, President Woodruff returned to the original question regarding women's participation, expressing regret as to "the course the sisters had taken, but now that they have gone so far," he concluded, "it will be better to let them finish this campaign on the lines which have been marked out for them."[60] For the future, it was agreed, both men and women in high church positions would be counseled to refrain from taking "a very active part" in politics.[61]

Afterward, the First Presidency met with the Relief Society General Presidency, along with Isabella Horne and Emily S. Richards, and counseled the women "as to the course they should pursue in their political relations and labors as suffragists and Democrats. Very clear, pointed & energetic instructions as to political principles and as to practice" were given to them, according to Elder Franklin D. Richards.[62] When Emmeline heard of the meeting, she was sure it would result in "the best good of all parties." She was pleased to learn that the women had been counseled in their political work "and the matter settled in part about talking Democracy." She was also confident that "Sisters Young Smith and Horne would be more moderate."[63] The counsel did not, however, appear to diminish the political activity of women in either party, as the following months attested.

Meanwhile, the question of the voting eligibility of women was progressing through the courts. The Utah Commission, in charge of Utah elections since 1882, had decided to remain neutral in the controversy and had instructed the registrars to use their own discretion in registering women to vote. A test case was brought in Ogden on August 6, 1895, by Sarah E. Anderson, who asked to be registered to vote both for state officers and ratification of the constitution. The registrar refused on the grounds that as a woman Sarah was ineligible to vote. She then sought a writ of mandamus to compel the deputy registrar, Charles Tyree, to register her. Her battery of attorneys were all Democrats, notably Franklin S. Richards, Samuel R. Thurman, and H. P. Henderson, who was also a district court judge. Their arguments convinced Judge H. W. Smith of the Ogden District Court, who found for the plaintiff and ruled that women were eligible to vote not only for state officers at the November election but also on ratification of the constitution. Tyree immediately appealed to the territorial supreme court through his attorney Arthur Brown, a Republican and husband of suffragist Isabel Cameron Brown.[64]

Though the *Woman's Exponent* had remained steadfastly neutral throughout the campaign, stressing only the need for women to study the issues and learn the political process, Wells took a definite stand when the question of women's eligibility to vote was judicially addressed. "The suffrage has been conferred upon the women of the territory by the delegates duly elected to the Constitutional Convention while assembled," she wrote in July, "and it does seem as though the right of suffrage ought to be exercised by them in having a voice and a vote as to the officers who shall govern and control affairs in the new state. It will make a very great difference in many respects if women are to be excluded from this first election."[65] Her opinion was shared by neither her party nor by newspapers outside the region initially. The *New York Sun* and the *San Francisco Chronicle* both suggested that, in the interest of statehood, women should not try to vote in November. Even suffragist Henry Blackwell urged the same position in a letter to Zina D. H. Young. Church leaders adopted a similarly cautious attitude and decided to use a "quiet influence to prevent the voting of women."[66]

The affirmative decision of the Ogden district judge, however, encouraged both parties to continue their courting of women and even converted Republicans. On August 22, while the case was still being deliberated by the territorial supreme court, the Republicans held their Salt Lake County convention. Emmeline attended not only as chair of the Woman's Republican League but as a delegate from the Farmer's Precinct—at that time she was a resident of the Waterloo area, a county precinct just south of the city limits. When she was named temporary chair of the convention, she applauded the delegates for the honor conferred upon "the women of Utah" by that gesture, stating that she considered it "a tribute to the work of the pioneers and to the mothers of the young men of the territory."[67] The *Herald* was willing to acknowledge the skill with which she presided and reported that the *Republican Catechism* (a pamphlet discussing the Republican platform), which she had prepared for distribution to Republican women, was available.[68] When Charles S. Varian was elected permanent chairman, she was elected one of the permanent vice chairmen.

On the second day of the convention, twenty-nine people were nominated for ten seats. It was a lengthy meeting, lasting until four the next morning. Emmeline, who was serving on the resolutions committee, was nominated for the House by Ruth May Fox. Her coworker, Lillie R. Pardee, was nominated for the Senate.[69] Hopeful that the territorial supreme court would affirm the district court's decision, the party made the two women official candidates along with Emma J. McVicker, nominated for state superintendent of schools a week later at the territorial convention.[70] In the event of a negative decision by the supreme court, the convention selected alternates for the three women candidates. As with her own nomination, Emmeline was especially pleased that Heber M., the son of her sister-wife Martha Givens Harris Wells, was the Republican nominee for governor.

After the convention, Emmeline continued organizing clubs, going south to Ephraim and then north to Brigham City and Logan, where the Logan women named the Republican club the Wells Club in her honor. From there she traveled to Richmond, Smithfield, Hyrum, and Wellsville, organizing clubs in each community, meeting friends, and preaching Republicanism.

When she returned to Salt Lake City, she found the peace of her home in Waterloo a soothing respite. The warmth of Indian summer lingered and the brilliance of the early autumn nights from "thousands of stars," softened by moon and clouds, stirred her poet's heart. "The feeling [is] indescribable that one has in gazing upon nature's beauties," she rhapsodized to her diary, especially "with the peculiar temperament I have," a temperament sensitive to the nuances of life as well as nature.[71] Her incisive, aggressive public persona seemed to find repose and a different mode of expression in nature's quiet sanctuary and in the private pages of her diary. In those quiet moments, she considered a political future that would be unthinkable to most women with whom she associated in the national suffrage movement. Utah women were clearly demonstrating that voting was merely an entry point to direct political involvement. Making the laws that governed them was the real prize. Partisan politics was proving to be an exciting arena for Emmeline Wells.

This chapter and the next have been reworked from a published article, "Schism in the Sisterhood: Mormon Women and Partisan Politics, 1890–1900," in New Views of Mormon History, *ed. Davis Bitton and Maureen Ursenbach Beecher (Salt Lake City: University of Utah Press, 1987), 212–41.*

Notes

1. Emmeline B. Wells, Diary, August 26, 1895, L. Tom Perry Special Collections, Harold B. Lee Library, Brigham Young University, Provo, Utah.

2. Reverend Shaw was both an ordained Methodist minister and a trained medical doctor. She left these professions to become a popular lecturer for temperance and suffrage. She served as vice president and later president of the NAWSA. Details of her life can be found in Eleanor Flexner, "Anna Howard Shaw," in *Notable American Women, 1607–1950: A Biographical Dictionary,* ed. Edward T. James, Janet Wilson James, and Paul S. Boyer, 3 vols. (Cambridge: Belknap Press of Harvard University Press, 1971), 3:274–77.

3. Katharine Anthony, *Susan B. Anthony: Her Personal History and Her Era* (Garden City, N.Y.: Doubleday, 1954), 428–29.

4. "Talking of Utah," Journal History of the Church, May 22, 1895, 2, Church Archives, The Church of Jesus Christ of Latter-day Saints, Salt Lake City, also available on *Selected Collections from the Archives of The Church of Jesus Christ of Latter-day Saints,* 2 vols. (Provo, Utah: Brigham Young University Press, 2002), vol. 2, DVD 19, microfilm copy in Harold B. Lee Library. See also Ida Husted Harper, *Life and Work of Susan B. Anthony,* 2 vols. (Indianapolis: Bowen-Merril, 1898), 2:825, who devotes nearly a page in her biography of Susan B. Anthony to the conference, noting that, while there, Anthony and Reverend Shaw "received the highest consideration" by the citizens of Utah.

5. The author is probably referring to Franklin D. Richards, an LDS Church Apostle, although she may have assumed his son Franklin S. Richards was a bishop.

6. Harper, *Life and Work of Susan B. Anthony,* 2:824.

7. "At the Tabernacle," Journal History of the Church, May 13, 1895, 2.

Schism in the Sisterhood   315

8. "Talking of Utah," Journal History of the Church, May 22, 1895, 2–3.

9. Governor Caleb West introduced the speakers and mentioned that Susan B. Anthony and Elizabeth Stanton had been introduced on their 1871 visit by the late Daniel H. Wells, then the Mayor of Salt Lake City and husband of the current chair, Emmeline Wells.

10. Emmeline Wells gave an account of the proceedings in various issues of the *Woman's Exponent*. See "The National Conference," 23 (May 15, 1895): 268–69; "Conference N.A.W.S.A.," 24 (August 15, 1895): 47–48; "Conference N.A.W.S.A.," 24 (September 1, 15, 1895): 53–54; "Conference N.A.W.S.A.," 24 (October 1, 1895): 62–63; "Conference N.A.W.S.A.," 24 (November 1, 1895): 77–79.

11. See "More Woman's Work," Journal History of the Church, May 14, 1895, 3–5, for a full account of their talks. The suffragists were not the only ones to denounce Roberts's stand on the suffrage question. Ruth May Fox noted in her diary on June 18, 1895, that at a social event a month later, which both Roberts and Joseph F. Smith attended, the party was "unusually fine but Oh!, the dressing down Mr. B. H. Roberts got from Joseph F. Smith. I really felt sorry for him." Ruth May Fox, Diary, Church Archives.

12. Wells, Diary, May 15, 1895.

13. "Woman Registration and Voting," *Salt Lake Tribune*, July 2, 1895, 4.

14. Details about the constitutional convention can be found in Jean Bickmore White, "Utah State Elections, 1895–1899" (PhD diss., University of Utah, 1968), 33–34; see also Jean Bickmore White, "Gentle Persuaders: Utah's First Woman Legislators," *Utah Historical Quarterly* 38 (Winter 1970): 31–49, especially 40–41.

15. Wells, Diary, May 21, 1895.

16. "A Call to Action," *Salt Lake Daily Herald*, June 2, 1895, 4.

17. Wells, Diary, June 15, 1895.

18. "To Recognize the Women," *Salt Lake Daily Herald*, June 16, 1895, 1; "Ladies to the Front," *Salt Lake Daily Herald*, June 16, 1895, 4; "The Political Arena," *Salt Lake Daily Herald*, June 25, 1895, 8; "The Political Arena," *Salt Lake Daily Herald*, June 26, 1895, 2; "The Political Arena," *Salt Lake Daily Herald*, June 27, 1895, 5; "The Political Arena," *Salt Lake Daily Herald*, June 28, 1895, 3.

19. "The Political Arena," *Salt Lake Daily Herald*, June 27, 1895, 5.

20. Wells, Diary, June 27, 1895.

21. "The Political Arena," *Salt Lake Daily Herald*, June 19, 1895, 8.

22. "To Recognize the Women," *Salt Lake Daily Herald*, June 16, 1895, 1.

23. "Right for Once," *Salt Lake Daily Herald*, June 19, 1895, 4.

316   An Advocate for Women

24. "We 'Note' It," *Salt Lake Daily Herald*, June 21, 1895, 4.

25. "The Political Arena," *Salt Lake Daily Herald*, July 11, 1895, 5.

26. "Political Talk," *Salt Lake Tribune*, July 15, 1895, 7; "Woman Registration and Voting," *Salt Lake Tribune*, July 2, 1895, 4; "Women's Clubs," *Salt Lake Daily Herald*, July 3, 1895, 4.

27. "Woman Registration and Voting," *Salt Lake Tribune*, July 2, 1895, 4.

28. Wells, Diary, July 2, 3, 5, 6, 1895.

29. Ruth May Fox, "My Story," 26, Utah State Historical Society, Salt Lake City.

30. Reference to Daniel H. Wells in the Journal of Jesse N. Smith puts him in "the same party as Abraham Lincoln." See Jesse N. Smith, Journal, "The Crowning Years of Pioneer Life," 1905, 455–56, Perry Special Collections. The *Salt Lake Tribune*, on January 7, 1896, referred to Wells as "that dear old man . . . still spoken of as the 'Father of Republicanism' in Utah"—a dramatic reversal from its characterization of him years earlier as a "one-eyed pirate" since he had one defective eye. See "City Jottings," *Salt Lake Tribune*, January 3, 1879, 4.

31. Wells, Diary, August 25, 1895. Though appalled at her mother's decision at that time and particularly her active partisanship, Annie herself later joined the Republicans and served in the state legislature for several years.

32. The Democratic Party and its Presidential candidate, William Jennings Bryan, supported the coinage of silver rather than gold, a position favored by most Westerners. Utah gave its vote to Bryan in the 1896 election.

33. Wells, Diary, July 6, 9, 1895. Whatever Wells's reasons for becoming a Republican, she made a thorough study of the party's platform and discussed political issues knowledgably and persuasively. As the auxiliary branches of the Republican League were organized, the members voted overwhelmingly to maintain the separate women's organizations, despite the criticism of the Democratic party. See "Address Women of Utah," *Salt Lake Tribune*, July 14, 1895, 1; "Women Republicans," *Salt Lake Tribune*, July 19, 1895, 7.

34. "The Political Arena," *Salt Lake Daily Herald*, July 11, 1895, 5.

35. "The Political Arena," *Salt Lake Daily Herald*, July 13, 1895, 8.

36. "Women Republicans," *Salt Lake Tribune*, July 19, 1895, 7. The *Tribune*'s shift from ridiculing Wells and her work to supporting and even lauding her public activity begins at this time, just as it did her husband.

37. "Woman Registration and Voting," *Salt Lake Tribune*, July 2, 1895, 4.

38. "The Political Arena," *Salt Lake Daily Herald*, July 18, 1895, 5.

39. The controversial and unique nature of this campaign was noted in the Boston *Woman's Journal* from July through September 1895. When Emmeline

was elected temporary chairman of the Salt Lake County Republican convention, which met on August 23, the paper noted that "this was no empty compliment, as her presiding continued through the entire day." See "Utah Democratic Convention," *Woman's Journal* 26 (July 27, 1896): 233, 240; "Utah Republican Women Organizing," *Woman's Journal* 26 (August 10, 1896): 256; "No Equal Suffrage in Utah," *Woman's Journal* 26 (September 7, 1896): 284; "The Press on the Utah Decision," *Woman's Journal* 26 (September 14, 1896): 292.

40. "The Coming Convention," *Salt Lake Daily Herald*, editorial, July 10, 1895, 4.

41. "The Political Arena," *Salt Lake Daily Herald*, July 9, 1895, 3.

42. "Democrats Name Women," *Salt Lake Tribune*, July 9, 1895, 1.

43. "It Was Democracy's Day," *Salt Lake Daily Herald*, July 14, 1895, 1.

44. Journal History of the Church, July 13, 1875, 6.

45. "The Political Arena," *Salt Lake Daily Herald*, July 13, 1895, 8; "It Was Democracy's Day," *Salt Lake Daily Herald*, July 14, 1895, 1.

46. "The Political Arena," *Salt Lake Daily Herald*, July 21, 1895, 3; "The Political Arena," *Salt Lake Daily Herald*, July 24, 1895, 8.

47. Wells, Diary, August 5, 1895.

48. Wells, Diary, August 8, 1895.

49. Wells, Diary, August 12, 1895.

50. Wells, Diary, August 1, 1895.

51. "Republicans Raised Cain," *Salt Lake Daily Herald*, July 28, 1895, 1; Wells, Diary, July 8, 27, 1895.

52. "The Political Arena," *Salt Lake Daily Herald*, July 31, 1895, 5.

53. Wells, Diary, September 9, 1895.

54. Wells, Diary, September 9, 1895.

55. Wells, Diary, September 9, 1895.

56. Wells, Diary, August 26, 27, 28, 1895.

57. Wells, Diary, August 26, 1895.

58. Abraham H. Cannon, Journal, July 30, 1895, Perry Special Collections; Wells, Diary, August 26, 1895.

59. The *Salt Lake Tribune* reported a talk by Isabella Horne in which she expressed her regard for "Democratic principles" and asserted that the "Prophet Joseph Smith loved them. He was a staunch Democrat," she added. "We were all Democrats in Nauvoo." "Democrats Name Women," *Salt Lake Tribune*, July 9, 1895, 1. See also *Nuggets of Truth* and *Nuggets of Truth, Hear Ye the Whole Truth*, ca. 1892, pamphlets, Perry Special Collections, which discuss the politics of Joseph Smith.

60. Cannon, Journal, July 30, 1895; Wells, Diary, July 26, 30, 1895.

61. Cannon, Journal, July 30, 1895; Franklin D. Richards, Journal, July 30, 1895, Richards Family Papers, Church Archives; see also White, "Utah State Elections," 81–85. This counsel did not persuade all Church leaders to refrain from politics. Both Moses Thatcher, an Apostle, and B. H. Roberts, a member of the Quorum of the Seventy, allowed themselves to be nominated for congressional offices at the Democratic convention. The furor following these nominations and the subsequent denunciation of the two Church officials in the Church's semi-annual priesthood meeting raised again the specter of Church involvement in political affairs and added another controversial measure to this final political act before statehood. For details of the preelection campaigning, see Edward Leo Lyman, *Political Deliverance: The Mormon Quest for Utah Statehood* (Urbana: University of Illinois Press, 1986), 265–85, especially 268–73.

62. Richards, Journal, July 30, 1895.

63. Wells, Diary, July 26, 30, 1895. She mentions nothing about restraining her own political activities. Invoking the politics of Joseph Smith may have been the primary complaint of Church authorities rather than their partisan activity.

64. The Republican Party and the *Tribune* had urged the Utah Commission to issue a directive to the registrars but were unsuccessful in their appeal. Its decline meant that the issue would have to be judicially decided. Sarah Anderson's suit against Tyree was a deliberate effort to have the issue resolved through the courts. See "The Political Arena," *Salt Lake Daily Herald,* August 7, 1895, 8; "The Political Arena," *Salt Lake Daily Herald,* August 9, 1895, 5; "Women Have a Right to Vote," *Salt Lake Daily Herald,* August 11, 1895, 1. See also White, "Gentle Persuaders," 40–42.

65. "Shall Women Vote in November?" *Woman's Exponent* 24 (July 15, 1895): 28.

66. Cannon, Journal, August 8, 1895.

67. "Republicans Meet," *Deseret Evening News,* August 22, 1895, 1. This was a typical response of Emmeline Wells to such recognition. She had already been instrumental in the appointment of Lillie Pardee as treasurer of the Territorial Executive Committee. When Pardee began her duties a few days later, Emmeline noted that it was a real achievement for the women of the party "and a most graceful compliment to them from Republican men." Wells, Diary, August 6, 12, 1895.

68. "Oquirrhs Made a Clean Sweep," *Salt Lake Daily Herald,* August 23, 1895, 1. Emily Richards responded with "The Republican Catechism Criticized

and Amended for the Benefit of the Women of Utah." A copy of this pamphlet is in the Church Archives and the Utah State Historical Society.

69. According to "The Political Arena," *Salt Lake Daily Herald,* August 24, 1895, 5, Wells had evidently hoped for a senate nomination but a miscue by her floor worker, Ruth May Fox, gave that honor to Lillie Pardee. This may have been a bit of journalistic sniping by the *Herald,* which had consistently baited Emmeline throughout the campaign. She was fifteenth on the first ballot at the convention, but only the top eight were elected. A proposal to give the two remaining spots to Emmeline and Lillie Pardee by acclamation was vetoed, but it was decided to give the county precincts and women more representation. Wells fit both qualifications.

70. Information on Emma McVicker is in Carol Ann Lubomudrov, "A Woman State School Superintendent: Whatever Happened to Mrs. McVicker?" *Utah Historical Quarterly* 49 (Summer 1981): 254–61.

71. Wells, Diary, September 8, 1895. While many of her newspaper articles and some of her diary entries demonstrate her effusive feelings about nature, her poetry is most expressive of her response to the natural world. In 1896 the first edition of a volume of her poetry, *Musings and Memories,* a particularly apt title, was published.

Rocky Mountain Woman Suffrage Convention (1895). Susan B. Anthony is seated third from right.

Church Archives, The Church of Jesus Christ of Latter-day Saints

Chapter 13

The Perils of Partisan Politics

'I am not sure which is the right course to pursue but am determined to stand for women.[1]

On August 31, 1895, while Emmeline Wells was on her travels for the Republican Party, the Democratic county convention convened. At the same time, the territorial supreme court delivered its ruling on *Anderson v. Tyree*. To the surprise of many and dismay of even more, the court reversed the judgment of the lower court and denied women the right to vote in the November election. Democratic convention chairman James H. Moyle concluded that the decision regarding the vote also denied women the right to run for office, though the ruling was not explicit. Thus, the Democrats did not nominate any women for office. The Republicans, however, already had three women candidates on their ballot.

When the Republican Party met two days later to ratify their nominations, U.S. Senate candidate Arthur Brown, a Republican who had successfully represented Tyree in the supreme court case, was the major speaker. He found himself in an awkward position, caught between defending his successful appeal to the supreme court and supporting the nomination of women by his party. He began by interpreting the ruling differently from Moyle, the Democratic chair. First, he chided the Democrats for "prating about their love for equal suffrage," but not daring "to put a woman upon their ticket when it came to the test." He then explained that "the right of women to vote has been questioned," in defense of his own position on the matter, but, he countered, "her right to hold office after the adoption of the constitution has never been questioned. I have never questioned that. The whole question is one of time. After the proclamation [of statehood] is issued women may hold office. . . . If you believe in woman suffrage," he concluded, "here is the only ticket with women upon it."[2] His controversial interpretation, however, did little to convince either his party or the people. This was not yet the time for women to participate in an election either as voters or candidates.

Emmeline felt constrained to respond to the court's decision. Feeling honored to speak for the women of Utah in the Republican convention, she wanted her fellow party members to know that though women could not yet vote, they could at least talk, and she, for one, hoped they would be allowed to speak during the campaign. She reminded them that the national woman suffragists were watching events in Utah with keen interest and would be disappointed in the decision of Chief Justice Samuel A. Merritt of the territorial supreme court. Like Brown, however, she did not feel that the decision proscribed her candidacy and concluded that if she should be defeated, she would not be disappointed since she was quite used to disappointment. She then closed her remarks by asking the convention delegates to "remember the women."[3] In response, her party, which had removed the names of the three Republican women candidates from a newspaper ad immediately following the supreme court's decision, reinserted them after the meeting.

In a curious reversal of positions, the Republicans were now defending the right of women to run for office. The Democrats were quick to take advantage of the precarious political stance the Republicans had taken. The *Herald*, in fact, directed an overtly hostile attack on the women candidates themselves, particularly Emmeline Wells:

> Of course now that the supreme court has decided that women cannot vote this fall, the ambition of Mrs. Emmeline B. Wells and Lillie Pardee must be nipped in the bud. They must be taken down

from their high pedestals, the salaries of $100 per month which they have been receiving as the price for relinquishing their previous Democratic ideas, and carrying on the evangelical and organization work of the Republicans, will be stopped and they will be relegated to a condition of innocuous desuetude into which the hum of ambition will penetrate but weakly.

It is truly a mournful spectacle. Here were two distinguished women who have always been understood to be Democrats until the time for organization of the Democratic women. Then neither happened to be invited to take a very high position in the Democratic ranks. The Republicans held out promises of honor and emolument, and they followed.[4]

Since Emmeline made no such observation in her diary, nor explained her choice of parties, it is impossible to know her actual motives, but it is also difficult to think the Democrats would not have welcomed her leadership abilities and political contacts as assets to the party. As she continued to campaign for the Republican Party, and for her own candidacy, public pressure mounted against her and doubts about the eligibility of women to run for office came up in Republican ranks. Party lawyers continued to argue over the full intent of the supreme court's decision. The question was clearly creating dissension in the party. At a planning meeting, the eligibility of Emma J. McVicker, the one woman on the Republican slate for a state-wide office, was discussed, with a final decision as to whether or not to retain her name deferred to a later public meeting. Before that meeting was held, however, McVicker, unwilling to be the subject of so much controversy, declared her own ineligibility.[5] By the end of September, Lillie Pardee, while still holding that women had the right to run for election, acknowledged lack of support from members of the party and thus also felt the need to withdraw.[6]

Of course, pressure was now intense against Emmeline's candidacy. Ever the fighter and the individualist, she was reluctant to follow the lead of her fellow candidates. The *Herald* was correct in claiming that "it will take a great deal of persuasion to clear the ticket of the last woman, though all possible pressure will be brought to bear on Mrs. Wells."[7]

When Joseph F. Smith, a counselor in the First Presidency of the LDS Church, expressed his disapproval of the political involvement of prominent Church officials during the priesthood session of the Church's October conference of that year, Emmeline took note. Remarking on the impact of his words, she observed that "there is quite an excitement over what was said at conference in reproof of men who go ahead without counsel & accept positions."[8] To what extent his disapproval influenced Emmeline's decision is not clear, but it may well have simply tipped the balance. She already felt tension from her daughter's ongoing disapproval over her political activity, the split in the party's ranks over her candidacy, the continuing harassment from the *Daily Herald*, and the slender basis on which her candidacy rested. "I suppose there is really no alternative but to withdraw," she reflected. But she was not happy to do so. This first election had a significance that no future election would have. Women on the ballot that selected the first officers of the new state would indeed be an event of historical significance. "I believe it is wrong," she fumed. "I do not believe it would really affect the party or statehood or cut any figure in the matter whatever, and I think moreover I have a right to be elected to the Legislature—as also other women—I yield unwillingly to the pressure brought to bear against the name of women on the Ticket."[9]

This period of indecision was marked by a growing antagonism with Emily Richards. Though separated by a generation, the two women had been essentially partners as LDS Church intermediaries with Congress. Emmeline may well have envied Emily's monogamous status, her husband's financial support, her comfortable life in Washington and in Utah, and the prominence she enjoyed in many circles, but the two women had worked well together, both making a significant impression on their eastern allies. Local politics, however, had put them on different sides, and each brought her own abilities and intense loyalties to bear on the present contest. On October 7, 1895, before Emmeline's resignation as a candidate, the *Herald* began printing a three-part reply by Emily Richards to the *Republican Catechism*, which Emmeline had authored and distributed earlier. In her reply,

Emily made a pointed reference to Emmeline's assertion that Governor Caleb West, a Democrat, and the last federally appointed governor of Utah, did not favor equal privileges for women because he failed to appoint any to territorial boards.[10] His refusal, Emily pointed out, resulted from the restrictions of the Edmunds-Tucker Act (prohibiting women from voting or holding office). That he was correct in that decision, she continued, "is demonstrated fully for Republicans in the resignations of Mrs. Pardee and Mrs. McVicker . . . for the reason that the decision of the court withholding from the women the right to vote disqualified them for holding office."[11] The implication was clear that Emmeline was simply delaying the inevitable.

On the day the first installment of the Richards critique was published, Emmeline and Emily met together in a woman suffrage meeting. Emmeline found it a "very unpleasant affair with Mrs. Richards, who had made up her mind to have some changes made." While not detailing the difficulties, Emmeline recorded that at the afternoon meeting "came the struggle with the faction from the County [suffrage association]," referring to the ongoing conflict between her and county president Ellen Ferguson, a Democrat, who was supported by Richards. "I suffered very much in my feelings," Emmeline lamented to her diary. Though she had encountered disagreements and power struggles before, she did not like to see a lack of unity among women dedicated to the same goals. Partisan politics, however, had altered the Mormon political landscape. Women, no less than men, became competitive in defense of their parties as well as their own ambitions. Though her bruised emotions were undoubtedly real, Emmeline was known as a determined, willful woman, not unfamiliar with the uses of either sarcasm or manipulation to achieve her own ends. The dispute was hardly a conspiracy against a vulnerable woman. Personal ambitions were nourished by the combative matrix of politics, and in the arena of party politics, Mormon women, like their male counterparts, were discovering, for the first time, the legitimacy—and unpleasantness—of dissent. It was not an easy transition. "Politics have divided us more than anything else that ever happened," Isabella Horne, regretfully but correctly, observed that year.[12] The experience of Mormon women, however, was not unique. The political conflict they encountered, which reflected both party and personal convictions, echoed the dissension that had beset the national suffragist ranks in 1867, dividing the suffragist movement for more than twenty years, while it also prefigured the aftermath of the 1920 passage of the Nineteenth Amendment, which gave the vote to all United States women. A unified woman's vote, or even a single-minded political platform, was never a realistic hope, despite suffragists' claims. Women were not only divided in the struggle for enfranchisement, they were divided after achieving it.

Only weeks before the election, Emmeline finally capitulated. In her letter of resignation, printed in the *Salt Lake Tribune*, she gave credit to the Republicans for being the "first to place women in nomination for offices of emolument and trust, expecting them to take an active part in the affairs of the new State," thus demonstrating "their appreciation of this new element in politics."[13] The day the letter appeared she once more turned to her diary to record her personal feelings. "I did not do it," she wrote, "without very great consideration and advice—likewise nevertheless I think my own judgment was best—and that was I should maintain the position—and make a test of the principle of woman's equality and see how successful I could be in the election."[14] She was not necessarily consoled in her decision when numerous supporters from the party, including former governor Arthur L. Thomas, told her that they felt she had made "the mistake of [her] lifetime."[15]

Despite her resignation, she continued to work for the party in the weeks left before the election.[16] She continued meeting with the Republican executive committee, entertained Kate Field, their former animus now behind them, watched the Republican Women's Club parade, and continued to encourage the suffrage organizations to campaign for the constitution. Finally, election day arrived. Unable to vote, women nevertheless showed their interest and support by serving lunches in all the precincts.[17] When the votes were finally tallied, the returns showed that 31,305 people had voted to ratify the constitution with 7,687 opposed. The Republicans swept the election of new state officers. This Republican sweep was especially satisfying to Emmeline, who had made a risky decision in giving her allegiance to the party primarily made up of Gentiles, but it was a particularly gratifying victory since the new governor was one of "our boys," Heber M. Wells, son of her sister-wife.[18]

The overwhelming acceptance of the constitution, however, was the sweetest victory, a well-earned reward for twenty years of personal struggle to hold, only to lose, and then regain the "blessed symbol." Visitors to Emmeline's office shared her excitement. "It seems almost too good to be true that we have equal suffrage," she exclaimed. "Junius [son of another Wells wife] has been in and several others of my friends, and all seems secure and no permanent ill feelings I trust."[19] That same day

Church Archives, The Church of Jesus Christ of Latter-day Saints

Heber M. Wells became governor of Utah Territory in 1895. He was the son of Emmeline's sister-wife Martha Givens Harris Wells but Emmeline considered him to be one of "our boys."

Emmeline Wells wrote a letter congratulating Elizabeth Cady Stanton on her eightieth birthday, which accompanied a gift from Utah women in the form of a ballot box made of Utah onyx, trimmed with silver and engraved with her name and the date, November 12, 1895.[20] The next day, she sent the happy news of the election to Susan B. Anthony and Carrie Chapman Catt. In response to Emmeline's telegram, Susan B. Anthony replied: "Oh, how good this little item makes me feel! Just to think that when I get to Washington Jan. 18, 1896, you and all of the dear women of Utah will be full-fledged citizens possessed of the right to vote on every question on equal terms with men. Well, I rejoice with you every day with every thought and every mention of Utah." She concluded by asking Emmeline for suggestions regarding the celebration of statehood for Utah at the National American Woman Suffrage Association (NAWSA) convention in Washington on January 23.[21]

U.S. President Grover Cleveland (1893–97) signed the order that admitted Utah to the Union on January 4, 1896. *Library of Congress*

President Grover Cleveland chose the first day of the new year, 1896, to formally accept the constitution and appointed January 4 as the day he would sign the statehood proclamation. Emmeline Wells again telegraphed Susan B. Anthony: "President signed Constitution of State of Utah today. Women are full-fledged citizens. Glory Hallelujah! Rejoice with us." Both Emmeline Wells and Emily Richards signed it. The reply was prompt: "We all rejoice with you that Utah is a State with her women free and enfranchised citizens."[22] After seventeen years of a precarious hold on the vote and nearly a decade without it, Utah finally won the honor of being the third state to permanently grant its women the right to vote. And after nearly a half century of trying, Utah was now to become a state, the forty-fifth to join the Union. The *Woman's Tribune*, noting that the new governor "did not forget to extend the hand of greeting to the women who are now voters," complimented them for their experience in managing "great enterprises as witness their Relief Associations" and for having shown in their membership in the suffrage association and particularly the National Council of Women (NCW) "their earnestness and ability."[23]

At dawn, on the clear, crisp fourth day of January 1896, guns were fired, whistles blown, and Utahns knew that the president of the United States had signed the proclamation of statehood. "All was joyous noise," Emmeline exclaimed, and the city was "streaming with flags and banners." When she reached her office that Saturday morning, she was soon joined by other women "anxious to participate in the demonstration of joy and gladness."[24] The inauguration of the new state officers occurred two days later. Again ringing bells and cracking gunfire heralded the beginning of a parade. Crowds filled the streets and "joy was everywhere," Emmeline exclaimed. The inaugural ceremonies were held in the Tabernacle, which had been festooned with red, white, and blue streamers everywhere. A large, illuminated American eagle surmounted the tower above the organ, and an immense flag, seventy-five by one hundred-fifty feet, covered the egg-shaped dome of the building with a large, illuminated star at one corner. Emmeline was happy to report to her readers that her friend and fellow suffragist, Margaret A. Caine, had been the principal designer of the decorations.

As the oath of office was administered to the new governor, the cannon was fired at Fort Douglas, after which the Mormon Tabernacle Choir sang "The Star Spangled Banner" and gave the premier performance of "Utah, We Love Thee," composed by the choir's conductor, Evan Stephens. The proceedings of the inauguration were solemn but impressive, Emmeline noted, bringing a tumultuous applause from the patriotic throng at their conclusion.[25] The inaugural ball later that evening lived up to all of its expectations. Emmeline sat in the governor's box with other members of the Wells family, while her daughter Annie and her husband, John Q. Cannon, participated in the grand march. Emmeline spent most of the evening at the side of her sister-wife Martha, the proud mother of the new governor, who received numerous demonstrations of her son's popularity. Electricity contributed to the brilliance of the decorations and lighting of the hall, which was also festooned with a large flag, a beehive, and a golden star.[26]

Capitalizing on both her political and familial relationship with the new governor, Emmeline Wells hoped to have more success now than in the past in creating opportunities for women in the new state government. A week after the November election, at the suggestion of George M. Cannon, chair of the state Republican committee, she wrote to each newly elected member of the senate and house proposing that they appoint a woman as chief clerk of the Senate, nominating Lillie R. Pardee for the position. When her efforts succeeded after the new legislature met, she was delighted to know "that the Certificate of the new

Senators had to be signed by a *woman* as well as a man." On the other hand, she had not been slow to complain to the inauguration planning committee that "it was noticable women were not considered in the proceedings or in any way recognized as a part of the new state."[27]

Denied the opportunity to create legislation herself, once statehood was obtained she resumed her legislative lobbying in earnest. She pressed for legislation to raise the "age of consent" (marriage without parental permission) to eighteen, a bill that "would not have been passed if we had not been present" during the debate, she maintained.[28] She also sat through a controversial discussion on jury service for women. While one state senator suggested that it be optional with the women, George Sutherland, elected to the state senate later that year, argued that it was neither "a right nor a privilege but a burden the same as military service." Therefore, he asserted, women should be exempt from jury service just as they were exempted from military service. The latter proposal won the day, and to Emmeline's chagrin, women would not be obliged to serve as jurors.[29] Throughout the year, she continued her lobbying efforts for a state-sponsored silk commission, state support of kindergartens, allocation of funds for public libraries, and the appointment of women to various state boards, the same issues that had received her attention in the past—but this time she met with greater success. Many of her editorials in the *Woman's Exponent* were appeals to the women of Utah to become alert to the issues the new legislature was discussing and to attend the sessions in order to directly express their own plans and hopes for the new state.[30]

Though she hoped that there would be no permanent ill feelings during this initial test of political schism, the Republican victory stirred the simmering feud between Emmeline Wells and Emily Richards. Both were involved in what was expected to be "the most brilliant affair of the season,"[31] a leap-year ball, planned by the Utah suffrage association as a fund-raising event while the new state was in a celebratory mood. The ball, however, became another occasion for discord. After days of planning and preparation and juggling unnumbered opinions on how to proceed, Emmeline was relieved that the event finally turned out to be "one of the most enjoyable and at the same time the least formal of any party given this season," according to one newspaper article.[32] Unaccountably, none of the Richards family attended. The next day, however, "Mrs. Richards was on hand to know all about the party," Emmeline noted, "and was very disagreeable when she learned that no more [money] had been made." Emily complained that if Emmeline had not been so involved in simultaneously planning the annual birthday party for Relief Society General President Zina Young, set for the next month, she "might have succeeded better."[33] The complaint seemed to be nothing more than a show of petulance reflecting her family's disappointment at the Republican sweep of the new state's officers.

More important than the leap-year ball, however, was the celebration of Utah's statehood at the forthcoming NAWSA convention in Washington, D.C. Anticipation was high regarding the choice of delegates to represent the voting women of the new state. On December 18, 1895, the Utah Woman Suffrage Association (UWSA) nominated a delegation of twelve.[34] Most of the active workers were among the nominees, but inexplicably, Emmeline's name was not among the number, her attendance simply assumed by the association. Recognizing her years of work in the cause and her representative position as president of the territorial and now state association, national suffragists also expected her to attend. One eastern correspondent, Margherita Hamm, of the New York *Mail and Express,* made that assumption clear in a pre-convention write-up:

> From far-off Utah will appear Mrs. Emmeline B. Wells, who has toiled thirty years for her principles, and now sees them triumphant in her own home. She will receive an ovation because long ago she foresaw and foretold what happened in the Great Basin last November. In fact, five years ago she laughingly said: "Women will vote and hold office in my poor little mountain State before they do in the rich and powerful states of the seaboard."[35]

As the time drew near, however, none of the nominees had made firm commitments to attend. Money was a problem for many of them, and the unexpected illness of a family member put Emily Richards's attendance in doubt as well. While Emmeline Wells was eager to attend, the way was even less clear for her. "My impressions have been all along that I should go, but how has not seemed to divulge itself. I cannot borrow the money with no prospect of paying immediately and so I am in doubt."[36] That neither the Church, nor the Relief Society, the state suffrage association, nor even her friends were either willing or able to provide the funds is incomprehensible. Though she had provided suggestions for the program and even been successful in changing the day of the Washington celebration to permit the newly elected Congressional delegation from Utah to attend, it appeared that Emmeline would not be among the women from Utah. As it turned out, that honor went to a Provo worker, Sarah Boyer, and to Emily Richards, no longer needed at home and expected to attend with her husband.[37]

"[I] can scarcely believe I am not going to Washington," Emmeline wrote on the day Emily and Sarah left. "It don't seem true at all."[38] Certainly that celebration, more than any other, would have been an appropriate culmination of her thirty-year effort in the suffrage cause. The expressions of regret proffered by ecclesiastical leaders were only salt in the wound. It is doubtful that LDS Church President Wilford Woodruff realized how painful his words were to Emmeline when he explained that his preference had been for Relief Society General President Zina Young and suffrage association president Emmeline Wells to attend, certainly the logical representatives. The common knowledge that Emmeline had no funds of her own to underwrite the trip and had always depended on Church or Relief Society support gave a hollowness to his regrets.[39] Her absence in Washington on this particular occasion was surely a great injustice in the woman suffrage story.

Emmeline kept busy while the festivities occurred in the nation's capital. She meticulously recorded the events as they were made known to her in the *Woman's Exponent* so that the grand occasion could be shared throughout the new state. The proceedings were also printed in the Boston *Woman's Journal* and the *Woman's Tribune*.[40] Both Anna Shaw and Susan Anthony paid tribute to Utah, which had joined Wyoming and Colorado as "the crown of our Union, those three states on the crest of the Rockies." Corinne Allen (wife of Utah's first Congressional representative Clarence Allen, a non-Mormon), Sarah Boyer, and Emily Richards all responded to the speeches of congratulations.[41] A talk by George W. Catt, husband of Carrie Chapman Catt, an officer in the NAWSA and budding new national suffrage leader, proved him to be an astute observer of how campaigns are won. His wife undoubtedly utilized his analysis of the Utah campaign when she became president of the NAWSA in 1900 and led the final march to attaining suffrage for all women in the United States in 1920.

Catt attributed Utah's success to "public opinion which ruled in Utah in engrafting liberty in its Constitution. It was not public opinion alone," he explained, "but organized public opinion." He observed that the Utah suffrage organization was nineteen times larger than New York's on the basis of population. "Behind every delegate in the Constitutional Convention," he noted, "there was an organized constituency demanding suffrage for women and men alike." He concluded by stating that "the Utah victory was won by organization. . . . The banner of victory which Utah unfurls to the breeze bears this device: 'Organize and Win.'" [42] This was no small tribute to the women of Utah, who had begun almost immediately after losing the vote in 1887 with plans to regain it at statehood seven years later. The campaign had indeed been a marvel of organization. A special tribute to Emmeline, "whose influence had been paramount in securing the franchise for the women of Utah," was heartily applauded and a telegram of congratulations sent to her, perhaps bringing her some measure of compensation.[43]

For days afterward, Emmeline received letters of congratulations, many of them giving "particulars of a good time and happiness, in the meetings or parties."[44] She hardly had time to dwell on her disappointment, however, since she continued to be involved in her two literary clubs, the Utah State Kindergarten Association (formed that year), Utah Federation of Women's Clubs, and Relief Society service. She could be found almost daily at the legislature, following the passage of bills of importance to her, annoyed that so many women "do not accept the responsibility of the franchise, and try to look into matters more deeply than they do."[45] She was particularly interested in the proposal to legitimate all the children of polygamous marriages born up to the time of the 1890 Manifesto. A long legislative debate ensued when the minority report changed the proposed cutoff date to statehood in 1896. To some, the later date suggested a willful disregard for the Edmunds-Tucker Act as well as LDS Church President Woodruff's Manifesto, but the date of statehood as the cutoff prevailed.[46] The discussion aroused some ill feelings, Emmeline noted. "It is rather unpleasant to wake up the old prejudices but unavoidable."[47] Once awakened old prejudices are harder to extinguish, as Emmeline would soon discover.

Despite her numerous religious and civic commitments, Emmeline Wells continued her compulsive letter writing. If anything, her correspondence with national leaders increased during this period, not only with the officers of the suffrage association but also with those of the NCW and National Women's Press Club, in which Emmeline served as a subcommittee member. She also corresponded with Corinne Allen and Isabella Brown, whose husband, Arthur, was elected senator from Utah. As a consistent correspondent, she never allowed a relationship to fade through lack of contact.

While the rivalry between Emily Richards and Emmeline persisted, there seemed to be an effort on both parts to keep it from assuming any great public notice, unlike the earlier rivalry between Emmeline and Charlotte Godbe Kirby. Both repeatedly appealed to the women of Utah "to maintain the best of feelings toward each other, despite party interests, to work for the benefit of woman-kind, and to put aside 'intense partisanship' in the interest of the public good."[48] As evidence of the sincerity of her own appeal, Emmeline Wells, on the last day of December 1896, recommended Emily Richards as a new member of the Reaper's Club, a conciliatory conclusion to their past differences. As they encountered the divisive demands of partisan politics, most Mormon women probably shared the sentiments of Ruth May Fox: "I do hope they will not engender bad feelings in their divisions on party lines," this active Republican worker wrote. "As for my part I care nothing for politics. It is Mormonism or nothing for me."[49]

Party rivalries, however, did not cease. These politically astute women had come alive to the excitement in working for the political principles and diverse goals of their individual parties. While strictly keeping political rivalry from the Relief Society meetings that brought many of these ambitious and dedicated women together, they continued individually to serve their own political interests. Emmeline's participation in partisan politics actually increased when George M. Cannon decided to resign as chair of the Republican State Central Committee. At the same time, the vice chair, E. K. Walton, also resigned "to give a permanent place on the Committee to some lady," now that women had the franchise. "The time for creating empty honors for women had ceased," the committee declared. After much debate, J. E. Dooley was elected to replace Cannon, Emmeline was elected first vice chair, and Walton was retained as second vice chair.[50] Lillie Pardee resigned as secretary but agreed to serve until a suitable replacement could be found. Emmeline's new office would keep her engrossed in politics throughout the year, particularly in arousing the interest of women, though she found some women no longer interested in party politics and despaired of trying to continue Republican women's meetings.[51]

However, the coming fall election, the first since 1887 in which women could vote, reversed some of the apathy as women not only anticipated voting again but also electing women to state office. A cautionary letter from Susan B. Anthony to the "newly-enfranchised women of Utah" advised them not to try to get women elected to office as much as "to get the best persons, whether men or women." She also advised them against acting too partisan, feeling that it would prove to be a strong objection to woman suffrage. This test of women voters naturally concerned her since their performance in the election preliminaries and at the polls would go a long way in winning supporters for the cause nationwide if they handled themselves judiciously. Emmeline concurred. "Whatever we do will help or hinder the cause elsewhere," she wrote, advising the women to use prudence in their return to suffrage.[52] She also advised her *Exponent* readers "to investigate for [themselves] and be sure [they] are right and honest in politics." She urged them not to allow any "individual caprice or ambitious desire for power or the spoils of office . . . to creep in and usurp the place of conscience" and warned them that they would be watched "with greater interest . . . than the women of Wyoming and Colorado" because of their greater number, and they should therefore set a good example for women in the other states.[53]

Despite their enfranchisement, members of the various branches of the UWSA continued to meet regularly, and by September 1896 they had formed themselves into women's leagues and civic clubs for the study of politics and civic government, thus removing those courses of study from Relief Society meetings.[54] Emmeline maintained her position as president of the suffrage association and continued to use the *Woman's Exponent* to urge restraint and thoughtful discussion in their meetings as they approached the coming election. This election was instrumental in introducing a new generation of women to the intrigue of politics and in inciting them to take over the reins of leadership. Susa Young Gates, who became a close associate of Emmeline's in support of the National and International Councils of Women, Ruth May Fox, Clarissa Spencer Williams, Alice Merrill Horne, and others from around the state found their own interests and ambitions fueled by the openings that Utah provided for local political activity along with representation in the national women's associations. Yielding her place to these intelligent, articulate, energetic newcomers would be a slow and painful process for Emmeline, which she resisted until well into her advanced years.

As this important election neared, the parties met to decide on their candidates for state office. The nomination of several women for the legislature pleased Emmeline Wells since it showed "the liberality of some honorable men who realize the justice of equal suffrage." She noted that a number of men were known to have changed from one party affiliation to the other and thus, she felt, women should not be criticized for doing so or for making some mistakes in the political process, clearly rationalizing her own alleged transfer of loyalties.[55] Wells continued to be a highly visible figure on the political scene, as did Emily Richards.

At the party conventions held that fall, both Emily and Emmeline were nominated by their respective parties for the state senate. While Emily declined, Emmeline agreed to run. Her friend and party supporter, George M. Cannon, optimistically claimed that Emmeline's name "would strengthen the ticket to the extent of 6000 votes."[56] The ballot for state senator in her district included ten candidates, five from each party, running "at large" for five seats. Voters could select any five of the ten. Among the five Republican candidates were Emmeline Wells, along with her Stake President Angus Cannon, who had evidently reversed his position on Church officials in politics. Angus Cannon's wife, Dr. Martha Hughes Cannon, was among the five Democratic candidates. It was an unusual contest, to say the least.

In early October, at the height of the campaign, Emmeline Wells left Utah for nearly a month's visit with her daughter Melvina in Idaho. She returned in time for the final weeks of campaigning, which included urging a revival of the struggling Women's Republican Clubs. But this time she seemed desultory and resigned, compared with the frenetic pace she had maintained the previous year. The intensity of her involvement in 1895, which had ended so disappointingly, had wearied her with the vagaries of politics, and she appeared reluctant to make a similar investment of time and emotion. On election day, however, she roused herself to the occasion, declaring it "extremely interesting considering the women's vote." Since the Republicans had made a clean sweep at the previous state election, Emmeline had some reason to feel optimistic about her candidacy this time around. But this year also hosted a presidential election, and many candidates would be able to ride the coattails of the favored presidential candidate, William Jennings Bryant, a silver man and a Democrat.

Emmeline spent the day at Republican headquarters in town, but by evening the crowds that had gathered to hear the final results had grown so large that confusion reigned everywhere. Weary of the whole procedure and undoubtedly nervous about the outcome of her own election, Emmeline went home and read throughout the night, her favorite pastime, especially during times of stress. She remained hopeful of the results, but being alone gave her time to think and rid herself of any delusions or unwarranted anticipation.

The next day Emmeline was devastated to learn that the local election turned out to be a clear-cut Democratic victory. The five Democratic candidates had all won senate seats. Dr. Martha Hughes Cannon

Senate and Staff of Utah's Second Legislature. Dr. Martha Hughes Cannon, first woman state senator in the United States, is standing between Senator John T. Caine and president of the Senate, Aquila Nebeker. The other two women are clerks.

Utah State Historical Society

trailed the Democrats on the ticket for state senator, but she garnered more votes than any of the Republicans, including her husband, Angus Cannon, who received the second highest number of votes of the Republicans. Emmeline came in last of all the ten candidates.[57]

Once again she was disappointed, humiliated, and embarrassed that she had not done better for her party. But once more she rallied to congratulate the victors and see the good in the outcome. Three women, all Democrats, won legislative seats, and eleven throughout the state were elected county recorders. Martha Hughes Cannon's victory crowned her as the first woman state senator in the country.[58] To her *Exponent* readers, Emmeline could not refrain from expressing a self-serving regret that "all the women [candidates] were not elected, for it would have been a much truer test of women's power had there been some women from each party." Her hopeful spirit not entirely extinguished, she concluded, "women as well as men must content themselves as best they can until another election, when things may be different."[59]

Though women had established a foothold in the politics of the new state, the outcome of the election would not prove to be a clear mandate for continued widespread involvement. Voting was one thing. Running for office was quite another. During the campaign, men who ran against women felt awkward in campaigning against them, and the men who lost to women felt humiliated. One can only imagine the embarrassment Angus Cannon, member of a prominent Latter-day Saint family and president of the Salt Lake Stake, felt in losing not only to a woman but to his own wife Martha. Women in politics in the nineteenth century were clearly an uncomfortable innovation. This "experiment in equality" would take time to find its niche in party politics. In fact, just two years after statehood the active Utah County Woman Suffrage Association denounced an "informal understanding" it had discovered to exist between the two political parties aimed at "eliminating women from the state and county tickets at the next election." The parties, the association said, claimed that "women were a weakness upon the ticket" since they lacked "executive ability and could not draw the votes of other women."[60] While this claim had not been tested and perhaps bore no basis in fact, the attitude that it bespoke reflected two persistent social and psychological barriers to woman's full political participation: namely, the reluctance of men to integrate women into the political system and the ambivalence of women themselves toward the propriety and capability of their sex in politics.

For Emmeline Wells, her adventure into partisan politics had been challenging and instructive. "What an experience this has been for me," she wrote at the height of her involvement. "It has been very exciting for me and quite new too—we are all beginners."[61] The "Americanization" process, leading to statehood, had introduced into the lives of Utah women—both Mormon and gentile—a new configuration of shared values and political goals to augment their individual religious or social bonds without seriously threatening them. Their female religious associations had fostered unity and conformity within them, and the common goal of the suffrage movement had insured a cooperative effort; now politics offered an arena for diversity, legitimate opposition, and new alignments.

In their transition from the UWSA to the political parties, however, women lost both power and autonomy as a collective body, to Emmeline's dismay. She found that 1895 was an exceptional year for Utah women—not a portent of a continued pattern of political involvement and notice. Nor was she happy about her own political fortunes. In her attempts to test the impact she might have in political office, she had been rejected first by the law, then by the voters, and lastly by her own party when not long after 1896 it reverted to prestatehood patterns by privileging male candidates. Some few women succeeded, however, and continued in small but respectable numbers to fill elected offices, mainly in the counties, but "the power of woman's vote" became illusory in the absence of a united female electorate. Woman's vote, it was discovered, was very little different from man's, and there were few specifically gender-based issues to force a coalition. Emmeline's continual effort to arouse women to claim a place in the political world went largely unheeded.[62]

The campaign to put woman suffrage in the Utah state constitution had been essentially a woman's campaign, planned and executed by women who had to convince the majority of one hundred four men in the constitutional convention that woman suffrage, which the legislatures of forty-two other states opposed, was good for Utah. But in leaving their suffrage association and moving into the political parties, these same women, capable, experienced, and energetic, moved back into traditional organizational relationships with men. They were vice chairs but not permanent chairs. They were delegates but not strategists. Their experience and ability were considered useful in the parties but not to lead them, conduct the campaigns, or develop political platforms and philosophies. And in that one exceptional year, 1895, it is probably fair to appraise the attention they received from both the press and the parties as political expedience.

But for the women who courageously became part of the drama, the experience was a taste of the "emancipation" promised by the vote. For Emmeline Wells, representation on any level in the political process marked a major step forward in the overall advancement of women. No amount of personal disappointment totally discouraged or disillusioned her. She came nearest to a sense of defeat when her last nomination as a candidate for the legislature failed to garner sufficient votes within her party. After the voting, she withdrew from the convention "weary of the proceedings." The satisfaction of attaining public office was not to be hers. Her optimistic spirit slowly mended, however, with the number of congratulations that her name had been considered as well as many expressions of sympathy that she had failed to win her party's nomination. Women, even from "the opposite party," thought it only right that she should be a Republican candidate. Despite her personal disappointment, however, achievement of the greater goal continued to lift and motivate her. "I am not sure which is the right course to pursue," she wrote, contemplating this turbulent period, "but am determined to stand for women."[63] At seventy, she still had two more decades and many more opportunities to fulfill that determination.

Notes

1. Emmeline B. Wells, Diary, September 24, 1898, L. Tom Perry Special Collections, Harold B. Lee Library, Brigham Young University, Provo, Utah.

2. "Republicans Ratified," *Salt Lake Daily Herald,* September 3, 1895, 3; "Republican Ratification," *Salt Lake Tribune,* September 3, 1895, 1.

3. Reported in "Republicans Ratified," *Salt Lake Daily Herald,* September 3, 1895, 3.

4. "The Political Arena," *Salt Lake Daily Herald,* September 2, 1895, 5. The only reference to payment for services in the party that Emmeline made was the following month, when she indicated that she had presented to the executive committee the "matter of money for the secretary [Lillie Pardee] and had the sum provided." Wells, Diary, October 9, 1895.

5. "Mrs. M'Vicker Withdraws," *Salt Lake Tribune,* September 15, 1895, 8; "Planned State Campaign," *Salt Lake Tribune,* September 12, 1895, 8.

6. See letter in "Withdrawal of Mrs. Pardee," *Salt Lake Tribune,* September 29, 1895, 4.

7. The paper also noted that U.S. Senate candidate Arthur Brown was pleased with Mrs. Pardee's withdrawal, since she was replaced by a "Brown" man, but evidently Mrs. Wells's possible replacement was not a Brown supporter, and thus he was not in favor of her withdrawal. See "Arthur Brown is Wrathful," *Salt Lake Daily Herald,* September 29, 1895, 1.

8. Wells, Diary, October 17, 1895. Whether or not Joseph F. Smith meant to include women in his remarks is unclear. He had not opposed their participation in the election campaign. The fact that Emmeline noted them in her diary suggests however that they had some impact on her decision.

9. Wells, Diary, October 16, 17, 1895.

10. See Emily S. Richards, "Republican Catechism," *Salt Lake Daily Herald,* September 25, 1895, 5; Emily S. Richards, "Republican Catechism," *Salt Lake Daily Herald,* September 27, 1895, 5; Emily S. Richards, "Republican Catechism," *Salt Lake Daily Herald,* September 30, 1895, 5. Wells had been a persistent lobbyist through the 1890s, not only to urge the legislature and the governor to create a permanent silk commission, which was eventually successful, but to appoint women to various territorial boards in which they had a vested interest. She was not successful in this endeavor until after statehood.

11. Emily S. Richards, *The Republican Catechism Criticised and Amended for the Benefit of the Women of Utah,* pamphlet (n.p., n.d.), 40, Utah State Historical Society, reprinted from Emily S. Richards, "Republican Catechism," *Salt Lake Daily Herald,* August 30, 1895, 5; Emily S. Richards, "Republican Sophistry," *Salt Lake Daily Herald,* September 1, 1895, 9; Emily S. Richards, "Republican Catechism," *Salt Lake Daily Herald,* September 7, 1895, 5; Emily S. Richards, "Republican Catechism," *Salt Lake Daily Herald,* September 21, 1895, 5.

12. "Convention in Atlanta," *Woman's Exponent* 23 (February 1, 15, 1895): 236.

13. "Mrs. Wells Off the Ticket," *Salt Lake Tribune,* October 20, 1895, 5.

14. Wells, Diary, October 20, 1895.

15. Wells, Diary, October 24, 1895.

16. In October 1895 the *Nephi Blade* reported on her visit with Emma McVicker judging it quite successful since the two women "confined their remarks to strict principles," leaving a discussion of personalities to others. "One good derived from having ladies in politics," it concluded. Emmeline Wells was identified as a "journalist," since she had withdrawn her name as a candidate. "Personalities," *Nephi Blade,* October 26, 1895, 4.

17. Wells, Diary, November 5, 1895.

18. Heber Manning Wells was the son of Daniel H. Wells and Martha Givens Harris Wells. He had served in the constitutional convention and had been active in civic affairs prior to that time. He was thirty-six when he was elected the first governor of the state of Utah in 1896. Orson F. Whitney, *History of Utah,* 4 vols. (Salt Lake City: George Q. Cannon and Sons, 1904), 4:619–20.

19. Wells, Diary, November 7, 1895. Junius was the son of Hannah Free Wells and Daniel H. Wells.

20. Wells, Diary, November 6, 1895.

21. From a *Deseret Evening News* article, December 28, 1895, in the Papers of Elizabeth Cady Stanton and Susan B. Anthony, Library of Congress, Washington, D.C.

22. Clipping from the papers of Elizabeth Cady Stanton and Susan B. Anthony.

23. From "The Third Star," *Woman's Tribune* 13 (January 18, 1896): 1, to which Emmeline Wells, Margaret A. Caine, and Zina Young Card responded with a telegram thanking Clara Colby, editor of the *Woman's Tribune,* for her recognition of events in Utah. "Complimentary Telegram," *Woman's Tribune* 13 (February 8, 1896): 14.

24. Wells, Diary, January 4, 1896.

25. Wells, Diary, January 6, 1896. For more details see "The Inauguration," *Woman's Exponent* 24 (January 1, 15, 1896): 100; and Edward Leo Lyman, *Political Deliverance: The Mormon Quest for Utah Statehood* (Urbana: University of Illinois Press, 1986), 281–82. See also "Inaugural," *Salt Lake Tribune,* January 7, 1896, 1; "Inaugural Ceremonies," *Deseret Evening News,* January 6 1896, 1.

26. Wells, Diary, January 6, 7, 1896.

27. Wells, Diary, January 1, 22, 1896.

28. Wells, Diary, February 5, 1896.

29. "With the Lawmakers," *Salt Lake Herald*, January 22, 1896, 5; Wells, Diary, January 21, 1896. That she was not judged by a "jury of her peers" was a complaint of Susan B. Anthony in her 1872 trial for attempting to vote. Jury duty for women remained a controversial aspect of enfranchisement for a number of years (varied from state to state).

30. See, for example, "Kindergarten Education," and "Appreciation of the Ballot," *Woman's Exponent* 24 (March 1, 1896): 124; "Women in Public Affairs," *Woman's Exponent* 24 (March 15, April 1, 1896): 132.

31. "The Leap Year Ball," *Deseret Evening News*, January 16, 1896, 1.

32. "Ladies Celebrate," *Salt Lake Daily Herald*, January 17, 1896, 8.

33. Wells, Diary, January 16, 17, 1896.

34. "Editorial Notes," *Woman's Exponent* 24 (February 1, 1896): 108; Wells, Diary, December 18, 1895.

35. "The Woman Suffragists," Journal History of the Church, January 23, 1896, 8, Church Archives, The Church of Jesus Christ of Latter-day Saints, Salt Lake City, also available on *Selected Collections from the Archives of The Church of Jesus Christ of Latter-day Saints*, 2 vols. (Provo, Utah: Brigham Young University Press, 2002), vol. 2, DVD 19, microfilm copy in Harold B. Lee Library.

36. Wells, Diary, January 15, 1896.

37. Wells, Diary, January 11, 15, 19, 21, 23, 1896.

38. Wells, Diary, January 19, 1896. Emmeline Wells was to suffer an additional unexpected slight. Evidently remarks reflecting "jealousy and envy and fear combined" over the Washington celebration disturbed Church leaders. At the end of the month, Emmeline was summoned to LDS Church President Wilford Woodruff's office, where he and his counselor George Q. Cannon made inquiries about the celebration. "The affair assumed gigantic shapes," she noted, and found the interview "frightful and overwhelming." "I cannot imagine that men in high places could listen to such frivolous misconstructions and misrepresentations," she wrote, "yet it is so and one must submit to such injustice which is nobler than to notice it." Wells, Diary, January 30, 31, 1896.

39. Emmeline received numerous expressions of regret from many quarters for her absence from Washington, including "all the brethren," as well as her Republican friends. For details of Emmeline's feelings during this period, see Wells, Diary, January 11, 15, 19, 21, 23, 1896. To her embarrassment, Emmeline, who was obligated to prepare the credentials for the two delegates, found she had incorrectly written Emily's and had to forward a new set "with an apology." Wells, Diary, January 20, 1896.

40. See, for example, "The Third Star," *Woman's Tribune* 13 (January 18, 1896): 1; "28th Annual National Convention," *Woman's Tribune* 13 (February 1, 1896): 9; "Minutes of 2nd Day of Conference," *Woman's Tribune* 13 (February 8, 1896): 13; "Report of NAWSA Convention," *Woman's Tribune* 13 (February 15, 1896): 17; "The Governor's Welcome," *Woman's Tribune* 13 (February 22, 1896): 23; and "The Utah Jubilee," *Woman's Journal,* January 11, 1896, 12; "Report on National Convention (NAWSA) Begins, Utah Welcomed," *Woman's Journal,* February 1, 1896, 33; "Woman Suffrage in Utah," *Woman's Journal,* February 8, 1896, 42; "A Utah Woman's View," *Woman's Journal,* April 25, 1896, 130–31. For reports in the *Woman's Exponent,* see "The Washington Convention," 24 (February 1, 1896): 109; "The Washington Convention," and "The Utah Evening," 24 (February 15, 1896): 113–14. The *History of Woman Suffrage* also includes a write-up of that celebratory convention. See "The National-American Convention of 1896," in *History of Woman Suffrage,* vol. 4, ed. Susan B. Anthony and Ida H. Harper (Rochester: Susan B. Anthony, 1902), 4:252–62.

41. The full text of Emily Richards' address is included in Brian H. Stuy, comp. and ed., *Collected Discourses Delivered by President Wilford Woodruff, His Two Counselors, the Twelve Apostles and Others, 1894–1896,* 4 vols. (Burbank, Calif.: B. H. S. Publishing, 1991), 4:419–23. Emily Richards makes no mention of Emmeline Wells in her review of woman suffrage in Utah.

42. George W. Catt, "Utah Suffrage Association," talk delivered January 24, 1896, in National American Woman Suffrage Association Papers, Library of Congress, Washington, D.C.

43. "Report of NAWSA Convention," 17.

44. Wells, Diary, February 7, 1896.

45. Wells, Diary February 4, 1896. She was particularly interested in pressing for women on state boards and getting state help for the silk industry. She was continually frustrated when she was prevented from attending the legislative session because of work and association commitments as well as the continual flow of visitors to her office. See Wells, Diary, February 25, 27, March 6, 11, 14, 17, 20, 24, 1896.

46. Details of the legislation affecting plural wives and their children can be found in Carol Cornwall Madsen, "'At Their Peril': Utah Law and the Case of Plural Wives, 1850–1900," *Western Historical Quarterly* 21 (November 1990): 425–44.

47. For details of the debate, see "Chance for the Exposition," *Salt Lake Tribune,* March 27, 1896, 5; "Evans Opposed the Bill," *Salt Lake Daily Herald,* March 27, 1896, 6; "Polygamous Issues," *Deseret Evening News,* March 28, 1896, 1; and Wells, Diary, March 27, 1896.

48. "S.L. Co. W.S.A.," *Woman's Exponent* 24 (March 1, 1896): 122; "Woman's Work and Duty," *Woman's Exponent* 25 (November 1, 15, 1896): 69.

49. Ruth May Fox, Diary, July 14, 1895, Church Archives.

50. "J. E. Dooly Chairman," *Salt Lake Daily Herald,* March 27, 1896, 3. Emmeline's name had been "cleared" by the First Presidency of the LDS Church when George M. Cannon had met with Counselor Joseph F. Smith requesting the presidency's opinion on her nomination. Wells, Diary, March 25, 1896.

51. Wells, Diary, May 8, 1896.

52. This information comes from two undated and untitled statements included in the Papers of Elizabeth Cady Stanton and Susan B. Anthony, Library of Congress. Emmeline picked up much of the language from the two statements in her editorial, "Suffrage in the West," *Woman's Exponent* 24 (May 1, 1896): 148.

53. "Suffrage in the West," 148.

54. "Suffrage Notes," *Woman's Tribune* (September 12, 1896): 82.

55. "Moderation and Self-Control," *Woman's Exponent* 24 (October 15, 1896): 58.

56. "Selected the Victims," *Salt Lake Daily Herald,* October 8, 1896, 2.

57. The top Democrat won 14,004 votes. Martha Hughes Cannon, fifth highest, gained 11,413 votes. Her husband came in second among the Republicans, gaining 8,742 votes. Emmeline Wells received 7,064. For a discussion of the election and the winners, see Jean Bickmore White, "Gentle Persuaders: Utah's First Women Legislators," *Utah Historical Quarterly* 38 (Winter 1970): 31–49.

58. The election became a *cause celebre* in Utah and throughout the country. It was not only highly unusual for a woman to be running for a political office but to run against her husband and *win* was truly a novelty, and tradition has it that the event was subject matter for Ripley's *Believe It or Not*. In its November 1897 issue, *Puritan Magazine* published an article entitled "Women Lawmakers in the West," which read: "A political woman was no new thing, but a woman fighting for a woman was a novelty, and the spectacle of a woman running for office against her own husband, and defeating him, created a positive sensation, not only in Utah, but throughout the land." "Women Lawmakers in the West," *Puritan Magazine* (November 1897): 50–51.

59. "Woman's Work and Duty," *Woman's Exponent* 25 (November 1, 15, 1896): 69.

60. "The Women Resolve," *Woman's Exponent* 27 (September 1, 1898): 33.

61. Wells, Diary, August 26, 1895.

62. A 1908 appraisal of woman suffrage in Utah revealed that fewer than twenty women had held elective office in the state since statehood, and a small number in county offices. Moreover, all women candidates garnered the fewest votes on their tickets, suggesting that women voters, who made up nearly 50 percent of those who voted, did not themselves vote for women candidates. See Parley P. Jenson, "Women's Enfranchisement in Utah," *Truth* 8 (March 29, 1908): 3.

63. Wells, Diary, September 23, 24, 1898.

Chapter 14

The "Blessed Symbol" for All

There is no other vitalizing force that can permeate every home and appeal to every individual citizen as the ballot can; therefore it must be the mightiest lever to uplift and to regenerate the world.[1]

Once it had achieved its goal to regain woman suffrage, the Utah Woman Suffrage Association (UWSA) turned its attention to encouraging women to vote and to educating them in the political process. Worried that women might not avail themselves of this newly won privilege, Emmeline Wells advised, encouraged, and instructed women in their political responsibilities now that they were once again voting citizens. More than her talks to the Relief Societies that she visited and the club meetings she attended, the *Woman's Exponent* was her primary conduit for her message. "Every sensible wide-awake woman should avail herself of the best opportunities possible to her . . . and get at least a general idea of the government under which she is living and how its affairs are conducted," she urged a few weeks before statehood was declared.[2] Though she still smarted from her election losses and particularly from the fact that history would not be able to record the name of any women in the first state legislature, Emmeline was optimistic about the future for women in the political activities of the new state, despite the claim of Provo women that they were not included in their local political parties just two years after winning the vote. That women took their voting privilege seriously at the outset was evident in the 1900 election year when Emmeline requested statistics for a history of woman suffrage in Utah, which she had agreed to write for Susan B. Anthony's massive *History of Woman Suffrage*.

Voting tallies at that time did not officially differentiate between male and female voters, but the Utah Council of Women (UCW) was able to persuade Governor Heber M. Wells to write a personal letter to each county recorder to secure the needed information. Though "eleven of the more remote counties did not respond," information was gleaned from sixteen counties showing that of 29,732 women who registered, 28,486 voted (95.8 percent). Male registrants numbered 31,571 with 29,738 voting (94.2 percent). In five counties, more women than men voted. Women comprised close to 50 percent of the vote, though the census indicated that males "comprised over 51 per cent. of the population."[3]

Whatever deterrents Provo suffragists faced in entering politics, women's initial political interest became evident in the numbers of women who sought county and state offices. For the first few years following statehood, women became elected members of both the state senate and house and in several county government posts.[4] With this kind of response, the political future for Utah women looked promising. However, neither Emmeline Wells nor Emily Richards, the two foremost workers in the suffrage cause, ever held an elective office. Nevertheless, for several years both remained active in their parties, Emily serving as an alternate delegate to the national Democratic convention in 1896 and Emmeline serving as vice chair of the state Republican Party.

After the grand National American Woman Suffrage Association (NAWSA) event in Washington, D.C., in 1896, celebrating Utah as the third woman suffrage state, Utah women felt a decided sense of achievement but also a correlative loss of enthusiasm to continue in the national suffrage movement. When officers of the UWSA met in an executive committee meeting later that year, they came face to face with the diminished interest in supporting the national struggle for the vote. The first order of business was to select representatives to the annual meeting of the NAWSA, scheduled for Des Moines, Iowa, the following January 1897.

Emmeline's problem was funding delegates. Many women felt they could not afford the trip, while others showed little interest in the convention, even though a barrage of letters from the national association urged them to attend. Emmeline herself had neither the time nor the money and, most unusual for her, little inclination to go. As president of the state suffrage association, however, she felt obligated either to go herself or to appoint someone else. For several weeks, she vacillated over her decision. "It looks selfish of us now we have the franchise not to help others," she acknowledged.[5] Finally, with no one else volunteering, Emmeline found the means to make the trip herself.

Des Moines reached −24°F (−31°C) that winter, but against its extreme cold radiated the warmth of Susan B. Anthony and her invitation to Emmeline Wells to introduce Anthony before she delivered her keynote speech. Most exciting for Emmeline, however, was the unexpected attendance of her daughter Melvina, who came to the convention representing the suffragists of Idaho, which had just come into the Union as the fourth woman suffrage state.[6] This was Melvina's first attendance at a national convention. Neither Emmeline nor Melvina had informed the other of her plan to attend, and they both were delighted to discover that they were lodged in the same hotel. When hearing of the mother-daughter suffrage duo, Susan B. Anthony called Emmeline and her daughter to sit with her on the stand during the meetings and invited them both to address the convention.[7] A highlight of the conference was the Iowa senate's invitation to several of the suffragists to speak before the state senators. Along with such prominent suffragists as Susan B. Anthony, Anna Howard Shaw, Clara Colby, and Alice Stone Blackwell to address the senate were Emmeline Wells and her daughter.[8]

At the convention proper, Emmeline, recognized as the woman "who has done more than any other person to secure woman suffrage in Utah," had been invited to speak about her experiences as a candidate for the Utah state senate. She reported, to laughter, that "a very young man had nominated her" and she explained that she did not win because she belonged to the wrong party. "The issue was silver," she said, and even Republicans voted the Democratic ticket, "and that was why I was not elected. They called me 'Mrs. Goldbug.'"[9] Making light of her political defeat was good catharsis. In her report, she described the voting pattern of women who, she was convinced, followed counsel to vote only for the best person, man or woman. Though not all women were totally comfortable participating in this formerly all-male political process, Emmeline boasted that she "was not afraid of men—not at all, not the least in the world. . . . We must stand up for the men. We could not do without them."[10] She had had far more experience than many women in working with men in influential positions, both the leaders of her church and those in the field of politics, locally and nationally. Moreover, she was pleased to report that even former opponents of suffrage were beginning to exercise their right to vote, swelling the number of women voters in Utah.[11] The stark reality that Utah had enfranchised its women twice while most other states had not yet seen fit to award it once was not lost on her hearers.

While applauding the success of the four Rocky Mountain states in gaining victory in the suffrage struggle, the association's treasurer also noted that none of them continued paying their dues to the national association thereafter. Emmeline had a ready response for Utah. She explained that Utah women "mean to work with the National, but we have not much money in Utah just now. In all other respects," she promised, "we mean to help as much as ever."[12] It was an uncertain promise, but it rested on a favorable history of prompt dues-paying as well as personal donations to the movement from its Utah supporters.

In addition to enjoying the company of her daughter, Emmeline Wells was delighted to meet the well-known journalist, feminist, lecturer, and newcomer to the convention from California, Charlotte Perkins Gilman.[13] Gilman and Wells struck up an immediate friendship, which led Gilman to make frequent visits to Utah and to develop associations with other Utah women, particularly Susa Young Gates.

Until 1899, two years after the Iowa meeting, the UWSA struggled to remain viable, but its leaders and active members had gradually redirected their efforts to the political parties. Thus, no organized body of women existed to send delegates to the conventions and lend support to the cause. Carrie Chapman Catt, the new president of the NAWSA, was not about to lose Utah workers or the enthusiasm that Utah women had given to their own fight for the ballot. In October 1899, she visited Utah with a plan to rekindle not only the interest but also the financial support of these enfranchised women. Drawing from the suffrage workers she had come to know, Catt organized the Utah Council of Women (UCW) to replace the suffrage association and to serve as an established resource to aid other states in their suffrage efforts. Her enthusiasm was infectious and reignited interest in the national movement, especially among younger suffragists. The council was comprised of Utah women representing multiple faiths and both political parties, with Emily Richards as president and the aging Emmeline, now seventy-one, as a member of the national executive committee.[14]

Charlotte Perkins Gilman (ca. 1900), an internationally known journalist, feminist, and lecturer, wrote the path-breaking feminist treatise *Women and Economics*. Photograph by C. F. Lummis.

For ten years, the UCW scheduled monthly meetings, with prominent suffragists speaking at some of them. Members participated in suffrage campaigns in other states and attended the national conventions of NAWSA. The UCW also proved to be a dependable source of financial aid to the national movement. After the first few years, however, interest in this organization also began to lag, and eventually meetings were held only as needed to assist with the latest strategy of the national association. The UCW frequently submitted petitions, for example, when the association sent out a call for the signatures of sympathetic citizens in behalf of the Sixteenth or "Anthony Amendment." Emily Richards remained an active worker, while Emmeline Wells

Carrie Chapman Catt (ca. 1909–32) served as president of the National American Woman Suffrage Association from 1900 to 1904 and from 1915 to 1920. Catt visited Utah in October 1899 to meet with the enfranchised women of the state. While in Utah, Catt organized the Utah Council of Women to replace the territorial suffrage association and to serve as an established resource to aid other states in their suffrage efforts.

Library of Congress

occasionally attended the meetings and continued to correspond with national suffrage leaders, though she was no longer the avid suffragist she had once been. By 1904, contrary to the aid she had promised at the 1897 Des Moines meeting, she was directing her public interests elsewhere. No longer needing to defend or advocate woman suffrage in Utah, she uncharacteristically commented, "It seems so ridiculous to me after we have succeeded in getting the suffrage to keep on as if the object had not been obtained." Her growing detachment also reflected her disenchantment with the UCW and Emily Richards at being "too small in her views" to be a good leader.[15] These remained private observations, however. She and Emily served as amicable co-workers in the UCW, whenever Emmeline attended its meetings, and in the Relief Society as well as several civic associations. Each felt a respect for the abilities of the other, however begrudgingly. Their differing politics had exacerbated the tension in their relationship, but time was an effective healer.

Though Emmeline restricted her attendance at national conventions, she retained a peripheral interest in suffrage developments around the country, writing occasional editorials on the subject for her paper. She enthusiastically joined with UCW members in sending a gift to Susan B. Anthony on her eightieth birthday in 1900. Their present was a length of black silk brocade, cultivated and spun entirely by Mormon women. Anthony later had it fashioned into a beautifully embroidered gown that she called her "Utah dress." Lucy A. Clark and Emily Richards, who represented the UCW at the NAWSA convention that year, presented the gift to Anthony. Of the many birthday presents she received, she was particularly delighted with this gift, she said, "because the silk worms—the mulberry trees were raised by Mormon women—the coloring—the spinning, the weaving, everything was done by the Mormon women in Utah . . . it is a very beautiful silk." She wrote an individual letter to each woman who had a part in its production. "My pleasure in the rich brocaded silk is quadrupled," she wrote to one of her friends, "because it was made by women politically equal to men."[16] Although Utah suffragists had honored Elizabeth Cady Stanton on her eightieth birthday five years earlier with a beautiful silver embossed onyx ballot box, Stanton felt slighted when she saw the array of gifts and well wishes that came to her co-worker. While Anthony received "thousands of dollars, jewels, laces, silks and satins," the elderly Stanton complained, she herself had received only "criticism and denunciation for my radical ideas."[17]

As vice chair of the state committee, Emmeline attended meetings of the local Republican Party and spoke at receptions and other political occasions. Assisting her was her daughter Annie Wells Cannon, a politically active woman, who had switched parties and would eventually serve as a Republican member of the state legislature. When the Republicans won most of the state offices in the November 1900 election, Emmeline mused that if she had been on the ticket that year, she might well have been elected.[18]

Emmeline's shift in attention from suffrage to the broader women's issues reflected in the goals of the National Council of Women (NCW) was facilitated by that organization's affinity to the NAWSA, which had given it birth. She attended only one more NAWSA convention but made an indelible name for herself in the movement when she agreed to write the chapter on Utah for the general history.[19] Though she felt she had given sufficient time and effort to woman suffrage to justify concentrating on other national causes, lingering memories and personal associations made it difficult for her to totally surrender her captain's post in the Utah suffrage movement. Yielding space for a new generation of activists seemed to be easier physically than psychologically. Emily Richards, who was twenty-two years Emmeline's junior, along with Susa Young Gates, Lucy A. Clark, and Ruth May Fox were among a younger generation for whom politics had proved to be a compelling public focus. These women and many other political and community workers were members of the Utah Woman's Press Club, organized by Emmeline in 1891, and had published their views in a variety of publications.[20] Emmeline Wells often resented what she saw as presumptuous behavior on the part of the newcomers.

Commencing work on her chapter of the *History* in October 1900 and devoting the early part of 1901 to completing it, Emmeline was moved to comment that there were some women "who didn't appreciate brain work." Many were certainly unaware of the kind of research and concentration involved in digesting more than thirty complex years of history into a brief twenty-page chapter. Like Susan B. Anthony, Emmeline Wells sometimes regretted the amount of time needed to research and write the chapter on Utah woman suffrage, knowing it took her away from the things that brought her the most personal satisfaction—her family, the Relief Society, her poetry, and the ever-pressing deadlines for her *Exponent* editorials.

Indicative of her broadening interests, Emmeline made an extensive trip to New York in April 1900. She attended a national convention of the Daughters of the Revolution, an organization that she had joined when a local chapter was organized in 1898, serving as its first regent.[21] She took the opportunity to make a brief visit to the offices of the NAWSA in New York before traveling on to Massachusetts for a brief reunion with family members. Returning to New York City, she attended the National Household Economic Conference, paying the requisite dollar to join. This was certainly a change for her, but in this period of expanding national women's organizations, Emmeline hoped to provide a Mormon presence, either by her own attendance or that of others.

Of most importance for the future, however, were the hours she spent with Fannie Humphreys Gaffney, president of the NCW, with whom she had become acquainted the year before.[22] Gaffney was typical of the younger women becoming active in national and international women's movements. She was an affluent, leisured, middle-class woman who could afford to travel to international conventions as well as devote time to the consuming task of heading national organizations. While Emmeline valued her time with Gaffney and would continue to enjoy the close relationship they developed, she found Gaffney's philosophy that "self-sacrifice is degenerating instead of uplifting" both uninformed and self-serving. Moreover, after reading an article by Gaffney published in the literary magazine *Harper's Monthly*, Emmeline was similarly unimpressed. "I am weary of so much nothingness," she complained. "We are so far ahead of these women, in almost every respect except money."[23] But "these women" were the leaders with whom she worked, and on other days she found many admirable qualities in them. The companionship she eventually developed with Fannie Gaffney stood her in good stead in her deepening relationship with the NCW.

A few months after Emmeline returned home, she was surprised and very pleased to receive an invitation from a woman's association to send her name to be embroidered in gold letters on a flag with those of "men and women makers of American history."[24] She also received another request, one of many invitations that began to arrive fairly consistently, to write an article for a national publication either about suffrage, Mormon women, the LDS Church, or some other contemporary issue.[25] As she set about to write the requested piece and to continue her work on the history of woman suffrage in Utah, evidently feeling that these efforts were unappreciated at home, she was once again moved to note that there were some women "who do not and cannot appreciate the mental labor of those whose brains are brought into service for the good of the community and in our case the Church as well."[26] She deeply regretted what she considered to be their narrow vision.

Besides suffrage, Emmeline's early interest in legislative proceedings continued with a greater likelihood of achieving results now that she was once again a voting citizen. In 1901 she was one of the chief lobbyists for the Utah State Kindergarten Association and a variety of other civic projects. She also closely followed the political jockeying over the delayed senatorial election, of particular interest since Utah had had only one senator for the previous two years because of a deadlock in the state legislature, which elected senators at that time. That year, after twenty-two ballots, the legislature finally elected Republican Thomas F. Kearns, an outcome that pleased Emmeline Wells. His victory came to have more personal implications when Kearns visited her in late January with an invitation to attend the inaugural ceremonies, at his expense, of newly elected U.S. President William McKinley.[27] Both LDS Church President Joseph F. Smith and Governor Heber M. Wells urged her to accept the invitation, and with Susa Young Gates, another guest, she was on her way to Washington by the end of February.

On the evening of their arrival, Emmeline and Susa attended a banquet for Republican Women at the Riggs House, where Susa Gates gave a "humorous and forceful" speech on "What protection has done for Utah in the way of industries," that, judging by the applause, evidently pleased the audience, Emmeline observed.[28] The evening provided Emmeline an opportunity to visit with some of her suffrage friends, including Clara Colby and Sara Spencer.[29] Emmeline and Susa also spoke at the congress of the International Press Union at the Riggs House, another global by-product of a national organization. Emmeline was made vice president for Utah. She and Susa spent several days meeting with some of the national women's leaders who were also visiting Washington for the inaugural events. J. Ellen Foster, president of the Press Union, arranged for a number of the Press Union Congress participants to travel to Glen Echo to visit American Red Cross founder Clara Barton, by this time an icon in women's circles whom Emmeline especially admired.[30]

Emmeline was not so admiring of all her new acquaintances, however. At a public reception, she was introduced to a Methodist minister, a close associate of the Reverend T. C. Iliff who served as a national spokesman for the antipolygamy movement and was still engaged in his crusade for a national amendment against the practice.[31] The unintimidated Emmeline invited the minister, who had once visited Utah, to visit once again, this time to "get the facts."[32]

The inaugural events proceeded in the midst of a rainstorm. They began on Monday morning, March 4, when Senator Kearns's party viewed the procession of federal dignitaries from the gallery of the Senate chamber. From that vantage point, they witnessed the swearing in of Theodore Roosevelt as vice president and new members of the Senate. Following that ceremony, the party adjourned to an outdoor platform for the inauguration of President McKinley, umbrellas their only protection from the downpour. The proceedings were nonetheless impressive, and the official swearing in of the new president was celebrated afterward with the traditional parade down Pennsylvania Avenue. Once again, the Kearns party, made up of members of the Kearns family and various Republican supporters from Utah, both Mormon and non-Mormon, had excellent vantage points from which to view the festivities, this time from the comfort of a group of rented rooms on Pennsylvania Avenue. That night the Utah party all went to the inaugural ball in the new pension building. The ball was too crowded for anyone to dance, Emmeline discovered, but an exciting event to attend. The round of activities continued throughout the week with concerts, visits to Alexandria and Arlington Cemetery, luncheons, receptions, and dinner parties.[33] For the guests from far-off Utah, this was a social event to be long remembered—and so very different from most of Emmeline's previous Washington visits.

It would be difficult to top any of the events to which Emmeline Wells was a guest, but a private interview with Vice President Theodore Roosevelt probably came close. She ostensibly met with him to convey the greetings of her son-in-law John Q. Cannon, who had served in the Spanish-American War as a lieutenant colonel, but she may have also been interested in expanding her political capital by adding another high-ranking United States leader to her list of influential Washington acquaintances. They discussed many topics, and Emmeline was pleased to note that he "spoke highly of Utah."[34]

The following year, 1902, marked the last time Emmeline Wells attended a national suffrage convention. It was a bittersweet experience for her, a less-than-satisfying conclusion to her association with NAWSA. Though Emmeline had redirected her primary interest from suffrage to the NCW, she was still a strong advocate, if passive participant, of the national association and was confident of the benefit of membership to Mormon women. But times had changed both the national and Utah movements. A new generation of activists had begun to replace the aging leaders of the first wave of the movement. Unlike their predecessors, the Utah advocates discovered that LDS Church leaders and some Relief Society members now questioned the value of Mormon representation at these annual suffrage conventions and were reluctant to contribute money for dues and delegate expenses.[35] "I have no heart to go on with the work I should like to take up because so much is being said—that hinders progress," Emmeline lamented.[36] She was, however, able to gather together the necessary means for this last suffrage excursion while beginning a personal crusade to educate women to the value of continuing national and international relationships. At the same time, she noted a loss of interest in the *Woman's Exponent*, resulting in a loss of subscriptions.[37] She recounted the good the periodical had done as a printed emissary for Latter-day Saint women and emphasized its important place among women's publications. Unfortunately, women of a younger generation did not become a major bloc of subscribers, despite the fact that some of them had developed an interest in participating in the associations so regularly chronicled in the paper.

Respecting the new retrenchment mood, many of the delegation from Utah who attended the 1902 suffrage convention in Washington, D.C., were self-funded. Among the delegates were two young women, Annie T. Hyde, serving as proxy for and counselor to newly installed Relief Society General President Bathsheba W. Smith, who had succeeded Zina D. H. Young, and Ida Smoot Dusenberry, also serving as Smith's counselor. Emmeline Wells had been invited to serve as general secretary. The three of them were to attend the convention representing the Relief Society. Before leaving, they all met with Bathsheba Smith for her counsel. Again reflecting her discomfort in yielding authority to younger workers, Emmeline felt embarrassed and probably a bit resentful at what she termed Hyde's "obstreperous" behavior during the meeting, feeling that it was "not her right or prerogative to domineer in that way." By the end of the meeting, Emmeline had already begun to anticipate continuing difficulties when they reached Washington and wondered how she, as the senior member of the delegation, would deal with them.[38]

The first test came upon arrival in Washington when they went directly to the Riggs House "to see some of the Suffrage people." To Emmeline's displeasure, Hyde and some of the others insisted upon staying there. Though it had long been the headquarters for the suffrage conventions, this particular year Emmeline had hoped to stay at the Fairfax Hotel, which headquartered the NCW, whose triennial convention was scheduled directly after the NAWSA convention. The Fairfax Hotel lodged many council delegates, and Clara Barton, whom Emmeline hoped to visit, was also staying there. This shift in lodging preference reflected Emmeline's shifting national interests. She made much of the incident. "I was much opposed to it but was finally persuaded much against my will to yield to those of the party much younger & unexperienced," Emmeline complained, regretting her surrender to these younger women, a concession she would always believe was wrong.[39] It was a situation hardly worth troubling over, but Emmeline's growing stature and status as "elder stateswoman" in national circles, as well as the deference she had come to expect from younger women who had accompanied her to previous conventions over the years, seemed undermined by this casual and relatively insignificant incident. But she was seventy-four, and however reluctant she was to share center stage with younger women, they were the new life of the movement and legitimately asserting their own wishes on these excursions. As was her wont, she soon reconciled herself to what she could not change and turned her attention to the longtime suffrage friends who attended the conference and with whom she had shared thirty years of suffrage experience.

At the opening session of the convention, Emmeline Wells was privileged to sit on the platform with the prominent women who addressed the delegates: Carrie Chapman Catt, NAWSA president; May Wright Sewall, president of the International Council of Women; Clara Barton of the International Red Cross; Susan B. Anthony; Anna Howard Shaw; and a guest, Madame Soffia Lenora Friedland of Russia.

This time Emmeline did not read the report for Utah, which she had written, but deferred to Annie T. Hyde, the Relief Society's designated delegate. Emmeline spoke at a later meeting.[40]

It had been nearly a decade since Elizabeth Stanton had actively participated in the NAWSA, and with Susan B. Anthony fighting the ills of advancing age, and several of the other suffragists Emmeline had once known now either gone or no longer active, she began to feel the emptiness that comes with the passing of a generation.[41] These women had given Emmeline entree into the national world of feminist politics and had never withheld their respect or friendship.

Despite Stanton's longtime absence, suffragists across the nation were saddened to learn of her death just a few months after this 1902 convention. Susan B. Anthony, Stanton's friend and closest colleague, was devastated to lose her partner in the cause that had consumed both their adult lives. "I cannot express myself at all as I feel," Anthony said in an interview. "I am too crushed to say much, but if she had outlived me she would have found fine words with which to express our friendship. I cannot say it in words." To the question, "What periods of your lives gave you the greatest pleasure?" she answered, "When we were digging together. When she forged the thunderbolts and I fired them."[42] The final letter Elizabeth Cady Stanton wrote, just twenty-four hours before her death, was devoted to woman suffrage. She sent it to Theodore Roosevelt, elevated to president after the death of William McKinley. As she had with presidents, Congress, and legislatures for half a century, she urged him to bring about "the complete emancipation of thirty-six million women." But like the national lawmakers before him, President Roosevelt turned a deaf ear to her plea.[43]

After Stanton left the suffrage movement in 1892 to concentrate on marriage and divorce reform, the presidency of the NAWSA fell to Susan B. Anthony who served until 1900, when she resigned in favor of the young and forceful strategist, Carrie Chapman Catt. Catt, however, was obliged to resign four years later because of the death of her husband. To Anthony's delight, her good friend, the well-respected Reverend Anna Howard Shaw was willing to take up the reigns and presided over the association until 1915. While Shaw was a revered

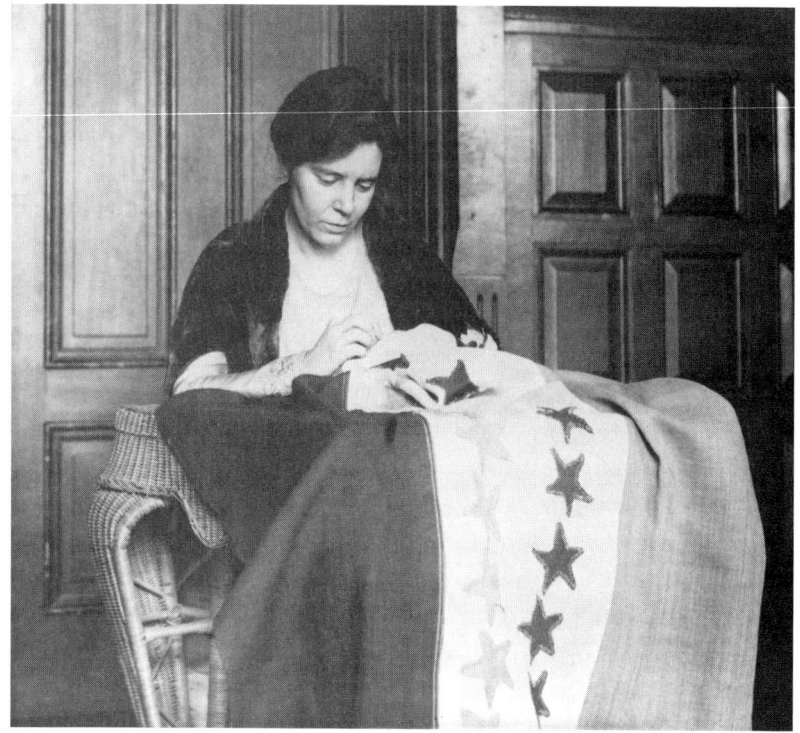

Alice Paul (ca. 1912–20), sewing a suffrage flag, organized the militant National Woman's Party in 1916 and in 1923 drafted an equal rights amendment.

minister, effective orator, and devoted suffragist, she did not possess the administrative skills of Catt, particularly essential when the offshoot National Woman's Party under Alice Paul threatened to overtake—and perhaps sink—the movement in 1913 because of its militant strategy. Catt agreed to resume the presidency in 1915 and led the more moderate NAWSA to success when the Anthony Amendment, by then the Nineteenth, was finally passed in 1920.[44]

Following the suffrage convention, Emmeline attended the annual meeting of the NCW, where she presented two papers and met with the executive council in her position as second corresponding secretary, the office to which she had been appointed three years earlier.[45] At the convention, she met other of her longtime eastern associates no longer active in the suffrage movement but, like Emmeline, still involved in women's issues through their connection with the NCW. They included Sara Andrews Spencer, who had been among the first to invite Mormon women to join the suffrage movement in 1878; Belva A. Lockwood, who had defended woman suffrage in Utah when Congress sought to repeal it; and Lillie Devereux Blake, who had also been a helpful advocate and intermediary during those difficult years. The proximity of the two national conventions facilitated the reunion of these old friends and co-workers. Many, however, would not meet again as time, age, and shifting interests diminished the close-knit sisterhood that the common goal of woman suffrage had created. Though equal suffrage had not yet been achieved for all their countrywomen, many of these early workers had taken their considerable experience and skills to other causes and yielded leadership in the suffrage movement to a younger generation.[46]

With her increasing involvement in the National and International Councils of Women, Emmeline felt relieved that the members of the UCW had taken up the banner of woman suffrage. For her, the convention of 1902 marked the closure of a long and satisfying association in a cause that had claimed many hours and years of effort by committed workers. By 1906, Emmeline's friend and colleague Susan B. Anthony had exhausted herself in the movement and succumbed to a "worn-out heart." Like Elizabeth Stanton before her, she too made a final plea shortly before her death that year to President Theodore Roosevelt, urging him to take his place in history "with Lincoln, the great emancipator," by submitting to the legislatures a constitutional amendment enfranchising women. She also received no response.[47]

Utah women held memorial services for Susan B. Anthony in the Assembly Hall in Salt Lake City on March 18, 1906, just three days after her death. A day earlier the state council of women met and proposed a number of resolutions in respect. Emmeline Wells and Emily Richards were among the speakers, and the invocation and a special tribute were offered by John T. Caine, a former Utah delegate to Congress and personal friend of Anthony.[48] The deaths of Stanton and Anthony, just four years apart, closed a long and significant chapter in the story of woman's rights. That Emmeline Wells, a distant Mormon woman, a plural wife, and oft-maligned crusader, had nonetheless entered the orbit of these women's world and found a respected and comfortable niche therein was a remarkable feat. It not only reflected her abilities, personality, and diplomacy but also demonstrated the depth of Stanton and Anthony's commitment to the ideal they all shared and the breadth of their vision of "equal privileges" for all. Of this threesome, only Emmeline would live to see that ideal come to pass.[49]

When Emmeline was appointed general president of the Relief Society in 1910 at the age of eighty-two, most of her travels from then until her death were associated with that organization. In the last few years in which she edited the *Woman's Exponent,* she did not abandon woman suffrage altogether as an editorial topic, however, and she occasionally met with the UCW. She also retained her longtime interest in legislative matters, though not as an active lobbyist. Her Relief Society responsibilities, her fading eyesight, and her deepening dependence on family members curtailed both her interest and activity in a cause that had claimed so much of her life in earlier years. Two years after Utah received statehood, Emmeline wrote a few thoughts about suffrage, one of the last editorials she would write on that subject. The editorial conveyed her confidence in the power of this political prize, so hard won in so few places by so many women. "When the franchise has been extended over more space, and embraces more people and peoples, or more nations," she wrote, "then we may be able to see what a powerful factor for the amelioration and purification of society it will become." Always making a heartfelt appeal to those women who had the franchise, especially those in her own state, she exhorted each of them "not to grow indifferent to the power she has in her own possession, the ballot . . . or toss aside the weapon of defense and of authority given her." She was convinced that there was "no other vitalizing force that can permeate every home and appeal to every individual citizen as the ballot can." Therefore, she concluded, "it must be the mightiest lever to uplift and to regenerate the world."[50] These were not empty words but rather the expression of the honest convictions of a woman who had won and lost and won again the use of that powerful civil right.

Several years later, Emmeline's daughter Annie Wells Cannon felt obliged to refute an article appearing in the *Ladies' Home Journal* that suggested that woman suffrage had failed to influence legislation for the well-being of and "protection of life" in the states where it had been granted.[51] In several long paragraphs, Cannon enumerated the statutes that Utah had enacted in behalf of women and its citizens in general. "Our statute books are full of improved laws for the safety of life, the comfort and protection of women and children," she wrote. "We have made many victories and expect to make more."[52] Six years after Utah received statehood, Governor Heber M. Wells wrote his own appraisal of the contribution women voters had made to Utah. "The plain facts are," he wrote, "that in this State the influence of woman in politics has been distinctly elevating.... Experience has shown that women have voted their intelligent convictions. They understand the questions at issue and they vote conscientiously and fearlessly."[53]

In June 1919, seventy-one years after the first woman's rights convention, the United States Senate finally passed the resolution submitting the Nineteenth Amendment to the states for ratification. The House of Representatives had passed the bill a year and a half earlier, at which Emmeline had exclaimed, "I rejoice!" It took several tries before the Senate cast the required two-thirds vote, however. Three constitutional amendments had been enacted since the national suffrage association had made its first bid for what it had hoped would be the Sixteenth or Anthony Amendment. Now the fate of the Nineteenth Amendment rested with the voters of thirty-six states, the number necessary for ratification. Several states, including Utah, called special sessions of their legislatures in order to ratify the amendment in a timely fashion. Utah did so on September 30, 1919. It was presented to the Utah state legislature by Elizabeth Hayward, the second woman state senator in Utah.[54]

Two months later, in November 1919, Carrie Chapman Catt, president of the NAWSA, visited Utah to meet with and formally merge the UCW with the newly organized Utah League of Women Voters (ULWV). Emily Richards, for twenty years president of the UCW, resigned her leadership to the chair of the ULWV, Mrs. Clesson S. Kinney. Catt also announced that a meeting of the League of Women Voters (LWV) would be held directly following the fifty-first annual convention of the NAWSA the following February in Chicago.[55]

While the nation awaited the outcome of the ratifying process, Emmeline Wells and her Relief Society board encouraged the ward and stake Relief Societies to "take steps to celebrate the Suffrage Jubilee" of Utah, on February 12, 1920. Though there had been a nine-year interval between the loss and regaining of the vote for Utah women, Emmeline desired recognition of the early point in the suffrage movement at which Utah women had first been enfranchised, 1870. "The educational value of this celebration is great," she exclaimed in her letter, "both as regards Pioneer History and the recognition of woman's place in civic life by the leading men of the Church and community." She invited the planners of the celebrations to make reference to historian Herbert Bancroft's statement about woman suffrage in his history of Utah. He wrote that from 1847 to 1850, "men and women voted by ballot in matters relating to government. Women had already voted in religious meetings by the uplifted hand," he acknowledged, "but this is probably the first instance in the United States, where woman suffrage was permitted." When Utah became a territory in 1850, he noted, the privilege was withdrawn.[56] Not to be outdone by the national celebration of woman suffrage when ratification occurred, Emmeline wanted to be sure that Utah was acknowledged as having been well in advance on the issue of woman suffrage. Unfortunately, the influenza epidemic that had claimed so many lives the year before still ravaged the Utah populace, and the celebration in Salt Lake City was cancelled.[57]

By the time the NAWSA convention convened in February 1920 in Chicago, only five of the needed thirty-six states had not yet ratified the amendment. While earlier suffrage conventions had been held "to disseminate the propaganda for a common cause, to cheer and encourage each other, to strengthen, organize, influence and to council [sic] as to ways and means of insuring further progress," this final convention was an occasion "to rejoice that their struggle was over, their aim achieved."[58] Obviously confident of victory, the association officers announced that this would be the last meeting of the organization. But even as the NAWSA suffragists in Chicago were turning the convention into a victory celebration, members of the National Woman's Party continued to work with local suffragists in those states that had remained neutral or even hostile to woman suffrage.[59] Until all thirty-six states had ratified, these suffragists were unwilling to declare victory.

Susa Young Gates and Donnette Smith Kesler were the official Utah representatives to the NAWSA convention, later joined by several other Utah women. In a highly emotional moment, the delegates passed a resolution dissolving the NAWSA and advancing the national League of Women Voters, a recent adjunct to the NAWSA, as a new and independent organization to succeed the NAWSA. Its primary objective for the first year would be to educate women voters in the political process. President Woodrow Wilson sent his congratulations to the convention, commending the women for their orderly transition to the League of Women Voters with "a wish for the new organization the same success and wise leadership" that had governed the NAWSA.[60] At the end of the convention, a victory banquet was held to which three thousand women were invited. Though neither the ninety-two-year-old Emmeline Wells nor Emily Richards attended this historic event, they were each awarded a gold pin for being among the "pioneers" of the movement.[61]

After a hard-fought battle, Tennessee, in August 1920, became the thirty-sixth state to ratify the Nineteenth Amendment, and woman suffrage across the nation became a reality. Emmeline Wells, the fifty-year veteran, rose to the occasion. "I rejoice and am exceedingly glad that the battle is over and the women of our nation have at last received their enfranchisement," she exclaimed. "When Miss Anthony was present at the last suffrage convention," she continued, "she said that she herself would not live to see the date but that suffrage would be gained in the twentieth century and her prophecy is now fulfilled."[62] An effusive letter in her name was then sent to Carrie Chapman Catt in New York City from the Relief Society, which stated,

> Utah's busy hive of Relief Society suffrage workers, some of whom have exercised their voting privileges for fifty years join the song of victory which rises from every enfranchised woman in these

United States of America today. As women wing their triumphant passage into every avenue of public and private endeavor may they bring back to their home lives only the rich essence of a sex purified and glorified by the fruit of life which shares liberty and the pursuit of happiness with every male voter in the land.

Her secretary affixed to the closing of the letter: "Emmeline B. Wells, Utah's Queen Bee."[63] Catt would probably have agreed.

On August 26, a message was sent across the wires announcing the signing of the national proclamation enfranchising nearly twenty-seven million women. The enthusiastic announcement noted that the proclamation had been signed by Secretary of State Bainbridge Colby "in the presence of a notable gathering of suffragists."[64] The reporter's assumption of a public signing was understandable but wrong. In one of those incomprehensible and politically insensitive blunders, Secretary Colby decided to sign the bill in the privacy of his own home at eight o'clock in the morning and then invited suffragists to meet with him in his office at ten o'clock to celebrate. Insulted by his callousness, members of the Woman's Party refused to accept the invitation. "I think it a very great pity that on an occasion so momentous to millions of American women, that no women should have been with Secretary Colby when he signed the proclamation," declared Mrs. Abby Baker of the National Woman's Party. "Representatives of all of the suffrage groups should have been present." Carrie Chapman Catt had not been notified in time for even the brief celebration in Colby's office later that morning and was thus not herself present for the event she had been instrumental in bringing to pass. Those who did attend, unaware of the previous signing, found their enthusiasm "somewhat dampened" upon learning of it, another newspaper reported in a monumental understatement.[65] Certainly, the private signing was one of the great inexplicable moments in the history of the woman suffrage movement.

Though Utah women had been voting for nearly twenty-five years since statehood and seventeen years before that, they staged a memorable victory celebration on August 30. It began with a parade that ended at the steps of the State Capitol, where Governor Simon Bamberger, former Governor Heber M. Wells, and other political dignitaries offered congratulatory messages. Emily Richards and several other veteran suffragists spoke of the early struggles to gain the vote, and members of the LWV urged the large gathering to value the precious right of citizenship. Emmeline Wells attended the proceedings and was described as "the most impressive figure on the platform." She did not address the crowd but was lauded as one who had waited and worked for this moment for half a century. "What those dim eyes had seen of history in the making, what those old ears had heard and what that clear brain had conceived and carried out only her close associates knew," a friend and co-worker observed. "She was the incarnate figure of tender, delicate, eternally determined womanhood, arrived and triumphant."[66] She not only had survived to relish this moment, but through her meticulous record keeping and through her letters, editorials, articles, and diaries, she left her own permanent account of this remarkable story.

Notes

1. "Thoughts," *Woman's Exponent* 27 (December 15, 1898): 76.

2. "Faith in the Future of Utah," *Woman's Exponent* 24 (December 1, 1895): 84.

3. Emmeline B. Wells, "Utah," in *History of Woman Suffrage*, vol. 4, ed. Susan B. Anthony and Ida H. Harper (Rochester: Susan B. Anthony, 1902), 951–52.

4. Susa Young Gates notes the women who participated in state government from statehood until 1920 in "Suffrage Won by the Mothers of the United States," *Relief Society Magazine* 7 (May 1920): 272–75; see also Susa Young Gates, "Utah," in *History of Woman Suffrage*, vol. 6, ed. Ida Husted Harper (New York: National American Suffrage Association, 1922), 646–49.

5. Emmeline B. Wells, Diary, January 22, 1897, L. Tom Perry Special Collections, Harold B. Lee Library, Brigham Young University, Provo, Utah.

6. Melvina Whitney Woods, a daughter of Emmeline and Newel K. Whitney, was married to Judge William Woods, a nephew of Daniel H. Wells, who settled in Wallace, Idaho, in 1888, and became a district judge soon thereafter. "Prominent Former Utahn [William Woods] Dies in Idaho," *Deseret News*, November 11, 1920, 1.

7. Wells, Diary, January 26, 1897. See also "About the Convention," *Woman's Exponent* 25 (February 15, March 1, 1897): 108. Mention of the attendance of Emmeline and her daughter was also made in "Woman's Suffrage: Annual Convention of National American Women," *Deseret Evening News*, February 2, 1897, 2; "The National Convention," *Woman's Journal*, February 6, 1897, 44; "The National Convention," *Woman's Journal*, February 18, 1897, 49; "An Object Lesson in Utah," *Woman's Journal*, February 20, 1897, 58; "Convention Report," *Woman's Journal*, February 20, 1897, 58; "The Senate Hearing," *Woman's Journal*, February 27, 1897, 66; and "The National Convention," *Woman's Journal*, March 6, 1897, 22; "National Plan of Work Committee," *Woman's Tribune* 14 (March 20, 1897): 74. See also Anthony and Harper, *History of Woman Suffrage*, 4:283–84, reprinted in *Battle for the Ballot: Essays on Woman Suffrage in Utah, 1870–1896*, ed. Carol Cornwall Madsen (Logan: Utah State University Press, 1997), 53–59.

8. "Annual Convention N.A.W.S.A.," *Woman's Exponent* 25 (January 15, February 1, 1897): 100.

9. "The National Convention," *Woman's Tribune* 14 (March 6, 1897): 19.

10. "The National Convention," 19. Wells had frequently been commended by admirers for the ease with which she could address both large and small assemblages of men in politics and on all levels of government.

11. "The National Convention," 19.

12. "The National Convention," *Woman's Journal*, February 18, 1897, 49. The *Salt Lake Tribune* also ran a daily account of the conference, though it seldom mentioned the names of either Emmeline Wells or her daughter.

13. Charlotte Perkins Gilman was probably one of the best-known feminist theorists of the late nineteenth century. Her book, *Women and Economics: A Study of the Economic Relation between Men and Women as a Factor in Social Evolution* (Boston: Small, Maynard and Company, 1898), brought her international fame. It decried women's economic dependence on fathers and husbands and asserted that emancipation came only with economic independence or self-reliance. For an extensive account of her life, see Carl N. Degler, "Charlotte Anna Perkins Stetson Gilman," in *Notable American Women, 1607–1950: A Biographical Dictionary*, ed. Edward T. James, Janet Wilson James, and Paul S. Boyer, 3 vols. (Cambridge, Mass.: Belknap Press of Harvard University Press, 1971), 2:39–42. A full biography is Mary A. Hill, *Charlotte Perkins Gilman: The Making of a Radical Feminist, 1860–1896* (Philadelphia: Temple University Press, 1980).

14. Gates, "Utah," 6:644–45. See also Wells, Diary, October 30, 1899.

15. Wells, Diary, December 15, 1904.

16. The dress has been preserved and is on display at the Susan B. Anthony home in Rochester, New York. The quotes are from Kathleen Barry, *Susan B. Anthony: A Biography of a Singular Feminist* (New York: New York University Press, 1988), 342. Receipt of the material was also noted in Anthony and Harper, *History of Woman Suffrage*, 4:390: "From the Utah Silk Commission composed of women came a handsome black brocade dress pattern, the work of women, from the tending of the cocoons to the weaving of the silk."

17. Stanton's edition of *The Woman's Bible*, her distrust of organized religion, and her advocacy of divorce and denunciation of marriage laws and practices did indeed bring her a reputation as radical and alienated numerous supporters of woman suffrage. The quote comes from Barry, *Susan B. Anthony*, 339.

18. Wells, Diary, November 6, 1900.

19. The chapter would be included in volume 4 (936–56) of what became a six-volume work on the history of suffrage up to 1920, when the Nineteenth Amendment gave suffrage to all United States women. Emmeline's chapter presented the Utah suffrage story from 1870 to 1896. Susa Young Gates completed Utah's story in the sixth volume of the *History of Woman Suffrage*, concluding with the passage of the Nineteenth Amendment. See 6:644–50.

20. Details on the club can be found in Linda Thatcher and John R. Sillito, "'Sisterhood and Sociability': The Utah Women's Press Club, 1891–1928," *Utah Historical Quarterly* 53 (Spring 1985): 144–56.

21. When Latter-day Saint women had attempted to join the Daughters of the American Revolution at that time, they were denied membership because of the LDS Church's history of polygamy. The ban remained in place until late in the twentieth century. The Daughters of the Revolution had no such proscription on membership.

22. Following the NCW annual meeting in 1899, Emmeline Wells traveled to New York to accept an invitation to meet Mrs. Gaffney at her home for a private dinner with Gaffney, her husband, and her sister. Afterward, Mrs. Gaffney accompanied Emmeline to visit Elizabeth Stanton, who registered her displeasure with the NCW's recent action against the seating of B. H. Roberts in Congress. Stanton also thanked Wells for the birthday gift sent by the women of Utah on her eightieth birthday. Wells, Diary, February 26, 1899.

23. Wells, Diary, May 5, 7, 1900.

24. Wells, Diary, November 19, 1900.

25. One such article, entitled "Why a Woman Should Desire to Be a Mormon," was written in 1903 at the request of several women's clubs of New York.

An Advocate for Women

Emmeline published it under that title in the *Woman's Exponent* 36 (December 1907): 39–40, and continued in *Woman's Exponent* 36 (January 1908): 46–48. In this article, she gives the genesis of Mormonism and its basic principles, her views on the relationship of Adam and Eve, an appraisal of the achievements of Latter-day Saint women, and her faith in the progress of women.

26. Wells, Diary, April 26, 1901.
27. Wells, Diary, January 25, 1901.
28. "In and About Washington," *Woman's Exponent* 29 (March 15, April 1, 1901): 90–91. To her diary, however, Emmeline admitted that the speech "greatly disappointed me." Susa evidently lost her voice "for the moment" which created a bit of a problem during her delivery. See Wells, Diary, February 28, 1901 (the day on which Emmeline often celebrated her February 29 birthday).
29. Wells, Diary, February 28, 1901.
30. Wells, Diary, March 1, 2, 1901.
31. Iliff, particularly active in the campaign that prevented B. H. Roberts from taking his seat in Congress in 1899 and 1900, remained a vocal and visible foe of Mormonism.
32. "In and About Washington," 91. In the same editorial describing their Washington visit, Emmeline Wells lists the names of the women with whom she mingled at this reception and other social events, all women of national and even international stature, who welcomed and sought out Emmeline as much as she did them. Other details about the Utah contingent in Washington can be found in "Utah Contingent in Washington," *Deseret Evening News*, March 4, 1901, 1; and "Utah at Inauguration," *Salt Lake Tribune*, March 5, 1901, 1.
33. References occur in all three publications in n32.
34. Wells, Diary, March 9, 1901.
35. Though the anti-Mormon crusade was ostensibly over, the fracas over B. H. Roberts's election in 1898, the continuing movement among a number of women's groups affiliated with the NCW against Mormonism, and the efforts toward passage of an antipolygamy amendment gave Church leaders some pause in supporting a continued relationship with these groups. Moreover, the Church was still dealing with the effects of the financial fallout from the Edmunds-Tucker Act and a period of recession during the last decade of the century, both of which left it struggling to maintain financial stability. Much thought was given to how the tithes of members were to be allocated.
36. Wells, Diary, January 30, 1902.
37. Carol Cornwall Madsen, "'Remember the Women of Zion': A Study of the Editorial Content of the *Woman's Exponent*, a Mormon Woman's Journal" (master's thesis, University of Utah, 1977), 45–49.

38. Wells, Diary, January 31, 1902.

39. Wells, Diary, February 9, 1902.

40. "Happenings Here and There," *Woman's Exponent* 30 (March 1902): 84.

41. Elizabeth Stanton had served as first president of the merged NAWSA from 1890 to 1892 but had removed herself from activity thereafter. Susan B. Anthony was eighty-two and suffering a variety of illnesses before her death four years after the 1902 convention. At Stanton's last appearance at a NAWSA convention in 1892, she gave what many considered her finest speech, entitled "The Solitude of Self," in which she asserted the absolute individuality of each human being and the need for each one to be fortified with all the skills necessary to traverse the shifting circumstances in the voyage of life. Excerpts are quoted in Miriam Schneir, *Feminism: The Essential Historical Writings* (New York: Vintage Books, 1972), 157–59. For the complete speech see Ellen Carol DuBois, *Elizabeth Cady Stanton, Susan B. Anthony, Correspondence, Writings, Speeches* (New York: Schocken Books, 1981), 246–54.

42. "Miss Anthony Interviewed," *Woman's Exponent* 31 (November 1, 15, 1902): 45–46.

43. Theodore Stanton and Harriot Stanton Blatch, *Elizabeth Cady Stanton as Revealed in Her Letters, Diary, and Reminiscences*, 2 vols. (New York: Harper and Brothers, 1922), 2:368–69. The women in Theodore Roosevelt's family had little use for woman suffrage and felt that leaders of the suffrage movement were "overzealous, and misguided." Their influence on Roosevelt, particularly that of his older sister, Anna "Bamie" Roosevelt Cowles, was especially evident on that issue. Roosevelt himself privately ridiculed the suffragists, but by 1911, he had become a "lukewarm" supporter. He continued to feel, however, that woman suffrage was a reform issue of far less consequence than many others of the time. See Betty Boyd Caroli, *The Roosevelt Women* (New York: Basic Books, 1998), 121–22.

44. Nancy Woloch, *Women and the American Experience*, 3rd ed. (New York: Alfred A. Knopf, 1984), 338–69.

45. One of the papers Emmeline delivered, entitled "The Age We Live In," makes an eloquent statement of her optimistic view of women's advancement in the nineteenth century and continued progress in the twentieth. It was first published as "The Age We Live In," *Woman's Exponent* 30 (April 1902): 89–90.

46. Details of the women who attended the NCW annual meeting, their accomplishments, and their dress, as well as the many social events, are found in "Happenings Here and There," *Woman's Exponent* 30 (March 1902): 84. On

the return trip, a visit to Hull House and a meeting with Jane Addams added to the pleasure of the journey home. Wells wrote an editorial describing the activities and success of Hull House in "Hull House, Chicago," *Woman's Exponent* 30 (April 1902): 92. She had opportunity to visit Hull House again some years later.

47. Barry, *Susan B. Anthony*, 351.

48. "Miss Susan B. Anthony, A Friend to Humanity," *Woman's Exponent* 34 (March 1906): 60.

49. Reed Smoot, who had made public early in his political career his interest in promoting women's associations and the affiliation of Latter-day Saint women with national women's organizations, became a strong supporter of woman suffrage. As early as 1913, seven years before the Nineteenth Amendment passed, he joined those who continued to urge Congress to consider it. He did not support the militancy that developed under the leadership of Alice Paul and the Woman's Party, however; he believed that the moderate tactics of Carrie Chapman Catt, president of the NAWSA, seemed more amenable and would ultimately prove to be more successful. See, for example, "Women Demand Votes for Women," *Deseret News,* July 31, 1913, 2; "Senator Smoot Discusses Suffrage," *Deseret News,* July 31, 1913, 2.

50. "Thoughts," *Woman's Exponent* 27 (December 15, 1898): 76.

51. The editorial on woman suffrage and its defense appears on the Editorial Page and the Editor's Personal Page, *Ladies Home Journal* 29 (April 1912): 1, 5.

52. Annie Wells Cannon, "Suffrage No Failure in Utah," *Woman's Exponent* 40 (May 1912): 69.

53. Published in Anthony and Harper, *History of Woman Suffrage*, 4:1089; reprinted in Madsen, *Battle for the Ballot*, 309–10.

54. Gates, "Utah," 6:649–50.

55. Mrs. Clarissa Smith Williams and Mrs. Amy Brown Lyman, "The Official Round Table," *Relief Society Magazine* 7 (January 1920): 39–40.

56. Emmeline B. Wells, Clarissa S. Williams, Julina L. Smith to Relief Society Stake Presidents, January 28, 1920, Church Archives, The Church of Jesus Christ of Latter-day Saints, Salt Lake City, also in Minutes of the General Board of the Relief Society, January 28, 1920, Church Archives. Hubert Howe Bancroft, a nineteenth-century historian, wrote *History of Utah* (San Francisco: History Company, 1890), one of the first histories of Utah, covering the period of settlement in 1847 to 1886.

57. "Woman Suffrage in Utah Is Fifty Years Old," *Deseret Evening News,* February 12, 1920, 1.

58. Donnette Smith Kesler, "Three Important Conventions," *Young Woman's Journal* 31 (May 1920): 271–76.

59. See "Final Chapter is Marked in Suffrage Drive," *Deseret News*, February 14, 1920, 3; and "Suffragists on 'Last Long Mile,'" *Salt Lake Tribune*, February 16, 1920, 1.

60. Kesler, "Three Important Conventions," 273–74.

61. Kesler, "Three Important Conventions," 271–76. See also Susa Young Gates, "Suffrage Won by the Mothers of the United States," *Relief Society Magazine* 7 (May 1920): 253–55.

62. "Utah Suffrage Workers Plan Commemoration," *Deseret News*, August 19, 1920, 1. See also "Suffrage Wins; Tennessee Clinches Victory," *Salt Lake Tribune*, August 19, 1920, 1.

63. Minutes of the General Board of the Relief Society, August 19, 1920.

64. "The Suffrage Victory for Women in the United States," *Young Woman's Journal* 31 (October 1920): 569.

65. "Colby Signs Proclamation for Suffrage," *Deseret News*, August 26, 1920, 1, 2. The subtitle to the article clearly states the problem: "Evades Fair Sex by Secretly Signing Historic Document in Privacy of His Own Home." He explained that because there was some antagonism between the NAWSA and the National Woman's Party, he wanted to avoid any unpleasantness that might occur in a public signing.

66. Gates, "Utah," 6:650.

Chapter 15

The Struggle for Inclusion

This work is bringing women into a nearness of contact that will increase confidence, and a more universal sisterhood will be established by the association and relations of this vast army of workers.[1]

At her eighty-second birthday celebration in 1910, Emmeline Wells was eulogized as a woman whose sphere of influence extended well beyond the community in which she lived. "She has traveled tens of thousands of miles to render service in defense of her Church and [her] sex," the tribute read, "and [she] enjoys the respect—in many instances the intimate acquaintance and affection—of the leading women not only of America, but of the world."[2] It was a fitting tribute, for by that time, after more than thirty-five years in the long crusade for woman suffrage, she had indeed traveled many miles, logged countless hours, and acquired many friends. Her years of activism had taken her across the country numerous times and would yet take her across the ocean.

After reclaiming the vote for Utah women at statehood in 1896, Emmeline Wells turned her attention to the National and International Councils of Women, adding even more miles to her travels. Her attendance at the first triennial meeting of the National Council of Women (NCW) in 1891 to her last in 1913 merged the goals and interests of the Relief Society of The Church of Jesus Christ of Latter-day Saints with the council's broad goals of betterment for women. Her overarching commitment in all her affiliations was to improve the status of women, an effort she had made her life's work for two decades. "We are engaged in a stupendous work," she told the readers of the *Woman's Exponent* in 1874, "the seed we sow will assuredly spring up, blossom and bear fruit in the future; and having the same prize to obtain, the same goal to reach, aiming at the same great result, the regeneration of women."[3]

The idea for the International Council of Women (ICW), organized in 1888, had originally grown out of Susan B. Anthony and Elizabeth Stanton's desire to internationalize the suffrage movement. Despite national differences, women from a host of nations, they believed, shared a common commitment to establish some form of political representation in their respective countries. They felt that collectivizing this shared goal would strengthen each nation's campaign with a global support system.

The concept of international alliances of women, however, did not originate with Stanton or Anthony, the architects of the ICW. A successful international temperance movement already existed, and the two women believed a similar suffrage alliance would formalize the loose-knit networks that linked women of the United States, England, France, and Germany in their shared feminist and social welfare goals.[4] Elizabeth Stanton's sojourn in England during 1882 and 1883 spurred the idea of allying with European suffragists. She did not act on the idea until 1887, however, when she engaged the organizing skills of Susan B. Anthony and assigned the indefatigable traveler May Wright Sewall, an eager internationalist, to elicit European interest. The convention convened a year later with an international celebration in Washington, D.C., coinciding with the fortieth anniversary of the 1848 Seneca Falls woman's rights convention.[5]

Anthony and Stanton had resolved to invite associations devoted to any aspect of the protection or advancement of women.[6] The two veteran activists recognized the need to include women from diverse reform movements, political equality being only one of their areas of concern. The organizations invited to participate represented "every department of woman's work," and included "literary clubs, art and temperance unions, labor leagues, missionary, peace, and moral purity societies, charitable, professional, educational and industrial associations." In fact, suffrage was not a priority in several national associations.[7]

Emmeline Wells and many members of the LDS Relief Society and Young Ladies' Mutual Improvement Association (MIA) found this diversity appealing. Wells thus gave vigorous effort to NCW and ICW work as a major vehicle for bringing to pass many of her own objectives. The aims in organizing paralleled her own, often thwarted, hope of achieving some form of universal sisterhood based on a union of interests and on overcoming the cultural limitations in all areas of life that tradition had imposed on women. "Much is said of universal brotherhood," the council idea noted, but "more subtle and more binding is universal sisterhood." The organizers hoped that through "an interchange of opinions on the great questions now agitating the world," women worldwide would be roused to "new thought," to an "intensify[ing of] their love of liberty," and to a "realizing sense of the power of combination."[8] Experience had shown that such advances could be made only through organized and concerted effort.

Emmeline was enthusiastic about the prospects of an international alliance. In a resounding endorsement of its organization, she declared that such a coalition would "give emphasis to the measures already advocated with such untiring energy and unflinching integrity, by advanced thinkers," and would develop new methods that would "lift the women of all nations into greater light, and bring them up to that relative position in the brotherhood of the world, that even-handed justice demands for them." Having already "broken down the iron gates that barred women out from the field of action where they might receive the full growth of stature, and development of talent," women, she believed, would by their numbers and abilities prevent the gates from being closed again. As "helpers in the world's great work," standing "side by side, and shoulder to shoulder, brother and sister, man and woman will advocate the triumph of right, in the momentous questions that are now agitating the world of thought."[9] These lofty expressions had found their way into numerous editorials in the *Woman's Exponent*, their force and sincerity undiminished by repetition.

It had not been and would not be an easy road to follow. On both the national and especially the international level, the NCW and ICW were continually obliged to recognize the autonomy of their constituents, as suffrage leaders had already discovered in their own organizations. National political rivalries, loyalty to differing ideologies, commitment to local causes, and varied priorities added subtle and sometimes overt conflict to the process of developing an international community of women. A particular rivalry between the upper-class women of the British suffrage movement and leaders from the United States often created organizational disputes.[10] Studies of internationalism have found that the interaction of conflict and consensus gave the movement vitality, enabled it to "define its common interests," and establish its identifying boundaries.[11] Though sometimes disparaged as a movement of elite, older, Christian women, mainly of Euro-American background, those identifying characteristics actually gave it cohesiveness, especially in these early years of internationalism, bringing together women who sought association with other women culturally and economically similar to better the lives of less-favored women.

The transnational women's movement of the late nineteenth century began a remarkable journey, after organization of the ICW, until it was disrupted by World War I. But its leaders had no illusions about the difficulties in creating a universal sisterhood, although they often utilized that aphorism in their public rhetoric. Such forthright idealism, however, helped to energize the collective conscience of adherents to the movement. Their mutual aims to achieve social justice and recognition for all women as participants in the global community provided a large measure of unity. The ideal of universal sisterhood, which privileged commonalities above differences, also fueled the movement's commitment to accept the individual goals of member associations while at the same time fostering "a sense of belonging to a great and irresistible current of world opinion, however much a minority they might be in their own country," wrote historian Richard Evans. The "sense of belonging" to something larger than their own association "gave them confidence in themselves and belief in the inevitability of ultimate victory" in achieving their goals.[12]

With all the liabilities presented by undisguised nationalism, however, the ideal of universal sisterhood was only a dream, reflecting the movement's goal, not its reality. Mormon women also tested the unity of both the NCW and ICW. Throughout the twenty-two years in which Emmeline Wells was involved in these two associations, there was a continual undercurrent and finally a rising wave of protest against Mormon membership that threatened the idea of inclusiveness as an overarching principle of these councils. From the outset in 1888, the admittance of Mormon women to the NCW became problematic. May Wright Sewall, who served at different times as president of both councils, recalled years later that "many good and noble women . . . thought of not accepting [Mormon] women," but she, Susan B. Anthony, and even the first NCW president, Frances Willard of the Woman's Christian Temperance Union (WCTU), had agreed to admit the women and their organizations "not as 'polygamists or as Mormon societies, but . . . as philanthropic and benevolent associations.'"[13] Their views prevailed, and the women representing the LDS Relief Society, the Young Ladies' MIA, and the children's Primary Association were permitted to attend and even address the international audience at that historic anniversary in 1888.

In 1891 at the first triennial meeting of the NCW, the Relief Society and Young Ladies' MIA became official members of the council. Though Emmeline Wells had not attended the 1888 organizational meeting, she was back in Washington three years later to formalize admission of the two Latter-day Saint organizations. With the moral support of LDS Church leaders and funding from the Relief Society, Emmeline and her associates left Salt Lake City on February 16. Besides Emmeline, the travelers included Jane S. Richards, representing the Relief Society; Carrie S. Thomas, representing the Young Ladies' MIA; along with Phebe Young Beattie; Electa Bullock; Sarah M. Kimball; and Katie Thomas. The large number of Utah women present entitled them to twenty votes at the meetings, the highest number from any state or territory.[14]

The meeting also brought together some of the most notable women of the East, occasioning a three-page editorial by Emmeline Wells identifying and describing them. Among the number were Lucy Stone, founder of the former American Woman Suffrage Association (AWSA); Julia Ward Howe, author of "Battle Hymn of the Republic" and president of the Association for the Advancement of Women; May Wright Sewall, secretary of the NCW at that time; Reverend Anna Howard Shaw; Isabella Beecher Hooker; and Bertha Honoré Palmer, president of the Board of Lady Managers of the upcoming 1893 Chicago World's Fair. Also in attendance were editor and abolitionist William Lloyd Garrison and several U.S. senators.[15]

Lucy Stone (ca. 1840–60), along with her husband, Henry Blackwell, fought for woman suffrage. Lucy organized the American Woman Suffrage Association in 1869.

After a sight-seeing tour of the capital city led by Emily Richards and her husband, the Mormon women, Sarah Kimball, Jane Richards, Carrie Thomas, and Emmeline Wells, armed with the required credentials for membership, met with May Wright Sewall. She "made a clear statement of the case," Emmeline reported.[16] Their admittance to the NCW, in other words, was not assured. Though LDS Church President Wilford Woodruff had issued his 1890 Manifesto prohibiting plural marriages and the conciliatory merger of the two suffrage associations had occurred that same year, some influential women still feared the taint of Mormon women if accepted to membership. The Mormons' ready admittance surprised them all and was attributed to the intervention of Susan B. Anthony.[17]

The three-day conference attracted enough people to fill Albaugh's Opera House in Washington, D.C., the site of the meetings. More than seventy-one women presented papers, including Carrie Thomas, Jane Richards, and Emmeline Wells. Both Thomas's and Richards's talks were brief, but Emmeline, speaking about the LDS Relief Society, gave "an extensive analysis of its work and organization."[18]

Emmeline Wells found she had not been forgotten after an absence of five years. Her suffrage friends gave her a special welcome, and the *Woman's Tribune* concurred with Emily Richards's claim that Emmeline was "one of the most interesting women at the Council," a woman who had been "chastened and spiritualized by suffering."[19] Concurrent with the NCW meeting was a meeting of the National Woman's Press Association scheduled at the Willard Hotel in Washington. Nearly five hundred women journalists assembled to discuss internationalizing the organization. Emmeline, among the number, was chosen to be on a seven-member committee to prepare a constitution for the proposed International Press Association for women.[20] Internationalism was infectious in the 1890s.

Some months after the NCW triennial meeting, Emmeline Wells reflected on the value of these national associations. For her personally, they gave her an appreciation as well as amazement at the intelligence, ability, and persuasive gifts of the women she encountered. One fact was immediately apparent to her as she sat through session after session addressed by educated and articulate women. "Women could teach publicly on the platform, not only common-place matters," she observed, "but also expound doctrine and principles, and even the Scriptures . . . as few men trained in this very calling could do." She recognized that women no longer had to "hide away in a corner knitting or darning socks. . . but they stand up and proclaim great moral and spiritual truths."[21]

One goal the NCW endorsed, and which all of the affiliated organizations shared, was to promulgate public civility. To the skeptics of national alliances of women, even the single-minded suffragists, this aim was appealing, and Emmeline Wells was quick to capitalize on it in her *Woman's Exponent* editorials. Moreover, she declared, "men and women must rise together, one cannot do without the other . . . therefore let woman as well as man do what she can do best" and use her influence to promote principled and ethical behavior.[22] Mingling with like-minded women, she was convinced, would benefit both the individual woman, as it had in her own life, and the associations in which they labored. These associations were even more important for

Mormon women, who had carried the burden of ostracism and calumny for more than half a century.

From 1891 on, Mormon women were represented at each of the triennial meetings of the NCW as well as at the quinquennial meetings of the ICW.[23] But Mormon women were dogged by continuing efforts to expel them, prompting both councils to issue statements invoking the "Golden Rule," as stated in the preamble to the constitution of the ICW. Organization leaders reminded the members of the "fundamental principles of the National Council" that no member council by joining made itself "liable to be interfered with in respect to its complete organic unity, independence, or method of work, or shall be committed to any principle or method of any other council."[24] The NCW and ICW leaders, who were generally not among the protesters, used their position to retain the membership of the two Latter-day Saint women's organizations. In 1895 the leaders of both councils went on record as protesting "against persecution of any people on account of religious belief or unbelief, or because of race or condition as contrary to the spirit and civilization of our time,"[25] a rebuke not only of the world at large but also of the behavior of some of the members of these councils. The enthusiasm, dependability, and dues provided by the Latter-day Saint organizations undoubtedly contributed to the cordiality of council leaders.

Support for maintaining a Mormon presence at these meetings also came from LDS Church and Relief Society leaders during these early years of membership. In an appeal for funding from Relief Society members, Emmeline Wells reminded them that "it was the mind of our leading brethren that we become a part of these great councils of women and it is a great advantage to us." She was persistent in reassuring those less convinced that "our money is not thrown away that goes to pay our membership in those councils."[26] Though supportive of their affiliation, Elder Joseph F. Smith nonetheless cautioned the appointed delegates, "Remember you go to teach and not to be taught. Learn all the truths you can, put them into active use when you return home, but remember that you are the light set upon a hill, and let your light so shine that all men will glorify God because of you."[27] Emmeline's purpose in maintaining membership may not have been quite so supernal, but she unreservedly believed that affiliation with such organizations could only work to the advantage of Latter-day Saint women.

By 1891 the social environment in Utah was finally conducive for concerted public activity among all the women of the future state. Church President Wilford Woodruff's 1890 Manifesto had brought hope to critics of Mormonism who detested the practice of polygamy, and Church members' adoption of national political parties augured well for a realignment of political power. Joining their mutual interests in the welfare of the community, Mormon and non-Mormon women enjoyed a period of détente that enabled them to move forward as "women of Utah" in a number of community projects.[28] The Columbian Exposition at the 1893 Chicago World's Fair, which was to be a showcase of women's cooperative enterprises, became both the catalyst and a stage for demonstrating the newfound cooperation of Utah women. The creation of a Woman's Department within the exposition's

Utah State Historical Society

Visitors outside the Utah Building at the 1893 Columbian Exposition.

administration, with a separate Board of Lady Managers, signaled the representation of women from every state and territory. The national exposition board was to be replicated in every state and territory. To display the industrial, artistic, and domestic achievements of the women of America, the board commissioned a Woman's Building, to be designed by a woman architect and decorated with paintings, statuary, and furnishings by women artists.[29]

The Board of Lady Managers, under Chicago clubwoman Bertha Honoré Palmer, held a competition to determine the architect. Sophia G. Hayden, a graduate of the Massachusetts Institute of Technology, received $1,000 for her winning design. The board also commissioned Mary Cassatt, expatriate American impressionist artist, to paint a large mural for the hall of the building. The left panel of the resulting three-part mural depicted young girls seeking recognition. The large center panel showed women picking fruit from the Tree of Knowledge and Science. The far right panel illustrated women participating in the various arts.[30] The woman's building was to be a monument to women's achievements across the spectrum of human endeavor.

Not everyone, however, was pleased with the idea of a separate exhibit for women. Particularly perturbed was Susan B. Anthony, who disdained the idea of a separate venue for women and urged American women to boycott the exposition unless women's work would be exhibited alongside men's. Bertha Palmer understood the motives behind the objections expressed by Anthony and her fellow dissidents, who called themselves "Isabellas," but Palmer was convinced that concentrating the displays in the woman's building more dependably assured that women would have full recognition and opportunity for representation.[31]

The women involved hoped that the exposition would not only provide a setting for women's industrial and artistic accomplishments, but also offer an arena to demonstrate how women's public work could promote their social status. The message to the nation's women was that collective action gave them a larger share in the "work of the world" and thus a distinct role in the shaping of that world.[32] That activists believed the notion of "separate but equal" did not convey this goal as well as the intermingled exhibits of men's and women's achievements in the individual state and country buildings, they did agree that the woman's building was a prominent showcase for their accomplishments. In the end, the woman's building turned out to be "a duplicate fair within the fair," one commentator concluded. The result was that with the exception of such industries as mining and those requiring heavy machinery, women were discovered to be "just as capable as men."[33]

The theme of the Woman's Department meshed smoothly with the aims of the newly organized National and International Councils, and the 1893 Chicago World's Fair proved to be a launching ground for development of both. In connection with the U.S. government's sponsorship of this Columbian Exposition, a World's Congress Auxiliary was planned to be an umbrella agency for individual congresses, each one devoted to a theme of social importance in connection with the fair. The Board of Lady Managers became the woman's branch of the World's Congress Auxiliary. Recognizing the "exceptional opportunity for convening representatives of all countries" afforded by the exposition and with the suggestion of the Board of Lady Managers, officers of the NCW invited members of the ICW to hold its first quinquennial meeting at the exposition.[34] Though it had originally been planned for London, since the current president of the ICW was Briton Millicent Garrett Fawcett, the British had not yet organized a national council. Thus, the Chicago World's Fair appeared to be a logical choice for the international convention. The NCW executive committee immediately began work to insure a positive response from member councils. The committee elected May Wright Sewall, one of internationalism's most avid workers, as its president and emissary, while also pledging to provide hospitality to all official foreign delegates, a proposition that ultimately proved to be more financially draining than the committee had anticipated. Appeals for donations were sent to all NCW members, to which the Latter-day Saint organizations promptly responded.[35]

The NCW mounted a massive recruiting effort to attract European visitors to the fair. May Wright Sewall twice traveled to Europe to arouse interest, securing enthusiastic responses from women's leaders throughout Europe and Russia. She obtained the names of every national women's organization and extended invitations to attend the congress. At the time of the exposition, member nations of the ICW were few. Besides the NCW, only a small number of representatives from nonfederated women's organizations in other nations were affiliated. Council leaders hoped the Congress of Women would encourage the organization of national councils in other countries.[36] It proved to be successful in attracting thousands of women to its weeklong series of sessions. The meetings began on May 15, 1893, and were held in the spacious and elegant Palace of Fine Arts, one of the large columned buildings that fronted the artificial lagoon designed by famed landscape architect Frederick Law Olmsted.[37]

Utah women enthusiastically responded to the invitation for each state and territory to participate in the fair's Columbian Exposition and, as requested, created their own territorial Board of Lady Managers. Emily S. Richards was president, assisted by Alice J. Whalen of Ogden and the chair of the Utah commission, Margaret Blaine Salisbury—a niece of Secretary of State James G. Blaine and also a personal friend of the president of the Ladies World's Fair Commission in Chicago, Bertha Palmer.[38] Both Whalen and Salisbury were non-Mormons appointed by Governor Arthur L. Thomas.

Emmeline served as chair of the Salt Lake County Board and assisted in organizing Columbian Clubs in each county to enlist workers and solicit handiwork to exhibit in the Utah and Woman's Buildings.[39] She was also instrumental in preparing several publications for the Woman's Building. One was a compilation of statistical surveys relating to women's employment, legal status, social activities, philanthropy and reform work, along with other notable achievements. She edited *Charities and Philanthropies* and *Woman's Work in Utah*,[40] and helped prepare a volume of poems by Utah poets, which was illustrated by Edna Wells Sloan, entitled *Songs and Flowers of the Wasatch*[41] and dedicated to Margaret Salisbury. Emmeline also assisted in the publication of *World's Fair Ecclesiastical History of Utah*,[42] in which representatives of the state contributed a history of their faiths. This volume was edited by Sarah M. Kimball.[43] The preface to the *Ecclesiastical*

History expressed the desire for more tolerance and unity than had been experienced in the past in Utah: "It is the earnest desire of members of the committee that a closer feeling of unity, and a broader desire for general helpfulness may result from the study of this little volume which we dedicate with love and prayers to the World's Columbian Exposition."[44] In addition, twelve Utah women submitted their books to the library of women authors in the Woman's Building, including, ironically, the anti-Mormon novels of Jennie Froiseth and Cornelia Paddock.[45]

As member organizations of the NCW, the LDS Relief Society and Young Ladies' MIA were invited to organize their own departmental sessions at the Congress of Women. Relief Society General President Zina D. H. Young, diffident at first, finally yielded to the appeals of Jane Richards and Sarah Kimball to send a representative group of Relief Society women; their expenses were covered by contributions from the individual ward societies. Zina Young agreed to attend along with Sarah Kimball, Jane Richards, Isabella Horne, Emmeline Wells, and Dr. Martha Hughes Cannon.[46] Emmeline presented papers at two sessions, the first touting the literary skills of western women, entitled "Western Women Authors and Journalists." In the other, "Grain Saving by Women," she described the unusual and successful welfare project of the Relief Society, which greatly interested her audience. The next morning an unexpected honor came to her. She was invited to preside over the General Congress in the Hall of Columbus at the Palace of Fine Arts, "an honor never before accorded to a Mormon woman," she noted. "If one of our brethren had such a distinguished honor conferred upon them," she wryly added, "it would have been heralded the country over and thought a great achievement."[47]

In her monthlong stay at the fair, Emmeline Wells met many of the European officers and members of the ICW, visited with officers of the NCW, and socialized with most of the prominent women of the National Women's Press Club, with participants in the Social Purity Congress, and other national organizations, including her suffrage friends, Susan B. Anthony, Reverend Anna Howard Shaw, Reverend Anna Garlin Spencer, and Mary A. Livermore.[48] Between sessions and socials, Emmeline somehow managed to write two editorials for her paper.

The preparatory work of members of the NCW in igniting interest and enthusiasm outside the United States proved successful. The women who attended the World's Congress of Representative Women came from 126 organizations in thirty-three countries. Six hundred of them contributed to the eighty-one sessions.[49] Bertha Honoré Palmer had the vision, the drive, and the will to give women full representation at the fair. She declared the Columbian Exposition had succeeded in promoting interest in the further advancement of women. "A community of interest has been created among women in every part of the world, such as has never heretofore existed," she exuberantly exclaimed. "We find that, as far as women are concerned, a new era is evidently beginning for them all over the world; that in every community opinions regarding the education, culture, business capacity, and their power for organized effort in useful directions are rapidly changing, and that their progress and development will move forward swiftly."[50]

A new ICW president was elected to head the next quinquennial meeting of the council scheduled for London in 1899, six rather than five years later. The thirty-six-year-old Countess of Aberdeen, Lady Ishbel, had all the credentials for assuming this new position. At the time of her election, she was living in Canada with her husband, the governor-general. Lady Ishbel, whose full name was Ishbel Marjoribanks (Marchbanks), had demonstrated her love for public service at an early age. Born to privilege, she moved in the highest circles of British nobility and acted from a lively sense of "noblesse oblige." She was instrumental in providing education for her servants, uniting disparate groups working for similar goals, and exhibiting, along with her husband, a strong social consciousness evident in the numerous causes they served. She became known as a proficient speaker and organizer and an inveterate reformer. Her heritage, experience, and social standing made her particularly well suited to preside over the ICW.[51] She ultimately served the ICW as president for three nonconsecutive terms, the last one completed when she was seventy-nine, only three years before her death.

Another tireless worker on behalf of the congress and the ICW was Rachel Foster Avery. Avery provided a consummate concluding tribute to the grand event in Chicago: "From the individual working alone, along one line of work, to the National Council and outward to the International, women had perfected a strong and flawless chain."[52] In reality, the actual solidarity of interests and universality of womanhood was limited. But neither the diversity in national backgrounds nor the member associations' individual goals prevented them from finding unity in their enthusiasm for internationalism as well as their shared dedication to bettering women's social condition.

Rachel Foster Avery gained notoriety as a national suffrage leader, serving as an officer in the National Council of Women and in the International Council of Women.

The Columbian Exposition spurred cooperative effort of women's associations not only in Utah but also throughout the country. Its theme of unity effectively blurred the differences in individual goals and methods of the diverse groups represented. The contagious appeal of "women's solidarity" also obscured the absence of working-class and minority women in the grand chorus of unified sisterhood.[53]

For the women's groups involved, however, especially those seeking validity for an international scope and agenda, the woman's congress reinforced their faith in the power of union and in their ability to transform society and to effect social justice. Independent goals of constituent members could be subsumed in the transcendent realization of woman's distinctive contribution to the "progress of civilization." Through the Chicago World's Fair and the woman's congress, women intended to capitalize on the potential of female solidarity, to surmount the role of passive onlooker on the world scene, and to exploit the moral authority granted women to implement their own social agendas and influence world affairs.[54] For Mormon women, the NCW and ICW provided a network of association with which they would affiliate for nearly another century.

The pervasive rhetoric of unity was not limited to the international forum that the woman's congress provided. During the strenuous months of preparation in Utah, Emily Richards advanced the hope that "while this work is divided between the territory, county and individual, it will all go to make one great whole and will be looked upon by visitors at the World's Fair as an exhibit from the women of Utah."[55] With virtually no capital, only "the active energy and enterprise" of willing women, the exhibitors hoped to make "a creditable showing" of Utah products, but more important, of cooperative hands.[56]

For Emmeline Wells, the woman's congress swelled her enthusiasm for expanding women's networks and convinced her of the social power of female combination. Echoing the objectives of the national board, Emmeline confidently asserted: "This work is bringing women into a nearness of contact that will increase confidence, and a more universal sisterhood will be established by the association and relations of this vast army of workers."[57] On Utah Day at the fair, Robert C. Chambers, Utah's World's Fair commissioner, reinforced the aura of conciliation so carefully nurtured by Utah women: "The people of Utah ... love the Union and the Union's flag, and, no matter what may have been said of them in the past, to-day they are marching in harmony with the men and women of this great Nation."[58] It was 1893, still three years before statehood, but within the next decade, Utah politicians B. H. Roberts and Reed Smoot would inadvertently set in motion events that would encroach on that harmony, seriously jeopardizing Mormon women's continuing affiliation with these emerging councils.

Though Utah women faced obstacles in maintaining unity with the National and International Councils, these associations had troubles of their own. The international recruiting efforts following the World's Fair exposed the almost insurmountable challenges in creating an international federation. The cost of membership, the difficulties of international travel, the language barriers, and the time involved in supporting local, national, and international groups taxed the abilities of many willing associations.[59] In some instances, husbands were not willing to give their wives either the time or the money to attend distant conventions. Few willing workers had independent incomes, legacies of their own, or control of trusts or foundations to assist in establishing an endowment fund for the councils or for their own travel as members of an international association.[60] Emmeline Wells's dependence on LDS Church or friends' financial support for all of her national and international work was indicative of some of these impediments.

In some countries, national politics hindered, if not prohibited, international alliances or women's political activism. Sweden's delegates, for instance, abstained from all votes at the 1899 quinquennial meeting relating to a resolution against militarism, since they were "not free to discuss political questions."[61] Competitive states and provinces in countries such as Austria, Hungary, South Africa, and Australia complicated efforts to form even a national federation.[62] Furthermore, some existing women's groups objected not only to the goals and personnel of the council, but also to the idea of formal alliance itself. These "violent feminists," as ICW secretary Teresa Wilson characterized them, "in their effort at independence, shook off all convention," being unwilling to collaborate with women whom they considered "aristocratic, orthodox, and 'devout doers of good works.'"[63] Their assessment was a fairly accurate, if dismissive, picture of the women involved in the international movement. Their goals did indeed reflect the values of primarily middle-class social activists devoted to social betterment around the world. They were women who believed their influence could make a difference. The ideals and goals of the Relief Society, in most instances, meshed comfortably with the objectives of these two councils, and the Relief Society's highly effective network and long experience in fundraising relieved it of many of the challenges faced by some of the newer women's groups.

In 1895, two years after the Columbian Exposition, Emmeline Wells attended the triennial convention of the NCW in Washington, D.C. Accompanying her were Martha H. Tingey, Minnie J. Snow, Susa Young Gates, Lillie T. Freeze, Maria Y. Dougall, Dr. Ellis B. Shipp, Sarah M. Kimball, and Elmina S. Taylor. Within this group were representatives from all three of the women-led LDS Church auxiliaries: Relief Society, Young Ladies' MIA, and Primary. All were community and religious leaders, and several had been active suffragists to whom national affiliation had great appeal. Emmeline was away from home for seven weeks, including a week in Atlanta prior to the NCW meeting to attend the National American Woman Suffrage Association (NAWSA) annual meeting with Marilla Daniels and Aurelia Spencer Rogers. During the ten-day interval between conventions, Emmeline visited members of the U.S. Congress to promote a silk experiment station in Utah, a remarkable departure from her earlier lobbying efforts, as was the affirmative response she received.

Though a relatively new member at this third meeting of the NCW, Emmeline Wells was as involved as she had been at the national suffrage meetings. She presided at one of the Mormon women's sessions, participated in several other sessions as a discussant, and presented a paper entitled "Forty Years in the Valley of the Great Salt Lake" in a session on philanthropy.[64] She was honored to be elected a patron of the council by her friend Rachel Foster Avery. Although the honor required an initial outlay of one hundred dollars, with an annual five-dollar remittance thereafter, Emmeline accepted and thus had the privilege of attending all business meetings and participating in every way, except voting. And as a frequent delegate from the Relief Society she had voting privileges as well. At the conclusion of the long but eventful trip, she returned home exhilarated and encouraged, only to face the unexpected hurdle that B. H. Roberts had persuasively erected in Utah's constitutional convention with his perorations against woman suffrage. Fortunately, the early groundwork done by the Utah Territorial Woman Suffrage Association, an effort that had united a number of gentile and Mormon women in a common cause, bore fruit. Utah suffragists enjoyed the success of years of labor when Utah became the third woman suffrage state.

The next year, 1896, with statehood finally achieved and woman suffrage permanently placed in the new state constitution, Emmeline Wells, as a patron of the NCW,[65] could give more of her time and attention to the council. She did not attend the next NCW meeting in Washington, D.C., in February of that year or the annual woman suffrage meeting but sent a greeting to the NAWSA relating to its commemoration of the fiftieth anniversary of the Seneca Falls convention. "What a testimony to the steadfastness of women in the work of humanity," she wrote, lauding the women who had given so much in the effort to achieve political equality.[66]

Though Emmeline did not attend the February meetings in 1896, she looked forward to representing the Relief Society at the NCW executive committee meeting in Omaha in October 1898. The attendance of Mormon women at this meeting did not occur without a struggle at home, however. At a business meeting of the Relief Society board, those members who hesitated using Relief Society funds to support membership in the NCW made their opposition clearly known. "If the sisters in general could have these matters explained to them, they would realize the importance of the connection that brought the women of Zion into such close relationship with the most famous and best educated women of the day," Emmeline argued, along with Jane Richards and Zina Card.[67] Emmeline and her friends won the day, but the discussion forewarned them of mounting opposition ahead.

Within ten minutes of Emmeline's arrival at the Omaha conference, Susan Anthony, May Wright Sewall (the president), and Louisa Robbins (corresponding secretary), visited her at the Paxton House and invited her to a small dinner party of eight to be followed by a meeting of the National Council of Jewish Women, which was affiliated with the NCW.[68] Pleased to be invited to such a select gathering, Emmeline was dismayed to find that hostility toward Mormon women persisted, ironically even among women who had experienced ostracism themselves. "One can easily comprehend the prejudice that must be met," she wrote in her diary, "when everyone you meet wants to know directly if you are a Mormon, and would not think of asking a woman from any other state, what church she belonged to."[69]

Despite her discomfiture at the social gathering, Emmeline Wells was pleased with the conference. Her ideas and resolutions were solicited, and the women who accompanied her were well received and enthusiastic about the work of the council.[70] Underlying Emmeline's enthusiasm for the meeting was her concern over the murmurings at home by those not committed to the "council idea."[71] When she returned, she wrote an editorial for the *Woman's Exponent* mildly chastising those women who "think it of little consequence and are hardly sufficiently interested to make themselves familiar with the standing of the National Council." Utterly dedicated to the importance of these associations to the acceptance of Mormon women in American society, Emmeline tried to impress on her readers her own convictions. "Woman's hour has struck," she insisted, "It is everywhere apparent and the time is hastening on when the women of this inter-mountain region will be able to prove the great intellectual and moral as well as spiritual strength that has come to them through the forces operating in their behalf to fulfill the prophecies that have been made in years gone by with regard to this chosen land."[72] There was no denying her enthusiasm and farsightedness in supporting the affiliation.

In the next twenty years, Emmeline Wells attended four of the seven triennial meetings of the NCW, five executive committee meetings, and one overseas convention of the ICW. During eleven of those years, she also served as Relief Society General President, and she held various offices of the local unit of the Mothers' Congress, the Daughters of Revolution, and the Utah chapter of the Federation of Women's Clubs, besides participating in Utah politics. She was anything but idle in her seventies and eighties. Despite the rocky path still ahead of her in her self-imposed mission to gain Mormon legitimacy in the sisterhood of American women, she had begun to feel the first blush of success, the best impetus to continue.

While the granting of statehood and the repossession of the vote culminated years of intense worry and work for Emmeline, she was now facing a number of other unexpected challenges that would have long-term effects on Mormon membership in the National and International Councils. One challenge began on September 15, 1898. That day

Emmeline recorded in her diary: "Roberts was nominated yesterday and the women of the State generally feel it is an insult." B. H. Roberts was a member of the LDS Church's Quorum of the Seventy, next in authority to the Quorum of the Twelve. It was Roberts's obstructionist tactics in the constitutional convention of 1895 that almost defeated woman suffrage, and now he was running once again for the U.S. Congress on the Democratic ticket. He was a controversial candidate, not only to women but also to non-Mormons because of his position in the general leadership of the Church and his continuing association with his plural wives. Since his polygamous status had caused no furor from non-Mormons the first time he ran for Congress (and lost) in 1895, Roberts had little reason to anticipate that it would draw any criticism three years later. But he did not reckon with the depth of antipolygamy fervor among some of the Gentile residents in Utah, nor the opposition of women who remembered his effective antisuffrage oratory in the recent constitutional convention.[73]

The day after he was nominated, visitors flooded Emmeline's office complaining and "wanting to know what to do." Among them were women from Roberts's own party, including Zina Young and Romania Pratt Penrose. The women hoped to enlist Emmeline's help in fighting Roberts's candidacy.[74] Not wishing to be openly hostile to an ecclesiastical authority, Emmeline decided to discuss the matter with newly sustained LDS Church President Lorenzo Snow and his counselor George Q. Cannon. She found them both opposed to Roberts's nomination for reasons other than his antisuffrage stance, and they were quite willing that the women should work to defeat him "either privately or publicly." They also talked "strongly" of a mass meeting, she noted. Their opposition to his candidacy reinforced her own indignation: "The idea that he should expect to be elected by women's votes after his anti-suffrage raid."[75]

During the 1895 election, the two partisan Salt Lake City newspapers debated Roberts's candidacy throughout the campaign, the *Herald* defending him and the *Tribune* beginning a strenuous campaign against him. The *Tribune* predicted that should he win the election, religious groups throughout the nation would protest and Congress would never seat him—predictions that were self-fulfilling[76]—and national women's groups would be instrumental in assuring that outcome.

Had the women of Utah either voted against Roberts or declined to vote, Roberts may not have been successful. But he won by a five-thousand-vote margin (32,316 to 27,108), and it was clear to Emmeline that women's votes had helped him win. If she had been vexed by Roberts's nomination, she was pained by his election: "It is a great disappointment to me that Roberts was elected—it cannot but be detrimental in every way. My heart is very sad. I cannot understand how the women of the State can be so unscrupulous as to vote for such a man."[77] A letter from Susan B. Anthony expressed her doubts that he would ever be seated and urged Emmeline to "publish an earnest protest" and to secure a statement from Roberts that he would not oppose woman suffrage when in Congress. Roberts agreed to this. Anthony also encouraged Emmeline "to combine the forces of your women into one voice, one action; that is your great need."[78] But the Roberts issue would deny them this kind of unity.

Whereas Mormon women failed to prevent Roberts from winning the election for Congress, women's organizations across the country took part in the successful national movement that blocked his seating. The movement began in Utah with protests from the officials of several Protestant organizations that opposed his continuing cohabitation with his three wives. Roberts was defying the 1893 Amnesty Act that had returned voting and other privileges to polygamists in exchange for obedience to the law prohibiting the practice of polygamy. Moreover, they feared, Roberts's high position in the LDS Church would compromise his objectivity in Congress, making him an unsuitable representative of all the people of Utah. The anti-Roberts movement swelled into a national crusade embracing the press, religious organizations, and a host of national women's associations, all protesting his seating. Many of these women's groups, such as the powerful Woman's Christian Temperance Union, the National Christian League for the Preservation of Moral Purity, the National Association of Loyal Women of America, and the Free Baptist Women's Missionary Society, were members of the NCW, scheduled to hold its 1899 convention in Washington, D.C., in the midst of the campaign against Roberts. Roberts's election had become a *cause célèbre* in the nation and would be a test of loyalty for LDS women when they attended the February meeting.

An earlier version of this chapter was published as "'The Power of Combination': Emmeline B. Wells and the National and International Councils of Women," BYU Studies 33 (1993): 646–73.

Notes

1. "Women and the World's Fair," *Woman's Exponent* 21 (December 1, 1892): 84.

2. "A Noble Woman," *Deseret Evening News,* March 5, 1910, 4.

3. Blanche Beechwood, "Bear Ye One Another's Burdens," *Woman's Exponent* 2 (March 1, 1874): 146.

4. Bonnie S. Anderson explores these informal associations and the individual efforts of women in three European countries and the United States beginning in the 1830s and continuing until the 1860s in *Joyous Greetings: The First International Women's Movement, 1830–1860* (New York: Oxford University Press, 2000). The American Civil War effectively suspended the woman's rights movement in the United States until the two national suffrage associations organized shortly after its close.

5. The origin and complete proceedings of the 1888 meeting are in *Report of the International Council of Women, Assembled by the National Woman Suffrage Association, Washington, D.C., March 25 to April 1, 1888* (Washington, D.C.: National Woman Suffrage Association, 1888). Other sources of the origins and development of the ICW are May Wright Sewall, comp., *Genesis of the International Council of Women and the Story of Its Growth, 1888–1893* (Indianapolis: n.p., 1914); Louise Barnum Robbins, ed., *History and Minutes of the National Council of Women of the United States, Organized in Washington, D.C., March 31, 1888* (Boston: E. B. Stillings, 1898), 1–7; Marie-Helene LeFaucheux and others, *Women in a Changing World: The Dynamic Story of the International Council of Women since 1888* (London: Routledge and Kegan Paul, 1966), 3–13. A feminist context and focus are given to the origins of the NCW and ICW by Richard J. Evans, *The Feminists: Women's Emancipation Movements in Europe, America and Australasia, 1840–1920* (London: Croom Helm, 1977), especially the appendix, 246–53; and Judith Papachristou, "American

Women and Foreign Policy, 1898-1905: Exploring Gender in Diplomatic History," *Diplomatic History: The Journal of the Society for Historians of American Foreign Relations* 14 (Fall 1990): 493-509.

6. Sewall, *Genesis of the International Council of Women,* 6-7.

7. See Robbins, *History and Minutes,* 3, 4.

8. Robbins, *History and Minutes,* 3; and *Report of the International Council of Women,* 10-11. In the *Report,* reference is made to the three Latter-day Saint women's organizations (Relief Society, Young Ladies' MIA, and Primary) in attendance on page 49, to the $100 donation each by Margaret Caine and Jane S. Richards of the Relief Society on page 455, and a condensed version of the talk given by Emily S. Richards on pages 107-9. The specific goals of the ICW, such as access to education, to the professions, and to industrial training, equal pay for equal work, and a single standard of morality, are listed on page 454.

9. "International Council of Women," *Woman's Exponent* 16 (January 15, 1888): 124.

10. According to Susa Young Gates, during the time May Wright Sewall served as vice president of the ICW and president of the NCW, Sewall "had met opposition in high social circles of Europe." Indeed, "European ladies" resented the American woman's supremacy in the two councils and were opposed to Sewall's ascending to the presidency of the ICW in 1899 when Lady Aberdeen decided to retire as president. See Susa Young Gates, "Lucy Bigelow Young," Susa Young Gates Papers, Church Archives, The Church of Jesus Christ of Latter-day Saints, Salt Lake City.

11. Leila J. Rupp, in *Worlds of Women: The Making of an International Women's Movement* (Princeton, N.J.: Princeton University Press, 1997), projects these ideas in her analysis of three international women's associations of the late nineteenth and early twentieth century, including the ICW. She discusses the attraction of internationalism to individual women, their strategies for making a difference on the world scene, and their persistent emphasis on their commonalities, especially their difference from men in global politics. She posits that the challenges "to the assumptions and structures of exclusion . . . ensured the continuation of the process of what it means to be a feminist internationalist."

12. Evans, *Feminists,* 252.

13. May Wright Sewall, "Purity of the Home," *Washington Post,* April 14, 1905, as quoted in Joan Smyth Iversen, *The Antipolygamy Controversy in U.S. Women's Movements, 1880-1925: A Debate on the American Home* (New York and London: Garland, 1997), 220.

14. Emmeline B. Wells, Diary, February 3, 16, 1891, L. Tom Perry Special Collections, Harold B. Lee Library, Brigham Young University, Provo, Utah.
15. "Representative Women of the Convention," *Woman's Exponent* 19 (March 15, 1891): 140–41.
16. Wells, Diary, February 21, 1891.
17. Wells, Diary, February 21, 1891. See also "A Glimpse of Washington," *Woman's Exponent* 19 (March 1, 1891): 132–33.
18. See Rachel Foster Avery, ed., *Transactions of the National Council of Women of the United States: Assembled in Washington, D.C., February 22–25, 1891* (Philadelphia: J. B. Lippincott, 1891), 258–60.
19. "National Council of Women," *Woman's Tribune* 8 (March 7, 1891): 75; reprinted in "A Glimpse of Washington," *Woman's Exponent* 19 (March 1, 1891): 132–33.
20. Wells, Diary, February 24, 1891.
21. "Woman's Special Mission," *Woman's Exponent* 19 (May 1, 1891): 164.
22. "Woman's Special Mission," *Woman's Exponent* 19 (May 1, 1891): 164.
23. The Relief Society withdrew its membership in 1971. Rebekah Ryan Clark has traced the history of Latter-day Saint women in the NCW in "An Uncovered History: Mormons in the Woman Suffrage Movement, 1896–1920," in *New Scholarship on Latter-day Saint Women in the Twentieth Century: Selections from the Women's History Initiative Seminars 2003–2004*, ed. Carol Cornwall Madsen and Cherry B. Silver (Provo, Utah: Joseph Fielding Smith Institute for Latter-day Saint History, 2005), 19–38.
24. Article II of the constitution of the NCW, adopted March 31, 1888, in Robbins, *History and Minutes*, 11. See also "The International Council of Women," *Relief Society Magazine* 8 (January 1921): 23.
25. Quoted in LeFaucheux, *Women in a Changing World*, 206.
26. "Relief Society Reports, Louisa Jones—Secretary," *Woman's Exponent* 23 (October 15, 1894): 199.
27. Susa Young Gates, "History of Women," National and International Relations of Women, Gates Papers.
28. Details of these activities can be found in Carol Cornwall Madsen, "Decade of Detente: The Mormon-Gentile Female Relationship in Nineteenth-Century Utah," *Utah Historical Quarterly* 63 (Fall 1995): 298–319.
29. A complete account of women's role in the Chicago Exposition is Jeanne Madeline Weimann, *The Fair Women* (Chicago: Academy Chicago, 1981). See also Judith Paine, "Sophia Hayden and the Woman's Building," *Helicon Nine: A Journal of Women's Arts and Letters* 1, no. 2 (1979): 28–47; and William D. Andrews, "Women and the Fairs of 1876 and 1893," *Hayes*

Historical Journal 1, no. 2 (Spring 1977): 173–84. Several dissertations and theses also address the subject of women and the Columbian Exposition.

30. *The Chicago World's Fair of 1893: A Photographic Record*, text by Stanley Applebaum (New York: Dover Publication, 1980), 69. For details of the preparations of the fair and the story behind the plethora of nineteenth-century world's fairs, see Reid Badger, *The Great American Fair: The World's Columbian Exposition and American Culture* (Chicago: Nelson Hall, 1979).

31. Noted in Betty Boyd Caroli, *The Roosevelt Women* (New York: Basic Books, 1998), 95–96. At the 1891 meeting of the NCW, the program listed two talks by members of the "Queen Isabella Association," taking its name from the dynamic queen who launched Columbus on his historic voyage. See Avery, *Transactions,* 8.

32. Gayle Gullett explores these ideas in "The Political Use of Public Space: The Women's Movement and Women's Participation at the Chicago Columbia Exposition, 1893," paper presented at the Berkshire Conference on Women's History, Wellesley College, June 1987, copy in possession of author.

33. Applebaum, *Chicago World's Fair,* 69.

34. See Fifth Resolution (actually the Sixth) of the National Council of Women, as reported in "National Council of Women," *Woman's Exponent* 19 (May 15, 1891): 170. A detailed account of the preliminary deliberations in the participation of the NCW and ICW at the 1893 Chicago World's Fair is Robbins, *History and Minutes,* 51–109. See also May Wright Sewall, *Genesis of the International Council of Women,* 46–75. A summary report is LeFaucheux, *Women in a Changing World,* 17–18.

35. The generous offer to provide "hospitality" for the foreign delegates to the Woman's Congress left the treasury of the NCW in arrears. A specific notice in the minutes of the May 22, 1893, meeting of the executive council indicates that the president announced to the committee that a large part of the money collected for the hospitality fund came from the women of Utah. The treasurer responded that "two hundred dollars besides their regular dues came from our two members in Utah (associations), sent most promptly as soon as the appeal went out." Robbins, *History and Minutes,* 88.

36. LeFaucheux, *Women in a Changing World,* 16–17.

37. Applebaum, *Chicago World's Fair,* 9.

38. "Women in the World's Fair," *Woman's Exponent* 20 (September 1, 1891): 36; and "Ladies Department of the World's Fair for Salt Lake County Organized," *Deseret Evening News,* September 27, 1892, 5. See also E. A. McDaniel, *Utah at the World Columbian Exposition* (Salt Lake City, 1894), 73.

39. Margaret Salisbury's special appeal to the legislature for funds to support Utah women's contribution to the Woman's Building was a brief synopsis of the broad range of industry and productivity in which Utah women were engaged "whether in the studio, counting house, schoolroom, factory, mill, dairy, or the farm." She noted the many employments and professions in which women were trained and urged the legislature to allow Utah women the opportunity "to meet their sisters of the different States and Territories in a manner highly creditable to the energy, intelligence and talent which charasterize [sic] the women of the West." See Margaret Salisbury, as quoted in "An Able Appeal," *Woman's Exponent* 20 (March 1, 1892): 125–26; and "To the Women of Utah," *Deseret Evening News*, April 17, 1893, 4, which announces the procurement of the funds requested for a silk display as well as a request for specimens of silk handiwork from women throughout the territory.

40. Emmeline B. Wells, ed., *Woman's Work in Utah* (Salt Lake City: George Q. Cannon and Sons, 1893).

41. Emmeline B. Wells, ed., *Songs and Flowers of the Wasatch* (Salt Lake City: George Q. Cannon and Sons, 1893).

42. *World's Fair Ecclesiastical History of Utah* (Salt Lake City: George Q. Cannon and Sons, 1893).

43. The *Deseret Evening News* regularly reported on the developments of the women's contribution to the fair. It noted the conference on charities, held in Salt Lake City on February 2, 1893, out of which came the pamphlet on charities, which it described in detail in "Conference on Charities," *Deseret Evening News*, February 2, 1893, 8. It noted the exceptional work of Margaret Salisbury in securing a silk exhibit from Utah women for the Woman's Building ("To the Women of Utah," *Deseret Evening News*, April 17, 1893, 4), and noted the impending Woman's Congress at which several Utah women were invited to speak, including Utah's "capable representative" Emmeline B. Wells ("The Woman's Congress," *Deseret Evening News*, April 3, 1893, 4).

44. Sarah M. Kimball, ed., *World's Fair Ecclesiastical History of Utah* (Salt Lake City: George Q. Cannon and Sons, 1893), vi–vii.

45. The other authors included were Eliza R. Snow, Hannah T. King, Augusta Joyce Crocheron, Mary Jane Tanner, Romania B. Pratt, Mrs. W. S. McCornick, Mary E. Almy, Emily B. Spencer, Hannah Cornaby, and Sarah E. Carmichael. "Editorial Notes," *Woman's Exponent* 21 (April 15, May 1, 1893): 156.

46. National Woman's Relief Society Record, November 8, 11, 1892; April 12, 1893; and undated meetings summarized after the November 11, 1892, meeting, Church Archives. See also Wells, Diary, November 3, 1892.

47. Wells, Diary, May 20, 1893.

48. Some of the other notable women Emmeline Wells met included Bertha Honoré Palmer of Chicago, president of the Board of Lady Managers of the fair; Ellen M. Henrotin, president of the General Federation of Women's Clubs; Isabella Beecher Hooker of the famous Beecher clan; and Julia Ward Howe, an outspoken critic of polygamy but highly acclaimed club woman.

49. LeFaucheux, *Women in a Changing World,* 17. Susa Young Gates, who attended, varied in her account, noting that 27 countries sent 528 delegates, the total attendance for the weeklong conference numbering 150,000 persons. Both sets of figures are probably estimates only. See Susa Young Gates, *History of the Young Ladies' Mutual Improvement Association* (Salt Lake City: Deseret News, 1911), 202.

50. From *Addresses and Reports of Mrs. Potter Palmer, President of the Board of Lady Managers, World's Columbian Commission* (Chicago: Rand McNally, 1894), 152–53.

51. After spending four years in Canada with her husband, she was elected president of the ICW as well as president of the newly organized Canadian Council. She had the unusual honor of speaking at the convocation exercises at the University of Chicago in 1898. For a full biography, see Marjorie Pentland, *A Bonnie Fecter: The Life of Ishbel Marjoribanks, Marchioness of Aberdeen and Tamair, G. B. E., LDD (honorary), J. P., 1857–1939* (London: B. T. Batsford, 1952).

52. LeFaucheux, *Women in a Changing World,* 17–18.

53. Gayle Gullett examines some of the flaws in this show of solidarity. The claim of universality, she writes, stemmed from the assumption of these middle- and upper-class reformers that they represented the interests of less advantaged women (working class and minorities) who were often the objects of their humanitarian efforts. See Gullett, "The Political Use of Public Space."

54. Rebecca L. Sherrick explores the motivations that brought so many women together and united them behind female internationalism, a monumental challenge for most of them, in "Toward Universal Sisterhood," *Women's Studies International Forum* 5, no. 6 (1982): 655–61.

55. Emily Richards, as quoted by May B. Talmage in "World's Fair Mass Meeting," *Woman's Exponent* 21 (November 15, 1892): 74.

56. "World's Fair and Silk Industry," *Woman's Exponent* 21 (December 15, 1892): 93.

57. "Women and the World's Fair," *Woman's Exponent* 21 (December 1, 1892): 84.

58. McDaniel, *Utah at the World's Columbian Exposition,* 5.

59. Minutes of the 1899 meeting of the ICW, London, July 6, 1899, in May Wright Sewall, ed., *The International Council of Women, 1899–1904, Report of Transactions of the Executive and Council* (Boston: n.p., 1909), xvii.

60. LeFaucheux, *Women in a Changing World*, 21.

61. LeFaucheux, *Women in a Changing World*, 21.

62. Sewall, *International Council of Women*, 8, 9.

63. LeFaucheux, *Women in a Changing World*, 19.

64. "The Women's Councils," *Deseret Evening News*, March 14, 1895, 5. See also "Second Triennial Session of the National Council of Women of the United States," February 17–March 2, 1895, Washington, D.C., Papers of the National Council of Women, New York Public Library. By this time Emmeline was feeling the satisfaction and comfort of genuine friendship with some of the leaders of both the NAWSA and NCW. See, for example, Wells, Diary, March 5, 6, 1895.

65. The privileges and responsibilities of patrons are explained in Robbins, *History and Minutes*, 225.

66. NAWSA, *Proceedings of the Thirtieth Annual Woman Suffrage Celebration of the First Woman's Rights Convention Held in Washington, D.C., 13–19 February*, ed. Rachel Foster Avery (Philadelphia: n.p., n.d.), 78.

67. National Woman's Relief Society Record, October 3, 1898, Church Archives. Zina Young Williams was then married to Charles O. Card.

68. Wells, Diary, October 22, 1898.

69. Wells, Diary, October 23–24, 1898.

70. Part of the business of the meeting was to elect a new roster of officers. Emmeline Wells had hoped to see Rachel Foster Avery elected president to succeed May Wright Sewall, but the honor went to Fannie Humphreys Gaffney, with whom Emmeline was less impressed. See Wells, Diary, October 30, 1898.

71. At a Relief Society meeting in Beaver, Utah, in 1894, just three years after joining the NCW, Emmeline found it necessary to endorse the affiliation of Latter-day Saint women with the NCW. "It was the mind of our leading brethren," she reminded them, "that we become a part of these great councils of women and it is a great advantage to us and our money is not thrown away that goes to pay our membership in those Councils." As quoted by Louissa Jones, comp., "Relief Society Reports, Beaver Stake," *Woman's Exponent* 23 (October 15, 1894): 198–99.

72. "Visit to Omaha," *Woman's Exponent* 27 (November 1, 15, 1898): 60.

73. Davis Bitton notes the anti-Mormon efforts during summer 1898 including the publications of an A. T. Schroeder, which charged Mormons

with still openly practicing polygamy, and the State Presbytery of Manti, which drew up a list of charges against the Church relating to the same offense. See Davis Bitton, "The B. H. Roberts Case of 1898–1900," *Utah Historical Quarterly* 25 (January 1957): 29–30.

74. Wells, Diary, September 17, 22, 1898.

75. Wells, Diary, September 20, 1898. It was generally considered by LDS Church leaders as well as the state's political leaders that it would be more beneficial to Utah to elect non-Mormons or at least monogamous Mormons to national office until time had extinguished the still-combustible anti-Mormon and antipolygamous feelings both locally and nationwide. These fears proved to be well founded. See Truman G. Madsen, *Defender of the Faith: The B. H. Roberts Story* (Salt Lake City, Utah: Bookcraft, 1980), 242–72.

76. "A Question for Voters," *Salt Lake Tribune,* October 5, 1898, 4, as quoted in Bitton, "B. H. Roberts Case," 34–35. Both Governor Heber M. Wells and LDS Church leader George Q. Cannon also publicly opposed his election.

77. Wells, Diary, November 10, 1898.

78. Susan B. Anthony to Emmeline B. Wells, December 5, 1898, Susan B. Anthony Papers, Library of Congress, Washington, D.C. See also B. H. Roberts, "The Political Status of Women in Utah," *Young Woman's Journal* 10 (March 1899): 104–5.

Chapter 16

The Power of Combination

That greater love and charity will prevail among womankind cannot be doubted when such a fraternal feeling is fostered and cherished as that which prevailed so largely during the entire sessions of the Council and Congress.[1]

In January 1899, three months after the election that sent B. H. Roberts to Congress, Emmeline Wells traveled to Washington, D.C., to attend the February meeting of the National Council of Women (NCW). Upon arrival she immediately sensed an undercurrent of ill will. Several member associations had been strengthened in their animus toward Mormon women by a growing national sentiment to prevent the seating of B. H. Roberts in Congress.[2] Though the usual number of papers was presented at the three-day triennial meeting, an inordinate amount of time was given to discussion of the Roberts election.

Pressured to add another resolution against Roberts to the large number already issued by other women's organizations, the NCW faced a dilemma. On the one hand, some of its most prestigious and supportive member associations had already published their own resolutions and wanted the council to collectivize the individual protests in a general resolution of its own. On the other hand, the council's charter allowed for a constituency of "diverse aims and varied activities," with its chief objective being "the overthrow of all forms of ignorance and injustice by the application of the Golden Rule to society, custom and law." To some members, the Roberts issue was outside the "specific work of the Council" and did not need to be addressed. The NCW was also concerned that if it did take a stance against Roberts it would offend two of its most supportive member organizations, the Relief Society and Young Ladies' Mutual Improvement Association (MIA), both affiliated with the LDS Church. The personal friendships that many of the council members had developed with Emmeline Wells and other Latter-day Saint representatives also deterred them from supporting a resolution. The position that the council would take on the issue, however, depended on the disposition of the resolutions committee, which held a four-hour meeting to deliberate the question. Emmeline Wells, representing the Relief Society, and Ann M. Cannon, a member of the Young Ladies' MIA board, were both members of the committee, as were representatives of the Woman's Christian Temperance Union (WCTU), the National League for the Promotion of Social Purity, and several other moral reform organizations.

On the opening day of the conference, there was little to suggest that this would be any different from previous triennial conventions. Of the ten Mormon women in attendance, four were delegates, and three of them, Emmeline, proxy for Relief Society president Zina D. H. Young; Martha Horne Tingey, proxy for Young Ladies' MIA president Elmina Taylor; and Zina Young Williams Card of the Young Ladies' MIA reported on their associations along with other organizational delegates.[3]

The following day, elections were held for the NCW's officers. Fannie Humphrey Gaffney was elected president, and unexpectedly Emmeline was honored to be elected second recording secretary, giving her a place on the executive committee.[4] But the palpable suspense regarding the Roberts case was evident throughout the meetings, abetted by reports from both Salt Lake City and eastern newspapers. "[The] matter is being looked forward to here with great interest," reported the *Tribune*'s Washington bureau, though only one member of the NCW had publicly spoken out against Roberts. Elizabeth B. Grannis of New York, who was president of the National League for the Promotion of Social Purity, had twice announced her hope that the NCW would produce a condemnatory resolution.[5] In later years, she would

Young Woman's Journal 10 (May 1899): 194, photographed by Johnson

Utah delegation to the Triennial National Council of Women, held in Washington, D.C., February 1899. Top row: *(left to right)* Martha Horne Tingey, Minnie J. Snow. Second row: *(left to right)* Ann M. Cannon, Emmeline B. Wells, Susa Young Gates. Third row: *(left to right)* Mabel Snow, Zina Young Card, Lula L. Greene Richards. Bottom row: *(left to right)* Lucy B. Young, Hana Kaaepa.

join Corinne Allen of Utah in keeping antipolygamy sentiment alive and subverting Mormon membership in the NCW.

The Mormon delegation soon became the focal point of the newspaper coverage. Delegate Minnie Snow (wife of LDS Church President Lorenzo Snow) was quoted as saying that she did not believe the council would be discourteous to the women of Utah, who were such an integral part of the organization, but if a "drastic measure is supported," it was "not at all unlikely that the Utah women will not only refuse to co-operate with the Council, but may leave it in a body."[6] This threat may have disturbed some in the NCW, but, ironically, the situation thrust the Mormon delegates into a dilemma of their own. None had supported Roberts in his bid for office, and they had foreseen the adverse reaction that his election would provoke. Their loyalty to their religion and to the principle for which he was being denounced, as well as his legitimately won election, however, compelled them to oppose the projected resolution.

For Emmeline Wells there was a double dilemma. Soon after Emmeline's arrival in Washington, NCW president May Wright Sewall, accepting her as head of the Utah delegation, took Emmeline aside to talk privately about the proposed anti-Roberts resolution. Sewall's advice was that the Utah women should vote for it, that it would be their "golden opportunity" to gain wider acceptance and prestige among the major women's organizations. She used "all her powers of persuasion to convince me it was the only course to pursue," Emmeline wrote,[7] but she said nothing of this interview to her fellow delegates.

The NCW leaders, recognizing the sensitivity of the issue, closed its business sessions to the public and refrained from putting any other kind of resolution to a vote, although the newspapers seemed privy to all that transpired. The Roberts question was the principal business of the resolutions committee, which maintained a strict silence on its proceedings.[8] Struggling for almost four hours to block passage of an anti-Roberts resolution, Emmeline Wells and Ann M. Cannon and their supporters compromised by formulating a resolution more generically worded and less personally incriminating than the original resolution. Surprisingly, their compromise resolution won the vote of the majority of the committee. But the opposition, led by representatives from the

WCTU, demanded that their views also be represented by means of a minority resolution. Both, it was finally agreed, would be presented to the entire council for a vote.[9] The snowstorm that raged outside during the meeting was hardly more threatening than the rhetorical storm that threatened within.

Described by the *Tribune*'s Washington bureau as "the most intense and exciting session of this convention, or any other which has been held in this city in a long time," the meeting began at ten in the morning and did not yield a vote until five o'clock in the afternoon. The report of the resolutions committee was the only topic to be considered and, according to the *New York Journal,* had been "the sole subject of debate since the convening of the council."[10] Discussion on the two resolutions created a spirited debate throughout the day. Amendments to the minority resolution were proposed and voted on but did not gather sufficient votes to pass.

The speakers seemed to be evenly divided between the two resolutions as they urged their respective views in strong, persuasive arguments. At the invitation of the chairperson, six Mormon women spoke, invoking restraint, tolerance, and sympathetic sisterhood among council members. The Mormon women insisted that polygamy should not be the issue and that the debate should center on the legality of Roberts's election. Ann Cannon, Minnie Snow, who read a letter from her husband LDS Church President Lorenzo Snow, Zina Williams Card, Susa Gates, Martha Horne Tingey, and Emmeline B. Wells along with supportive council members all made their case for the majority resolution.[11] Though the *Washington Post* described the debate as a "battle royal between the opposing forces," it hastily added that the discussion "was carried on with the greatest dignity and consideration, and at no time degenerated into anything akin to a squabble in spite of the fiery arguments that were made and the intense feeling displayed."[12]

Except when asked to comment, the Utah delegation quietly listened to the various speakers, showing plainly "the strain under which they suffered," according to the *New York Journal*. However, never once, it observed, "did they lose the thread of any argument and when, from time to time, they rose and, in response to the demand of the presiding officer, went upon the stage to speak, their bearing plainly showed they had the courage of their own convictions."[13] The Utah women were surprised at the strength of the support of Susan B. Anthony, Reverend Anna Garlin Spencer, and J. Ellen Foster, all prominent leaders in the National American Woman Suffrage Association as well as in the NCW, who, along with various members from other associations, lent their voices in favor of the majority resolution.

Finally, after the lengthy discussion, a vote was taken on the minority resolution. It was defeated thirty-one to sixteen, leaving the majority vote before the convention. At this point, Emmeline Wells decided to speak, declaring that "the seating of Mr. Roberts need not be regarded as any menace on the part of the people of Utah. Previous to his nomination," she explained, "I did all I could to defeat him. I did this as a Republican and a suffragist." But, she continued, he had been elected by the citizens of Utah and should be allowed to take his congressional seat. She concluded by expressing her regret that "the Mormon question should have been made the main work of the convention," joining the others voicing the same objection.[14] When a rising vote was called in favor of the majority resolution, twenty-four delegates stood. When the negative vote was invited, none stood. The majority vote had won the day. "There is little doubt," the *Salt Lake Tribune* reported, "that the final result was attained by the weight of the representatives from the National Women's Relief Society and the Young Ladies' Mutual Improvement society of Utah, whose arguments and emotional appeals led" to the favorable outcome.[15]

A final vindication for the Mormon women was a new resolution of the council, presented by Anna Garlin Spencer of the resolutions committee, which stated that "at succeeding sessions of the National Council of Women, no resolution or petition be presented, except such as bear upon the objects, policy or work of the Council itself, in its internal administration or in its relation as a body to other organizations, or to some specific representation of the Council in national or international enterprises or meetings."[16]

When Emmeline Wells visited Elizabeth Cady Stanton, who was not active in the NCW, in New York following the convention, Stanton, who had read of the controversy, confided in Emmeline her disapproval of the resolution against Roberts. She "thought it very bad taste and wrong in principle [and] ridiculed May Wright Sewall and especially her desire for popularity."[17] Emmeline felt that Stanton's opinion vindicated the courageous stand the Utah women had taken against Sewall's advice.

Susan B. Anthony expressed sentiments similar to Stanton's. Anthony scorned the NCW's proposed action. She triggered a stream of invective from the New York State Federation of Women's Clubs. Accused of being "soft" on polygamy because of her evident support of Mormon women, particularly on this issue, Anthony explained that she could see no reason to protest the seating of a Mormon "who had violated the law of monogamy" while ignoring those of other faiths who were "known to be violators of that law and many others for the protection of women and girls outside of Utah." Because his life choice adhered to a religious principle, Roberts, she declared, "is less a sinner than those men who live in violation of the teachings of the society in which they move." Anthony further explained that, although Congress may try to unseat Roberts after he had taken office, it was not its prerogative to prevent Roberts from taking his seat, and any motion or resolution to do so from women's organizations would only make them look ridiculous. She reiterated what she had said in the past, that though she abhorred polygamy, she detested "even more the license taken by men under the loose morals existing in what the Mormons call the Gentile world. . . . I think the wives and mothers of the country might better enter into a crusade against the licentiousness existing all around us and polluting our manhood, and leave it to our lawmakers to settle the matter of Roberts' fitness to be their associate in Congress."[18]

Few women shared Anthony's position or dared to publicly admit to it if they did. Women's organizations from all over the country joined their voices with congressmen, national and local clergymen, moral reform organizations, newspapers, and outraged citizens against Roberts and his polygamous status. The anti-Roberts movement snowballed across the nation, claiming seven million signatures protesting his seating by the time of the hearings in January 1900. Even as the NCW held its meetings, the Daughters of the American Revolution (DAR) and the National Congress of Mothers were writing their own resolutions of protest.[19] "The shadow of the Roberts case" clearly hung over "all the women's meetings in Washington," declared the *Salt Lake Tribune*.[20]

A key player in the antipolygamy protest was Corinne Allen, wife of Clarence Allen, Utah's first representative to Congress, against whom Roberts had unsuccessfully run for the congressional seat in 1896. At the annual meeting of the DAR, she proposed a resolution against Roberts, which, when voted on by the organization, was met with overwhelming support.[21] This approval fueled Allen's crusade for all the national women's organizations to support her campaign for a constitutional amendment prohibiting polygamy in all the states. These women's organizations received a hearty endorsement from another Utahn, Dr. T. C. Iliff of Salt Lake City, who was lecturing around the country against Roberts. He lauded the women of America whose action has always been against Mormonism, he asserted, and was confident Roberts's bid for office would be defeated, the women of America having raised up their voices to demand it.[22] And he was right.

To most observers, it was the Roberts case that marked the end of the brief period of deténte in Utah and triggered the postmanifesto antipolygamy movement, re-igniting the campaign for a constitutional amendment. The legal issue over Congress's right to prevent Roberts from taking his seat, as opposed to unseating him, raised a number of constitutional issues that spurred discussion of a sweeping law that would prevent any future political debacles such as this one. Thus, the movement for a constitutional amendment forbidding polygamy gathered enough force for the Congressional House Committee on Election of President, Vice President, and Representatives to initiate a bill prohibiting polygamy in all of the United States and disqualifying polygamists from holding federal office.[23] Though the bill did not pass Congress, the issue would continue to smolder for another decade.

The relationship between B. H. Roberts and Emmeline Wells had its own unresolved elements. They had been political adversaries even before the Utah constitutional convention showdown in 1895. He was a Democrat, an antisuffragist, and a candidate heedless of the political and social realities that surrounded his bids for a congressional seat. His election in 1898 had been the cause of much chagrin to Emmeline, who witnessed with deep regret the breakdown of relations between the Mormons and other members in the national women's organizations. As an outspoken, active Republican, as a leader of the woman suffrage battle in Utah, and as a "strong-minded" woman's rights advocate, Emmeline Wells epitomized all that Roberts opposed.

Strangely, during this period of nearly two decades when they knew one another as forceful opponents, the two had never formally met. Nearly fifteen years after Utah's constitutional convention in 1895, they had their first personal encounter on the occasion of Emmeline's eighty-second birthday. On February 28, 1910, the Relief Society, for which she was then general secretary, fêted her with a large public reception in the newly constructed Bishop's Building in Salt Lake City. Following the afternoon reception, which more than six hundred guests attended, was a private program attended by family members, Relief Society board members, and several high-ranking leaders of the Church, including Anthon H. Lund (a member of the First Presidency of the Church), Heber J. Grant (a member of the Quorum of the Twelve Apostles), Colonel Willard Young, and B. H. Roberts (a member of the Quorum of the Seventy), along with J. Golden Kimball (also of the Quorum of the Seventy). As one of the six gentlemen who spoke, "all congratulatory and commenting upon the life and work of 'Aunt Em,'" Roberts offered a brief tribute and presented her with a bouquet of white roses.[24]

Almost a month later, Emmeline Wells wrote a letter to express her thanks. The letter combines her spirit of conciliation and the sentiments of age, with a definite air of coquetishness:

> Ever since the evening of the 28th of February last I have contemplated penning a few words to you—and others, who were so gracious to me on that occasion.
>
> I have written to two or three ladies since, to whom I felt under special obligations, but not to my gentlemen friends—not even those dearest to me. I resolved that night, that I would write a few words of appreciation in grateful acknowledgement of your delicate gift of

roses pure and white—and tell you that of all the flowers given me on that happy occasion, that bouquet was the most beautiful by far—and coming from one who knew me so distantly (in a way) it was such a surprise that it was really like discovering a treasure—finding a beauty disguised in one, where we had only anticipated a quantum of reserve.

I feel now that I know you better, if only because of the selection of the flowers, that I love most of all—white roses.

But I pass on to the eloquent, but brief address and I must say—what others have said to me, (tho' I deprecate repeating the sentiments of others, and making them my own)—"It was the gem of the evening's entertainment."

You will see how crooked my lines are and my penmanship is very uneven—but if I wait longer, your letter would not be the first as I promised myself it should be,—nevertheless there are others, but say what you will,—there is something in being <u>first</u>. Some day—sometime, if I should live on and on, I may converse with you—as I only do to a few choice souls—not that I can give you new thoughts—you get those from the depths of the font in your own heart—but to exchange, or interchange thoughts with one of superior intelligence is a luxury in this barren world of cold communication. . . .

And now again I must express my simple heartfelt thanks for your excellent choice of the <u>roses</u> that fade all too soon and a wish for you and your dear ones, that you may revel in the gardens of paradise where the roses bloom eternally and where there are joys supernal forevermore.[25]

The letter was a tender and genuine, if mannered, expression of Emmeline's regard for her former opponent. Time had smoothed the edges of their political differences and they had turned their energies back to their shared religious commitment, now resistant to former political incursions.

The tumultuous beginning to the last year of the century gave way to one of the great adventures of Emmeline's life, attendance at the quinquennial meeting of the International Council of Women (ICW) in London, scheduled for June 1899. It was assumed that Emmeline, as an officer of the executive committee of the NCW, would attend, but money, as usual, was the uncertain element. In this new international venture she was joined by a fellow worker just as zealous and, unfortunately, just as impecunious as Emmeline. Nearly thirty years Emmeline's junior, Susa Young Gates, who was making her own name as a public activist in national circles, had been appointed to the press committee of the NCW. An ardent suffragist as well as an avid supporter of the NCW, Susa Gates soon became Emmeline's colleague. In 1889, Susa Gates had founded and was still editing the *Young Woman's Journal*, a young woman's version in monthly magazine form of the *Woman's Exponent*. The two editors thus had much in common.[26] Since Susa Gates lived in Provo, Utah, forty-five miles south of Salt Lake City, the two women maintained a lively correspondence, which revealed their shared interest in the NCW.[27]

Both women experienced the embarrassment of depending on outside funding for their involvement in the councils, an unpleasant situation which did not, however, deter them from their commitment to the "Council Idea" and their shared sense of the importance of keeping Mormon representation in these two important organizations. Both women hoped to attend the second quinquennial meeting of the ICW in London, but neither, by January 1899, had any assurance that funding would be forthcoming. While seldom disclosing who or what organization underwrote her travel expenses, Emmeline probably depended on the largesse of friends as much as on Relief Society or Church funding. This year proved to be particularly challenging for her. Because she had had difficulty obtaining the means to attend the February NCW meeting in Washington, she was thus less than optimistic about obtaining more funds to travel to England. Susa Gates, a devoted acolyte of Emmeline's at that time who was less pressured to attend, was adamant that means should be found for Emmeline to make the trip. "Zion has never needed your wise help more than now," she assured Emmeline."[28] But Susa Gates, as it turned out, was the first one to obtain funding. Through the generosity of the Young Ladies' MIA and its general president, Elmina Taylor, Gates, a member of the board, was guaranteed a place at the international meeting.

Not only was Emmeline's trip to London still in doubt as late as May, so was her participation on the program, though she was a patron and officer of the NCW. When a second "World's Congress of Women," similar to the one held at the Columbian Exposition at the 1893 Chicago World's Fair, was proposed to be held in conjunction with the ICW London meeting, Emmeline sent to May Wright Sewall, vice president of the ICW and candidate for president, suggestions for several department meetings with subjects and speakers, similar to those held in Chicago six years earlier. But department meetings featuring individual organizations, as had been the previous pattern, were not to be the format of this congress, Emmeline learned. Sessions were to be arranged around the social themes of importance to the ICW with participants in each drawn from a variety of organizations. She therefore proposed a paper on the Relief Society that would be appropriate in a session dealing with humanitarian work.

To the surprise of Emmeline Wells, May Wright Sewall indicated that only one national representative could participate on any one theme, and she had already invited Margaret A. Caine, who would speak on the Relief Society's commitment to sericulture, to be that person. Susa Gates, eager to see that her friend was on the program, decided to submit Emmeline's name as a discussant in one of the sessions, and Sewall condescendingly invited Emmeline to participate in a session on charitable nursing. Emmeline was stunned by Sewall's rejection of her proposal and was unwilling to be a discussant in a session only ancillary to her primary interests.[29] But she was additionally perplexed a month later when Sewall invited Gates to be a presenter. These were slights Emmeline had never encountered before. Though Sewall later apologized for the "pain" she had caused her, Sewall's actions were inexplicable to Emmeline, who had presented papers or addressed the delegates at every convention she had attended.[30]

In the meantime, repercussions from the NCW debate over B. H. Roberts in January of that year made their way across the ocean to London, resurrecting anti-Mormon sensibilities there and causing May Sewall to sternly if unrealistically warn Susa Gates that the Latter-day Saint women who attended the international meeting should exercise the "utmost care" not to allow any discussion to occur that would reveal their association with Mormonism. There were many people, she believed, who had "not yet learned to disassociate from the Mormon Church the idea of plural marriage" as she herself had been able to do. Sewall reminded Gates that she had repeatedly supported Mormon women in the various organizations when efforts were made to exclude them. But she was emphatic about wanting to avoid any embarrassment caused by Gates's often ebullient public support of polygamy or by similar sentiments from any other Utah women who might attend the London meeting. Though she had appointed Gates acting chair of the press committee for the NCW meeting earlier that year, having developed a high regard for her abilities, Sewall was mortified when the *New York World* quoted Gates as saying before that meeting began that "she wished plural marriage were still within the law in Utah" so that her husband, who was only forty-two, "could now take a young wife."[31]

By the end of April, Emmeline Wells could "see no opening whatever [to go to London] unless the Lord puts it into the hearts of some who have means to assist me."[32] Having secured funding for herself, Susa Gates was still hopeful that means would be found for her friend. "I will go to the Presidency myself," she promised Emmeline. "Who better deserves favor, if it could be called a favor this act of justice than the woman who has labored incessantly for the good of the kingdom."[33] Justice in such matters, Emmeline knew by then, often rested on material means to obtain it. But ever philosophical about disappointment, Emmeline thought of the work involved in arranging for such a long absence and was half inclined to give up the search for funds. Yet, at age seventy-one, she knew this was an opportunity that would probably not come again. "Another quinquennial five years later would not be available to me," she wrote. But, she added, "I must be satisfied in my case."[34]

At virtually the last day in which she could make the necessary reservations to travel, she finally secured the amount necessary for the long voyage and time away. The Relief Society board voted to raise six hundred dollars for the trip, three dollars from each contributing ward.

Any additional money it raised would assist Margaret A. Caine to go as well.³⁵

Emmeline Wells attended a preparatory meeting of the NCW's executive committee in June before departing for England. The meeting was held in New York at the home of Fannie Humphreys Gaffney, the newly elected NCW president, with such women's leaders attending as Kate Waller Barrett, outgoing NCW president May Wright Sewall, Mary Lowe Dickinson, Elizabeth Grannis, and Sadie American. When nominations for subcommittee members were requested, Emmeline Wells nominated Emily Richards as a member of a committee to bring her on board the NCW, and Emmeline was nominated for the peace committee, an area of work that commanded much of her attention during the next few years.³⁶

When she finally embarked on the long voyage across the Atlantic, Emmeline was pleased to find on board Mrs. Gaffney with some of her family as well as an actress of some renown, Mary Chase. With particular pleasure, Emmeline Wells struck up a conversation with Rudyard Kipling, who was traveling with his wife and family to Europe. Only a few days of seasickness marred an otherwise pleasant crossing.³⁷

Emmeline was the last of sixteen Utah women to travel to England for the quinquennial. Six of them were participants: Susa Young Gates and Margaret A. Caine were presenting papers; Elizabeth C. McCune, Lucy B. Young (Susa's mother), and Jean Clara Holbrook were patrons of the NCW and therefore entitled to attend the ICW meetings in a nonvoting capacity; Emmeline would be busy in her position as second recording secretary of the NCW.³⁸

Though neither Susa Gates nor Emmeline Wells felt that the new NCW president, Fanny Gaffney, had either the brilliance or authoritative manner of her predecessor, the two were heartened by Gaffney's genuine offer of support in London. She would be adamant, she promised, about putting "her foot firmly on any attempt to discriminate against American women."³⁹ The titled women of Great Britain did indeed show disdain for the Americans, officers and delegates alike, as was clearly demonstrated when May Wright Sewall gave a plenary address in Queen's Hall. Last on the program, she spoke to a clearly diminished audience. When those who remained began clapping loudly before she had concluded, the Americans were at first nonplused, but they quickly discovered that the clapping was a signal that the audience had heard enough.

As Utah delegate Elizabeth McCune readily observed, there was "quite a jealousy between the two nations." Susa Gates described this tension in a letter to Young Ladies' MIA General President Elmina Taylor. "Mrs. Sewall, Miss Anthony, and in fact all of them are treated very queerly by these English high-born dames. I tell you there is serious trouble here in regard to getting Mrs. Sewall elected president of the ICW; these English women feel it would be an insult for a plain American woman to be Pres. over the heads of Countesses and titled women." Moreover, she complained, "there was a strong effort made to prevent all of us from getting any invitations to social functions." They were thus gratified when the hospitality committee rectified that intended social snub, and all of the women received "far more invitations than they could accept."[40] All but Emmeline, according to Susa's account. "Aunt Em has suffered everything. No invitations, no notice, nothing but coldness."[41] Emmeline's own account, however, seems to belie this observation. Though she did spend much of her free time alone, by preference, exploring the streets of London, she also attended a number of social functions between meetings. Moreover, her diary reveals a woman enjoying herself immensely.

For nine days, meetings of the ICW alternated with sessions of the congress. Emmeline Wells eagerly attended both. She supported her two Mormon friends when they delivered their papers and perfunctorily noted that Susa Young Gates read hers on "The Scientific Treatment of Domestic Service," to "much applause," but was sorry to note that Margaret Caine "gave her address [on sericulture] and made a failure."[42]

Wells declined a last-minute invitation to speak at a session chaired by May Wright Sewall. Still smarting from the earlier slight, she chose not to participate without sufficient notice or preparation. Despite Sewall's exhaustive work for the National and International Councils,

Emmeline was well aware that she was not a favorite among the women of either group.[43] Emmeline did, however, agree to participate as a discussant in a session addressing the work and importance of benevolent societies, a field she loved and about which she was well suited to speak without extensive preparation.[44] Drawing a large crowd, the session was held in Convocation Hall in the Dean's Yard of Westminster Abbey, "the most select and noted of all the places of meeting," according to Susa Gates.[45] The session was chaired by Beatrice Webb, widely known in both Great Britain and America as a socialist reformer.[46] "There," Emmeline recorded in her diary, "I had the opportunity to speak and to explain our Relief Society fully its date of organization its thorough practical work its halls and buildings in this and other countries [and] its practical work for those needing assistance."[47] "She was listened to with marked attention," Susa Gates observed, "and the Chairman offered her an increase of the allotted time at the close of her remarks, which, however, was not accepted."[48] Emmeline had not been a "presenter," but she took full advantage as a discussant to say her piece on the Relief Society.

The intermingling of sessions and socials, of entertainment and education, inadvertently denied the congress a clear-cut identity. Its objectives, however, were noble enough. Vying for the participants' favor, time, and attention were sixty-four sessions held in five different halls. During the sessions, more than two hundred fifty papers on various topics were read in front of a total audience of more than twenty-five hundred. The ICW meetings themselves brought two hundred delegates from twenty-four countries.[49]

The plenary sessions on peace and woman suffrage introduced the Utah representatives to unfamiliar audience responses: cheering, hissing, and the now familiar impatient clapping to silence lengthy speakers.[50] Nothing short of a standing ovation, however, could reflect the respect and admiration an audience of three thousand showed for eighty-year-old Susan B. Anthony. While woman suffrage was not a high priority for all the delegates, even the British recognized the international stature acquired by the stately Anthony in her crusade for woman's rights in America.[51]

The newspapers did not fail to notice that, even as this large gathering of women was making a claim for political equality, the British Parliament rejected a proposal permitting women to be elected as counselors or aldermen in the new borough councils.[52] Though unable to participate on the borough level of government, British women and, indeed, all of the executive committee members demonstrated their gift for politics in the business meetings of the ICW. Because of her own political experience, Emmeline Wells was not surprised to discover that behind closed doors women were not above adopting the political machinations commonly associated with local politics. While they recognized the formidable abilities and experience of ICW vice president May Sewall, a logical successor to the ICW presidency, she was not a unanimous choice to succeed the popular Countess of Aberdeen. Though Sewall was ultimately elected, that closed-door session revealed a competitive and aggressive spirit in the committee, a strong strain of nationalism, and unpleasant wrangling over every issue. The whole procedure exposed Emmeline to the political realities in bringing together highly nationalistic delegates to an international arena.[53] Nationalism was a traditional impediment to global agreement, particularly in politics and economics. These reformers found that social welfare added its own challenge in creating universal sisterhood through the ICW.

Aiding in the creation of international personal relationships, however, were some of London society's most lavish receptions, given by British nobility and ICW officers. In addition, various British clubs and societies sponsored more than forty teas, luncheons, and receptions for individual groups of delegates and participants. Journalists covering the congress could hardly ignore the inordinate number of European nobility in attendance nor slight the splendor of the grand soirees held in some of London's most elegant homes and finest establishments. Their detailed descriptions of the events, the elegant settings, and the apparel and jewelry of the hostesses probably attracted more readers than the back page reviews of the papers presented and important global issues discussed. Even the *Deseret News* succumbed to the wired reports of the splendor of the socials, placing an Associated

Press interview with Susan B. Anthony and the Countess of Aberdeen under the headline, "London Society for the Week." The brief dispatch did manage, however, to convey how important these two leaders were to the congress.[54]

Most of the Utah delegates were captivated by the display of wealth and high culture they encountered at these affairs. Emmeline Wells, already moved by the collective intelligence, political savvy, and self-confidence demonstrated at the congress, came to acknowledge the power of wealth and social position. The pageantry of nobility, a stunning packaging for the London meeting, introduced her to another arena of female status and influence. Her usual aplomb in unfamiliar social settings deserted her temporarily in the presence of such studied opulence and the deference it commanded. The great houses, the marble-and-gold interiors, the magnificent antiques and paintings, the elegant dinners and teas, the handsome clothing, and the exquisite jewels bedazzled her. "It does seem remarkable," she mused, "that we should have such an opportunity given to us—from the very far away but we feel the Lord has done it."[55]

The opening reception at the elegant Stafford House, with its splendid display of titled ladies—including the Duchess of Sutherland, the Countess of Aberdeen, and the Countess of Warwick—made an impressive beginning. More than a thousand guests met the distinguished hostesses at the foot of a grand staircase and were then ushered up the marble stairway, lit at every step by huge candelabra. Charlotte Perkins Gilman, whose path-breaking feminist treatise, *Women and Economics,* was the talk of the congress, arrived just after Emmeline Wells and Susa Gates, whom she had met two years earlier in Omaha, Nebraska. Drawing near the grand stairway, she observed the two women "plainly dressed and looking timidly up at the array of tiaras on the landing." Undaunted by the regal panoply herself, she offered to accompany them.[56] Wells had been impressed with Gilman at their first meeting, considering her to be "one of the brightest women of [the] nineteenth century," and was grateful to see that Gilman "really seemed to take extra pains for some of our Utah party."[57]

More receptions and socials followed, but none quite equaled that given by Lady Rothschild and her daughter-in-law Mrs. Leopold de Rothschild at Gunnersbury Park, their elegant residence and private park on the outskirts of London. The gathering was "the most magnificent . . . of all we have attended" declared Emmeline. "Everything was on the grandest scale imaginable."[58] The newspapers agreed, describing the event in alluring detail, as did Emmeline Wells and Susa Gates in their respective publications. Four bands, strolling magicians, trained dogs, and a circus ring with "lady performers" entertained the twelve hundred guests, who enjoyed delicacies of every kind served under the large, colored tents that dotted the grounds. It was all "beyond description," Emmeline wrote, "in mind and brain and heart forever engrafted."[59]

The *piece de resistance*, however, was the unexpected invitation to visit Windsor Castle, where Queen Victoria had agreed to greet the guests from the congress. About two hundred women boarded a special train to Windsor, where they walked up the long drive to the castle and waited until it was time for the queen to take her afternoon ride. Lining the driveway leading from the castle to the entrance gates, the visitors eagerly awaited a glimpse of the queen. Finally she emerged in her carriage, waving to the women, stopping to speak to Lady Aberdeen and to view a group of Hindu and Parsee women dressed in their native costumes. After she had passed out of the drive, the guests were invited into St. George's Hall for tea. "It was a fitting close to the great International gathering of women," Emmeline Wells observed.[60]

While the major London papers gave primary coverage to the closing days of Parliament, which coincided with the congress, such a gathering of women could not be entirely ignored. It particularly drew the attention of London's numerous women's and working-class newspapers, which covered the congress in detail. The *Humanitarian*, a monthly review of "sociological science," gave its "Notes and Comments" column repeatedly to news of the congress, perhaps because of the personal interest of its editor, Victoria Woodhull Martin, the controversial figure in the American suffrage movement of some years earlier.[61] "A quarter of a century ago it was hardly possible for a woman to be heard in public," the *Humanitarian* noted, asserting that "the fact that such a Congress has been possible is an evidence of the ground gained by the woman's movement . . . and a tribute to those early pioneers who suffered so much for the cause."[62]

The *Englishwoman's Review* characterized the congress as youthful, impatient, voluble, and perhaps too diverse and extensive to be as effective as it might have been. As an organ for social and industrial questions, the *Review* focused on the political and legislative sessions, especially those addressing legislation relating to working-class women.[63] Though industrial workers did not represent themselves at the congress, issues relating to their employment had long been on the agenda of social reformers. Class and gender intersected as many of the middle- and upper-class women of the convention had devoted themselves and their organizations to aid working-class women.

Back in Utah, the *Deseret News* rehearsed the wide range of topics under discussion, recognizing that women were now engaged in debating questions in the realms of science, emigration, the professions, and even "politics with the same enthusiasm with which they would take up questions pertaining to education and social affairs." Though it praised Utah's delegates and had been supportive of the strong advocacy by Mormon women for a variety of causes, it incongruously claimed to be worried about "women with rather pronounced views," who were "not representative of womankind in general" and who, if given "too much latitude," might hinder rather than advance woman's cause. The paper seemed more comfortable with the sessions on international peace, a topic unifying the commitment of the conference delegates more than any other. Women's influence as wives and mothers, the *News* optimistically affirmed, would solve "all the problems connected with that question."[64]

For those who first envisioned and then executed the plans for the congress, it was nothing short of a triumph. The personal and national quibbling faded against the excitement and enthusiasm of the participants. Nor could the detractors who derided its unevenness in presentation, its lack of a consistent underlying principle, or who felt its scope of issues "unwomanly" or its claims to "universal sisterhood" ephemeral and idealistic, diminish the general euphoria of the congress's planners or the enlarged vision of its participants.[65]

Understanding the questions of "national autonomy" and "racial independence" as well as the differing agendas of its constituency, the ICW had chosen to emphasize its policy of restraint in exercising power over auxiliary members and their own policies and programs. With organizations ranging from moral reform societies and religious auxiliaries to the highly politicized woman suffrage associations, seeking consensus on procedure and objectives, strained the most ecumenical vision and diplomacy. As newly elected ICW president May Wright Sewall discovered, adjudicating both personal and political differences among the affiliated groups "really forced the entire Executive, nay, the Council itself, to study large questions of the kind that engage statesmen."[66] Internationalism would not be easy.

Emmeline Wells was ecstatic about the conference and certain of its influence and the future of the ICW. "That greater love and charity will prevail among womankind cannot be doubted," she wrote, "when such a fraternal feeling is fostered and cherished as that which prevailed so largely during the entire sessions of the Council and Congress." She was convinced that "ultimately a great federation of the sisterhood of the world will come to pass," and the world would be the beneficiary.[67]

Sometime later Emmeline Wells was alarmed to learn that Elmina Taylor had begun expressing doubts about the value of maintaining membership in the NCW. "I do hope that sentiment will not gain ground," Wells wrote to Susa Gates.[68] This fear would be her call to arms in the challenging decades ahead.

This two-month overseas excursion had been both a private and professional venture of extraordinary meaning and value to Emmeline Wells. It was in many ways a personal triumph, a vindication of sorts, of the causes to which she had spent her mature years. Her forum had moved beyond Utah, beyond Washington, to London, and to the world outside through the representation that gathered on that significant occasion. To an international audience she had been given opportunity to explain her people, to praise their good works, and to commend their intelligence and capability in directing humanitarian projects. Moreover, she had spoken as a woman who possessed a political advantage, the right to vote, something that few other women enjoyed, achieved to a large extent through her own leadership and unflagging determination.

On the homeward-bound ship, Emmeline reflected on the two months that had just passed and the years that had preceded them. "How many years have flown and what stirring events have transpired during the last few years. My life seems wonderfully changed and developed. What further changes are yet to come I know not. Certainly a remarkable destiny and a most romantic life."[69]

At age seventy-one, Emmeline could well have enjoyed the ICW congress as a climax to a full and contributing life and looked forward to the quiet years of old age—but she would be found in the trenches for two more decades.

An earlier version of this chapter was published as "'The Power of Combination': Emmeline B. Wells and the National and International Councils of Women," BYU Studies 33, no. 4 (1993): 646–73.

Notes

1. "Home Again," *Woman's Exponent* 28 (August 15, September 1, 1899): 45.
2. See chapter 15 for details of B. H. Roberts's 1898 election.
3. The other members of the Utah delegation were Carrie S. Thomas, Emily S. Richards, Minnie J. Snow, Mae Taylor, and Susa Young Gates.
4. The *Salt Lake Tribune* reported on each day's activities. See "Women Fight Roberts: National Council Will Discuss His Case—Lively Session Promised," *Salt Lake Tribune*, February 14, 1899, 1; "Salt Lake Women Heard: Deliver Address before National Council of Women," *Salt Lake Tribune,* February 15, 1899, 1; "Women in Council," *Salt Lake Tribune,* February 16, 1899, 1; "Mrs. Wells is Honored," *Salt Lake Tribune*, February 16, 1899, 3; "Fight over Roberts: National Council of Women Discusses His Case—Contest Was a Fiery One," *Salt Lake Tribune*, 1; "Women in Council: Final Public Meeting of National Gathering in Washington," *Salt Lake Tribune,* February 20, 1899, 2. See also the *Deseret News,* February 16, 1899, for more about Wells's election and the events of that day's discussion.
5. Elizabeth B. Grannis would be a major player in the prolonged effort of several women's groups to obtain a constitutional amendment against polygamy. See "Fighting for Roberts: Utah Delegation Working for the Polygamist," *Salt Lake Tribune*, February 18, 1899, 1.

6. "Women's Council Votes to Bar Out Roberts," *New York Journal*, February 18, 1899, 1. See also "Women and Polygamy," *Deseret News*, February 18, 1899, 5. The *Woman's Tribune* 13 (February 25, 1899): 14, however, responded to Snow's threat of withdrawal: "That any organization would withdraw from the Council because its own thought on every topic was not adopted would indicate a retarded development which would practically unfit the body for inclusion in the Council idea."

7. Emmeline B. Wells, Diary, February 11, 1899, L. Tom Perry Special Collections, Harold B. Lee Library, Brigham Young University, Provo, Utah.

8. "Fighting for Roberts: Utah Delegation Working for the Polygamist," *Salt Lake Tribune*, February 18, 1899, 1. There is some ambiguity about Emmeline's membership on the committee because of contradictory statements in the various reports of the meeting. Most indicate she was involved.

9. The minority resolution stated: "Whereas As the passage of the Edmunds Bill (so-called) established the law of monogamic marriage as binding upon all citizens of the United States; therefore, Resolved, That no person shall be allowed to hold a place in a law-making body of the nation who is not in this, and in all other matters, a law-abiding citizen." It was signed by representatives of the WCTU, National Association of Loyal Women of American Liberty, the National Free Baptist Woman's Missionary Society, and National Christian League for the Promotion of Social Purity. The majority resolution presented by Emmeline Wells and Ann Cannon read: "Whereas the National Council of Women of the United States stands for the highest ideals of domestic and civic virtue, as well as for the observance of law in all the departments, both State and national; therefore Resolved, That no person should be allowed to hold a place in any law-making body of the nation who is not a law-abiding citizen." As quoted in Susa Young Gates, "The Recent Triennial in Washington," *Young Woman's Journal* 10 (May 1899): 204–6; "Women's Council Votes to Bar Out Roberts," *New York Journal*, February 18, 1899, 1; and "Fought over Roberts: National Council of Women Discusses His Case—Contest Was a Fiery One," *Salt Lake Tribune*, February 19, 1899, 1, which includes a description of the "fierce struggle over this issue."

10. "Women's Council Votes to Bar Out Roberts," 1. See also "Women's Great Fight Today—National Council Divided as to Disposition of the Roberts Issue," *New York Journal*, February 14, 1899.

11. Gates, "The Recent Triennial in Washington," 208–9.

12. Quoted in Gates, "The Recent Triennial in Washington," 209.

13. "Women's Council Votes to Bar Out Roberts," 1.

14. "Fought over Roberts," 1.

15. "Fought over Roberts," 1. Susa Young Gates, it was reported, in particular, resorted to an emotional appeal, weeping during her argument and appealing to the friendship and compassion of the council members.

16. "Women's Council Votes to Bar Out Roberts," 1.

17. Wells, Diary, February 26, 1899.

18. Ida Husted Harper, *Life and Works of Susan B. Anthony*, 3 vols. (Indianapolis: Hollenbeck, 1908), 3:1150–53; see also "Miss Anthony on Roberts," *Woman's Exponent* 28 (November 15, December 1, 1899): 80.

19. "Fight against Roberts," *Salt Lake Tribune*, February 26, 1899, 1.

20. "Condemning Roberts," *Salt Lake Tribune*, February 21, 1899, 1.

21. "Opposition to Roberts," *Deseret News*, February 20, 1899, 2; "Denounce the Polygamist," *Salt Lake Tribune*, March 4, 1899, 4.

22. "Facts about Roberts," *Salt Lake Tribune*, February 28, 1899, 1; "The Roberts Agitation," *Salt Lake Tribune*, March 7, 1899, 4; "Condemn Roberts," *Salt Lake Tribune*, March 17, 1899 1.

23. The full text of the House Committee report is in "Antipolygamy Amendment," *Salt Lake Tribune*, March 6, 1899, 2. For additional comments, see "Condemning Roberts," 1; "The Roberts Amendment," *Salt Lake Tribune*, March 5, 1899, 12; and "The Roberts Case," *Salt Lake Tribune*, March 10, 1899, 4.

24. Details of the event are in "Public Reception," *Woman's Exponent* 38 (March 1910): 61–62.

25. Emmeline B. Wells to B. H. Roberts, March 20, 1910, B. H. Roberts Papers, Special Collections, J. Willard Marriott Library, University of Utah, Salt Lake City.

26. Susa, a daughter of Brigham Young, had earlier requested a creative partnership with Emmeline on the *Woman's Exponent,* but Emmeline had declined her assistance. Susa was born in 1856 in Salt Lake City and pursued a multitude of public causes in addition to bearing thirteen children, six of whom lived to maturity. For short biographies, see Rebecca Foster Cornwall, "Susa Y. Gates," in *Sister Saints,* ed. Vicky Burgess-Olson (Provo, Utah: Brigham Young University Press, 1978), 63–93; and Andrew Jenson, ed., *Latter-day Saint Biographical Encyclopedia: A Compilation of Biographical Sketches of Prominent Men and Women in the Church of Jesus Christ of Latter-day Saints,* 4 vols. (Salt Lake City: Andrew Jenson History, 1901–36), 2:626–29.

27. Their correspondence is catalogued under the Susa Young Gates Papers, Church Archives, The Church of Jesus Christ of Latter-day Saints, Salt Lake City.

28. Susa Y. Gates to Emmeline B. Wells, January 23, 1899, Gates Papers.

29. May Wright Sewall to Susa Young Gates, January 10, February 28, and April 1, 24, 1899; Emmeline B. Wells to Susa Young Gates, January 21, 1899; Susa Young Gates to Emmeline B. Wells, January 23, 1899, Gates Papers. Sewall's rejection may have related to the fact that Emmeline Wells was well known as a plural wife and as a defender of polygamy. The Roberts affair had also thrust polygamy into the spotlight again, just six months before the meetings began and her role in the controversy was well publicized.

30. May Wright Sewall to Susa Young Gates, April 1, 1899, Gates Papers. Susa Gates, as a member of the press committee, had become the chief correspondent between Sewall and Mormon women during this period.

31. May Wright Sewall to Susa Young Gates, January 10, 31, 1899, Gates Papers. Sewall was adamant in her feelings that B. H. Roberts had no place in Congress and that polygamy was a detestable practice.

32. Emmeline B. Wells to Susa Young Gates, April 25, 1899, Gates Papers.

33. Susa Young Gates to Emmeline B. Wells, April 26, 1899, Gates Papers.

34. Wells to Gates, April 25, 1899, Gates Papers.

35. Special Meeting of the Board of Directors, May 17, 1899, 269–70, National Woman's Relief Society Record, Church Archives.

36. Wells, Diary, June 7, 1899.

37. Wells, Diary, June 14–21, 1899.

38. The other Utahns were Priscilla Jennings, her daughter May, and her granddaughter Lucille Jennings; Carrie Thomas and daughter Kate; Josephine Booth; Amanda Knight and daughter Inez; Lydia Dunford Alder; and Emma Lucy Gates, Susa Young Gates's daughter. Susa Young Gates, "International Council of Women," *Young Woman's Journal* 10 (October 1899): 437–38.

39. Susa Young Gates to "Beloved friend [Elmina Taylor]," June 13, 1899, Gates Papers.

40. Susa Young Gates to Elmina Taylor, June 29, 1899, Gates Papers. Particularly disdainful of the American women was the wife of the Bishop of London. She was openly hostile to May Wright Sewall and showed her displeasure with Susa when meeting her. One British woman, however, who befriended the Mormons was a Mrs. Montefiore, wife of the nephew of Moses Montefiore, the great benefactor of the Jews in Jerusalem.

41. Gates to Taylor, June 29, 1899.

42. Wells, Diary, June 28, July 3, 1899. Susa Gates's talk was summarized in "Report on International Council and Congress," *Woman's Tribune* 16 (September 1899): 65.

43. Wells, Diary, June 30, 1899.

44. Wells, Diary, July 1, 1899.

45. Gates, "International Council of Women," 443.

46. Beatrice and Sidney Webb had visited America, including Salt Lake City, the previous year, a visit that Beatrice recorded. She was particularly interested in meeting Utah state senator Martha Hughes Cannon and noted in her journal Cannon's election victory over her husband, Angus, and Emmeline Wells, both of whom had opposed Cannon. She was, therefore, acquainted at least with Emmeline's name and with Mormonism before the London meeting. See David A. Shannon, ed., *Beatrice Webb's American Diary, 1898* (Madison: University of Wisconsin Press, 1963), 126–36.

47. Wells, Diary, July 1, 1899. See also "Women in Social Life," *The Transactions of the Social Section of the Congress of Women,* 7 vols. (London: T. Fisher Unwin, 1900), 7:192.

48. Gates, "International Council of Women," 443.

49. Handbook of the International Congress, International Council of Women, 1899.

50. Wells, Diary, June 27, 1899; Gates, "International Council of Women," 443; "Women Are in Council Today," *Deseret News,* June 27, 1899, 1.

51. "The International Congress of Women," *Queen, the Lady's Newspaper,* July 1, 1899, 36, and July 8, 1899, 99, Faw.cett Library, City of London Polytechnic, London; and "Strike! Fear Not! Strike and Slay!" *Shafts: A Paper for Women* 7 (July–September 1899): 52–71, Fawcett Library.

52. *The Englishwoman's Review of Social and Industrial Questions* 30 (July 15, 1899): 156, Fawcett Library; see also "No Office Holding for Women," *Deseret News,* June 27, 1899, 3.

53. Wells, Diary, June 29, July 4, 1899.

54. "London Society for the Week," *Deseret News,* July 8, 1899, 1.

55. Wells, Diary, June 28, 1899.

56. Charlotte Perkins Gilman, *The Living of Charlotte Perkins Gilman* (New York: D. Appleton-Century, 1935), 263–64. For details of this and other socials, see "International Congress of Women," *Queen,* 36; Gates, "International Council of Women," 439; Susa Y. Gates, "Biography of Lucy B. Young," typescript, Utah State Historical Society, Salt Lake City; and *The International Council of Women, Report of Council Transactions,* 7 vols. (London: T. Fisher Unwin, 1900), 7:286–92.

57. "Home Again," *Woman's Exponent* 28 (August 15, September 1, 1899): 45.

58. Wells, Diary, July 4, 1899; "Home Again," 45.

59. Wells, Diary, July 4, 1899; "Home Again," 45; Gates, "International Council of Women," 446.

60. "Home Again," 45; Gates, "International Council of Women," 449–50; Wells, Diary, July 7, 1899.

61. Victoria Woodhull's liberal and often shocking proposals in the name of women's liberation, especially her advocacy of free love, quickly became a detriment to the suffrage cause in the United States. For a brief overview of her life, see Geoffrey Blodgett, "Victoria Claflin Woodhull," in *Notable American Women, 1607–1950: A Biographical Dictionary,* ed. Edward T. James, Janet Wilson James, and Paul S. Boyer, 3 vols. (Cambridge: Belknap Press of Harvard University Press, 1971), 3:652–55.

62. "Notes and Comments," *Humanitarian* 15 (July 1899): 65; "Notes and Comments," *Humanitarian* 15 (August 1899): 139, Fawcett Library.

63. "The International Congress of Women," *Englishwoman's Review* 30 (July 15, 1899): 153–54, 158. The paper was particularly impressed with the arguments of Alexandra Gripenberg of Germany, who elicited the strongest response from the audience for her "extremely powerful paper" on the rights of working women. "Women cannot ask for equal rights," the baroness argued, "and at the same time claim indulgence on the score of sex. Grownup women ought to have the right to protect themselves." At that time, protective legislation for women was heatedly debated in the United States and spawned an opposing movement two decades later, centered on an equal rights amendment, which would eliminate any distinction between men and women workers.

64. "Council of Women," *Deseret News,* June 29, 1899, 4.

65. See, for example, Frances H. Low, "A Woman's Criticism of the Women's Congress," *Nineteenth Century* 46 (August 1899): 192–202, British Library, London; "Council of Women," *Deseret News,* June 29, 1879, 4; and "Notes and Comments—The International Congress of Women," *Humanitarian* 15 (August 1899): 139.

66. May Wright Sewall, ed., "International Council of Women," *Report of Transactions of the Executive Council, 1890–1904* (Boston: n.p., 1909), xviii, xix.

67. "Home Again," 46.

68. Emmeline Wells to Susa Young Gates, undated letter, 1900, Gates Papers.

69. Wells, Diary, August 8, 1899. Her return home with Susa Gates was noted in "Utah Women Return Home," *Deseret News,* August 22, 1899, 8.

Chapter 17

The Elusive Sisterhood

*If our sisters could only comprehend that
we can never be "polished stones, etc" without some preparation—
and that we must meet and mingle with people
to remove prejudice.*[1]

As a new century dawned, Emmeline Wells looked back on the previous half-century with pride in the accomplishments of women. "American women have brought about great changes in the last fifty years," she wrote as the nineteenth century closed, "the advance toward a higher civilization, a purer and better government is largely due to the women reformers and educators, not only here, but in other countries." With great optimism she envisioned "the future business of the world conducted by men and women in co-operative movements and institutions.... There will be greater improvement," she was convinced, "when women not only give advice and lend their influence, but when they actually manipulate side by side the *modus operandi* of the great schemes now almost entirely in the hands of men."[2]

Utah had been in the union of states for four years, and, with the exception of the Roberts election, Utahns had moved forward once again in a cooperative effort to develop the state and remove the points of contention of the past century. Emmeline Wells had been more than a spectator of the tumultuous events that had altered the Mormon way of life in Utah and at seventy-two did not intend to concede to age.

She could not have anticipated, however, that her work on behalf of women would continue for another twenty-one years.

Though the woman suffrage campaign was successfully behind her and most of the old-guard suffragists were leaving or had left the scene of national activity, she had chosen not to diminish her public work but rather to shift it to the new and wider field of activity that the National and International Councils of Women offered. The newly formed Utah chapter of the Daughters of the Revolution (DR) (1896) and the Mothers Congress (1898) as well as the Daughters of Utah Pioneers (1901) also claimed a portion of her time and interest. Though no longer serving as their president, she still attended meetings of the two literary associations she had organized in Salt Lake City, the Reapers Club and the Utah Women's Press Club, and she participated in the Utah Federation of Women's Clubs. Though inclusive of their older members, most of these organizations were led by a younger generation of workers. Emmeline had entered the ranks of highly respected and valued elder stateswomen whose intelligence and experience were readily recognized. "It does seem quite remarkable," she mused in 1901, "that I should have had the attention of so many noted people & be sought after by those of our own faith as well after the obscurity in which I had lived during the time of raising my family & really when apparently it would have been more to my life and helped to awaken and develop ideas and sentiments to aid others, but God knows the best and withheld from me much others enjoyed."[3]

In April 1900 Emmeline traveled to New York to attend the national meeting of the DR. "I do not know how we shall be received," she worried, "as the Roberts case is in everybody's mouth and people seem to have no regard for our feelings whatever but we can hold our own nevertheless."[4] Repeated tests of this determination awaited her. Barred from membership in the older and more prestigious Daughters of the American Revolution (DAR), in November 1898 Mormon women had organized a chapter of the DR, which had welcomed their membership. Always more than just a member of any organization to which she belonged, Emmeline served first as regent and later as chaplain of the Wasatch branch.[5] For this, the eighth annual meeting of the DR,

Emmeline wrote the report of the Utah Society that was presented by Mabelle Snow, another representative from Utah. The delegates were treated to visits to the historic sites in and around New York and a trip to Philadelphia, and several delegates visited the nation's capital and Mount Vernon. Always cautious in her expectations, Emmeline found the reception tendered to the Utah women far more cordial than she had anticipated and her report of their Utah activities fully in line with those of other chapters. The principal business of the meeting centered on the possibility of a merger with the DAR. Emmeline doubted the consummation of such a union under the plan proposed since the DR, she felt, "would gain very little for what they would have to surrender."[6] Others felt the same and the merger did not take place.

While in New York, Emmeline visited Fanny Gaffney, president of the National Council of Women (NCW), and held a "confidential conversation with her." Together they also attended the Domestic Household Science National Conference. Ever a joiner, Emmeline became a member of the association.[7] Though she found Fanny Gaffney to be affable and socially well connected, an advantage for a NCW president, she was, as previously noted, less impressed with her leadership or intellectuality. She had dismissed Gaffney's article in *Harper's Monthly* as "really nothing new at all" and found Gaffney's denigration of "self-sacrifice" to be demeaning to her hard-working constituents.[8]

Emmeline traveled east again in November that year, accompanied by Elizabeth McCune, to attend the executive committee meeting of the NCW in Minneapolis, where she was scheduled to make a presentation. She was also designated the investigating commissioner to the Philippine Islands. The assignment required her to study and report on the country's social and domestic conditions affecting women and families. It was part of the International Council of Women's (ICW) intention to do similar studies in all of the island possessions of the United States. Although this new responsibility would not require travel to the islands, Emmeline approached it vigorously, seeking information from all the sources to which she had access and filing her reports as requested.[9] While in Minneapolis she spent time again with Fanny Gaffney, reinforcing a friendship that would earn Gaffney's support of Latter-day Saint membership in the NCW.

After her memorable visit to Washington in February 1901 as a guest of Utah Senator Thomas F. Kearns, she was dismayed when he later became a moving party in the reinvigorated anti-Mormon movement. Returning home from that adventure in April 1901, Emmeline immersed herself in the popular peace and international arbitration movement supported by the NCW. The delay of a much-anticipated visit of May Wright Sewall, now president of the ICW, allowed Emmeline time to travel extensively for the Relief Society. By early July, however, she was back in Salt Lake City concentrating on finalizing plans for Sewall's visit later that month.

Emmeline Wells, as second recording secretary, and Susa Young Gates, as a member of the press committee of the NCW, shared responsibility for the visit. Since Susa lived in Provo, many of the arrangements fell to Emmeline. Sewall was herself eager to visit Utah, a stop on her way to the Pacific Coast. "I believe there are true hearts—not a few—in Utah who wish very much for me to come," she had written to Susa Gates earlier that year. "I believe if on the whole the sentiment of solidarity, which is at the very core of the Council, would be nurtured and strengthened by my visit to Utah, that the conditions for making the visit will arrive."[10]

Emmeline Wells carried the load of providing a reception commensurate with Sewall's international stature. Her friends and allies rallied and planned a full schedule of meetings and socials.[11] This included a visit with President Lorenzo Snow of The Church of Jesus Christ of Latter-day Saints (LDS Church), at which time Sewall told him how much good was being done by the Church's delegates to the council, especially Emmeline Wells, Susa Gates, and, of course, his wife, Minnie J. Snow.

Sewall's arrival on July 12 was heralded with the usual collection of prominent women. She was then escorted directly to the temporary home of her hostess, Elizabeth McCune, who was living in the Gardo House, a lovely mansion in Salt Lake City built by Brigham Young, while her own new home was being constructed. Banquets, receptions, and the customary excursion to Saltair filled the social hours. But Sewall was in Salt Lake City to preach internationalism and this she had opportunity to do in the Salt Lake Tabernacle to a standing-room-only audience, again in the Assembly Hall to an invited audience, and once more to an equally enthusiastic audience in Provo as the guest of Susa Gates, who was responsible for writing a report of the visit for members of the NCW.[12] At Sewall's request, Wells made sure that a number of Gentiles were invited to all of the scheduled events.[13]

When the public activities ended, Emmeline and Sewall spent a quiet evening alone discussing the many experiences that had brought them together. Despite Emmeline's hard feelings toward Sewall relating to the London ICW convention, the two women had put that unpleasantness behind them. "Needless to say," Emmeline wrote of their visit, "we considered it a 'red letter day'—a time we had both looked forward to for many years."[14] The visit also helped to underscore Sewall's support of the Latter-day Saint women's organizations against the nascent movement to exclude them from membership in the two councils. She was also anxious to secure a commitment from Mormon women for their continuing support of the work of the councils. The two Latter-day Saint women's organizations, Relief Society and Young Ladies' Mutual Improvement Association (MIA), had proven to be dependable dues-paying members and diligent agents of the goals of the councils. While Emmeline did not raise much money to compensate her guest for her expenses, she was hopeful her visit would awaken the dormant interest in affiliating with the National Council.

Out of Sewall's visit Emmeline found a need for putting "new ideas into the work." This included "a progressive woman's paper along all lines, and not confine[ing] itself to clubs or any one organization." Though regretting the lack of funds to launch such a venture, she envisioned a publication transcending the boundaries that defined the mission of the *Woman's Exponent,* a paper that represented "the women of the world in a large and broad sense."[15] She had evidently caught the enlarged vision of May Wright Sewall, whose work for women now rested on the possibilities of an international alliance of women even more comprehensive than the ICW. Apprising Susa Gates of this aspiration, Emmeline found her eager to capitalize on the idea, offering to co-edit such a publication or, alternatively, helping Emmeline expand the horizon of the *Woman's Exponent,* despite her continuing association with the *Young Woman's Journal,* which she had founded in 1889. Susa, in fact, asked Emmeline for permission to represent the *Exponent* as *her* magazine during her residency in New York while her husband served a mission there. Susa further suggested that Emmeline mention her name in connection with the *Exponent* whenever she met with Joseph F. Smith, a member of the First Presidency of the Church. Not waiting for Emmeline to make such an overture to President Smith, Susa wrote to him herself, expressing their ideas about a paper and receiving his unqualified support in every way but financial. Susa then suggested that Emmeline move to New York and publish an expanded *Woman's Exponent* there.[16] Nothing came of any of the suggestions, but the strong journalistic bent of these two women complemented their equal enthusiasm for bringing Mormon women more closely in touch with life beyond Utah's borders. Publications and participation in national women's groups, Emmeline still claimed, offered the best opportunity for diminishing the parochialism she feared.

The year concluded sadly for Emmeline Wells, however, with the death of LDS Church President Lorenzo Snow along with her friend, the well-loved Relief Society leader Zina D. H. Young. Both Snow and Young had been visionary and supportive of Emmeline's work. Emmeline and Zina Young had spent years together working on the central board of the Relief Society, and Emmeline had frequently served as her proxy at national women's meetings.

These two leaders were replaced by individuals both named Smith: Joseph F. Smith, successor to Lorenzo Snow as President of the LDS Church, and Bathsheba W. Smith, widow of Elder George A. Smith and successor to Zina D. H. Young as Relief Society General President. Emmeline was apprehensive about their interest in her work. "I doubt very much if Prest. Smith [Joseph F.] has as much confidence in what women can do, as Prest. Snow, or Prest. Cannon [Counselor George Q.]," Emmeline confided to Susa Gates. "There are so many things that want righting." And Bathsheba "can't understand these matters," Emmeline wrote, because "it is all new to her."[17] In the next few years she found herself frequently longing for "such women as Aunt Zina-Aunt Eliza [R.

Snow], Mother [Elizabeth Ann] Whitney." And Sister Isabella Horne, she added, "is worth a dozen of this younger lot."[18]

Bathsheba Smith called Emmeline Wells to be general secretary, a much more burdensome job than correspondence secretary. Emmeline, however, saw it as an opportunity to deepen her relationship with the new Relief Society president and perhaps convince her of the value of national affiliation for Latter-day Saint women. But this was not to be. Only occasionally did Bathsheba allow Relief Society funds to underwrite attendance at the national conventions nor did she ever attend herself.

Emmeline immediately felt the change of leadership styles from one of patience, conciliation, and vision to one of benign caretaking and reluctance to become involved in anything beyond local religious matters.[19] The makeup of the Relief Society board also changed as new and younger members were called to serve. Ironically, at a time when anti-Mormonism was invading the agenda of national women's organizations more than ever before, some of the older board members preferred to withdraw rather than defend Latter-day Saint membership in these organizations. Wanting to prove the Relief Society as independent from and equal to any other national association, they found many converts to this point of view. For Emmeline, maintaining membership was mandatory for Mormon women to achieve a standing among other women, to enjoy the respect from a national presence, and to erase the negative views they had so long sustained. From her exposure to national women's leaders Emmeline had learned that Mormon women were just as capable, intelligent, and forceful as other women and wanted them to be recognized for these qualities. She thus drew on her store of influence with ecclesiastical leaders to counter opposition at home, and she counted on the good will of national leaders to offset the well-orchestrated drive of influential national women's groups to force Mormon women out of their organizations. For many, however, polygamy still defined Latter-day Saint women.

Fighting on these two fronts, Susa Young Gates and Emmeline Wells led the battle to maintain connection, fearful of the detrimental effect of a return to isolation. Only with the defense of such prominent women as Susan B. Anthony, Elizabeth Cady Stanton, and Sara Andrews Spencer in the early days and May Wright Sewall, J. Ellen Foster, and Carrie Chapman Catt in later years could they succeed on the national level. These women lent their support not because they had been tolerant of polygamy; they had always been adamantly opposed to it. But the former supporters had disparaged all forms of marriage as the unequal yoking of men and women, a condition supported by law, and all of them found polygamy no worse than the promiscuous behavior of the very men who condemned it.[20] Moreover, these women held their organizations to their "collective" (credo) to accept all women's groups devoted to their goals. The loyalty of these national leaders would prove to be a deciding factor in the years to come.

The Roberts election four years earlier had ignited this new and long-lasting antipolygamy movement. A Utah clergyman, Reverend William Campbell, among others, was deeply committed to totally eradicating plural marriage, which still persisted despite Wilford Woodruff's 1890 Manifesto. He had used the election to initiate a well-planned campaign against the practice, recruiting women from the various home missions to cooperate with him in his crusade. Their success in arousing and influencing public opinion in the Roberts affair expedited Campbell's campaign for a constitutional amendment forbidding plural marriage in all the states. By 1899 he had enlisted most of these organizations into a coalition to front the movement.[21] When the Woman's Christian Temperance Union (WCTU), already a formidable force in the social purity movement, joined the coalition, it was successful in persuading thirty state chapters to adopt resolutions in support of an amendment.[22] Elizabeth B. Grannis, head of the National Christian League for the Promotion of Social Purity, and Utahn Corinne Allen became key players in this renewed attack on Mormon polygamy.

Church leaders were dismayed at this move to make polygamy once again a national issue, especially since Latter-day Saints were still struggling to adjust to the effects of Woodruff's 1890 Manifesto. Drafting a petition of their own, leaders urged both Mormons and sympathetic non-Mormons to sign it. Church leaders also attempted to refute erroneous statistics concerning the number who practiced polygamy and presented their own statistics showing the decrease of polygamous families since the 1890 Manifesto.[23]

The persistent agitation by national women's groups kept the sentiment alive, however, and by 1902 this second and more militant antipolygamy crusade publicly erupted, once again bringing Mormons into the national spotlight. With the help of antipolygamy women, both locally and nationally, Reverend William Campbell and numerous lobbyists from Utah took up their vigil in Washington, organizing petition drives and speaking before Congressional committees.[24]

With such persistent hostility to his religion, it was understandable that President Joseph F. Smith was reluctant to use LDS Church funds for Latter-day Saints to attend national women's conventions. But Emmeline Wells regretted his response to this latest crusade and confided to Susa Gates that he may have been influenced at home. "His wives are not like us," she complained to Susa, "they do not believe in the things we are doing; and neither do many others of our good blessed sisters."[25] How much she wanted them to know what she had learned in mingling with those national figures and how pleased she was to have Susa, a daughter of Brigham Young, though twenty-eight years younger than she, as her co-worker. Both women were journalists and used their publications to advocate the cause that informed their activism. Their commitment to bringing Mormon women into the national sisterhood often made them scapegoats and objects of derision. But their shared vision fueled their optimism. The two of them engaged in an epistolary conversation for nearly a decade, sharing ideas, worries, advice, and strategies. Much like her work with the younger Emily Richards in the suffrage movement, Emmeline Wells now looked to Susa Gates as her partner in their drive to protect and promote the interests of Mormon women.

Writing to each other weekly, and often more during the time Susa lived in Provo and New York, they freely expressed their frustrations, their disappointments, their hopes, and the importance of their work, which required so much effort against such formidable resistance. "If our sisters could only comprehend that we can never be 'polished stones, etc.' without some preparation—and that we must meet and mingle with people to remove prejudice," Emmeline wrote to Susa after one frustrating day. There is so much, she added "that <u>we know, and they don't</u>."[26]

The two women were not totally alone in their commitment. If indeed there is strength in numbers, the Relief Society and Young Ladies' MIA sent a large contingent of enthusiastic representatives to Washington in February 1902, using primarily their own resources, to attend both the convention of the National American Woman Suffrage Association and the triennial meeting of the NCW. The group went without the blessing of their Relief Society president, who felt the large Mormon representation had ignored the counsel of their leader, Joseph F. Smith. President Smith, however, upon learning of the women's determination to attend the two conventions, relented his disapproval but advised them to remember that "you go to teach and not to be taught. Learn all the truths you can, put them into active use when you return home."[27]

Emmeline keenly felt the new order of things. "I have no heart to go on with the work I should like to take up," she wrote, "because so much is being said—that hinders progress."[28] For the first time she seemed to be cut loose from the shared ideals that had tied her to former Relief Society president Zina D. H. Young. Emmeline Wells would have to make her own way in the future.

Four of the women who traveled east in 1902 represented the Young Ladies' MIA and ten were there as Relief Society representatives. Each organization had as official voting members at the convention just one proxy for its absent president and one delegate. Emmeline attended the triennial in her capacity as second recording secretary of the NCW. Understanding the capricious financial base on which Emmeline's attendance depended, Susa, in her account of the meeting in the *Young Woman's Journal,* was particularly effusive in stating Emmeline's value to such excursions: "The party [of Utah women] was led by that gracious and great little woman," she wrote. "Every Utah woman owes this indomitable soul a great debt of gratitude for the public work which she has so ably and untiringly performed these many years." Moreover, no one could be quite certain just how many more years the seventy-four-year-old Emmeline would be able, though willing, to devote to the strenuous work of the Relief Society at home, her editorship of the *Woman's Exponent,* and the constant requests for her service by local and national associations. The time seemed propitious to acknowledge her accomplishments. "She was honored on this occasion," Susa Gates continued, "not only by our own Utah women, but also by the great women of the nation convened in Washington."[29]

Emmeline Wells may have been a bit skeptical about how well Utah women honored her since this was the trip at which the Utah delegation she headed chose to stay at the famous Riggs House rather than the Fairfax Hotel, headquarters of the NCW and Emmeline's choice. But Emmeline commanded the attention of the delegates and national leaders. Always invited to speak when she attended these meetings, she delivered one of her more acclaimed talks, "The Age We Live In," an eloquent tribute to the achievements of women, which was included in the first Relief Society handbook, printed later that year. She focused on the part she believed women were destined to play in the world's work and her belief that the nineteenth century had liberated women to fulfill that destiny. She declared that "this awakening of woman and her co-operation with man in the world's great work" is one of the "tremendous forces recently brought into active exercise." This was the opportune time for woman to take her place in the work of the world, for the world needed her service, "and she has come to stay," Emmeline confidently asserted.[30]

Emmeline Wells spent a memorable hour at the triennial when she was invited to visit Clara Barton in her rooms at the Fairfax Hotel "talking Mormonism and answering her questions about our people and the past history and future outlook." It was a "rare opportunity and very unexpected," Emmeline noted.[31] Like her visit with May Wright Sewall the year before, she relished these opportunities for intimate conversations with women she admired.[32]

Despite these satisfying but momentary distractions, the "labors of the Utah women in the Council were not all pleasant, nor was their path all sunshine," Susa Gates reported. The moral reform members of the NCW expressed their concern that polygamous marriages were still being performed in Utah. In fact, during the same month that the NCW met, a number of representatives from the home mission societies, along with members of the Federation of Women's Clubs, the National and International Councils of Women, and "kindred associations" appeared before the House Judiciary Committee "in favor of a stringent constitutional amendment against polygamous practices." The women expressed alarm at the growth of the LDS Church through its missionary activity, fearful of the spread of polygamy. Noncommittal about proposing an amendment, the Judiciary Committee did promise to send an investigative team to Utah to ascertain the facts, as requested, but actually failed to take any final action.[33]

As chairman of the NCW press committee, appointed in March 1902, Susa Gates became the personal object of criticism from the evangelical women in the council, who felt she deliberately ignored the activities of their organizations. Elizabeth B. Grannis, one of the strong voices for an antipolygamy amendment, was particularly perturbed at a slight she perceived as deliberate. Chafing at the lack of publicity given to a speech she had given in Wisconsin or to any other of her organization's activities, she accused Gates of extreme partiality. Grannis complained that she had lost hope for fair coverage and with Susa Gates at the helm, Grannis no longer expected the press committee to take note of her organization. "I have received letters," Grannis wrote, "in which the sentiment is expressed by the authors that I have no idea, and am quite incapable of appreciating the depth of intrigue of the Mormon Chairman of the Press Committee."[34]

In defense, Susa Gates first excused herself on the basis of not being fully acquainted with the requirements of her new position and on her desire to serve the interests of all members but succeeding, evidently, only in failure to do so. Then, Gates offered a stinging rebuttal to Grannis's accusation. Gates pointed out that her own organization had received less than impartial treatment by the council. "You little realize," she replied, "the long struggles made by Mrs. Wells, to include our women to come out of their seclusion and join in the national movement. They feel very deeply the suspicion and scorn with which they are met by many women of the world." Voicing a familiar complaint of her Mormon co-workers, she added, "Not one of you women would think of accusing any other woman in the Council because she was a Methodist, or Catholic, or a Rathbone Sister, or a Colored woman, of injustice and partiality." Expressing misgivings about service and loyalty to the council, Gates explained that "her friends often question the desirability of keeping membership in the Council and paying their money to do so when confronted constantly with these very misrepresentations."[35] In this standoff, Grannis and Gates were just beginning an adversarial relationship that reflected the long-held antithesis of the social purity organizations toward Mormon women. Gates would depend on the support of May Wright Sewall, ICW president, and Ida Husted Harper, chair of the International Council's press committee who, despite others' criticism, admired Gates's amazing self-confidence and assurance, her commanding presence, her total dedication to the council, and, of course, her journalistic and argumentative skills.

Meanwhile, as Susa Gates was defending her position as press committee chair, the more immediate problem for Emmeline Wells and Susa, and those Latter-day Saint women who hoped to maintain a close connection with the National Council, was the source of funding—a problem intensified by the growing local opposition to membership in national organizations. The LDS Church's generosity of the 1870s and 1880s was, in large measure, a matter of self-preservation. That emergency had seemingly passed with the 1890 Manifesto and statehood in 1896, so other programs now claimed the Church's attention and funds. The 1893 financial panic and recovery from the Edmunds-Tucker Act also made claims on the Church's resources. Thus, those women, like Emmeline, who could not afford the cost of membership and travel on their own, depended on the dues from the women's organizations of the Church to underwrite their expenses.[36]

Just how strong the opposition to affiliation was emerged later that year when Emmeline Wells and Susa Gates searched for funds for Susa to attend an executive committee meeting of the ICW in Copenhagen preparatory to the quinquennial meeting to be held in Berlin in 1904. ICW press secretary Ida Husted Harper had requested Susa Gates to

Senator Reed Smoot (1903–33) supported the membership of Latter-day Saint women in national organizations. *Library of Congress*

be her surrogate at the meeting. This was an opportunity not to be missed, and Emmeline was as pleased as Susa that Harper was willing to send a Mormon woman to act in her stead. Moreover, only days before sailing, Susa learned that May Wright Sewall, ICW president, was unable to attend this preliminary meeting and requested Susa to read her message to the committee and report back to her its deliberations.[37] The recurring issue was who would pay Susa's expenses.

The answer still was not yet in place only a few weeks before the meeting was to convene. Finally, Emmeline Wells, Susa Gates, Anthon Lund (of the First Presidency of the Church), and Elder Reed Smoot (who was a candidate for the senate that year) met together in President Joseph F. Smith's office to discuss the matter. "Reed Smoot," Emmeline noted, "sees the advantage of our taking every opportunity offered of making friends with women of prominence in the world."[38] But, of course, she lamented "it is a question of money." She continually found it strange "that the brethren should hesitate when such advances are made toward us as a people—really the woman's day is dawning and means must come as well for the work cannot be done without it."[39] Susa Gates then proposed a plan. If the *Deseret News* would pay her transportation costs to New York, for which she would supply the paper with correspondence, and if the Relief Society and the Young Ladies' MIA would each contribute a hundred dollars, she would be able to make the trip. President Smith expressed the "mind of the council" in giving his support to her scheme, and she was successful in carrying it out.[40] It was clear, however, that financial resources for these excursions would no longer come from the general fund of the Church but from the auxiliary organizations, when they were willing, and from private means.

Funding for Susa Gates's trip was only one of many hurdles that she detailed to Emmeline Wells. Susa confided that when May Sewall mentioned Susa's role at the meeting, "there was a general howl went up all over the globe." Even Susan B. Anthony doubted the wisdom of sending a Mormon woman to Europe as the only U.S. delegate, fearing that the decision would "taint the Council in the eyes of other nations." The common consensus, Susa explained to Emmeline, is that "we are, as a people, the shrewdest advertisers of our religion on earth" and that Susa herself was dangerous because she was "extremely shrewd and polite."[41] It was clear that neither the 1890 Manifesto, Utah's achievement of statehood, nor the defeat of B. H. Roberts was sufficient to dispel hostility toward Mormons, even monogamous members, and toward the LDS Church. The brief period of détente during the 1890s had ineluctably drawn to a close over the Roberts affair, despite efforts to revive it afterward.

Rather than reconsidering her appointment, the ever loyal Sewall inexplicably, in view of these concerns, simply counseled Susa Gates not to mention her Mormonism to the foreign delegates. "Why should they ask me to go, if they fear me so much!" Susa queried Emmeline. Susa did not make any promises to Sewall, however. Though Susa clearly chafed at the necessity of traveling "incognito, as it were," she nevertheless felt obliged to fulfill the assignment.[42] Emmeline was deeply suspicious of Sewall's motive when so many objections surfaced. "It seems very mysterious," she replied to Susa, but with her characteristic faith in Providence, Emmeline noted, "If the daughters of Zion are to become the head as we have been foretold and as we actually believe, it has to begin sometime—somewhere."[43]

Susa Gates's evasiveness at the Copenhagen meeting, however, seemed to work. She was impressively fêted during the executive meeting, as befitted the only United States representative, and invited to country homes and villas, making many admiring friends along the way. Afterward, however, she garnered only criticism. The first barb was directed to her press notes, which the European members found to be "too personal," especially in contrasting Danish women with their northern and southern neighbors and in describing other individual characteristics of some of the delegates. In the same vein, others felt the notes had not been dignified enough for an official document.[44]

By the end of the year, so many protests about Susa Gates's activities in Copenhagen had poured in to May Wright Sewall's office that she unleashed her embarrassment and disappointment in a long letter to Susa. Sewall explained the chagrin of the delegates upon learning that a Mormon had represented the United States and that she had flaunted her religion by speaking at meetings of the local Relief Society and Young Ladies' MIA after the executive meeting. Clearly irritated, Sewall felt betrayed by Susa's impolitic press notes and the disclosure of her identity by her actions following the executive committee meeting. Sewall made it very clear to Susa that, despite allegations to the contrary, she had not commissioned Susa to be her proxy and that Susa had attended only as a surrogate for international press chair Ida Harper. Though Susa was the only U.S. delegate, Sewall explained, she was authorized only to take notes of the meeting. With so much criticism directed at Sewall herself and the embarrassment the incident had caused her personally, Sewall's continual defense of her association with Susa was perplexing. This Sewall could do, she had evidently convinced herself and hoped to convince others, because she recognized that Mormonism and polygamy were not identical, insisting that her warm reception and defense of Latter-day Saint women were tokens of her belief in the ecumenical nature of the council. The goal of the "council idea," she told Susa, was to bring together women of all faiths and political persuasions, not to promulgate their views but to cooperate in the great work of the council.[45]

Sewall's many-paged explication of her approach to Mormonism, her faith in the "council idea," and her displeasure with Susa's actions moved Susa to send an equally long response. She reminded Sewall that it was her request, not Susa's desire, to attend the executive meeting and keep her identity hidden. She had never agreed to the latter, she explained, and her participation in meetings of the Relief Society and Young Ladies' MIA fulfilled the expectations of the two organizations' general boards, which had paid her way to the executive meeting. She spoke to these Latter-day Saint groups only on the significance of the council, she assured Sewall, and wished that all the members of the executive committee could have been in attendance when she spoke. Moreover, Susa declared, her attendance at Relief Society and Young Ladies' MIA meetings was perfectly legitimate since both organizations were members of the council. Finally, Susa explained, to think of her as a proxy of the president of the ICW was absurd, and she never thought of herself in such a way. "You are responsible," she wrote, "for whatever there was of that."[46] This was an inexact disclaimer since Gates had identified herself as acting as proxy earlier.

Though generally unknown among the women at home, this unpleasant episode caused Susa Gates great concern. "It is no light matter," she wrote to Emmeline Wells after receiving Sewall's letter, "the fact that the highest circles of European women are stirred to such deep agitation over a Mormon woman's actions and words."[47] Emmeline was "the only woman in Zion," Susa explained, to whom she could disclose the letter and a report of her actions there. Emmeline was dumbfounded upon learning of it since there had been no inkling of the incident in Copenhagen until Sewall's letter to Susa, written five months after the meeting.

Emmeline Wells expressed surprise to learn that the problems of the summer executive committee meeting were still simmering five months afterward. She was surprised at Sewall's chastisement of Susa Gates and in her even more stringent indictment of the Countess of Aberdeen, the vice president and former president of the International Council, who had castigated Susa as well as Sewall.[48] Though Emmeline ill advisedly gave Susa's responding letter to Bathsheba Smith, Emmeline at least restrained from giving it to either of the general boards or to Church President Joseph F. Smith. "It would so prejudice Prest. Smith," she wrote Susa, "that any future association or affiliation would be impossible." Not surprisingly, Bathsheba Smith was more persuaded than before that withdrawal was the only course to pursue. The incident reinforced her opposition and made her even more sympathetic to those "who cannot see outside a narrow groove," Emmeline lamented. "They do not know the a.b.c. of Council work, nor what it stands for in the great world of humanity." She concluded, "I really stand as it were <u>alone</u> in the matter." Setbacks were inevitable, she reasoned, and resigned herself, in typical fashion, to the situation. "We must be still," she advised Susa, "and await the right time, because there will be a right time."[49]

Emmeline Wells remained busy in Salt Lake City as Susa Gates represented their interests while living in New York. An invitation from a Mrs. Church in Wellsville, New York, perhaps at Susa's instigation, to write a paper on Mormonism resulted in one of the most extensive of Emmeline's expositions of doctrine and the place of women in the theology of the LDS Church. The "lecture," Mrs. Church explained, was to be read at a number of New York women's clubs. In the piece, which Emmeline titled "Why a Woman Should Want to be a Mormon," she explained how Mormonism was advantageous to women in both its theology and practice and outlined some of its basic tenets, including her own conviction of the eventual removal of the "curse" placed on Eve (making her subject to Adam), which was a pivotal issue in the woman movement.[50] Other honors followed. Emmeline was informed that she had been reelected one of the international vice presidents of the International Press Union, more an honorary than a working position. She also received a copy of a laudatory London magazine article about her. While she enjoyed this kind of recognition, her pleasure was always tinged with a touch of resentment and need for self-justification. "I have not had so many privileges as many of the sisters with whom I have been associated," Emmeline wrote, "but," she added, "I have enjoyed my own gifts of mind and heart and tried to make myself useful in spreading the truth."[51]

In March 1903, Bathsheba Smith unexpectedly notified Emmeline Wells that the general board had selected her to represent the Relief Society at the next executive committee meeting of the NCW scheduled for New Orleans, which to Emmeline's surprise the Relief Society would be willing to fund. Susa, still press committee chair, was unable to attend, so Emmeline agreed to prepare the press notes for her. It turned out to be a difficult meeting, fraught with knotty problems from the beginning and testing, in another arena, the nondiscriminatory position of the council toward its members. Much discussion centered on the admission of "colored women" to the New Orleans chapter. Though the NCW included the National Council of Colored Women as well as the National Council of Jewish Women as members, the councilwomen of New Orleans expressed concern that its members would be socially ostracized if they mingled with local black groups. After much debate the New Orleans members finally decided "to do without the Southern hospitalities and be entirely independent," regardless of the consequences.[52] If the Mormon delegates felt empathy toward the "colored women," whose situation paralleled their own, it was not recorded.[53]

Emmeline Wells had been accompanied to the meeting by two of the younger Mormon activists, but these two, Clarissa Spencer Williams and Ruth May Fox, unlike some of the others, shared Emmeline's Republican Party sympathies and had the literary and political background to provide a satisfying exchange of ideas and sharing of compatible interests.[54] Clarissa Williams later became a counselor to Emmeline in the Relief Society General Presidency, while Ruth May Fox turned her attention to the young women of the Church, becoming the Young Ladies' MIA General President. Their companionship helped to offset the disturbing effects of the meeting, which had been a scene of confusion and excessive prejudice. It was a warning to Emmeline. "If we are to continue our relations to the Council," she cautioned Susa, "you and myself must do some <u>wise</u> planning."[55]

Though Emmeline's life work and singular goal seemed to be continuously thwarted by opposition at home and away, she was adamant about establishing Mormon women on the same footing as other women. Though pillared by the constancy of the influential May Wright Sewall and other national leaders, as they had been earlier by Susan B. Anthony and Elizabeth Cady Stanton, Emmeline's efforts were almost derailed by reactions to the election of Elder Reed Smoot of Utah to the

United States Senate earlier that year and the widespread movement to unseat him.[56] Coming on the heels of the Copenhagen fiasco, it triggered an intense and prolonged campaign against him, the Church, and Latter-day Saint membership in national women's associations.

Susa Gates and Emmeline Wells corresponded at length about the Smoot hearings, recognizing that some Mormons felt uncomfortable with the idea of an Apostle entering the world of politics. Emmeline felt differently. "You see" she admitted to Susa, "I believe in our leaders being in Congress, and would even welcome the nomination of Joseph F. Smith to the presidency of the United States."[57] Pleased with Smoot's election to the Senate, she felt assured that he would be a great influence in behalf of his religion. It did, however, become a rallying point of antipolygamists, whose mission now was three-fold: to unseat Senator Smoot; to achieve a constitutional amendment to outlaw polygamy; and to expel Mormon women from all national women's groups.

Within the National Council, Elizabeth Grannis, who had led the opposition to B. H. Roberts, took the lead again. At the outset of this second campaign, however, she played both sides. Even as she denounced the seating of Reed Smoot and questioned the impartiality in the press notes of Susa Gates, Grannis inexplicably told Susa how much she admired the success of Mormon women in "removing prejudice" and particularly praised their cohesion and strength. Susa was flattered with the compliments. But Emmeline was unmoved. "Whatever professions [she] has made to you," she warned, "I would not trust [her] not at all."[58] Despite the flattery, Susa was keenly aware of the hostility toward her, promoted by Mary Lowe Dickinson (candidate for National Council president), who, Susa believed, was egged on by Dr. Sarah J. Elliott, a traveling lecturer for the antipolygamists. Elliott had lived in Utah for eight years and had identified herself as a doctor, though she had not practiced while living there.[59] But Grannis's antagonism was unflinching and led to the next challenge Emmeline and Susa would encounter in their preparations for the quinquennial meeting of the International Council in Berlin, scheduled for summer 1904.

While the new state of Utah was accommodating itself to the broader American culture, Mormon women were still clearly fighting to be fully accepted into mainstream American society. The hopes of diminishing prejudice during the last decade of the nineteenth century had been demolished with the renewed antipolygamy campaign. Mormon women continued to be ostracized, criticized, and even vilified. The furor over one political election in Utah had set the stage for an even more lengthy and widespread turmoil over a second. Unlike the 1880s, in which affiliation with national women's groups benefited Mormon women as well as the LDS Church, these connections now seemed less beneficial. Emmeline Wells and her cohorts thus found themselves struggling both at home and abroad to maintain the hard-won acceptance. Fighting on both fronts to hold on to that female association, Emmeline felt like an unwelcome agitator. Nevertheless, she would not be discouraged. "If we are to take the prominent places prophesied of concerning our women," she wrote to her friend Susa Gates, "we should certainly not let go of what we have already obtained."[60] The years ahead would repeat the calumny and derision that Mormons had experienced two decades earlier, but Emmeline and her fellow workers were determined to hold firm to their achievements. Yet it would take patient commitment to do so.

Notes

1. Emmeline B. Wells to Susa Young Gates, March 25, 1902, Susa Young Gates Papers, Church Archives, The Church of Jesus Christ of Latter-day Saints, Salt Lake City.

2. "The New Century," *Woman's Exponent* 29 (November 15, December 1, 1900): 52.

3. Emmeline B. Wells, Diary, August 3, 1901, L. Tom Perry Special Collections, Harold B. Lee Library, Brigham Young University, Provo, Utah.

4. Wells, Diary, April 19, 1900.

5. "Daughters of the Revolution," *Deseret Evening News,* November 17, 1898, 7; "Daughters of Revolution Elect Officers," Journal History of the Church, March 25, 1916, 11, Church Archives, also available on *Selected Collections from the Archives of The Church of Jesus Christ of Latter-day Saints,*

2 vols. (Provo, Utah: Brigham Young University Press, 2002), vol. 2, DVD 33, microfilm copy in Harold B. Lee Library. A plaque located in Zion's Bank in Salt Lake City inadvertently confuses the DR with the DAR, indicating that the DAR was founded November 16, 1896, on the spot where the bank stands, with Emmeline Wells and a number of other LDS women as charter members. The DR was founded on that day two years later in Room 208 of the Templeton Building.

6. A. W. Sterling, "Daughters of the Revolution," *Woman's Exponent* 29 (June 1, 1900): 3.

7. Wells, Diary, May 4, 1900.

8. Wells, Diary, May 5, 7, 1900.

9. This assignment augmented her work on the peace committee of the NCW.

10. May Wright Sewall to Susa Young Gates, April 26, 1901, Gates Papers.

11. Emmeline B. Wells to Susa Y. Gates, July 10, 1901, Gates Papers.

12. Susa Gates wrote a press release describing Sewall's itinerary while in Utah for "State Correspondence: Utah," *Woman's Journal,* August 15, 1901, 278. She also included a short article about her visit in "Mrs. May Wright Sewall," *Young Woman's Journal* 12 (August 1901): 377–78.

13. Wells, Diary, July 10, 1901. These included Mrs. Eliza Kirtley Royle, "known as the mother of clubs in the West," Mrs. Mooney, president of the Utah Jewish Women's Council, Mrs. Coulter, president of the Utah Federation of Clubs, and Mrs. McVicker, regent of the University of Utah, among others.

14. "Mrs. Sewall's Visit," *Woman's Exponent* 30 (August 1, 1901): 20.

15. Emmeline B. Wells to Susa Young Gates, September 20, 1901, Gates Papers.

16. Susa Young Gates to Emmeline B. Wells, December 12, 1901, Gates Papers.

17. Wells to Gates, March 25, 1902.

18. Wells to Gates, March 25, 1902.

19. In her maiden address as Relief Society General President Bathsheba Smith, who was also serving as "presidentess" of female temple workers, indicated that she had not been able to travel much among the sisters. "It had been her calling to work for the dead," and she "was happy in that work." "Annual Conference Relief Society," *Woman's Exponent* 30 (December 1901): 54.

20. On several occasions Susan B. Anthony noted the hypocrisy of the men in Congress denouncing B. H. Roberts, or any other polygamous husband, of immorality. "At least Mormon men marry their mistresses," Anthony averred on one occasion. See, for example, "Susan B. Anthony on Love of

Impure Men," Journal History of the Church, November 25, 1899, 8–9; "Miss Anthony on Roberts," *Woman's Exponent* 28 (November 15, December 1, 1899): 80; "A Brave Woman's Words," Journal History of the Church, December 2, 1899, 6; "Miss Anthony Is Grossly Insulted," Journal History of the Church, December 14, 1899, 11–12.

21. Joan Smyth Iversen presents the details of the origins and development of this campaign in *The Antipolygamy Controversy in U.S. Women's Movements, 1880–1925* (New York: Garland, 1997), 189–200.

22. Iversen, *Antipolygamy Controversy,* 189–200. The fervor with which the WCTU waged its antipolygamy battle continued unabated until the American public finally lost interest in the social purity ideals it represented. By 1913 the Utah chapter of the WCTU, which included both Mormons and Gentiles, threatened to withdraw from the national movement unless the organization stopped its campaign against Mormons. In fact, the secretary of the Ogden chapter, Lillie Frey, a Gentile, announced that if the state chapter did not withdraw, "she and many other gentiles in Utah will drop out of the organization personally." "Mrs. Walker Deplores Trouble Begun by the Antimormon Agitators," *Salt Lake Herald Republican,* October 15, 1913, 3. The national WCTU maintained its drive against Mormons while the Utah chapter focused on other social problems.

23. *Messages of the First Presidency of the Church of Jesus Christ of Latter-day Saints,* comp. James R. Clark, 6 vols. (Salt Lake City: Bookcraft, 1970), 4:40–42.

24. A comprehensive analysis of this twenty-year campaign is Iversen, *Antipolygamy Controversy,* 185–211.

25. Wells to Gates, March 25, 1902.

26. Wells to Gates, March 25, 1902.

27. Susa Young Gates, "History of Women—National and International Relations of Mormon Women," mss., Gates Papers.

28. Wells, Diary, January 30, 1902.

29. "The National Council of Women," *Young Woman's Journal* 13 (June 1902): 246–51. See also "Happenings Here and There," *Woman's Exponent* 30 (March 1902): 84.

30. Emmeline B. Wells, "The Age We Live In," in *The General Relief Society: Officers, Objects and Status* (Salt Lake City: General Officers of the Relief Society, 1902), 72–73. See also "The Age We Live In," *Woman's Exponent* 30 (April 1902): 89–90.

31. "Happenings Here and There," 84.

32. "Happenings Here and There," 84.

33. "To Count the Wives in Utah Homes," *Journal History of the Church*, February 25, 1902, 2.

34. Elizabeth B. Grannis to Susa Young Gates, April 26, 1902, Gates Papers.

35. Susa Young Gates to Elizabeth B. Grannis, May 4, 1902, and June 19, 1902, Gates Papers. See also Grannis to Gates, April 26, 1902.

36. Membership in the Relief Society required monthly dues ranging from ten to fifty cents beginning in 1898. Occasionally, special fund-raising drives helped to raise money for specific society or community needs.

37. Susa Young Gates to Emmeline B. Wells, June 23, 1902, Gates Papers. Sewall's confidence in Gates prompted her to adopt Gates's suggestions to improve the message she had written, which Gates was to deliver to the committee.

38. Despite the verbal attacks lodged against him by national women's groups, Reed Smoot continued to advocate the value of Latter-day Saint women's participation in national associations. For details of his election, see Milton R. Merrill, *Reed Smoot: Apostle in Politics* (Logan: Utah State University Press and Department of Political Science, 1990), esp. 22–30. A more recent analysis of the election of Reed Smoot is Kathleen Flake, *The Politics of American Religious Identity: The Seating of Senator Reed Smoot, Mormon Apostle* (Chapel Hill: University of North Carolina Press, 2004).

39. Wells, Diary, June 10, 1902.

40. Journal History of the Church, June 12, 1902.

41. Gates to Wells, June 23, 1902. The public presence of Emmeline Wells for more than two decades and the membership of Mormon organizations or individuals in a variety of national women's organizations had given them a place of both admiration and disparagement in the nation's press. This kind of public notice along with the LDS Church's vigorous proselytizing program caused suspicion and worries among many critics of Mormonism.

42. Gates to Wells, June 23, 1902.

43. Emmeline B. Wells to Susa Young Gates, July 9, 1902, Gates Papers. Relief Society General President Eliza R. Snow consistently sermonized that Mormon women were "at the head of all womankind," speaking religiously rather than politically. She took her cue from Joseph Smith who told the women of the Nauvoo, Illinois, Relief Society that some day "this society would have power to command Queens in their midst." *A Record of the Organization, and Proceedings of the Female Relief Society of Nauvoo,* April 28, 1842, Church Archives.

44. Henni Frochhammer to Susa Young Gates, September 20, 1902, Gates Papers; Susa Young Gates to Froken Henni Frochhammer, September 2, 1902, Gates Papers.

45. May Wright Sewall to Susa Young Gates, December 31, 1902, Gates Papers. See also J. Ellen Foster to Susa Young Gates, March 19, 1902, Gates Papers. Ellen Foster was a loyal supporter of Mormon membership and expressed a personal friendship with both Emmeline Wells and Susa Gates.

46. Gates to Wells, June 23, 1902; Susa Young Gates to May Wright Sewall, January 25, 1903, Gates Papers. Despite Gates's disclaimer, the *Woman's Exponent* identified her as proxy. See "Mrs. Gates' Trip to Europe," *Woman's Exponent* 31 (August 1, 15, 1902): 20.

47. Susa Young Gates to Emmeline B. Wells, January 19, 1903, Gates Papers. A report of Susa Gates's trip to Copenhagen and the gracious way in which she was accepted initially as the representative from the United States is "Mrs. Gates' Trip to Europe," 20. Gates made several reports of her trip abroad, the most significant one at the Beehive House in Salt Lake City at which the entire First Presidency of the LDS Church was in attendance. Remarks by President Joseph F. Smith were unexpectedly encouraging when he indicated his pleasure with all that had been accomplished. See "Mrs. Gates Return," *Woman's Exponent* 31 (September 1, 15, 1902): 28.

48. The two women were not only competitive in their roles as ICW president, but the Countess also displayed a common British disdain for the American women in the council.

49. Emmeline B. Wells to Susa Young Gates, January 25, 1903, Gates Papers.

50. The lecture was published under the same title in *Woman's Exponent* 36 (December 1907): 39–40, and 36 (January 1908): 46–48.

51. Wells, Diary, July 19, 1903.

52. Wells, Diary, March 23–31, 1903, especially March 25, 1903. A brief report of the meetings is in "General Conference Relief Society," *Woman's Exponent* 31 (May 1903): 94. The *Exponent* account is taken from a talk Wells delivered to the Utah Woman's Press Association on April 25, 1903.

53. Ruth May Fox noted the dilemma of the local council over the "colored problem" as well as admission of the Ladies of the Grand Army of the Republic, an equally difficult problem for the Southern members of the NCW. Fox noted that both groups of women were finally admitted. Ruth May Fox, "My Story," 34–35, Utah State Historical Society, Salt Lake City. More information on Ruth May Fox can be found in Linda Thatcher, "'I Care Nothing for Politics':

Ruth May Fox, Forgotten Suffragist," *Utah Historical Quarterly* 49 (Summer 1981): 239–53.

54. Ruth May Fox found the sessions "less impressive" than she had anticipated but interesting nonetheless. In all, according to her autobiography, she attended twelve meetings of the NCW and served as auditor of the council from 1919 to 1921 and again in 1925. As president of the Young Ladies' MIA, she became an official delegate. See Fox, "My Story," 34, 35.

55. Emmeline B. Wells to Susa Young Gates, March 30, 1903, Gates Papers.

56. Reed Smoot was elected on the Republican ticket in 1902 and seated in March 1903. He had been appointed an Apostle of the Church in 1900 at the age of thirty-eight. Unlike B. H. Roberts, who was never seated as the Congressman from Utah, Smoot was seated but underwent a four-year battle to retain his seat, winning his right to office in 1907. He served until 1933. Despite intense protests against him, he continued to support Mormon membership in the various national women's organizations. See Merrill, *Apostle in Politics*, and Flake, *Politics of American Religious Identity*.

57. Emmeline B. Wells to Susa Young Gates, February 5, 1903, Gates Papers.

58. Susa Young Gates to Emmeline B. Wells, January 30, 1903, Gates Papers; Emmeline Wells to Susa Young Gates, February 24, 1903, Gates Papers. Grannis made clear the following June that it would be politic on the part of Susa to resign as Press Chairman of the National Council, especially if Mary Lowe Dickinson, avidly opposed to Mormonism, became president.

59. For a brief sketch of Dr. Elliott, see "Where She Spent Her Time Here," *Deseret Evening News,* April 4, 1903, 4.

60. Emmeline B. Wells to Susa Young Gates, undated letter (but sometime in 1900), Gates Papers.

Chapter 18

"A Fine Soul Who Served Us"

*I have not followed anyone else,
but I hope I have kept within the radius of the true light.*[1]

Even as contention and wrangling plagued the members of the National Council of Women (NCW), threatening disbandment of the council altogether, plans for the third quinquennial meeting of the International Council of Women (ICW) were underway. Like the London meeting five years earlier, this was an event Emmeline Wells eagerly anticipated. As an officer of the NCW and regular delegate to the executive committee meetings, she was expected to travel to the conference, scheduled for Berlin in summer 1904. But there would be obstacles. By the end of 1903, she sensed May Wright Sewall's fears of repeating the 1902 fiasco in Copenhagen and Sewall's concern that Wells, well known as a plural wife and defender of her faith, would ignite the same consternation from the European members as they had displayed toward Susa Gates.

Besides May Wright Sewall's reservations, other rumors circulated that some women at home in Utah might hinder Emmeline Wells from going to the Berlin meeting. Convinced of her own indispensability, she tried to dismiss these rumors as being from those "who like to make mischief and really could not do the work possibly." She was relieved that nothing was said in the Relief Society board meetings, which she attended as general secretary, though some board members exhibited what Emmeline felt was an "awful spirit." "Perhaps we may be able to overcome those rebellious spirits," she hoped.[2] Her age, experience, and place in national circles made it increasingly difficult for her to give way to a less-experienced, though eager, corps of younger activists, and she chose to see them as more rebellious than ambitious.

It was not only the "rebellious spirits" that threatened Emmeline Wells's participation in the Berlin conference, however. Early in January 1904, Relief Society General President Bathsheba Smith received a mandate from Joseph F. Smith, president of The Church of Jesus Christ of Latter-day Saints, that she was to send to Germany only those women who were able to pay their own way.[3] He had finally come to terms with his own feelings about the relationship of the Relief Society and Young Ladies' Mutual Improvement Association (MIA) with the National Council. Even Bathsheba Smith was ruffled at the news since she had nominated her granddaughter, Alice Merrill Horne, a member of the Relief Society board, to be her proxy. Alice Horne was herself upset enough to complain to President Joseph F. Smith, which prompted him to attend the next board meeting.[4] As he explained his decision, it became clear to the board that those women who objected to using Relief Society dues to send representatives to the council meetings had the stronger voice.[5] Moreover, the explosion of anti-Mormonism in these national groups over Elder Reed Smoot's election to the Senate the year before, was a convincing reason to withhold Church funds. Emmeline was thus energetic in seeking some other source of funding, while her friend Susa Gates, unable to attend herself, disclosed a spiritual manifestation she received confirming Emmeline's participation.[6]

Meanwhile, Emmeline Wells made preparations to attend the February executive committee meeting of the NCW in Indianapolis, the home of honorary president May Wright Sewall. If resistance to the seating of B. H. Roberts, debated in the 1899 triennial meeting of the council, was difficult for the Utah delegates, the 1904 executive committee meeting offered even stronger and more successful resistance against Reed Smoot. The expressed objection was that Smoot's first allegiance was to the LDS Church and its principles, thus preventing him from acting independently or freely sustaining the Constitution. Some opponents, unable to disassociate Mormons from polygamy, even went so far as to claim that Smoot was a polygamist as well.[7]

Before the Indianapolis meeting began, the delegates had been briefed that there would be important reports from the standing committees, "especially from the Committee on Resolutions, which has had before it, during the last year, a question of exceptional importance."[8] During the first few days of the meeting, the agenda proceeded as usual, the committee and delegate reports interspersed with luncheons, teas, and socials by the local women's organizations. The committee on resolutions was the last to be heard.

The chair of this committee, Elizabeth B. Grannis, read the seven resolutions, six of them reinforcing the aims of the council in improving women's status. The last one, however, reflected the intensifying movement against Reed Smoot. It specifically objected to his representation in the Senate, while identifying polygamy as a threat to "the foundation of family life." According to the resolution, people should "protest and petition against the seating in our national Congress any man who may practice or subscribe to it." The resolution's supporters explained that the resolution had been sent from Utah by people who were aware of the continued practice of polygamy, and the committee urged the NCW to endorse the resolution.[9] This time Emmeline Wells and Maria Y. Dougall, her co-delegate, succeeded only in tabling the resolution, explaining that the matter had already been brought up in the United States Senate which, they argued, was sufficiently able to settle its own affairs.[10] As Emmeline had reminded them, Senate hearings on whether Senator Smoot should be allowed to retain his seat were scheduled to begin the following month. No one could have predicted at that point, however, that the hearings would continue over three different Congressional sessions until finally being resolved in February 1907 in Smoot's favor.[11]

The Reed Smoot election rallied the same opposing factions as had coalesced around the election of B. H. Roberts. Even before the Congressional hearings on Smoot, the Salt Lake Ministerial Association had expressed irritation at what it felt was a violation of both the Edmunds-Tucker Act, the 1890 Manifesto, and the state constitution by a segment of LDS Church members who refused to accept these barriers to plural marriage.[12] The Ministerial Association was the Utah base of the amendment movement and engaged the ready response of the Woman's Christian Temperance Union (WCTU) and other evangelical women. The Daughters of the American Revolution, the Interdenominational Council, and the National Christian League for the Promotion of Social Purity also joined the coalition. All had united under an umbrella association, the National League of Women's Organizations, determined to be as successful against Smoot as they had been in the campaign against Roberts, who was never seated.

Even more than the individual clergymen, who fervently lectured and published to permanently abolish polygamy, the leading spirit in this new anti-Mormon offensive was Corinne Allen of Utah.[13] Like Angelina Newman two decades earlier, Corinne Allen became a strategist and indefatigable leader in the ensuing conflict. Allen had once been an ally of Emmeline Wells's in various civic undertakings and in the local Republican Party. But Allen's long-standing intolerance of plural marriage found a ready object in Reed Smoot, who, she was convinced, was a practicing polygamist like Roberts. As president of the Utah chapter of the popular National Congress of Mothers, Allen convinced the national association to join the anti-Mormon crusade, and for more than a decade she attempted to expel Mormon women not only from that organization but also from the National Federation of Women's Clubs and finally from the NCW and ICW.[14]

Plans for the Berlin conference began to unfold in January 1904 against this backdrop of anti-Mormonism and the imminence of the first round of hearings to unseat Reed Smoot. While sympathetic to the feelings of Bathsheba Smith, president of the Relief Society, and those Relief Society members who opposed affiliation, Emmeline Wells had fashioned an entire career around gaining acceptance for her people in the larger American society, exerting individual diplomacy, meeting opposition on its own turf, and mounting, through her words but even more through her person, an impressive defense of her Mormon sisters. Moreover, she had made friends in all of these national organizations, particularly of the leadership, and she was confident of their loyalty and support. Without some financial help from the Church, however, many Latter-day Saint women would be precluded from future association and the opportunity to personally refute the slanderous publicity. Moreover, it would appear that the anti-Mormon forces had succeeded in driving out the Mormons.

Emmeline Wells, fortified by Susa Gates's prophetic dream, remained hopeful of going to Berlin. Even May Wright Sewall came to acknowledge that Emmeline was a logical delegate. Prospects looked brighter in April 1904 when Emmeline was appointed an American delegate to the conference and invited to make stops in Boston to attend the national convention of the Daughters of the Revolution and in Paris to attend the executive committee meetings of the NCW. These appointments, she was certain, would elicit the necessary funding. Unfortunately this did not happen, although Emmeline explored every possibility. A visit with Elder George Albert Smith, newly appointed member of the board of the Young Men's Mutual Improvement Association, was disheartening. He was favorable toward her going but did not wish "to have any say in the matter of raising money." "I felt he was more or less powerless," she concluded, "when I thought him strong."[15] An unexpected endorsement, however, came the next day from her friend Mrs. Sol Siegel of Salt Lake City. In a visit to Emmeline, at which Bathsheba Smith was present, Mrs. Siegel told Bathsheba of the "estimation in which the ladies in Berlin and Dresden held me [Emmeline] as a woman of merit," and urged Bathsheba Smith to send her to the conference. But Emmeline noticed that Bathsheba stiffened at the suggestion. "She is not in favor of women who tell her what she ought or ought not to do," Emmeline observed, and worried that Siegel was offended by Bathsheba's imperious manner. Bathsheba Smith, Emmeline regretted, "does not present the best side to strangers."[16] Despite Sewall's reversal and Mrs. Siegel's flattering words, albeit no financial aid, Emmeline's fruitless search for funds was the decisive factor. Her hope of going to Germany quietly faded, and by early May, Berlin was no longer on Emmeline's horizon.

Alice Merrill Horne, as it turned out, became the appointed proxy for her grandmother, Bathsheba Smith, who supported her granddaugher's desire to attend the conference. Lydia Alder would attend as delegate. There would not be as large a company of Mormon women as had attended the Woman's Congress in London five years earlier. Only Emily Richards and Ida Dusenberry joined the two delegates in Berlin. Indeed, times had dramatically changed in that short span of time, as had Church leadership, its auxiliary women's leaders, along with officers of national organizations, all of whom had set their own priorities, relationships, and direction.

As the Berlin conference grew near, Emmeline Wells prepared the statistical and financial report of the Relief Society that would be presented as well as the credentials for Alice Horne to the annual meeting of the Daughters of the Revolution.[17] She also wrote a long article for the *Deseret News* outlining the sessions of the conference and noting the special commendations to be given to May Wright Sewall, retiring president of the ICW.[18] When the day of departure arrived, Emmeline went to the depot to see Alice "as she goes to Berlin & Paris across the water," giving her a bouquet of carnations as a departing gift and once more hiding the familiar broken heart behind the well-practiced amiable front. Later she poured from that heart her deep disappointment: "Today I was to have spoken in the Woman's International Congress in Berlin—in Philharmonic Hall on Elementary Education and Co-education," she reflected. "No one knows how disappointed I have felt over this affair. It makes me feel so bad that I am not good company for those around me. . . . The women who have caused the opposition do not value the Council as I do nor do they know how to estimate and appreciate its benefits—so cannot know how I feel."[19] At various social gatherings many of her friends expressed their disappointment that she had been unable to attend, only exacerbating her distress. Even more disheartening was to learn a month later that an acquaintance, Dr. Seymour B. Young, would have provided funds if he had known of her situation, as would have two other friends, Nelson Empey and T. G. Webber. She was stung with regrets. "All these offers came too late to do any good," she lamented, while wondering why she was "hindered & if it was best."[20]

Had Emmeline Wells been there, she would have confronted Corinne Allen, now her bitter critic, who was then living in Germany with her daughter. Allen attended the Berlin conference as a member of the National Congress of Mothers and was as determined there as at home in the United States to disaffiliate Mormon women from the organization. The two Utah delegates encountered her when they attended a session on social purity. Elizabeth Grannis, who still headed the National Christian League for the Promotion of Social Purity, presented a paper that, rather than addressing the subject in general, singled out the LDS Church for her criticism. "It was a bitter attack upon our religion," Lydia Alder reported. As the respondent to the paper, Allen continued the attack in her own remarks until the chair of the session finally cut her off. Anna Howard Shaw, Carrie Chapman Catt, and May Wright Sewall all expressed their regrets over this unforeseen verbal assault.[21]

Emmeline Wells published news of the Berlin Congress in her paper, noting the popularity of Charlotte Perkins Gilman and the prestige of Susan B. Anthony among the European delegates. Anthony had truly achieved legendary status around the world and never disappointed her devotees in her now limited appearances.[22] Emmeline did not, however, record the unhappy incident with Elizabeth Grannis and Corinne Allen.

Seven years elapsed before Emmeline Wells attended another meeting of the NCW. Even Susa Gates had turned her attention to other pursuits and her correspondence with Emmeline had generally declined. With the national effort to unseat Reed Smoot and the unflagging determination of the antipolygamists, it seemed propitious to keep a low profile and was virtually impossible to raise funds for travel. But their adversaries continued in their obsessive drive. In 1905, Elizabeth Grannis mounted another strong effort to expel the Latter-day Saint women's organizations from the NCW at its triennial convention and to issue a resolution aimed specifically at Smoot. This time, according to one newspaper report, the resolution passed because of the absence of "that potent trio from Utah, Mrs. Emmeline B. Wells, Mrs. Lorenzo (Minnie) Snow and Mrs. Susie Young Gates." They had proven themselves "politicians enough to defeat any action by the congress concerning Mormonism," the article continued. The resolution encouraged people "by petition and otherwise" to protest against the seating of "any man in our National Congress or allowing any man to hold such a seat, who may practice or subscribe to the doctrine of polygamy."[23] Ever supportive, the aging Susan B. Anthony condemned the resolution, asserting that Reed Smoot was not a polygamist and had a constitutional right to retain the position to which he had been legally elected. As a result of their opposition to such resolutions, however, Anthony, along with May Wright Sewall, who had successfully blocked a move to expel the Mormons from the NCW the summer before, had to answer charges of being polygamy sympathizers.[24] In the debate at the council meeting, Anthony said that she had more respect "for a Mormon who imagined that he had a religious sanction for his deeds, than . . . for a nominal Christian who lived an immoral life." May Wright Sewall argued that Mormon women could benefit by their association with women holding "a higher ideal of monogamic marriage" and reminded the council that even Frances Willard, president of the WCTU, had favored their membership.[25] Unable to win enough votes to expel the Latter-day Saint women's organizations, the anti-Mormon faction now focused its energies toward amending the constitution.

During her seven-year absence from national conventions, Emmeline turned her attention to the many local committees on which she served. Once again she gave time to the Relief Society, visiting local units throughout the western states. She also worked tirelessly to keep her paper afloat, which by that time she issued just once a month. Though she was still active on the executive committee of the Republican Party, she had begun to find local politics disconcerting. She was deeply disappointed when Heber M. Wells lost the nomination for another term as governor of Utah, wondering how anyone could defeat a man "with the personal magnetism and magnificent presence of our dear Hebe." The Smoot hearings were equally dismaying to her. "It seems a perfect burlesque more than a court of inquiry of a dignified body," she lamented. To most Mormons the proceedings appeared to be a "witch hunt" and an attack on the LDS Church rather than a legitimate inquiry into Smoot's qualifications to hold office. The intense and protracted interrogation of Church President Joseph F. Smith elicited some equivocating and unapologetic answers, not only perturbing the Senate Committee but some Latter-day Saints as well. Though certain that "the Lord will defend his people," Emmeline recognized that "all [in the hearings] have not been blameless."[26]

Emmeline also was astute enough to see that despite the fervent move to unseat Smoot, the mood of the country was beginning to shift from that of twenty years earlier, and that this time despite persistent effort, the anti-Mormon campaign would not be as successful in capturing the nation's full attention. It is strange, she observed, that those who were pressing so hard in their crusade against polygamy "are doing more harm to the cause they are bolstering up than against our people."[27] Their claims seemed strident and increasingly anachronistic, as was the national purity crusade itself. Initially capitalizing on the Smoot hearings, the campaign could not maintain its intensity over the long period of the hearings nor regain momentum afterward. Social mores and moral values were changing and polygamy had lost its titillating appeal.[28]

During the next few years, only proxies for the presidents and delegates from the two LDS Church's women's organizations attended the various meetings of the NCW. Emmeline, now in her late seventies, continued to write the report of the Relief Society, delivered by the current representative, but she did not attend herself. At the 1906 meeting, Rebecca E. Little and Clarissa S. Williams represented the Relief Society. One of the telling acts of the council at that meeting was its remarkable about-face from the year before, voting this time to add an amendment to its constitution to the effect "that in the future no matters political or religious should be discussed at the council meetings."[29] Moreover, May Wright Sewall, former NCW president, and Mary Wood Swift, current council president, both seconded a motion that a letter should be sent to Susa Young Gates and Emmeline B. Wells "thanking them for the excellent assistance they had given the association in the past and expressing their regrets that they were unable to be present at the meeting."[30] Whether this was a personal or organizational gesture, the effect was the same. The council had formally recognized two women who had been loyal supporters of the work of the council in Utah despite the resolutions and actions against them. From that time on, efforts to remove Mormon women from membership were futile. Diehard crusaders such as Corinne Allen and Elizabeth Grannis thus took another direction and lobbied for a college marriage course on the "sanctity of monogamic marriage," though they did not give up their drive for a constitutional amendment.

An unexpected ally in Utah, however, promised renewed interest in the antipolygamy crusade. For most of the years between 1900 and 1916, the Republicans controlled Utah politics; but from 1905 to 1911, a third political group, which called itself the American Party, dominated Salt Lake City government. The *Salt Lake Tribune,* which had recently been purchased by Thomas Kearns, a non-Mormon Republican, supported the American Party during its years of political prominence.[31] Established by a number of disgruntled Utah Gentiles who had made their animosity and distrust of the LDS Church the basis of their platform, the American Party attracted the support of antipolygamy women.[32] At the party's first major victory in Salt Lake City in November 1905, several months after antipolygamy forces in the NCW were successful in passing a resolution against Reed Smoot, the National Congress of Mothers and National League of Women's Organizations, claiming to represent all the women of America, sent a telegram to the Utah party which the *Tribune* printed in a boxed setting above the columns of its front page. The telegram congratulated the American Party "on behalf of womanhood and childhood, for love of home and freedom and our country." It then expressed the hope that the party would "hold its banner aloft until it gathers into its ranks every local law-abiding citizen" that "Utah may be redeemed from the conditions which have aroused the horror and indignation of millions of American citizens."[33]

Though the purity campaign made little headway nationally, it quickly attached itself to the new political party in Utah. Local support had been instrumental in passing Congressional antipolygamy measures, and Grannis and Allen anticipated the same from Utah's American Party.

Three years later, in 1908, Reed Smoot's reelection campaign caused another flurry of controversy. While some Republicans and all Democrats hoped to quash his candidacy, Smoot's decision to run forced an expedient alliance of Republicans and Democrats to thwart an American Party statewide election.[34] Alarmed at the party's previous successes in Salt Lake City and its endorsement of the antipolygamy societies, Emmeline decided to return to political activity.

Securing the help of numerous women, Emmeline passed out literature and canvassed neighborhoods to inform people of the importance of the vote and ensure the reelection of Republican Reed Smoot. On voting day, two of her grandsons drove about in a carriage, collecting women voters and driving them to the polling places. When the returns came in, the news was good. "We are rejoicing," Emmeline declared, "but not making demonstrations." She was hopeful there would not be any untoward celebrating by "our people."[35] A small gathering, however, took place at the Beehive House, a former residence of Brigham Young, that afternoon at which Susa Gates, Emmeline Wells, and several Republican women met with Reed Smoot, George H. Brimhall, LDS Church President Joseph F. Smith, and other Republicans to celebrate their victory quietly.[36]

By 1908 the "backlash"[37] against the antipolygamy movement clearly had taken hold. To everyone's surprise, the NCW invited Relief Society president, Bathsheba W. Smith, never a fan of national organizations, to serve on a committee on marriage and divorce (of all topics), and Emmeline's daughter Annie Wells Cannon, a member of the Relief Society board, to serve on the resolutions committee.[38] A number of honors also fell to Emmeline that year. In February, Utah Governor John C. Cutler sought Emmeline's advice on delegates to send to the International Congress of Mothers, a longtime foe of Latter-day Saint women, and later that month Emmeline received a London newspaper featuring her picture and a sketch of her life. "Not all correct but all favorable," she reported, the second time she had been so noted in London. In April she received an invitation to attend the International Conference on Woman Suffrage to be held later that year in Amsterdam,[39] and she and Bathsheba Smith were also invited by Lillian M. Hollister,

Bathsheba W. Smith, Relief Society General President (1901–10), appointed Emmeline Wells to be her general secretary. Together the two women addressed various suffrage and other political issues. When Smith died in 1910, Wells succeeded her as president.

corresponding secretary as well as chair of the press committee of the NCW (and also national president of the Ladies of the Maccabees), to assist with the Peace Congress to be held in London in July. They agreed to help and arranged to have Romania Pratt Penrose attend and her husband, Charles W. Penrose, an Apostle then serving as president of the LDS Church's European Mission, to serve as a delegate. In fast succession, Mormon women had been brought in from the periphery of national sisterhood.

In addition, as an active member of the newly organized prohibition movement in Utah, Emmeline Wells was invited to preside at a meeting of "Mormons and Gentiles," which included both Democrats and Republicans who were supportive of the movement. Capitalizing on her Washington, D.C., contacts, the committee delegated her to send letters on prohibition to various senators and other prominent politicians, including U.S. President Theodore Roosevelt, whom she had twice visited several years earlier.[40] When Utah Governor William Spry, a Republican, vetoed a local option liquor control bill in 1909, for which she had lobbied, Emmeline was extremely disappointed. "It means very much for us," she lamented.[41] Two years later, however, the governor signed the local option bill, and in 1917 the legislature enacted statewide prohibition.

That year brought a new set of challenges to Emmeline Wells. Her disappointment at being denied the trip to Berlin for the ICW meetings gave way to hope that she might attend the ICW quinquennial scheduled for Toronto, Canada, in June 1909.[42] But she was slated for another disappointment when the Relief Society board selected Alice Merrill Horne and Elizabeth Wilcox to represent the organization. When Bathsheba Smith insisted that Emmeline attend the NCW meeting in Seattle, she petulantly refused. "When I really desired to go to Toronto I was not encouraged and now when others have been named [to the NCW meeting] I am not going to be forced into it when others are ready. . . . I am not in the mood."[43] Emmeline prepared the credentials for the Mormon delegates, as she usually did, and wrote the report of the Relief Society, another task she always performed for such meetings.[44]

Emmeline Wells corresponded with officers of the international council, however, most of their exchanges relating to the postconference visit to Utah by some of the international delegates a month after conclusion of the Toronto meeting. Lillian Hollister, corresponding secretary of the ICW, had invited Emmeline to serve as chair of the reception committee for the prominent women who would be traveling to Utah as part of a cross-country tour. Hollister listed several names of Mormon and non-Mormon women to serve with Emmeline. All member clubs in Utah would be assisting.[45] Emmeline looked forward to the coming visit but was most pleased when she learned that she and Susa Young Gates had been elected patrons of the International Council.[46] The old animosities appeared to have given way to a new period of détente.

Emmeline spent the early summer of 1909 with the reception committee preparing for the one hundred ICW visitors who would be descending on Salt Lake City. When they arrived in July, members of the Relief Society and Young Ladies' MIA boards met the visitors at the train station in Ogden and escorted them to Salt Lake City, where they were treated to an organ concert in the Tabernacle and a tour of Temple Square. After the sightseeing, they were hurried off to the train to Saltair, where they tested the buoyancy of the Great Salt Lake before lunch, which was served on the Saltair pavilion.[47] Members of the committee were invited to bring their husbands and individual "head ministers." Joseph F. Smith, president of the LDS Church, was both a husband of a board member, Julina, and also her "head minister." But the careful planning went awry when Corinne Allen, chair of the committee for interpreters, decided to boycott the festivities, drawing several other members of the welcoming committee with her. She informed Emmeline Wells by letter that the invitation for Joseph F. Smith, a principal witness in the Reed Smoot hearings, to attend the dinner made it impossible for her to participate.[48] "It was most unpleasant," Emmeline noted, "however it was unavoidable on my part as in no case would I leave out Joseph F. Smith."[49] The withdrawal of Allen and her associates left primarily Mormon women in charge of the affair, though several non-Mormon women remained on the committee.

Emmeline Wells served as toastmistress and welcomed the guests. Elder John Henry Smith also greeted the guests. Joseph F. Smith did not speak and stayed only briefly before returning to the city. The company then heard from the presidents of the National Councils of Great Britain, Germany, Belgium, Norway, Sweden, Holland, and Italy with a special greeting from Rabbi Charles Freund. Longtime worker in the National American Woman Suffrage Association, Sadie American and her mother, along with Charlotte Perkins Gilman, a frequent visitor to Utah, were also among the number who attended.

The next morning the *Salt Lake Tribune* reported the visit on its front page. It faulted the Mormon members of the committee for deception in meeting the guests in Ogden an hour earlier than scheduled, for using their time alone with the guests on Temple Square to fill them with Mormonism, but primarily for including Joseph F. Smith among the guests. Corinne Allen submitted a copy of a letter she sent to Emmeline to the *Salt Lake Tribune,* citing her reasons for abandoning the committee at the last minute. She noted that she had respected Emmeline in the past and would be happy to ignore all differences of opinion in carrying out the plans for the entertainment, but she did not want to put herself in a position of honoring "a man who stands for the violation of the law which the National [Purity] League is organized to uphold." She also felt that Elizabeth Grannis, president of the National League, was slighted for not being invited to speak at the luncheon.[50]

Allen used the *Tribune* article to vent her scarcely controlled antagonism and her renewed desire to cancel Mormon membership in the council. She was pleased to announce that Hollister, the newly elected ncw president, "will prove that Mormons cannot affiliate with us," and that the former president, May Wright Sewall, "betrayed her trust and disgraced pure womanhood by dealing with the Mormons." Hollister, she concluded, "has firmly announced her determination to drive all Mormon organizations out of the International Council of Women, and we are now in the majority, so they must get out." She further opined that Susa Gates and Emmeline Wells would never go to Europe again as delegates from the ncw.[51] Emmeline read the "wicked stories" printed in the *Tribune* that morning and then, after writing a long editorial about the event for her paper, put it behind her as she prepared to listen to the lectures of Charlotte Perkins Gilman scheduled for the next two days.[52]

The *Deseret News*, however, felt obliged to respond to the *Tribune*'s accusations and called Allen's behavior "an exhibition of the intense partisan hatred with which everything pertaining to the people of the State of Utah" is held by some Mormon critics. It emphasized the fact that all members of the committee had been urged to invite their husbands and that President Smith was there merely as a guest, not an honoree. The newspaper wondered why Corinne Allen, knowing that Smith would very likely be invited, waited until the last moment to register her complaint and in such a dramatic way.[53] What the final impressions of the European visitors might have been was not made public, but the actions of Corinne Allen reminded Mormons that antipolygamy sentiment still lingered.

In September 1909, Emmeline Wells learned that one of the last of the original suffrage workers, Henry Blackwell, husband of Lucy Stone, had died. He had attended a national suffrage meeting in Seattle but had become ill shortly thereafter. Blackwell and Stone had been adversaries to Wells over polygamy, but their mutual fervor for woman suffrage always transcended the issues that divided them.[54]

The antipolygamists received a spurt of energy when the phenomenon known as muckraking broke onto the national scene in 1911.

Among those the journalists targeted, even at that late date, were the Mormons. Primarily directing their attacks against Reed Smoot, now well into his second term in office, they represented the LDS Church as being subversive of the traditional family with designs for national, political, and economic dominance. Magazines and newspapers published their accusations, but with only a short-term effect.[55]

Another flurry of anti-Mormonism occurred in 1913 when the longtime foe of Mormons, the WCTU, feeling secure in its drive for a prohibition amendment, focused once again on polygamy. Helen Hood of the Illinois chapter was particularly voluble in denouncing the practice, classifying it with "white slavery, cocaine, morphine, and other institutions of evil." Resolving to "rid our communities of their [LDS Church] books and missionaries" and "deploring the seating of Reed Smoot," Hood was rebuffed by the Utah chapter, made up of women of all creeds, who threatened to withdraw from the national organization unless the attacks were stopped.[56] Reconciliation had finally been achieved among women's groups in Utah, a development that eroded the Utah base of the antipolygamy movement.[57]

In 1910, Bathsheba Smith died. Though she and Emmeline Wells viewed the importance of maintaining a connection with national women's organizations differently, their devotion to the Relief Society, their shared experiences as first-generation Latter-day Saints, and their years of friendship mitigated that difference. As secretary to Bathsheba Smith in the Relief Society for nine years, Emmeline had proven her loyalty. She had helped make decisions, fulfilled assignments, and counseled with Bathsheba on all aspects of Relief Society work. Emmeline had spent may quiet hours with her and she grieved at her passing.

Despite those nine years, and fourteen earlier years as a general officer of the Relief Society, the eighty-two-year-old Emmeline Wells was overwhelmed when she was elected by the Relief Society board as a successor to Bathsheba Smith. Others found it a natural succession. "As to the business and the purposes of the Relief Society," the *Deseret News* effused, "she has come to be looked upon well nigh as an oracle, so familiar is she with all its workings down to the smallest detail. She accordingly brings to the high position she now occupies all the qualifications necessary to crown her service to it with a generous measure of success."[58] Emmeline viewed the unexpected honor as the crowning point of her work for women.

Even with her new responsibilities, her conviction of the importance of maintaining national affiliations did not wane, and she decided to attend the executive meeting of the NCW in Chicago in November 1911, this time as the Relief Society's official delegate. Ironically, the Utah women "received marked attention" even as the council held memorial services for the late president Lillian M. Hollister,[59] who had been so determined to expel them. Hollister was replaced at the meeting by Kate Waller Barrett, a friend of Mormon women and longtime associate of Emmeline Wells in the suffrage and council conventions. Mormon women could expect smooth sailing in the council under her presidency.

However, by 1913, national leaders observed an ebbing enthusiasm among their once avid Utah supporters. May Wright Sewall, still a leader in the National Council, visited Salt Lake City that year to request Joseph F. Smith's endorsement of Mormon representation in the council. Recognizing the important ecclesiastical position Emmeline Wells now held, Sewall used her name as a lever—she informed Smith that Wells "had done much to create the good feelings now existing" toward Latter-day Saint women and noted that she had proposed that a bust of Emmeline Wells be placed in a hall of statues of the great women of the United States, then in the planning stages by the NCW. "President Wells," Sewell said, "was the connection between the women of the Council and the women of the Church," implying the need for others to continue that relationship.[60] President Smith refrained from outright acquiescence, preferring, he said, to leave membership decisions to the two auxiliaries.

The eighty-five-year-old Emmeline Wells, newly energized by Sewall's appeal, thus attended the executive committee meeting in November of that year in New York with Sarah McLelland, a younger Relief Society board member, and Martha H. Tingey, representing the Young Ladies' MIA. The Utah women participated in the discussions, and Emmeline was elected chair of the council's advisory committee, her dynamism superseding her age. Her editorial the following month conveyed the depth of her commitment to national affiliation. "The influence gained in the world by association with women of note and ability to devote their lives to causes of humanity is helpful to our women, and the Latter-day Saint women yield an influence that is beneficial to others." As one of the chief mediators, no one knew better than Emmeline Wells that "much prejudice has been allayed through this affiliation and the true position and condition of the 'Mormon' women has been made plain."[61] Membership, she asserted, yielded reciprocal benefits. Though she was no longer to be one of the delegation, she appealed to her successors to keep this affiliation alive.

By 1914, the First Presidency of the LDS Church, however, seemed less agreeable to maintaining these relationships. In February the presidency advised the Relief Society to "remain as it is for the present, at least," explaining that they "did not want to interfere in its corporate life." But the Presidency reminded the board that national affiliations were but "a passing incident in the life of the Society, an incident which may be terminated at any time without affecting in any way the Society itself. The Society must be regarded as paramount in importance to everything else now connected with it, or which may hereafter be connected with it," the presidency reiterated, "and its meetings must be conducted in the spirit of a religious organization, as though no affiliation at all with the National organization had been entered into."[62]

Now, four years into her Relief Society presidency, Emmeline Wells conceded the preeminence of the Relief Society, though she could not retreat from maintaining national ties. Her goal in seeking national affiliations had always been to create a niche for Mormon women, and while their objectives were generally compatible with those of the Relief Society, coat-tailing their programs had not been her driving force. Having weathered the storms of prejudice successfully, she, with the help of many others, had secured a place for Mormon representation in the prominent women's associations of the nation. Membership in these groups, she believed, gave prestige to the Latter-day Saint women's organizations while providing a forum for them to engage in an equitable dialogue on women's issues. That the Relief Society would be able to retain its autonomy and determine its own course while participating in a national network she had no doubt. Thus, in the remaining years of her life, she felt comfortable in giving her full attention to the Relief Society.

Joseph F. Smith took the occasion of the seventy-second birthday anniversary celebration of the Relief Society to remind the sisters of the basis of its membership in these associations. You are "the head and not the tail," he reiterated. "I want it distinctly emphasized that the Relief Societies of the Church of Jesus Christ of Latter-day Saints cannot afford to yield their prerogative to stand at the head of any other self-made, self-constituted female or male organization in the world."[63] He did not advise the Relief Society to drop its national affiliations, which pleased Emmeline, and both agreed that the Relief Society was not to adjust its own programs to accommodate those of any other woman's organization. Only as they corresponded with those of the Relief Society were the objectives of these councils to be adopted in the Church's program for women.

The roots of President Smith's position on Latter-day Saint membership and his restraint in the use of Church money and auxiliary leaders' time used in facilitating these national connections are easily discernible. He valued the independence and integrity of the Relief Society and its significant place within the Church. He recognized the important place it had in the lives of Latter-day Saint women. He did not want its identity to be subsumed within that of any other women's consortium. Even more, however, his wariness was understandable when considering the personal abuse he experienced from these same groups and the calumny they heaped on him and the LDS Church during the Smoot hearings and afterward.[64]

Emmeline Wells was missed by her friends in the National Council. As president of one of its member organizations, she received repeated requests to attend the executive committee meetings as well as the triennial meetings. "We need women like you who are fearless in expressing themselves and who believe in the Council idea," wrote Emma Bower, the first vice president, in 1915.[65] But Emmeline did not attend any more national meetings. She did, however, fund the attendance of representatives from the Relief Society, sending a check for $100 to board member Elizabeth McCune "for all the comforts and conveniences you may desire" as Relief Society delegate to the 1916 meeting, a gesture of principle, not need, since Elizabeth McCune was one of the wealthiest women in Utah. That same year, the Relief Society General Secretary assured Emmeline's many friends in the council that even in her eighty-eighth year, she could be found at her desk each day, though much of the business of the Relief Society was now done by committees.[66]

One of her last contacts with council women occurred in December 1915. The Countess of Aberdeen, president of the International Council of Women and onetime critic of Mormon women, was on a lecture tour of the United States accompanied by her husband. Relief Society leaders had invited them to include Utah on their itinerary. Graciously accepting, they were scheduled to give their lectures in four Utah cities. Both Mormon and gentile women were on the committee of arrangements. Susa Gates was the general chair of the event, with Emmeline Wells as honorary chair. Emmeline accompanied the Aberdeens as they visited the historic sites in Salt Lake City and the meetings in which Lady Aberdeen was scheduled to speak. Lady Aberdeen, who would eventually serve as ICW president for thirty-six of its first fifty years, concluded her Utah visit by noting that "it is seldom that one has the honor of being introduced twice in one day by a queen, but that honor has come to me today. For in my brief visit here I have quickly observed that 'Aunt Em' is the Queen of Utah."[67]

Emmeline Wells was beginning to taste the fruits of her long and challenging personal commitment to better the lives of Mormon women. In 1909, she ruminated about the work she and her friend Susa Gates had done over the years. "We have found favor with some of the most eminent women of the age," Emmeline wrote, "and this has certainly removed much prejudice, and how far reaching it may yet be, neither you nor I can determine."[68]

Finally, Emmeline Wells was ready to yield her place to a younger generation of women who would now carry the responsibility of representing their people. As president of the Relief Society, she was absorbed in its challenges and objectives, traveling to women's conferences, attending meetings of the various local women's groups to which she belonged, and conducting board meetings and annual Relief Society general conferences. She directed the Relief Society in its World War I work and acknowledged the personal appreciation of U.S. President Woodrow Wilson for selling the Relief Society wheat, which had been stored by the women as an early welfare project, to the government during the war. Though her body began to fail her, her mind stayed clear, and she was able to preside over the Relief Society board meetings until a month before her death at age ninety-three. Though she always lamented the lack of time to write all that she wanted, others were particularly disappointed that she had been unable to write a book she had promised on the important people she had met. It is unfortunate for later generations that the book was not written, for it would have been the best evidence of the far ranging influence of this Mormon woman, small in form but large in accomplishment.

With age came many honors. Public receptions on her birthday and newspaper tributes, even from the once antagonistic *Salt Lake Tribune,* filled her final years, along with honorary citations from the various women's groups with which she was associated, including the Lady Maccabees, the Council of Jewish Women, the Utah Council of Women, the Authors and Cleophan literary clubs, along with the two clubs she organized in 1891, the Reapers and Utah Women's Press Club.

In 1912, Emmeline Wells became the first woman recipient of an honorary degree from Brigham Young University in Provo, Utah. Accepting the degree as a tribute not just to herself but also to the women of Utah, she rejoiced that her literary talents had been recognized with an honorary doctor of literature. The next year, she again was honored by an invitation from LDS Church leaders to unveil the newly sculpted Seagull Monument on Temple Square, a recognition of the life-saving presence of seagulls who helped preserve one of the first harvests in the Salt Lake Valley from an infestation of crickets. "I wore my best silk dress," Emmeline wrote, "and I stood with head uncovered holding the long streamers that held the vail [sic] in place while I spoke the few words that were very significant of the event sixty-five years ago." Long before, in her native Massachusetts, people in her small village seemed to sense that she was "a child of destiny," and this was but one of the events that made this impression a reality. "I cannot describe the sensations that thrilled my soul as I stood in the midst of that vast multitude assembled on that memorable occasion," she wrote in her diary, "one that helps to make history. And—so in my later life much that seemed impossible has come to pass and the gift of foretelling events has been verified in what has really transpired in these later years."[69]

At her death in April 1921, Emmeline Wells was honored with a funeral in the Salt Lake Tabernacle, which was filled to overflowing with thousands who had been touched in some way by her dedication to improving the lives of women. Flags were flown at half mast on all LDS Church buildings. "She had the mental force which caused her to be a pilar [sic] of strength perhaps more than has been given any other woman of her day," declared the Church's Presiding Bishop, Charles W. Nibley, just one of the remarkable tributes delivered at her funeral.[70] Seven years later, on the centenary of her birth, a life-size bust of her, commissioned by the women of Utah of all faiths and persuasions, was placed in a prominent niche in the rotunda of the Utah State Capitol, the lone woman so honored for seventy years. It carried a most felicitous inscription: "A Fine Soul Who Served Us." Far from consigning her to anonymity and isolation,

Bust of Emmeline B. Wells in the Utah State Capitol Building.

Mormonism opened the way for this New England child to become an influential actor on the world stage, a champion of her religion, and a devoted advocate for the rights of women.

Notes

1. Emmeline B. Wells to Susa Young Gates, September 1, 1909, Susa Young Gates Papers, Church Archives, The Church of Jesus Christ of Latter-day Saints, Salt Lake City.

2. Emmeline B. Wells, Diary, December 4, 1903, L. Tom Perry Special Collections, Harold B. Lee Library, Brigham Young University, Provo, Utah.

3. Wells, Diary, January 6, 1904.

4. Wells, Diary, January 6, 7, 8, 1904. Though generally unsupportive of affiliation with national organizations and reluctant to use Church or Relief Society funds, both President Smiths were also hesitant about breaking all connections.

5. Wells, Diary, January 11, 1904.

6. Wells, Diary, January 14, 1904.

7. The Woman's Christian Temperance Union (WCTU), which withdrew from the NCW that year because the Council would not endorse the antipolygamy movement, initiated a petition campaign against Smoot indicating that whether or not he was a polygamist, he represented the LDS Church, which claimed and taught "superior authority, divinely sanctioned to control its members in civil as well as religious affairs." See "WCTU after Reed Smoot's Scalp," *Salt Lake Herald,* September 13, 1903, 1. A complete report of the resolutions drawn up by the WCTU is in, "Onslaught on Senator Smoot," Journal History of the Church, September 17, 1903, 3, Church Archives, also available on *Selected Collections from the Archives of The Church of Jesus Christ of Latter-day Saints,* 2 vols. (Provo, Utah: Brigham Young University Press, 2002), vol. 2, DVD 26, microfilm copy in Harold B. Lee Library. Dr. Sarah Elliott had been a principal speaker at the WCTU meeting. See also Susan B. Anthony to Susa Young Gates on the antipolygamy question, August 23, 1905, and December 21, 1905, Gates Papers.

8. "Executive Session of the National Council of Women," *Young Woman's Journal* 15 (March 1904): 134.

9. On the incidents of post manifesto polygamy, see D. Michael Quinn, "LDS Authority and New Plural Marriages, 1890–1904," *Dialogue: A Journal of Mormon Thought* 18 (Spring 1985): 9–105; Kathryn M. Daynes, *More Wives Than One: Transformation of the Mormon Marriage System, 1840–1910*

(Urbana: University of Illinois Press, 2001); and B. Carmon Hardy, *Solemn Covenant: The Mormon Polygamous Passage* (Urbana: University of Illinois Press, 1992).

10. "Executive Session N.C.W., Indianapolis, Indiana," *Woman's Exponent* 32 (February 1904): 68. Only six members were against tabling the resolution while forty were in favor. A few months later, in May, Alice Louise Reynolds, a faculty member of Brigham Young University in Provo, Utah, and a delegate to the annual convention of the Federation of Women's Clubs, also spoke against a number of resolutions proposed by that organization at its annual meeting in St. Louis. When expressing her objections, she found her voice was lost in the unanimous chorus in favor. "Defended the Mormon Faith," *Salt Lake Herald,* May 26, 1904, 1.

11. A full discussion of the Smoot hearings is in Kathleen Flake, *The Politics of American Religious Identity: The Seating of Senator Reed Smoot, Mormon Apostle* (Chapel Hill: University of North Carolina Press, 2004).

12. Utah's state constitution, Article III, Section 1 (First), drawn up in 1895, expressly forbids the practice of polygamy in the state.

13. Joan Smyth Iversen details this major assault on Mormonism in the last three chapters of her book, *The Antipolygamy Controversy in U.S. Women's Movements, 1880–1925: A Debate on the American Home* (New York: Garland, 1997), 185–267. The Smoot hearings are detailed on pages 216–21. For more information on Corinne Allen's personal campaign against polygamy, see Iversen, "Corinne Allen and Post-Manifesto Antipolygamy," *Journal of Mormon History* 26 (Fall 2000): 110–39.

14. Iversen, "Corrine Allen," 110–39. The influence of May Wright Sewall, president at different times of both the NCW and ICW, and her efforts to bring others to recognize the distinction between Mormonism and polygamy were major supports to Mormon women. See "A Vigorous Defense," *Deseret News,* June 8, 1904, 4.

15. Wells, Diary, April 27, 1904.

16. Wells, Diary, April 28, 1904.

17. According to Alice Merrill Horne's diary, the meeting of the Daughters of the Revolution discussed the issue of Reed Smoot's election to the Senate, expressing much anti-Mormon sentiment. In a show of indignation, Horne walked out of the meeting after announcing the withdrawal of the Utah chapter from the national association. I am indebted to Harriet Horne Arrington for this anecdote.

18. Bertha Karr, "Greatest International Congress of Women, German's Fair Sex Engineering a Great Conclave in the Imperial Capital as a Slap in

the Kaiser's Face for His Opposition to the Woman's Movement in the Fatherland—America's Delegates," *Deseret News,* May 21, 1904, 13.

19. Wells, Diary, April 18, June 14, 1904.

20. Wells, Diary, June 4, July 20, 1904.

21. This incident was not reported in the published accounts of the conference but is explained in some detail in Lydia Dunford Alder's personal record of the conference prepared for the First Presidency of the Church. See Lydia Dunford Alder, "Report: International Congress of Women, Berlin, 1904," Church Archives, also referenced in Iversen, "Corrine Allen," 110–39.

22. See "International Quinquennial," *Woman's Exponent* 32 (April 1904): 87, 88; "International Quinquennial (concluded)," *Woman's Exponent* 32 (May 1904): 95, 96; "Notes and News," *Woman's Exponent* 33 (June 1904): 3; "Items from Berlin," *Woman's Exponent* 33 (June 1904): 7; "The Berlin Meetings," *Woman's Exponent* 33 (June 1904): 7, 8; "Homeward Bound," *Woman's Exponent* 33 (July 1904): 11; "Mrs. Horne at Home," *Woman's Exponent* 33 (July 1904): 12–13. Most of the articles were taken from other women's papers.

23. The information, taken from an undated and unidentified newspaper clipping written by John E. Jones, appears to be a report of the 1905 National Council of Women meeting. The clipping is in the Corinne Allen Papers in the Schlesinger Library, Radcliffe College, Cambridge, Mass.

24. Iversen, "Corinne Allen," 129.

25. "Miss Anthony and Polygamy," *Woman's Exponent* 33 (February 1905): 60–61.

26. Wells, Diary, August 21, December 20, 1904. Kathleen Flake analyzes the various testimonies of witnesses in the hearing, some of which were more evasive than enlightening. Joseph F. Smith's declaration of a second manifesto in 1904 clearly bore the imprint of the Smoot hearings. Flake, *Politics of American Religious Identity*. For a complete record of the Smoot hearings, see *Proceedings before the Committee on Privileges and Elections of the United States Senate*, Senate Document 486, Fifty-ninth Congress, 4 vols. (Washington, D.C.: Government Printing Office, 1906).

27. Wells, Diary, December 19, 1904.

28. Joan Iversen describes the slow demise of this campaign and particularly the unsuccessful efforts of Corinne Allen in *Antipolygamy Controversy*, 239–67, and "Corinne Allen," 131–39.

29. "National Council of Women," *Salt Lake Tribune*, April 13, 1906, 14. A similar resolution had been proposed at the 1899 NCW meeting but had evidently been ignored.

30. "National Council of Women," 16.

31. Thomas Alexander explains that the American Party was "an irritant to the two major parties and to the Mormon Church" and was unsuccessful in winning statewide elections, dying out before World War I. Not only had it been supported by non-Mormons, it also had the support of members of the Reorganized Church of Jesus Christ of Latter Day Saints, now the Community of Christ Church. Thomas G. Alexander, "Political Patterns of Early Statehood, 1896–1919," in *Utah's History,* ed. Richard D. Poll, Thomas G. Alexander, Eugene E. Campbell, and David E. Miller (Provo, Utah: Brigham Young University Press, 1978), 417.

32. An editorial in the *Woman's Exponent* details the concerns Emmeline Wells felt of extreme importance in the 1909 election, particularly the boast of the American Party that if victorious, it would rid the state of the notorious "twenty-six," meaning the general authorities of the LDS Church. Temperance and prohibition were other issues at stake in the election. See "The Political Situation in Utah," *Woman's Exponent* 37 (October 1908): 20.

33. "Women of America Send Congratulations," *Salt Lake Tribune,* November 9, 1905, 1.

34. Thomas G. Alexander, *Mormonism in Transition: A History of the Latter-day Saints, 1890–1903* (Urbana: University of Illinois Press, 1996), 30–34.

35. Wells, Diary, November 4, 1908.

36. The electoral politics of Smoot's senatorial campaigns and the political involvement of LDS Church leaders are discussed in Alexander, *Mormonism in Transition,* 16–36. See also Flake, *Politics of American Religious Identity.*

37. The term is used in the title of chapter 8 in Iversen, *Antipolygamy Controversy.*

38. Wells, Diary, April 21, May 20, 1908.

39. Emmeline Wells invited Romania Pratt Penrose to respond to Reverend Anna Howard Shaw's address at a similar conference of the International Woman Suffrage Alliance to be held in London in 1909, which she did. Penrose's report of the conference and her remarks are in "The Quinquennial, The International Woman's Suffrage Alliance Congress, held in London, April 26th to May 1st inclusive, 1909," *Woman's Exponent* 38 (June 1909): 1–2. See also Emmeline B. Wells to Romania Pratt Penrose, March 31, 1909, Romania Pratt Penrose Papers, Church Archives.

40. In 1906 a number of Evangelical Protestant groups initiated a prohibition movement that coincided with an emphasis by LDS Church leaders on the Word of Wisdom, a health code for Latter-day Saints prohibiting the use of tea, coffee, tobacco, and liquor. The Protestant Evangelical prohibition movement came to Utah in December 1907. The movement had political as

well as religious ramifications for the Church. While some Republicans and most Democrats supported prohibition, many Republicans opposed it for fear it would alienate business and manufacturing interests usually supportive of the Republican Party. Church leaders feared another political division based on religious lines but offered no consensus. This prompted a three-year legislative debate until 1911, when a local option bill passed. In 1917 a Democratic-controlled legislature, dominated by Mormons, enacted statewide prohibition. For a more detailed explanation, see Alexander, *Mormonism in Transition,* 34, 38, 258–64.

41. Wells, Diary, January 15, 16, 25, February 21, 1909. See also Alexander, *Mormonism in Transition,* 34.

42. Notice of the Quinquennial meeting appeared in Lillian Hollister, "International Council Quinquennial," *Woman's Exponent* 37 (May 1909): 59. Hollister was not a friend of Mormon women and would later join a new campaign to expel them.

43. Wells, Diary, June 26, 1909.

44. See "Triennial Report of the National Woman's Relief Society," *Woman's Exponent* 38 (August 1909): 14–15.

45. The Utah clubs that had membership in the NCW included the Maccabees, Woman's Relief Corps, the Jewish Council, Woman's Suffrage Council, and National Christian League as well as the Relief Society and the Young Ladies' MIA, seven groups all together.

46. Wells, Diary, August 10, 1909.

47. Details of the convention were announced in "Prominent Women to be in City Today," *Salt Lake Tribune,* July 16, 1909, 14.

48. President Joseph F. Smith, a polygamist, had been a major witness in the Smoot hearings and in defense of Reed Smoot and the LDS Church he had elicited the personal ire of antipolygamist women.

49. Wells, Diary, July 16, 1909.

50. "Salt Lake City Visited by Distinguished Women," *Salt Lake Tribune,* July 17, 1909, 1–2.

51. "Salt Lake City Visited by Distinguished Women," 1–2.

52. Wells, Diary, July 17, 18, 19, 20, 1909.

53. "Mrs. Allen Criticized," *Deseret Evening News,* July 17, 1909, 1. Emmeline's editorial in the *Woman's Exponent* also rebutted the *Tribune.* "International Council Delegates," *Woman's Exponent* 38 (August 1909): 12.

54. Emmeline Wells wrote a long obituary for him in her paper. She noted among other things that he had known a number of Mormons in Ohio, particularly "Hyrum Kimball and Joseph L. Heywood," with whom he had

had some business transactions. See "Henry Browne Blackwell," *Woman's Exponent* 38 (October 1909): 32, 35.

55. James B. Allen and Glen M. Leonard, *The Story of the Latter-day Saints* (Salt Lake City: Deseret Book, 1976), 472-73.

56. "Classes Mormonism with White Slavery and Similar Evils," *Herald Republican*, October 11, 1913, 2; "Commercial Club Is Indignant over the Antimormon Sayings," *Herald Republican*, October 14, 1913, 2; and "Mrs. Walker [President of the Utah Chapter] Deplores Trouble Begun by the Antimormon Agitators," *Herald Republican*, October 15, 1913, 3. Both associations were comprised of Mormon and non-Mormon women of all faiths and affiliations.

57. Iversen, *Antipolygamy Controversy*, 239-67.

58. "President of Relief Society," Deseret News, October 8, 1910, 4.

59. A. W. C. [Annie Wells Cannon], "Utah Women at Chicago," *Woman's Exponent* 40 (November 1911): 29.

60. Minutes of the General Board of the Relief Society, April 17, 1913, Church Archives.

61. "The National Council," *Woman's Exponent* 41 (December 1913): 84.

62. The First Presidency to the Relief Society Presidency, February 6, 1914, Minutes of the General Board of the Relief Society, October 3, 1914. Corinne Allen, in a 1912 article or speech entitled "Power of the Mormon Church in National Organizations of Women," declared that "the Mormon Church formed a distinct plan of placing their women in Gentile women's organizations for the purpose of conciliating public opinion, of proselyting and securing social recognition of polygamy." Her concern was that if left unchecked, even at this late date, "these organizations may ultimately become subservient of the Mormon Church." Allen discounted the efforts of the Church to suspend further practice of plural marriage and maligned the individual women who had served as representatives of Utah to national women's conventions, blending truth with half- and non-truths in her accusations. Her remarkable persistence and large following attest to her dedication and appeal in her single-minded crusade against Mormons. The document is in the Corinne Allen Papers, Schlesinger Library, Radcliffe College, Cambridge, Mass.

63. Minutes of the General Board of the Relief Society, March 17, 1914.

64. Subsequent LDS Church leaders encouraged activity in the councils, not so much for the good they would do the Relief Society and Young Ladies' MIA as for the good these Latter-day Saint organizations could do for the councils and their members. Relief Society General President Belle Spafford's presidency of the NCW and leadership in the ICW between 1945 and 1970 represented the climax of Mormon membership. The Relief Society dropped its membership in 1971.

65. Emma E. Bower to Emmeline B. Wells, October 15, 1915, Emmeline B. Wells Papers, Church Archives. Although Joseph F. Smith gave conditional approval to LDS membership in the National and International Councils, Reed Smoot was a champion of these affiliations. At a Relief Society conference in 1913, "he spoke of the great good accomplished by women of the Church when they attended the Eastern Conventions . . . and referred in glowing terms to President Emmeline B. Wells and her influence among these women. . . . Nearly all noted women knew Mrs. Wells, and always asked after her. We hope the association with the eastern women in their mammoth conventions would not be given up, but continued with unabated vigor, for the educational value was incomparable." "Speeches in Relief Society Conference," Minutes of the General Board of the Relief Society, October 3, 1913.

66. Amy Brown Lyman [General Secretary] to Elizabeth McCune, January 4, 1916, Lyman Papers, Perry Special Collections.

67. "Prominent Woman Approaches Majority—'Aunt Em' Wells Nears Important Event," *Salt Lake Tribune,* January 9, 1916, 10. Details of their visit can also be found in a letter to the First Presidency of the LDS Church from Susa Gates, outlining the schedule of their brief visit to Utah and its success. Susa Young Gates to President Joseph F. Smith and Counsellors, December 19, 1915, Relief Society Executive Papers, Church Archives. See also "Lord and Lady Aberdeen in Utah," *Relief Society Magazine* 3 (January 1916): 13–17.

68. Emmeline B. Wells to Susa Young Gates, September 1, 1909, Gates Papers.

69. Wells, Diary, October 1, 1913.

70. "Glowing Tributes Paid at Bier of Beloved Woman," *Deseret News*, April 30, 1921, 10.

Epilogue

Honors and accolades filled the last years of Emmeline Wells's life, justifiably deserved by her unflinching and enduring work in behalf of women and her faith. The plaudits came from national as well as local leaders, men as well as women, and from Mormons as well as those outside the faith. Not many women in her religion could look back on interviews with four U.S. Presidents, one in her own home, appearances before Congressional committees, and a close working relationship with five presidents of The Church of Jesus Christ of Latter-day Saints. In later years, her birthdays were always publicly celebrated, and her death was noted not only in Utah newspapers but also in the *New York Times*. Though her role in the many organizations to which she gave so much of herself slipped from active to honorary, her presence energized and encouraged those who picked up the standard she had carried so enthusiastically for so long.

Perhaps her greatest achievement was integrating the many facets of her personality and life experiences. She brought passion and purpose to her personal as well as her public life. One is not conscious of ideological, social, or political boundaries that might have isolated these many strands of experience and interests from one another. She wove her domestic, religious, and public commitments into a design in which each thread was essential though distinct but also interdependent and complementary, and she managed to keep them all in balance. Emmeline Wells designed the fabric of her own life.

Her focus remained clear and unwavering throughout her life: the advancement of women and the defense of her church. As this volume repeatedly attests, the circumstances of her time and place provided a perfect setting for the conflation of these two commitments. She was never deterred by continuing disappointments, personal affronts, or unforeseen setbacks. Nor did she alter her convictions to gain acceptance among others who did not share her religious beliefs. She never yielded her position on plural marriage. She never yielded her faith in the sisterhood of women. She never yielded her advocacy of women's rights. Yet she was not a revolutionary. She believed that the social order of American life, as then existed, was functioning at only half throttle. She knew it could be far more effective and powerful if it were fueled by all of its human resources.

That the nineteenth century was "woman's era" Emmeline Wells had no doubt. That the world was stirring out of its complacency with an incomplete social order and wishing to make it whole was evident to her in the dramatic changes she saw all about her. And that her religion both explained and promoted this momentous phenomenon was a fundamental truth to her.

Emmeline Wells did not allow the vicissitudes that marked her life to rule or divert her. In that one area she carefully shielded the private from the public woman. Always willing to see a providential hand in the disappointments and sorrows that punctuated her life, Emmeline knew that through those trials she would acquire the personal discipline that would enable her to best perform her service to women. Her transition in the *Salt Lake Tribune* from "polygamic concubine" to "beloved leader" was a consequence not only of the social changes that occurred during her lifetime but of the integrity and fidelity she gave to her commitments.

In a rare, dual role Emmeline Wells both influenced and chronicled the historic period in which she lived. Her life story provides a different image of Mormon womanhood than the oft-used pioneer stereotype. As the foremost Latter-day Saint woman of her time, she, ironically, remains virtually unknown today. Hopefully, this volume will acquaint a new generation with an earlier one to which it owes so much.

Abbreviations of Organizations

AWSA	American Woman Suffrage Association
DAR	Daughters of the American Revolution
DR	Daughters of the Revolution (Utah chapter)
ICW	International Council of Women
LDS	The Church of Jesus Christ of Latter-day Saints
LWV	League of Women Voters
MIA	Mutual Improvement Association
NAWSA	National American Woman Suffrage Association
NCW	National Council of Women
NWSA	National Woman Suffrage Association
UCW	Utah Council of Women
UTWSA	Utah Territorial Woman Suffrage Association
UWSA	Utah Woman Suffrage Association
WCTU	Woman's Christian Temperance Union

Index

agency, 7, 80–81
Alder, Lydia D., 249, 464, 465
Allen, Corinne, 285, 302, 304, 305, 332, 334, 413, 440, 462, 465, 472, 472–73
amendments. *See* constitutional amendments; National Woman Suffrage Association (NWSA): and constitutional amendment
American, Sadie, 419, 472
American Association for the Advancement of Women (AAAW), 195
American Party, 468, 469
American Woman Suffrage Association (AWSA), 118, 155, 220, 243–44, 251
Anderson, Finlay, 123
Anderson, May, 307
Anderson, Sarah E., 311
Anderson v. Tyree, 311–12, 321
Anthony, Lucy, 279
Anthony, Susan B.
 and anti-Roberts movement, 397, 412
 attended ICW quinquennial meeting, 421
 attended NAWSA convention, 360
 and Columbian Exposition, 385
 and creation of ICW, 377
 death of, 363
 defended LDS women's membership, 380, 411
 eightieth birthday of, 354
 friendship of, with Emmeline, 220, 267, 276, 278, 350, 388
 and *History of Woman Suffrage*, 195–96, 198–200
 as president of NAWSA, 361
 and Smoot resolution, 466
 and suffrage amendment, 117
 on suffrage and plural marriage, 119
 against Susa Gates going to Copenhagen, 447
 and union of national suffrage organizations, 251
 visited Utah, 126, 128–29, 293–97
 and woman suffrage in Utah, 271, 327, 328
 on women holding office, 189, 335
anti-Mormon sentiment, 122, 161, 182, 195, 219–21, 397–98, 406–11, 417, 436, 447–48, 451–53, 460–62, 472–73

antipolygamy legislation, 120, 166, 223, 224
antipolygamy movement, 133, 158, 160, 182, 190–91, 212–15, 413, 440–41, 444, 465–67, 468–69, 473–74
Anti-Polygamy Society, 158, 167, 182, 212, 213
Atkins, Annie, 308
Avery, Rachel Foster, 198, 279, 390, 393
Ballot Box, 154. *See also* National Citizen and Ballot Box
Bamberger, Simon, 368
Bancroft, Herbert, 366
Barrett, Kate Waller, 419, 475
Barton, Clara, 357, 360, 443
Baskin, Robert N., 224
Beattie, Phebe Young, 380
Bennett, Charles, 302
Bennett, Isabella, 285, 301
birthdays
 of Brigham Young, 114
 of Elizabeth Cady Stanton, 327, 354
 of Emmeline Wells, 9, 18, 185, 376, 414
 of Relief Society, 268, 477
 of Susan B. Anthony, 279, 354
Bishop, Olive, 19
Blackwell, Alice Stone, 350
Blackwell, Henry B., 117, 219, 226, 312, 473
Blake, Lillie Devereux, 160, 226, 363
Board of Lady Managers, 385, 386, 387
Bower, Emma, 477
Boyer, Sarah, 332
Bradford, Mary C. C., 294
Brown, Arthur, 312, 321–22
Brown, Isabel Cameron, 183, 197, 244, 247–48, 334
Bullock, Electa, 295, 306, 380
Caine, John T., 224, 241, 306, 309, 310, 363
Caine, Margaret A., 329, 417, 419, 420
Caine, Margaret N., 183, 197, 241, 249, 271
Campbell, William, 440, 441
Cannon, Angus, 310, 337, 339
Cannon, Annie Wells, 20, 45, 239, 329, 354, 365, 469
Cannon, Ann M., 409, 410
Cannon, George M., 302, 329, 335, 336

Index

Cannon, George Q., 122, 153, 155, 188–89, 193, 196–97, 285, 303, 310, 396
Cannon, John Q., 239, 303, 329, 358
Cannon, Martha Hughes, 299, 306, 337, 339, 388
Card, Zina Young Williams. *See* Williams, Zina Young
Cassatt, Mary, 385
Catt, Carrie Chapman, 327, 351–52, 360, 361, 362, 365, 368, 465
Catt, George W., 333
Chambers, Robert C., 391
Chase, Mary, 419
Chicago World's Fair in 1893, 25, 384–87, 391
The Church of Jesus Christ of Latter-day Saints. *See also* Relief Society; Young Ladies' Mutual Improvement Association (MIA)
  changes by, after Edmunds-Tucker Act, 254–55
  1895 conferences of, 285, 324
  and female self-sufficiency, 7–8
  leaders of, question membership in women's organizations, 394, 426, 439, 445–46, 450, 460, 476
  leaders of, support membership in women's organizations, 383
  leaders of, support woman suffrage, 188, 247, 251
  in Nauvoo, 18–19, 27, 83
  and opportunities for women, 25, 84–86
  petitions of, to Congress, 15, 153, 165, 223–24, 393
  and political activity of leaders, 298, 310–11
  theology of, and feminism, 24–25, 80–82, 450
Clark, Lucy A., 354, 355
Clayton, Cornelia H., 249
Cleveland, Grover, 223, 270, 328
Cleveland, Rose, 220–21
Cobb, Augusta Adams, 128
Colby, Bainbridge, 368
Colby, Clara Bewick, 198, 225, 245–46, 350, 357
Colfax, Schuyler, 131
"colored women," 451
Columbian Exposition, 25, 268, 384–85, 387–88, 389, 390
Congress
  and antipolygamy legislation, 15, 119–21, 165–66, 201–2, 222, 224
  House Judiciary Committee, 165–66, 224, 444
  and Industrial Christian Home, 223
  petitioned by Latter-day Saints, 15, 165, 223–24, 393
  seating of Latter-day Saints in, 397–98, 406, 451–53, 460–62, 466–67
  and Utah statehood, 131, 132
  and woman suffrage, 119, 160, 201–2, 216
Congress of Women. *See* World's Congress of Representative Women
constitutional amendments
  Fourteenth, and woman suffrage, 154–55
  on antipolygamy, 413, 440, 444
  on woman suffrage, 117, 326, 365, 367. *See also* National Woman Suffrage Association (NWSA): and constitutional amendment
Cook, Harriet, 123

Cooke, Sarah A., 183, 197, 216
Countess of Aberdeen. *See* Marjoribanks, Ishbel
Crane, Charles, 302
Cullom Bill of 1870, 120–24
Cutler, John C., 469
Dalton, Lucinda, 188
Daniels, Marilla, 276, 278, 393
Daughters of the Revolution (DR), 355, 434–35
Democratic Party, 255, 298–99, 305–6, 310, 321
Deseret News, 74, 75–76, 119, 156, 168, 271, 294, 422, 425, 464, 473
Devens, Charles, 165
Dickinson, Mary Lowe, 419, 452
disfranchisement, 108, 133, 155, 160, 164, 190–91, 201–2, 215–16
divorce, 129
Dooley, J. E., 335
Dougall, Maria Young, 252, 393, 461
dower right, 131. *See also* equality; rights
Dusenberry, Ida Smoot, 359, 464
Dwyer, Margie, 249
East, Willmirth, 43
Edmunds, George F., 165
Edmunds Act of 1882, 166, 212, 213, 215, 223, 224
Edmunds Bill of 1881, 153, 197, 201–2, 212, 213
Edmunds Bill of 1885, 219, 224, 227
Edmunds-Tucker Act of 1887, 223, 227, 230, 237, 238, 249, 254, 297–98, 301, 325, 445, 462
education, 9, 25, 74–75, 97, 102, 107, 108
elections, 124, 125, 131, 190–91, 213, 237, 238, 253, 297–99, 312, 321–22, 324, 326–27, 335–39, 349, 354, 357, 396, 469
Elliott, Sarah J., 452
Emery, George, 186
Empey, Nelson, 464
Enabling Act, 270, 297, 306
Englishwoman's Review, 425
equality, 72–73, 78, 81–82, 97, 189. *See also* dower right; rights
Evans, John Henry, 302
Eve, 81, 450
Fairfax Hotel, 360, 443
Fawcett, Millicent Garrett, 386
Felt, Louie B., 307
feminism. *See* woman movement
Ferguson, Ellen, 193–95, 222, 223, 248, 272, 299
Field, Kate, 214–15, 280, 309, 326
Foster, J. Ellen, 357, 411
Foster, Rachel G. *See* Avery, Rachel Foster
Fox, Ruth May, 269, 272, 302, 308, 313, 334, 336, 355, 451
Freeze, Lillie T., 393
Freeze, Mary Ann, 285, 307
Freund, Charles, 472
Friedland, Soffia Lenora, 360
Froiseth, Jennie, 158, 183, 197, 213, 216, 244, 245, 246, 248, 250, 285, 308, 388
Fuller, Margaret, 78–79, 96–97, 100, 101
Gaffney, Fannie Humphreys, 356, 407, 419, 435
Gage, Matilda Joslyn, 164, 166, 191, 196
Garden of Eden, 81–82

Garrison, William Lloyd, 381
Gates, Susa Young
    attended ICW quinquennial meetings, 416, 417–18, 419–21, 445–50
    attended McKinley inauguration, 357
    attended NCW triennial meeting, 278, 393, 410
    as editor, 416, 437–38
    friendship of, with Emmeline, 441, 442–43
    as NCW press secretary, 416, 436, 437, 444–45, 452
    as patron of ICW, 471
    and politics, 336, 355
    and *Woman's Exponent*, 45
Gentiles. *See* non-Mormons, in Utah
George Reynolds v. the United States, 162
Gibbs, George F., 310
Gilman, Charlotte Perkins, 351, 423, 472, 473
Godbe, Annie Thompson, 38, 41, 128, 197, 215
Godbe, Charlotte Ives Cobb, 38, 41, 128, 149–53, 168, 246, 249
Godbe, Mary Hampton, 38, 41, 128
Godbe, William, 126, 127, 149
Grannis, Elizabeth B., 407, 440, 444, 445, 452, 461, 465
Grant, Heber J., 29, 247, 251, 287, 414
Greene, Louisa (Lula), 38, 41
Hamm, Margherita, 331
Hardy, Josephine B., 295
Harper, Ida Husted, 445–46
Harris, Elias, 18
Harris, Eugene Henri, 19
Harris, James Harvey, 18, 19
Harris, Lucy Stacy, 18
Hayden, Sophia G., 385
Hayes, Lucy B., 158, 166–67
Hayes, Rutherford B., 164, 166, 167, 182
Henderson, H. P., 306, 311
Hill, Sam, 308
History of Woman Suffrage, 195, 198, 349, 355
Hoar, George F., 216
Holbrook, Jean Clara, 419
Hollister, Lillian M., 469, 471, 473, 475
home life, for women, 105–7. *See also* marriage
Hood, Helen, 474
Hooker, Isabella Beecher, 199, 381
Hooper, William, 119
Horne, Alice Merrill, 336, 460, 464, 471
Horne, Cornelia H., 43
Horne, Isabella, 191, 221–22, 299, 306, 310, 311, 325, 388, 439
Howard, Elizabeth, 248
Howe, Julia Ward, 195, 244–45, 380
Humanitarian, 424
Hyde, Annie T., 359, 361
Hyde, Ella, 272
Iliff, T. C., 357, 413
Industrial Christian Home, 223, 246, 274
Industrial Christian Home Association, 241
International Council of Women (ICW)
    and Chicago World's Fair, 25, 386, 389
    executive committee meeting of, 445, 447–48
    goals of, 378, 379, 426, 435

membership of, 378–79, 380, 383, 387, 391
members of, visit Salt Lake City, 471–72
organization of, 240, 377
quinquennial meetings of, 26, 417, 419–22, 459
International Press Union, 357
Julian, George Washington, 119
jury service, 330
Kane, Elizabeth, 132
Kane, Thomas L., 132
Kearns, Thomas F., 357, 436, 468
Kesler, Donnette Smith, 367
Kimball, J. Golden, 414
Kimball, Prescindia, 125
Kimball, Sarah M.
    and antipolygamy movement, 121, 221–22
    attended NCW triennial meeting, 267, 380, 381, 393
    corresponded with national newspapers, 38
    edited *World's Fair Ecclesiastical History of Utah*, 387
    and Relief Society, 295, 388
    and Republican Party, 302
    and UTWSA, 247, 252, 270, 271
    and woman's rights, 125, 186
King, William H., 310
Kinney, Mrs. Clesson S., 365
Kipling, Rudyard, 419
Kirby, Charlotte I. Godbe. *See* Godbe, Charlotte Ives Cobb
LaBarthe, Eurethe K., 306, 307
Ladies' Home Journal, 365
Latter-day Saint women
    on antipolygamy legislation, 121, 123–24
    on enfranchisement, 125–26
    petitions of, 132
    protested indignities, 221–22
    rally of, 40, 121, 123–25, 158, 222
    and results of battle over plural marriage, 228–29
    self-image of, 217–18
    on women holding public office, 187–88
leadership, 107
League of Women Voters, 367
Lewis, Mrs. Juan, 191
Liberal Party, 127, 186, 190–91, 253
Little, Nellie, 281
Little, Rebecca E., 467
Livermore, Mary A., 388
Lockwood, Belva A., 155, 161, 226, 363
Lund, Anthon H., 27, 414, 446
Lyman, Francis M., 274
Maginn, Eli P., 18
Manifesto of 1890, 254, 384, 440–41, 445, 462
Mann, Stephen A., 124, 125
Marjoribanks, Ishbel, 389, 478
marriage, 98–105, 129, 238, 330. *See also* home life; motherhood; plural marriage
Married Persons Property Act of 1872, 131
Maxwell, George R., 190–91
McCune, Elizabeth C., 419, 420, 435, 436, 478
McKinley, William, 358
McLelland, Sarah, 475

Index

McVicker, Emma J., 285, 295, 313, 323
memorials. *See* petitions and memorials
Merritt, Samuel A., 322
Miner, J. A., 302
Minor, Francis, 154
Minor, Virginia, 154–55
Minor v. Happersett, 155
moral reform, 106, 200, 443–44. *See also* social purity
Mormon Tabernacle Choir, 329
Morrill Act of 1862, 120, 161, 162, 165, 166, 169, 182, 193
motherhood, 106. *See also* marriage
Mott, Lucretia, 73, 117
Moyle, James H., 321
Murray, Eli H., 189
Musings and Memories by Emmeline B. Wells, 29, 35
National American Woman Suffrage Association (NAWSA), 251, 276, 278, 293, 332–33, 349–51, 354, 358–61, 361–62, 366–67, 393, 394, 442
National Citizen and Ballot Box, 164, 196. *See also Ballot Box*
National Council of Jewish Women, 394, 451
National Council of Women (NCW)
  and Chicago World's Fair, 386–87, 389
  executive committee meetings of, 394–95, 419, 435, 450–51, 460–61, 475
  goals of, 354, 376, 378, 382
  membership of, 267, 279, 378–79, 380, 381, 383, 391, 397, 451, 465–66
  organization of, 240, 243
  triennial meetings of, 25, 266, 278–79, 362–63, 380–82, 393, 406–11, 442–43, 465, 467
nationalism, 419–20, 422
National Woman's Press Association, 382
National Woman Suffrage Association (NWSA)
  annual conventions of, 25, 183, 200
  and Congress, 225
  and constitutional amendment, 117, 154–56, 161
  1879 convention of, 15, 163–64, 168
  1885 convention of, 215
  1888 convention of, 243–44
  1889 convention of, 249, 251
  formation of, 117–18
  and fortieth anniversary of Seneca Falls convention, 240, 242–43
  LDS attendance at meetings of, 15, 25, 163–64, 168, 183, 196, 197, 198, 243, 249
  membership and associations of, 117–18, 118–19, 126, 154, 199–200, 212, 229, 241, 244, 249, 251
  merger of, with AWSA, 199, 244, 251
  objectives of, 117
  and organization of International Council of Women, 240, 243
  supported woman suffrage in Utah, 229
Newman, Angelina (Angie), 216, 222, 223
newspapers, 36, 38, 39, 122, 124, 169, 226, 299–301, 304, 305, 312, 396, 407, 409–10, 422, 424–25
New York Graphic, 169
New York Herald, 123
New York Journal, 410
New York Sun, 312
New York Times, 119, 488
New York Woman Suffrage Association, 195
New York World, 418
Nibley, Charles W., 480
non-Mormons, in Utah, 127, 130–33, 158, 246, 253, 384
Nuttall, L. John, 247, 256
Paddock, Cornelia, 133, 183, 197, 213, 216, 388
Palmer, Bertha Honoré, 381, 385, 389
Pardee, Lillie R., 285, 304, 305, 313, 323, 329, 335
Paul, Alice, 362
Penrose, Charles W., 186–87, 287, 470
Penrose, Romania Pratt. *See* Pratt, Romania B.
People's Party, 26, 186, 192, 253, 255
Perkins, Sarah M., 200
petitions and memorials, 15, 154, 156, 165, 166, 186, 197, 216, 222, 274, 281–82, 287, 352, 440
plural marriage
  court cases about, 162, 225
  defended in *Woman's Exponent*, 38–39, 48–49, 53
  demeaning to women, 9
  as model marriage, 101
  results of battle over, 227–28
  solved by natural attrition, 150–51
  and statehood, 130–34
polygamy. *See* plural marriage
Pomeroy, Samuel C., 119
Powers, Orlando, 269
Pratt, Romania B., 26–27, 194, 195–96, 221–22, 245, 248, 299, 470
priesthood, 84–86
prohibition, 470
property rights, 131, 191
pseudonyms, 51
public life, women in, 103–6
public office, women holding, 186–90, 313, 321–24, 336–40, 422
Queen Victoria, 424
Rawlins, J. L., 306
Reaper's Club, 269
Relief Society
  and Congress of Women, 388
  and funding of attendance at conventions, 418, 439, 446, 449, 460
  jubilee of, 268
  and LDS female community, 4–5
  membership of, in national women's organizations, 25, 241, 243, 244, 380, 392, 394, 407, 437, 476–77
  organization of, 27, 83
  and organization of UTWSA, 247
  representatives of, at 1902 NAWSA convention, 442
  and spiritual gifts, 84
  and Utah suffrage jubilee, 366
  and women's rights, 83–84
  work of, 27–28, 392, 421
Relief Society Magazine, 27, 45
Republican Party, 15, 26, 117, 118, 229, 255, 299–302, 304, 308, 312–13, 321, 322–23, 354, 466. *See also* Territorial Republican Women's League
Revolution, 38, 76, 122, 150

Reynolds v. the United States, 162
Richards, Emily S.
　attended ICW quinquennial meeting, 464
　attended NAWSA convevtions, 331, 332, 333, 354
　attended NCW triennial meeting, 267
　attended NWSA convevtions, 183, 197, 241, 243
　and Columbian Exposition, 387, 391
　conflict of, with Emmeline, 324–25, 330–31, 334
　and Democratic Party, 298, 311, 336, 349
　and politics, 355
　and Relief Society, 285, 295
　as UCW president, 352, 353
　as Utah representative to NWSA, 244
　and UTWSA, 247–49, 252, 271–72
　in Washington, D.C., 222, 381
　and woman suffrage, 281, 369
Richards, Franklin D., 85, 247, 287, 298, 311
Richards, Franklin S., 224, 282, 283, 297, 298–99, 309, 311
Richards, Jane S., 241, 246, 247, 248, 295, 298–99, 306, 380, 381, 388, 394
Richards, Lula Greene. *See* Greene, Louisa (Lula)
Riggs House, 162, 163, 357, 360, 443
rights, 286–27. *See also* equality; *See also* dower right
Riter, Priscilla Jennings, 249
Robbins, Louise Barnum, 279
Roberts, Brigham H. (B. H.), 274, 282–83, 396–98, 406–15
Robinson, Harriet H., 244
Rogers, Aurelia Spencer, 276, 278, 393
Romanticism, 78–80
Roosevelt, Theodore, 358, 361, 363, 470
Salisbury, Margaret Blaine, 285, 302, 303, 387
Salt Lake Herald, 40, 283, 299–301, 304, 305, 306, 322, 396
Salt Lake Ministerial Association, 461–62
Salt Lake Tribune, 42, 127, 151, 162, 166, 168, 280, 281, 282, 300, 305, 396, 411, 468, 472–73, 479
San Francisco Chronicle, 312
San Francisco Mission Mirror, 169
Sargent, Ellen C., 156
Saxon, Elizabeth Lyle, 198, 245–46
Sears, Isabel. *See* Whitney, Isabel (Belle)
Sears, Septimus, 239, 303
self-reliance, 97–98, 99
Senate. *See* Congress
Severance, Caroline, 151
Sewall, May Wright
　and anti-Roberts resolution, 409
　and Chicago World's Fair, 386
　and creation of ICW, 377
　elected ICW president, 422
　as former NCW president, 466, 467
　friendship of, with Emmeline, 198, 279
　and ICW 1899 convention, 417, 419–20, 420
　as ICW president, 446, 447, 448–49, 459, 465
　as NCW corresponding secretary, 267, 381
　as president of ICW, 360, 380
　visited Salt Lake City, 436–37, 475
Shattuck, Harriet, 243

Shaw, Anna Howard, 279, 293–97, 332, 350, 360, 361, 381, 388, 465
Shipp, Ellis B., 278, 393
Siegel, Mrs. Sol, 463
sisterhood, universal, 71, 158, 160, 267, 378, 379, 390, 391, 426. *See also* womanhood
Sloan, Edward L., 40–41
Smith, Bathsheba W.
　corresponded with national newspapers, 38
　death of, 474
　and Democratic Party, 299, 306
　as Relief Society counselor, 295
　as Relief Society General President, 26, 359, 438–39, 449, 460, 463, 469
　and UTWSA, 247, 248
　and woman suffrage, 125
Smith, George A., 42
Smith, George Albert, 463
Smith, H. W., 311
Smith, Hyrum, 19
Smith, John Henry, 247, 472
Smith, Joseph, Jr., 17, 19, 83, 84
Smith, Joseph F.
　called Emmeline to be Relief Society General President, 27
　and Emmeline, 303, 357
　and national women's associations, 475, 477
　and national women's conventions, 383, 441, 442, 460
　and political involvement of Church leaders, 324
　and reception of ICW visitors, 471–72
　supported woman suffrage, 251, 285–86
　and Susa Gates, 438
Smoot, Reed, 446, 451–53, 460–61, 465, 466–67, 469, 474
Snell, Nettie Young, 241
Snow, Eliza R.
　and antipolygamy movement, 121, 123
　and Charlotte Godbe, 152
　death of, 228
　and Emmeline, 27
　poetry of, 36
　as Relief Society General President, 41, 184
　and strong-mindedness, 68
　and *Woman's Exponent*, 43
　and woman's rights, 75, 125
Snow, Erastus, 80
Snow, Lorenzo, 225, 396, 436, 438
Snow, Mabelle, 435
Snow, Minnie J., 278, 393, 409, 410, 436
social purity, 200, 228, 252, 377, 445, 465, 467, 468. *See also* moral reform
Spencer, Anna Garlin, 388, 411
Spencer, Louisa King, 187
Spencer, Sara Andrews, 156, 157–58, 161, 162, 164, 165, 166, 195, 357, 363
spiritual gifts, 84
Spofford, Jane, 163
Spry, William, 470
Stansbury, Lyle Meridith, 294

Stanton, Elizabeth Cady
  and anti-Roberts resolution, 411–12
  and creation of ICW, 377
  death of, 361
  defended LDS women's membership in NWSA, 164
  eightieth birthday of, 327, 354
  and *History of Woman Suffrage*, 198–99
  and Seneca Falls convention, 73, 117
  and union of national suffrage organizations, 199, 251
  visited Utah, 126, 128–29
  and woman's rights, 159
statehood. *See* Utah Territory
Stenhouse, Fannie, 133
Stephens, Evan, 329
Stone, Lucy, 117, 118, 218–20, 243, 380
Stowe, Harriet Beecher, 194–95
Sutherland, George, 330
Swift, Mary Wood, 467
taxes, 191, 280
Taylor, Elmina S., 278, 279, 302, 393, 416, 426
Taylor, John, 153, 166, 168, 170, 188, 194, 222, 228
temple worship, 84
Territorial Republican Women's League, 303. *See also* Republican Party
Thomas, Arthur L., 326, 387
Thomas, Caroline, 267
Thomas, Carrie S., 380, 381
Thomas, Katie, 380
Thurman, Allen G., 165
Thurman, Samuel R., 287, 297, 309, 311
Tingey, Martha Horne, 393, 407, 410, 475
Trumbo, Mrs. Isaac, 302
Tucker, John Randolph, 224, 227
Tullidge, Edward, 42
Tyree, Charles, 311
U.S. Supreme Court, 15, 155, 162, 177, 182, 193, 225
Utah Council of Women, 352
Utah League of Women Voters (ULWV), 365
Utah Territorial Woman Suffrage Association (UTWSA), 248–49, 251–52, 270, 271–72, 273
Utah Territory. *See also* woman suffrage: in Utah
  achieved statehood, 326–29
  changes in, after Edmunds-Tucker Act, 238, 254
  constitutional convention in, 270–71, 275–76, 280–85, 297, 340–41
  enfranchised women, 40–41, 76, 116, 120, 124–25
  governance of, 116
  statehood attempts of, 41, 130–33, 192–93, 237–38
  supreme court of, 191, 312, 313, 321
Utah Woman's Press Club, 355
Utah Woman Suffrage Association (UWSA), 331, 336, 348, 349, 351
Utah Women's Press Club, 269, 287
Varian, Charles S., 313
Victorianism, 5–6
voting pattern, of women, 349, 351
Walton, E. K., 335
Wasatch Literary Association, 21
Washington Capitol, 169

Washington Post, 266, 410
Watchman, 108
Webb, Ann Eliza, 214
Webb, Beatrice, 421
Webber, Nellie, 249
Webber, T. G., 464
Wells, Daniel H., 20, 114, 168, 238–39, 303
Wells, Elizabeth Ann (Annie). *See* Cannon, Annie Wells
Wells, Emma, 20, 22
Wells, Emmeline B.
  association of, with *Woman's Exponent*, 22–23, 24, 28, 43, 44–45, 46–58, 115–16, 153, 302
  attended ICW quinquennial meeting, 26, 415–27
  attended McKinley inauguration, 357–58
  attended NAWSA conventions, 276, 278, 350–51, 358–61
  attended NCW executive committee meetings, 394–95, 419, 435, 450–51, 460–61, 475
  attended NCW triennial meetings, 266–68, 278–79, 362–63, 380–82, 393, 406–11, 442–43
  attended NWSA conventions, 15, 25, 162–70
  attended NWSA executive committee meeting, 198
  as Aunt Em, 3, 54–55
  baptism of, 18
  birth and childhood of, 16–18
  as Blanche Beechwood, 3, 51–54
  broadened focus beyond suffrage, 353, 355, 376–77, 434, 437
  candidacy of, for House, 313, 323–24, 326
  candidacy of, for Senate, 336–37, 339, 350–51
  causes of sorrow for, 19, 22, 67–68, 103, 217, 239–40, 242
  and Columbian Exposition and Congress of Women, 387, 388, 391
  death of, 29, 480
  defended the Church and plural marriage, 24, 53, 69, 115, 160, 190, 462–63, 489
  description of, 23
  determination of, 18, 22, 275, 287, 307, 441–42, 453, 459–60, 489
  did not attend conferences, 220, 242, 331–32, 459–60, 462–63, 464, 467, 470–71, 477
  diplomacy of, 8–9, 26, 462
  and dower rights, 131
  entertained visitors to Utah, 151, 213, 214, 250, 297, 326, 436–37, 471–72, 478
  feminist philosophy of, 70, 80, 81–84, 95–110
  held office in women's organizations, 25, 163, 270, 271–72, 303, 355, 387, 407, 434
  home of, 21, 239
  honors given to, 28–29, 185, 356, 388, 450, 469, 479–80, 488
  joined Republican Party, 301–2, 303
  marriages of, 18, 19, 20
  met presidents, 166, 223
  met vice president, 358
  on international alliance, 378
  as patron of ICW, 471
  as patron of NCW, 270, 393–94
  petitioned Congress, 165, 222–23, 393

Wells, Emmeline B. (cont.)
  poetry of, 17
  on political divisivness and unity of women, 256, 268, 271–74, 276, 325
  was politically active, 26, 186, 192, 237, 274, 301–2, 303–4, 304–5, 307–9, 312–13, 322, 326, 329–30, 333–34, 335, 340, 348, 349, 354, 356, 466, 469, 470
  and political parties, 255–56
  public and private life of, 3–4, 186, 488–89
  qualifications of, as representative of the Church, 153
  as Relief Society General President, 26–28, 364, 474, 476, 478–79
  Relief Society service of, 26–28, 30, 184, 268, 439, 474
  and Roberts, 396–97, 409–11, 413–15
  and Rocky Mountain NAWSA convention, 294–97
  self-reliance of, 7–8, 19, 22, 22–23, 57, 97–98
  and statehood festivities, 328, 330–31
  strong-minded, 68–70
  taught school, 18, 19, 20
  on trials, 22, 53, 217, 489
  and UTWSA, 248–49
  on value of national associations, 382, 439, 450, 476
  visited New England, 218–19
  visited New York, 355–56, 434–35
  and woman suffrage, 134, 154, 156, 163, 186–87, 191, 218, 250, 268–69, 270, 270–271, 273, 280, 281, 283, 284, 335, 351, 352–53, 359, 364, 366, 367–68, 369
  and women holding office, 186, 187, 322, 324
  worked toward acceptance of LDS women, 394–95
  worldview of, 7–8, 22, 68–70, 76–78, 85–86, 159–60
  writings of, 10, 23, 34–35, 50–55, 108, 148–50, 151, 154, 183–84, 185, 356, 450
Wells, Heber M., 313, 327, 349, 357, 365, 368, 466
Wells, Louisa, 20, 22, 239
Wells, Martha Givens Harris, 329
West, Caleb W., 225, 306, 325
West, Josephine, 223, 248
West, Joseph A., 224
Whalen, Alice J., 387
Whitney, Elizabeth Ann, 19
Whitney, Isabel (Belle), 20, 239
Whitney, Melvina, 20, 22, 239, 350
Whitney, Newel K., 19
Whitney, Orson F., 251, 283, 284, 303
Wilcox, Elizabeth, 471
Wilcox, Hamilton, 119
Willard, Frances, 200, 212–13, 243, 252, 380, 466
Williams, Clarissa Spencer, 302, 336, 451, 467
Williams, Zina Young, 15, 25, 162–70, 394, 407, 410
Wilson, Teresa, 392
Wilson, Woodrow, 28, 367, 479
Wollstonecraft, Mary, 78
womanhood, 6–7, 8, 52, 56, 68, 79, 96–100, 102–3, 159–60. *See also* sisterhood, universal
woman movement, 7, 47, 56, 70–77

Woman's Christian Temperance Union (WCTU), 161, 200, 212, 241, 244, 252, 410, 440, 462, 474
Woman's Congress. *See* World's Congress of Representative Women
Woman's Exponent, 34–58, 77, 114, 115, 133, 134, 157, 184, 270, 271, 302, 312, 332, 348, 359, 437–38
Woman's Home Mission Society (WHMS), 216
Woman's Journal, 38, 39, 41, 53, 122, 128, 134, 149, 151, 154, 155, 157, 161, 164, 216, 219, 249, 332
Woman's Tribune, 225–26, 266, 328, 332, 382
woman suffrage. *See also* public office, women holding
  achievement of, 365–69
  court cases about, 154–55, 311–12, 321
  and *Deseret News*, 75–76
  and political parties, 340–41
  publications advocating, 38, 39–40
  as solution to plural marriage, 119
  in states where already granted, 335, 351, 352, 359, 364–65
  in Utah, 49, 121–22, 124–26, 133–34, 159, 164, 186–91, 201–2, 215–16, 227, 247–51, 268–69, 273–74, 275–76, 280–88, 297–98, 300–301, 311–12, 321–22, 327–28
Woman's Words, 148, 154, 156, 157, 160
women, "real." *See* womanhood
Woodhull, Victoria, 95, 118, 424
Woodruff, Phebe, 124
Woodruff, Wilford, 247, 254, 285–86, 311, 332
Woods, Melvina Whitney. *See* Whitney, Melvina
Woods, Ruth, 241, 243, 244
Woods, William, 239
Woodward, David, 16
Woodward, Diadama Hare, 16, 69
World's Congress Auxiliary, 386
World's Congress of Representative Women, 387, 388, 389, 390–91
  Second, 417, 421, 422, 424–25
World's Fair Ecclesiastical History of Utah, 387–88
Young, Amelia Folsom, 246, 305, 310
Young, Brigham, 25, 27, 41, 42, 115, 121, 126–27, 158
Young, Brigham, Jr., 247
Young, Lucy B., 419
Young, Luella Cobb, 241
Young, Seymour B., 464
Young, Willard, 414
Young, Zina D. H.
  death of, 438
  and Democratic Party, 298–99, 306
  hosted Francis Willard, 213
  as Relief Society General President, 278, 295, 388
  spoke, 246
  supported *Woman's Exponent*, 47
  and UTWSA, 247, 248
  visited East Coast for lecture tour, 193–95, 197
  and woman suffrage, 312
Young Ladies' Mutual Improvement Association (MIA), 25, 26, 243, 244, 380, 388, 407, 416, 437, 442, 446, 449, 460
Young Woman's Journal, 45, 416